SIXTH EDITION

The Family Dynamic

Canadian Perspectives

Margaret Ward
Cambrian College (retired)

Marc Bélanger
Vanier College

1914–2014: Nelson Education celebrates 100 years of Canadian publishing

NELSON / EDUCATION

The Family Dynamic: Canadian Perspectives, Sixth Edition

by Margaret Ward and Marc Bélanger

Vice President, Editorial Higher Education:
Anne Williams

Executive Editor:
Maya B. Castle

Marketing Manager:
Terry Fedorkiw

Developmental Editor:
Jacquelyn Busby

Photo Researcher:
Melody Tolson

Permissions Coordinator:
Melody Tolson

Production Project Manager:
Claire Horsnell

Production Service:
Cenveo Publisher Services

Copy Editor:
Sheila Wawanash

Proofreader:
Pushpa

Indexer:
BIM Indexing Services

Design Director:
Ken Phipps

Managing Designer:
Franca Amore

Interior Design:
Cathy Mayer

Cover Design:
Johanna Liburd

Cover Image:
Ian Nolan/Getty Images

Compositor:
Cenveo Publisher Services

Library and Archives Canada Cataloguing in Publication

Ward, Margaret, 1935-, author
The family dynamic : Canadian perspectives / Margaret Ward, Cambrian College (retired), Marc Bélanger, Vanier College. — Sixth edition.

Includes bibliographical references and index.
ISBN 978-0-17-653192-8 (pbk.)

1. Families—Canada—Textbooks. 2. Families—Textbooks. I. Bélanger, Marc, 1967-, author II. Title.

HQ560.W37 2014
306.850971   C2013-905700-5

PKG ISBN-13: 978-0-17-666087-1
PKG ISBN-10: 0-17-666087-9

In Memory of

John Albert (Jack) Ward, 1928–1990
Devoted physician and family man

Denise Papadatos-Bélanger, 1965–2011
A wonderful wife and mother

BRIEF CONTENTS

CONTENTS

PREFACE

The Family Dynamic serves as a basic introduction to family studies, particularly for people who are interested in finding employment in a human services field. As such, it provides a firm theoretical grounding. In addition, because postsecondary students, like all of us, learn best if they can relate concepts to their own experience or that of others, we have provided many examples throughout the text, as well as in boxes and in questions at the end of each chapter.

The Family Dynamic is set up to help students approach the subject matter, and the full colour design in this edition helps capture interest. Each chapter begins with learning objectives and an opening vignette to stir interest and curiosity, as well as to introduce the topic of the chapter. New to this edition is a section headed "Where Do I Fit In?" that asks students a few personal reflection questions to get them thinking about how the topic of the chapter relates to them. Also new is a series of sections throughout each chapter called "Time to Review." These include both factual and critical-thinking questions that allow students to review and think about the material as they finish reading a section. Each chapter ends with a case study, a chapter summary, and questions for personal reflection or group discussion. Within the chapters, boxes are included to amplify points made within the text or to present issues—some of them diverting—for class discussion. Definitions of key terms are in the margin next to the paragraph in which the term is explained. An appendix summarizes various sociological theories for students who do not already have this background, and a running glossary allows quick reference to key terms. On the website associated with this text, students will also find quiz questions, a full glossary, flashcards, and other resources to assist them in their studies.

The ancillary package includes an Instructor's Manual, a PowerPoint® presentation, and a Test Bank. These can be accessed at **www.nelson.com/site/ thefamilydynamic6e**. Please contact your Nelson representative, who will gladly provide you with access to the instructor's resources online.

As with previous editions, we have not attempted to write an exhaustive study of Canadian families but rather to open up the subject and present the variety in our family experiences. We have also introduced challenges and issues to stimulate thought and discussion about the current state and the future direction of families. When exploring these issues, we have tried not to take sides, although we do have beliefs and opinions; rather, we have sought to lay out arguments for competing positions to encourage students to form their own opinions. The orientation of the book is practical and tries to show how the theory relates to students' lives and their future work situations.

Early in this book's history, one reviewer referred to it as a "smorgasbook," a term we consider a compliment. In this edition, as in earlier ones, we have tried to spread out a sampling of the rich fare of information available on Canadian families in the hope that readers will be tempted to feast where they have tasted.

New to the Sixth Edition

An advantage of a new edition is the chance to benefit from the feedback of those who have used the text. In addition to updating the statistics and references, the following improvements have been made:

- For the first time, the text is in full colour.
- Several new and helpful pedagogical features have been added. Each chapter has a new section titled **"Where Do I Fit In?"** that encourages students to connect personally with the story, character, or situation discussed in the vignette. Each chapter also has two or three **"Time to Review"** sets of questions to recap the material. The definitions of **key terms** have been placed in the margins next to the paragraphs in which they are explained. A full glossary of key terms is available on the book's website.
- A **case study** has been added to the end of each chapter. These illustrate the issues and topics presented in the chapter in a real-world scenario. This feature will help students see the connection between the theoretical and the applied aspects of the topics. They may also serve as points of discussion.
- Mary Crea-Arsenio of the University of Guelph has contributed three excellent boxes in Chapter 6 ("Supportive School Environments: Students Fight Back"), Chapter 8 ("Healthy Aging: What Is the Government Doing?"), and Chapter 15 ("Hunger and Its Impact on Children").
- The growing diversity of families is reflected throughout the text. In Chapter 2, there is a greater focus on ethnic diversity and immigrant families. In Chapter 4, we have expanded the discussion of same-sex marriages, and in Chapter 8, there is more discussion of immigrant and Aboriginal seniors.
- Other areas have also been expanded. In Chapter 3, some theories of mate selection have been added, as well as the concepts of "the field of eligibles" and "assortative mating." In Chapter 5, the value of children (VOC) framework has been added. In Chapter 8, we added Kübler-Ross's five stages of psychological reactions to death. In Chapter 10, we added information about patterns of adjustment to divorce and about stressors and protective factors for children during divorce. In Chapter 12, we updated the sections on childcare and eldercare and work–family balance. We also added the cost of childcare in each province.
- We have updated the material on the impact of technology, especially social media, on mate selection (Chapter 3), on socialization of children (Chapter 6), and on the interface between the family and workplace (Chapter 12).
- We have also updated our discussion of federal and provincial laws and policies throughout the book. For example, in Chapter 5, we discuss Quebec's challenge of the *Assisted Human Reproduction Act* on constitutional grounds and the closing of the Assisted Human Reproduction Agency of Canada (AHRC). Marriage fraud is discussed in Chapter 4. There are updated sections on policies about

employment benefits and childcare (Chapter 12) and social assistance to needy families (Chapter 15).

- Some of the 2011 Census data on families was released in September 2012. These new data have been included wherever possible – for example, new data on foster children have been incorporated.

Acknowledgments

It is a joy to be able to thank people publicly for their many private kindnesses. We offer our gratitude

- foremost, to our students over the years, who both infuriated and challenged us in ways impossible to catalogue through their questions, arguments, comments, and stories;
- to our colleagues at Cambrian College and Vanier College for their past and continuing support;
- to Mary Crea-Arsenio, University of Guelph, for writing the excellent boxes in Chapters 6, 8, and 15;
- to the editors and marketing manager at Nelson Education—Maya Castle, Jacquelyn Busby, Claire Horsnell, Terry Fedorkiw, and Sheila Wawanash—for their expertise, patience, and helpfulness;
- to Ann Renee Belair of Vanier College, who provided many helpful comments and suggestions for this edition;
- to our relatives, friends, and colleagues for demonstrating so many variations on family living.

Margaret Ward especially recognizes her grandchildren, Andy, Victoria, Kimi, Robin, and Kodi, part of the generation who will be creating their own family forms and stories.

Marc Bélanger thanks Tommy and Katerina for being such wonderful kids. You always make me proud.

Finally, we thank Jim Douthit (MW) and Christine Lavoie (MB) for their generous practical help, unfailing interest, and encouragement. We dedicate this book to them with love.

We would also like to thank the reviewers for their insightful feedback.

Alan Brown, Mount Saint Vincent University

Pearl Crichton, Concordia University

Marissa Fleming, Georgian College

Cheryl Fraelich, University of Manitoba

Anthony Iafrate, Lambton College

Scott R. Miller, University of Windsor

Mary Murphy-McHenry, Lambton College

Laura Pao, Vanier College

Penny Poole, Fanshawe College

Lori E. Weeks, University of Prince Edward Island

Elaine Weiner, McGill University

Special Features

The text contains valuable pedagogical features that enhance learning:

- **Learning Objectives:** Each chapter begins with a set of learning objectives to set the stage for what follows. These take the form of questions about the intended knowledge that students should be able to demonstrate following a thorough reading of the chapters.

LEARNING OBJECTIVES

What are the implications of an aging population for the future?

What forms will families likely take in the future and what changes in roles will follow?

How does technology affect on the family?

How do government policies affect families?

Will the family survive?

Adela and her granddaughter, Sara, are looking at a photo album.

Sara speaks first. "It's been fun looking at all the old pictures with you, Nana, and hearing about our families. I think I can write an interesting family tree assignment now. I didn't know that your grandfather homesteaded in Manitoba or that Grampa's ancestors left Ireland during the potato famine. It's nice to see what a good normal family we come from. Parents stayed married and looked after their children. Not like some of my friends."

"That's not the whole story, you know. Yes, Grampa and I got married when we were young and had your mom and your aunt and uncles, and we did all stay married," replies Adela. "But not all our relatives had lives like that.

"Look at these pictures. There's Marilyn, my cousin's daughter. Poor Marilyn! Marrying an alcoholic, becoming a widow when he crashed his car. She was only 35. She managed to raise her girls pretty well alone. Now she's living with Rodolfo, who's 12 years younger."

"Who are these two women holding hands?" asks Sara.

"That one's Sue, your second cousin on your grampa's side. It's odd to call Andrea her wife. But they got married once it was legal. Sue's parents never expected grandchildren through artificial insemination. But here's a picture of the twins, Josh and Brendan."

"Who's this dark-skinned man, Nana?"

"That's Mohandas. The women in the picture are his wife, Kate, and Kate's grandmother, Marty. Marty's my oldest friend—almost like a sister. His parents picked out a wife for him in India, but he wouldn't agree to an arranged marriage. Maybe his parents will forgive Kate and Mo now that they're expecting a baby.

"Here's a picture of my niece Pauline and her husband, Brian. Her parents almost disowned her when she married a Roman Catholic, especially when she had to become a Catholic too. And they were good Presbyterians. It seems narrow now with so many people marrying across religious lines. Pauline complains her children will never make her a grandma—Stephen's a priest. And.

Where Do I Fit In?

Do you think that the family in the opening vignette is unusual or is it a fair representation of many families in Canada today?

Think about your own family . . .

1. Who do you consider to be in your family?
2. Are the people in your family different from other people you know? If so, in what ways?

- **Vignettes:** Each chapter opens with a vignette followed by questions headed **"Where Do I Fit In?"** These are "reflection" questions that encourage students to connect with the story, character, or situation discussed in the vignette.

- **New—Running Glossary:** Also new to this edition is a running glossary where key terms are highlighted and defined on the page where they first appear. The full glossary, which can be found on the book's website, allows students to quickly review the chapter's material: names, terms, and theories.

monogamy: marriage to only one person at a time

serial monogamy: a series of marriages to different partners, although to only one at a time

polygamy: marriage of one person to more than one person of the opposite sex

polygyny: marriage of one man to several wives

sororal polygyny: marriage of one man to several wives who are sisters

polyandry: marriage of one woman to several husbands

Canada, the only legal kind of marriage is **monogamy**, which is marriage to only one person at a time. In a society such as Canada in which there is a high rate of divorce and remarriage, sociologists have coined the term **serial monogamy** to describe a series of marriages to different partners, although to only one at a time.

In other social groups, the family has been based on one person married to several others of the opposite sex. The term for this practice is **polygamy**. The most frequent form is one man married to several wives. Strictly speaking, this arrangement is called **polygyny**, but since it is the most common form, many polygynous marriages are mistakenly called polygamous. Polygyny is the practice in many Muslim countries, in some African societies, and was also encouraged among the early Mormons in the United States. Sometimes all the wives are biological sisters, and this arrangement is called **sororal polygyny**. A very rare form of polygamy is one woman with several husbands, and this arrangement is called **polyandry**.

The practice of polygyny gives rise to ethical arguments based on freedom of religion. However, it is important to note the distinction between religious *belief* and religious *practice*. While Canadian laws do not restrict religious belief, they may restrict religious practices that violate an individual's rights and freedoms. Under international human rights law, there is a growing consensus that polygyny violates women's right to be free from all forms of discrimination (Department of Justice, 2012a). Critics say that polygyny encourages patriarchy and devalues women (Bala, 2004), but supporters dub the practice "the ultimate feminist lifestyle." One plural wife suggests that being one of several not only lightens the burden of housework and childcare, but also provides co-wives with an exceptionally skilled husband (Joseph, 1997). Some supporters of polygyny use the term "compersion" to refer to the act of sharing their lover's happiness with another (Luscombe, 2012). On the negative side, authorities have investigated the Bountiful commune, along with other communities of the sect in Utah, Arizona, and Texas, over charges that underage girls have been married to much older men (Bramham, 2008; Matas, 2008) (see Box 4.1 below).

- **Boxes** present examples, charts, and graphs to illustrate points in the text. These exhibits engage students in questions that probe their understanding. Many exhibits ask students to reflect on their personal views on a topic.

- **New—Time to Review** questions at the end of each major section highlight key points and provide students with a built-in test of their understanding of the material before they proceed to the next section.

- **New—Case Studies** appear at the end of each chapter and include focus questions that help students think through a challenging family situation.

- **Chapter Summary:** Each chapter ends with summary points that review the key concepts and facts covered in the chapter.

- **Class and Personal Assignments** These assignments include questions for group discussions and individual reflection.

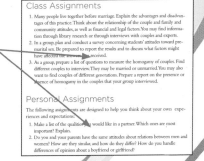

About the Authors

Margaret Ward holds a B.A. degree in English from the University of Toronto, a master's degree in Child and Development Studies from Laurentian University, and a Ph.D. in Human Development and Family Systems from the Union Institute in Cincinnati, Ohio. She has written extensively on issues that have an impact on the family, especially adoption.

Outside of her academic pursuits, Margaret served as a member and secretary of the board of Sudbury Juvenile Services from 1981 to 1983. She also served on the board of directors of the Children's Aid Society for the Districts of Sudbury and Manitoulin from 1974 to 1982. The mother of 11 children, 8 of whom are adopted, she has received two Adoption Activist Awards for her writings on adoption. Currently she serves on the Foster Care Review Board for Pima County, Arizona.

Before her retirement in 1996, Margaret was a member of the Cambrian College faculty, where she had taught since 1985. During her tenure, she presented several courses, including Marriage and the Family, Developmental Psychology, and Introductory Behavioural Science. Before joining Cambrian, she taught at a number of high schools in the Sudbury and Toronto areas.

Margaret now lives in Arizona with her second husband and four cats that enjoy the quilts she makes.

A natural curiosity about why people do the things they do and a passion for anything academic led **Marc Bélanger** to study sociology. He holds both B.A. and M.A. degrees from McGill University in Montréal. Following an unintended career in the food service business, Marc has been teaching at Vanier College for over 10 years. Now that he is a teacher, he wants to more effectively transmit knowledge and passion to students, so he has nearly completed a master's in education degree from the Université de Sherbrooke. Marc lives on the South Shore of Montréal with his two wonderful children.

About the Nelson Education Teaching Advantage (NETA)

The **Nelson Education Teaching Advantage (NETA)** program delivers research-based instructor resources that promote student engagement and higher-order thinking to enable the success of Canadian students and educators. To ensure the high quality of these materials, all Nelson ancillaries have been professionally copy-edited.

Be sure to visit Nelson Education's **Inspired Instruction** website at http://www.nelson.com/inspired/ to find out more about NETA. Don't miss the testimonials of instructors who have used NETA supplements and seen student engagement increase!

Planning Your Course: NETA Engagement presents materials that help instructors deliver engaging content and activities to their classes. **NETA Instructor's Manuals** not only identify the topics that cause students the most difficulty, but also describe techniques and resources to help students master these concepts. Dr. Roger Fisher's *Instructor's Guide to Classroom Engagement* accompanies every Instructor's Manual.

Assessing Your Students: *NETA Assessment* relates to testing materials. **NETA Test Bank** authors create multiple-choice questions that reflect research-based best practices for constructing effective questions and testing not just recall but also higher-order thinking. Our guidelines were developed by David DiBattista, psychology professor at Brock University and 3M National Teaching Fellow, whose research has focused on multiple-choice testing. All Test Bank authors receive training at workshops conducted by Prof. DiBattista, as do the copy-editors assigned to each Test Bank. A copy of *Multiple Choice Tests: Getting Beyond Remembering*, Prof. DiBattista's guide to writing effective tests, is included with every Nelson Test Bank.

Teaching Your Students: *NETA Presentation* has been developed to help instructors make the best use of Microsoft® PowerPoint® in their classrooms. With a clean and uncluttered design developed by Maureen Stone of StoneSoup Consulting, **NETA PowerPoints** features slides with improved readability, more multi-media and graphic materials, activities to use in class, and tips for instructors on the Notes page. A copy of *NETA Guidelines for Classroom Presentations* by Maureen Stone is included with each set of PowerPoint slides.

Technology in Teaching: *NETA Digital* is a framework based on Arthur Chickering and Zelda Gamson's seminal work "Seven Principles of Good Practice in Undergraduate Education" (AAHE Bulletin, 1987) and the follow-up work by Chickering and Stephen C. Ehrmann, "Implementing the Seven Principles: Technology as Lever"(AAHE Bulletin, 1996). This aspect of the NETA program guides the writing and development of our **digital products** to ensure that they appropriately reflect the core goals of contact, collaboration, multimodal learning, time on task, prompt feedback, active learning, and high expectations. The resulting focus on pedagogical utility, rather than technological wizardry, ensures that all of our technology supports better outcomes for students.

Instructor Resources

All NETA and other key instructor ancillaries are provided on the *Instructor's Resource* CD (ISBN 0176582452) and the Instructor Companion Site at www .nelson.com/site/thefamilydynamic6e, giving instructors the ultimate tool for customizing lectures and presentations.

NETA Test Bank: This resource was written by one of the authors of the textbook, Marc Bélanger, Vanier College. It includes over 1000 multiple-choice questions written according to NETA guidelines for effective construction and development of higher-order questions. The Test Bank was copy-edited by a NETA-trained editor. Also included are 180 completion, 170 short answer, and 100 essay questions.

The NETA Test Bank is available in a new, cloud-based platform. **Testing Powered by Cognero®** is a secure online testing system that allows you to author, edit, and manage test bank content from any place you have Internet access. No special installations or downloads are needed, and the desktop-inspired interface, with its drop-down menus and familiar, intuitive tools, allows you to create and manage tests with ease. You can create multiple test versions in an instant, and import or export content into other systems. Tests can be delivered from your learning management system, your classroom, or wherever you want.

NETA PowerPoint: Microsoft® PowerPoint® lecture slides for every chapter have been created by Jaime Nikolaou, University of Toronto. There is an average of 40 slides per chapter, many featuring key figures, tables, and photographs from *The Family Dynamic: Canadian Perspectives, Sixth Edition.* NETA principles of clear design and engaging content have been incorporated throughout, making it simple for instructors to customize the deck for their courses.

Image Library: This resource consists of digital copies of figures, short tables, and photographs used in the book. Instructors may use these jpegs to customize the NETA PowerPoint or create their own PowerPoint presentations.

NETA Instructor's Manual: This resource was also written by Marc Bélanger, Vanier College. It is organized according to the textbook chapters and addresses key educational concerns, such as typical stumbling blocks student face and how to address them. Other features include a chapter overview, chapter outline, learning objectives, terms and concepts, engagement strategies for use in class or online, multimedia resources, and sources for further information.

DayOne: Day One—Prof InClass is a PowerPoint presentation that instructors can customize to orient students to the class and their text at the beginning of the course.

CourseMate

Engaging. Trackable. Affordable.

Nelson Education's *The Family Dynamic* CourseMate, authored by Penny Poole, Fanshawe College, brings course concepts to life with interactive learning and exam preparation tools that integrate with the printed textbook. Students activate their knowledge through quizzes, flashcards, and short answer questions, among many other tools.

CourseMate provides immediate feedback that enables students to connect results to the work they have just produced, increasing their learning efficiency. It encourages contact between students and faculty: you can select to monitor your students' level of engagement with CourseMate, correlating their efforts to their outcomes. You can even use CourseMate's quizzes to practise "just in time" teaching by tracking results in the Engagement Tracker and customizing your lesson plans to address students' learning needs.

Engagement Tracker: How do instructors assess their students' engagement in the course? How do instructors know their students have read the material or viewed the resources assigned?

Good practice encourages frequent contacts between students and faculty: with CourseMate, instructors can use the included Engagement Tracker to assess student preparation and engagement. Instructors can use the tracking tools to see progress for the class as a whole or for individual students. This helps instructors identify students at risk early in the course, uncover which concepts are most difficult for the class, monitor time on tasks, and keep students engaged.

Interactive Teaching and Learning Tools

CourseMate includes interactive teaching and learning tools:

- Quizzes
- Flashcards
- Chapter overviews
- Case studies
- Critical-thinking questions
- And more

The variety of tools in CourseMate respects diverse ways of learning and give students ample opportunity to actively engage with the course concepts. Students receive prompt feedback, which helps them focus their learning efforts on the concepts they have yet to master. Time plus energy equals learning, and CourseMate offers an engaging way for students to increase their time on tasks.

Interactive eBook: In addition to interactive teaching and learning tools, CourseMate includes an interactive eBook. Instructors can use it as a supplement to the printed text, or as a substitute. Students can take notes, highlight, search, and interact with embedded media specific to their book. To access CourseMate, please ask your Nelson sales representative for an SSO account. To provide your students with access to CourseMate, please direct them to **www.nelsonbrain.com**

THE FAMILY

Chapter 1
What Is a Family?

LEARNING OBJECTIVES

What are some definitions of the family?

What are the main theories used to study the family?

How do researchers get information about families?

Adela and her granddaughter, Sara, are looking at a photo album.

Sara speaks first. "It's been fun looking at all the old pictures with you, Nana, and hearing about our families. I think I can write an interesting family tree assignment now. I didn't know that your grandfather homesteaded in Manitoba or that Grampa's ancestors left Ireland during the potato famine. It's nice to see what a good normal family we come from. Parents stayed married and looked after their children. Not like some of my friends."

"That's not the whole story, you know. Yes, Grampa and I got married when we were young and had your mom and your aunt and uncles, and we did all stay married," replies Adela. "But not all our relatives had lives like that.

"Look at these pictures. There's Marilyn, my cousin's daughter. Poor Marilyn! Marrying an alcoholic, becoming a widow when he crashed his car. She was only 35. She managed to raise her girls pretty well alone. Now she's living with Rodolfo, who's 12 years younger."

"Who are these two women holding hands?" asks Sara.

"That one's Sue, your second cousin on your grampa's side. It's odd to call Andrea her wife. But they got married once it was legal. Sue's parents never expected grandchildren through artificial insemination. But here's a picture of the twins, Josh and Brendan."

"Who's this dark-skinned man, Nana?"

"That's Mohandas. The women in the picture are his wife, Kate, and Kate's grandmother, Marty. Marty's my oldest friend—almost like a sister. His parents picked out a wife for him in India, but he wouldn't agree to an arranged marriage. Maybe his parents will forgive Kate and Mo now that they're expecting a baby.

"Here's a picture of my niece Pauline and her husband, Brian. Her parents almost disowned her when she married a Roman Catholic, especially when she had to become a Catholic too. And they were good Presbyterians. It seems narrow now with so many people marrying across religious lines. Pauline complains her children will never make her a grandma—Stephen's a priest. And

Becky, who they adopted from Vietnam, has become a career woman without time for a husband and children."

"Look at the size of this family!" exclaims Sara.

"Alan's my youngest brother's son. This is his second wife, Angie. I think they met through the Internet. I remember how unhappy he was before his divorce from Sandra. Here are his children, Stephanie and Jan, and hers, Melanie and Sean, and theirs, Miranda, in the wheelchair. They've had a rough time with Miranda and her cerebral palsy, but she is so sweet and loving. They're worried about Stephanie, now that she's moved in with her friend Louis. They'd like it better if they'd got married first.

"And this one is Roger, Grampa's cousin's son. He works for some help agency in the Third World—I can't remember its name. Here's a picture of his wedding to Anna in Colombia. She's Australian. Anna says they won't have children because they move too often. It would be hard on kids and interfere with their work.

"Oh, there's your mom in the driveway, Sara. Maybe you can show me your assignment tomorrow."

● ● ● ● ○

What is a family? Almost all of us have been members of at least one family. We see families all around us, both in real life and in the media. We all know what families are, though not all are as complex as Adela and Sara's. Yet when we try to define "family," the task is not so simple. Do we include only the people who live with us? Should we count all of our relatives? One difficulty in defining "family" is that we use the word for many different things—our ancestors, our parents, brothers, sisters, our spouses and children, and all of our other relatives.

Where Do I Fit In?

Do you think that the family in the opening vignette is unusual or is it a fair representation of many families in Canada today?

Think about your own family . . .

1. Who do you consider to be in your family?
2. Are the people in your family different from other people you know? If so, in what ways?

What Is a Family?

Definitions of the family change according to time and place. When the French and English arrived in Canada, they encountered First Nations groups with family structures quite different from those found in Europe. For example, Wendat (Huron) families consisted of many people living together in a longhouse. The residents were often all descendants of a senior female (Baker, 2001). Nowadays we would tend to think of such a grouping as a **household** rather than a single family. According to Statistics Canada (2012a), a household refers to people who occupy

household: a person or group of persons who occupy the same dwelling

the same dwelling and can consist of one or more families, a single person, or a group of related or unrelated people, for example siblings, a live-in nanny, or apartment mates.

communal living: a group of people, who may or may not be related by birth or marriage, sharing financial resources and living arrangements

Communal living, which exists in Canada among some groups, provides another image of family. Acting on their religious beliefs, Hutterites traditionally share financial resources, work assignments, and even meals on a community basis. Accommodation, furniture, and clothing are provided according to need. From about the age of three, children spend most of their days in school. They eat their meals in the communal dining hall, seated separately from their parents, according to their age and sex. Although family ties are recognized, community takes precedence over the family unit (Smith & Ingoldsby, 2009).

The Legal Family

census family: a legal definition of the family used by Statistics Canada

In Canada, the term "family" differs according to who is defining it. A variety of legal definitions exist. The census, which is taken every five years, counts what it calls the **census family** (see Box 1.1) (Statistics Canada, 2012b). Family members are also defined in a host of Canadian laws and regulations. For example, people cannot marry certain categories of relatives, such as parents or brothers and sisters, because they are too closely related. Child welfare laws define parents and specify which relatives are close enough to be allowed to adopt a child without agency approval (Ministry of Children and Youth Services, Ontario, 2011). Immigration law considers certain relatives close family members and thus to be given preference in entering the country (Citizenship and Immigration Canada, 2012a). Government regulations determine family for services, such as medical and family benefits, bereavement leave, and special visiting programs in penitentiaries (Correctional Service of Canada, 2011). In fact, everyone who works in a social services field must learn specific legal definitions of the family in the course of their work.

Kinchip or kit → a family relative

BOX 1.1   Some Definitions of the Family

Statistics Canada

Census family is defined as a married couple and the children, if any, of either or both spouses; a couple living common-law and the children, if any, of either or both partners; or a lone parent of any marital status with at least one child living in the same dwelling and this child or these children. All members of a particular census family live in the same dwelling. A couple may be of opposite or same sex. Children may be children by birth, marriage, or adoption regardless of their age or marital status as long as they live in the dwelling and do not have their own spouse or child living in the dwelling. Grandchildren living with their grandparent(s) but with no parents present also constitute a census family.

Source: Adapted from: Statistics Canada. 2007. *2006 Census Dictionary*. Statistics Canada Catalogue No. 92-566-XWE. Ottawa, Ontario. February 14. http://www12 .statcan.ca/census-recensement/2006/ref/dict/fam004-eng.cfm (accessed February 14, 2007).

Correctional Service of Canada

Family members eligible to participate in the Private Family Visiting Program are spouse, common-law partner, children, parents, foster parents, siblings, grandparents, and persons with whom, in the opinion of the institutional head, the inmate has a close familial bond, provided they are not inmates.

Source: Correctional Service of Canada. Private Family Visiting Program. 2007.

Air Canada

The Bereavement Fare Policy allows people to fly at the last minute in the event of a death or imminent death in their immediate family. Immediate family includes spouse (common-law as well as same-sex partners), child (includes adopted, step, grand, and great-grand), parent (includes step, grand, great-grand, in-law, and common-law in-law), daughter, son, father, mother (includes legal, in-law, and common-law in-law), brother, sister (includes step, half, in-law, and common-law in-law), aunt, uncle, niece, nephew (includes those of spouse and common-law spouse), legal guardian (with proof of judgment), and spouse of legal guardian. All above include in-laws of same-sex partner.

Source: Air Canada, 2009.

Vanier Institute of the Family

The Vanier Institute of the Family defines family as any combination of two or more persons who are bound together over time by ties of mutual consent, birth, and/or adoption or placement and who, together, assume responsibilities for variant combinations of some of the following: physical maintenance and care of group members; addition of new members through procreation or adoption; socialization of children; social control of members; production, consumption, and distribution of goods and services; and affective nurturance—love.

Source: Vanier Institute of the Family. Found at: http://www.vanierinstitute.ca/ definition_of_family

Children's Aid Society of Toronto

CAST defines family to include anyone with a meaningful relationship to a child either through blood ties, community, or culture.

Source: Children's Aid Society of Toronto, 2009.

If you look carefully at the definitions above, you can see that some of them (Statistics Canada, Correctional Service of Canada) define a family by who is included. Others (the Vanier Institute of the Family, Children's Aid Society of Toronto) define a family as a particular kind of relationship. Sociologists look at both aspects when studying families—which people make up a family, and what is the nature of their relationship.

Legal definitions are not fixed; they have changed as a result of court cases and legislation. For example, in most provinces, common-law spouses have been given many of the rights and responsibilities of married couples as to financial support, employment benefits, and custody and support of children. In 2005, the federal government passed a law making same-sex marriages legal across Canada. Legal definitions are not consistent across the country, or even within provinces, and may lead to confusion about rights and responsibilities. As well as deciding which government services will be provided to individuals, legal definitions also determine what individuals are legally entitled to within their relationship. In Quebec, for example, programs such as worker's compensation and the Quebec Pension Plan treat de facto, or common-law, couples like legally married couples. Yet de facto couples in Quebec have no property or support rights (Gouvernement du Québec, 2012a).

Social Definitions of the Family

Various groups and social institutions also define the family. A number of churches and religious organizations have studied the family and, in the process, have stated how they define a family (Canadian Conference of Catholic Bishops, 2006; Canadian Society of Muslims, 2005). Hospital intensive-care units usually permit visits by immediate family members only. Schools accept permission and absence notes from parents only, unless they are informed otherwise. Even restaurants, museums, and amusement parks offer special deals only to families. Of course, they often have some kind of definition of what constitutes a family.

Various ethnic groups may regard family membership in different ways. Aboriginal peoples in Canada tend to have a very broad definition of family membership, and children are often cared for by relatives. If child welfare workers define a family as consisting of parents and children only, then they may feel that some Aboriginal parents are neglecting or even abandoning their children, when these parents believe that their offspring are safe within their family circle. Such misunderstandings have led to unnecessary removal of children from their families (Fox, 2005).

Underlying many of the differences in the way people regard families are two basic concepts: the nuclear family and the extended family. The **nuclear family** is usually regarded as married parents and their children. Sometimes called the "standard North American family," or SNAF (Smith, 1993), it forms the basis for what advocates call "traditional family values" (Erera, 2002). Nuclear families come in two forms, depending on our perspective: **family of orientation** is one that we are born into and raised in; **family of procreation** is one that we form through marriage or cohabitation, and in which we raise our children. We can imagine society made up of interlocking sets of nuclear families with many individuals being members of both forms; however, this pattern works neatly only if all couples get married, have biological children, and never divorce.

In reality, many families do not fit this description. Children may have more than one family of orientation. When parents divorce, their children may have two families to which they are connected, with one parent in each. Adopted children

nuclear family: a family consisting of a husband, a wife, and their children

family of orientation: the family that we are born into and raised in

family of procreation: the family that we form through marriage or cohabitation, and in which we raise our children

start out in one family and are raised in another. With the current trend toward making contact with birth relatives, adoptees may resume membership in their birth families. Some adults have more than one family of procreation. This situation occurs most often with parents who later have children with another partner. Occasionally, two families of procreation result when someone enters an illegal, bigamous relationship or lives common-law while still married to someone else.

The second concept is the **extended family**, which encompasses the nuclear family and all other relatives. Once again, there is variation in what constitutes membership. Some people include more distantly related cousins, while others include only first cousins. In the past, most families that lived in small rural communities in Canada were related through marriage or descent. For these individuals, the entire community could be considered their extended family. In both nuclear and extended families, genetic and "blood" relationships are important, although other types of relationships, such as marriage or adoption, are recognized by most people.

extended family: the nuclear family and all other relatives

Personal Definitions of the Family

Some definitions of the family are quite personal. In some families, a close friend is counted as a member. In other cases, such as those where there has been a high level of conflict and where there is continuing bad feeling, a family may not consider one member as belonging, even though he or she is a legal or biological member. This is especially true when parents have disowned a child or when a marital partner has disappeared, but no divorce has occurred. Different family members may have separate ideas of who belongs. For example, a child may include her divorced father, while her mother does not.

Ideas about the family fall along a continuum with biological and legal definitions at one end, and social and personal ones at the other. For most people, biological and social definitions coexist and are used to fit the circumstances. In stepfamilies, the term "father" can refer to both biological father and stepfather. The concept of family usually includes biological and legal ties as well as emotional attachment (Holtzman, 2005).

Intentional Families

Modern society often encourages frequent and dramatic changes, such as moving to another city or getting a new job. This reality makes stable and long-term relationships a challenge. In response to this, some people have decided to form **intentional families**. The members, though not related by blood or marriage, call themselves a family and may share residence, finances, and a common lifestyle. Intentional family members may also live apart but meet regularly for meals, holidays, and milestones such as birthdays. Because of relocation, separation, divorce, or the death of a loved one, a person may feel alone and isolated. The decision to join an intentional family often arises from the need for human companionship and the emotional connection that comes from shared experiences. The first intentional family was formed in Providence, Rhode Island, in 1972; it is now into its second generation (Graham, 1996).

intentional family: two or more individuals, not related by blood or marriage, who call themselves a family and may share residence, finances, and a common lifestyle

Thinking about Families

Just as there are many definitions of the family, so there are many theories about what makes families work and how they relate to society as a whole. A theory provides a general framework of ideas that can be used to answer questions about the world. Sociologists have used a number of approaches, either singly or in combination, to look for some order and meaning to questions about the social world. Understanding the theories is important because these theories help shape government policy, agency regulations, therapy methods, and other ways society relates to families. Each approach tells us something of interest about families; each, however, also has limitations on how much it can explain. As we discuss theories, we should keep in mind the following questions:

1. How does the theory account for both change and continuity in family patterns?
2. Does the theory show how society and the family influence each other?
3. What does the theory say about relationships within the family?
4. How has the theory affected the policies and practices of government, social agencies, and others who deal with families?

How Does Society Influence Families?

Families do not exist in isolation—they are part of a vast social network. Through membership and participation in neighbourhoods, schools, work, religious organizations, and social and recreational groups, family members are part of the larger society in which they live. The influence of society operates through social institutions, such as schools and religious groups, laws, political and economic factors, pressure from activist groups, and the mass media. Society provides expectations for behaviour. For example, family members are supposed to look after one another physically and emotionally, and are not supposed to harm one another. They are expected to socialize children to meet certain standards of behaviour. Society also limits family behaviour by means of laws such as those against violence, by the benefits provided through social assistance, and through stigma and labelling of those who do not meet societal expectations.

Macro or Micro?

Theoretical perspectives are broadly separated according to whether they take a macro or a micro perspective. **Macro** theories look at the big picture. They principally study the values of a society and the way those values affect the family. The structural functionalist and conflict theories are macro perspectives. **Micro** theories focus on individuals or small groups and emphasize relationships within individual families. These include symbolic interactionist theory, family systems theory, and exchange theory. The feminist perspective has both macro and micro branches, as does the ecological theory.

macro: a theoretical perspective that looks at the big picture and studies how the values of a society affect the family

micro: a theoretical perspective that focuses on individuals or small groups and emphasizes relationships within individual families

The Family as an Institution

The structural functionalist theory views the family as an institution among other social institutions, such as schools, the workplace, and the healthcare system. According to this view, the family has a number of important functions in society. George Murdock was an anthropologist who studied societies around the world. From his vast collection of data, he identified four basic functions that families perform—the sexual, the economic, the reproductive, and the educational (Murdock, 1949). Current theorists have expanded on Murdock's functions and identify five basic functions—reproduction, socialization, social placement, economic support, and emotional support (Berns, 2013). Families may also perform other functions, but these are fundamental. And while other social institutions may share in some of these functions, they can never entirely replace the family. For structural functionalists, when the family performs all these functions well, social stability results.

Knowledge of the "proper" way of doing things in society—mainly, how to survive and how to take part in social life—is passed on to each generation through the process of **socialization**. Talcott Parsons and Robert Bales claimed that the family has two basic and irreducible functions—the primary socialization of children, and the stabilization of adult personalities (Parsons & Bales, 1956). The cultural rules that outline what, where, when, how, and why we should do something are referred to as **social scripts**. If people don't behave in the expected way, they leave themselves open to criticism or pressure to conform.

Structural functionalists generally believe that role specialization increases the efficiency of family functioning. In particular, they state the husband/father is an instrumental (active or doing) specialist and the wife/mother is an expressive (emotional) specialist. In other words, the man is responsible for economic support of the family members and the woman for their psychological and emotional nurture.

socialization: a lifelong process in which the cultural knowledge of how to survive and how to take part in social life is passed on to each generation

social scripts: the cultural rules that outline what, where, when, how, and why we should do something

Evaluation of Structural Functionalist Theory

The most important strength of the structural functionalist theory is its explanation of how the family is related to other institutions and how it contributes to society as a whole. It also emphasizes family strengths, such as cooperation between members, rather than weaknesses. However, there are a number of difficulties with the structural functionalist approach. Although this theory usually provides good explanations of why society maintains values across generations, it is not as clear in explaining why families and society change. The structural functionalist theory often focuses on stability. This conservative approach ignores topics such as family violence and sexual abuse.

Another difficulty is that this view is not very tolerant of differences from the **SNAF (standard North American family)**. Anything that departs from the breadwinner–father and homemaker–mother raising their children—in other words, the majority of Canadian families—is regarded as abnormal or defective in some way (Smith, 1993). Margrit Eichler has called this the **monolithic bias**, the tendency to treat all families the same, with one correct form and universal functions (Eichler, 1983).

Nevertheless, because it has long been the basis for providing social services to families, understanding structural functionalist theory is important for anyone involved in social services delivery. If a man, woman, and children are living together, they are assumed to be a family. The father/husband is still often seen as responsible for the financial support of the family, while the mother/wife is seen as responsible for the personal care of family members, especially children. It is therefore often easier for a man to receive household help when no woman is present in the home, and for a woman to receive financial support when no man is present. In all provinces, welfare benefits used to be restricted to single mothers and their children. Single fathers were not eligible until the regulations were successfully challenged in the courts as unconstitutional (Baker, 1995).

Finally, the structural functionalist view tends to assume that society has one set of **norms** and **values**, something that is not true of a multicultural society such as Canada. Different groups have their own norms for choosing marriage partners, for deciding whether the new couple should live with relatives or by themselves, for dividing labour between husband and wife, and for many other aspects of family life.

The Family in Conflict

Like structural functionalism, conflict theory is a macro perspective that views the family from the perspective of its relationship to the wider society. But instead of emphasizing positive aspects of the relationship, they stress negative influences. Conflict theory is particularly concerned with power relationships and inequality. According to Marxist theory, the economic system of a society has a profound influence on all social groups, including the family.

Friedrich Engels was a colleague of Marx, and he argued that throughout human history, as the economic system changed, so did the family. During the early stages of human evolution, groups survived through hunting and gathering. The means of production were collectively owned and the family as we know it did not exist. There were no rules limiting sexual relationships and the entire society was a family. As groups began to settle and the mode of production turned

standard North American family (SNAF): a term used to describe a family form based on a breadwinner–father and homemaker–mother raising their children

monolithic bias: the tendency to treat all families as being the same

norms: culturally defined rules for appropriate social behaviour

values: cultural standards by which we determine what is good or bad, right or wrong

to agriculture, the concepts of private property and ownership began to emerge. The state created laws to protect private property, and a system of monogamous marriage developed to solve the problem of inheritance. Property was usually owned by males, and to pass it on to their heirs, they had to be certain of the legitimacy of those heirs. They needed control over their wives so that there would be no doubt about the paternity of the offspring. The monogamous family provided the most efficient arrangement for this purpose (Engels, 1884).

While some conflict theorists write about conflict between family members, a more revealing use of the conflict perspective is its focus on how families compete with other social institutions for scarce resources. For example, companies would prefer that employees not be absent to take care of their sick children or to bring their elderly parents to doctor appointments. Conflict theorists would look at how family benefits in the workplace are negotiated between these groups.

Evaluation of Conflict Theory

Conflict theory explains why families and societies change as a result of shifts in the balance of power. It also reveals how the interactions between families and other social institutions are not always harmonious. Conflict theory is not strong, however, in demonstrating how families contribute to society as a whole. Neither is it good at explaining why society's norms and values for families tend to change slowly (White & Klein, 2008).

The Family as Interacting Members

In contrast to structural functionalism and conflict theory, symbolic interactionism uses a micro approach to family relationships. Interactionists feel that the best way of understanding relations between family members is to examine the meanings each sees in other members' words and actions. Such meanings affect behaviour directly (Burgess & Locke, 1960). For example, one spouse may say to the other, "Why are you reading that book?" The partner might interpret the question to mean "Why are you wasting your time?" or "Why did you choose that book and not another?" The response will differ according to the meaning read into the question. Interpretations develop in this way out of ongoing interactions between family members. Behaviour and objects gain meaning, or become symbols, through this process of interaction (Ingoldsby et al., 2004).

A major contribution of interactionist theory is an expansion of the concepts of **status** and **role**. In contrast to structural functionalists, who study status and role from the viewpoint of society, symbolic interactionists study these from the viewpoint of the individual. People develop a sense of self through the attitudes of others and through relationships with parents, peers, and others who are significant to them. Through interaction, individuals can anticipate the behaviour of others and can tailor their own to match. This putting oneself in another's place is called **role-taking**. Knowledge of role expectations comes from prior experiences. For example, husbands and wives may have different notions of how they

status: a social position that carries a set of expectations concerning suitable behaviour

role: the behaviour expected of a person who has a particular status

role-taking: putting oneself in another's place

role strain: a sense of discomfort or tension felt by one who has difficulty meeting role expectations

should behave in marriage based on experiences in their families of origin. As a result, they may have problems because their role expectations clash. **Role strain** is a sense of discomfort or tension felt by one who has difficulty meeting role expectations (White & Klein, 2008). An example is the stepmother. The only roles available are either the biological mother or the stereotypical wicked stepmother, neither of which fits the reality of most families (Church, 2004). When such a situation occurs, people are described as experiencing role strain.

Evaluation of Symbolic Interactionist Theory

The value of the symbolic interactionist theory is the emphasis it places on peoples' responsibility in shaping their view of the world. Since the theory focuses on interactions between individuals, it has been used as a basis for family therapy. If a therapist can help family members change their interpretations of behaviour, the quality of their interaction can be improved. However, symbolic interactionism has been criticized for the micro view that is its main strength; it pays little attention to the impact of wider society on family relationships. Symbolic interactionism ignores factors such as laws, economics, social class, or values and does not explain society-wide changes in families (White & Klein, 2008).

The Family as a System

system: a set of interrelated and interacting parts

The systems approach to the family also looks at how individual members interact, but views this interaction as a system. A **system** contains a set of interrelated and interacting parts. Like all systems, anything that affects one part of the family will affect all parts (Bowen, 1974). For example, if a parent is stressed or angry, this will likely have an impact on all family members.

In the family system, there is a complementarity of roles. If, for example, one person is in the role of parent, another must be in the corresponding role of child. Society expects certain patterns of behaviour from a person in a particular role. A parent is expected to be nurturing and self-sacrificing, while a child is expected to be loving and reasonably obedient. Difficulties may arise if the individual, for example a stepmother, does not fit the role, or if a person has no recognized role.

subsystem: smaller groupings within a system

Families also contain **subsystems** (Montgomery & Fewer, 1988), or smaller groupings of members within the family. The most common are the spouse, parent, and sibling subsystems. In large families, the sibling subsystem may be further subdivided into smaller groupings based on age, sex, or interest (Bossard, 1975). In families where the separation of gender roles is marked, there may be clear male and female subsystems. Chores may be divided along gender lines, with men and boys doing outside and maintenance work, and women and girls responsible for housekeeping and childcare.

boundaries: imaginary lines marking who belongs to a system

Systems and subsystems have **boundaries** (Bowen, 1974) that mark who is a member and who is not. In our society, boundaries have to be open enough to allow interaction with the outside world. For example, most of us would have difficulty surviving physically without income from a job or some other source. Other input sources include school, friends, and religious and social organizations

(Broderick, 1993). The same holds true for subsystems within the family. Children need to interact with adults to receive adequate nurture and have appropriate adult behaviour modelled for them.

Most families operate in much the same way from day to day; that is, they have a steady state made up of familiar routines, rituals, and patterns of interaction. Every family develops its own rules for regulating how members interact. This fact helps explain why families behave in completely different ways in similar situations, for example the loss of a job or a parent–adolescent argument. Some rules are explicit—in other words, they are stated. Rules of this sort include curfews and who drives the family cars. Although other rules are implicit, or unstated, members are still expected to follow them. Such rules might govern how fights are settled or control other forms of family interaction (Broderick, 1993).

When new circumstances or problems arise in families, members often use tried-and-true methods to bring the situation back to the normal steady state (Bowen, 1974). At times a family system is pushed further and further from its steady state by changes in the family, such as maturing children or chronic illness, or changes in the environment, such as job loss. Family members suddenly find that their usual ways no longer work. At this point, some families fall into confusion, while others change rapidly.

Evaluation of Family Systems Theory

The main strength of family systems theory is its ability to account for the impact of the behaviour of one individual on all members of the family. It also explains why behaviour continues in destructive patterns, even through generations. For these reasons, many therapists use it as a basis for their work with families.

There have been criticisms of this theory, however. First, the concentration on the family system as a whole overlooks the experience of individuals, something that is particularly true in cases of spousal assault. Systems theory assumes that destructive behaviour is the result of a vicious cycle. This explanation comes suspiciously close to blaming the victim for her or his own misfortune. Second, theorists often make little or no reference to important social factors, such as unemployment, that affect family life, even though systems theory is quite capable of including such influences (Cheal, 1991).

Fair Trade within the Family

According to exchange theory, much of family life can be viewed in terms of costs and benefits. Costs are factors that discourage certain behaviours; rewards are a person's pleasures. Most of us have an idea of our worth in terms of our abilities, personality, appearance, and even possessions. We expect to get the best return for what we provide in relationships at the least cost to ourselves. For example, if we feel we are reasonably attractive, we usually choose as a mate someone who is also good-looking, or we look for another benefit, like an exceptionally pleasant personality. We also go by the rule that when we receive favours, they must be repaid. Similarly, we expect favours we have given to be returned (Brinkerhoff & Lupri, 1989).

Evaluation of Exchange Theory

Exchange theorists have helped us understand decision making in families, especially in husband–wife relationships. For instance, they have studied marital interaction as a bargaining process used by one member who wishes to change family rules. Power in families is not shared equally by the spouses; in many families, the husband has the advantage in education, income, prestige, social status, and even size. As a result, he has more resources with which to bargain. In such situations, the exchange is not equal; rather, one spouse exerts power over the other (White & Klein, 2008).

Exchange theory is limited, however, in its ability to explain family dynamics because it is based on individual rather than on family needs. It also assumes that people behave with self-interest, something that is not always true. For example, people keep having children even though children are a financial drain on the family (White & Klein, 2008).

The Role of Gender in the Family

Feminist theory looks at issues from both macro and micro perspectives. Although feminist thinkers differ in their views on other issues, they generally agree that family relations, and society as a whole, are based on the power and authority of men, a system called **patriarchy**. As a result, women are limited in their choices and denied opportunities to develop themselves (Fox & Murry, 2000; White & Klein, 2008). While feminist theory will be presented here as a single perspective, in fact there are several variations of feminist theories, including Marxist, liberal, and radical feminism (see Appendix for more details).

patriarchy: a social system based on the power and authority of men

Feminist thinkers criticize structural functionalism for supporting the patriarchal view of the family. They state that the political and social control men hold over women is tied to the belief that a man is naturally head of the family. Within the family, as in the wider society, men tend to have more power and control than women and tend to receive more benefits (Fox & Murry, 2000). This situation is reflected, for example, in the imbalance in responsibility for household work that often occurs when both spouses are employed (Marshall, 2006). Focusing power in the hands of one family member can also lead to abuse of that power, including the use of violence.

gender socialization: the process by which individuals learn the socially defined behaviour appropriate for males and females

The values that support men in a power role are widespread in our society. The inequality between men and women begins with **gender socialization**. Boys are expected to be active and aggressive, and girls to be nurturing and sensitive to others. Often, the differences that result from gender socialization are pointed to as "natural" differences between men and women (Fox & Murry, 2000). For example, the idea that a woman can be fulfilled only as a wife and mother still has widespread acceptance (Douglas & Michaels, 2004).

Feminists also point to higher levels of pay in traditionally male-dominated occupations, such as construction, law, and medicine. Traditional "female" occupations, like providing childcare, preparing and serving food, and cleaning, tend to be lower paid. Part of the original basis for lower pay was the notion that women's work provided

luxuries for the family; it was the man who supported the family. Furthermore, w
are expected to take time off from work for childcare. Doing so, in turn, reduces th
ability to advance their careers and makes them more dependent on men.

Evaluation of Feminist Theory

Feminist thought is the driving force for much current research on the family, by
both men and women. The feminist perspective tends to focus on family issues
that are of greater concern to women, such as abuse. Another example already
mentioned is the study of the difference in the amount of housework done by
men and women. Feminists have also supported equity in the workplace, including
pay and promotion opportunities (White & Klein, 2008). Critics of feminist
theory claim that this perspective places too much emphasis on the role that
gender plays in social interaction.

The Wider Social Context

The ecological theory looks at the relationship between family and society. Uri
Bronfenbrenner has provided the broad outline of this approach (Bronfenbrenner,
1979). According to this theory, families are a part of interlocking systems that
influence each other at five levels (see Figure 1.1).

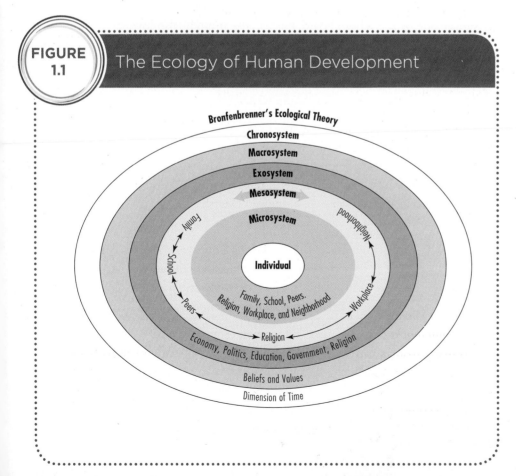

FIGURE 1.1 The Ecology of Human Development

Bronfenbrenner's Ecological Theory

Level 1—The Microsystem

The **microsystem** consists of the small groups in which people interact face to face. For adults, this might involve family, workplace, and organizations to which they belong. The microsystem most directly affects the quality of life through relationships with individuals; therefore, its nature and quality are important. Each family member has a different microsystem; for example, those of young children may include friends and daytime caregivers.

Level 2—The Mesosystem

The **mesosystem** is made up of the relationships between two or more groups of which the individual is a member. A child's mesosystem might consist of the relationship between family and daycare centre or between family and school. For parents, the mesosystem might consist of the relationship between family and workplace. The quality of the connections is important—whether they are weak or strong, negative or positive.

Level 3—The Exosystem

The **exosystem** is a setting in which individuals do not take an active part but which has an effect on them through the mesosystem or microsystem (Garbarino, 1992). For children, this could consist of expectations in a parent's workplace or decisions made by the school board. For parents, it might also involve the school board, which can close the school on a workday for staff development, thus forcing the parents to make special arrangements for childcare.

Many of the important decisions that exosystems make and that affect the family are not even thought of as family related (Garbarino, 1992). Some, such as daycare subsidies for low-income families, obviously are. In the workplace, fringe benefits are clearly family oriented; even these are affected, however, by which definitions of the family are used. Other policies, in both the government and the private sector, although not seen as "family" issues, also affect families. Governmental decisions, such as the location of major highways, can affect children's routes to school or travel time to the daycare centre or workplace. Policies and assumptions in the workplace can also affect family life. One assumption, for instance, is that those on the executive track will work long hours and "move to move up." The time demanded can interfere with family life, and relocating, which is often required for moving up, can disrupt support networks, such as the extended family.

Although the exosystem may seem made up of immovable institutions, individuals and groups have often been successful in changing it. For example, unions have affected working conditions, parent groups have prevented closing of local schools, and many groups working together have forced government to increase funding for daycare.

Level 4—The Macrosystem

The **macrosystem** consists of a society's ideology and culture. These shared beliefs and ways of doing things are, taken together, the basis on which policy decisions are usually made (Garbarino, 1992). Most social policies are based on assumptions concerning relationships between the sexes, such as the division of labour between males and females both inside and outside the family. Such policies tend to be adjusted in response to problems that arise out of changing economic or political situations; however, adjustments like these are often slow in coming.

Level 5—The Chronosystem

The **chronosystem** includes the dimension of time as it relates to the social environment (Bronfenbrenner, 1993). "External influences" refer to historical periods and cohorts. For example, the opportunities for women to pursue education and careers have increased during the past 40 years. "Internal influences" refer to changes that occur as an individual matures. As children get older, they react differently to external events and may be better able to control how those events influence them. For example, researchers have found that negative effects of divorce on children often peak in the first year after the divorce, but by two years after, family interaction is more stable and the negative effects are less.

chronosystem: includes the dimension of time as it relates to the social environment

Evaluation of the Ecological Theory

Although the ecological theory does address family relationships in the microsystem, its real strength is in its explanation of how society interacts with the family. The ecological view, for example, can help service providers understand how minority families differ from mainstream families in their relationships with their extended families and with organizations such as schools, police systems, and social service agencies (Phenice & Griffore, 1996). In addition, the awareness that a policy in one area may have quite unintentional effects on the family can be important if service is provided by several social agencies.

The Family through Time

Looking at the family using one of the frameworks we have discussed is rather like looking at a snapshot that has frozen a moment in time. As we leaf through a photo album, we develop a different perspective on families. Over the years, old faces change or disappear and new ones are added. Often, pictures mark special events—birthdays, weddings, graduations, visits, and trips. Some theorists take the "album" approach to studying the family rather than that of a single snapshot.

Developmentalists look at the entire life cycle of the family from its formation to its end. They divide the cycle into stages. At each stage, the family changes in predictable ways. Having a baby, for instance, calls on parents to accomplish certain **developmental tasks**. The idea of tasks was borrowed from child development theory. According to Robert Havighurst (1952), a developmental task is something an individual is expected by society to achieve at a particular stage of development. Success in this task leads to happiness and success in later tasks; failure brings unhappiness, social disapproval, and difficulty completing later tasks. Developmental theorists of the family have borrowed this idea, but here it is the

developmental tasks: tasks that an individual or a family is expected to achieve at a particular stage in development

family that passes through developmental stages (Carter & McGoldrick, 2005). New parents, for instance, must adjust their family arrangements to meet the physical and emotional needs of the baby as well as their own. If they do not, the family will often experience difficulties at later stages.

social time clock:
socially approved timetable for certain life events

The stages and tasks are related to the **social time clock**; that is, to a socially approved timetable for certain life events. If individuals or families are significantly off-schedule, they may experience difficulties. For example, our society is not geared to provide for adolescent parents. They probably have not finished school and have difficulty supporting themselves financially. If they wish to continue their education, the system is usually not very supportive and flexible regarding childcare and school attendance. Social prejudice is reflected in such expressions as "children raising children" (Luker, 1996).

Evaluation of Developmental Theories

Several criticisms of developmental theories have been made. First, the theories have been described as providing a form of idealized model that real families do not fit. For example, if stages are determined by the age of the eldest child, as with Duvall and Miller (1985), families with "caboose" babies or other large variations in age between oldest and youngest child do not really fit the category (Ingoldsby et al., 2004).

A second criticism is that such theories depend on the concept of the nuclear family. Early developmental theorists assumed that the family consisted of the husband/father, wife/mother, and children who were born at a suitable interval following their parents' marriage. In the 1940s, when the theory was developed, most families did follow this pattern (Aldous, 1996). Other types of families were considered defective in some way; for instance, a single-parent family was considered to be missing the second parent. Of course, many present-day families do not fit the two-parents-plus-children pattern. Originally, developmental theorists also treated men's and women's family experiences as being similar; we now know that they are not (Cheal, 1991).

Developmental theorists are responding to changing family forms. Carter and McGoldrick (1999) initially proposed six stages: leaving home; the joining of families through marriage; families with young children; families with adolescents; launching children and moving on; and families in later life. They later added developmental stages for divorce, the post-divorce family, and remarriage (Carter & McGoldrick, 2005). They also describe family life cycles of women that are distinct from men's. There has also been some discussion of family life cycles or life courses of lesbians and gay men (Cohler, 2006). A somewhat different approach has been taken by Aldous (1996), who describes family careers or paths. These include marital career, parental career, and sibling career. Not all families include all these paths or follow them in the same order. For some families, parenthood may come before marriage; for others, it may never arrive. Within each path, however, certain things can be expected, for example the increased demands on a parent's time in looking after a new baby. The family career approach answers the "inflexibility" criticism of family development theories.

A third criticism is that developmental theories focus on a single generation and thus overlook intergenerational relationships. For example, if we concentrate on midlife, we may ignore young adults or the grandparent generation. This problem can be overcome through using a combination of systems and developmental views (Laszloffy, 2002b).

In spite of its drawbacks, the developmental view has advantages. It allows researchers to compare family life in different cultures, even those as similar as the United States and Canada. In both countries, for example, fertility rates fell sharply from the mid-1960s until the mid-1970s. Then the birth rate for the United States began to rise again while the Canadian rate continued to drop (Bélanger & Ouellet, 2002). Also, the developmental perspective is fairly easy to relate to the stages in both child and adult development, such as those described by Erik Erikson (1982).

And Other Theories . . .

We have presented the most popular sociological theories used to study the family and its dynamics. However, other theoretical perspectives are also used. If you wish to learn more about these, please consult the Appendix.

BOX 1.2 The Approach of This Book

Much of this book will follow the developmental view of the family, using the family career approach. We will look at how couples get together and consider their relationships in several variations—unmarried cohabitation, marriage, and same-sex unions, among others. After examining the decision to become parents and the process of raising children, we move on to discuss the middle and later years. Next, we explore recent changes in family trends, such as divorce and remarriage, and the family's relationship to the workplace.

Despite its drawbacks, the developmental view offers some benefits: it enables us to tie the events in family life to studies in human development, and it allows comparisons of present-day families with those of other times and places. Insights from other theories can also help our understanding. To overcome some of the developmental view's drawbacks, we will need to pay attention to the variations that are common in our society, such as single-parent families and stepfamilies. We will meet many people like those in Adela and Bill's extended family. Some issues, such as family violence and poverty, affect all age groups, and these will be discussed separately. Finally, we will need to consider how governments and social institutions affect family life.

In addition to the various theoretical approaches, we will also explore three different themes. The first theme is diversity. Canadian families show a rich diversity in their form, in their cultural practices, and in how they respond to everyday situations. But as anyone who works with families can appreciate, this diversity can sometimes make it challenging to find standardized policies and responses. The second theme is the social context. Canadian society is constantly changing, and changes in the wider society inevitably have an impact on families. It is important to recognize how the family influences, and is influenced by, other social institutions. The third theme is interactions within the family. The family is the site of our most intimate relationships, and it is fascinating to see how these interactions unfold.

Time to Review

As you have seen, many different theories are used to study families.
1. Which theory most appeals to you?
2. Write a brief summary of this theory and explain why you find it most appealing.

Researching the Family

Where do we get all the information we have about families? Sociology, including family studies, uses many of the same methods of research as other social sciences. There are two main approaches in studying the family. **Quantitative research** is based on collecting data that are presented in the form of numbers and analyzed using statistical techniques. Yet "the things we can easily count are not always the things that count most for families" (Coontz, 2000, p. 292). **Qualitative research** is concerned more with verbal descriptions of behaviour based on reports from people being studied, on observation, and on the analysis of patterns. This type of research often helps identify questions that are then studied quantitatively.

A common quantitative method is the **survey**, which involves approaching people for information face to face, over the telephone, by mail, or over the Internet (Greenstein, 2006). One of the most important survey researchers is Statistics Canada. As well as conducting a census every five years (see Table 1.1 for information based on the 2011 Census), Statistics Canada investigates many areas of Canadian life on a continuing basis. For example, it provides annual estimates of poverty in families. Many sociologists are also involved in survey research. The survey method has the advantage of getting answers from a large number of people; on the other hand, it is difficult to investigate a topic in any depth using this method. Researchers must pay attention to how well the individuals surveyed represent the group they want to study. For example, depending only on calls to land-line telephones for a survey leaves out people who use only cellphones (Pew Research Center, 2006).

Magazines often publish the results of questionnaires completed by their readers. However, we must be careful about accepting the opinions they report as typical

quantitative research: based on collecting data that are presented in the form of numbers and analyzed using statistical techniques

qualitative research: concerned more with verbal descriptions of behaviour based on reports from people being studied, on observation, and on the analysis of patterns

survey: a method of research that involves getting information from many individuals

TABLE 1.1 — Structure of Families in Canada, 2011 Census

	Number	Percentage
Total families	9 389 700	100.0
Couple families	7 861 860	83.7
Married families	6 293 950	67.0
Common-law families	1 567 910	16.7
Lone-parent families	1 527 840	16.3
Female parent	1 200 295	12.8
Male parent	337 545	3.5

Note: In 2011, the largest percentage growth was among common-law couples. Numbers may not add up due to rounding.

Source: Adapted from: Statistics Canada. 2011. *Distribution (number and percentage) and percentage change of census families by family structure* (table). "Portrait of Families and Living Arrangements in Canada." 2011 Census. Catalogue no. 98-312-X2011001. Ottawa, Ontario. Statistics Canada. http://www12.statcan.ca/census-recensement/2011/as-sa/98-312-x/2011001/tbl/tbl1-eng.cfm

of Canadians because many of them originate in the United States, and the opinions and experiences of Americans may differ from ours. There is also no way of knowing how well magazine questionnaires represent all ages and classes of people. Another problem is that with any kind of research that involves self-reporting, participants may knowingly or unknowingly distort the facts. On one questionnaire, teenagers mischievously said they were adopted when they were not and reported they had serious problems (Fan et al., 2002).

An **experiment** involves changing conditions deliberately and observing any changes in behaviour that result. In some cases, researchers perform experiments to test relationships, for example the physiological arousal of couples during arguments as measured by instruments similar to lie detectors (Gottman, 1991). In spite of the ability to control factors, experiments do have drawbacks. Since the research laboratory is not a natural setting, the behaviour there may not be typical of everyday interaction. It is also unethical to conduct experiments that may damage a person physically or emotionally, such as isolating a baby from its mother to learn the effects of maternal deprivation (Greenstein, 2006).

Probably the most common form of qualitative research is the in-depth **interview**. This type of research involves more detailed and lengthier face-to-face questioning than the survey method. Interviews are often too time-consuming and costly to involve huge numbers of subjects (Patton, 1990). The interview method is often used when the researcher is looking for information that cannot easily be transformed into numbers. One such study concerned how rural women felt about the benefits and challenges of holding jobs (Ames et al., 2006). At times,

experiment: a research method that involves changing conditions deliberately and observing any changes in behaviour that result

interview: a research method in which the researcher asks questions face to face

direct observation: a research method in which the researcher watches and records behaviour

focus group: a research method in which group members discuss a particular issue

content analysis: a research method based on analyzing documents or other kinds of records

correlation: a mathematical method for showing the direction and strength of a relationship between variables

cross-sectional research: a research method that studies individuals of different ages and compares them in relation to the factor under investigation

cohort effect: characteristics or attitudes that result from the period of history in which people have lived

longitudinal research: a research method in which the same individuals are studied for a period of time

interview research is used as a basis for questionnaires that can be given to a larger number of individuals.

Direct observation by researchers avoids the problems found in self-reporting. In one form, naturalistic observation, the researcher tries to watch and record normal activities as unobtrusively as possible. Sometimes, recordings are made and later analyzed in the office or laboratory. For example, in one study of marital relationships, researchers videotaped couples discussing a problem topic and coded their facial expressions. They found that couples who later separated were more likely to have miserable smiles and to show disgust (Gottman, 1991). In another form of observation, the investigators take part in the activities of the subjects and report on their experiences. This method is often used when researchers, more often anthropologists than sociologists, study different cultures. By living in the society, it is possible to observe small details that the outside observer might miss and to understand the meanings of certain activities (Daly, 2007b).

Focus groups bring together people who share some experience. Through discussions, members help researchers understand key issues of their situation (Daly, 2007b). One focus group, for example, talked about challenges of their mixed-race marriages (Lowe, 2006).

In doing **content analysis**, researchers might look at the forms of communication used during the period they are studying (Patton, 1996). Sheila Kieran (1986), in her book on family law in Ontario, quotes letters and diaries; sources like these help bring dry official documents to life. Researchers have even examined changes in how fathers have been portrayed in comic strips over a period of 60 years (LaRossa et al., 2000).

Once the researchers have gathered data, they often perform statistical analysis. Doing this is, of course, a characteristic of quantitative research, but it may also be used by qualitative researchers following many interviews or observations. One of the simplest and most common forms of analysis is **correlation**, which attempts to find a relationship between two or more factors or variables (Greenstein, 2006). Correlations cannot, however, prove that one factor or event caused another. For example, in a study of marital satisfaction, researchers found a correlation between life events such as the birth of a child or children leaving home and the level of satisfaction (Lupri & Frideres, 1981).

In comparing life stages or historical periods, it is important to keep in mind two different approaches to research. **Cross-sectional research** studies individuals of different ages and compares them in relation to the factor under investigation. A major problem with comparing attitudes (toward sexuality, for example) among people of different age groups is that these are affected by different historical events and values, and the differences in attitude may not be the result of age but of changing times. This is referred to as a **cohort effect**. The findings of Lupri and Frideres (1981) concerning marital satisfaction may be showing cohort influences rather than the effect of the life stage. Cohort influences can be overcome by **longitudinal research**—that is, by following the same people over a long time. Human Resources Canada and Statistics Canada, for example, are jointly studying the way children grow and develop from birth to adulthood. The first group, aged zero to 11 in 1994, numbers about 15 000, with younger children being added to the study (Statistics Canada, 2010a). One difficulty with longitudinal studies is the many years needed before results are available. In the interval, subjects may lose interest or disappear. Sometimes, to get information faster and yet reduce cohort effects, a combination of cross-sectional and longitudinal studies is used (Baltes et al., 1977).

Whatever method of investigation is used, the results are affected by the theoretical approach to the family because the approach determines which questions are asked. If a structural functionalist wished to study decision making in the family, the question may be, "How is decision making related to traditional roles?" A feminist, however, would ask, "How is decision making related to power in the family?" A family systems theorist might want to know the impact of decision making on subsystems in the family, and a developmentalist how decision making differs at various stages.

Time to Review

As you have seen, many different methods are used to study families.
1. Which method most appeals to you?
2. Write a brief summary of this method and explain why you find it most appealing.

Immediate Family Members Only

Canadian families show amazing diversity and complexity. This can sometimes make it challenging to apply general, standardized policies that assume a simple and universal family form. Imagine that you are a nurse and the hospital where you work has a strict visitation policy. All visitors are welcome throughout the day, but after 7 p.m. only immediate family members are allowed to stay. Now imagine you have this group of people visiting poor Jean-Guy in the hospital. It is five minutes before 7 p.m. and you have to ask some people to go. Who would you ask to leave, and who would be allowed to stay?

Jean-Guy has four biological children—Marie, Steve, Lisa, and Pei-Li. Marie is Jean-Guy's eldest daughter. She is 18 years old and has lived with Jean-Guy since her mother, Pauline, left when she was three years old. Neither Jean-Guy nor Marie has seen Pauline since she left. Marie has been dating Robert for three years, and since last year, Robert and Marie have been living together in the basement of Jean-Guy's house. Jean-Guy met Sally 12 years ago. They married and had two children together—Steve and Lisa. Since their divorce five years ago, Steve lives with Jean-Guy during the week but goes to Sally every weekend. Lisa lives with Sally during the week but with Jean-Guy every weekend. Jean-Guy is now married to Min. Min has two daughters—Melinda and Marlene—from a previous marriage. Melinda lives full-time with Al, Min's ex-husband, and Marlene lives full-time with Min and Jean-Guy. Min and Jean-Guy have a biological daughter—Pei-Li. She is two years old. Jean-Guy has legally adopted Marlene, but Min has not legally adopted any of Jean-Guy's children. Min's elderly grandmother lives with her and Jean-Guy.

Imagine that everyone mentioned in this scenario (with the exception of Pauline) is visiting Jean-Guy. You may want to draw a diagram to visualize all the complex relationships in this group.

1. How many nuclear families are there?
2. How many households are there?
3. Who is in Jean-Guy's *immediate* family—who is allowed to stay past 7 p.m.?

Summary

What Are Some Definitions of the Family?

Families have been defined in different ways according to time and place. In Canada today, there are several legal definitions of family, as well as social and personal definitions. Two ideas of family common in North America are the nuclear family, consisting of parents and children, and the extended family, which includes other relatives.

What Are the Main Theories Used to Study the Family?

Sociologists have suggested a number of theories to explain what happens in families. Macro theories look at the big picture. Micro theories emphasize relationships within individual families.

1. The structural functional theory views the family as an institution among other social institutions. Families fulfill five important functions in society—reproduction, socialization, social placement, economic support, and emotional support. When the family performs all of these functions well, social stability results. The cultural rules that outline what, where, when, how, and why we should do something are referred to as social scripts.
2. Conflict theory is concerned with power relationships. It is based on the assumption that the economic system of a society has a profound influence on all social groups, including the family. Throughout human history, as the economic system changed, so did the family. This perspective focuses on how families compete with other social institutions for scarce resources.
3. Symbolic interactionists feel that the best way of understanding relations between family members is to examine the meanings each sees in other members' words

and actions. They study roles from the viewpoint of the individual. Symbolic inter-actionists use the concepts of role-taking, role expectations, and role strain.

4. Systems theory regards a family as a set of interrelated parts in which anything that affects one part affects all other parts. Families also contain subsystems, which are smaller groupings. Boundaries set out who belongs to a family or its subsystems. Families operate according to rules. When new circumstances or problems arise in families, members often use tried-and-true methods to bring the situation back to the normal steady state.

5. Exchange theorists look at the costs and benefits of family life to family members. They have been especially concerned with how husbands and wives make decisions.

6. Feminist theory believes that family relations, and society as a whole, are based on the power and authority of men, a system called patriarchy. The inequality between men and women begins with gender socialization. The theory focuses on how men and women may have different experiences within a family.

7. The ecological view regards families as part of interlocking systems that influence each other at five levels: the microsystem, made up of small groups with face-to-face interaction; the mesosystem, made up of relationships between two or more small groups; the exosystem, which affects families through the mesosystem or microsystem; the macrosystem, or a society's culture and ideology; and the chrono-system, which adds the element of time to the system.

8. The developmental view considers families from their formation to their end. At each stage of the family life cycle, members must accomplish developmental tasks. These are related to the needs of members and to social expectations. More recently, developmental theories have expanded to include couple and parent "careers." This perspective forms much of the basis of this book.

How Do Researchers Get Information about Families?

Researchers use two approaches to studying families—quantitative and qualitative. Typical quantitative methods are surveys and experiments, which are followed by statistical analysis. Qualitative research uses in-depth interviews, direct observation, focus groups, and content analysis. Cross-sectional research compares people of different ages at the same moment in time. Longitudinal studies follow the same individuals for a period of time.

✓ Class Assignments

✓1. Select an occupation that deals with families. Do some research or interview someone who is familiar with that occupation. Try to learn how knowledge of the family is important in the occupation. You should find out how people in this pro-fession define families, how they think families function, and how they get infor-mation about families.

2. Often, cultural differences can be observed in religious customs. Interview a friend, neighbour, acquaintance, or classmate about the religious event most important to

his or her family. Find out what practices are followed. These may include worship, family events, and special foods or clothing. Learn how these have affected the person's relationship with others of the same faith and with people of other faiths. Discover the values the individual sees in this event.

Personal Assignments

The following assignments are designed to help you gain insight into your own experiences:

1. Think about your own family. What are some of the events that have occurred that might affect your ability, either positively or negatively, to provide service to others? Are there any individuals you might have difficulty helping? Why?
2. Make a list of the many statuses that you fill (e.g., student, friend, son/daughter, employee, parent). Which statuses are most important to you? Why? What is the role expectation for each status? Do you have any role conflicts or role strain related to family life?

Chapter 2

History, Culture, and Canadian Families

LEARNING OBJECTIVES

What is the difference between race and ethnicity?

What are some characteristics of the Canadian population?

What are some of the patterns of immigration to Canada?

What are some of the experiences of immigrants in Canada?

FIRST NATIONS

by Robyn Montour

Family History

I am a part of the people of the First Nations. I am a Mohawk, from the tribes of the Six Nations, also known as North American Indian or Iroquois. Both my parents are from within the Six Nations. My father, who is a Chief in the Mohawk council, is Mohawk and was born in Kahnawake, a Mohawk reserve. My mother was born in Detroit because of the iron working trade that many Mohawks were and still are a part of today, but she is also from Kahnawake. My family did not immigrate from anywhere, we only moved from different native lands, such as the Mohawk and Hudson River valleys and also along the St. Lawrence River. We were the first people to inhabit, occupy, and roam the lands of North America. The Creator, Shonkwaiah'tison, put us here.

Both my parents have full-time jobs and they share the household responsibilities. This is different from the past, because in the old days the men hunted and the women stayed home to care for the kids and the crops, but it is somewhat the norm nowadays. Throughout my childhood, I was taught my culture and the belief system of the traditional Mohawk, which is the ways of the longhouse: ceremonies, singing, dancing, and festivals. I was also taught some of the ways of the Catholic Church because my father's mother was one of the converted Catholics. But I was told that I could follow whatever I wanted, so I choose the traditional Mohawk way, and this is what I truly believe in, the creator, Shonkwaiah'tison. I was also taught to be respectful to whoever was around me and especially my elders because they were the ones with all the knowledge. I was taught not to discriminate against other people and to ignore others if that was what they wished to do. I feel that my family is different from the Mohawk families of the past, but this goes for almost everyone who lives in the modern world. With all the new technologies and so on, most families have changed in one way or another from the old days. Despite all the technological changes in my family, it is certain that one thing stayed the same, and that is that we still have the common beliefs and cultural backgrounds as other Mohawk families did in the olden days. I am very proud of my family and I feel that I was raised in a healthy and safe environment and I was always well taken care of. I am also very proud of my ethnic background despite the discrimination or negative actions taken against us. I would not change my family or my ethnic background for anything in the world.

Source: Robyn Montour/Vanier College. Found at: http://www.vaniercollege.qc.ca/tlc/publications/native-circle/native-circle-2003/robyn-montour.pdf

Canadian families have changed over time, and will continue to change, because the family, like all social institutions, is influenced by the larger social context. In the ecological model of the family (described in Chapter 1), this larger social context is called the macrosystem. The social context of Canada is a history of cultural change. The first people to inhabit this land were the various Aboriginal groups, from the Haida and Nisga'a of the West Coast to the Inuit of the North, the Blackfoot and Cree of the plains, the Iroquois and Mohawk of central Canada, and the Mi'kmaq of the East Coast. About 500 years ago, Europeans began to arrive and settle, first in the east, but gradually moving west across the country. The first colonists were the English and the French, and they brought with them their own cultures and family forms. Ever since, Canadian culture has been influenced and has evolved as a result of various waves of immigrant groups arriving and settling here.

In this chapter, we will examine the fascinating cultural diversity of Canadian families. The ever-changing mosaic that has defined Canadian society has also defined what is seen as a "normal" family. Many social policies reflect this image, and may have a negative impact on families that don't meet this standard. We will conclude by looking at the importance for all of us of differences and social attitudes.

Where Do I Fit In?

How is Robyn Montour's family different from your family? How is her family similar to yours?

Think about your own family . . .

1. What is your ethnic or cultural background?
2. In what ways would you say that your family is similar to or different from most Canadian families?

Racial and Ethnic Differences

Race and ethnicity are important social categories that can define who we are and how we are treated. While they are often grouped together, they are not the same thing. **Race** refers to physical differences between groups of people. The most common feature used to distinguish different races is skin colour—black, white, brown, yellow, or red. However, these categories are just as inaccurate as the simple colour scheme used to describe them. There is not enough genetic difference between people of different races to justify placing them in them separate groups. The reality is that there is just one human race (see Box 2.1). Another way to classify people is based on their culture. **Ethnicity** is the term used to refer to a group of people who share a common cultural heritage. Some examples of ethnic groups are Chinese, Italian, Haitian, or Ukrainian. While cultures are more real than races, classifying people by ethnicity can still be a complex undertaking, especially in a multicultural society such as Canada. Think of all the people who identify themselves as Greek-Canadian, Polish-Canadian, or Vietnamese-Canadian. With a growing number of relationships between people of different ethnicities, we can expect this cultural complexity to increase even more.

race: a system of classifying people based on physical characteristics such as skin colour

ethnicity: term used to specify a group of people who share a common cultural heritage

BOX 2.1   American Anthropological Association Statement on "Race" (May 17, 1998)

In the United States both scholars and the general public have been conditioned to viewing human races as natural and separate divisions within the human species based on visible physical differences. With the vast expansion of scientific knowledge in this century, however, it has become clear that human populations are not unambiguous, clearly demarcated, biologically distinct groups. Evidence from the analysis of genetics (e.g., DNA) indicates that most physical variation, about 94%, lies within so-called racial groups. Conventional geographic "racial" groupings differ from one another only in about 6% of their genes. This means that there is greater variation within "racial" groups than between them. In neighboring populations there is much overlapping of genes and their phenotypic (physical) expressions. Throughout history whenever different groups have come into contact, they have interbred. The continued sharing of genetic materials has maintained all of humankind as a single species . . .

Historical research has shown that the idea of "race" has always carried more meanings than mere physical differences; indeed, physical variations in the human species have no meaning except the social ones that humans put on them. Today scholars in many fields argue that "race" . . . was a social mechanism invented during the 18th century to refer to those populations brought together in colonial America: the English and other European settlers, the conquered Indian peoples, and those peoples of Africa brought in to provide slave labor . . .

Source: American Anthropological Association, AAA Statement on "Race," May 17, 1998. Found at: http://www.aaanet.org/stmts/racepp.htm

Census Definitions of Race and Ethnicity

In the first census, which was conducted in 1871, Canadians were asked questions about their age, sex, religion, and race. In the following years, the choices for "race," "ethnicity," and "ancestry" changed many times. In the 1891 Census there was no question about race, but then it reappeared, and from 1901 to 1941 Canadians were asked to identify their race. Eventually, the race question was dropped and Canadians were instead asked to identify their ethnic origin (Boyd et al., 2000).

Collecting data on ethnicity and interpreting the results is complicated and challenging due to a number of factors. First, the concept of ethnicity is fluid and difficult to define. Second, respondents' understanding or views about their ethnicity, awareness of their family background, number of generations in Canada, the length of time since immigration, and the social context at the time of the census can all affect the reporting of ethnicity from one census to another. Third, increasing intermarriage or unions among various groups has led to an increase in the reporting of multiple ancestries. Fourth, changes in the format of the census question and the examples provided on the questionnaire have affected reporting patterns over time. For example, the inclusion of "Canadian" as an ethnic choice has led to an increase in this category (Statistics Canada, 2010b).

In the 1996 Census, for the first time, people were asked whether they were a member of one of the population groups defined as a visible minority. A **visible minority** is a person, other than an Aboriginal, who is non-Caucasian in race or non-white in colour (Statistics Canada, 2012c). In Canada, the visible minority population consists mainly of the following groups: Chinese, South Asian, black, Arab, West Asian, Filipino, Southeast Asian, Latin American, Japanese, and Korean. An **Aboriginal** person is one who is First Nations, Inuit, or Métis (Statistics Canada, 2012d). In Canada today, the Aboriginal population is divided into four categories: North American First Nations people registered under the *Indian Act*, North American First Nations people not registered under the *Indian Act* (the non-status population), Métis, and Inuit (Statistics Canada, 2009i). Just as we have seen with the definition of the term "family" in Chapter 1, there are many different ways to describe groups of people. Although Statistics Canada still uses the term "Indian" as part of its definition of Aboriginal, many in the Aboriginal population prefer the term "First Nations." The legal definition may differ from social definitions, and individuals may have their own personal definitions of their racial and ethnic identity. The 1996 Census was also the first in which "Canadian" was included as one of the ethnic origin choices. These constant changes to the census categories confirm that race and ethnicity are social constructs rather than biological categories.

visible minority: a person, other than an Aboriginal, who is non-Caucasian in race or non-white in colour

Aboriginal: a person who is First Nations, Inuit, or Métis

Minority and Dominant Groups

A **minority group** refers to any group that holds less power than the **dominant group**. Sometimes, having a numeric majority doesn't necessarily make this the dominant group. For over 50 years, whites, who were a numeric minority in South Africa, passed apartheid laws that discriminated against blacks, the native majority. But usually the dominant group tends to be a country's numeric majority as well.

minority group: any group that holds less power

dominant group: a group that has the greatest power but not necessarily the greatest numbers

The Canadian Population

From the first Aboriginal people, who arrived thousands of years ago, the area that is now Canada has been populated by waves of immigrants. The social structure and cultural norms and values have changed with each passing wave.

Aboriginal Peoples

Historically, First Nations families in North America did not have just one pattern of family relationships. Clan lineages, such as Iroquoian and Pacific Coast societies, held rights to specific tracts of land for farming, hunting, or offshore fishing and controlled specific trading routes. In the Iroquois Confederacy, conflicts and other issues were settled by consensus rather than force. Pacific Coast societies used feasts or potlatches as a way of handling conflicts and settling such issues as inheritance rights (Ray, 1996). Under the rules of clan membership, individuals were required to marry outside the clan to which they belonged. Over generations, every family in a community was related by descent or marriage to every other family in the community (Royal Commission on Aboriginal Peoples, 1996).

Small migratory hunting groups developed in the subarctic and Arctic and included the Inuit, northern Anishinaabe, and Swampy Cree. These groups consisted of a few closely related hunters and their wives, children, parents, and grandparents. These societies were based on social bonds rather than rigid territorial boundaries (Ray, 1996).

Plains buffalo-hunting societies, such as the Blackfoot, resembled both the clan and migratory groups. For most of the year, their organization was similar to that of the nations of the northern forests. During late summer, the buffalo-hunting and sun-dance camps were as large as the winter villages of the Iroquoian and Pacific Coast nations. In these societies, status was earned not through gift-giving or holding territorial rights, but through men's prowess in fighting and hunting (Ray, 1996).

To Aboriginal people, the family signifies parents and children living together in a household. But it also has a much broader meaning. Family also means an extended network of other relatives, such as grandparents, aunts, uncles and cousins (Royal Commission on Aboriginal Peoples, 1996). The traditional means of teaching proper behaviour and community-held values is through storytelling. By attending and observing such activities as weddings, funerals, and namings, children learn the customs and values of their community (Pepper & White, 1996).

Extended family networks often take responsibility for the care and nurture of their members. These networks provide a stable base for young people who leave reserves for education or employment. Especially in cities, "families of the heart"—that is, voluntary groups that aim to preserve traditional ways—are assuming some of the functions of extended family members. Community services on reserves are also filling part of the role of the extended family, for example by providing home care for the elderly. Aboriginal child and family services provide prevention, protection, and foster care services, and are more successful than provincial agencies in finding Aboriginal foster homes. However, legal jurisdiction for child welfare often does not rest with these agencies (Castellano, 2002; National Council of Welfare, 2007a).

During the 18th century, the expanding fur trade resulted in a growing number of mixed children of First Nations and European parentage. These people established communities separate from those of First Nations and Europeans and generally married among themselves. A new Aboriginal people emerged—the Métis—with their own unique culture, traditions, language (Michif), collective consciousness, and sense of nationhood (Métis National Council, 2012). In 1982, the repatriated Constitution recognized the Métis people as one of the three Aboriginal peoples of Canada.

In recent years, the Aboriginal population has been growing nearly six times faster than the Canadian population as a whole and has passed the one-million mark. There are three reasons for this trend. First, Aboriginal people as a group are younger; therefore, more are of child-bearing age. Second, more individuals are identifying themselves as Aboriginal. Third, residents of reserves have been more completely counted. The largest increase has been among those who said they were Métis. Although the largest number of Aboriginal people lives in British Columbia and Ontario, the proportion of the population is higher in Manitoba, Saskatchewan, and the territories. Over half (54 percent) live in cities. As a whole, the opportunities of Aboriginal people are more limited than those of the general Canadian population, but the gap is decreasing (Statistics Canada, 2009).

Aboriginal cultural practices are also showing new life. In non-reserve areas, about one-third of Aboriginal children are involved in traditional cultural activities, such as learning from elders and taking part in drum and dance groups. There is also evidence that many individuals are learning an Aboriginal language (O'Donnell, 2008). And Idle No More, a grassroots social movement whose issues include the sovereignty, rights, and respect for the treaties of First Nations people, hopes to reduce environmental damage and social inequality (CBC, 2013).

English Canadians and French Canadians

The character of English Canadian society had roots in Britain. Canada became part of the British Empire as a result of conquest and colonization. In order to further expansionist goals, the traditional "masculine" characteristics were encouraged—enterprise, aggression, and responsibility for the weaker or less civilized (Mann, 2001). Many emigrants from the British Isles were troublemakers who were "sent to the colonies" or younger sons whose families could not support them. They thus had incentives to seek their individual fortunes. Many were members of various Protestant denominations and sects. This religious diversity did not encourage community-wide cooperation, as did the Roman Catholic Church in Quebec or Aboriginal cultural and religious practices. English Canadians have always seen the family as responsible for its members. The chief responsibility was to nuclear family members. Aboriginal families, and to a lesser degree French-Canadian families, usually value ties with extended family members more than English Canadians do.

In Quebec, the French government encouraged a society that mirrored the homeland and discouraged dissidents. The *Quebec Act* of 1774 defined the borders of Quebec and preserved the French civil law tradition and the *seigneurial* system of land ownership (Foulds, 2012). Traditional Quebec society, which continued until about 1960, emphasized four elements. First, the Roman Catholic Church defined both family roles and educational goals. Second, a rural lifestyle was central. Third, large families were idealized. Men were patriarchs and women found their chief glory in motherhood. The fourth underpinning was the French language and culture (Valois, 1993). If English Canadians valued "masculine" qualities, French Canadians were perceived as "feminine"—religious, elegant, and civilized (Mann, 2001).

A new definition of Quebec identity blossomed during the Quiet Revolution of the 1960s. Gone was the authority of the Roman Catholic Church. Education replaced religion as the chief authority on values. A modern industrial economy replaced the rural lifestyle. The large family lost its prestige under the influences of the sexual revolution and the contraceptive pill. Only the importance of the French language remained unchanged, but it was made central only to Quebec society, rather than to French Canadian culture as a whole (Laplante, 2006; Valois, 1993). The provincial government took over social services, and Quebec's family support programs have become the strongest in Canada (Conseil de la famille et de l'enfance, 2008). There are other differences between Quebec and the rest of Canada; for example, more couples in Quebec choose to live together instead of marry (Milan et al., 2007). Even though they speak the same language, francophones living outside Quebec differ from Quebeckers because they do not have the same official supports for language and culture.

Other Immigrant Groups

The 1901 Census recorded about 25 different ethnic groups in Canada. People who reported Aboriginal, British, or French ancestries, were the majority of the population at that time. Over the next century, successive waves of immigration to Canada have increased the cultural diversity of the nation's population. The 2006 Census enumerated more than 200 different ethnic origins, and 11 had passed the one-million mark. A little over 10 million people reported Canadian as their ethnic ancestry, making this the largest group (Statistics Canada, 2010).

The diversity of Canada's population will continue to increase significantly over the next couple of decades. By 2031, between 25 percent and 28 percent of the population will be foreign-born, about half in Asia, and between 29 percent and 32 percent will belong to a visible minority group, nearly double the proportion reported by the 2006 Census. The visible minority population is likely to increase rapidly among the Canadian-born, many of whom are children and grandchildren of immigrants (Statistics Canada, 2011).

The vast majority of people belonging to a visible minority group will live in cities. By 2031, visible minority groups will make up 63 percent of the population of Toronto, 59 percent of the population in Vancouver, and 31 percent of the population in Montreal. By 2031, nearly half of Canadians aged 15 and over will be foreign-born or will have at least one foreign-born parent (Statistics Canada, 2011).

Multiracial Families

Multiracial families have nearly always existed, though at times they were hidden or made illegal. They have recently received increased attention, especially since the election of Barack Obama in 2008 as president of the United States. His relatives have Indonesian and Malaysian as well as Kenyan and white American roots (Marcovitz, 2009). An increasing number of people report that they belong to more than one ethnic group (Austin, 2004; Statistics Canada, 2013d). Mixed-race families have several variations: marriage and common-law unions between visible and non-visible minority individuals; children born to such parents, both within and outside marriage; and children adopted internationally or transracially within Canada.

Ethnic Origin	Total Responses	Single Responses	Multiple Responses
Canadian	10 563 805	5 834 535	4 729 265
English	6 509 500	1 312 570	5 196 930
French	5 077 215	1 170 620	3 710 675
Scottish	4 714 970	544 440	4 170 530
Irish	4 544 870	506 445	4 038 425
German	3 203 330	608 520	2 594 805
Italian	1 488 425	700 845	787 580
Chinese	1 487 580	1 210 945	276 635
North American Aboriginal	1 836 035	628 460	1 207 575
Ukrainian	1 251 170	276 055	975 110
Dutch (Netherlands)	1 067 245	297 885	769 355
Polish	1 010 705	255 135	755 565
East Indian	1 165 145	919 155	245 985
Russian	550 520	107 300	443 220

TABLE 2.1 Ethnic Origins of Canadians, 2011

Source: Adapted from: T. Chui, K. Trans, & H. Maheux. Statistics Canada. 2007. *Top 10 countries of birth of recent immigrants, 1981 to 2006* (table 1). "Immigration in Canada: A Portrait of the Foreign-born Population, 2006 Census." Catalogue No. 97557-XIE. Ottawa, Ontario. Statistics Canada.

Notes:

1. Respondents who reported multiple ethnic origins are counted more than once in this table because they are included in the multiple responses for each origin they reported. For example, a respondent who reported "English and Scottish" would be included in the multiple responses for English and for Scottish.
2. Only groups with more than 500 000 total responses are included.

The 2006 Census found, over a five-year period, mixed marriages and common-law unions had increased five times faster than all unions combined. Most (247 600) involved a person from a visible minority paired with someone who was not. Nearly 42 000 were couples from different minority groups (Statistics Canada, 2008d). Research in the United States found that the most common combination there involved black men and white women (Batson et al., 2006). Mixed-race couples may experience difficulties arising from their different cultural traditions or from the prejudice of relatives. Indeed, some interracial marriages are more likely to end in divorce than those of same-race partners. Marriages of Asian–white couples, however, tend to be stable (Zhang & Van Hook,

2009). "Firsts" are a challenge for any couple—first serious disagreement, first child, first death of a parent or sibling. They are more stressful for interracial or intercultural couples because of the difference in their perspectives. In successful unions, both partners usually need to adjust their cultural expectations (Lowe, 2006; Roer-Strier & Ben Ezra, 2006; Rosenblatt, 2009).

No one knows how many multiracial children are in Canada because they are not counted as a specific category. In general, both mixed-race and same-race couples have children at the same rate (Fu, 2008). Brothers and sisters in multiracial families may assume different racial identities based on their appearance, their attachment to a particular parent, and their experiences with racial groups. Sometimes they identify with their visible minority parent because that is how society and sometimes their parents see them. Often they feel as if they don't belong to either group (Austin, 2004; Harris, 2003; Laszloffy, 2002a).

Many children have been adopted internationally and transracially. The first agency-sponsored interracial adoptions took place in 1959 in Montreal. International adoptions have increased in the years since then (Ward, 1984). Many of the children from abroad have been members of visible minorities. From 1995 to 2004, nearly 20 000 such adoptions took place. Most children went to families in Quebec, followed by Ontario. In recent years, China has been the main source country. Inter-country adoptions have declined from a high of 2180 in 2003 (Adoption Council of Canada, 2005; Hilborn, 2009). Parents adopt internationally and transracially mainly because they want young children. Some also give humanitarian reasons (Cole, 1984). After a terrible earthquake in Haiti in early 2010, immigration departments acted to fast-track the foreign-adoption approval process of orphans (Canadian Press, 2010).

Since the 1970s, transracial adoptions have been condemned for a number of reasons. For example, they have been labelled a form of genocide—the removal of a people's children. There have also been concerns about adoptees' identity development when neither parent is racially similar. Parents' colour-blindness can leave children feeling racially undecided (Morrison, 2004; Ward, 1984).

We will be taking another look at some of these issues in later chapters.

Time to Review

1. What is the difference between race and ethnicity?
2. Name some characteristics of Aboriginal families.
3. What are some of the qualities of English Canadian and French Canadian families?
4. What are some of the features of the families of other immigrant groups?
5. Describe some characteristics of multiracial families.

Patterns of Immigration to Canada

It is impossible to talk about immigrants as a single group. Many factors have affected who was allowed to immigrate from where and how many could come in a particular period. While each individual family made the decision to immigrate, the social context at the time had a significant impact on how easy or difficult it was for them to do so and what their experience likely was when they arrived. Over the last century, key factors have included the desire to maintain the "British" character of Canada, the need for labour to develop the country, and humanitarian motives.

The Desire to Retain Canada's "British" Character

Before 1900, many newcomers came from the British Isles and the United States, including many who were loyal to the British at the time of the American Revolution. For many years, both federal and provincial governments placed many barriers to the immigration of non-whites, members of certain religious groups, and others regarded as being hard to assimilate into British-based culture. For example, Chinese people, who originally came to Canada because of labour shortages in mining, railway construction, and domestic services, faced growing prejudice. The result was passage of numerous bills to restrict the civil rights of the Chinese, such as the right to vote, to enter certain professions, or to reside in a provincial home for the aged and infirm. The infamous Head Tax was imposed to discourage Chinese immigrants. In 1923, the federal government passed the *Chinese Immigration Act*, which made it nearly impossible for Chinese individuals to enter Canada and thus prevented family reunification until it was repealed in 1947—the result was a society of "married bachelors." Concerned that many Asians were coming to Canada by way of Hawaii, the federal government ruled that immigrants had to come from their lands of origin in a continuous journey. Because there were no ships coming directly from India, potential immigrants were automatically disqualified. At various times, Ukrainians, Mennonites, Jews, Hutterites, and Doukhobors were discouraged or banned from immigration (Knowles, 2000; Li, 1998). Black people originally came to Canada as slaves; slavery existed in Eastern Canada until the early 1800s. Some came as black Loyalists. Although they were promised land and adequate food and shelter, many did not receive them (see Box 2.2). In 2001, over 80 percent of black people living in Halifax were at least third-generation Canadians (Milan & Tran, 2004).

BOX 2.2   Africville: A Community Displaced

The community of Africville was started by black immigrants who were former slaves and had fought for the British Crown during the War of 1812 with the promise of freedom for their participation. When the war ended, they were relocated to Nova Scotia.

From the very beginning, the people of Africville lived in a society that was overtly racist toward people of African descent. In the 1850s, railroad tracks were laid straight through the community and land was expropriated from Africville residents for this purpose. City service facilities not wanted elsewhere were dumped on Africville. The city closed its sewage disposal pits in the south end of Halifax and relocated them to the edge of Africville in 1858. An infectious diseases hospital was built on a hill overlooking the community in the 1870s. Finally, the city moved the large open city dump, labelled a health menace by the city council and resisted by residents in other areas, to a site just 100 metres from Africville homes.

All these things could be done because the Africvilleans were black and poor. They had no social, political, or economic power to stop the city from using their community as a dump, in every sense, and from taking their land.

Between 1965 and 1970, the community of Africville was bulldozed. The first building to be destroyed was the community church—and this happened at three o'clock in the morning. Some residents had their homes demolished while they were in the hospital. Others were given only a few hours to pack their belongings before the bulldozers roared in. Africville disappeared and its people scattered—some into public housing in Halifax and others to different areas of the province.

The attitude of white Haligonians to Africville is reflected in the following newspaper announcement as the community was being bulldozed: "Soon Africville will be but a name. And in the not too distant future that too, mercifully, will be forgotten."

Source: Irvine Carvery, Africville: A Community Displaced, Library and Archives Canada. Found at: http://www.collectionscanada.gc.ca/northern-star/033005-2601-e.html

There are many other examples of prejudice and racism. Between the two world wars, the Ku Klux Klan recruited members in Canada. In addition to visible minorities, they were against Jews, Catholics, and French Canadians (Appleblatt, 1976). Just before World War II, one group in Toronto, the Pit Gang, flaunted the swastika at a sports event involving a Jewish team; the result was a riot (Levitt & Shaffer, 1987). In the 1930s, Jews fleeing Nazi Germany were turned away by Canada. During World War II, Japanese from the West Coast were interned inland, losing their businesses, houses, and other property in the process. They were not released until after the war. Even then, many were encouraged to return to Japan, even though they were born in Canada and were citizens (Knowles, 2000). More recently, following the attacks on New York and Washington on September 11, 2001, Muslims and those perceived as Muslims suffered discrimination and attacks (McDonald & Quell, 2008; Sykes, 2008).

The Need for Labour

Often, the desire to keep Canada "British" conflicted with the need for labour, for example in mining, lumber, and railway construction, and the desire to develop agriculture across the Prairies. Chinese, Sikh, and Japanese workers were brought in because they would accept low wages and primitive conditions in work camps, which British immigrants would not. From about 1890 to 1914, Ukrainian farmers were encouraged to settle in clusters across the Prairies. In part, this strategy was designed to attract still more immigrants. Eventually, their communities stretched from Manitoba to Alberta. Later, Ukrainians became a source of cheap labour in other types of work. Italians worked in mining and manufacturing. After World War II, some companies were allowed to bring groups of workers into Canada in a "bulk-labour" program (Knowles, 2000).

In boom times, such as the early 1900s or after World War II, both employers and the federal government supported the influx of workers. During recessions and the Great Depression, immigration was discouraged. Unions opposed bringing in cheap labour because of its impact on wages. During the recession immediately following World War I, there was pressure on companies to release foreign labourers so as to provide jobs for returning veterans. One company that complied was International Nickel in Sudbury, Ontario; it fired 2200 of 3200 employees, most of them foreign-born (Knowles, 2000). Thus, preferential treatment for certain groups in the population had dire results for immigrant families.

Humanitarian Motives

Many groups have been admitted to Canada for humanitarian reasons. For example, fugitive slaves who escaped from the United States came to Canada once slavery was banned here in 1793 and abolished in 1834. The principal end of the Underground Railway, as the escape network came to be called, was in southwestern Ontario (Prince, 2004). Doukhobors, persecuted by the Russians for refusing military service and for their communal ways, migrated to Saskatchewan and then British Columbia. Others included Jewish war orphans and Jews expelled from Romania during the inter-war period; Estonian boat people after World War II; Vietnamese boat people in the late 1970s; Hungarians fleeing an unsuccessful uprising against their Communist government in 1956–57; American draft dodgers and deserters during the conflict in Vietnam; and Asians expelled from Uganda in 1972. Between 1947 and 1962, nearly 250 000 refugees and people displaced by World War II, mainly European, were admitted to Canada, more than to all other overseas countries combined. More recently, the Minister of Citizenship, Immigration and Multiculturalism announced that Canada would make a commitment to resettle up to 1300 Syrian refugees displaced by the crisis in Syria (Citizenship and Immigration Canada, 2013).

Sometimes, strings were attached. Polish war veterans were required to work on a farm for a year. Some refugees were well educated. Several Hungarians, for instance, had comprised a large part of the faculties of forestry and mining engineering at the University of Sopron; they were integrated into the University of British Columbia and the University of Toronto (Knowles, 2000).

Changes to Citizenship and Immigration since World War II

Before 1947, Canadians were officially regarded as British subjects. In addition, married women automatically assumed the nationality of their husbands, an easy way to bypass standard requirements but also a way to lose citizenship. The *Canadian Citizenship Act* of 1947 changed that. It created the category of Canadian citizen and permitted married women to be citizens in their own right. In the early 1960s, limitations were placed on which relatives could be sponsored for immigration. New regulations nearly eliminated racial discrimination among unsponsored immigrants, as long as they had a job waiting for them or could support themselves while they found one, were not criminals or terrorists, and did not have a disease that was a danger to public health. Immigration appeals, allowed on many grounds, created a logjam in the system. In 1973, appeal rules were made tighter. To reduce the backlog, in what amounted to an amnesty, about 39 000 legal and illegal immigrants were granted landed immigrant status.

The *Immigration Act* that was introduced in 1976 established four categories of immigrants. The latest revision to the act, in 2008, defined 12 categories of immigrants in four classes: (1) the family class, whereby nuclear family members and aging parents and grandparents can be sponsored; (2) the economic class, which admits skilled workers, entrepreneurs, and investors; (3) the refugee class; and (4) other immigrants, which includes those admitted on humanitarian and compassionate grounds (Citizenship and Immigration Canada, 2012b). In 2008, the federal government also passed Bill C-50, which gives greater power to the Minister of Immigration and Citizenship to designate who should and should not be allowed into Canada. A major criticism of the bill is that it bypasses parliamentary oversight of the fairness and practicality of who comes to Canada (Rotberg, 2012).

Thus, the pattern of immigration to Canada has shifted dramatically over the past several years. Before 1967, immigration rules favoured those from Europe or countries of European heritage, such as the United States. Now nearly three-quarters of immigrants come from Africa, Asia, the Caribbean, and Latin America, and only 16 percent from Europe. Currently, the largest group of recent immigrants is Chinese, especially those from the People's Republic of China (Statistics Canada, 2013d). (See Table 2.2.) In 2006, South Asians were the largest visible minority group (Statistics Canada, 2013f).

Most newcomers settle in Ontario, British Columbia, and Quebec, and especially in the large cities of Toronto, Vancouver, and Montreal. Many newcomers move into particular neighbourhoods in large cities. Some of these minority neighbourhoods have replaced earlier enclaves such as "Little Italy" or "Little Greece" (Chui et al., 2007). Under the Canada–Quebec Accord, Quebec is the only province that has independent authority in selecting and integrating newcomers to the province. Immigrants settling in Quebec are more likely to come from French-speaking countries (Citizenship and Immigration Canada, 2012c).

A new law amending the *Citizenship Act* came into effect on April 17, 2009. Under the old rules, it was possible for Canadians to pass on their citizenship to endless generations born outside Canada. To protect the value of Canadian citizenship for the future, the new law limits—with a few exceptions—citizenship by descent to one generation born outside Canada (Citizenship and Immigration Canada, 2010b).

TABLE 2.2 — Top 10 Countries of Birth of Recent Immigrants, 2011 and 1981

	Order 2011	1981
1	People's Republic of China	United Kingdom
2	India	Vietnam
3	United Kingdom	United States of America
4	Philippines	India
5	United States of America	Philippines
6	Italy	Jamaica
7	Hong Kong	Hong Kong
8	Germany	Portugal
9	Vietnam	Taiwan
10	Pakistan	People's Republic of China

Source: Adapted from T. Chui, K. Trans, and H. Maheux. 2007. Statistics Canada. *Immigration in Canada: A Portrait of the Foreign-born Population.* 2006 Census. Catalogue No. 97557-XIE. Pg. 10, Table 1.

Time to Review

1. What are the different factors that have influenced immigration in Canada?
2. How have these factors influenced the nature of immigration in Canada?

The Experience of Immigrants in Canada

Many immigrants have seen Canada as the "promised land" with many opportunities for bettering themselves. For some, the promise takes a long time to be fulfilled. Whatever their status in their home country, immigrants to Canada immediately become part of a minority group. The types of policies in place at the time of their arrival can either facilitate or complicate adaptation. So too can the existence of other social networks, such as family or an established cultural community. Immigration is often a stressful event, and this can affect family members differently. In this section, we will look at how immigration affects families economically, culturally, and socially, as well as how the experience can affect each family member differently.

Officially, the Canadian government supports the integration of immigrants. Federal, provincial, and municipal governments offer public assistance by subsidizing classes to learn English and French or programs to find a job. At the same time, an official policy of multiculturalism is promoted through the public recognition—and funding—of ethnic diversity (Bloemraad, 2006).

Soon after they arrive, most immigrants want to find work. But getting hired can be challenging. A study of immigrants who arrived between October 2000 and September 2001 found that, six months after their arrival, 72 percent had tried to find jobs, but only 43 percent were successful. Four years after arrival, the proportion looking for work dropped to 49 percent, suggesting improved employment status over time, but the unemployment rate of 19 percent was still higher than the Canadian average of 6.8 percent in 2005. In spite of substantial gains in terms of increased employment, new immigrants still faced challenges in finding work (Xue, 2007). Even when they do find work, many immigrants do not find work in the same field as in their former country. Reasons include a lack of Canadian experience; problems in having their qualifications recognized, especially if these were obtained in a developing country; and lack of fluency in English or French.

Despite the fact that immigrants are increasingly better educated and more highly skilled, most take longer to achieve employment and income levels similar to those of the Canadian-born population. One possible explanation for this discrepancy is immigrant's low social capital—that is, the personal and professional networks they are able to mobilize in their economic interests (Thomas, 2011). Social capital plays an important role in helping immigrants find work. Friendship networks are the most important resource on which newcomers rely for employment, especially on first arriving. After six months in Canada, only 11 percent of newcomers have received help from government agencies, but this doubles to 22 percent after four years (Xue, 2007).

On average, incomes are lower for immigrants than for Canadian-born workers (see Figure 2.1). In 2008, the average hourly wage of a working age Canadian-born employee was $23.72, while the average hourly wage of a Canadian immigrant employee was $21.44—a gap of $2.28 per hour. The gap was even wider for employees with university degrees. When comparing immigrants aged 25 to 54 with university degrees with their Canadian-born counterparts, there was a $5 hourly wage gap in 2008 (Gilmore, 2009). Refugees have the poorest employment rate, probably because of severe problems in their home countries and language barriers. The disadvantage both in finding work and in level of income may continue for many years. Even if they do find a job, many new immigrants find it difficult to balance work and family for reasons ranging from lack of knowledge about daycare and public transportation to rigid and unusual work schedules (Lochhead, 2003; Picot et al., 2007; Schellenberg & Maheux, 2007). For adults wanting to work, finding a job that pays well has an important effect on the experience of an immigrant family. Later in this book, we will discuss the many ways poverty affects family life.

Although many immigrants live with relatives or friends at first, most move to their own houses or apartments soon after arrival (Chui et al., 2007). Many live in ethnic neighbourhoods that support their cultural traditions. Yet there can be a

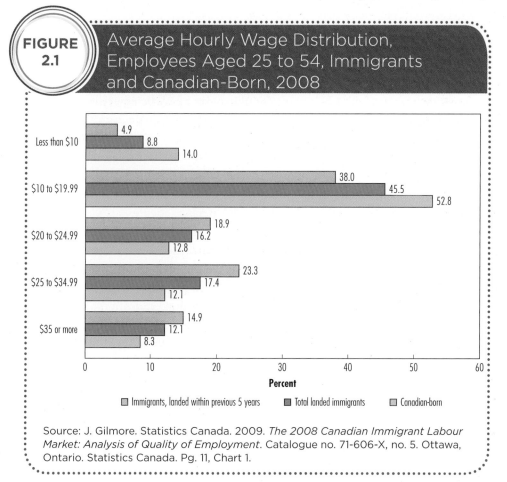

FIGURE 2.1

Average Hourly Wage Distribution, Employees Aged 25 to 54, Immigrants and Canadian-Born, 2008

Source: J. Gilmore. Statistics Canada. 2009. *The 2008 Canadian Immigrant Labour Market: Analysis of Quality of Employment*. Catalogue no. 71-606-X, no. 5. Ottawa, Ontario. Statistics Canada. Pg. 11, Chart 1.

misfit between accustomed family roles and Canadian realities. One such area is in gender roles. When men cannot find work that will support their families, their wives will also need to work. Thus, women become co-providers, with a resulting growth in their power in making family decisions. Their husbands do not always welcome this change. In addition, women may still be expected to fulfill their traditional homemaker role, with the danger of overload and exhaustion (Kim & Woolfolk, 2007). Older members are an important resource for immigrant families. Women do housework and care for grandchildren to allow their children to work full time. Men more often do outside work such as gardening (Treas, 2008). Both South Asian and Chinese seniors usually live in family-oriented households, either their own or those of relatives (Chui et al., 2005; Tran et al., 2005). Life there is not always peaceful, however. Many Asian elders are upset by their children's and grandchildren's lack of respect (Parker, 2004).

Immigration can also mean separation from family members. Female domestic workers, for example, may leave children and extended family members behind when they come to Canada on temporary visas. Children may feel abandoned and want to stay with caregivers to whom they have become attached. Both caregivers in the original country and immigrant parents may have problems with authority and discipline. Once they are reunited with their children, mothers may have difficulties developing relationships with them (Dreby, 2007; Kim & Woolfolk, 2007; Tyyskä, 2007). Some form family-like relationships with others in their situation. Many keep in touch through letters, phone calls, and email (Tran et al., 2005). The immigrant woman who comes to Canada with her husband's family and leaves her own relatives behind in the old country may be especially isolated and have few sources of support if she has conflicts with his parents or siblings. It is even more difficult for her if she does not know English or French, because she cannot gain access to services outside her ethnic community (Bush et al., 2010; Tyyskä, 2007).

Many immigrants, especially the more recent newcomers, retain a strong sense of belonging to their ethnic or cultural group. A person's identity as "Canadian" increases with the number of generations since immigration. Many families keep their ethnic identity in various ways—food preference is a common example. Other practices are tied to dress codes, for instance the hijab (head covering) of Muslim women or the turbans of Sikh men. Cultural practices are often modified in North America. A newspaper story described a Muslim graduation prom that included dinner, entertainment, and prayers, with males and females in separate rooms (Anderssen, 2009). Arranged marriages may be combined with individual choice, with parents suggesting several suitable candidates and the individual making the final selection (Saleem, 2003).

Sometimes, cultural practices arouse more substantial condemnation if they violate mainstream Canadian values. Two practices that have received much publicity in recent years are female genital mutilation and "honour" killings, whereby men kill female relatives who have "shamed" them. These are culturally based practices in parts of Africa, the Middle East, and South Asia (Hollinger, 2007). A study at the University of Sherbrooke found that there have been 12 victims of honour killings in Canada since 1999 (Daly, 2012).

Differences of experience within ethnic groups may arise from the individual's social class, religion, level of education, and which part of the home country the person came from. Some immigrants closely follow traditional ways, while others keep some customs from their homelands but otherwise blend in with mainstream society (Tran et al., 2005). Immigrants who left their former countries by choice differ from refugees, who were forced to leave their home countries. The former, for example, can keep up family connections in their homeland. Not all refugees are from visible minorities—for example, those from the former Yugoslavia and Serbia, who, like most other refugees, experienced terror and violence that can continue to affect their family relationships in Canada (Beiser et al., 1995).

Children of immigrants may have difficulty growing up in two cultures. At school and by their friends and the media, they are encouraged to be independent, spontaneous, and outspoken. At home, many are expected to be modest, respectful, and concerned with the family as a whole. Thus, there can be a clash of values. Parents may emphasize thrift and saving so that the family can get ahead economically, while children hope for luxuries like designer clothing and cellphones. Some feel pressure from their parents to excel in school and extracurricular activities. As they settle into Canadian ways, some children become less willing to speak the language they share with their parents. As much as parents may want them to integrate, many feel sad when they see their children losing the language and culture of the homeland. Even if children continue to speak to their parents in the native language at home, their ability to communicate in this language may stay at a childish level while their fluency in the mainstream language improves (Harris, 2009). Immigration is a difficult experience and often leads to an increased need for interdependence as parents and children rely on each other to successfully cope with the pressures of adapting to a new society (Chen et al., 2006). As a result, there may be problems in communication within the family and with maintaining the parents' authority. The experience of children of immigrants will be further discussed in Chapter 6.

Time to Review

1. What are some of the challenges faced by immigrants when they first arrive in Canada?
2. What factors can facilitate or hinder the adaptation of new immigrants?

Is Being Different Acceptable?

In theory, Canada is a country that has valued acceptance and embraced diversity. In practice, there are many regrettable examples that these principles have not always been followed. Many of the first missionaries and government officials saw Aboriginal customs as backwards, and they tried to wipe them out. One way was by taking children from their homes and educating them in residential schools, where the children were isolated from their families and culture. They were often subjected to a harsh, military-like regime in the schools, and many suffered emotional, physical, and sexual abuse. The schools cut them off from models of healthy family interaction, so institutional graduates had few skills and little knowledge when they came to raise their own families (Sinclair, 2007).

Earlier in this chapter, we defined minority and dominant groups, but we need to look at several aspects of the relationship between these groups if we are to understand its impact on families. According to structural functionalists, when large numbers of people share the same values and beliefs, change will happen slowly. New immigrants are encouraged to absorb the dominant social scripts from many sources in society and to base their lives on them. From the conflict perspective, social inequality comes about because those with power resist change. People who do not fit the accepted social script and who do not have power can encounter serious difficulties. As a minority group, immigrants have little influence to compel the powerful majority to change. Feminist theorists focus on gender inequalities, both in Canadian culture and in the culture of origin. They will examine the particular challenges that immigrant women face. It is also enlightening to examine the communication and interaction between individuals. Each new immigrant has a unique experience and has his or her own story to tell. Symbolic interactionists focus on these personal narratives in order to better understand the immigrant experience.

Prejudice and Discrimination

prejudice: a negative attitude toward an entire group of people

Many Canadians accept and even encourage differences. We point with pride to our federal *Charter of Rights and Freedoms*, provincial legislation recognizing the fundamental rights of all people, and our multicultural society. Nonetheless, there are limits to what we view as socially acceptable. **Prejudice** is a negative attitude toward an entire group of people. Over the years, many groups of immigrants have faced prejudice.

discrimination: negative treatment of a group of people based on prejudice

People who are prejudiced may express their intolerance. Members of a minority group may experience negative actions, or **discrimination**, by the majority, and thus be denied political, economic, and social rights. During World War II, for instance, Japanese Canadians were interned far from the West Coast because they were seen as dangerous aliens (Knowles, 2000). Even recently, 20 percent of visible minority individuals, blacks and Japanese more than others, reported that they have experienced discrimination (Sykes, 2008). Women have been discriminated against throughout much of history, as when they have not been allowed to own property or to vote. In fact, many argue that women are still disadvantaged with respect to pay and opportunities for promotion. In much of Canada, social acceptability is based on white, middle-class, and male norms, and relies on values that have come from Canada's British and Christian heritage (Kallen, 2003; White & Klein, 2008).

Discrimination based on majority values can profoundly affect the family life of minority group members. Child welfare workers who belong to the majority group may regard the traditional child-rearing methods of some minority groups as poor parenting. Churches and educational and social service organizations have provided programs, often with the best of intentions, that worked to destroy family life and family ties among Aboriginal people. For example, the gift-giving that accompanied traditional Kwakiutl marriage practices was interpreted by missionaries as bride selling; therefore, they tried to stamp out the custom (Ray, 1996). One aspect of family that differs across cultures is the extent to which extended family members are considered part of the immediate family. Many misunderstandings about the caring and competence of parents have centred on this difference. In the case of Aboriginal families, many social workers felt that the custom of allowing grandparents or other relatives to care for children showed indifference and neglect on the part of the parents. They removed the children and placed them with families who followed the majority cultural practices. The Aboriginal parents, however, felt that they were behaving responsibly because caring family members were looking after their children (Sinclair, 2007).

stigma: a trait or an attribute that is used to differentiate individuals and has a negative value

Stigma

A **stigma** is a trait or an attribute that is used to differentiate individuals and has a negative value. Members of minorities are often stigmatized by the majority.

Many immigrants face the stigma that they are taking jobs from "real" Canadians or that they can't speak "our" language. Stigmas are not intrinsic attributes but rather are socially constructed and acted upon. The stigma may change value over time, or it may disappear and a new one emerge. When a person carries a stigma, it is negatively responded to by some or all segments of society, and thus one of the consequences is that these individuals become marginalized in the larger society (Frideres, 2005). If a particular characteristic is regarded as unnatural, it is considered particularly dangerous. For example, Aboriginal peoples were (and sometimes still are) regarded as "savages" in need of civilizing (Blackstock, 2009).

A stigma can also spread to others outside the minority group. If one associates too much with members of a minority group, one is regarded as being just like them. This attitude is reflected in proverbs like "A man is known by the company he keeps." If a person works with an Arab community group, for example, he or she may be suspected of having sympathy for terrorists.

The degree of stigma attached to a particular status sometimes changes with time. For example, the first Italian immigrants to Canada worked in factories or in the construction industry as unskilled tradesmen. Italians, along with many other groups, were listed as "non-preferred" immigrants. During World War II, many faced discrimination and were accused of being sympathetic to fascist ideals. After the war, a need for labour made Italians once more welcome in Canada. Since then, the image of the Italian community in Canada has improved (Sturino, 2012).

The Majority's Sense of Superiority

Central to the discussion of immigrants and other minorities is the majority's sense of superiority—the notion that its way is the right way and that any other is somehow wrong, or at best inferior. In part this is a power issue—changes in norms may threaten the majority's control over much of social life (Kallen, 2003). Since many regard the family as the heart of society, they see any differences or changes in family patterns as a threat to society itself. Around the world, people have developed unique and fascinating forms of the family. When they immigrate to Canada, they naturally bring these practices and values with them. These may be quite different from the dominant Canadian form and may arouse ridicule and condemnation from the majority. This sense of superiority and the fear that what we value most will be destroyed provokes the most violent forms of prejudice.

Responses to Stigma and Discrimination

When immigrants arrive in a new country, they identify—or are identified—with the status of immigrant. They often lack financial resources (a job and money), social resources (personal and professional networks), and cognitive resources (knowledge of the language and norms of Canadian culture). However, much of their disadvantage stems from their minority status (Lalonde & Cameron, 1993). From the immigrant's perspective, there are four main responses to minority status: separation, assimilation, integration, and marginalization (Güngör, 2011). These **acculturation strategies** can be located along two dimensions: acceptance or

acculturation strategies: psychological and behavioural changes in individuals as a result of migration

FIGURE 2.2 Acculturation Strategies

Culture of Origin	New Culture	
	Accept	**Reject**
Accept	Biculturalism	Cultural maintenance
Reject	Assimilation	Marginalization

rejection of the new culture, and acceptance or rejection of the old culture (see Figure 2.2).

separation: an acculturation strategy based on the voluntary rejection of the dominant culture or involuntary exclusion from the dominant culture

Separation is a collective rather than an individual acculturation strategy (Lalonde & Cameron, 1993). It can occur by choice or be forced on a particular group (Cook, 2003). For example, the Hutterites, whom we discussed in Chapter 1, have chosen to stay apart from mainstream society. New immigrants may also choose to live in ethnic enclaves. On the other hand, Muslims have emphasized their Islamic identity in the face of discrimination after the destruction of the World Trade Center in New York City on September 11, 2001 (Sykes, 2008). Chinese workers who came to Canada during construction of the Canadian Pacific Railway faced so much discrimination that they were forced to live in ghettos. The First Nations reserve system is another example of separation. Forced separation also includes segregation and, at the extreme, genocide (Cook, 2003). Separation is more likely when the immigrant cultural group is perceived to be more distinct from the dominant group (Lalonde & Cameron, 1993).

assimilation: an acculturation strategy based on rejection of the heritage culture and full and exclusive orientation toward the dominant culture

Assimilation occurs when an individual rejects his or her heritage culture and adopts a full and exclusive orientation toward the dominant culture (Güngör, 2011). Like separation, assimilation can be voluntary or be forced on a minority, and may occur unevenly, with "bumpy" progress in some areas (Brown & Bean, 2006). Immigrants may choose to take on the customs and values of the majority culture in Canada. For example, immigrants from India may opt to choose their own marriage partners instead of agreeing to arranged marriages. In general, minority members choosing to assimilate regard this as a road to opportunity (Cook, 2003). On the other hand, the original purpose of residential schools was to force Aboriginal children to change from so-called "savages" to "civilized" beings; that is, to forcibly assimilate them into non-Aboriginal society (Blackstock, 2009).

passing: trying to hide the fact that one is a member of a minority group

Due to discrimination, members of minority groups sometimes attempt to pass as a member of the majority group. Assimilation is one form of **passing**. One problem with trying to pass is that it forces the individual to live a double life.

This, by itself, causes a strain. Often, there will be uneasy moments as children or other relatives ask questions. Family members sense that this is a taboo subject. Such secrets can have long-lasting and quite unintentional effects on family relationships because they interfere with openness in family communication (Imber-Black, 1993; Kirk, 1984). In addition, there is fear that the secret will be discovered. A great deal of anxiety and role strain are experienced in the attempt to pass.

A third acculturation strategy is **integration**, in which high levels of engagement in both the heritage and the mainstream cultures are sought (Güngör, 2011). An example of this is the hyphenated Canadian (e.g., Polish-Canadian, Chinese-Canadian). Integration depends on inclusion, the removal of barriers so that all individuals can fully take part in society (Brown & Bean, 2006; McDonald & Quell, 2008). Integration is also argued to be the most adaptive pathway because it implies bicultural competence and flexibility. The heritage culture is maintained through family life and within the ethnic community, whereas contact with the mainstream culture often takes place in more public arenas such as at school or work. For example, individuals will speak their mother tongue and celebrate the holidays of their heritage culture with their family but speak the national language and participate in national festivities at school or at work (Güngör, 2011).

A fourth type of acculturation—**marginalization**—occurs when there is little possibility or interest in maintaining the heritage culture and little interest in having relations with others in the dominant culture. Marginalization is often associated with significant loss of the heritage culture and the appearance of a number of dysfunctional and deviant behaviours, such as delinquency, substance abuse, and family abuse (Berry, 2005).

We can also describe the interaction between immigrants and the dominant society from the perspective of social policies. **Acculturation policies** are strategies for integrating or excluding immigrants that are promoted or enforced by the dominant group through laws or other official programs.

integration: an acculturation strategy in which high levels of engagement in both the heritage and mainstream cultures are sought

marginalization: an acculturation strategy that occurs when there is little possibility or interest in maintaining the heritage culture and little interest in having relations with others in the dominant culture

acculturation policies: strategies for integrating or excluding immigrants that are promoted or enforced by the dominant group through laws or other official programs

FIGURE 2.3   Acculturation Policies

Minority Culture		Dominant Culture	
		Accept	**Reject**
	Accept	Multiculturalism	Segregation
	Reject	Melting pot	Exclusion

multiculturalism: an acculturation policy that accepts diversity and includes all ethnic and cultural groups

melting pot: an acculturation policy that encourages individuals to assimilate into the dominant culture

segregation: an acculturation policy based on forced separation from the dominant group

exclusion: an acculturation policy that marginalizes immigrants

When diversity is an accepted feature of the society as a whole, and includes all the various ethnic and cultural groups, this is an acculturation policy of **multiculturalism**. In 1971, Canada became the first country in the world to adopt a multiculturalism policy (Citizenship and Immigration Canada, 2008). When assimilation is the strategy preferred by the dominant acculturating group, this is termed the **melting pot**. When separation is forced by the dominant group, this is called **segregation**. Finally, marginalization, when imposed by the dominant group, is called **exclusion** (Berry, 2005).

Time to Review

1. What is the difference between prejudice and discrimination?
2. What are the different acculturation strategies used by immigrants?
3. What are the different acculturation policies used by dominant groups?

Providing Services to Immigrants

Canadians have a long history of community involvement in assisting newcomers to adapt to life in Canada. Organizations exist that can help immigrants find a place to live, look for a job, obtain a social insurance number and health insurance card, enrol children in school, get language training, find a family doctor, access government and community services, learn about banking, shopping, and other everyday tasks, and meet other Canadians (Citizenship and Immigration Canada, 2010b). The demand for service agencies to develop policies that are sensitive to the cultural traditions of their clients has been growing. Furthermore, the need for such policies will probably increase, for a variety of reasons. Since most immigrants are young adults with children, the adults are concerned with government and agency policies regarding childcare and education. Many go to relatives or small ethnic organizations for help rather than to mainstream agencies, such as Children's Aid Societies or child welfare departments that they fear do not respect the values of their group (Unger et al., 2007). Provincial agencies may be unwilling or unable to provide culturally sensitive services. For example, Muslims criticized an Ontario agency for placing Muslim children with Christian foster parents who did not support their religious and dietary practices (Van Harten, 2004). Agreements between Aboriginal bands and provincial and federal governments have permitted formation of child welfare and family service agencies that are culturally sensitive; however, such services are not available nationwide and are not always successful (Blackstock, 2009; Castellano, 2002). Immigrant groups do not have even this level of legal protection. They could, however, be better served by developing closer ties between mainstream agencies and existing or new ethnic organizations.

Differences and the Study of the Family

Why is it important for us to be aware of differences between families? First, we need to understand that *different* does not equal *inferior*. Rather, we must realize that we have all been shaped by our family and cultural heritage, our wider social context, and our past experiences. These have helped us develop our knowledge, strengths, vulnerabilities, and expectations as we go through life. They have also shaped how we perceive others. For example, if we have been subjected to prejudice by a particular group, we may be suspicious of its members in the future. On the other hand, we may see others like us as allies.

Second, as we have seen, the Canadian population is becoming more diverse. The growing visible minority population is challenging governments and communities to identify and remove barriers to equitable participation in social and economic life—particularly those barriers rooted in racial discrimination. Immigration has forced open the whole question of what constitutes family and how it should be defined. Religious and cultural practices governing how families are formed and what rights and responsibilities family members have for each other have come into conflict with mainstream Canadian laws and traditions, prompting an important debate about the roles of government and religion with regard to the family (Vanier Institute of the Family, 2012b).

In much of the remainder of this book, we will be looking at the stages of the family life cycle. It is important for us to remember that many individuals and families do not go through the stages in a neat, orderly manner. Some take detours. Others vary the order in which they move through stages, while still others may miss some completely. These variations contribute to the richness of human experience.

Merry Christmas, Xiao Bo

The children of families who immigrate can face many difficulties. At home, they are still surrounded by familiar language, customs, and values. But going to school can be a traumatic experience. They may not understand what people are saying, and some of the behaviours that are so natural to Canadian-born children may seem strange and even rude.

Imagine you are an elementary school teacher in Guelph, Ontario. All the children in your class speak only English, and most live in nuclear families with married parents and one or two siblings. In October, Xiao Bo was placed in your class. His family had just come to Canada from Shanghai. You were told that neither of his parents had found work yet and that the family is living with his father's brother and his family, who came to Canada five years ago. At first, some of the children teased Xiao Bo because of his name and his poor English. They especially teased him about the lunches he would bring—not the standard fare of sandwiches and juice boxes, but plastic containers with rice, different kinds of fishy sauces, and a thermos of water. After a few weeks, the children either became used to Xiao Bo or lost interest in teasing him. In fact, Xiao Bo was generally ignored by the rest of the class.

Now it is December 15. The school has been decorated with Christmas bows and lights, and a big Christmas tree has been set up and decorated at the main entrance of the school. As you have done every year since you started teaching five years ago, you have organized a Christmas party for the class. This includes a gift exchange and a pot luck party of seasonal goodies—hot chocolate, candy canes, and sugar cookies in the shape of stars, Christmas trees, and snowmen. On the day of the party, the children were naturally more excited than usual. They were loud and boisterous throughout lunch. No one seemed to notice Xiao Bo sitting quietly in a corner eating his rice. After lunch, the children sang carols—"Jingle Bells," "Deck the Halls," and "Frosty the Snowman." It seemed that each child was trying to make his or her voice stand out over the others. Xiao Bo stared at the children in wide-eyed wonder. Then it was time for the highlight of the party—the gift exchange. Each girl had drawn a name of one of the boys from a hat, and this was her partner for the gift exchange. Sarah McCormick had drawn the name of Xiao Bo. When it was her turn, she rudely thrust a small gift at the boy. He shyly took the gift, and carefully unwrapped it. It was a snow globe of a house and a few trees. He gently shook it and watched in wonder as the snow floated about. Very quietly, he whispered, "Thank you." Xiao Bo then ran to his school bag and took out what looked like a small cake, delicately wrapped in cellophane. He proudly held it out to Sarah. She took one look at it and said, "Yuck—that looks disgusting!" Xiao Bo turned away so that the children would not see him crying.

We all become so used to our own customs that we cannot imagine that others might not share them. In mainstream Canadian culture, Christmas is a significant holiday and is celebrated with much tradition. Yet for many Canadians (and not just recent immigrants), Christmas is not part of their cultural heritage.

1. If you were the teacher in this scenario, what would you have done differently?
2. To what extent should teachers, and others who deal with culturally diverse groups, consider traditions other than those of the mainstream Canadian culture?
3. What is the mainstream Canadian culture?

Summary

What Is the Difference between Race and Ethnicity?

Race and ethnicity are important social categories that can define who we are and how we are treated. While they are often grouped together, they are not the same thing. Race is a system of classifying people based on physical characteristics such as skin colour. Ethnicity denotes a group of people who share a common cultural heritage. In Canada, we use the term "visible minority" to refer to a person, other than an Aboriginal, who is non-Caucasian in race or non-white in colour. An Aboriginal is a person who is First Nations, Inuit, or Métis. A "minority group" refers to any group that holds less power than the dominant group.

What Are Some Characteristics of the Canadian Population?

Canada has been populated by waves of immigrants. To Aboriginal people, the family signifies parents and children living together in a household. Family also means an extended network of other relatives. In recent years, the Aboriginal population has been growing nearly six times faster than the Canadian population as a whole. The character of English Canadian society has its roots in Britain. English Canadians have always seen the family as responsible for its members. In Quebec, the French colonial government encouraged a society that mirrored the homeland and discouraged dissidents. The 2006 Census enumerated more than 200 different ethnic origins. The diversity of Canada's population will continue to increase significantly over the next 20 years. Multiracial families have nearly always existed, though at times they were hidden or made illegal. Many Canadian children have been adopted internationally and transracially.

What Are Some of the Patterns of Immigration to Canada?

Before 1900, many newcomers came from the British Isles and the United States. Federal and provincial governments placed many barriers to the immigration of non-whites, members of certain religious groups, and others regarded as being hard to assimilate into British-based culture. In boom times, both employers and the federal government supported the influx of workers. During recessions and the Great Depression, immigration was discouraged. Many groups have been admitted to Canada for humanitarian reasons.

Before 1967, immigration rules favoured those from Europe or countries of European heritage. Now, nearly three-quarters of immigrants come from Africa, Asia, the Caribbean, and Latin America. Most newcomers settle in Toronto, Vancouver, and Montreal.

What Are Some of the Experiences of Immigrants in Canada?

Immigrants to Canada immediately become part of a minority group. The types of policies in place at the time of their arrival can either facilitate or complicate their adaptation. Most immigrants want to find work but often face challenges. Many do not find work in the same field as in their former country. On average, incomes are lower for immigrants than for the Canadian-born workers. Although many immigrants live with relatives or friends at first, most move to their own houses or apartments soon after arrival. Children of immigrants may have difficulty growing up in two cultures.

Canada is a country that has valued acceptance and embraced diversity. However, there are many examples that these principles have not always been followed. We need to look at several aspects of the dominant group–minority group relationships if we are to understand their impact on families. Prejudice is a negative attitude toward an entire group of people. Members of a minority group may experience negative actions, or discrimination, by the majority. Discrimination based on majority values can profoundly affect the family life of minority group members. A stigma is a trait or an attribute that is used to differentiate individuals and has a negative value. From the immigrant's perspective, there are four main responses to minority status: separation, assimilation, integration, and marginalization. Acculturation policies are strategies for integrating or excluding immigrants that are promoted or enforced by the dominant group through laws or other official programs.

Class Assignments

1. Try to find out how many ethnic groups are represented at your school. Make a list of all of them, as well as the population of each group, if this information is available. What policies does your school have for accommodating different ethnicities and religions? For example, what happens if a student has to miss a test because of a religious holiday? Make a list of the different policies.
2. Examine an occupation that involves working with people. What changes have occurred already and may occur in the future because of changes in families, the racial and ethnic makeup of the community, or both?

Personal Assignments

The following assignments are designed to help you gain insight into your own experiences:

1. If you were filling out the census, what would you indicate as your ethnicity? Would you indicate a single or multiple responses? When, how, and why did you or your family or ancestors first arrive in Canada?

2. How do you think the census question on ethnicity should be asked? Why do you think Statistics Canada collects data on people's ethnicity? What factors should Citizenship and Immigration Canada consider when accepting immigrants to Canada?

3. List the areas in which you consider yourself part of a minority. Have you experienced any discrimination because of this? Explain. In what ways might this experience help or hinder you as you interact with others?

THE COUPLE RELATIONSHIP: MERGING DIFFERENCES

Chapter 3
Getting Together

LEARNING OBJECTIVES

How are families formed?

How do people select their mates?

How is sexuality part of intimate relationships?

What are some aspects of intimate relationships?

What are the alternatives to marriage?

As the king's handsome son came up to the forest, the thorn branches burst into bloom and parted to let him pass. He climbed the tower stairs as the legend told him he should. Then he opened the door to the chamber where Briar Rose lay sleeping, still as lovely as the day she fell under the witch's spell. Immediately he loved her and gently kissed her. As soon as his lips touched hers, Briar Rose opened her eyes and smiled. As soon as the wedding festivities could be arranged, Briar Rose and her prince were married in royal splendour. The witch's curse was forgotten, and they lived happily ever after.

In the story of Briar Rose, we have the essentials of romance—the beautiful princess needing rescue, the handsome prince who rescues her, and above all something magical, including love at first sight and living happily ever after. This story, and those of Snow White, Cinderella, and their sisters in spirit colour our imagination of love and courtship. In North American society, according to popular myth, man meets woman, they fall passionately in love, and then they fade into misty shadows to the tune "The Wedding March." Yet for many people, living "happily ever after" is just an illusion. The reality is both more ordinary and more complex.

Where Do I Fit In?

Do you think that the story of Briar Rose is just a fairy tale, or is that how some people *do* fall in love?
  1. Think about the family you were raised in. How did this family begin?
  2. Would you like to start your own family, or have you started your own family? If so, how did you do this?

All societies have families, and therefore all societies have norms and customs for starting families. In our society, marriage is still the norm—most people marry at some point in their lives. **Marriage** refers to a socially, legally, and/or religiously recognized union of people who commit to one another. It is also used to refer to the ceremony by which this union is formally endorsed. The ceremony is also called a wedding. Society encourages marriage in a number of ways. Relatives and friends may ask, "Why aren't you married yet?" and may try matchmaking. More subtle pressures are seen in advertising and popular culture. When most people you know are married, social life is organized around couples. If you are unattached, you may not fit in.

In Chapter 1, we saw that there are many definitions of family. Often, a new family begins when two people decide to form a relationship. This may be a legal union, as in a marriage, or a social union, as in introducing someone as your partner. The process of deciding who will be your partner is called **mate selection**. In many societies, mate selection is often accomplished by the family rather than

marriage: a socially, legally, and/or religiously recognized union of people who commit to one another

mate selection: the process by which partners are selected

arranged marriage: a type of marriage in which the partners are selected by a third party rather than by each other

romantic love: a strong emotional attachment often including a mixture of sexual desire, tenderness, affection, and playfulness

the individual. **Arranged marriages** were and continue to be considered unions of whole groups; thus the extended family is involved in the couple's relationship. If marriages are not arranged by families, couples need some basis for selecting their own partners. In European and North American society, **romantic love**—defined as a strong emotional attachment between adolescents or adults, or as a mixture of sexual desire and tenderness, of affection and playfulness (Regan, 2008)—has become the standard. Psychologists define the criteria for love as physical arousal, the presence (real or imagined) of someone to love, and the belief that you are in love (Pines, 2005).

In this chapter, we will examine the different ways families begin. Like all human behaviour, such a complex task has many different aspects. For many, choosing a husband, wife, or life partner may seem like a highly personal decision, yet social forces inevitably exert a powerful influence. Sex is necessary for human reproduction, and sexuality is often an essential part of mate selection, but a great variety of social and cultural practices are associated with choosing a mate. We will examine some of these, including the fascinating and sometimes surprising interactions that occur between couples.

Setting the Family Cycle Turning

Mate selection is the most common way of starting the family life cycle. Pairing may be heterosexual or, less frequently, homosexual. In either case, individuals go through a process of choosing a life partner. The next steps vary: some couples live together and never marry; others marry before living together; and many begin with premarital cohabitation and eventually marry.

Despite the diversity in individual experiences, mate selection is divided into two basic streams—those decided by the couple and those decided by the families of the couple. Both forms are closely tied to the values and traditions of the cultures that support them. In many societies, families provide the principal social security system. Family membership and responsibilities of individuals are key to such a system. In South Asian families, for example, men are expected to provide financial support for their families of procreation as well as other relatives. If a father dies, his oldest son or brother will support his widow and children. Because they are not regarded as wage earners, women are devalued as a financial liability. The well-being of the family as a whole takes priority over individual happiness. In addition, a traditionally rigid system of social and occupational status has existed for centuries. It should be no surprise that marriages are arranged, both to maintain appropriate status and to increase family economic well-being (Medora, 2003; Rastogi, 2009).

In contrast to South Asian society, mainstream North American culture values individual achievement. All people are responsible both for their own success and for the well-being of their families of procreation. Both males and females are valued as individuals. In this system, "family" tends to be defined more narrowly than in South Asian society. When the individual social security system fails, there is little formal expectation that extended family members will help. Rather, society as a whole is expected to fill the gap. This expectation is part of a long-standing trend of shifting responsibility from the family to society—for example, for education and health care (Thornton et al., 2007). Picking one's own mate fits this culture of individuality and self-sufficiency.

There are close links between the macrosystem, or wider culture, and the exosystem, mesosystem, and microsystem. This is an important point to remember when looking at how families are formed. The various sociological perspectives each offer distinct insights for understanding how and why particular partners are selected. For structural functionalists, mate selection, regardless of the method used, is necessary to maintain social order and perpetuate society. This perspective focuses on how mate selection is functional for society. According to conflict theorists, the norms of mate selection tend to reproduce the existing class structure of society. This perspective focuses on how mate selection really involves exploitation and the exercise of power. The feminist perspective suggests that women are often considered objects of exchange, and mate selection serves to reduce women to objects based on appearance while disregarding their other statuses, such as personal accomplishments and occupational success. Symbolic interactionists focus on the communication that occurs between the couple as they develop and maintain their relationship.

According to psychiatrist Erik Erikson (1982), the most important developmental task in young adulthood is the establishment of intimacy, in the sense of a close emotional relationship with another. A key aspect of intimacy is the ability and freedom to disclose one's innermost self to another. This aspect can be expressed in friendship or in a sexual-romantic relationship. Intimacy develops when both people in a relationship feel understood, cared for, and valued by the other. Self-disclosure and intimacy are related to relationship satisfaction and stability (Regan, 2008). In much of North American society, development of intimacy is considered a prerequisite for marriage. Of course, not all intimate relationships, or even all formal engagements, lead to marriage.

A second developmental task is building the foundation for the couple's relationship (Carter & McGoldrick, 2005). Not only do the individuals have to negotiate and define their own relationship, they also have to realign their relationships with each partner's family and friends. The pattern of relationships, if we follow symbolic interactionist thought, is established from the earliest interchanges between partners. For example, when professionals counsel victims of spousal assault, they often discover that the abusive relationship began during courtship. The same pattern holds true for other aspects, both good and bad, of a couple's relationship. The interaction patterns that are formed while dating often continue throughout the relationship.

In societies where couples do not have free choice of a partner, the basis of the relationship is also established before marriage. The shared experiences of the couple include the expectations of their families and society at large. Personal aspects of their relationship may not develop until after marriage (Rastogi, 2009). In countries where traditional values are the norm, such as China and India, men place a high value on women's chastity, their desire for a home and children, and their abilities as a cook and homemaker. In these same societies, women value men with ambition, good financial prospects, and favourable social status (Myers et al., 2005).

For many, a serious relationship is expected to result in marriage. But there is a growing recognition that marriage may not meet every person's needs. Acceptance of relationships that do not include marriage is growing. The number of people living together without marriage or before marriage (cohabitation) is increasing (Vanier Institute of the Family, 2012b). Individuals are becoming more open about homosexual relationships, and these are consequently more visible (Bigner, 2006). And a person no longer has to be married to have children. Women can adopt a child, use reproductive technologies, or find a man willing to father a child (Hertz, 2006). Single men do not have as many options as women, but some adopt or raise a child they have fathered. These parents often cannot be distinguished from those becoming single parents through divorce or widowhood. Among ethnic groups, however, there is still great variety in the extent to which an unmarried person is accepted (Thornton et al., 2007).

Arranged Marriages

In most societies and historical periods, marriage has been at least partly arranged and has been based on a series of familial considerations rather than on the desires of the individuals concerned (Buunk et al., 2010). In some societies, as in India, social caste and family descent are important. Such societies consider the choice of a husband or wife too important to be left to mere children. Instead, marriages are arranged by parents and matchmakers. Some of the criteria used in selecting the individuals to be joined as a couple include practical skills, family alliances, economic arrangements between the families, and overall health of the individuals (Myers et al., 2005). They may also consider eligibility, similarity of background, horoscopes, financial and social position, and, if the couple is fortunate, the personalities of the prospective bride and groom (Medora, 2003).

Arranged marriages occurred in Canada and still do. In both New France and Upper Canada, young people were encouraged by wealthy landowner parents to marry not for love but for family and property (Kieran, 1986; McKie et al., 1983). The government in France wished to make New France a copy of French society. However, since few marriageable French women were available, men formed long-term relationships with Aboriginal women. To curb this trend, about 800 French women, known as "*les filles du roi*" (daughters of the king), were persuaded to sail to North America in the late 1600s, for which they received a dowry and essentials for starting farm life. Marriage became compulsory in New France, and the unmarried lost privileges. These unions were not arranged in the strict sense of the term, but prospective grooms had relatively little choice (Huck, 2001; Landry, 1992).

In the early part of the 20th century, Sikh immigrants to British Columbia were not allowed to bring wives and children with them. Given that there was prejudice against them, unmarried Sikh men could not seek white women for wives. Following changes in immigration laws in 1951, many Sikh men depended on relatives in the Punjab to arrange marriages for them; others advertised in Indian newspapers (Das Gupta, 2000).

Although arranged marriages have become rarer, they continue to occur in many parts of the world and among many immigrant groups in Western societies. Usually, an exchange of benefits is involved. In some cases, the bride or groom sees marriage as a route to immigration; in return, they offer their ability to earn a living and keep up religious and cultural traditions. In a study of second-generation South Asian immigrants living in North America, 25 percent of the participants indicated that their parents would likely arrange their marriage (Buunk et al., 2010). Relatives still advertise in newspapers published for Indians living in North America or on the Internet, hoping to find spouses for young people in their family. Even when not directly arranging their children's marriages, parents often attempt to influence their choice of a mate. There may be pressure on children of new Canadians to marry within their ethnic group. A common strategy used by parents is to restrict the social interactions of their children. Because they may want to follow customs they have learned in Canada instead of those of their ethnic group, second-generation immigrants indicate that conflicts with their parents in the realm of dating and marriage are common (Buunk et al., 2010).

A **forced marriage** occurs when people are coerced into a marriage against their will. It is very different from an arranged marriage, in which the free and informed consent of both parties is present. Forced marriage often affects young people who may be taken abroad on false pretexts or pressured to marry to sponsor their new spouse for immigration purposes. In many if not all instances, it is the parents who are forcing the young person to marry. Every major faith condemns the practice, and it is considered a human rights violation. Many countries have taken both legislative and non-legislative routes to combat the practice (Department of Justice, 2011).

forced marriage: a marriage in which people are coerced into marrying against their will

The Shift toward Free Choice

Western society has gradually shifted from arranged marriages toward free choice. But the shift has not been smooth, and movement has occurred more quickly in some parts of the population than in others. Also, some rapid shifts in attitudes have been followed by periods of reaction. Many changes, including attitudes toward premarital sexual experience, reflect changing social conditions and even increases in scientific knowledge.

The Road to Romantic Love

During the 12th century in Provence, in southern France, many young knights did not have the financial resources for marriage, especially if they were younger sons. They diverted their sexual energy by worshiping the lady of the manor and by doing deeds to prove themselves worthy of love. This emotion became known as "courtly love" and provides the origin of the term "courtship" (Lee, 1975).

Over time, sex and romantic love became gradually linked. During the Industrial Revolution, emphasis on individuality grew. Young people wanted the right to choose their own mates and love came to be used as the basis for marriage (Coontz, 2005). The earliest settlers from Europe brought this tradition with them to North America, where this focus on romantic love and free choice was combined with the emphasis on individual achievement.

Early Years of Settlement

The conditions on the North American frontier encouraged choosing one's mate. Actual practices were related to three phases: (1) the exploration of the wilderness, (2) the establishment of new settlements, and (3) the growth of larger towns and cities. Since the phases occurred at different times in different places, dates are hard to attach to them. For example, European settlements were established earlier in the East than on the Prairies, and earlier near major waterways than in the hinterland.

In the exploration phase, survival depended on an individual's initiative and resourcefulness. Added to harsh conditions was an extreme shortage of white women. Many European men formed unions with Aboriginal women. These were often established on the basis of an exchange of goods for expertise in wilderness travel and survival or to cement trading or military alliances (Ray, 1996). It is difficult to know what part, if any, romantic love played.

This phase was followed by a transitional period during which settlers moved into areas already mapped by the traders and explorers. Although many travelled in family groups, many also left relatives behind. The frontier saw an influx of unattached males because it provided opportunities for enterprising young men. In mate selection, practical matters were important. Was the prospective partner strong and healthy? Was he or she a hard worker? Life in the remote parts to which they were going was not easy. Both partners would have to put in long, hard labour to make their new farm productive (Azoulay, 2001; Coontz, 2005). And, although everyone worked long hours, there were occasions to meet, such as after church or at barn raisings. Courting occurred in the parlour, and young couples were often left alone there to become acquainted (Coontz, 2005).

Life in cities also tended to encourage individuals to choose their own spouses. As young people became less dependent on their parents for financial survival, they had more freedom of choice. On the family farm worked by father and sons, parents had relatively high control over marriages because they controlled their children's livelihood. This is still true when a person works in a family business, especially in times when jobs are scarce. In the cities, where a greater variety of jobs was available, parents' control weakened and young people could please themselves more (Coontz, 2005).

The Relationship Continuum

Usually, arranged and self-chosen marriages are treated as if they are quite different; however, they lie along a continuum, with completely arranged marriages at one end and completely self-chosen unions at the other. Most fall in between, although they tend to one side or the other. For instance, most individuals who choose their partners take some account of their parents' feelings about their prospective mates. In arranged matches, the couple often will not be forced to marry if either is opposed.

There is also a continuum for the idea of marriage as exchange and marriage as shared emotion. Arranged marriages tend to pay more attention to the overall benefit of the new union to both families, while free choice tends to emphasize shared emotions, such as the love and companionship of the specific individuals.

In North America, most couples are at the romantic love end of the scale, something that is encouraged in many ways. We are socialized from childhood to believe in love matches. There is also the constant media and advertising message—love is the mountaintop of experiences. The **complementary needs hypothesis** states that individuals feel most attracted to potential partners who complement them, an assumption that reflects the saying that "opposites attract." Complementary individuals are assumed to be so attractive because they enhance the likelihood that one's needs will be gratified. These needs may be emotional. For example, a person who has a strong, dominant personality may be attracted to someone who is submissive. The complementary needs may also be practical. Young women who lack economic resources may feel attracted to older men who have acquired economic resources and may therefore be good providers (Dijkstra & Barelds, 2008). Needs can also be influenced by social values. In the example just given, for instance, there are signs of a double standard that may reflect certain social scripts for gender roles (Pines, 2005).

complementary needs hypothesis: individuals feel most attracted to potential partners who complement them, as reflected in the saying that "opposites attract"

Social exchange theory suggests that individuals evaluate the potential success of a relationship based on a number of comparisons made both according to one's own standards and comparisons with one's peers. Researchers have repeatedly found that men prefer physical attractiveness in a female partner, while women value status and resources in their male partner (Li et al., 2002). For example, a male will evaluate his potential success in forming a relationship with a particular female based on his own standards of physical attractiveness, the cultural standards of physical attractiveness, and the likelihood that she will want to form a relationship with him. As long as both partners feel they are getting something positive from the relationship, they will stay together.

social exchange theory: a theory based on the idea that individuals evaluate the potential success of a relationship based on a number of comparisons

People tend to fall somewhere between the two extremes, often using both exchange values and emotional appeals, such as complementary needs, to attract a mate. Love, apparently, isn't blind. Couples often wait until they are financially and educationally ready to marry (Smock et al., 2005), while several studies demonstrate exchange theory acting during courtship. Men, more than women, show off their "material" assets, such as education, job, or car, as a way of attracting a mate. Women tend to emphasize physical appearance. Increasingly important, however, is women's ability to contribute financially because many families need two incomes. On the emotional side, both men and women display sympathy, kindness, and helpfulness. They also use good manners and humour as means of attraction (Coontz, 2005; Regan, 2008). Power in relationships has also long interested researchers. If a man and woman date each other for different reasons, their relationship may be in trouble. The person who has the least to lose can usually control the relationship (Bogle, 2008).

Freedom of Choice?

field of eligibles: people who are considered acceptable as potential partners, both by the individual and by society

Theoretically, we can marry almost anyone we choose. We are, however, limited in many social and cultural ways. Most of these factors apply to both heterosexual and homosexual couples. We select our mates from a **field of eligibles**, people who are considered acceptable as potential partners. This field is defined both individually and collectively. On a personal level, an individual may have specific criteria that they are looking for—a university graduate, for example (Quah, 2009). But there are many social factors that also dictate the field of eligibles.

incest taboo: a social norm that prohibits mating between closely related individuals

To begin with, there are legal barriers. In Canada, there is a law about being in only one marriage at a time. In many parts of the world, people must marry someone of the opposite sex. Other restrictions are based on the **incest taboo**, which appears in some form in every society and which prohibits mating between closely related individuals (Coontz, 2005). Thus we are barred from marrying certain relatives, such as parents, grandparents, and siblings. Society does not, however, know exactly how to deal with the "irregular" relationships occurring in adoptive and stepfamilies. The situation of brothers and sisters by adoption was clarified in 1991—they cannot marry each other. (See Box 3.1.) Stepsiblings are not legally related, but society frowns on marriages between them, especially if they were raised together.

BOX 3.1   A Quiz: Can You Marry Me?

Here is a list of relatives, extended family members, and other closely connected people. According to Canadian law, which ones can you marry?

I am your

1. Adopted child or parent
2. Former husband's or wife's parent
3. Stepbrother or stepsister
4. Aunt, uncle, niece, or nephew
5. Adopted sister or brother
6. First cousin
7. Deceased spouse's aunt or uncle
8. Half-brother or half-sister
9. Grandfather or grandmother
10. Former stepchild

At Confederation, the federal government was given responsibility for marriage, but no new law was enacted. Rather, the rules of the various provinces continued. Although these rules varied somewhat, all but Quebec's were based on English law. In 1563 (during the reign of Henry VIII), Archbishop Parker of the Church of England drew up a table of prohibited marriages. In 1835, this list became law. So Canadian regulations were based on the 1563 list, with only a few changes. Quebec's rules were similar.

Although there were some changes, the law (or lack of it) led to confusion about several relationships. You could marry your deceased spouse's brother, sister, niece, or nephew, but not an aunt or uncle. The situation following divorce wasn't at all clear. You could, however, marry an adopted brother, sister, or even child. Every year, a few individuals petitioned the Senate to pass a private member's bill so that they could marry a closely related person—an uncle, for example, or a nephew.

A new law, the *Marriage (Prohibited Degrees) Act*, came into effect on December 17, 1991. It does not permit marriage between people who are closely related biologically (grandparents, parents, children, grandchildren, siblings). It treats adoptees as if they had been born into their new family and therefore bans marriages on the same basis as biological relatives. Half-brothers and half-sisters also cannot marry. But aunts or uncles and their nieces or nephews can, as can relatives of former spouses. First cousins and stepbrothers and stepsisters were able to marry even before the 1990 legislation.

Therefore, the answers to the quiz are (1) no, (2) yes, (3) yes, (4) yes, (5) no, (6) yes, (7) yes, (8) no, (9) no, (10) yes.

Sources: Hurley, 2005; *Marriage (Prohibited Degrees) Act*, 1990; Standing Committee on Justice and Solicitor General, 1987; "Some notes on prohibited degrees," 1984; Standing Senate Committee on Legal and Constitutional Affairs, 1987; Vienneau, 1990.

Much as we might like to deny it, families have both direct and indirect influence on mate selection. In fact, approval by people important to them, such as family and friends, has been found extremely important in young adults' decisions (Pines, 2005). Sometimes approval or disapproval is openly stated; at other times it is communicated through the attitudes and nonverbal messages of relatives. Families and friends may also introduce us to the people we eventually marry. When there are a number of brothers and sisters close in age, for example, one of the girls may fall in love with a brother's friend. Adolescents are more likely to engage in romantic relationships within their immediate social groups, as opposed to searching for mates outside of their social circle (Boutwell et al., 2012).

The former caste system in Hindu India allowed marriage only to a person at the same social level. This type of marriage is referred to as **endogamy**, or marriage within the group. Systems of this kind may allow some choice of the marriage partner. Often, parents seek approval of the young people before final plans are made and select another candidate if the first fails to please the prospective bride or groom (Medora, 2003; Rastogi, 2009). Some cultures have adopted the practice of **exogamy**, or marrying outside one's group. In many Aboriginal North

endogamy: the practice of marrying someone from within one's own social group

exogamy: the practice of marrying someone from outside one's own social group

American societies, it was forbidden to marry someone from your clan, or sometimes even from your village (Frazer, 2010).

The influence of families can be more subtle. Our parents choose where the family lives; this, in turn, determines who our neighbours are, where we go to school, and the proximity of people our own age. Parents may also influence whether we continue our education and where we do so, either directly or through factors such as income level. One of the great mixing places is the post-secondary institution. Here, people with similar interests from a variety of places have an opportunity to meet. **Propinquity** refers to physical closeness. People generally select their partners from among those who live nearer to them geographically (Pines, 2005). This is because it is easier to get to know people who live nearby than those who live far away. In part because many immigrants live in enclaves, or groups within the larger society, they tend to marry people of the same ethnic origin.

Sigmund Freud proposed that romantic attraction is strongly influenced by the personality traits of one's parents. Men are more likely to choose women who resemble their mothers and women are more likely to select men like their fathers. Our parents may have an influence on our choice of partners, but this does not mean that we necessarily choose a partner who resembles our parents. Three researchers examined the correlations between personality traits in spouses and their in-laws in a large sample of Dutch twins and found little evidence of similarity between spouses and their parents-in-law (McCrae et al., 2012). Sociologists have discovered that we are likely to marry those similar to ourselves in intelligence, education, socioeconomic status, physical attractiveness, age, religious and ethnic background, and personal habits (Pines, 2005). The process of choosing a mate on the basis of certain traits is called **assortative mating** (Boutwell et al., 2012). In recent years, women's earnings have become more important to their marriage prospects. As a result, partners are becoming more similar in income as well (Amato et al., 2007). The tendency to marry someone similar to oneself is called **homogamy**.

Geographical and social factors outside our control also influence our selection of mates. Anyone who lives in a small community can tell you that the choice of a partner is quite limited, as only a few people in the community are of a suitable age. In the metropolitan areas of southern Canada, one can be more selective because many more people live there. In many cities, for example, there are gay/lesbian communities where same-sex partners can meet through friends. Opportunities in smaller places are scarcer. As a result, homosexual individuals often enter serious courtship later than heterosexual people (Brown, 2006). When a city becomes too big, however, it may become difficult to find someone with similar values. This is one reason for the growing use of Internet dating services.

If the male/female ratio is not balanced, one sex may have a wider choice of partners. *Les filles du roi,* for example, had available a number of potential partners because of the shortage of women in New France. One woman broke engagements to two men before marrying a third, all within a few days (Landry, 1992). Currently, Yukon, Nunavut, and the Northwest Territories have the reputation of

propinquity: physical and geographical closeness

assortative mating: the process of choosing a mate on the basis of certain traits

homogamy: the practice of marrying someone similar to oneself

being good places for marriage-minded women because of an abundance of men. According to the 2011 Census, men slightly outnumbered women in the territories, with Alberta following close behind (Statistics Canada, 2012f).

Individuals usually partner with someone about the same age. When there is a substantial age difference, women tend to be younger than their male partners (Boyd & Li, 2003). When the first members of the baby boom generation reached marrying age, women were at a disadvantage because there were fewer men slightly older than themselves. However, as the last of the baby boomers matured, men found that they outnumbered eligible younger women (Kettle, 1980).

The values we have learned from our families, friends, and acquaintances affect who we marry. A study of dating and mate selection among young adults from immigrant families found that they were influenced by parents who held endogamous views on marriage partners in order to maintain cultural, linguistic, and intergenerational ties within the family (Nesteruk & Gramescu, 2012).

Most people prefer to marry someone from their own racial group. Racial differences are much more conspicuous than religious and ethnic ones. Prejudice, of course, plays a part in this preference. The **status-caste exchange theory** was proposed in the 1940s for understanding patterns of black–white intermarriage in the United States. Given the caste-like racial divisions prevalent at the time, the theory predicted that blacks of low socioeconomic status would hardly ever marry whites, but high SES blacks would sometimes marry lower-status whites through a process of status-caste exchange. The high SES status of the black partner would compensate for the presumed loss incurred socially by the white partner as a result of marrying into a lower caste. A recent study found support for this theory in the United States, but not among Canadian interracial couples (Hou & Myles, 2011).

status-caste exchange theory: a theory proposed in the 1940s that blacks of low socioeconomic status would hardly ever marry whites, but high SES blacks would sometimes marry lower-status whites

The larger the racial group in the area, the less likely people are to intermarry, since they have a wide choice among people of similar background and only a limited choice of others. People with ethnically diverse friends are more likely to marry across ethnic and racial lines. So are members of the second and third generations (Clark-Ibañez & Felmlee, 2004; Stevens et al., 2006). And some groups intermarry more often than others. For example, among visible minorities, people of Japanese background are more likely to marry someone from another ethnic or racial group than are blacks or other Asians. This is probably related to the long history of Japanese people in Canada, as well as their relatively small number (Milan & Hamm, 2004). Sikhs, Muslims, and Hindus are least likely to marry a person of a different religion (Rastogi, 2009).

Time to Review

1. What are the two types of mate selection?
2. How does each of the sociological perspectives explain mate selection?
3. What are the developmental tasks associated with mate selection?
4. What are some of the factors considered in selecting a partner?

The Love Ideal

The Wheel of Love

How can we combine the evidence about homogamy in marriage with the ideal of romantic love? Sociologist Ira Reiss (1980) described what he called the "wheel of love" (see Figure 3.1). According to this theory, all forms of love and friendship develop through four processes. The first is a feeling of rapport. When people feel comfortable with each other, they reveal aspects of themselves such as their experiences, hopes, and fears. The second phase, self-revelation, can cover many areas of life, or it can expose private feelings and ideas. Usually, only close relationships involve deep revelation—these often encompass sexual activity. The third phase is the development of mutual dependencies. Individuals begin to rely on each other to share ideas, jokes, and intimate feelings. Thus the fourth process—personal-need fulfillment—comes into play. If needs are fulfilled, there is growing rapport, and the circular process is renewed. Since women often tend to be more attuned to relationships, they may move more quickly to self-revelation and mutual dependency. Growing trust is an important aspect of the developing relationship (Regan, 2008).

These four processes are related to various factors involved in mate selection. If a couple has similar experiences and values, they are likelier to feel rapport. Cultural background helps determine what each individual regards proper to

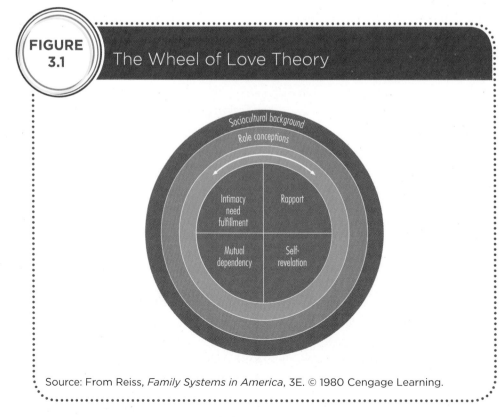

FIGURE 3.1

The Wheel of Love Theory

Sociocultural background

Role conceptions

Intimacy need fulfillment

Rapport

Mutual dependency

Self-revelation

Source: From Reiss, *Family Systems in America*, 3E. © 1980 Cengage Learning.

reveal. Some topics may be taboo. Certain sexual activities may be approved or discouraged.

A New Custom—Dating (and Beyond)

Dating

World War I transformed Canadian society, and one of the changes was the rise of dating. Before World War I, when a young man called on a young woman, it was assumed that his attentions were serious. Courtship took place mainly at community activities and in the parents' home. In 1914, Canada was mainly a country of farms and small towns; by 1918, it had become an industrial nation. For the first time, single men and women went out alone together without any particular intention of marrying each other. In most cases, the young man would pay the costs for the date (Coontz, 2005). In this and other societies that allowed individuals some choice in selecting a marriage partner, steady dating frequently became a part of mate selection. As dating crept into the social life of younger teens, so did going steady. People far too young to be planning marriage started "going" with each other, a custom that arose partly through a desire for security in social life. If you didn't have someone you could rely on, you might be left at home while all your friends were at the social event of the year (Bogle, 2008).

During the 1960s, dating patterns shifted to more varied and egalitarian practices. Sexual freedom increased. "Hooking up" includes a wide range of sexual behaviours, such as kissing, oral sex, and penetrative intercourse, that often occur without any promise of or desire for a more committed romantic relationship. Much research suggests that these encounters are becoming increasingly popular among adolescents and young adults in North America, representing a marked shift in openness and acceptance of casual and uncommitted sex (Garcia et al., 2012). First-semester college men, in a recent study, were more likely to report hooking up with penetrative sex if they had experienced it during high school, especially if they also engaged in binge drinking (Olmstead et al., 2012). In spite of these varied practices, most adolescents do expect to marry. Many, however, don't expect to go straight from dating into marriage. Rather, they consider cohabitation a step along the way (Manning et al., 2007). Those in a romantic relationship at high school graduation are likelier to marry in early adulthood. If they have a non-romantic sexual relationship, they are likelier to cohabit (Raley et al., 2007).

The most common dating goals of adolescents are identity, intimacy, status, and sex. For many youth, dating is an important activity in self-exploration and identity formation. Intimacy goals involve the pursuit of committed, exclusive relationships that foster self-disclosure, emotional intimacy, interdependence, and emotional attachment. Status goals focus on the social validation of the self, the partner, and the relationship as ways to enhance social status. For many, dating is also an initiation into sexual experience and fulfillment (Kelly et al., 2012).

The widespread popularity of the Internet has also affected dating. Emails, chat rooms, message boards, and webcams have become more than mere forms of communication as individuals seek to satisfy their need for interpersonal relatedness virtually, sometimes even anonymously, on the web (Mahfouz et al., 2008). Four main social forces appear to be driving the rapid growth of online dating. First, a growing proportion of the population is composed of singles, who are the main pool for online dating. Second, for this group especially, career and time pressures are increasing, so they need more efficient ways of meeting others for intimate relationships. Third, single people are more mobile. This is an advantage in the job market, but it also makes it more difficult to meet people for dating. Finally, due to growing sensitivity about sexual harassment, workplace romances are on the decline (Brym & Lenton, 2001).

Perhaps the greatest social change is that online dating offers access to potential partners whom people would be unlikely to meet through other avenues. The field of eligibles for an individual was once limited to members of that individual's social network. The Internet now affords access to a vastly wider network of potential partners. Another change is that the choice of a mate once relied largely upon the individual's intuitions and personal opinions. Online dating, with complex and "scientific" processes for matching couples, promises to create matches between suitable partners using new tools that draw upon data provided by thousands, even millions, of users. However, there is little evidence that the current "compatibility formulas" are especially effective (Finkel et al., 2012).

In 2008, 16 percent of Canadians reported finding love online (Calgary Herald, 2008). Dating sites, such as Lavalife, eHarmony, and Plenty of Fish, either match users based on personality profiles or allow users to search for prospective partners with certain characteristics. A twist reflecting the arranged marriage practice invites family and friends to participate in online matchmaking (Barraket & Henry-Waring, 2008).

Same-sex dating may be difficult for teens and young adults. A Canadian study found that there was no difference in the dating goals of same-sex and other-sex attracted youth (Zimmer-Gembeck et al., 2012), but some delay coming out because they fear their parents' reaction. Homosexual youth are often harassed and sometimes physically abused at school. There are few rituals of the "boy meets girl, boy dates girl" type available to gay male and lesbian individuals. Often, dating is postponed until adulthood. Because of social expectations and stigma, it is rarely acceptable outside gay and lesbian society to bring a date of the same sex. In addition, if one partner is unsure of his or her homosexual identity or wishes to remain closeted, it can be quite risky if the other partner tells others (Brown, 2006).

Now that there are more unattached people over age 40, researchers are looking at their dating behaviour. One of the challenges when examining the literature on dating in later life is that dating is often assumed to be a precursor to marriage and not a goal in and of itself (Watson & Stelle, 2011). The most significant factors affecting the likelihood of dating later in life are gender and age—women are less likely to date than are men, and both men and women are less likely to date as age increases. Factors that increased the likelihood of older adults dating are driving ability, living in a single-family residence, being relatively healthy, and participating in social activities. Specifically for women, health and mobility are the most significant predictors of dating. Companionship is the most cited reason for dating in later life. Another reason for dating is the pursuit of physical affection (Watson & Stelle, 2011). Those close to family and friends are less interested in finding a romantic partner (Carr, 2004).

Love can be an elusive target.

Source: Barry Maguire.

The Disadvantaged in Romance

Some people have difficulty finding partners because they do not fit the standards of physical eligibility promoted through popular media. Desirable men and women are portrayed as young, slim, good looking, and in control of their bodies and their lives. People who differ substantially from this stereotype may have problems establishing an intimate relationship (Carmalt et al., 2008).

One such disadvantaged group has been referred to as "people of size." Especially when their weight exceeds 150 kg (unless, of course, they look like a football player), they may be regarded as somewhat obscene or as objects of ridicule, rather than as romantic partners (Carmalt et al., 2008). In Internet relationships, however, appearance may not be mentioned or may be misrepresented. A Canadian poll conducted by Brym and Lenton (2001) found that 25 percent of online daters misrepresent themselves.

Another disadvantaged group includes those with visible physical differences, such as a physical deformity or a crippling disorder. In addition to the physical differences, these individuals are too often seen as little more than their "disability" and thus as not being full participants in society. Since they are often regarded as marginally employable, they may have difficulty finding jobs that would allow them to support families (Feng et al., 2007; Torjman, 2007). Besides, they are not "supposed" to be interested in sex, marriage, or child-rearing. Thus, in the competition for partners, such individuals are disadvantaged in multiple ways.

A third disadvantaged group is older people, especially older women. The chance of marrying for the first time drops off dramatically after a person reaches 30 years of age (Crompton, 2005). There are a number of reasons. Since most people are married by their 30s, their choice of partners becomes more limited after that age. Women who have devoted themselves to their careers are often seen as aggressive and unfeminine (Kingston, 2004) and have to either overcome this stereotype or find someone not threatened by their success. Among gay men, those who are young, physically fit, and middle or upper class are favoured. Older gay men often have lower sexual status and may suffer from poor self-esteem and depression. Some agree to unsafe sex to please a more desirable partner (Green, 2008).

The number of eligible over-30s is swelled by the growing number of people who are divorced. These people may have problems getting back into the stream of searchers. The social networks of younger people are organized so that meeting eligible individuals is quite easy. Since most people over 30 are married or cohabiting, social life is based on couples. Meeting someone is therefore more difficult. Women have the hardest time meeting eligible people. Men usually have more economic and social power than women, which makes up for their age. In addition, women more often have custody of children after divorce, and many men do not wish to accept the complications of a stepfamily. Some choose younger women, with whom they can renew a sense of their youthfulness. Women usually do not have this option because society scorns the older woman–younger man relationship, though the media have recently portrayed the "cougar"—the woman who pursues younger men—with a mix of favour and distaste. Finally, men die younger than women. In 2011, women aged 55 and older living alone outnumbered men. As they aged, the differences became even greater (Statistics Canada, 2012f).

The Never Married

The 2011 Census counted more unmarried people in Canada aged 15 and older than those who were legally married (see Table 3.1 on page 73). This statistic reflects the increase of divorced, and especially of the never-married individuals (Statistics Canada, 2012f). While many of these will eventually marry, many will

TABLE 3.1

Never-Married Men and Women, Not Living Common-Law (Selected Age Groups), 2011

Age Group	Male	Female
15–19 years	99.3%	97.3%
35–39 years	23.5	16.6
55–59 years	8.4	6.9
75–79 years	5.5	5.5

Source: Adapted from: Statistics Canada. 2011. *Legal Marital Status (6), Common-law Status (3), Age Groups (17) and Sex (3) for the Population 15 Years and Over of Canada, Provinces, Territories, Census Metropolitan Areas and Census Agglomerations, 2001 and 2006 Censuses 100% Data* (table). "Topic-based tabulation." 2011 Census. Catalogue No. 97-552-XCB2006007. Ottawa, Ontario. Statistics Canada. Accessed Sept. 12, 2007. (With calculations by the authors)

not. Indeed, marriage statistics are boosted by those marrying for the second or more times.

In spite of these trends, our society still believes in marriage. Marriage is generally seen as a natural and necessary state for individuals to reach full development. A stigma is particularly attached to being an unmarried woman, which is reflected in the expression "old maid." The stigma is greater because singlehood is seen as chosen rather than as involuntary; it also tends to increase with age (Crompton, 2005; DePaulo, 2006). A recent study found that in most of Canada, women who did not expect marriage had, on average, less education than those who did expect to marry; they were also over 40 and had children. Men with poor employment prospects expected to remain single. Quebeckers were less likely to expect marriage than other Canadians (Crompton, 2005).

The degree of pressure to get married also depends on relatives, ethnic background, and personal circumstances. Parents and grandparents may want to see another generation. As an ethnic group, the Irish, for instance, accept singleness fairly readily, but South Asians do not. How comfortable an unmarried person feels with his or her state also depends on whether it is chosen or imposed. If individuals hope to marry, they may feel doubly disadvantaged; they are alone and they do not feel in control of their fate (Schwartzberg et al., 1995). Unattached gay and lesbian individuals face many of the same issues as heterosexual singles. In addition, they may have difficulties developing close family-like relationships with friends, the result partly of social stigma and partly of limited opportunities, especially in small towns (Schwartzberg et al., 1995).

A special group of the unmarried includes those who choose to be celibate: who choose to make "an honest and sustained attempt to live without direct sexual gratification" (Sipe, 1990, p. 58). Celibacy is encouraged in both Hinduism and Buddhism as an aid to meditation and spiritual liberation. It can also allow those with religious vocations to serve others better. The Roman Catholic Church requires celibacy for priests and for members of religious orders. For many, the life is satisfying and they may come to regard members of their religious community as family members. Some individuals, however, do not keep their vows of celibacy (Abbott, 1999). Over several years, there has been much publicity in Canada concerning sexual abuse in schools and other institutions run by religious organizations, especially when staff members have faced criminal charges.

We must not assume that unmarried means uncoupled. The unmarried include homosexual and heterosexual cohabiting couples. A number of these relationships are long-standing and satisfying.

Sexuality

In the early period of European exploration, values regarding sexuality were often contradictory. Many of the early European settlers of North America had a puritanical outlook—anything that was fun was probably sinful, especially sex. This attitude is reflected in the "marital standard" for sexual behaviour: sex is permissible only in marriage and only to produce children (Reiss, 1960). One of the chief advocates of this stance has been the Roman Catholic Church. Actual practices may have been more permissive.

sexual double standard: a term used to describe the social principle that men are allowed more sexual freedom than women

The **sexual double standard**, whereby men are allowed more sexual freedom than women, has been common at various times. During the late 1800s, women were idealized as being pure and sexless (Reiss, 1960). Men were permitted much greater sexual freedom than women. This double standard has continued for a long time. Parents, especially immigrants from countries with conservative values, still allow sons more freedom than daughters. If young men engage in sexual activity, it's "natural"; however, if girls have sexual partners, they are viewed as "promiscuous."

The sexual revolution was a central element of North American culture in the 1960s. During the 1960s and 1970s, sex among dating couples increased. Not surprisingly, studies conducted during the 1960s found that younger people had more permissive attitudes than their parents. Many college students of that generation considered premarital sex acceptable for engaged couples. The sex-for-fun standard, which had already been accepted for men, became more acceptable for women (Rothman, 1987). Part of the change came from the general rejection of parents' values during the 1960s. In addition, the new availability of the pill reduced the risk of pregnancy. It has been argued that the birth control pill marked a significant turning point in women's choice and control over their own sexuality. Others have argued that because the pill ensures that the user is always ready for sex without reproduction, this in fact reflects patriarchal values. Nevertheless, the pill remains a popular form of birth control. A recent poll found that over 84 percent of Canadian women have at some point in their lives used the birth control pill (Granzow, 2007).

Attitudes toward premarital sexual activity continued to become more permissive until the 1980s and then stayed at about the same level (Bibby, 2001). Based on a sample of 15- to 19-year-olds, the proportion of teens who had had sexual intercourse at least once declined between 1996 and 2005. As well, the proportion who reported becoming sexually active at a very early age decreased. However, among those who were sexually active, there was no significant change in the likelihood of having multiple partners or, for males, using condoms. So while some adolescents have adopted measures to reduce their risks of sexually transmitted infection and unwanted pregnancy, others report high-risk behaviour (Rotermann, 2008). The younger they have sex, the higher the risk of an unwanted pregnancy or a sexually transmitted infection.

Sexual activity among teenagers appears to relate to a number of factors. Individuals with more permissive attitudes and those using alcohol engage in more sex. Peer group attitudes are also important (Garriguet, 2005; Hampton et al., 2005). It is commonly accepted that males, in general, are more likely to be sexually promiscuous, while women more often become romantically attached first. Men tend to initiate sexual relations more often than women do. Because men are socialized to be independent and unemotional, it may be harder for them to become committed to a relationship, while women tend to try to maintain the relationship. The differences, though, are not large. Young men, for example, also have sex for love, and women get physical pleasure (Regan, 2008).

Michel Foucault has argued that "homosexuality" is a relatively recent invention distinct from earlier forms of same-sex love and lust (Valverde, 2006). Prior to 1969, homosexuality was a criminal offence in Canada. Those accused of homosexual activities were charged as sex offenders and, if convicted, could be sentenced to long prison terms (Makarenko, 2007). Although the law and social opinions have changed substantially since then, same-sex partners still face many challenges. Like women and men in general, lesbians and gay men tend to move into relationships in different ways but face the same basic challenges as heterosexual couples. Lesbian couples usually begin by forming an emotional connection, and gay men start with a sexual relationship. Traditionally, gay males are thought to be more likely to practise **polyamory**, or having more than one relationship at a time, including both long-term and short-term (Bettinger, 2006). Nevertheless, many form long-term exclusive partnerships. AIDS (acquired immune deficiency syndrome) has complicated the issue: one partner's affairs may be life-threatening to the other.

polyamory: having more than one romantic relationship at a time

Today, sex is increasingly central to mainstream culture, in large part due to the Internet. Sexual images have always been closely linked with technological developments, and the proliferation of the Internet has resulted in both a significant growth in the amount and increased ease of access to online pornography (Garlick, 2011). There are signs, however, that attitudes are swinging toward more control of sexual behaviour. Some sex education programs for teens advocate, with varying degrees of success, no sex until the individual is in a committed relationship (Rosenbaum, 2009; Uecker, 2008). Others promote "safe sex" to avoid HIV (human immunodeficiency virus), the virus causing AIDS, and other sexually transmitted infections. Indeed, both men and women theoretically prefer sexually inexperienced partners over experienced ones (Garcia, 2006).

There are questions, however, over how much young people's behaviour has been influenced by these trends. Sexually transmitted infections have increased among both sexes. It was estimated that at the end of 2008, there were approximately 65 000 people in Canada living with HIV, including AIDS. New cases increased at about the same rate for several years. Since 2005, the greatest number of new cases, as well as the largest number of total cases, has been among men having sex with men; however, the number of infected heterosexual individuals is increasing (Public Health Agency of Canada, 2012a).

Risk-taking—that is, not using condoms during intercourse or using them inconsistently—is more likely among young people with multiple partners and those who have a poor relationship with parents, belong to a sexually active peer group, or use alcohol or drugs. Individuals involved in prostitution are less likely to use protection if they are street youth or male. Many teens hold two disturbing beliefs: that they are unlikely to be infected with HIV and that a vaccine can prevent HIV/AIDS, a view also held by many adults (Boyce et al., 2006; Garriguet, 2005; Public Health Agency of Canada, 2012a).

The past hundred years or so have seen great changes in attitudes toward sexual behaviour. Given this large shift in attitudes, the potential for misunderstanding and conflict between the generations is high. Recently, teens have begun using communication technologies, such as cellphones and the Internet, in their dating practices. While their parents may worry about online predators, studies have found that most adolescents protect themselves effectively (Maticka-Tyndale, 2008).

Time to Review

1. When and why did the practice of dating begin?
2. What are the goals of dating?
3. Who are the disadvantaged in love? What kinds of challenges do they face?
4. What are some of the issues regarding sexuality in mate selection?

Obstacles to Love Relationships— The Communication Gap

Many difficulties in intimate relationships are related to the gender-role socialization of men and women. Men tend to use communication to achieve goals, establish authority, and compete for attention and power. Women, on the other hand, are more likely to use communication to build connections and solve problems. For them, closeness is built on communication. For men, however, closeness comes more from shared experiences. Thus, both can become baffled and hurt by the lack of understanding they perceive in their partner. When conflict occurs, women more often want to discuss problems, while men are likelier to deny them or to leave the relationship (Driver et al., 2003; Regan, 2008; Wood, 1996). Same-sex couples tend to adopt more equal communication in their relationships than heterosexuals (Gotta et al., 2011). In both types of couples, communication about feelings more often occurs nonverbally than verbally and misunderstandings are common (Nowicki, 2003). Often, we are afraid to reveal our innermost feelings to others for several reasons. We may not want to risk being misunderstood or having our emotions used against us; we may also fear making others uncomfortable.

Individuals come to new relationships with expectations. They may have learned these in their families of origin or through relationships with friends or lovers. Some expectations can result in warped communication and crippling relationships. One example is treating another as property. In some cases, one partner may see the other as someone from the past, like a parent or previous lover. Others try to make the partner fit a fantasy ideal. In the early stage of the relationship, people may deliberately misrepresent themselves because they are afraid the person they are seeing will not like the real person they think they are. In other relationships, one partner tries to absorb the other, sometimes even telling outsiders the partner's "real" feelings (Sieburg, 1985).

The quality of a relationship and a couple's communication during the process of mate selection are important for the marriage or cohabitation that follows. Once they have been established, patterns of communication are difficult to change.

Thorns in the Relationship

Two major problem areas in relationships are "love gone bad" and "sex gone bad" (Regan, 2008, pp. 161, 217). Both suggest a failure to achieve the kind of intimacy Erikson (1982) describes. As with communication, patterns set during dating and cohabitation may continue into marriage if the relationship survives.

Problems with love include unrequited passionate love and obsession with the loved person. The latter may include spying and stalking. Couples may break up because of mismatched love styles. For example, a partner who is sexually expressive may feel unfulfilled by someone who shows love through sharing activities. Passion normally fades over time, with the result that some individuals believe they have "fallen out of love" rather than entering a new relationship dimension (Regan, 2008).

Sex gone wrong includes sexual dissatisfaction, which may result from poor communication about sexual desires or from incompatibility. Infidelity can range from flirting and kissing to sexual intercourse, and it often breaks the trust and commitment expected in a love relationship (Regan, 2008). Infidelity can also include emotional rather than physical involvement. For example, Internet relationships can become so intense as to interfere with face-to-face ones (Hertlein & Piercy, 2006). The reasons given for infidelity in premarital relationships are similar to those for infidelity in marriage—dissatisfaction, revenge or jealousy, desire for variety, and sexual incompatibility. Adolescents also cite insecurity, immaturity, and lack of communication. One difference in premarital and marital infidelity is that people are more likely to end a premarital relationship than a marriage because of infidelity, perhaps because they are not as strongly committed (Branden, 2008; Roscoe et al., 1988). A comparative study of heterosexual, lesbian, and gay male relationships warned couple therapists about presuming that all gay male relationships naturally evolve to non-monogamy. Their findings revealed that some gay couples maintained a monogamous relationship (Gotta et al., 2011).

Problems in sexuality may also result from mistaken cues. In spite of "no means no" campaigns, the belief that women offer token resistance to sex—that they say no even though they mean yes—is still common. Studies have found that about one-third of women have engaged in this kind of token resistance. The most frequent reason they gave was that they did not want to appear promiscuous. In other cases, individuals may do the opposite—agree to sex even when they do not want it. In one Canadian study, for example, 42 percent of women and 24 percent of men had unwanted sex (C. Struckman-Johnson & D. Struckman-Anderson, 2003). In another Canadian study, 6 percent of boys and 11 percent of girls in grade 11 reported having sex when they did not want it (Boyce et al., 2006).

A more serious problem is dating violence. The forms it takes are similar to those in marriage. The only exception is that date rape is reported more often than marital rape, perhaps because sexual relations are regarded as the right of a husband or wife. Sexual aggressiveness is more common among single men than single women. For men, it is related to their acceptance of rape myths, especially the belief that women, even when raped, enjoy sexual activity (Christopher et al., 1998; Davis, 2008; Kelly, n.d.; O'Keefe, 2005). Violence also occurs in lesbian and gay relationships. The little evidence available suggests that such violence is similar in both frequency and type to that between heterosexual partners (Kirkland, 2004; Ristock & Timbang, 2005). We will look at violence against partners in more detail in Chapter 14.

Alternatives to Marriage

In Canada, the majority of couples will marry. However, a growing number are choosing alternative living arrangements while still maintaining an intimate relationship. Cohabitation without marriage is the preferred alternative, especially among young Canadians. Another choice is "living apart together."

Living Together

cohabitation: a relationship in which the partners live together but are not married

Moving in together has become increasingly common at all ages. There seem to be two forms of **cohabitation**, or living together. In one, the couples do not see it as a way of forming a family with children. For these people, living together may be a trial run at marriage, and many do eventually have traditional weddings (Regan, 2008). Some couples, however, do see children as having a place in their relationship, even if they are not formally married. This form of cohabitation is very similar to marriage. Predictions see even more couples living together before or without marriage. We will consider unmarried cohabitation in more detail in Chapter 4.

Living Apart Together

living apart together (LAT): a relationship in which the partners do not live together

A type of relationship described quite recently is non-resident partners, referred to as **living apart together** (LAT). LAT partners regard themselves as a couple, and so do others. About 8 percent of Canadians are in such a relationship. While most are under 30, 45 percent are older (Milan & Peters, 2003). European researchers have found that a LAT relationship often leads to cohabitation or marriage. Younger couples live with parents until they can afford to set up a separate household. However, many, especially older individuals, have no plans to move in together. Some have responsibilities for children or parents. Others may receive social subsidies such as the Guaranteed Income Supplement for seniors. They may also value their independence (Castro-Martín et al., 2008; De Jong Gierveld, 2004; Haskey, 2005; Trost & Levin, 2005).

Time to Review

1. What are some of the obstacles encountered in relationships?
2. What are the alternatives to marriage?

Briar Rose Revisited

We have come a long way from Briar Rose, the symbol of romantic love. Relationships between couples are far more complex than her story would have us believe. They involve the impact of our society and its values and norms. Families influence our choice. Relationships are a mix of our past history and our ability to communicate. They bring intimacy and conflict. For most couples, the relationship patterns developed during mate selection form the basis for the rest of their family life.

Marriage Prospects

Carlos has been an engineer with a construction company for nearly a year and has already earned a promotion. Juli-Anne's job arranging conventions is as secure as the next contract. Because his prospects are good, Carlos is anxious to get married. Juli-Anne isn't so sure, even though Carlos is now paying most of their living costs.

They have lived together for two years. At first, things seemed to go well. They would text each other maybe 30 times a day, more if they were having a long conversation. They'd check in just to say hello, to plan errands and chores, to report on what they were doing with friends or family, or to decide how they'd spend the evening. Sometimes it was easier to text about minor issues like scheduling conflicts or dirty clothes on the floor than to talk about them. They were always only a few clicks away from each other. When they were at home, even during meals, they would text their friends and share messages with each other.

Recently, Juli-Anne feels that things have changed. The couple spends more time with Carlos's family, who immigrated recently from Mexico. They don't have many relatives in Canada, but they share traditions with other immigrant families. Carlos and his four sisters are expected to be present for every celebration. Juli-Anne enjoys the good-natured fun, the Mexican food, and the lively music. But she finds customs like remembering family members with a shrine on the Day of the Dead or elaborately celebrating the *quinceañera* (15th birthday) of Carlos's youngest sister a bit peculiar. Her own family's practices around birthdays and Christmas are low-key and often involve eating at an upscale restaurant. Carlos complains that these aren't celebrations at all. The last time they were with Carlos's family, his mother spoke openly about wanting a grandson and looked pointedly at Juli-Anne. Carlos didn't seem aware of how uncomfortable Juli-Anne was.

Now, whenever Carlos texts her, he wants to know what she's doing, where she is, and who she's with. He gets upset when she doesn't answer right away, even though she tells him that she can't interrupt a meeting with an important client. He checks on her Facebook postings. He wants to know whom she's friended and demands that she unfriend males who are not relatives. When she complains, he tells her that his actions show how much he loves her and how much he wants her to himself. Carlos accuses Juli-Anne of being secretive because she has started to limit her posts on Facebook.

Juli-Anne wonders what will happen once they're married.

1. Discuss the relationship of Carlos and Juli-Anne in terms of the Wheel of Love theory.
2. Nonverbal communication can be important for couples. To what degree do you think this couple has developed skills in such communication? Explain your answer.
3. What benefits and problems do you foresee for Juli-Anne and Carlos if they do marry?

Summary

How Are Families Formed?

Despite the growing variety in family types, most begin with mate selection, which is related to the developmental task of forming an intimate relationship.

How Do People Select Their Mates?

Mate selection is closely related to the values and traditions of the societies of which they are part. Relationships fall along a continuum between arranged and self-chosen. At one end of the scale are arranged marriages, which are planned by parents to link two families. In North America, there has been a shift toward choosing one's own mate.

The idea that romantic love is the basis for marriage developed gradually from the "courtly love" tradition of the 12th century. The complementary needs hypothesis posits that individuals feel most attracted to potential partners who complement them, an assumption that reflects the saying that "opposites attract." Social exchange theory suggests that individuals evaluate the potential success of a relationship based on a number of comparisons made both according to one's own standards as well as comparisons made against one's peers.

Theoretically, we can marry almost anyone we choose. In practice, we select our mates from a field of eligibles, people who are considered acceptable as potential partners. The incest taboo prohibits mating between closely related individuals. Endogamy refers to marriage within one's group, while exogamy means marrying outside one's group. The process of choosing a mate on the basis of certain traits is called assortative mating. The tendency to marry someone similar to oneself is called homogamy.

During the 1920s, the practice of dating emerged. During the 1960s, dating patterns shifted to more varied and egalitarian practices. The most common dating goals of adolescents are identity, intimacy, status, and sex. The widespread popularity of the Internet has also affected dating. Perhaps the greatest social change is that online dating offers access to potential partners whom people would be unlikely to meet through other avenues. Same-sex dating may be difficult for teens and young adults. The most significant factors related to the likelihood of dating later in life are gender and age.

Some people, such as those with visible disabilities and older women, are at a particular disadvantage. Some people choose to be celibate, sometimes as part of religious vows.

How Is Sexuality Part of Intimate Relationships?

The past hundred years or so have seen great changes in attitudes toward sexual behaviour. Values regarding sexuality were often contradictory. The sexual double standard, whereby men are allowed more sexual freedom than women, has been common at various times. During the 1960s and 1970s, sex among dating couples increased. Attitudes toward premarital sexual activity continued to become more permissive until the 1980s and then stayed at about the same level. When young couples first have sex, women tend to do it to express love and men for physical satisfaction. Today, sex is increasingly central to mainstream culture, in large part due to the Internet. Michel Foucault has argued that "homosexuality" is a relatively recent invention, distinct from earlier forms of same-sex love and lust. Sexual activity among teenagers appears to relate to a number of factors. Sexually transmitted infections have increased among both sexes. Risk-taking sexual behaviour and misconceptions about HIV are worrisome.

What Are Some Aspects of Intimate Relationships?

Many difficulties in intimate relationships are related to the gender-role socialization of men and women. Men tend to use communication to achieve goals, establish authority, and compete for attention and power. Women, on the other hand, are more likely to use communication to build connections and to solve problems. Individuals come to new relationships with expectations learned in their families of origin or through relationships with friends or lovers. Communication about feelings more often occurs nonverbally than verbally. Once they have been established, patterns of communication are difficult to change.

Two major problem areas in relationships are "love gone bad" and "sex gone bad." Problems with love include unrequited passionate love and obsession with the loved person. Sex gone wrong includes sexual dissatisfaction, which may result from poor communication about sexual desires or from incompatibility. Infidelity breaks the trust and commitment expected in a love relationship. Problems in sexuality may also result from mistaken cues.

A more serious problem is dating violence. The forms it takes are similar to those in marriage. The only exception is that date rape is reported more often than marital rape.

What Are the Alternatives to Marriage?

In Canada, the majority of couples will marry. However, a growing number are choosing alternative living arrangements while still maintaining an intimate relationship. Cohabitation without marriage is the preferred alternative, especially among young Canadians. Another choice is "living apart together."

Class Assignments

1. Many people live together before marriage. Explain the advantages and disadvantages of this practice. Think about the relationship of the couple and family and community attitudes, as well as financial and legal factors. You may find information through library research or through interviews with couples and experts.
2. In a group, plan and conduct a survey concerning students' attitudes toward premarital sex. Be prepared to report the results and to discuss what factors might have affected the answers you received.
3. As a group, prepare a list of questions to measure the homogamy of couples. Find different couples to interview. They may be married or unmarried. You may also want to find couples of different generations. Prepare a report on the presence or absence of homogamy in the couples that your group interviewed.

Personal Assignments

The following assignments are designed to help you think about your own experiences and expectations:

1. Make a list of the qualities you would like in a partner. Which ones are most important? Explain.
2. Do you and your parents have the same attitudes about relations between men and women? How are they similar, and how do they differ? How do you handle differences of opinion about a boyfriend or girlfriend?

Chapter 4
Wedding Bells . . . or Not

LEARNING OBJECTIVES

What are some of the different marriage arrangements?

How does society affect marriage?

How is cohabitation different from marriage?

What do we know about same-sex marriages?

What factors are involved in marital happiness?

What is the possible future of marriage?

While weddings are a universal practice, every culture has its own traditions surrounding the ceremony, for example the old English rhyme "something old, something new, something borrowed and something blue." Here are some wedding traditions from around the world that go beyond the white dress and veil.

- During the Greek Orthodox wedding ceremony, the bride and groom are given crowns called *stefana* that are connected by a ribbon. This signifies the union of the couple as well as indicates that they "rule" over their household.
- An important part of Chinese weddings is the tea ceremony. In fact, there are several. On her wedding day, the bride serves tea to her parents as a token of appreciation for the love and care they have given her. This ceremony is done before the bride leaves her parents' house and is usually not too elaborate. The tea ceremony for the groom's family takes place after the wedding and is much more elaborate. This ceremony also includes lotus seeds and two red dates to symbolize the early arrival of children from the newlyweds.
- Before an Indian bride gets married, she and her female friends and family decorate their hands and feet with elaborate designs called *menhdi*. These temporary designs are made from the plant dye henna, are incredibly intricate, and take hours to apply.
- In Jewish weddings, the groom crushes a glass under his foot at the end of the ceremony, with wedding guests calling out "Mazel tov" (good luck) after the glass shatters.
- In traditional Zulu culture, the bride selects her groom. The number of cattle that will be given to her father in exchange for her is then negotiated. For the wedding ceremony, the bride is decorated with red and white ocher designs on her legs and arms. Bags of pebbles are tied to her ankles; these will rattle when she dances. She wears a veil made of beads and twisted leaves, and oxtail fringes are tied to her elbows and knees and around her neck.
- In Russia, there is a touch of comedy before the wedding. The parents of the bride pretend to "steal" the bride and refuse to let the groom see her. The poor young man then pays a small symbolic ransom called *vykupnevesty* to get his beloved back. Of course, the entire event is played out only to amuse the guests.
- Cengizhan Celik and Candan Canik married in Üsküdar, Istanbul, with each tweeting "Evet," the Turkish word for "I do," from an iPad. The local mayor officiated the tech-friendly ceremony and even asked the bride and groom if they took each other as husband and wife by tweeting as well.

Source: Golijan, 2012.

The wedding ceremony has two social functions. First, it is the public acknowledgment that a new family has been created. Second, it is a ritual marking the change in status and roles among all family members (Kalmijn, 2004). Many wedding customs are reminders of earlier practices. Does the father give the bride away? Does the groom give her a ring? Both traditions are remnants from a time when a daughter was considered a financial asset who could be purchased. The wedding ceremony still contains the traces of property transfer and the bride price.

Does the bride wear white? In many Western cultures, this colour symbolizes virginity, which was valued in arranged marriages. Do we throw rice or its substitute, confetti? Whatever we throw, we are wishing the couple fertility. In the past, the production of children, especially an heir, was one of the reasons marriages were arranged (M. Baker, 2007).

In Canada, the proportion of married people has been declining over the past decades while the proportions of those who are divorced and those who have never married have been increasing. Cohabitation is also becoming more acceptable and popular than in the past, especially among young adults. Nevertheless, it is still true that in Canada, the majority of couples will marry.

Historically, the family has been the central organizational unit in almost all societies. Families were formed through marriage, and marriage was viewed as both an important event and a part of the natural progression of the life course for both women and men. Marriage often had religious and spiritual significance as well (Thornton, 2009a).

In this chapter, we will look at marriage as a social practice that both influences and is influenced by the wider society. While in Canada we often talk of marriage as if there were only one kind; in fact marriage occurs in many different forms, and we will examine some of these different arrangements. We will also look beyond the traditional image of marriage and examine other forms of couple relationships. While marriage between a man and a woman used to be the only legitimate way to form a family, this is no longer the case. Cohabitation is an increasingly popular alternative. Since 2005, same-sex marriages have been legal in Canada, and although there is not yet much research on these marriages, we will look at some of the issues faced by these couples. After looking at marital happiness and the factors associated with long-term success in marriage, we will conclude by asking the question "What is the possible future of marriage?"

Where Do I Fit In?

1. Think about the wedding ceremonies you have attended. What do you remember about them? What rituals were performed?
2. Do you plan to get married, or are you already married? What led you to make this choice?
3. If you do not plan to marry, what are your reasons for making this choice?

Married to One . . . or Many

Marriage is a legally and socially recognized union. The federal government has two acts dealing with marriage. The *Marriage (Prohibited Degrees) Act* identifies people, such as brothers and sisters, who cannot marry because they are too closely related by blood or adoption. The *Civil Marriage Act* defines marriage as "the union of *two people to the exclusion of all others*" [emphasis added]. This means that in

marriage: a legally and socially recognized union

monogamy: marriage to only one person at a time

serial monogamy: a series of marriages to different partners, although to only one at a time

polygamy: marriage of one person to more than one person of the opposite sex

polygyny: marriage of one man to several wives

sororal polygyny: marriage of one man to several wives who are sisters

polyandry: marriage of one woman to several husbands

Canada, the only legal kind of marriage is **monogamy**, which is marriage to only one person at a time. In a society such as Canada in which there is a high rate of divorce and remarriage, sociologists have coined the term **serial monogamy** to describe a series of marriages to different partners, although to only one at a time.

In other social groups, the family has been based on one person married to several others of the opposite sex. The term for this practice is **polygamy**. The most frequent form is one man with several wives. Strictly speaking, this arrangement is called **polygyny**, but since it is the most common form, many polygynous marriages are mistakenly called polygamous. Polygyny is the practice in many Muslim countries, in some African societies, and was also encouraged among the early Mormons in the United States. Sometimes all the wives are biological sisters, and this arrangement is called **sororal polygyny**. A very rare form of polygamy is one woman with several husbands, and this arrangement is called **polyandry**.

The practice of polygyny gives rise to ethical arguments based on freedom of religion. However, it is important to note the distinction between religious *belief* and religious *practice*. While Canadian laws do not restrict religious belief, they may restrict religious practices that violate an individual's rights and freedoms. Under international human rights law, there is a growing consensus that polygyny violates women's right to be free from all forms of discrimination (Department of Justice, 2012a). Critics say that polygyny encourages patriarchy and devalues women (Bala, 2004), but supporters dub the practice "the ultimate feminist lifestyle." One plural wife suggests that being one of several not only lightens the burden of housework and childcare, but also provides co-wives with an exceptionally skilled husband (Joseph, 1997). Some supporters of polygyny use the term "compersion" to refer to the act of sharing their lover's happiness with another (Luscombe, 2012). On the negative side, authorities have investigated the Bountiful commune, along with other communities of the sect in Utah, Arizona, and Texas, over charges that underage girls have been married to much older men (Bramham, 2008; Matas, 2008) (see Box 4.1 below).

This is not simply a philosophical debate; it also has practical implications. For example, if a family consisting of one husband and several wives applies for immigration to Canada, should they all be accorded marital status? If so, are these marriages considered legal? If not, who becomes the sole wife, and what happens to the "extras"? Is it fair to exclude polygamous families as immigrants?

BOX 4.1   Bountiful Polygamy

In the reign of James the Second
It was generally reckoned
A rather serious crime
To marry two wives at one time

—W. S. Gilbert (1875/1996, pp. 33, 35)

It is illegal in Canada to be married to more than one husband or wife at once, but the case of the Bountiful community in Lister, British Columbia, challenges this law. The group, part of a sect that broke away from the Mormon Church, openly practises polygamy. About 1000 men, women, and children live in the community, first established in the 1940s. Although he won't confirm the numbers, former leader Winston Blackmore is speculated to have 26 wives and more than 100 children.

Officials have long been concerned over reports of sexual and physical abuse of women and children in Bountiful. But for many years, B.C. authorities decided not to prosecute sect members for polygamy. They believed the law banning it could be challenged under the guarantee of religious freedom under the *Charter of Rights and Freedoms*. More recently, federal authorities stated that the Charter does not protect polygamists (Bailey, 2007; Bramham, 2008). After the successful conviction for polygamy of Warren Jeffs, a polygamous Mormon leader, in Utah in 2007, Canadian authorities decided to react. In January 2009, B.C. Attorney General Wally Oppal charged two of the leaders of the Bountiful community with one count each of practising polygamy. In the fall of 2009, the charges were thrown out after the men's lawyers successfully argued in court that the decision of a previous special prosecutor not to lay charges was final. The latest development occurred on November 23, 2011, when Justice Bauman of the B.C. Supreme Court ruled to uphold Canada's polygamy laws as constitutional. In his ruling, Justice Bauman said the law violates the religious freedom of fundamentalist Mormons, but the harm against women and children outweighs that concern.

Sources: Bailey, 2007; Bala, 2004; Bramham, 2008; Oziewica, 2000; National Post, 2009.

Society and Marriage

The **marriage rate** measures marriages that occur in a given year. It does not include common-law unions or already existing marriages. In 2008, there were 147 288 marriages in Canada. At 4.4 marriages per 1000 people, the marriage rate was at the lowest level it has been in the past century (see Figure 4.1) (Human Resources and Skills Development Canada, 2012a). Unfortunately, these are the last data we will have on the number of marriages in Canada. Statistics Canada no longer collects information on marriage and divorce rates. (*Globe and Mail*, 2011).

Social, economic, and legal factors determine the age at which individuals marry for the first time. During the Great Depression, marriages were delayed. After the Depression, the rate reached almost 11 marriages per 1000 people in the first years of World War II. One explanation is that, fearing the uncertainty of war, young men hurried to get married before they were sent overseas. During the prosperous times following the war, the ages of both men and women marrying for the first time reached a low for the century. The marriage rate peaked

marriage rate: a measure of marriages that occur in a given year

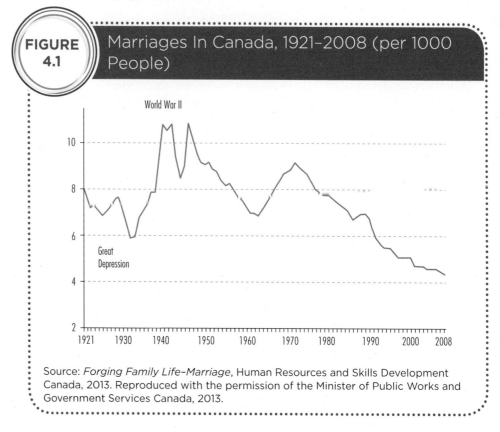

FIGURE 4.1 Marriages In Canada, 1921–2008 (per 1000 People)

Source: *Forging Family Life-Marriage,* Human Resources and Skills Development Canada, 2013. Reproduced with the permission of the Minister of Public Works and Government Services Canada, 2013.

again in the 1970s, as the baby boom generation entered adulthood (Human Resources and Skills Development Canada, 2012a). Now, first marriages are once again occurring later in life. Indeed, since 1991, first marriage rates have closely followed economic upswings and downturns. Three factors may be involved: women's greater education levels, poor opportunities for young workers, and an increase in the proportion of couples living together before marriage (Statistics Canada, 2008j).

Canadians who do marry are doing so at an older age than ever before. While there is a popular belief that people in the past married at a younger age, in fact the average age of first marriage has fluctuated. In 1950, the average age at first marriage was 28.5 years for men and 25.9 years for women. Between 1972 and 2008, the average age at first marriage increased from 22.5 to 29.1 for women and from 24.9 to 31.1 for men (Human Resources and Skills Development Canada, 2012a). What has remained stable over time is that grooms are generally around two years older than brides. This has implications both during the marriage and toward its end. Because women, on average, live longer than men, a woman is more likely to die a widow while a man is more likely to die a husband (Eichler, 2012).

One explanation for the trend to postpone marriage is that extended schooling among women delays the timing of life transitions, including family formation. Furthermore, in the past, female university graduates were less likely to marry than women who did not have a university education. In 1981, 65 percent of women with a university degree were married, compared with 76 percent of women who did not have a university degree. But this is no longer the case. In 2006, 57 percent of women with a university degree were married, compared with 53 percent of women without a university degree (Statistics Canada, 2010c).

There are also regional differences. In 2008, the marriage rates of Nunavut, the Northwest Territories, and Quebec were all significantly below the national average (Human Resources and Skills Development Canada, 2012a). Historically, the marriage rate has been lower in Quebec than in Ontario. According to researchers at Statistics Canada, one reason may be the celibacy rule for Roman Catholic priests and nuns, a greater number of whom live in Quebec than in Ontario (Dumas & Bélanger, 1996). This trend also has its roots in the Quiet Revolution of the 1960s, when Quebeckers began rejecting marriage because of its religious overtone and more and more people began choosing common-law unions (Statistics Canada, 2009j).

The Law and Marriage

Because marriage is a legal contract, it is governed by laws. The Canadian Constitution divides jurisdiction over marriage. As we noted previously, the *Civil Marriage Act* gives Parliament responsibility for the legal definition of marriage, while the provinces are responsible for licensing and registering marriages, and the *Marriage (Prohibited Degrees) Act* lays out rules about who can marry. In Canada, brothers and sisters cannot marry, although such marriages were popular among ancient Egyptian royalty. Marriage to more than one person at a time is not allowed. A divorce or annulment is necessary before a married person can be married again. Religious annulments are not recognized by Canadian law and are valid only to the extent that they may be recognized by the church that performed the marriage ceremony. The provinces and territories each set their own laws concerning the legal age for marriage. Across the country, both partners must be 18 years old (19 in British Columbia), but one or both may marry as young as 16 with parental consent. Marriages may be voided (their legal status is as if they had never occurred) if they are afflicted with a flaw that nullifies the marriage, for example if one of the spouses is already married or the spouses are closely related. Marriages have to be consummated by sexual intercourse between the couple and may be voided if they are not. Attempts to void marriages done on a bet, on a dare, or to get a gift, have all failed (Duhaime, 2012). Under Canadian law, a **marriage of convenience**, which is a marriage where the sole purpose is for the spouse to immigrate to Canada, is illegal (Citizenship and Immigration Canada, 2012d).

marriage of convenience: a marriage where the sole purpose is for the spouse to immigrate

The law also governs who may perform a legal marriage. Marriage ceremonies are performed either by clerics during a religious ceremony or by judges or justices of the peace during a civil ceremony. At the beginning of the 21st century, 76 percent of marriage ceremonies were religious. Religious ceremonies were most common in Ontario (98.5 percent), while in British Columbia more than half the ceremonies were civil (Eichler, 2012).

Before 2003, same-sex marriages were barred in Canada. Under pressure, several provinces enacted a "registered domestic partnership" law, giving each partner the status of "spouse" for many purposes, regardless of sex. Alberta went further, passing the *Adult Interdependent Relationships Act*, effective in June 2003, which applied to unmarried same-sex and opposite-sex partners but might include other close relationships, such as parent and child. Same-sex couples argued that even though they could register their partnerships, denying them the right to marry was discriminatory. Court rulings in several provinces led to a patchwork of laws and regulations, allowing same-sex marriage in some jurisdictions but not in others.

The federal government drafted legislation legalizing same-sex marriage and referred the proposed law to the Supreme Court of Canada for an opinion on four questions:

1. Can Parliament alone pass laws concerning marriage?
2. Is the section of the draft bill that permits same-sex couples to marry consistent with the *Charter of Rights and Freedoms*?
3. Does the freedom of religion guaranteed by the Charter protect religious officials who refuse to perform same-sex marriages?
4. Is the opposite-sex requirement for marriage consistent with the Charter?

In December 2004, the Supreme Court answered yes to only the first three questions. It did not answer the fourth because the federal government intended to proceed with the legislation. In the midst of heated controversy, the *Civil Marriage Act* became law on July 20, 2005. The central provision of the act was the definition of marriage as "the lawful union of two persons to the exclusion of all others" (Bala, 2004; Hurley, 2005).

A marriage brings with it both rights and duties. Partners have the right to sexual access to the other; they have the right to be treated kindly; they have the right to expect faithfulness from each other. A divorce can be granted if one partner refuses sex, if he or she has sexual relations with someone other than the spouse, or if he or she is cruel toward the other. Laws against assault apply to spouses as much as to unrelated individuals. Both partners have the right to use family assets, although the individual who owns a car or cottage may sell it without the consent of the other. They have a right to the matrimonial home, which is usually treated in law as a special case. They have a responsibility to support each other and any children they might have. They also have the right to decide the kind of upbringing they want for their children—for example, which schools they should attend and in which religious faith they should be raised (Cochrane, 2007; Kronby, 2006).

Some couples draw up a marriage contract, sometimes called a prenuptial agreement—that is, a legal document that alters the effect of the law, usually as it applies to property. Some couples go as far as to include the number of children they will have and who will take out the garbage. One lawyer suggests that if couples need to include such details, their relationship may well be in trouble (Cochrane, 2007; Kronby, 2006). Couples may decide to enter into these types of agreements so that they have control over who gets what in the event of a breakup. Even though the property rights of each partner in the event of a divorce are defined by law, couples sometimes disagree over who should get which debts and assets.

A marriage contract can create problems. If the financial situation of one or both partners changes, it may impose an unfair settlement on the couple. For instance, both partners may be working when they marry. If they have a child and one spouse stays home to care for the child, that person may not be in a good position to support himself or herself if the couple splits up. Contracts may be set aside in court if they are clearly unfair or if deception was involved (Cochrane, 2007).

If a couple that is living together in a common-law relationship breaks up, their rights and obligations regarding their assets and liabilities are often not very well defined by law. Because of this, some unmarried couples choose to sign a cohabitation agreement so that they both know who is entitled to what if they break up (Financial Consumer Agency of Canada, 2012). Property is not automatically shared, and untangling who is entitled to how much can lead to costly legal battles. And not every province provides for support for common-law partners. Quebec is a notable example. In that province, common-law partners are known as de facto partners and no statutory provisions give them rights regarding property division, the family residence, and spousal support (Common Law Separation Canada, 2007). The other provinces vary in the length of time the unmarried couple must live together before spousal rights are recognized.

A cohabitation agreement also provides a way to ensure that a partner can inherit from the other partner. Unlike in marriage, an earlier will does not become void when two people become a cohabiting couple. Thus, a former spouse or other person may inherit if rights are not clarified by a contract or will. A final reason for a cohabitation agreement is to protect partners from future changes in the law. For example, if common-law spouses are granted the same property rights as legally married couples, a contract could exempt them from these provisions (Bala, 2004; Cochrane, 2007).

Talking about laws and contracts in general terms is difficult, since legislation differs from province to province. In most provinces, legally married spouses have an equal share in the family home and in assets gained during the marriage. When an individual remarries, a contract may be used to protect the interests of the children from the first marriage. The new spouse may be barred from inheriting property, such as a house, that was acquired during the first marriage. In one case, a woman who had been in extreme poverty following a divorce saw the marriage contract as a sign of love from her second husband. Under the contract, her new husband has no legal right to the house she bought with her own money; she is thus assured that she will not lose financially as a result of her second marriage. When a wealthy spouse marries someone with little money, a contract may be drawn up limiting the share the poorer one can get if the marriage breaks up. Business owners may draw up contracts excluding the business from the assets of the marriage: under equal-sharing rules, the spouse would be entitled to half of the business assets if the marriage ends. If there are several business partners, that might jeopardize the business. A contract can head off such difficulties (Cochrane, 2007).

Marriage in the Family Cycle

In the past, marriage was a rite of passage that marked the fact that an individual had reached adulthood. With marriage came approved sexual relations, cohabitation, and parenthood (Amato et al., 2007). Marriage was closely related to the economic and social organization of society; for example, in traditional Aboriginal cultures men and women had different roles based on sex and family status. In patriarchal cultures, men work to support the family and women provide physical and emotional care for its members.

The symbolic meaning of marriage is changing. It is no longer the official signal that an individual has adult status. In fact, marriages are being delayed until later in life, and individuals are not waiting for the ceremony before they have sexual relations or live together. The ability to support oneself financially has become a more common criterion of adulthood. Since more women are now in the workforce, they are not necessarily dependent on men for support. In addition, widely available contraceptives mean that parenthood can often be postponed indefinitely (Arnett, 2007; Coontz, 2005).

From the developmental perspective, the transition to a successful marriage requires completing four tasks. Each married couple must establish a couple identity, define their boundaries, maintain a household, and manage their relationship. The couple must develop a variety of strategies for accomplishing these tasks effectively (Brotherson & Moen, 2011). Marriage also requires commitment to a new family system (McGoldrick, 1999a). It often involves separating emotionally from the family of origin, learning to accept the roles of husband and wife, and gaining a sense of identity as a new and distinct family. This sense of being a couple is referred to as "we-ness" (Driver et al., 2003). The couple needs to learn to depend first on each other for satisfaction of their needs. Even couples who have lived together before marriage report that their relationship changes after marriage. Many find this fact surprising, but men and women often bring to marriage expectations learned in their families of origin that they did not have of the living-with relationship. They may have the security to act naturally for the first time, but each spouse brings a history of traditions and expectations. The couple must decide which of these to keep, change, or drop (McGoldrick, 1999a).

The wife and husband have individually been members of various microsystems—family of origin, friends, workplace. Now they must renegotiate as a couple their relationships with these groups. Even if they have been living together, the partners may not have related to the extended families as a couple; each may have visited her

Finding a spouse is hard work.

Source: Barry Maguire.

or his family alone. Changes that couples make in visiting patterns, in social activities such as a night out with friends, or in family rituals and traditions affect others—some may become hurt or angry. The new marriage partner is often the first new member of the extended family system in many years. The stress of change may lead to conflict with in-laws and friends. Some issues may be put on hold by the couple. For instance, they may not deal with sex-role-related issues, such as the responsibility for childcare, until they become parents (McGoldrick, 1999a).

Ethnic couples may face additional adjustment stresses due to differences between the messages that the media, schools, and other institutions of the white Christian majority give off about families and the values of their ethnic group. Minority groups may have family boundaries different from those of the majority. For example, many Italian families put more emphasis on the extended family and less on the nuclear family. In traditional South Asian culture, the well-being of extended families takes precedence over individual or couple happiness. A couple may not separate from one or both families of origin to the same degree as in the dominant North American culture. Nevertheless, partners also need to deal with issues related to "we-ness" and their relationship with extended family members. Conflict over the definition of sex roles may also exist. Immigrants from Muslim countries, for example, may expect more subservience in women than is usual among English or French Canadians; if women begin to accept new values, serious conflict may arise between spouses. Standards among cultures over the degree of emotional intimacy between spouses also vary. In cultures where marriages are usually arranged, less intimacy may be expected than in the dominant culture, with its emphasis on the self-sufficient nuclear family (Bush et al., 2010; Hines et al., 1999).

mixed couple: opposite-sex or same-sex, common-law or married couples in which one spouse or partner is a member of a visible minority group and the other is not, as well as couples comprised of two different visible minority groups

With the increasing ethnic diversity of the Canadian population, it is hardly surprising that the number of couples in mixed unions has been on the rise since the early 1990s. In 2006, nearly 4 percent of Canadian couples were mixed. **Mixed couples** are defined as opposite-sex or same-sex, common-law or married couples in which one spouse or partner is a member of a visible minority group and the other is not, as well as couples comprised of two different visible minority groups (Milan et al., 2010). Compared to couples who were not in mixed unions, people in mixed unions were younger, did better socioeconomically, and were more likely to live in large urban areas. A higher proportion was Canadian-born, and the proportion increased with the number of generations in Canada. The impact of mixed unions will certainly change the dynamic and nature of Canada's ethnic diversity in future generations, with consequences such as the choice of language within mixed households, as well as how children in mixed families report their ethnic origins and identify with visible minority groups (Milan et al., 2010).

Mixed marriage may make adjustment more difficult for a couple. An important source of conflict may arise if one partner focuses on individualism and the other on family and community ties. Because partners lack the same cultural expectations, conflict can be harsh and unpleasant. Relations with in-laws can also lead to disagreements that may vary from the amount of time spent with relatives to inviting a widowed mother to live with the couple. Some issues, perhaps religion, may be brushed aside until children are born (Bratter & King, 2008; Daneshpour, 2009; Lowe, 2006; Zhang & Van Hook, 2009).

Why Marry?

Although fewer individuals in their 20s are marrying now than even 15 years ago, many people will marry at some time during their lives, so there must be reasons for the institution's continuing popularity. Over the centuries, marriage has served a number of purposes, most of which are still relevant today.

Status

Getting married gives one a social status, and for some, this gives them a sense of place and belonging in society. Although most Canadians do not marry for money or position, they do consider whether their prospective partner earns enough

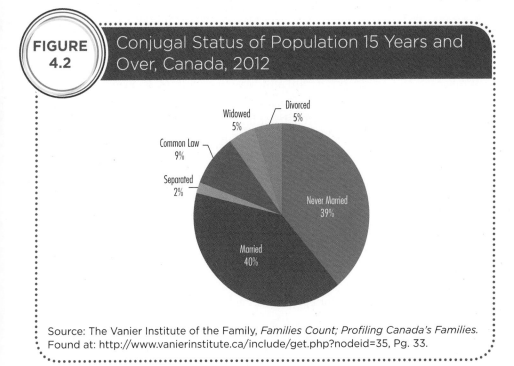

FIGURE 4.2

Conjugal Status of Population 15 Years and Over, Canada, 2012

Source: The Vanier Institute of the Family, *Families Count; Profiling Canada's Families.* Found at: http://www.vanierinstitute.ca/include/get.php?nodeid=35, Pg. 33.

TABLE 4.1

Conjugal Status of Population 15 Years and Over, by Province, 2012

	Never Married	Married	Separated	Common-Law	Widowed	Divorced
Canada	13 788 492	13 833 655	767 550	3 002 058	1 798 662	1 690 074
Newfoundland and Labrador	183 855	238 095	8 639	30 784	33 428	17 858
Prince Edward Island	55 823	63 654	3 812	8 681	8 462	5 673
Nova Scotia	356 067	390 512	23 632	72 863	60 314	45 307
New Brunswick	277 510	317 789	21 286	63 022	45 990	30 353
Quebec	3 203 412	2 542 181	124 989	1 282 292	441 078	460 804
Ontario	5 296 062	5 781 190	356 911	781 201	696 815	593 721
Manitoba	537 007	506 881	24 905	76 849	67 153	54 208
Saskatchewan	455 976	432 382	19 669	69 339	60 347	42 245
Alberta	1 583 685	1 596 139	77 450	284 893	146 134	185 444
British Columbia	1 782 758	1 933 751	103 816	315 880	235 850	250 518
Northwest Territories	21 407	12 015	926	6 348	1 201	1 452
Yukon	15 378	11 657	1 069	4 778	1 156	2 063
Nunavut	19 552	7 409	446	5 128	734	428

Source: The Vanier Institute of the Family, *Families Count; Profiling Canada's Families.* Found at: http://www.vanierinstitute.ca/include/get.php?nodeid=35, Pg. 33.

money so that they can have the lifestyle they want (Regan, 2008). Marriage continues to give couples a legal and social status they do not gain by cohabitation (Roy, 2005).

Immigrants to Canada may find that the marriage customs and laws in their home country differ from those in Canada. Many countries allow marriage before the age of 18, especially for girls, but according to Citizenship and Immigration Canada, a person is considered a spouse only if the marriage is valid under the law of the country where it took place and under Canadian law (Citizenship and Immigration, 2009b). Various religions, such as Islam, permit multiple marriages; however, families that arrive from countries such as Saudi Arabia and Pakistan that allow men to marry more than one wife will have only one wife recognized under Canadian law.

Economics

There are economic reasons for getting married and starting a family (Coontz, 2005). When homesteaders went west, both men and women had to put in long hours clearing stumps and breaking the soil. After their children were born, the wife's responsibilities centred more on the house they had built. Once old enough, the children helped out with farm chores. This pattern continued into the 20th century in rural Canada. A study of a Quebec parish in the 1930s found that for a farm to be productive, the labour of all family members was required (Miner, 1939/1974). In current Canadian family law, the two partners have a duty to support each other financially, either by making money or by caring for the home and children (Cochrane, 2007).

Nowadays, marriage is not necessarily a financial benefit. For example, the Old Age Security pension is given by the federal government to individuals rather than to families. Because they can cut costs by sharing accommodation, married and cohabiting couples are less likely to be poor than a single person. Marriage does, however, grant rights to support and to property division.

Sex

adultery: the act of having sexual relations with someone other than your spouse

Marriage is designed to regulate sexual behaviour. Usually marriage limits sexual relations to an exclusive partner. This expectation is reflected in Canadian divorce law, in which **adultery** is grounds for divorce. In the past, it was considered important that a bride be a virgin and that she have sexual relations only with her husband. This stricture ensured that land and titles were passed on only to biological descendants of the husband. It mattered less, however, if the man had sexual experience before and outside marriage. With improved contraception, child-bearing can be separated from sexual activity. Although sexual access to the partner is presumed, it is not always present in marriage, such as when illness prevents it or when one or both partners do not choose to have sexual relations. When this occurs, divorce may be granted on grounds of cruelty or marriage breakdown (Cochrane, 2007; Coontz, 2005; Donnelly & Burgess, 2008).

Children

Marriage is also designed to care for children. Since they need parents' care for so many years, the stability of the marriage relationship allows children to survive physically and to become socialized and productive members of society (Amato, 2005). In Canada, children are entitled to financial support regardless of the marital status of their parents (Department of Justice, 2006). Higher levels of female employment and social benefits have made it possible for single parents to raise children, although usually not in luxury.

Identity

Particularly for women, marriage has provided an identity over the years. In the past, the wife has taken her husband's name. In Quebec, since 1981, spouses have been required to keep their birth surnames unless there are exceptional circumstances (Directeur de l'état civil Québec, 2007; Justice Québec, 2003). During daily living, the couple forms a unique family culture and worldview. These aspects of the family identity also provide a sense of purpose and meaning for each individual. With current opportunities to build a career, women no longer need to depend on a husband for economic identity.

Love and Support

Finally, marriage serves to look after the emotional needs of the partners, a requirement that arises from the idea of romantic love. No matter how wrong things are in the rest of the world, partners expect their husband or wife to be loving, sympathetic, and encouraging. In marriage, a person expects to find unfailing love and support (Amato et al., 2007; Lasch, 1979). As we can tell from the levels of marital violence and divorce, however, not all partners are kind and loving. And the unmarried can also have their emotional needs met by extended family members, friends, and lovers.

Other Reasons

Most functions traditionally considered part of marriage can be met in other ways. So why marry? Obviously, marriage has appeal, as witnessed by the drive to legalize same-sex unions.

First, marriage provides what one theorist calls an "enforceable trust." That is, the legal provisions for support and sexual fidelity provide the couple a degree of security (Coontz, 2005). Because marriage assumes a long-term contract between spouses, they may feel secure enough to incur short-term costs for long-term benefits (Waite, 2003). For example, one partner may support the other during postsecondary schooling because he or she expects family income to eventually be higher. Married partners also have greater financial rights if their union is dissolved (Cochrane, 2007).

Second, marriage has been regarded as superior to other kinds of adult relationships, such as nonsexual friendships, domestic partnerships, long-term cohabitation, and single-parent families (Ellison, 2004). Although current trends in divorce and single-parent families show an increase, most of us have been socialized to believe that marriage is the "natural" state for adults. A good deal of pressure is still put on couples who are dating or living together to get married. Often, parents and grandparents wish to be grandparents and great-grandparents and see marriage as a desirable step toward parenthood. Once most people of a particular age group, or cohort, are married, social life tends to be organized on a couples basis, thereby putting further pressure on individuals to marry. Marriages tend to occur in waves. Once a couple has attended several weddings, they may marry as a way to repay social obligations. Ethnic and religious groups differ, however, in how much they value and expect marriage (Le Bourdais et al., 2003).

The whole romantic view of love may also be involved in individual decisions to marry. For those who are having problems, such as loneliness or difficulties with their family of origin, marriage may beckon as an instant cure (McGoldrick, 1999a). As we can see by the present high rate of divorce, such hopes are often dashed. Indeed, the first same-sex partners granted a divorce in Canada spoke of their unrealistic expectations that marriage would "fix" their problems (Makin, 2004).

In spite of the pressures to marry, the marriage ideal has changed. It is no longer seen as the principal career for a woman or solely as a financial partnership. Nor is it seen as the only setting in which to raise children. Rather, individuals come to marriage looking for self-fulfillment and for emotional growth and satisfaction. Ideally, each partner is willing to work at making their relationship worthwhile. The result is a greater emphasis on equality and sharing (Coontz, 2005).

Changes in Marriage over Time

From the structural functionalist perspective, the family is a unit that ensures the survival of its members through separate roles for men and women. Exchange theorists point out trade-offs in these roles. For example, men's big-game hunting was important in providing protein; in return, women prepared and preserved the meat for family use. Feminists add that, in societies where status and power are granted to men, women are exploited. This problem was particularly true of Victorian society. Women traded child-bearing, as well as household and family care, for the financial support and status provided by men. This pattern was also present in rural Quebec and in at least some Aboriginal societies.

Today, couples look forward to a much more democratic marriage. The wife usually plans to keep working after marriage, since her income is important in maintaining the couple's standard of living. In turn, many husbands do more housework. This change has been gradual, though. Sociologists point to the effect of the two world wars, in which women had to replace men in the factories and offices. After the wars, most women returned to their traditional role—the ideal of the breadwinner husband and homemaker wife and mother was still strong. One outcome of the acceptance of the "traditional" family was the baby boom; it was as if the couples were making up for lost time, and more. This period has been called the "golden age of the nuclear family" (Coontz, 2005). Nonetheless, the principle that respectable women could work outside the home had been established. Women who continued to work after marriage did so to help buy houses or new furniture. Once children were born, mothers stayed home, at least until the children were in school. Since women often worked part time, their pay was seen as an extra, something to help buy luxuries; their real business was looking after the family (Coontz, 2005).

By the 1970s, income was not keeping pace with inflation and a wife's pay was often necessary to prevent the family's purchasing power from declining. In addition, a growing number of women chose to follow their own career goals. In 2011, about 58 percent of all women aged 15 and over had jobs. Among those aged 15 to 24, a higher proportion of women (56.4 percent) than men (54.5 percent) were employed (Statistics Canada, 2012h) (see Table 4.2).

Roles in Marriage

The shift from single-income to dual-income families has created conflicts concerning men's and women's roles in the family. Values and expectations about what their roles should be have not changed as fast as families have. As seen in Table 4.3, men spend more hours than women on paid work, but women outperform men in the number of hours they devote to housework and to childcare. As might be expected, at present no single pattern of marriage roles exists. In fact, four have been described by sociologists.

Conventional Roles

The first role pattern, usually referred to as **conventional roles**, is based on the structural functionalist notion that men and women have separate spheres of action, and that the home is the proper place for women, just as the labour force is for men. This pattern originated among the middle class in the 19th century. Since the man held the power base in the family, the woman gained her status from her husband (Coontz, 2005). Such a view in an extreme form is represented by the

conventional roles: a marriage with a homemaker wife and breadwinner husband

---

TABLE 4.2 Employment Rates of Women and Men, by Age, 2011

	Women	Men
All ages	57.9%	65.9%
15–24 years	56.4%	54.5%
25–54 years	77.2%	84.8%
55 years and over	29.1%	39.6%

Source: Statistics Canada. 2012. *Table 282-0002—Labour force survey estimates (LFS), by sex and detailed age group, annual (persons unless otherwise noted),* CANSIM (database). Ottawa, Ontario. Statistics Canada. http://www5.statcan.gc.ca/cansim/pick-choisir?lang=eng&p2=33&id=2820002

expectation that a wife should be "barefoot, pregnant, and in the kitchen." This type of family is now a minority in Canada (Marshall, 2006).

As long as the marriage lasts and employment is secure, the conventional pattern has distinct advantages. The specialization in tasks allows the partners to become expert in specific areas. A particular strength is that it provides for specialized care of children and home. This division of labour reflects the organization of society, where paid employment tends to become more and more specialized. It also fits in with the socialization children receive in most families concerning gender roles—that girls and boys are expected to behave in different ways.

There are, however, disadvantages to the conventional model. With only one wage earner, families have less security in poorer economic times. In addition, there is little security for women if partners separate. Furthermore, the role for women is isolating, since housework tends to be done alone. Wives' hunger for adult companionship may lead to demands on husbands, and perhaps to marital dissatisfaction and conflict. It may also be difficult for a woman to move from the workforce to being at home alone. She may miss the companionship and challenges she had on the job. Instead of having her own work identity, she now takes her status from her husband (Coontz, 2005).

Shared Roles

shared roles: a marriage in which both partners work and share household responsibilities

Currently, the most common roles in marriage are **shared roles**, where both partners work and share household responsibilities. Many more women are sharing the provider role, although, on average, they contribute less than half the family income because of their lower hourly earnings. Almost two-thirds of couples have similar weekly work hours. Now that women are sharing the provider role, men are spending more time in chores and childcare. The general notion that men "help" with housework and women "help" with the provider role still persists, though to a lesser degree than before (Daly, 2004a; Marshall, 2006, 2009). We will look at the relationship between family and workplace more fully in Chapter 12.

Dual-Career Roles

dual-career roles: a marriage in which both partners are committed to their careers

A third pattern is **dual-career roles**, in which both partners are committed to their careers (Beaujot, 2000; Nett, 1988). This is sometimes difficult to distinguish from shared roles. The difference is the priority set on the career. Some women start working to help out financially, and what was originally just a job becomes a career. By definition, careers exclude interrupted or part-time work, so the proportion of women employed in them is small. When wives have an income of $100 000 or more, paid work and housework are more likely to be split evenly (Marshall, 2006). In a small study of such families, couples often shared chores based on other factors, such as who likes to cook, while neither partner seemed to be in a better bargaining position (Risman & Johnson-Sumerford, 1998). The arrangement may work very well until the couple has children, often later than other families because of the desire to get careers established. The presence of a child makes long workdays and business trips much harder to schedule. These couples may thus be faced with sacrificing one career, at least for a while, or

TABLE 4.3

Average Hours per Day Spent on Paid Work, Housework, and Other Unpaid Work*

	1992	1998	2010
Men			
Total paid and unpaid	13.3	13.3	13.4
Paid work and related	8.8	8.8	8.5
Housework	2.9	2.8	3.0
Childcare	1.6	1.7	1.9
Women			
Total paid and unpaid	14.7	14.4	14.9
Paid work and related	7.6	7.7	7.7
Housework	4.8	4.3	4.3
Childcare	2.3	2.4	2.9

* Averaged over one week

Source: Statistics Canada. 2010. *Average time spent per day on various activities, for the population and participants aged 15 and over, by sex, Canada, 2010* (table). "General Social Survey - 2010: Overview of the Time Use of Canadians." Ottawa, Ontario. Statistics Canada. http://www.statcan.gc.ca/pub/89-647-x/2011001/tbl/tbl11-eng.htm and http://www.statcan.gc.ca/pub/89-647-x/2011001/tbl/tbl12-eng.htm and http://www5.statcan.gc.ca/cansim/a26

purchasing household services and nanny care for children. High-income households are more likely to pay for domestic help, especially if the woman makes more money (Marshall, 2006; Treas & de Ruijter, 2008). They may also face difficulties such as deciding whose job has priority in the event that the transfer of one partner and not the other comes up. Such decisions may be made on the basis of income earned or availability of jobs in the two fields.

Reverse Conventional Roles

A fourth pattern, in which there is a breadwinner wife and a homemaker husband, is referred to as **reverse conventional roles** (Nett, 1988). In 2005, only 11 percent of Canadian families fit this pattern (Marshall, 2006). The househusband appears in popular culture, for example in the comic strip *Adam@Home* (Bassett, n.d.) and the reality-TV show *Househusbands of Hollywood*. This arrangement is often temporary. Some couples opt for the husband to stay at home with young children because the wife's pay is higher or more secure. Currently, parental benefits can be claimed by one parent or shared between the two partners (Service Canada, 2009). More fathers are therefore choosing to stay home with their new children when their wives return to work (Marshall, 2003). Sometimes wives are

reverse conventional roles: a marriage with a breadwinner wife and homemaker husband

forced to become primary breadwinners if their husbands are laid off, injured, or recovering from an illness.

During economic downturns, as reported by the media (e.g., Kershaw, 2009), the numbers of "Mr. Moms" may increase. According to Statistics Canada, when employment fell each month from October 2008 until March 2009, men aged 25 to 54 were harder hit than their wives (Statistics Canada, 2009e). Many men report how rewarding it is to develop a close relationship with their children. Although stay-at-home fathers experienced social stigma in the past, that may be lessening as more men in general are increasing their involvement in housework and childcare.

Time to Review

1. How does marriage fit into the life cycle?
2. What challenges do mixed couples face?
3. What are some of the reasons for getting married?
4. How have marriages changed over time?
5. What are the patterns of roles in marriage?

Together, but Not Married

Many couples live together before or in place of marriage. Unmarried cohabitation is not new. In some parts of the world, especially in Africa and Sweden, it has been common for centuries (Ambert, 2005a; Coontz, 2005). In many countries, it has society's partial blessing as a stage in couple formation and courtship, but as one that should lead to formal marriage.

In Canada, cohabitation is increasingly accepted, especially among younger people. A 2009 survey of young people aged 15 to 19 found that over three-quarters approved of cohabitation, and at least one-third stated explicitly that they planned to live with someone at some point in their lives (Vanier Institute of the Family, 2010). The majority of Canadian men and women still wish to have a lasting relationship as a couple, and the decline of marriage has been mostly offset by the growth of cohabiting unions (Le Bourdais & Lapierre-Adamcyk, 2004). Young adults, francophones, those who do not attend religious services, and Canadian-born individuals are more likely to approve of cohabitation. In addition, those who had lived through family disruption as children were more apt to be in favour of cohabitation (Milan, 2003).

common-law union:
a union of two partners in a lasting relationship resembling marriage

According to the 2011 Census, 2.8 million people aged 15 and older were in a **common-law union** (see Table 4.4). Common-law families now make up 15.4 percent of all census families, a proportion that has more than doubled over the past two decades (Vanier Institute of the Family, 2010). Most of those forming families through a common-law relationship eventually marry. This suggests that Canadians generally view cohabitation as a prelude to marriage rather than a substitute for it. A notable exception is in Quebec, where many believe that common-law is a distinct alternative to marriage (Vanier Institute of the Family, 2010).

TABLE 4.4	Proportion of Common-Law Families as a Percentage of All Families, 2011
Canada	16.7%
Newfoundland and Labrador	12.9%
Prince Edward Island	11.2%
Nova Scotia	14.2%
New Brunswick	16.0%
Quebec	31.5%
Ontario	10.9%
Manitoba	11.9%
Saskatchewan	12.5%
Alberta	13.6%
British Columbia	13.0%
Yukon	25.1%
Northwest Territories	28.7%
Nunavut	32.7%

Source: Adapted from: A. Milan, M. Vézina and C. Wells. 2007. *Table 4.* "Family Portrait: Continuity and Change in Canadian Families and Household in 2006, 2006 Census." *Census.* Catalogue No. 97-553-XIE. Ottawa, Ontario. Sept. 12, 2007.

This trend is rooted in Quebec's Quiet Revolution, during which the Roman Catholic Church's influence on family life declined and contraception became more available. However, cohabiting couples in Quebec tend to have the same characteristics as married couples in the rest of Canada—they have strong labour force participation, higher incomes, and lower rates of poverty (Mohs, 2012).

For cohorts born before 1960, the proportion of cohabiting couples is also increasing. This suggests that many people are choosing to cohabit instead of remarrying after divorce or widowhood (Ambert, 2005a; King & Scott, 2005; Wu, 2007). In addition, those who have cohabited before marriage are more likely to do so after the marriage ends (Wu, 1995).

Living Together and the Law

Even though couples living together may behave as if they are married—for instance, by calling each other "husband" or "wife"—and may be considered married by relatives and friends, by law they are not married.

To be considered a common-law union, the couple must live together for a certain period of time (see Table 4.5). For federal issues such as federal government

TABLE 4.5 — Criteria for Common-Law Status

Province/Territory	Criteria for Common-Law Status
Alberta	Alberta does not have common law marriage. Instead they have created a category of relationship known as adult interdependent partner. An adult interdependent partner is someone living in a relationship of interdependence for a period of at least three years, or a relationship of some permanence if there is a child. You can also become an adult interdependent partner by entering into a written adult interdependent partner agreement.
British Columbia	You must cohabit for two years in a marriage-like relationship.
Manitoba	You must cohabit for three years, or for one year if you have a child together.
New Brunswick	You must cohabit continuously in a family relationship for three years and one person must be substantially dependent on the other for support, or live together for one year and have a child together.
Newfoundland	You must cohabit for one year and have a child together.
Nova Scotia	You must cohabit for two years.
Ontario	You must cohabit for three years, or have a child and a relationship of some permanence.
PEI and NWT	You must cohabit for a period of at least two years, or have cohabited in a relationship of some permanence and together you are the natural or adoptive parents of a child.
Quebec	Quebec, unlike the other provinces has a Civil Code, and it has never recognized common-law partnership as a kind of marriage. In Quebec, common-law partners are known as de facto partners. Many laws in Quebec explicitly apply to de facto partners in much the same way as spouses. Currently there is no clear timeline for becoming de facto partners.
Saskatchewan	You must cohabit continuously for a period of not less than 24 months.
Yukon	You must cohabit in a relationship of some permanence.

Sources: CommonLawRelationships.ca; Regie des Rentes Quebec, Definition of Spouse. Found at: http://www.rrq .gouv.qc.ca/en/vie_a_deux/couple/Pages/definition_conjoint.aspx

pensions, the required period of cohabitation is one year. Each province sets its own conditions for common-law status. In Ontario and New Brunswick, the period is three years, while in British Columbia and Nova Scotia, the period is two years. Some provinces, such as Ontario, also consider a couple to be common-law if they have a child together and are living together, regardless of the length of time. A common-law union can be either between people of the same sex or opposite sex; it does not make a difference for legal purposes (Canadian Divorce Laws, 2012a).

In 1995, the Supreme Court of Canada ruled that marital status and sexual orientation are prohibited grounds of discrimination under the *Canadian Charter of Rights and Freedoms*. Following the ruling, many laws and amendments have been passed that extend the rights and benefits of marriage to unmarried cohabiting couples (Bailey, 2004). Yet there are still differences. To receive spousal support, cohabiting partners must stay together for the eligibility period to be considered a common-law union. Married couples get this right as soon as they are married. If one partner in a common-law union dies without a will, there are no automatic inheritance rights for the other partner (Canadian Divorce Laws, 2012a).

Cohabiting couples still do not have the same property rights as married couples (Cochrane, 2007). Whoever owns something—house, car, or business— keeps it without sharing if the couple separates. Former partners may be able to claim a share if they are able to prove that they made a contribution to gaining the asset. In one case heard by the Supreme Court of Canada, a couple that had lived together for about 20 years had in that time built up a successful farm and bee-keeping business, which was registered in the man's name. The Court decided that the woman had contributed equal work and effort, and gave her half the property and business assets (Kronby, 2006). In each of several other such cases, the cohabiting partner needed to prove his or her contribution. As we have seen, some of these difficulties can be overcome by making a cohabitation agreement.

But spousal status carries burdens as well as rights. Some legal challenges have been made by those seeking to avoid the legal penalties associated with spousal status. For example, some social assistance payments are given based on the joint incomes of married or common-law couples. For individuals, it would be more advantageous to be considered as separate rather than joined (Bailey, 2004).

Quebec is a special case. Persons there "living in common-law unions may as well be strangers to each other, as far as the Quebec Civil Code is concerned" (Dumas & Bélanger, 1996, p. 126). Cohabitants have no specific legal obligations to each other, such as support or shared property rights. Their relationship is governed only by their private contracts, such as cohabitation agreements, joint purchase of a house, or a will. In social law, however, de facto (common-law) and married spouses are treated the same. They have the same rights and responsibilities around social assistance, benefits from the Quebec Pension Plan, and tax laws (Justice Québec, 2008; Roy, 2005).

Cohabitation and Marriage

In some ways, cohabitation and marriage are alike. Both involve romantic and sexual relationships in which individuals live together. Many couples regard cohabitation as a stage in courtship or as a trial marriage. Others choose it as an alternative to marriage. Part of the growing similarity between marriage and cohabitation is the result of changes in marriage. In addition, cohabitation is becoming accepted as a setting in which to raise children (Thornton et al., 2007).

There are, of course, differences between marriage and cohabitation. Marriage tends to be more permanent. There is no waiting period for legal rights and responsibilities to apply, as when couples live common-law. Cohabitation is not governed by the same social expectations as marriage, and the costs of leaving are seen as lower than marital separation or divorce (Musick & Bumpass, 2012).

Although much research suggests that cohabitation before marriage is associated with lower subsequent marital quality, this is not always so. Some research has found that cohabiting and non-cohabiting couples who eventually marry do not differ in terms of marital stability or dissolution rates. A number of studies also found that premarital cohabitation does not have a significant effect on marital quality (Jose et al., 2010). Some studies that looked specifically at physical abuse found that violence is more common among cohabiting couples (Statistics Canada, 2006a).

There are also differences between those choosing cohabitation rather than marriage. Young people who had romantic relationships and sexual intercourse at a younger age are more likely to cohabit, especially if they have had many sex partners (Thornton et al., 2007). One of the few longitudinal comparisons of cohabiting and married couples found that for females, higher levels of education and income were associated with a greater likelihood to choose cohabitation. For males, there was no significant difference in income between those who married and those who cohabited (Lachance-Grzela & Bouchard, 2009).

Cohabitors tend to be less religious and less traditional than non-cohabitors (Jose et al., 2010). Married people generally have more confidence in the future of their relationship and have less accepting attitudes toward divorce. Cohabiting partners are more likely to share housework equally. They are also more likely to share paid work, and cohabiting women are more likely to work. By contrast, married couples are more inclined than cohabiting partners to pool their financial resources (Le Bourdais & Lapierre-Adamcyk, 2004).

Only a minority of women cohabit with more than one partner. If serial cohabitors marry, they tend to have high divorce rates, about twice as high as women who lived only with their eventual husbands (Lichter & Qian, 2008). These trends suggest that some cohabitors have problems making a commitment or in making a long-term relationship work (Ambert, 2005a; Popenoe, 2008).

It is difficult to make general statements about the happiness of cohabiting couples. Why? Cohabitation covers a wide range of relationships, from steady dating, through trial marriage, to a substitute for marriage, including a setting for raising children. The social context has also changed. In the 1970s, many couples living together were free thinkers who did not accept social norms. These norms are now changing; cohabitation is more widely accepted socially (Wu, 2008). So what was true in the past may not hold for present-day couples. Research indicates, however, that part-time cohabitors tend to have greater conflict in their relationship than full-time ones (Madsen et al., 2012). Older cohabitors tend to be more satisfied with their relationship than younger individuals. They are also more likely to consider cohabiting as a substitute for marriage (King & Scott, 2005). Another way of measuring satisfaction is looking at how often couples separate. One Canadian study showed that cohabiting-couple families are more prone to break down than married families—two and a half times more likely in Quebec and five times more likely in the rest of Canada (Le Bourdais & Juby, 2002). This difference is probably the result of a lower sense of commitment, a weaker sense of we-ness, and less desire for the relationship to last for a long time (Popenoe, 2008).

Does living together before marriage affect the quality of the marital relationship? Early studies suggested yes. One theory argues that cohabitation changes people and their relationships so that they are not as committed to their marriage. Spouses who cohabit before marriage are less likely to be happy and more likely to divorce than those who have not cohabited. (Hohmann-Marriott, 2006; Stanley et al., 2006). Another explanation suggests that cohabitors might be less skilled in keeping relationships going over a long time (Popenoe, 2008). Many of these studies were biased by the fact that they only looked at young couples early in their relationships. When comparing married and cohabiting couples who were in long-term relationships, the levels of satisfaction were similar for both groups (Lachance-Grzela & Bouchard, 2009). Other studies suggest that premarital sex and cohabitation have become part of normal romantic relationships. Couples who regard cohabitation as a step toward marriage tend to have happier relationships than those who do not (Bond et al., 2012). Women who had sex or cohabited only with their future husbands were no more likely to divorce than those who married without premarital sex or cohabitation. Only if they had had more than one such relationship was there greater risk of separation (Teachman, 2008). Marital relationships are poorer for those who bore a child premaritally (Tach & Halpern-Meekin, 2009), but cohabiting couples with a child or children are more stable than childless unions (Le Bourdais & Lapierre-Adamcyk, 2004).

The social acceptability of cohabitation may cause marriage and cohabitation to become more alike. Research from Europe and Australia shows that when half the population cohabits, divorce rates are the same for individuals who do or do not live together before marriage (Hewitt & de Vaus, 2009; Reinhold, 2007). In Quebec, marriages following cohabitation are at the same risk of disruption as those entered directly (Le Bourdais & Lapierre-Adamcyk, 2004).

Same-Sex Marriages

Until recently, there was a major difference between homosexual and heterosexual couples—although same-sex couples had gained many of the same rights as other cohabitors, lesbians and gay men had no further stage possible in their relationship because they were not allowed to marry. On July 20, 2005, Parliament passed the *Civil Marriage Act*, which redefined marriage in Canada as "the lawful union of two persons to the exclusion of all others." To appease the opposition of some religious groups, it also states that "officials of religious denominations may refuse to perform marriages that are at odds with their religious beliefs" (Bowal & Campbell, 2007).

Same-sex couples choose marriage for the same reasons as heterosexual couples. An important motive is the legal recognition and benefits that come with marriage. These include the opportunity to create families through adoption, to automatically have the right to care for a partner in the case of illness or injury, and to act on other legal matters (Macintosh et al., 2010).

The legalization of same-sex marriages seems to have made it more socially acceptable. Before 2005, a national poll found that 49 percent of Canadians supported the legalization of same-sex marriage. A more recent poll, conducted in 2009, showed that 61 percent of Canadians supported the legalization of same-sex marriage. Some family members who were opposed to a same-sex couple cohabiting were less negative and more inclined to support it if the couple was legally married. This is important, because, as is the case for heterosexual couples, same-sex couples who have greater support from family and friends are more likely to have higher levels of commitment to their relationship (Macintosh et al., 2010).

Because same-sex marriages have only recently become legally recognized, research is limited. Among the studies that have been done, researchers have found that similar factors predict relationship satisfaction in both heterosexual and same-sex couples. Most married same-sex partners report a level of satisfaction at least equal to that reported by spouses from married heterosexual couples. If the same factors that influence heterosexual marriages also affect same-sex marriages, institutionalized support might be expected to enhance the stability of these relationships (Kurdek, 2005).

A qualitative study of the first cohort of same-sex couples to marry in Canada sought to describe the impact of marriage on the couples. Ninety-two percent mentioned the impact of the language of marriage. Words such as "spouse," "marriage," "wife," "husband," and "daughter-in-law" made them feel more understood by their friends and families. Three-quarters of participants commented on the fact that legalized marriage had an impact on their level of being "out." Three-quarters also indicated that they felt that they and their relationships were full participants in society and that marriage had given them a newfound sense of empowerment and inclusion in a system that they had been restricted from in the past (Macintosh et al., 2010).

A study on how same-sex couples divide housework drew three conclusions. First, same-sex couples did not assign tasks based on the traditional husband and wife roles. Second, same-sex couples were more likely to have a more equitable division of household tasks. Finally, over time, partners became more specialized in certain tasks (Kurdek, 2005).

Surveys of same-sex couples have found that many are able to resolve conflict more effectively than heterosexual couples. However, the frequency of disputes was the same as for heterosexual couples. They also disagreed over the same issues—finances, affection, sex, being overly critical, driving style, and household tasks (Kurdek, 2005).

Married Happiness

In spite of worries that marriage is going downhill, married people's level of happiness has changed little since 1980. Nevertheless, the level of interaction between husbands and wives has declined (Amato et al., 2007). There are problems with measuring the success of marriage. What criteria do we use? Do we consider the number who stay married? Some researchers have done just that and have identified risk factors associated with higher levels of divorce (Amato et al., 2007); yet not all unhappy marriages end in divorce. Do we ask couples how satisfied they are? Researchers found that most people report being happily or fairly happily married. Do we look for signs of conflict? Couples who do not fight may be avoiding almost all interaction with each other. In spite of these research difficulties, it is possible to consider several aspects of happiness. We will look at four influences on marital satisfaction: what individuals bring to marriage, how couples interact, how they deal with conflict, and how extended families and neighbourhoods affect couples (Bradbury & Karney, 2004).

Individual Qualities and Marital Happiness

When we enter a relationship, we bring our personality and past history with us. These shape how we approach interactions with others. How people perceive relationships depends on whether their outlook on life is basically positive or negative (Goldberg & Sayer, 2006). Expressiveness, or the ability to show one's feelings, can increase marital satisfaction. This behaviour tends to bring out the best in the partner. These good feelings, started early, extend many years into marriage (Amato et al., 2007; Miller et al., 2003). Perfectionism, especially if an individual is trying to live up to his or her notion of others' opinions, can be destructive (Haring et al., 2003). If a person has a negative outlook on life, the level of happiness of both partners is reduced. When a partner has an insecure attachment, needing constant reassurance, the stability of the marriage is higher, but satisfaction declines (Bradbury & Karney, 2004; Hollist & Miller, 2005).

Sex-role identity appears to be associated with adjustment in marriage. "Masculine" persons of either sex tend to have high levels of drive and ambition. In the past, these qualities have been associated with men, especially as they compete in the workforce. "Feminine" people usually have a strong sense of responsibility and are attuned to interpersonal relationships. Both men and women have different blends of the two characteristics. They can be high in one, high in both, or low in both. Those who are predominantly masculine or feminine have a range of qualities that they can bring to solve marital problems. An androgynous individual, one high in both characteristics, has even more to offer, while an undifferentiated individual, low in both, has the least to offer. Researchers explain this in terms of exchange theory; that is, androgynous partners bring more resources to help solve problems than predominantly masculine or feminine individuals, while the undifferentiated bring the fewest (Baucom et al., 1990). A decline in traditional gender roles is related to greater marital happiness (Amato et al., 2007).

Partners who are emotionally healthy have higher levels of empathy and interpersonal skills and more accurately interpret the messages that their partner is sending. These skills help them maintain their marriage and increase their happiness (Goodwin, 2003). Those who are high in all these factors establish conflict resolution styles early in marriage that lead to a strong relationship. Those who are low in these factors are more likely to have a troubled marriage (Schneewind & Gerhard, 2002).

Interaction between Partners

The relationship style of couples is related to both problem solving and marital satisfaction. It appears that the pattern of interaction first developed by a couple tends to continue (Schneewind & Gerhard, 2002). Each partner's perception of the relationship and the other person is also important. For example, if wives think their marriage is good, they are more likely to consider low-level anger in their husband as due to a bad day or some other neutral cause. Those who rate their marital bond low are apt to think such negativity is personal (Driver et al., 2003).

As we saw in Chapter 3, the quality of communication is important to a relationship, since it directly affects the way in which couples make decisions and solve problems. Couples with a high level of communication are less likely to have problems and more likely to solve those they experience than couples that communicate less well. This observation is especially true concerning husband–wife relations and problems to do with child-rearing. For instance, couples who decide together to have children are more likely to remain happy with their marriages than those marriages in which the pregnancy was an accident or where the partners disagreed over having a child (Cowan & Cowan, 2003). Couples in two-career families, especially when one or both travel a great deal, also depend on frequent and clear communication to keep their marriages healthy (Holmes, 2009; Rhodes, 2002).

Spending a long time talking, however, does not necessarily mean that a couple's communication is effective. When emotions such as anger get mixed up with factual messages, much misunderstanding may result. Couples can get caught in a vicious cycle where ambiguous messages are seen as negative or threatening. In turn, this leads to further emotional distance between the partners (Driver et al., 2003). When a spouse is supportive during conflict, there is less stress on the marriage. It is therefore important for a person to concentrate on what his or her spouse is saying, rather than planning a response. Thinking about how one's words will affect a partner's feelings is also important (Cornelius & Alessi, 2007; Fincham et al., 2007).

Nonverbal communication may be more important than what a couple says. If a person can read his or her partner's nonverbal messages, the marital quality is probably high. The person is likely aware of what his or her spouse is feeling, since nonverbal messages often communicate emotion more accurately than words (White, 1989). In cultures that emphasize family over the individual, subtle nonverbal cues are used to express feelings and opinions. For these couples, a spouse's sensitivity to such clues is particularly important (Ting-Toomey, 2009).

Effective communication depends on continued use of maintenance strategies, such as being positive or helpful when one's partner is tired, cross, or otherwise negative. Such sensitivity helps promote resilience in a marriage—that is, the ability to successfully overcome difficulties (Canary et al., 2002).

Generally, we expect that marriage partners who agree with each other are less likely to break up. Researchers have found that the more agreement there is between spouses, the greater the stability of the marriage. Disagreement in marriage is probably reduced by homogamy. If we marry someone with a similar cultural background, educational level, religion, and values, we are more likely to agree on major issues (White, 1989). If one spouse views the other positively, both feel more satisfied. Fondness, admiration, and trust all help to create a climate where marital satisfaction can grow (Driver et al., 2003; Goodwin, 2003).

Conflict in Marriage

Predictably, verbal disagreements tend to be higher when the couple is having problems in their marriage. Determining which is cause and which is effect is difficult, however (White, 1989). Are they having problems because they fight? Or are they fighting because they have basic problems in their relationship? Conflict occurs in every marriage—it is a sign that something in the relationship needs attention. What is important is the way the couple deals with conflict. Relationship personality—that is, level of interpersonal competence and empathy of both partners—leads to positive or to damaging solutions (Schneewind & Gerhard, 2002). In addition, couples need to recognize whether a problem is solvable. If it is unsolvable, they may work out a system that allows their marriage to continue, even if they disagree (Driver et al., 2003).

Individuals have different conflict styles. Some are non-assertive; that is, they do not defend their own position but give in to the other person. Others use direct aggression or violence to force their opinions on their partners. Still others use indirect means of communication. Some appear to agree but manage to make things turn out wrong, a strategy called passive aggression. Others hint or use non-verbal messages and expect to be understood (Kurdek, 1995). In dealing with conflict, couples face the challenge of striking a balance between emphasizing their own individuality and protecting their togetherness. Those who are most successful in dealing with differences are those who de-escalate their conflict instead of feeding anger. Those who trade anger for anger are more likely to set off a vicious cycle. As a result, such couples are more likely to divorce (Driver et al., 2003).

The balance between conflict and the pleasant aspects of marriage is also important. Researchers have found, for example, that every negative interaction is balanced by four or five positive ones in stable marriages (Gottman, 1993). The level of conflict and satisfaction appears related to how couples perceive their relationship. Wives who are happy and committed to their husbands are more likely to work actively to keep their marriage positive, particularly if they believe their efforts will work (Myers & Booth, 1999; Weigel & Ballard-Reisch, 1999). Men and women, according to a Quebec study, are happier in relationships where they idealize each other (Bouchard et al., 1999).

Influence of Others

Extended family members can have an impact on a couple's marital happiness in several ways. First, family-of-origin experiences affect both husbands' and wives' satisfaction, probably as a result of the ways they have learned to communicate (Sabatelli & Bartle-Haring, 2003). More directly, parents can create stress in their children's marriages. An Ontario study identified five areas of possible conflict: first, balancing time spent with nuclear and extended families; second, changing family roles and rules; third, pleasing parents or spouse; fourth, struggling with power; and fifth, fearing future obligations to older relatives (Beaton et al., 2003).

Conflict with in-laws can erode happiness, even in long-term marriages (Bryant et al., 2001). Extended families may have a greater effect on minority group members. Relationships with in-laws are more important for some ethnic groups than others (Goodwin, 2003; Root, 2001). Relatives of gay and lesbian individuals may project negative social stereotypes and completely reject their child and his or her partner. Others are more accepting (Connolly, 2006).

The social environment in which couples find themselves is also influential. Couples in interracial marriages and gay and lesbian partners may have to rely for social support more on friends than on families (Hunter, 2005). Thus, the area in which these couples live can affirm or devalue their relationship. Couples who live in areas with high levels of welfare and poverty may suffer from chronic stress. In good times, their marriages may be satisfying. In times of crisis (e.g., a transit strike with no other means of transportation, or a daycare closing), their relationship may suffer. It is hard to be kind and loving when you are under acute stress (Bradbury & Karney, 2004; Murry et al., 2008; Neff &Karney, 2007).

Long-Lasting Marriages

A number of sociologists have tracked marital happiness across the life span and report similar findings. For example, Lupri and Frideres (1981) studied married couples in Calgary. They found that levels of happiness were high early in the marriage, rose at the birth of the first child, and then dropped to an all-time low when there were teenagers in the family. Gradually, satisfaction with the marriage rose as the children left home and the couple lived together without them. However, happiness never again matched the high level experienced early in marriage. Another study suggested that parents got a respite between preschoolers and adolescents, when marital happiness rose slightly before dropping again (Walker, 1977).

There are several criticisms of the life-cycle view of marital satisfaction. Some of these are based on the fact that the surveys were conducted by asking people of different ages about their feelings, rather than following the same couples over the years. There may thus be differences in what different generations consider satisfaction. For example, older couples are shyer about discussing sex with their partners than younger couples are. It may also be that more couples who are older report happiness than couples with children at home because those with unhappy marriages have separated or divorced, and more of the satisfied ones are still together.

Recent longitudinal studies show a somewhat different picture. Two studies tracked changes in couples' happiness during a 20-year period. Both found that happiness declined over the time span. However, the amount of decrease was related to the couples' happiness at the beginning of the research. Those who were happiest to start with showed the least decline; those who were least happy showed the most (Amato et al., 2007; Kamp Dush et al., 2008). Several short-term longitudinal investigations have looked at stressful points in the family cycle. A small qualitative study learned that newlywed couples, even those who had lived together before marriage, experienced surprising aspects of their marriages that were worse than they expected (Hall & Adams, 2005). All marriage partners must adapt to

each other in many ways, for example in a matter as commonplace as sharing
a bed (Rosenblatt, 2006).

Types of Marriage

Marriage is a complex relationship, and a single measure of marital satisfaction
does not capture the complexity and variety of relationship patterns. Lavee and
Olson (1993) collected data from 8 383 heterosexual married American couples
and measured the spouses' evaluation of their relationship along nine dimensions:
personality issues, communication, conflict resolution, financial management, leisure activities, sexual relationship, children and parenting, family and friends, and
religious orientation. They then identified seven types of marriage.

The largest marriage type (40 percent) was the devitalized marriage. This type
is characterized by dissatisfaction with all nine dimensions of the marital relationship. At the other end of the spectrum, 9 percent of the couples were classified as
having a vitalized marriage. These couples show a high level of satisfaction with
every dimension of their relationships.

Couples in financially focused marriages are characterized by having a single
relationship strength, financial management, and dissatisfaction with other relationship issues. Money holds this type of couple together. Conflicted marriages are
low on many of the internal aspects of their relationship, such as personality issues,
communication, conflict resolution, and sexuality. They may avoid or fail to settle
issues between them and focus instead on external issues, such as leisure activities,
the children, and their religious life. Balanced couples communicate well and are
highly satisfied with their problem-solving strategies. These couples place a lot of
value on their nuclear family, with a balance of quality relationship in both internal
and external matters. Financial management, however, is often a specific problem
in the relationship. Harmonious couples are highly satisfied with each other, but

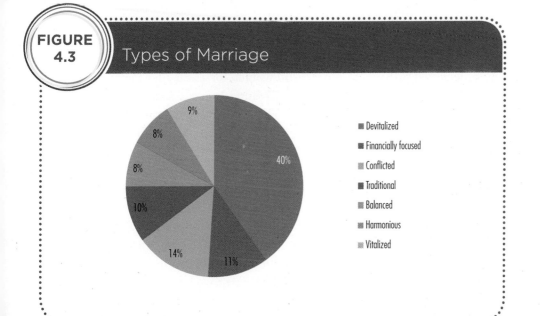

FIGURE 4.3 Types of Marriage

- Devitalized — 40%
- Financially focused — 11%
- Conflicted — 14%
- Traditional — 10%
- Balanced — 8%
- Harmonious — 8%
- Vitalized — 9%

the children may be seen as a burden and the parenting role as a source of distress. Traditional couples are dissatisfied with their sexual relationship and with the way they communicate, but they have strong and satisfactory relationships with the extended family and friends.

Children and Marital Happiness

A number of studies confirm a drop in love and happiness and an increase in conflict when couples, both heterosexual and homosexual, become parents. This trend is probably related to the quality of their relationship before their child is born. The quality of the time they spend together is also important (Goldberg & Sassler, 2006; Kluwer & Johnson, 2007). Similarly, parents, especially mothers, report lower marital happiness when their children go through puberty (Whiteman et al., 2007).

Several explanations are offered for the drop in marital satisfaction when children are in the home. The birth of the first child is usually experienced as a high, in many ways similar to a honeymoon. New parents, however, soon need to face the realities of day-to-day living with an infant. Family life changes with each new child, whether through birth or adoption. Relationships become more complex as first-time parents make the transition to a threesome. If there is more than one child, sibling relationships are also involved. Furthermore, one parent may be jealous of the baby's relationship with the other parent. Especially if both are working outside the home, each partner may become so tied up with the new daily tasks that he or she has less time to know what the other is thinking and feeling (Belsky & Kelly, 1994; Cowan & Cowan, 2003). On average, parents are not as happy with their marriages as nonparents—and the more children, the lower the satisfaction. Mothers of infants are the least satisfied (Twenge et al., 2003).

The demands the new child puts on the parents can affect their relationship. In the first months, sleep is often interrupted, so that parents do not get adequate rest. If both partners work, time demands are more extreme. They may be so tired that they either do not have the energy to spend on each other or may become extremely irritable. If they do not take time to keep lines of communication open, their intimacy, including their sexual relationship, may suffer. For example, couples report decreased sexual responsiveness in women for a year after the birth of the first child (Elliott & Watson, 1985). Marital satisfaction and sexual satisfaction go hand in hand (Gossman et al., 2003). A baby's continuing demands can reduce a mother's energy and responsiveness. If that happens, the husband may feel that he isn't appreciated for the effort he puts into helping around the house and supporting the family. Dissatisfaction is higher if there is a combination of risk factors. These include depression after the birth, an unplanned pregnancy, disagreement about having a child at all, and poor problem-solving abilities (Cox et al., 1999).

Children can have other effects on the marriage. Conflicts over child-rearing may arise, especially if one parent is more permissive than the other. One baby-sitter, for instance, reported that a mother found it cute that her children tied her pantyhose together to make a rope for lowering a basket up and down stairs, while the father forced the sitter, as well as the children, to eat two helpings of vegetables before any of them could have dessert.

The presence of children significantly influences decisions about jobs or careers and about where the family lives, as well as the nature of the husband–wife relationship. If, for instance, one of the children has serious medical problems, the parents may refuse a job relocation to remain near an excellent children's hospital or a trusted physician, even if such a choice limits the chance of promotion (Day et al., 1985). More commonly, the family may think about the distance from a school when choosing where to buy a house or rent an apartment.

A number of explanations are possible for the drop in marital satisfaction when children are teenagers. Parents now have children who are keeping adult hours, so privacy takes some planning. Teenagers, especially when parents disagree on how to deal with the challenges they present, can strain a marriage. Some families taking part in a study of marital stability in large adopting families reported that their marriages had been in danger of failing because of the stress placed on them by one or more very difficult children. For example, if a girl defied and challenged the mother and acted like a sweet innocent around the father, the parents often disagreed about the best way of handling her. In extreme cases, this disagreement resulted in such serious marital difficulties that the parents considered separation (Ward & Tremitiere, 1991). Children may also impose a financial strain if they go on to postsecondary education.

Once children have left home, couples are required to adjust to living without children again. Frequently, they must rebuild common interests. Yet once the adjustment is made, husband and wife can develop a closeness that was lost when they had children at home; thus, marital satisfaction increases. A research study that followed middle-aged couples for 18 years discovered that the shift to an empty nest increased marital satisfaction. The main reason was an increase of women's enjoyment of time with their partners (Gorchoff et al., 2008).

Beyond the demands posed by children, a couple's parents may also require more assistance if their health is failing—further strains are thus placed on the family. These years have sometimes been called the "sandwich years" because couples are squeezed by both the older and the younger generations (Williams, 2005).

Infidelity in the Relationship

Whether a person is sexually unfaithful depends on individual and social values and on opportunity. If the individual or his or her social group condemns infidelity, it is less likely. In general, society regards sex outside a committed relationship as wrong and as worse among women than men (Blow & Hartnett, 2005; Day, 2005). Infidelity is more likely where opportunity for an undiscovered encounter presents itself; for example, a person is working out of town or has an Internet affair. Sex outside a committed relationship ranges from a one-night stand to a long-term relationship. It can be only sexual, only emotional, or a combination. Although actual physical contact may not occur, interaction with an Internet lover may lead to emotional withdrawal from a partner (Blow & Hartnett, 2005; Hertlein & Piercy, 2006).

Varying definitions of infidelity make it difficult to know how common it is. Most researchers state that men are more likely to be unfaithful, though recent studies show that the rates for men and women are becoming more alike. When transgressions other than intercourse, such as emotional connection or kissing, are taken into account, women report as many acts of infidelity as men. For men, being married or cohabiting has no significant effect in predicting infidelity, but married women are less likely to be unfaithful (Mark et al., 2011). The length of relationship matters. For both men and women, infidelity decreases in long-term unions, though there are some risk periods. There is a peak for women in the seventh year of marriage and, for men, in about the eighteenth year (Blow & Hartnett, 2005; Brand et al., 2007; Thornton et al., 2007). Characteristics of individuals, regardless of their marital status, are related to the likelihood of having an affair. People who are interested in sex and who have greater sexual experience are more likely to be unfaithful. So are those who are uncomfortable with emotional closeness (Blow & Hartnett, 2005). There are suggestions that use of sex-enhancing drugs such as Viagra may lead to affairs (Tuller, 2004). People who often attend religious services tend to have fewer affairs (Atkins & Kessell, 2008). Several studies have found that education is associated with infidelity—highly educated people are more likely to report engaging in infidelity than less educated individuals (Mark et al., 2011).

Once infidelity has been revealed, the primary relationship is, of course, affected. A cross-cultural survey found that infidelity was the single most-cited cause of divorce. In Western countries, it has been estimated that infidelity is the primary cause of between 25 and 50 percent of divorces (Mark et al., 2011). Cohabitors are more likely than the married to part. There can be rage, loss of trust, fear, and lower self-esteem. Men are more likely to be angry and jealous over the sexual aspects of infidelity; women are likelier to be jealous of the emotional aspects (Blow & Hartnett, 2005; Edlund et al., 2006; Thornton et al., 2007).

Married Happiness throughout Life

Marital happiness and conflict alone do not explain why some unions survive for many years and others do not. Some moderately happy couples divorce (Amato & Hohmann-Marriott, 2007). Others who are very unhappy stay together and describe their marriage five years later as happy (Fincham et al., 2007). And some couples stay together after one partner has been unfaithful.

One study looked at why couples stayed together for 50 years. Happy couples spoke of the importance of respecting each other and treating each other with dignity. They agreed on a comfortable level of closeness; for some, there was a lot of togetherness, for others a lot of individual activity. They had a shared vision of what their life together should be, although they may not have put it into words. Unhappy couples married for 50 years, like the happy ones, believed that divorce was not an option for them and that they just had to make their marriages work. They did this by doing many things on their own and keeping enough distance to avoid conflict. The pattern for long-term marriage was probably set in the early days of their relationship. Like other couples, those who were happy in the beginning were more likely to stay happy. Unhappy people remained unhappy (Dickson, 1995). More recent studies have confirmed these findings (Amato et al., 2007; Kamp Dush et al., 2008).

Another study compared heterosexual couples with same-sex relationships that had lasted for at least 15 years. Sexual orientation apparently was not important for satisfaction with their relationships. The factors that mattered most were ability to contain major conflicts and to develop psychologically intimate communication. The two factors are related. Openness and honesty between partners helps them find ways of talking about conflict so that negativity is kept to a minimum. For those who had difficulty showing affection openly, loyalty, kindness, faithfulness, and sharing counted with their partners (Mackey et al., 2004).

When a marriage encounters rough times, other factors become important. The first is commitment (Fincham et al., 2007). Commitment empowers couples to work at solving problems rather than separating, and may involve sacrifice. For example, one partner's illness or injury may interfere with the quality of the other's life (Rosenblatt, 2006). Some couples stay together, even when one member does not wish to or cannot have sexual relations (Donnelly & Burgess, 2008). Moderately happy couples who divorce probably lack a strong commitment to their marriage (Amato & Hohmann-Marriott, 2007). When commitment is not enough, forgiveness becomes important in repairing a marriage, especially when there has been a serious betrayal, such as infidelity.

Scholars have also identified sanctification as a factor in some long-lasting marriages. That is, the marriage is seen as having a higher purpose (Fincham et al., 2007). One study of enduring unions of African Americans, for example, found that the church community provided support for the marriage (Marks et al., 2008). Indeed, support by friends and relatives bolsters relationships. The pattern may be circular: happy marriages receive more approval and the approval encourages happiness (Amato et al., 2007). A good marriage can give a couple a sense of meaning. This feeling may come because both partners are happy individuals who like being together.

Does Marriage Have a Future?

Canadian sociologist Robert Brymhas made an interesting reply to this question: "The family is not a crumbling institution. What is happening, however, is that people are freer than they once were to establish the kinds of family arrangements that best suit them" (Vanier Institute of the Family, 2010, p. 32).

Whether marriage has a future depends on the viewpoint you take. Statistically, marriage is on the decline. In part, the decline is likely due to delayed marriages; it is also partly because of tighter economic times and partly because of the increase in cohabitation before marriage. The growing rates of cohabitation and divorce, and the raising of children outside marriage, are signs that marriage is becoming deinstitutionalized; that is, that there are fewer norms and values in society telling married people how they should behave.

From another perspective, marriage is changing to meet the needs of a changing society (Cherlin, 2004). It is moving from a patriarchal, husband-led system to a more egalitarian partnership between husband and wife. More couples are sharing both wage-earning and the provision of home- and childcare. This trend has come about partly in response to economically hard times. In part, however, it also reflects a movement in society to preserve the rights of minorities, including women. The high divorce rate does not necessarily mark the end of marriage as an institution. Many divorced persons remarry (Statistics Canada, 2008j). If anything, marriage is valued more highly now than in the past. After all, same-sex couples lobbied strongly to have the right to marry. If there is a marriage crisis, it may arise from valuing it too highly, rather than not enough. Part of the delay in marrying comes from the desire to have everything just right before making a commitment. Part comes from the desire to avoid divorce (Edin & Reed, 2005; Thornton et al., 2007).

Do the changes in families mean that marriage is on the way out? Most same-sex couples choosing to marry are in stable, long-term relationships little different (apart from sexual orientation) from heterosexual married couples (Ambert, 2005b; Kurdek, 2004). Cohabitation, because of the many couples involved, has had, and probably will have, a significant impact on marriage; however, there is little sign, except perhaps in Quebec, that it will become an alternative to marriage in the near future (Le Bourdais & Lapierre-Adamcyk, 2004; Seltzer, 2004).

Marriage has changed and is changing. The love revolution (marriage for love rather than to meet family and clan needs) started the shift by altering rules and making marriage more satisfying. There is no going back to older ways (Coontz, 2005). Because of the value still placed on marriage, it will in all likelihood survive.

Time to Review

1. How is cohabitation different from marriage?
2. What do we know about same-sex marriages?
3. What factors are involved in marital happiness?
4. What is the possible future of marriage?

An Unhappy Bride

Most of the time, a wedding is a happy event. Family and friends gather to give their best wishes to the couple and to acknowledge this legal and symbolic transition. For some, though, a wedding may be an unhappy event.

One semester, there was a bright young student named Hafsah. A few weeks into the semester, Hafsah suddenly stopped coming to class. It was only in the last week of the semester that she reappeared. Her teacher was concerned and wanted to help, so he asked her to stay after class. This is the story she told:

> I haven't been able to come to class because I'm afraid that my brother will see me and force me to go back home. I have been living with my aunt, and I hardly leave her house at all. I don't want to go back home because, if I do, my parents will send me to Pakistan to get married. For over a year now,

they have been telling me that I must marry a nice man and that, at my age, it would be shameful not to marry. They tell me that the whole family will reject me if I don't get married soon. They tell me that I will dishonour them as parents. Three years ago, they sent my sister to Pakistan for an arranged marriage. She was only 16, and he was much older. I don't even want to know who my parents have picked for me.

When I was at home, the only computer was in my father's office, and I was not allowed to use it. I got a cellphone, but when my father found it, he took it away from me. He told me that I only wanted it to call Canadian boys and he called me a dirty whore. I don't want to get married, especially not to someone I don't even know. I think that everyone has the right to choose who they want to marry. For now, I just want to be a normal 18-year-old girl and hang out with my friends. I really want to go to school because I want to become an accountant. I once told my father that if I studied accounting, I could help him with his business. He laughed at me and told me that girls can't understand numbers. He thinks that education is a waste of time for girls. He didn't even let my sister finish high school. I don't know what to do. I don't want to shame my family, but I am too young to get married, and I really want to get an education so that one day I can support myself.

1. If you were the teacher and one of your students told you this, what advice would you give her?
2. What if you were a friend or co-worker? How would you react to this story?
3. Forced marriage is a crime in Canada. Do you think that teachers or other service providers who work with young women have an obligation to report it if they hear about a forced marriage? Explain your reasons.

SUMMARY

What Are Some of the Different Marriage Arrangements?

Marriage is not merely a private event. It marks both the legal creation of a family and changes in social status and role. In Canada, the proportion of married people has been declining over the past decades. Nevertheless, it is still true that the majority of couples will marry. In Canada, the only legal kind of marriage is monogamy, which is marriage to only one person at a time. In other social groups, the family has been based on one person married to several others of the opposite sex. The term for this practice is polygamy.

The marriage rate measures marriages that occur in a given year. Social, economic, and legal factors determine the age at which individuals marry for the first time. There are also regional differences. Because marriage is a legal contract, it is governed by laws. A marriage brings with it both rights and duties. Some couples draw up a marriage contract, which is a legal document that alters the effect of the law, usually as it applies to property.

How Does Society Affect Marriage?

From the developmental perspective, the transition to a successful marriage requires completing four tasks: establishing a couple identity, defining boundaries, maintaining a household, and managing the relationship. From the systems theory perspective, the wife and husband have individually been members of various microsystems—family of origin, friends, workplace. Now they must renegotiate as a couple their relationships with these groups. Ethnic couples may face additional adjustment stresses and may have family boundaries different from those of the majority. Conflict over the definition of sex roles may also exist. Mixed couples are defined as couples in which one spouse or partner is a member of a visible minority group and the other is not, as well as couples comprised of two different visible minority groups. Mixed marriage may make adjustment more difficult for a couple.

Getting married gives one a social status, and for some, this gives them a sense of place and belonging in society. There are economic reasons for getting married and starting a family. Marriage is also designed to regulate sexual behaviour by limiting sexual relations to an exclusive partner and to care for children.

Particularly for women, marriage has provided an identity over the years. Marriage serves to look after the emotional needs of the partners. Marriage provides what one theorist calls an "enforceable trust" and has been regarded as superior to other kinds of adult relationships. The romantic view of love may also be involved in individual decisions to marry. Today, couples look forward to a much more democratic marriage.

Historically, there has been a clear division between men's and women's roles. The change to greater equality in roles has been gradual. Married women have become a large part of the paid workforce, especially since the 1970s, when many families found two incomes necessary for economic survival. Families usually fall into one of four role patterns: conventional, shared, dual-career, and reverse conventional. Both the conventional and the reverse conventional patterns have a clear division of roles between spouses, while shared and dual-career role patterns do not make such a strong distinction. In many of these families, however, women are still expected to assume the major responsibility for family care.

How Is Cohabitation Different from Marriage?

This choice is becoming more approved and practised as a lifestyle, especially among younger people and Quebeckers. Most of those forming families through a common-law relationship eventually marry. This suggests that Canadians generally view cohabitation as a prelude to marriage rather than a substitute for it. Although cohabitation resembles marriage, partners have fewer legal rights. To be considered a common-law union, the couple must live together for a certain period. Couples who lived together before marriage are more likely to divorce, perhaps because they are less traditional in their beliefs. As more people cohabit, however, the rate of separation becomes more like that of people who marry without prior cohabitation. The social acceptability of cohabitation may cause marriage and cohabitation to become more similar.

What Do We Know About Same-Sex Marriages?

Same-sex couples choose marriage for the same reasons as heterosexual couples. An important motive is the legal recognition and benefits that come with marriage. The legalization of same-sex marriages seems to have made it more socially acceptable. Researchers have found that similar factors predict relationship satisfaction in both heterosexual and same-sex couples. Most married same-sex partners report a level of satisfaction at least equal to that reported by married heterosexual couples. Surveys of same-sex couples have found that many are able to resolve conflict more effectively than heterosexual couples, though the frequency of disputes was the same. They also disagreed over the same issues—finances, affection, sex, being overly critical, driving style, and household tasks.

What Factors Are Involved in Marital Happiness?

Several methods are used for measuring success in marriage, for instance levels of agreement between husband and wife or positive and negative communication. Marriage is a complex relationship. Lavee and Olson measured marital satisfaction along nine dimensions and identified seven types of marriage. Marital satisfaction is affected by personal qualities of the partners, by their interactions, and by their extended families and wider society. Happiness appears greatest early in marriage, drops with the arrival of children, is at its lowest point when adolescents are in the home, and increases with the empty nest. Some reasons given for this pattern are the added stress of having more family members and the greater opportunities for disagreement. Whether a person is sexually unfaithful depends on individual and social values and on opportunity. A cross-cultural survey found that infidelity was the single most-cited cause of divorce. Long-lasting marriages are not necessarily happy. When they are, couples usually respect each other and have common goals.

What Is the Possible Future of Marriage?

Whether marriage has a future depends on the viewpoint you take. Statistically, marriage is on the decline. In part, the decline is likely due to delayed marriages; it is also partly because of tighter economic times and the increase in cohabitation before marriage. From another perspective, marriage is changing to meet the needs of a changing society. Because of the value still placed on marriage, it will in all likelihood survive.

Class Assignments

1. Think about two television shows that present family life. What roles do men and women play in them? Do you think these roles are typical of society today? Explain.

2. Interview two individuals about the division of responsibilities, chores, and privileges in marriage. Do you feel that their answers are related to their age or cultural background? Why or why not? Compare your information with that gained by your classmates.

Personal Assignments

The following assignments are designed to help you think about your own family experiences:

1. Describe the kind of marriage your parents have, if they are currently married. How has this affected your ideas about the roles of husbands and wives in marriage? Why?
2. If you had a marriage contract or prenuptial agreement, what would you choose to include? Why? Would you want such a contract? Give your reasons.
3. What do you think are the greatest challenges marriage faces today? What are the greatest opportunities? Give reasons for your answer.

PART 3

THE EXPANDING FAMILY

Chapter 5
Children—Yes or No?

LEARNING OBJECTIVES

Why do people decide to have children?

How has the Canadian fertility rate changed over time?

What are the choices for those who do not want the children they conceive?

What options are available to those who are childless involuntarily?

What issues are faced by atypical families?

iStockphoto

Daddy and I wanted a little boy so much. We tried and tried, but we couldn't start a baby growing. Then we went to see Dr. Mason. He did lots of tests. He found Daddy didn't have the special seeds that make babies grow and that I didn't have the eggs. We were very sad. So Dr. Mason borrowed seeds from another man and eggs from another woman. He started a baby growing from them in a dish. Then he put that baby inside Mommy in a special operation so it could grow until it was big enough to be born. Mommy and Daddy were very happy. And you know what? That baby was you!

Does this scenario seem farfetched? Not something we talk about, especially with children? We are much more comfortable with the more usual method of producing children, through sexual relations between a husband and wife. This has been the ordinary course of events for millennia. Often in the past, the first child was one of many. Sometimes the success of a marriage was calculated by the number of children a couple had, sometimes by the number of sons.

Where Do I Fit In?

1. What did you think when you read the opening vignette? How did you feel?
2. Do you want children? Why or why not? How many?
3. If you already have a child, why did you become a parent?

Enlarging the Family Circle

Societies can continue only if people have children. In many cultures, having children is seen as a natural part of adult life. While the decision to have a child is individual, or is made between a couple, many social factors have a powerful influence on this decision. It is most useful to look at personal factors in the context of a social structure that dictates when and how many children a person should have (Mayer & Trommsdorff, 2010).

Having a child results in an important change in status and is a marker event. This occasion may be the first time the parents have to take full responsibility for another person. In a conventional-role marriage, husband and wife have clearly defined roles. When both partners are employed, however, the household and work responsibilities are shared. Once a child is born, husband and wife roles often need to be renegotiated to allow for the child's care (Cowan & Cowan, 2003). For young single parents, the transition may mean a sudden shift from childhood to adulthood, from being looked after by parents to looking after a child.

In this chapter, we will look at the various reasons, both personal and social, for having children. Over the past 50 years, the fertility rate has dropped significantly in Canada. From a high of 3.93 children per woman in 1959, the fertility rate underwent a sharp decline in the 1960s and continued to drop until it reached a low of 1.49 children per woman in 2000. After that, the rate increased to reach 1.7 children per woman in 2009 (Human Resources and Skills Development Canada, 2012b). Having a child means not just giving birth but also caring for and raising that child. Sometimes, a child who has been conceived is not wanted, and there are several choices available to these parents. Other times, a couple may dearly want a child but be unable to conceive. These parents also have a variety of options. Finally, reproductive technologies offer new alternatives for conceiving a child. We will look at some of the legal and ethical issues surrounding these technologies.

The Social Script

At some point in their lives, nearly all Canadians will consider having children. Table 5.1 shows that only 7 percent of Canadian women do not intend to have any children.

TABLE 5.1

Fertility Intentions, Females Aged 20-39, 2006

20-39	Females by Age Group				
	20-24	25-29	30-34	35-39	Total aged
Number (millions)	1.1	1.1	1.1	1.2	4.5
How many children have you given birth to?					
None	88%	61%	31%	20%	50%
One	9%	20%	24%	22%	19%
Two	2%	13%	31%	38%	21%
Three or more	1%	6%	14%	20%	10%
Do you intend to have a/another child?					
Yes	87%	75%	42%	19%	55%
Don't know	3%	7%	13%	7%	7%
No	10%	19%	45%	74%	38%
What is the total number of children you intend to have (including those you have now)?					
None	7%	5%	5%	9%	7%
One	7%	7%	9%	15%	10%
Two	45%	46%	45%	45%	45%
Three	23%	23%	15%	17%	19%
Four or more	11%	7%	9%	5%	8%
Don't know	7%	12%	17%	9%	11%
Average number intended	2.3	2.3	2.2	1.9	2.2

Source: Vanier Institute of the Family, *Fascinating Families*, Figure: Fertility Intentions, Females Aged 20-39, 2006, Canada, Issue 13, Dec. 2008. Found at: http://www.vanierinstitute.ca/include/get.php?nodeid=813

There is still a great deal of social pressure to have children. One pressure is the myth of motherhood. According to the myth, motherhood is an instinct that can fulfill a woman in a way no other experience can. Of course, much of the notion is true. Bearing and raising a child can provide satisfaction unlike any other life experience. Another part of the myth is the importance of having a child of each sex for a well-rounded family. This belief accounts for a number of families who have a string of boys or girls before one of the other sex is finally born or adopted. Some unmarried women in their 30s or 40s hear their biological clock ticking and decide to have a child while they still physically can, even if they do not have a partner. They may seek out a temporary partner for the sole purpose of becoming pregnant, or they may resort to artificial insemination; still others adopt (Hertz, 2006).

Sociological Perspectives on Having Children

Naturally, the different sociological perspectives focus on the social aspects of having children. Each perspective offers different insights into the process. Here are examples of some of the issues each perspective might examine.

Structural functionalists focus on having children as a necessary function of families in perpetuating society. The developmental approach tends to see having children as a developmental task of most families. Conflict theorists suggest that the social pressure to have children is a reflection of the prevailing ideology. They might also look at how families with children have greater social advantages than families without children. The systems theory looks at how the decision to have a child or children creates different subsystems that affect the family dynamic. The ecological approach will look at how the wider social context, which includes the mesosystem, the exosystem, and the macrosystem, influences a family's decision to have children, and also determines the experiences of families with children. Symbolic interactionists focus on the personal reasons for having or not having children, while feminist theorists tend to study child-bearing as an issue reflecting women's control over reproduction.

Fertility Rates in Canada

Before the days of old age pensions, the family allowance, and welfare, the family provided almost the only social security system. If it failed, people were dependent on charity. Since many infants died, it was important to have a large family so that two or three children might survive to look after the parents when they were old or disabled.

total fertility rate: the average number of births per woman over the course of her reproductive life

Although the pressure on couples to have children is almost as strong as ever, the size of the Canadian family has been steadily shrinking. To replace the population, each woman must have 2.1 children—Canada has been below this level since 1977. (See Figure 5.1 on page 127.) In Canada, the **total fertility rate**, or total number of children a woman is expected to have, has been stable since 1993 at about 1.6 children. This pattern followed a slight increase in births in the early 1990s as women who had postponed having children gave birth. The **crude birth rate** is a measure of the number of births in a given year. There have been periods in which the birth rate dropped, for example during the Great Depression. The "baby boom" from 1946 to 1964 saw a dramatic increase in birth rates for those years. From one generation to the next, there has been a decrease in fertility at the youngest ages and an increase in fertility among older women. However, postponing births into their 30s does not make up for the drop in fertility in their 20s (Statistics Canada, 2008j).

In Canada, births to unwed mothers were classified as "illegitimate" until 1974; since then, the term "out of wedlock" has been adopted to refer to these births. In the past, such children were often born to single mothers not living with the father of the child. This is no longer the case: the majority of children born "out of wedlock" now have both parents present, but the parents are not married. The greatest increase came for children born to common-law partners (Department of Justice Canada, 2012b). As we saw in Chapter 4, the cohabitation rate is highest in Quebec. Since June 2002, Quebec has recognized same-sex parental kinship, so, for example, a baby can have two mothers declared as parents on the official birth registry (Duschesne, 2004).

A number of approaches to increasing the birth rate to replacement levels have been tried or suggested. The family allowance program in Canada began in 1945 and gave benefits for children under the age of 16. The benefits received

crude birth rate: the number of births per 1000 population

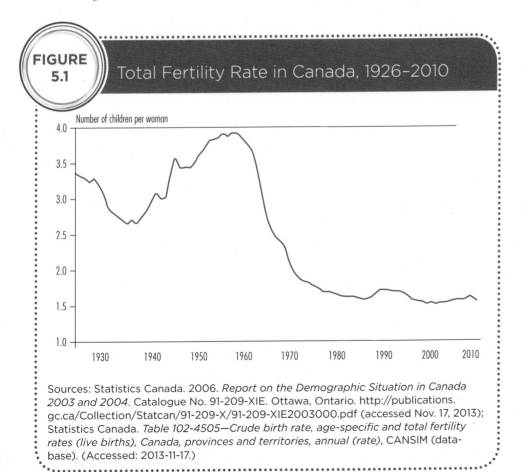

FIGURE 5.1

Total Fertility Rate in Canada, 1926–2010

Sources: Statistics Canada. 2006. *Report on the Demographic Situation in Canada 2003 and 2004*. Catalogue No. 91-209-XIE. Ottawa, Ontario. http://publications. gc.ca/Collection/Statcan/91-209-X/91-209-XIE2003000.pdf (accessed Nov. 17, 2013); Statistics Canada. *Table 102-4505—Crude birth rate, age-specific and total fertility rates (live births), Canada, provinces and territories, annual (rate)*, CANSIM (database). (Accessed: 2013-11-17.)

by families were relatively modest. Since this was also the baby boom generation, it is difficult to say whether the family allowance had an independent effect on the birth rate. In the past, Quebec offered incentive payments to parents, but the birth rate showed only a slight increase before dropping again (Parent & Wang, 2007). More recently, theorists have suggested that increases in fertility depend on providing conditions to increase young people's confidence in their future (Roy & Bernier, 2007). Others suggest that encouraging immigration of young people who are of an age to have children will help stimulate the sagging birth rate and offset the aging population of Canada (Samuel, 1990). Immigration is, in fact, helping to maintain the Canadian population (Chui et al., 2007). Yet the longer immigrant women are in Canada, the more the birth rate among them tends to resemble that of Canadian-born women (Bélanger & Gilbert, 2003).

While most women are able to conceive and give birth by the age of 15, teenage pregnancy is generally seen as a social problem requiring efforts to prevent it. It is assumed that most teenage pregnancies are unintended, so changes in teen pregnancy rates may reflect more effective contraceptive use, greater access to reproductive health services, exposure to higher-quality sexual health education, or a shift in social norms. The teen pregnancy rate in Canada has declined in each consecutive year from 1996 (44.2 per 1000 women aged 15–19) to 2006 (27.9 per 1000). Many teens who become pregnant choose abortion; those who decide to have the child are counted in the teen birth rate. The Canadian teen birth rate decreased from 22.1 per1000 in 1996 to 13.7 in 2006 (McKay & Barrett, 2012).

Why Is the Canadian Family Shrinking?

A number of factors have led to Canadians choosing to have smaller families, including medical advances, general economic trends, and various psychosocial reasons.

Medical Advances

Medical science has had two major effects on the birth rate. First, infant mortality, or the death of a child under one year of age, declined steadily in Canada since the early 1960s, tapering off recently. Currently, the mortality rate is one of the lowest in the world (CIA World Factbook, 2013). As a result, it is no longer necessary to have a large number of children to ensure the survival of two or three. Most children born today in Canada will live to adulthood. Second, contraception has become more convenient and effective since the birth control pill became available in 1961.

Changes in Law

Until July 1, 1969, contraception was illegal in Canada. Under the 1892 *Criminal Code*, birth control was thought obscene and likely to corrupt morals. A Toronto druggist was jailed in 1960 for selling condoms. The first family-planning clinics in Canada operated illegally. Many women relied on folk recipes and illegal abortion to control fertility. Since it was legal, however, to use contraceptive devices to prevent illness or to treat disorders, sympathetic doctors provided many prescriptions (McLaren & McLaren, 1997). The birth rate showed its sharpest drop following the legalization of birth control (Dumas, 1987).

The availability of abortion, when a woman's life or health (including mental health) is in danger, was also legalized in 1969. In 1988, the Supreme Court of Canada found the complex procedure required to obtain an abortion unconstitutional. As a result, abortion was, in effect, no longer criminal (Statistics Canada, 2008j). This change has made it possible to avoid having children after birth control fails. Although the pill was very popular in the 1960s, many couples have turned to sterilization once they have as many children as they want. Among Canadian married couples, where the wife is over 35, nearly two-thirds are protected by sterilization (Balakrishnan et al., 1993).

Economic Trends

As in all countries that have undergone industrialization, the shift from a resource-based economy to a manufacturing-based one has had an impact on the Canadian birth rate. The birth rate is also connected to national and global economics. During the Great Depression, families became smaller. The economic boom following World War II saw an increase in the birth rate that lasted until the 1960s and produced the baby boom. The inflation and recession of the 1970s and 1980s, with the greater number of women in the workforce, led to smaller families once again. News reports suggest that abortions and sterilizations increase during hard economic times (e.g., Kebede, 2009). Part of the variation in fertility is related to the age at which women have their first child; in boom times it is earlier and in bust times later. Since women have a limited number of years in which they can bear children, the total number they have is related to the age at which they have the first child.

The relationship between the economy and the birth rate, however, is far from simple. The late-20th century drop in the birth rate is also connected to women's participation in the workforce. Part of the phenomenon of working wives and mothers is related to the need of families to have two incomes and to the growth of single-parent families. Several studies in Canada and in other industrialized countries have found that there is an inverse relationship between the female labour force participation rate and the total fertility rate—as more women enter the workforce, the fertility rate declines. The role incompatibility hypothesis states that this is because of the strain of performing the roles of both employee and mother (Mishra & Smyth, 2010).

Since education is more important for employment than in the past, many women put off having children until they are through school and able to support them. Being a student and a mother are both time-intensive roles, making it difficult to do them simultaneously. Better-educated women are more likely to pursue careers and may postpone child-bearing until they are well established on their career path. Those with higher education levels might delay child-bearing until they feel they can "afford" children (Mills et al., 2011). Some researchers argue that even when people are economically successful, the cost of raising children has become so high in terms of lost career opportunities that having more than two children may be undesirable (Crompton & Keown, 2009).

Children are expensive. Including housing and daycare, families spend from 10 percent (Quebec) to 15 percent (Ontario) of their income on the first child (Douthitt & Fedyk, 1990). According to one estimate, raising a child to age 18 cost nearly $167 000 in 2004 (Manitoba Agriculture, Food, and Rural Initiatives, 2004). Costs vary across regions. For example, Ontario has higher prices for goods and services and a greater proportion of married women who work. Some of the variation between regions may be accounted for by different standards of what families feel they ought to provide for their children. The increased need to educate children for the technically demanding workplace also places demands on family income.

Psychosocial Reasons

People decide to have children for many reasons. One attempt to systematically describe these reasons is called the value of children (VOC) framework. This classification scheme includes three satisfactions (or values) of children, including instrumental assistance (help in old age), rewarding interactions (companionship, love), and psychological appreciation (living through children). The VOC scheme also includes four costs of children, including financial costs (the cost of education), child-rearing demands (emotional strain and pregnancy), restrictions on parents (being tied down), and costs to social relationships (marital strain) (Miller, 2009).

Child-Free through Choice

Despite the social pressure to have children, why do some couples choose to remain childless? About 7 to 8 percent of Canadians make this choice. Some may fear that the husband–wife relationship will be damaged. Once the couple introduces another person into the family, the partners may not be able to remain as close as they wish. Women may also fear having to give up the equality they have established in their marriage relationships if there are children who require care.

Some women do not wish to sacrifice a career to which they are dedicated. Having children may mean a conflict between family responsibilities and long hours, travel, or moves for work. Some individuals wish to keep their options open, to be able to change to a job they will enjoy more but that will pay less. The financial commitment a child demands can remove this freedom.

Three more reasons may lead a couple or an individual not to have children. First, some couples want to keep their options open for new experiences of all sorts. They may look at parenthood as such an experience, but reject it because of the commitment involved. Second, the voluntarily childless are more interested in learning about the world than in rearing the young. Finally, some individuals do not have a partner with whom they want to have children.

In spite of the growing acceptance of family differences, however, women choosing not to have children face disadvantages. For example, some workplaces may give scheduling priority to women with children. In addition, outsiders may become intrusive, wanting to know why someone remains childless

(Abma & Martinez, 2006; Stobert & Kemeny, 2003). Women who choose not to have children are often considered antisocial or psychologically defective in some way (Douglas & Michaels, 2004). Their marriages are expected to be unsatisfying. Couples who decide to remain childless are sometimes perceived as being selfish (O'Connor, 2012).

Time to Review

1. How do the different sociological perspectives look at having children?
2. Describe the trends in Canadian fertility rates.
3. Why is the Canadian family shrinking?

Unwanted Children

Some pregnancies, including those of both single and married individuals, are unwanted. Basically, an expectant mother has three options: not having the baby, giving the baby to someone else to raise, or raising the baby herself. Most of the discussion here is concerned with choices made by unmarried women because little information about unwanted children of married women is available.

Until the mid-1970s, unmarried women who became pregnant had to live with the shame of being labelled promiscuous. Few choices were available for so-called fallen women. Life was difficult for both mother and child. Unmarried parenthood was stigmatized. Abortion was illegal, costly, and often dangerous. Often, adoption was offered as a form of rescue for both mother and child. The mother could keep her secret and the child, it was hoped, did not have to bear the stigma of illegitimacy (Strong-Boag, 2006). Due to medical, legal, and social changes, women today have more choices.

Not Having the Baby

An abortion is the medical termination of a pregnancy. In Canada, abortions have been legal under certain circumstances since 1969 and with no restrictions since 1988. The Box 5.1 timeline shows important milestones in the abortion debate in Canada.

BOX 5.1

Abortion Rights: Significant Moments in Canadian History

1892: The first *Criminal Code* of Canada prohibits abortion except when the mother's life or health is endangered. Abortions must be approved by a doctors' panel and occur in a hospital.

1969: Abortion activist Dr. Henry Morgentaler opens a private abortion clinic in Montreal. The clinic is the first of several.

June 1970: Dr. Morgentaler's clinic is raided. He is charged with several offences, including performing abortions without approval from a therapeutic abortions committee.

March 1975: Morgentaler begins serving an 18-month sentence after being found guilty.

January 1976: Morgentaler's original conviction is set aside and a retrial is ordered.

September 1976: Morgentaler is acquitted. In November, Quebec's new Parti Québécois government drops all charges against him.

1981: Quebec sets up abortion clinics as part of its community health services system.

1982: Canada enacts the *Charter of Rights and Freedoms*.

1988: On January 28, the Supreme Court of Canada strikes down Canada's abortion law as unconstitutional. The law violates section 7 of the *Charter of Rights and Freedoms* by infringing on a woman's right to "life, liberty and security of person." Canada now has no law restricting abortion; it becomes a medical procedure like any other.

1989: The Supreme Court rules that a man cannot veto a woman's abortion decision.

1990: The federal government introduces Bill C-43, penalizing doctors for performing abortions when a woman's health is not at risk. The bill passes the House of Commons, but dies in the Senate after a tie vote.

1992: Morgentaler's Toronto clinic is firebombed.

1994: A Vancouver doctor is shot for performing abortions. Two related shootings follow in Ontario and Manitoba. None are fatal.

1995: Access to abortions outside hospitals remains inconsistent. Some provinces cover the cost in non-hospital clinics; others don't. Some women must pay the cost themselves.

2008: On July l, Morgentaler, now 85, receives the Order of Canada, an honour sparking outrage and demonstrations among anti-abortion advocates. Some return their Order of Canada medals.

2012: A majority of MPs reject a motion for review of "when life begins." Another motion asks the House of Commons to condemn the practice of sex-selective abortions.

Sources: AbortionInCanada.ca. History of Abortion in Canada. Found at: http://www.abortionincanada.ca/history/ (Accessed Feb. 2, 2010); CBC, Abortion Rights: Significant Moments in Canadian History. Found at: http://www.cbc.ca/canada/story/2009/01/13/f-abortion-timeline.html (Accessed July 4, 2009); L. Duhaime, *Abortion Law in Canada.* Found at: http://duhaime.org/LegalResources/FamilyLaw/LawArticle-27/Abortion-Law-in-Canada.aspx (Accessed Feb. 3, 2010); National Abortion Federation. (2010), *History of Abortion in Canada.* Found at: http://www.prochoice.org/canada/history.html (Accessed Feb. 3, 2010); K. Mackrael, (2012). *New Debate Looms Over Sex-Selective Abortion Motion.*

The number of abortions in Canada has decreased slowly in recent years (see Table 5.2). In the mid–1990s, there was one abortion for every three or four live births. Most were performed on women in their late teens and 20s. In Yukon, there were more than two abortions for every five births, the highest rate in Canada, with the level a bit lower in Quebec. Since 1996, both the total number and the

TABLE 5.2	Total Number of Reported Abortions in Canada by Selected Year, 1974–2010
Year	**Number of Abortions in Canada**
1974	52 435
1984	69 449
1988*	72 693
1989	79 315
1990	92 901
1997**	111 526
2004	100 763
2009	93 755
2010***	64 64

*Abortion legalized
** Peak year
*** Quebec did not report

Sources: Statistics Canada. 2000. *Induced abortions, by age group, Canada, provinces and territories*. "Therapeutic Abortion Survey." Ottawa, Ontario. Statistics Canada; Canadian Institute for Health Information. Table 1: Induced Abortions Performed in Canada.

rate have fallen slightly. While several factors are involved, many think that better access to contraception has resulted in fewer unwanted pregnancies and therefore fewer abortions (Women's Health Research Institute, 2011).

Like other aspects of reproduction, abortion has raised many questions. First, there is debate over when human life begins. Is it at the moment of conception, the moment the child breathes on its own, or some point between these extremes? Second, there is the issue of whose life is to have priority. Is it to be given to the pregnant woman or to the fetus with the potential of living as an independent being? The answer to this is related to the first issue. Third is the issue of a woman's having the right to control her reproductive system. Should an adolescent require her parents' consent before having an abortion? Should a wife have her husband's consent? A fourth area involves the timing of abortion. With medical advances in helping premature infants survive, the time gap between the last date an abortion could be performed safely and the date at which a fetus could survive is becoming shorter. How late should an abortion be permitted? Should access be restricted to the first trimester because such abortions are safer and do not raise the question of the potential survival of the child? Religious groups, in particular, have taken positions on the morality of abortion. Part of the controversy has been expressed in repeated demonstrations outside abortion clinics.

Some women are selective about which child they want to give birth to and raise. With more sensitive prenatal diagnosis, it is possible to tell if a child will be born with a chromosomal or genetic disorder. For example, Down syndrome, a chromosomal disorder that results in low intellectual functioning, can be diagnosed through amniocentesis, a procedure in which some of the fluid surrounding the fetus is drawn off through a large syringe and examined under a microscope. We will look in more detail at prenatal diagnosis later in this chapter.

female feticide: the practice of aborting a female fetus

Parents may choose to abort or keep a fetus based on its sex. **Female feticide** happens in India and China by the millions, but it also happens in North America in numbers large enough to distort the male-to-female ratio in some ethnic groups. The strongest evidence of sex selection occurs if previous children were girls. Couples who have several daughters and no son may selectively get rid of female fetuses until they can ensure that their next child is a boy. The College of Physicians and Surgeons of British Columbia has stated that the termination of a pregnancy because of an undesired sex is repugnant and that it is unethical for physicians to facilitate such action. The College in Ontario also stated that it is inappropriate to use ultrasound solely to determine the sex of the fetus. Therefore, doctors should be allowed to disclose this information only after about 30 weeks of pregnancy—in other words, when an unquestioned abortion is all but impossible (Kale, 2012).

infanticide: in the Canadian *Criminal Code*, a female person commits infanticide when she causes the death of her newly born child

In rare and extreme cases, mothers kill their babies soon after birth, often after they have tried to conceal their pregnancies (Kramar, 2005). In Canada, this act is called **infanticide** and it is identified as an offence in the *Criminal Code*. A defence of diminished responsibility applies: "A female person commits infanticide when by a wilful act or omission she causes the death of her newly-born child, if at the time of the act or omission she is not fully recovered from the effects of giving birth to the child and by reason thereof or of the effect of lactation consequent on the birth of the child her mind is then disturbed" (Department of Justice, 2008b). Note that only the mother of a child can commit infanticide, seen as the result of a mental disturbance following childbirth.

Giving the Child to Someone Else

Foster Care

foster care: the provision of care by a family, other than a parent or guardian of a child, approved and arranged by a child welfare authority

In the 19th century, when children could be a financial asset, one option for children who were orphans or whose parents could not care for them was to be placed in **foster care**. In exchange for room and board and some education, the children were expected to assist in the foster household. Many children went from orphanages to these homes, often on farms where boys helped with farm work and girls helped indoors. Usually the families were not well screened, and unfortunate placements occurred. Once the children were in homes, there was little supervision. *Anne of Green Gables,* by Lucy Maud Montgomery, is based on a mix-up that occurred when orphanage staff acted on a request sent through a third party. Although Anne is a fictional character, many young people in Canada went to work in homes. A large group was sent from England to Canada. The practice of fostering was praised for providing opportunities for young people, known as Home Children, who had no prospects in England. In reality, however, many children were exploited. In addition, many lost ties with birth relatives, especially siblings (Strong-Boag, 2011).

In such a society, infants were a liability. In New France during the 1700s, a number of women gave their illegitimate babies to Aboriginal people to raise because they felt this was better than exposing them to the elements and thereby allowing them to die (Moogk, 1982). Many children were abandoned. Foundling homes, which were set up to care for abandoned children, had mortality rates of between 85 and 90 percent, partly because of problems with contagious diseases—it was before the days of immunization and the development of modern medicines—and partly because people did not understand how much attachment and stimulation mattered to infant development and survival (Rooke & Schnell, 1983). Foster homes often provided temporary substitute care during family crises. Some institutions limited the children they would accept to those past infancy from respectable families experiencing hardship like the death of a husband and father. Others served populations like children of members of fraternal orders (Strong-Boag, 2011). Mothers who could not take advantage of institutional care for their children sometimes turned to "baby farmers," women who would take unwanted children for a small one-time fee and try to place them for adoption. Many of these children died. The baby farmers were then accused of killing the babies in their care, which gave them more space for babies, so that they would be able to charge fees over again (Zelizer, 1985).

By the turn of the century, foster homes were seen as the best substitute for the natural home. Foster parents were compensated for children who were hard to place—the very young, the sickly, and those with mental and physical challenges. Eventually, virtually all foster parents received boarding payments to help meet the costs of providing for the children in their care (Strong-Boag, 2011). A study of Romanian orphans found strong evidence that young children placed into foster care were better able than those in institutions to form strong attachments to their carers. The younger a child was when placed in foster care, generally up to the age of three years, the more likely the child would develop an attachment (Smyke et al., 2010).

The trend in foster care is now away from baby care and long-term placements. Advances in medical science mean that children in Canada are unlikely to be orphaned, and with the improvement in benefits available for single parents, children are also less likely to enter foster care because of their parents' death or extreme poverty. Instead, they are more likely to be in foster care because they have behavioural problems or because they are victims of neglect or abuse. Children entering care tend to be older than before, and to have many more emotional and physical problems (Sumner-Mayer, 2006). For the first time, the 2011 Census counted the number of children in foster care. Foster children aged 14 and under represented 0.5 percent of children in this age group in private households (Statistics Canada, 2012j). Aboriginal children are overrepresented among children in foster care, and many children in care have special needs requiring specific attention (Farris-Manning & Zandstra, 2003; Strong-Boag, 2011). The best estimate from two studies is that between 76 000 and 85 000 kids are in foster care in Canada. Foster care rates differ by province, but tend to range between $23 and $30 a day, depending on the age of the child (Canadian Press, 2012a). Foster parents are required to have special therapeutic and child-management skills (Bass et al., 2004). Given the problems foster children can bring into the family, and given increased employment of mothers outside the home, foster families are in short supply.

Canada does not yet have a national strategy to address issues related to foster care, leaving many children in care in a state of limbo (Farris-Manning & Zandstra, 2003). Since foster care is seen as a temporary stop away from home, contact between the children and their birth parents is encouraged so that the move home will be smoother. It is therefore difficult for foster parents to feel that the child is theirs. There is also an emphasis on adoption planning for children who cannot return home (Elmore, 2003). If they want the child to stay, foster parents may have to adopt him or her.

Adoption

For many years, the comfort offered the childless was, "You can always adopt." Unlike foster care, in **adoption**, legal rights and responsibilities are transferred from the birth parents to the adoptive parents. Once parental rights have been terminated, biological parents cannot regain custody of their children. **Open adoption** refers to a situation where the adoptive parents and the birth parents know each other and exchange information such as family, medical, and social histories. In a **closed adoption**, the biological and adoptive parents know little or nothing of each other. Records are often sealed, preventing the child from tracing his or her roots and the birth parents from knowing what became of their child (Canada Adopts, 2001).

In early 20th-century North American society, adoption was regarded with suspicion. It was feared the child would have inherited "bad blood" from inadequate parents. At this time, adopting children who were somewhat older was considered safer because you could better judge their character. In 1873, New Brunswick became the first Canadian province to pass adoption legislation, followed in 1896 by Nova Scotia. The remaining provinces passed similar laws between 1920 and 1930. Before that time, birth and adoptive parents might sign an indenture of adoption, but this document was not binding and the child could be returned to the biological parents at any time if he or she proved unsatisfactory to the adoptive parents. Frequently, adoptions were informal and without legal protections (Strong-Boag, 2006).

Over time, attitudes evolved. In the 1930s, adoption became more respectable. Agencies tried to place children like those the adopters might have had, matching them for race, religion, and even hair and eye colour. During the 1950s, adoption specialists stated that it was in the children's best interests to sever ties with birth parents and closed adoptions became the norm. In the 1970s and 1980s, the number of adoptions dropped off. Given improved contraception and a greater

adoption: the legal transfer of parental rights and obligations from birth parent or parents to adoptive parent or parents

open adoption: a form of adoption where the adoptive parents and the birth parents know each other and exchange information

closed adoption: a form of adoption where the biological and adoptive parents know little or nothing of each other

social acceptance of single mothers, fewer babies were being placed for adoption (Grotevant, 2008).

Currently, single mothers who keep their babies are more likely to come from situations where raising such a child is not stigmatized. In fact, some mothers experience considerable pressure from their family and peers to raise the child themselves. They also tend to have a deep need for a close relationship and a desire to demonstrate their love for the child or their ability to raise a child. Those who surrender a child for adoption are less likely to come from single-parent homes, are more likely to have professional parents, and are more likely to see adoption as giving their baby a better chance in life (Moore & Davidson, 2002).

Mothers who do make this choice are now offered various degrees of openness in adoption. Often, they are able to select the adoptive parents. Some agencies arrange meetings; others offer the mother descriptions of several suitable families and allow her to make a choice (Sobol et al., 2000). Usually, the decision to give up a child for adoption is extremely painful for the birth mother. Many experience a continuing sense of loss and desire for contact with the adoptee (Fravel et al., 2000). Extended family members may also experience a similar loss (Ward, 2005).

All provinces and territories have policies regarding the release of information to adoptees and birth parents. Most provinces have adoption reunion registries that enable contact once both parties register. Most will also search for birth relatives on request. Identifying information, including original birth and adoption records, is provided by all the provinces. However, adoptees and birth parents can deny access to such information (Canadian Council of Natural Mothers, n.d.; Gouvernement du Québec, 2008; Ontario Ministry of Community and Social Services, n.d.). In black-market adoption arrangements, the suitability of the adoptive parents is not regulated, especially if they choose never to legalize the adoption.

Many children are raised for part or all of their lives by members of their extended family (Grotevant, 2008). Although their biological parents may be unable or unwilling to care for them, they may be much wanted by other relatives. This practice is more common among some ethnic groups than others; for example, Aboriginal people have customarily used the extended family for childcare and informal adoption. **Aboriginal custom adoption** is a privately arranged adoption between two families within the Aboriginal community. It is an open process that involves many people in a child's life, including the birth parents, the extended family, and the Aboriginal community. The goal of Aboriginal custom adoption is to ensure Aboriginal children are raised in Aboriginal families so that they retain their language and cultural identities. Aboriginal custom adoptions are recognized in Canadian courts. Families often have a custom adoption ceremony and the adoption is considered legal when a child is physically transferred to the adoptive parents (Adoptive Parents, n.d.). Aboriginal children retain their First Nations status even if they are adopted by non-First Nations parents (Strong-Boag, 2006).

Aboriginal custom adoption: a privately arranged adoption between two families within the Aboriginal community

Adoption and child welfare come under provincial jurisdiction, so each province has its own laws and regulations. Although some provincial agencies have certain rules and regulations regarding issues such as religion, race, age, marital status, or sexual orientation, in general, as long as you are a Canadian citizen over 18 and do not have a criminal record, you have the right to adopt (Canada Adopts, 2001). There are thousands of children, including babies, available for adoption in Canada. However, the majority of these children are age six and older (Adoption Council of Canada, n.d.). Many eligible children are not adopted. According to the director of the Adoption Council of Canada, it is difficult to know how many domestic adoptions occur in Canada. Each province and territory has its own method of reporting, and these cannot be compared. One estimate gives 30 717 children waiting for adoption but only 2336 placed (Pedersen, 2009).

intercountry adoption: a process that recognizes an individual or couple as the legal and permanent parent or parents of a child from another country

During the 1950s and 1960s, **intercountry adoptions**, also known as international adoptions, grew in popularity, especially in Ontario and British Columbia. More recently, foreign adoptions increased from 320 children in 1991 to 2180 in 2003. Since then, adoptions dropped to 1535 in 2006 and 1908 in 2008. The largest numbers in 2008 came from China, South Korea, and Haiti. About two-thirds were girls. The majority were placed with families in Ontario and Quebec (Hilborn, 2009). Intercountry adoption is regulated under provincial and foreign adoption laws. Either the provinces or private licensed agencies may arrange the adoptions (Human Resources and Skills Development Canada, 2012c). The agencies provide a range of pre- and post-adoptive services, and the adopting parents are responsible for all costs, such as travel, medical expenses, and agency fees. These expenses can be $25 000 and more (Canada Adopts, 2001).

An important consideration in intercountry adoption is that it may produce a racially mixed family. Parents thinking of adopting a child of a different race may consider such factors as their own ethnicity and the racial makeup of their neighbourhood. As they get older, the children often increasingly recognize that the biological and racial differences from their parents carry social weight (Dorow, 2006).

Attitudes toward intercountry adoption vary. Individuals choose intercountry adoption partly because they want to be parents and partly because babies from abroad are often more available. But many are also concerned about the welfare of children in danger because of war or extreme poverty. Critics see intercountry adoptions as exploitation and imperialism, and many foreign governments are now trying to place children in local homes (Hilborn, 2009). The pop singer Madonna, for example, came under criticism after adopting two orphaned children from Malawi (Mponda, 2009). There is also a fear of political repercussions from governments in developing nations that perceive they are being robbed of a valuable human resource (Cole, 1984). Many countries, including Canada, subscribe to the *Hague Convention on Protection of Children and Co-operation in Respect of Intercountry Adoption,* which sets out principles designed to protect the rights of the children, their birth parents, and the adoptive parents from corruption or illegal practices (Hague Conference on Private International Law, 2012).

BOX 5.2 | Multiple Sibling Adoption

Our saga started quite innocently. We thought we needed another boy; we had three daughters and only one son. Adoption looked good. We were delighted with the one girl we had adopted as an infant, and were ready to try a boy a little younger than she was, perhaps aged 5 or 6. We submitted to the usual procedures for approval.

Mother's Day changed everything.

"Let's get them!" said our son as he opened the paper to see "Today's Child," a publication column presenting children needing adoption. Sure enough, there was our little boy, $4\frac{1}{2}$ years old. As a bonus, he would bring his four older brothers.

In about 2 months we were parents of six sons and three daughters, acquiring our first teenager, looking forward to a glorious year with eight teenagers, [and] explaining [to people] our three 7-year-olds, our lifestyle completely transformed.

Source: Margaret Ward, *Full House: Adoption of a Large Sibling Group*. Child Welfare. 1978.

Like foster care, adoption still carries a stigma (Kline et al., 2006). The blood tie is seen in our society as indissoluble and of a mystical nature. There are numerous accounts of children adopted as infants later finding their "real" parents—it is as if society considers the adoptive parents who have raised them as somehow less parental. The belief that the biological tie is important for the bonding of mother and child is strong; therefore, attachment in adoption is regarded as second best (Erera, 2002). These notions of adoption being second best make some adoptive parents feel they are not fully entitled to the child they are raising (Ward, 1979). As a result, they have problems functioning like real parents in areas such as discipline. This emphasis on blood ties and genetic heritage also underlies the recent flood of adoptees seeking contact with their birth parents. "Resemblance talk," or looking for similarities between children and parents, may place those who are adopted at a disadvantage (Becker et al., 2005; Miall, 1987).

Raising the Child Oneself

The number of people who resort to abortion, foster care, or adoption are relatively easy to discover because many are involved with hospitals and social service agencies; however, finding out how many people keep and raise unwanted children is impossible. There are several reasons for this. Any child born within a marriage is assumed to be wanted, but this may not be the case. Married women do have abortions and do place their children with other families despite a stigma attached to those who do not raise their biological children. In addition, many children who were unplanned and initially unwanted eventually become much loved.

Even knowing the number of unmarried mothers who raise their own children does not provide us with an accurate count, since some women in their 30s or 40s with no opportunity or no desire to marry choose to have a child rather than never experiencing the pleasures of motherhood. Included among these are lesbians who adopt or use new reproductive technologies. In her study of lesbian mothers in Alberta, Fiona Nelson (1996) learned that many women assumed they would have children and being lesbian did not change this. The real decision involved how to go about having a child, because they could not become pregnant as simply as heterosexual women. Many additional decisions were involved, for example which partner should have the baby (Chabot & Ames, 2004). Because of stigma against lesbian women in many fertility clinics and because of the cost of having one of the few willing doctors perform artificial insemination, not covered under Alberta's health plan, many chose self-insemination. In these cases, the child is very much wanted even though the mother is single.

A group virtually ignored are the unmarried fathers who wish to raise their children. Until 1970, they had virtually no rights. In 2006, nearly one-fifth of lone-parent families were headed by fathers. Many are divorced rather than never married (Milan et al., 2007). Even today, when men are more involved in raising children, unmarried fathers receive relatively little social support (Miall & March,

Source: Stuart Carlson/Universal Uclick.

2005). Gay men have fewer options for parenthood than women. A few adopt. Some may father a lesbian's child through artificial insemination and become actively involved in parenting, or they may enlist the help of a surrogate mother (Barret & Robinson, 2000).

The unwanted child who is raised by a parent is at risk for physical or emotional abuse (Duffy & Momirov, 1997). In Chapter 14, we will look at this and other factors involved in child abuse. Single-parent families, who now make up a growing proportion of the population, are discussed in more detail in Chapter 9.

Time to Review

1. What issues are raised by abortion?
2. How does foster care work?
3. What are the different kinds of adoption?
4. What do we know about parents who keep their unwanted children?

"Desperately Seeking Baby"

While some parents have children they don't want, others cannot have the children they do want. Infertility can pose a major crisis for a couple. Since our society has as a norm that married couples have children, infertile couples may have a sense of being defective, which reduces their overall sense of self-worth. The medical investigation of infertility is intrusive and often uncomfortable. The couple is asked intimate questions about their sexual activity. Sex may lose spontaneity as the couple plans intercourse when the woman is most likely to be fertile. If the treatment is successful, the woman may experience a very anxious pregnancy because she is afraid to believe she is really going to have a baby. If the treatment is unsuccessful, the couple mourns not being able to have children. Often, the people around them may not be supportive because they do not understand the severity of the loss. After all, no one has died—someone just didn't exist (Jacobs & O'Donohue, 2007). The couple is forced to rethink what parenthood really means to them. Should they plan a life without children or find some other way to become parents?

Women usually feel the lack of children more than men: they have been socialized to believe that they achieve full worth as human beings only if they are mothers. Their feelings of loss are made worse by others' unthinking questions about childlessness (Jacobs & O'Donohue, 2007). Men may see their own infertility as an assault on their manhood. Many experience a temporary impotence when they first learn that they are infertile. Many wives experience rage at their husbands. The balance of power in the family may change (Berger, 1980). Fertile partners may feel that if they were married to someone else, they could have children; thus, childlessness is part of the price of monogamy.

The knowledge that the spouse might have children in another union further undermines the self-esteem of the infertile partner. The tests and procedures a couple undergo during a fertility investigation, such as keeping track of when and how intercourse occurred and undergoing tests after having sex, can make them feel as if the doctor is watching them over their bedpost. Sex life can suffer (Jacobs & O'Donohue, 2007; Pawson, 2003).

In the past, the only choices available to infertile people were to find a child someone else did not want to raise or to remain childless. The options are wider now. They still include foster care and adoption; added to these, however, are the new reproductive technologies.

Assisted Reproductive Technologies

Some would-be parents dream of having a child who has their own genes. Others want a child who won't inherit a lethal gene they carry, such as the one for Tay-Sachs disease, which leads to progressive brain deterioration. Such individuals may turn to one of the three basic forms of assisted reproductive technologies (ART): artificial insemination, surrogacy, and in vitro fertilization. These have many variations and can be used alone or together.

Types of Technologies

Artificial Insemination

artificial insemination: the practice of using sperm from a donor to fertilize an egg

This method has been around for many years. **Artificial insemination** (AI) involves placing the male's sperm inside the woman's vagina or uterus with a syringe so that she can become pregnant. Donor sperm is used when the husband is infertile or carries a genetic disorder. It has also been used for unmarried women who wish to have children. There is now a donor sibling registry to arrange contact between children fathered by the same sperm donor (Freeman et al., 2009).

Since insemination is relatively simple, there are reports of do-it-yourself efforts. For example, in pre-AIDS days, some lesbians wishing to have children sometimes used sperm donated by gay men. The technology to freeze sperm allows it to be stored before use, sometimes for years. It also allows donors to be tested for HIV before their sperm is used. Some men preserve sperm before undergoing chemotherapy or when they have a terminal illness so that they can father children after treatment or death. In some cases, sperm has been removed from men who are in a coma or even after death (Andrews, 1999; Gosden, 1999; Mundy, 2007). The development of sperm banks allows prospective parents to screen potential donors for qualities they want in their child. One extreme example was the Repository for Germinal Choice in California, now closed, which preserved sperm from outstanding scientists and professionals, including Nobel Prize winners. More than 230 children were born from these donors to women who had been pre-screened for intelligence (Goodwin, 2000).

Surrogate Mothers

When the woman cannot conceive or carry a child to term, some couples turn to **surrogate mothers**. In the simplest form of surrogacy, a fertile woman bears a child for another person. The surrogate mother is often paid and signs over the baby at birth. Historically, surrogacy involved sexual intercourse, but nowadays artificial insemination is routine. Surrogacy also permits single men, gay males for instance, to become fathers. The embryo may have developed from the egg of the prospective mother or a donor, fertilized by her partner's or a donor's sperm. In such cases, the situation is called a "host womb" (Gosden, 1999). One much-publicized case involved a mother giving birth to her daughter and son-in-law's triplets (Levin, 1987).

surrogate mother: a woman who agrees to artificial insemination, usually for a fee, with a view to turning over the resulting child to the biological father and his wife

In Vitro Fertilization

In vitro fertilization (IVF) became news with the birth in 1978 of Louise Brown, the first "test-tube baby," in England. This procedure involves removing ripe eggs from the woman's body and fertilizing them with the man's sperm in the laboratory. One or more of the embryos are then placed in the woman's uterus with the hope that one will become implanted and produce a baby. This procedure is usually used when the fallopian tubes leading from the woman's ovaries to her uterus are blocked. Success rates, as measured by live births, can be disappointing. They vary depending on many factors: a woman's age, her medical history, use of her eggs or a donor's, use of a donor embryo, the number of embryos transferred, and reliance on a host womb. Often, less than one-third of IVF cycles are successful (Centers for Disease Control, 2008). Excess embryos are routinely frozen so that they can be thawed and implanted later if the first try is unsuccessful. Donor eggs have been used when the woman is infertile (following menopause, for example) or is carrying a genetic disorder (Cowan, 2003; Gosden, 1999).

in vitro fertilization: the technique of fertilizing a woman's eggs with her partner's sperm in a lab dish, and later placing the embryo(s) in her uterus

Because the embryo used for IVF develops in a lab dish for the first few days, it is open to examination. With advances in DNA technology, it is possible to test embryos for sex and for a variety of inherited diseases (Sandel, 2007). Scientists are also studying ways to determine which eggs, sperm, and embryos are healthiest. Once a woman is pregnant, with or without assistance, the fetus's development can be monitored through ultrasound, amniocentesis, examination of cells from the placenta, or tests of the mother's blood. The assumption is that a child with a defect can be aborted (Ormond & Ross, 2006; Sandel, 2007). A few parents have sued when they bore a child with disabilities because they had neither been warned of the risk nor offered prenatal diagnosis (Weil, 2006). In cases where the use of fertility drugs or IVF has resulted in a multiple pregnancy, parents may opt for selective reduction, a procedure that destroys "excess" fetuses to allow one or two a better chance to develop (Mundy, 2007). Some couples, when they learn the child is the "wrong" sex, will go to another doctor for an abortion.

Cloning

In 1997, Scottish scientists announced that they had made a **clone**—a genetically identical copy—of a sheep, which they named Dolly, using a cell from the udder

clone: a genetically identical copy of a cell or an organism

of a six-year-old ewe. Other animals have also been cloned. In 1999, scientists at Nexia Biotechnologies, near Montreal, cloned three goats from a single cell (CBC, 1999). Theoretically, it is possible to clone a human being using the same technology.

Social and Ethical Issues

As former McGill University professor Roger Gosden says, "Reproduction is something that individuals do and the rest of society cares about" (1999, p. 5). Conceiving a child is usually a private matter; however, assisted reproductive technologies have opened it to public scrutiny. Attitudes in society range from condemning all such technologies as unnatural to accepting them wholeheartedly as progress. Most people care to some degree about the ethics of their use.

The Canadian Assisted Reproductive Technologies Register (CARTR) was first established in 1999 for the collection of data from Canadian fertility centers that were using assisted reproductive technologies (ART). In 2007, 13 482 treatment cycles involving ART were reported to the register. Overall, 32 percent of these cycles resulted in pregnancy and nearly 26 percent resulted in a live birth (Gunby et al., 2011).

The Financial Side

ART procedures are expensive and often not covered by medical insurance. One cycle of in vitro fertilization costs approximately $7750 to $12 250. Only 15 percent of couples affected by infertility can afford IVF treatment (Canadian Agency for Drugs and Technologies in Health, 2012). This raises some questions: Is it right to allow better-off people to have children and deny them to the poor? Will women with lower incomes become the providers rather than recipients of such services? Will the cost widen the gulf between super-advantaged children and those who are not? There are reports that clinics in developing countries provide surrogacy services for relatively low rates (Dolnick, 2007). In some places, large payments are made to egg and sperm donors and to surrogate mothers. Does this amount to baby selling? Some individuals regard paying a surrogate's fee as a type of prostitution because the woman is paid for the use of her body. Even if donors and surrogates are banned from making large profits, are they entitled to compensation for their time and discomfort? (Freundlich, 2001; Spar, 2006). Should public insurance cover ART procedures? In 2009, under a new plan, a minimum of two cycles of IVF were remunerated in Quebec. Ontario and Alberta are also considering such policies (Canadian Agency for Drugs and Technologies in Health, 2012).

Contracts

Since 2004, surrogacy in Canada has been regulated. The *Assisted Human Reproduction Act* provided national guidelines for many new reproductive techniques, including surrogacy. According to the act, it is illegal to pay or offer to pay a woman to serve as a surrogate. The act does not, however, determine whether surrogacy agreements are legally valid, and it opens the door to custody disputes (Reilly, 2007). Fortunately, such cases rarely arise. In Canada, a birth mother cannot consent to the adoption of her child before a specified time following the child's birth. This limit may hold when the surrogate is also the genetic mother of the baby.

One well-publicized custody case was that of "Baby M" in the United States. The surrogate decided to keep the child. The matter was finally resolved, based not on contract law but on the best interests of the child. Custody was granted the biological father and his wife, who adopted the baby. The surrogate-biological mother was given visiting rights (Freundlich, 2001; Spar, 2006).

What should be the position when the surrogate provides only a host womb and not the egg? Can she be forced to follow certain health restrictions (e.g., no alcohol)? If she doesn't, can she be held liable for damage to the baby? Can contracting parents be forced to assume responsibility if the child fails to satisfy them? In one case, the father and his wife claimed only one of a set of twins—a girl—and refused to take the boy ("Surrogate mother furious," 1988).

Consent
Problems with surrogacy contracts may also involve consent. Did the surrogate truly understand what she was agreeing to? Consent issues arise in other areas. Is it legal, for example, to use sperm or eggs taken from comatose or dead individuals? They are in no position to consent. What about frozen embryos? How long should they be kept? Can embryos be destroyed or donated to others without permission from the contracting individuals? What should be done with embryos if the prospective parents both die? Or what should happen if the couple divorces and one ex-partner, as has happened, no longer wishes to have a child (Maranto, 1996)? Pro-life advocates insist that embryos are potential human beings and should not be destroyed. Who owns embryos, eggs, and sperm?

Splitting and Multiplying the Parent
In a bizarre case, a California judge ruled in September 1997 that a two-year-old girl had no legal parents and was thus not entitled to child support. She was born following egg and sperm donation and growth in a host womb. The husband, however, did not sign the contract until the surrogate was already pregnant. The couple separated shortly after the baby's arrival. When the mother sued for child support from her ex-husband, he argued he should not be held responsible. The judge's decision was the result. A later decision freed the husband from support obligations and required the wife to adopt the little girl (Freundlich, 2001). This case prompts a critical question: Who precisely *are* the parents?

Provincial laws do not provide an adequate definition of legal parenthood when reproductive technologies are involved (Leckey, 2009). Two other cases provide examples. A little boy was determined to have three legal parents—his birth mother, his sperm donor father, and his birth mother's lesbian partner. On January 2, 2007, the Court of Appeal for Ontario determined that all three were acting as the child's parents (Court of Appeal for Ontario, 2007). On the other hand, a Quebec judge refused to let the social mother adopt a child carried by a surrogate, even though her husband provided the sperm, because paid surrogacy is illegal (Baudoin & Blaikie, 2009).

To discuss the issue, we need to develop a new vocabulary because ARTs have separated conception and pregnancy from parenthood. One proposed set of terms is as follows: (a) *intentional mother and father,* the woman and man who want to have a child; (b) *genetic mother and father,* the woman and man who supply the egg and sperm; (c) *gestational mother,* the woman who carries the embryo and gives birth to the baby; and (d) *nurturing mother and father,* the woman and man who raise the child (Hinman, n.d.). In ordinary situations, these different types of parenthood are combined in just one man and one woman. In cases like Baby M or the child without legal parents, where various parent figures are involved, the matter becomes crucial to the well-being of the child. A side issue concerns inheritance rights of children born using frozen sperm or embryos (with or without the father's consent) following his death (Andrews, 1999).

The Vanier Institute of the Family also raises concerns over the growing use of DNA testing to determine a child's biological father and refers to a "Genes R Us" attitude. Under Canadian divorce law, an adult who has acted as a parent and treated the child as his or her own is regarded as the child's legal parent, whether biologically related or not. Provincial laws may, however, differ in cases of unmarried and separating parents (Knoppers, 2000). In such cases, as well as those involving ARTs, protecting the welfare of the child is important. How best to do so depends on the answer to the question, who is the parent?

The Dream Child

Science originally helped couples overcome infertility. Now it can let them choose the kind of baby they want through genetic testing of embryos and prenatal diagnosis of disabilities. Questions arise, however, over prenatal diagnosis solely for purposes of sex-selection, as is reported in China and India, where males are valued and female fetuses often aborted. There are also concerns about how severe a disability needs to be to justify abortion. For instance, does cleft palate, a correctable defect, qualify? It follows that society may become less tolerant of disability and underachievement (Glover, 2006; Sandel, 2007).

When prospective parents use reproductive technologies, they can try to create a child with some wished-for characteristics (Glover, 2006). They may do this by selecting a donor with particular characteristics. For instance, one couple offered US$50 000 for a tall, athletic, clever college student to be an egg donor (Ehrensaft, 2005). Or they may try sperm-sorting techniques prior to artificial insemination to improve their chance for a child of the "right" sex (Mundy, 2007).

Making designer babies is uncertain in any case. Although there is no scientific follow-up of people conceived through the Repository for Germinal Choice, at least one child experienced learning difficulties (Goodwin, 2000). We all carry genes that, in the wrong combination, can produce surprise disabilities. Genetic accidents and mutations lurk as well. Of course, development is also affected by the environment in which we live.

Tampering with DNA

In the quest for designer children, scientists have looked ever closer at human genes and the DNA sequences they contain. Now that the human genome has been mapped, even more techniques may become possible. Should cloning be permitted? If so, what will it do to family relationships? Will it put a new twist on the song "I'm My Own Grandpa"? Germ-line therapy promises to eliminate genetic disorders from a family line. Should this be allowed? Is such manipulation preferable to abortion following prenatal diagnosis? If science is to advance along these lines, it will need to engage in experiments with eggs, sperm, and embryos. Should human ones be used? (Glover, 2006; Spar, 2006).

Genetic Information

Although we are not solely our genes—even identical twins differ—most of us value genetic information. For some, it involves life and death. How much information should individuals resulting from ART receive, and how best should it be stored? Should donors be warned about being a carrier of a genetic disorder that turns up in a child? For a long time, parents were advised to keep the fact of artificial insemination secret. Some may also hide use of donor eggs or embryos out of a desire to conceal their infertility. Providing genetic information was hampered both by secrecy and by poor record-keeping in the past. Yet social workers point out that family secrets are bad for children. Telling children they are adopted, for instance, is related to better adjustment later in life. Other individuals are concerned that children may grow up without valuable genetic information (Ethics Committee of the American Society for Reproductive Medicine, 2004b; Freundlich, 2007).

Individual Rights versus Social Policy

Finally, where should the line be drawn between individual rights and what is good for society as a whole? For example, should the government or some other body decide who can be a parent? Should IVF be available for women over 55 years old? Should the number of children be limited? Should prospective parents be tested to determine whether they are qualified to raise a child? Life expectancy is increasing, and many seniors raise their grandchildren. Should sexual orientation or marital status matter? Should payment for procedures be made legal? How should contracts be interpreted? The questions multiply, and answering them will involve ethical, social, and legal principles. One guiding principle is that it is essential to protect family relationships, especially those involving children.

The Royal Commission on New Reproductive Technologies and the *Assisted Human Reproduction Act*

Until the *Assisted Human Reproduction Act* came into force, the market and the views of individual physicians largely determined what services might or might not be available and to which women (Baylis, 2011). As a result of concerns over the many problems and ethical issues surrounding the new reproductive technologies, the federal government created the Royal Commission on New Reproductive Technologies in 1989 to look into these methods and to make recommendations for policies and safeguards. The commission issued its report, which contained 293 recommendations, in November 1993. Its major conclusions were that unethical use of reproductive technologies should not be permitted and that regulations were needed to protect all individuals involved, as well as society as a whole (Health Canada, 1999). After two attempts, Parliament passed the *Assisted Human Reproduction Act* (Bill C-6). (See Box 5.3 below, which provides more information.) Most of the law came into effect on April 22, 2004, with the exception of some provisions that depended on the drawing up of new regulations. The act also established the Assisted Human Reproduction Agency of Canada (AHRC) to oversee the whole subject (Hébert et al., 2004). Health Canada is now responsible for developing policy and regulations under the *Assisted Human Reproduction Act* and for administering and enforcing the act and its regulations (Health Canada, 2013).

In December 2004, the Quebec government—with the support of Alberta, Saskatchewan, and New Brunswick—challenged some sections of the act on constitutional grounds. The Quebec Court of Appeal gave its opinion on June 19, 2008, that those sections dealt with provincial rather than federal powers. The federal government appealed to the Supreme Court of Canada. In December 2010, the Supreme Court released a 5–4 decision that upheld the right of provinces, with some exceptions, to regulate ART and fertility clinics (CBC, 2012). The federal prohibitions against such activities as human cloning, creating in vitro embryos for research purposes, manipulating embryos to increase the probability of a particular sex, and payment for surrogacy or for the purchase of embryos remained in force. However, Canada now has a fragmented, province-by-province approach to the regulation of assisted human reproduction (Baylis, 2011), and in 2012 the federal government announced that it would close AHRC (Assisted Human Reproduction Canada, 2012).

BOX 5.3 — Regulating Reproductive and Genetic Technologies

The *Assisted Human Reproduction Act* is based on several principles: It is important to protect the health and well-being of children and of women. The use of reproductive technologies must involve free and informed consent. There should be no discrimination based on sexual orientation or on marital status. These technologies should not be commercialized. Finally, the human genome must be protected.

Certain activities are banned; these include

1. Human cloning
2. Combining human and animal genetic material

3. Germ-line therapy
4. Use of cells of embryos, fetuses, anyone under 18 years of age, or a corpse, to create an embryo, fetus, or person
5. Sex diagnosis for sex selection, except for purposes related to the health of the embryo or fetus
6. Maintenance of an embryo outside the human body after the 14th day following fertilization (excluding time spent in the frozen state)
7. Implantation of a human gamete, embryo, or fetus in an animal, and vice versa
8. Advertising and commercialization of any of the above practices; commercialization of surrogacy
9. Commercial transactions involving human genes, cells, embryos, and fetuses

Source: *Assisted Human Reproduction Act*, published by the Minister of Justice.

The Future

A factor that affects all atypical families is the lack of a social script. Society still considers a married couple and their biological children the norm. From early childhood, we learn how biological mothers and fathers ought to act. Yet few norms exist for adoptive parents, foster parents, and surrogate mothers. Since these are not the standard relationships, there are some areas where social expectations of families do not fit. Consequently, families may feel considerable discomfort that may interfere with their ability to parent the child.

Psychologically, members of these families have all suffered significant losses of some kind. Children have been separated from one or both genetic parents, even if this separation occurred before birth. Infertile parents have lost the ability to have their own biological child. Even fertile parents who have resorted to the new technologies have not been able to conceive in the "normal" way, through sexual intercourse. All members of the family have some degree of pain and a sense of being different with which they must come to terms. There may also be ambiguity about who is considered a family member. For example, is an adoptee considered part of the birth mother's family? Such ambiguity can be a source of continuing stress (Boss, 2002; Kim, 2009). Experts predict that more couples than ever before will have children because of the new birth technologies. We cannot predict, however, what impact other factors will have on these families, so any prediction is at best only an educated guess.

Time to Review

1. What are the different kinds of assisted reproductive technologies?
2. What issues arise from the use of ARTs?
3. How are reproductive technologies regulated in Canada?

Difficult Choices

We have developed and continue to develop methods that allow us to significantly influence the process of reproduction. However, there is a gap between what we can do and what we should do. The issues are complex, and there are no easy answers. The case study that follows illustrates just some of the questions that arise when discussing the use of ARTs.

> ### The Case of Rebecca and Joshua
>
> Rebecca and Joshua are a married couple. They know that they each carry the gene that causes Tay-Sachs disease, a disease of the nervous system. When both parents carry the Tay-Sachs gene, their child has a 25 percent chance of developing the condition. The nerve damage usually begins while the baby is still in the womb, and symptoms may appear when the child is three to six months old. The disease tends to progress very quickly, and the child usually dies by age four or five. Rebecca and Joshua want to have a child, but Rebecca has blocked fallopian tubes. In vitro fertilization would be an effective way for her to get pregnant, but Rebecca's gynecologist warns the couple of the high risk for the child having Tay-Sachs and tries to discourage them. She suggests adoption as an alternative, but they refuse. The doctor then proposes prenatal genetic testing, but again Rebecca and Joshua refuse. Because of their religious beliefs, they feel that it is their duty to have their own child and that the result will be in God's hands.
>
> 1. What are the ethical issues in this scenario?
> 2. What principles can you use to help you decide what to do?
> 3. If you were the doctor, what would you do?
> 4. If you were a friend of Rebecca and Joshua's, what advice would you give them?

Summary

Why Do People Decide to Have Children?

While the decision to have a child is individual, or made between a couple, many social factors have a powerful influence on this decision. Having a child is often regarded as the mark of adulthood. There is much pressure on couples to have children. Since motherhood is considered necessary for personal fulfillment, women who choose not to have children are stigmatized.

How Has the Canadian Fertility Rate Changed over Time?

The total fertility rate, or total number of children a woman is expected to have, has been stable since 1993 at about 1.6 children. From one generation to the next, there has been a decrease in fertility at the youngest ages and an increase among older women. Teenage pregnancy is generally seen as a social problem requiring efforts to prevent it. The teen pregnancy rate in Canada has declined in each consecutive year from 1996 to 2006.

In the earlier, rural economy in Canada, children provided labour for the family enterprise and social security for the elderly. For a variety of reasons, the birth rate has dropped markedly in the past few decades. First, medical advances have reduced infant mortality and provided more effective contraceptives. Second, despite opposition on moral and religious grounds, both contraceptives and abortion have been legalized. Third, economic factors encourage smaller families. Child labour is no longer a necessary part of our economy. Poor economic times and women's growing participation in the workforce, as well as the cost of raising children, also foster smaller families. Many women put off having children until they are through school and able to support them. The value of children (VOC) framework helps identify the satisfactions and the costs of having children. Finally, many couples believe that large families may damage the marital relationship and have an adverse effect on child development. About 7 to 8 percent of Canadians make the choice to remain childless.

What Are the Choices for Those Who Do Not Want the Children They Conceive?

There are three basic approaches to the unwanted child. First, a woman may choose not to have the baby; that is, she has an abortion. This choice has produced controversies on moral grounds. Second, a parent may give the child to someone else to raise. In foster care, people other than the parents or guardians care for a child. It is not usually intended as long-term care and the children are generally older and have more behavioural problems. Adoption involves the permanent transfer of parental rights to other adults. There is growing openness in adoption, which allows continuing contact with birth parents and the possibility of later contact with adult adoptees. A growing trend is international adoption. A third choice is to raise the child oneself. There is stigma against married people who give up a child. Single-parent families have recently gained wider acceptance.

What Options Are Available to Those Who Are Childless Involuntarily?

If a couple cannot have children, they may experience stress and loss of self-esteem, both because of their childlessness and because of the investigation and treatment of their infertility. Birth technologies, such as artificial insemination, in vitro fertilization, and surrogate motherhood, offer other choices, although some procedures have a low success rate. Assisted reproductive technologies have given rise to many social and ethical issues. Only 15 percent of couples affected by infertility can afford IVF treatment. When prospective parents use reproductive technologies, they can try to create a child with some wished-for characteristics. Other questions involve the line between individual rights and what is good for society as a whole. The *Assisted Human Reproduction Act* of 2004 provided national guidelines for many new reproductive techniques, but in 2012 the government of Canada announced that it would close Assisted Human Reproduction Canada.

What Issues Are Faced by Atypical Families?

All families in which children are not raised by both biological parents face a number of issues. A factor that affects all atypical families is the lack of a social script. Psychologically, members of these families have all suffered significant losses of some kind. Experts predict that more couples than ever before will have children because of the new birth technologies.

Class Assignments

1. In small groups, discuss different options for dealing with an unwanted pregnancy. Design questions for a brief survey. Individually, interview 10 people each and compare your results. Were there any surprises?
2. For a month, keep a scrapbook of stories that appear in newspapers and/or magazines about having children. You may also wish to keep a log of any news stories you hear on the radio or television. What were the main issues?

Personal Assignments

The following assignments are designed to help you think about your own family:

1. If you had your wish, how many children would you have? Why? Would your answer be affected by your marital status? Explain.
2. If for some reason you could not have a biological child, what options would you consider? Why would you choose to use or not use particular methods of having children? If you would decide not to have a child, give your reasons.

Chapter 6
Bringing Up Baby

LEARNING OBJECTIVES

What is the place of socialization in the family life cycle?

What role do parents play in the socialization of children?

In what ways do cultural groups differ in parenting styles?

In what ways do other family members influence the socialization of children?

How do society and the family interact in socialization?

What is gender socialization?

What are age cohorts?

The "pacifier" habit—the habit of sucking a rubber nipple—is an inexcusable piece of folly for which the mother or nurse is directly responsible. The habit when formed is most difficult to give up. The use of the "pacifier," thumb-sucking, finger-sucking, etc., make thick boggy lips, on account of the exercise to which the parts are subjected. They cause an outward bulging of the jaws, which is not conducive to personal attractiveness.

Source: Department of Public Health, *The Care of the Infant and Young Child* (Toronto: 1922). Pg. 30.

A pacifier is helpful for fretfulness or to prevent thumb sucking. . . . A baby who has periods of mild irritability can often be entirely quieted by having a pacifier to suck. We don't know whether this is because the sucking soothes some vague discomfort or simply keeps the baby's mouth busy. . . . Most of the babies who use a pacifier freely for the first few months of life never become thumb suckers, even if they give up the pacifier at 3 or 4 months.

Source: *Baby and Child Care* by Dr. Benjamin Spock. Pocket Books, a division of Simon & Schuster Adult Publishing Group from *Baby and Child Care* by Dr. Benjamin Spock. Copyright © 1945, 1946, 1957, 1968, 1976, 1985, 1992 by Benjamin Spock, M.D.

Over the years, there has been little change in the physical development of children. All newborn babies need care for survival. Most children sit up before they stand, and stand before they walk. But society has changed in what it regards important, and in the kind of behaviour it expects of its members. The use (or nonuse) of a pacifier is one minor example.

Socialization in the Life Cycle

Socialization is the process of passing on to new members a culture's ways of thinking and acting. It occurs mainly in childhood, and by the time they are adults, people are expected to share the values and norms of society. As children, we learn rules for behaviour, for example that we must not bite people. As young people, we learn how to behave in school and college, and what is expected on the job. We learn to be partners and parents. We learn what behaviour is suitable for the middle-aged and elderly and for the separated or widowed. Socialization is a cradle-to-grave process.

Most theories of the family look at how cultural values and norms are passed on to new members; in other words, they are concerned about how society reproduces itself. Predictably, some take a macro view. Structural functionalist thinkers are interested in how transmission of cultural norms ensures the stability of both families and society. The ecological approach looks at how the various levels of the social context affect families. Conflict theorists and feminist thinkers look at the way inequities in society are maintained from one generation to the next. Others approach the topic from a micro perspective, looking at how family relationships shape individual experiences. According to symbolic interactionists, this shaping occurs through day-to-day interactions among family members. Parents and children shape one another through their interaction. Systems theorists emphasize family subsystems and boundaries in shaping children.

The socialization of children often begins with parents and soon includes other family members. The circle expands to more distant relatives, babysitters, daycare personnel, other children, school, television, Facebook, and other aspects of society. Learning can occur through explicit instruction but occurs most often through subtle interactions and observation of others' behaviour. Through socialization, individuals develop a sense of their identity, status, and roles in society. They learn how to survive physically in society and acquire skills needed for social life. While every society socializes its members, how they are socialized can be quite different. To take a simple example, the proper distance between people varies. In North America, it is greater than in Latin American countries. There, people talk comfortably with each other at about the distance that here would be seen as revealing either sexual or hostile feelings (Hall, 1973).

In this chapter, we will look at how families and other social institutions influence child development. From the micro perspective, we will look at how daily interactions between family members help teach children the norms and values of their culture. Since Canada is a multicultural society, there is a diversity of social scripts regarding the socialization of children. We will look at the outcomes of certain parenting practices on child development and how sometimes the practices of a particular group may challenge the dominant cultural norm. From a macro perspective, we will look at how the wider social context also influences the socialization of children. Social institutions such as schools play a major role in the development of most children. Government policies regarding daycare determine how many children will be placed, and this too has widespread social impacts.

Where Do I Fit In?

1. The opening vignette gives two different opinions about the use of a pacifier. What do you think about using a pacifier?
2. Think about your own socialization. Which people have had the biggest impact on you? In what ways did they affect you and why?
3. Imagine that you had been born into a different family. How might your life have been different? How would you be different?

The Socialization Smorgasbord

Socialization experiences are something like a buffet. You can eat only what is placed on the table, but you don't need to take everything. Thus, children are presented with a variety of experiences out of which they form individual identities and value systems.

Socialization does not take place in a vacuum. The child participates actively in the process. The levels of physical maturation, intellectual development, and social experiences help determine whether a child can understand and comply with socially approved behaviour (Maccoby, 2007). For example, toilet training depends on the ability of the child to understand what is expected, as well as on nerves and muscles sufficiently mature to control elimination. Similarly, if a child cannot "read" social cues, he or she cannot respond appropriately. Such a failure can result from impaired vision or hearing, from delayed intellectual development, or from unfamiliarity with particular cultural norms. The child's developmental stage also affects ability to profit from experiences. In general, a child needs to move from a close relationship with one or two people to interaction with a widening social circle (see Table 6.1 below). Children also make choices about their behaviour. These factors help explain why children from the same family can turn out so differently.

Defining Children

How we socialize children reflects what we expect of their future and the value we place on them. If we feel children are an economic resource, child labour makes sense, especially if the family needs the money to survive. If we value the closeness and love children bring to parents, we will emphasize their emotional development and sensitivity.

In Canada's early years, children were often employed. Those on farms shared in daily chores and seasonal labour. In cities, children helped in home-based businesses, such as boarding houses, or delivered laundry. Boys worked in street trades: polishing shoes or selling newspapers. Some were their parents' only support (Bullen, 1992). One report showed that as recently as 1882, many children aged 5 to 15 were working in manufacturing, and some as young as 2 had been hired in the past (Kieran, 1986). These were not safe and easy jobs. One 12-year-old lost his arm and leg in a mill accident; his employer gave him $10 compensation and paid his hospital but not his doctor's bill. Better technology, cheap immigrant labour, and compulsory school attendance combined to reduce paid child labour (Gaffield, 1982).

TABLE 6.1 Children's Developmental Stages and Expanding World Stages

Developmental Stages	Psychosocial Crises	Radius of Significant Relations
Infancy	Basic trust vs. basic mistrust	Maternal person
Early childhood	Autonomy vs. shame, doubt	Parental persons
Play age	Initiative vs. guilt	Basic family
School age	Industry vs. inferiority	Neighbourhood, school
Adolescence	Identity vs. identity confusion	Peer groups

Source: *The Life Cycle Completed: A Review* by Erik H. Erikson. Copyright © 1982 by Rikan Enterprises, Ltd. Used by permission of W. W. Norton & Company, Inc.

The 20th century saw the arrival of the economically worthless but emotionally priceless child, who was expected to provide emotional satisfaction for the parents (Zelizer, 1985). Being a mother was seen as "the greatest duty allotted to woman-kind" (Department of Public Health, Toronto, 1922, p. 3). Experts offered advice to mothers on how to raise healthy children. Most theories were based on observations of white middle-class children. In the past, women had asked advice from their mothers and other experienced women; now, traditional methods were devalued by professionals. Parents' anxiety over child-rearing increased (Stearns, 2003).

This intrusion into family life by experts affected poor and minority families, especially those receiving welfare. Professionals visited such families to ensure that only the "deserving" poor received help. If childcare methods did not conform to scientific standards, families were given unwanted advice. If they did not comply, they could lose their children, something that still holds for cases of child abuse and neglect. The case of the Dionne family and their quintuplets in the 1930s and '40s was one of the most publicized examples of intrusion by professionals (Nihmey & Foxman, 1987). The children were made wards of the province, separated from their parents, and raised according to the best standards of experts in Toronto. These standards went counter to the traditions of the rural French Canadian society to which the family belonged. Eventually, the children were returned to the care of their parents, but there was a gulf between their early socialization and the family's values and customs. Only quite recently has the public focused on the thousands of Aboriginal children separated from their biological families and put in residential schools and foster and adoptive homes (Richardson & Nelson, 2007).

Childhood came to be regarded as a special time, increasingly differentiated from adulthood. This process led to the development of specialized children's institutions. Children attended school regularly to help provide a skilled and educated labour force. Children's recreational and medical facilities were created. Children had their own courts and justice systems (Brennan, 2012), and the training school, a combination prison and educational facility, was established to teach out-of-control and criminal children socially approved behaviour.

Parents—The First Socializers

Parents are the single most powerful influence in the socialization of children (Grusec & Davidov, 2008). This reality is especially true during early stages of development. Parents directly influence their children both by who they are and through day-to-day interaction. They also exert indirect control over much of their children's environment. For example, by selecting the neighbourhood where they live, they affect their children's peer groups. Parents also bring their own history and experiences to child-rearing.

Family Structure

Structural functionalists, as well as conflict theorists and some feminist theorists, look at how a child's family structure has an impact on his or her socialization.

The number, marital status, gender, sexual orientation, education, and age of a child's parent figures help shape the child. A growing number of studies have looked at how children fare in different types of families. Researchers have used a variety of criteria to determine their well-being. These include school performance and plans for higher education, level of delinquency, early first sexual experience and teen parenthood, risk of later divorce, and relationship with parents (Amato, 2005).

One, Two, or More Parents

While the law in Canada states that a child can have just two legal parents, in 2007 an Ontario court said the biological mother of a five-year-old boy and her same-sex partner could both be legally recognized as mothers of the child. The boy's biological father was still recognized as his dad (CBC News, 2007). The reason given for the ruling was that if the birth mother died, her partner would not be recognized as also being a mother to the child. The term "triparenting" refers to such family arrangements. Triparental situations typically involve a teenage mother and her parents. Another example might be the genetic father, the mother, and her male partner who in their day-to-day life all act as parents of the child (Cutas, 2011).

In general, children living in single-parent homes face a higher risk of low academic achievement and of dropping out than do children who live in two-parent families. One explanation stresses the inter-parental conflict that is too often generated as a marriage dissolves and inflicts psychological stress on children. Another explanation emphasizes the weak material resources of most single parents and the fact that time pressures on single parents make them less able to participate in their children's schooling. Lending support to these explanations is the finding that, when monetary and non-monetary resources are statistically controlled, the effect of single parenthood is reduced and even disappears in some studies (Pong et al., 2003).

Marital Status

The proportion of children living in households with married parents decreased between 2001 and 2011. However, the total figures do not show the changes individual families go through. We can record the number of children currently living with married parents, for example, but this does not indicate whether this is a second, third, or even fourth marriage, or how much time was spent in a single-parent household following a divorce and before the remarriage (Raley & Wildsmith, 2004). Children seem to have more difficulties if they grow up with never-married, divorced, or remarried parents. But it is important to distinguish between the family structure and the changes that led to a particular situation. Studies on the negative effects associated with divorced, single-parent, and step-parent families have found that disparities are often greatest during the period immediately following the change in family structure (Potter, 2012). We will look at single-parent families in greater detail in Chapter 9.

On average, children living with both biological parents married to each other do best, with adoptees with married parents coming a close second. Children in cohabiting families where either both parents are biological or one is a stepparent also tend to have more problems. Children living with neither biological parent—except adoptees—have the most difficulties (Amato, 2005; Feigelman, 2001). A number of studies have reported that children in cohabiting families fare more poorly than their counterparts in married families. A longitudinal study of family situation and academic performance found no differences in level of school engagement between children in married families and children in cohabiting families. However, there was a difference in perceived achievement. Some possible explanations are that cohabiting parents may be less directly involved in school-work and may spend less time learning about children's school activities, assisting with the selection of courses, monitoring homework completion, or communicating with school personnel (Zheng et al., 2012).

Gender and Sexual Orientation of Parents

Research has not identified any significant gender-exclusive parenting abilities (Biblarz & Stacey, 2010). Children with lesbian parents do at least as well as those in single-parent families. They are not more likely to be homosexual than the general population (Ambert, 2005b; Meezan & Rauch, 2005). Studies on adolescents reared by same-sex parents have found that they did not differ from adolescents with different-sex parents on psychological well-being, peer relations, school variables, substance use, delinquency, or victimization (van Gelderen et al., 2012). Some research has found that two lesbian parents seem to outperform comparable married heterosexual biological parents on several measures (Biblarz & Stacey, 2010). However, since public opinion generally holds that it is better for children to be reared in a traditional mother–father family, many young children and adolescents have reported that they experience stigmatization because they have lesbian mothers (van Gelderen et al., 2012).

Parents' Education and Employment

Parents' jobs affect the family in several ways: hours worked, work demands, and income. Parents in occupations requiring a higher education are more likely to be employed and have fewer periods of unemployment (Morissette & Picot, 2005; Parcel & Menaghan, 1994). They also tend to receive higher pay (Chung, 2006). Parents' income can affect the area in which a family lives. Canadian children in affluent neighbourhoods, it has been found, score higher on tests of school readiness than children living in poorer areas. The school, recreational facilities, and peer groups are different from one part of a city to another and from one part of a province to another (Kohen et al., 2008). Income also determines, in part, both children's clothing and activities. For example, music or competitive sports require lessons and/or expensive equipment as well as transportation costs. Clothing and activities can help decide the child's peer group. Children from poorer families have less success in school, on average, than children from wealthier families. Parents with higher education and income tend to encourage learning and provide more resources, including books and computers (Conger & Dogan, 2008; Davis-Kean, 2005; Gauvain & Perez, 2008). When parents have less education, their pre-school children tend to watch more entertainment programs and have less contact with books. Later school performance is related to early experiences with books (Kirkorian et al., 2008). Several studies have also found that children from a higher socioeconomic status continue to learn during the summer months of elementary school, but lower-SES students tend to stagnate or lose ground. This phenomenon has been called the "summer slide" (Slates et al., 2012).

The impact of jobs does not stop at income. When parents, both mothers and fathers, have complex occupations, children do better in school. Complex work provides a variety of tasks and involves qualities such as people skills, knowledge, and the ability to deal with changing circumstances. This work is what teachers, doctors, and business managers do, not what dishwashers and low-level data entry clerks handle. American researchers have also found that employed mothers tend to be authoritative with their children, a parenting style leading to academic and social success. Young Canadian children with working mothers, on average, showed less hyperactivity, more pro-social behaviour, and less anxiety. The advantages of having parents in more complex occupations are lower when money and time are stretched by a large family or new baby (Hoffman & Youngblade, 1999; Nomaguchi, 2006; Parcel & Menaghan, 1994).

Adolescent Mothers

Teenage motherhood has generally been associated with negative and long-term consequences for these women and their children (Statistics Canada, 2008l). Many studies show that, while individual adolescent mothers may manage quite well, their children are often at risk for developmental problems. First, pregnancies of young teens are highly risky: babies are more likely to be premature. Second, young mothers lack the financial and social resources to overcome the physical disadvantages. Third, to develop best, a child needs a stable, loving relationship with at least two adults. Adolescent development is in many ways the opposite of that needed for good parenting. Teens are finding their own identity and may be impatient with limits on their activities. Babies are very limiting.

Many adolescent mothers live with their parents. In some cases, grandparents are understanding and helpful; in other cases, disagreements may arise over who can take care of the child. The question then becomes "Whose child is this?" The young mother may give in or rebel. If she rebels, she may cease taking care of her baby or move out, taking her child with her (Ambert, 2006; Anderson, 2003). In either case, the baby loses a parent figure. In addition, living with parents can be filled with conflict and detrimental to the development of both the young mother and her child. Teen mothers living in romantic relationships are less harsh with their children than other young mothers. It may be that more competent and well-adjusted young mothers live with a male partner (Abell et al., 2003).

"Late" Parents

In 2008, the average age of mothers was 29.8 years. The primary reasons for the delay in child-bearing are the pursuit of higher education, increased labour force participation, and delayed union formation (Milan, 2011). These women's children typically have the advantages of a stable home, favourable income, and good neighbourhood environment. Older women, however, are at greater risk for problems in pregnancy. Because they are less fertile than younger women, they are likelier to use reproductive technologies. As a result, they are at risk for multiple births. Such babies are often premature and more prone to developmental problems (Bushnik & Garner, 2008; Mundy, 2007). Others have "caboose" children or children in a second marriage.

How does child-rearing by older parents differ from that by younger parents? Their children do as well as others, though their life experiences are different (Boivin et al., 2009). Studies have found that older fathers are less physically active but are likelier to spend time reading and playing pretend. Because mature parents are more apt to be financially stable, they can often provide enriching experiences, such as museum visits or travel. On the other hand, children in such families may fear their parents will die (Morris, 1987; Recker, 2007). Some late-born children may have much more adult attention than children in the family born earlier. One mother reports that her caboose son thought he had six parents, including his four older siblings. It is possible that with more women delaying child-bearing, having older parents will not be regarded as particularly different in the future.

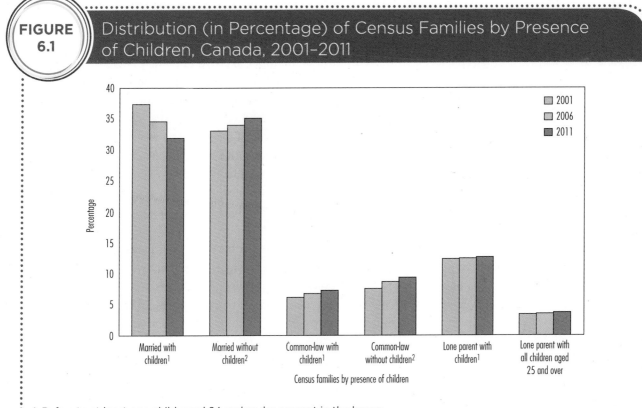

FIGURE 6.1

Distribution (in Percentage) of Census Families by Presence of Children, Canada, 2001–2011

1. Refers to at least one child aged 24 and under present in the home.
2. Includes families with all children aged 25 and over.

Source: Adapted from: Statistics Canada. 2011. *Distribution (in percentage) of census families by presence of children, Canada, 2001 to 2011* (table). "Portrait of Families and Living Arrangements in Canada." 2011 Census. Catalogue no. 98-312-X2011001. Ottawa, Ontario. Statistics Canada. http://www12.statcan.gc.ca/census-recensement/2011/as-sa/98-312-x/2011001/fig/fig1-eng.cfm

What Accounts for Differences in Child Well-Being?

No single explanation accounts for differences among families. Even families within a single category are quite different. For example, single-parent mothers vary by age, by the route to single parenthood (unmarried, separated, divorced, widowed), by life experiences before and after becoming a parent, and by the length of time single parenting lasts. It is important to acknowledge that most children in non-traditional families grow up without major problems. According to one calculation, about 10 percent of children living with married biological parents have serious problems, while 20 percent of those in single-parent or step-families do—twice the level. From another perspective, 80 percent manage quite well (Greene et al., 2003). Instead, what seems to matter for children's emotional well-being is family process. Successful parenting also depends on factors such as level of education, income, and views on parenting, as well as on the quality of the parent–child relationship (Cutas, 2011).

However, some children do face greater challenges. Risk factors for children include economic hardship, exposure to stress, conflict between parents, poor parenting quality, and lack of contact with non-residential fathers. In addition, boys tend to have a harder time than girls (Amato, 2005). Let's look at some of these factors.

Children who live in poverty are more likely to develop a range of diseases and to die earlier. Children born into poor families often continue to experience deprivation later in life. They may also suffer developmental delays that have a lasting impact on their subsequent health (Raphael, 2011). Single parenthood, separation, and divorce often mean a loss of income. As a result, families may be forced to move away from friends and other social supports into areas with poorer-quality housing and higher crime. Here, children experience less favourable peer influences. Poverty and stressful life events, such as separation and low quality of parental functioning, work together to create less favourable environments for children.

Children who experience severe conflict between their parents fare poorly. This finding is true for families with married biological parents, as well as cohabiting parents and stepfamilies. Adolescents with divorced parents, for example, do not do well when they are caught in the middle of parents' battles. In fact, children often do better once high-conflict parents separate (Feinberg et al., 2007; Schoppe-Sullivan et al., 2007; Stahl, 2007). One study found that interactions within families have greater impact than family structure by itself (Lansford et al., 2001).

The quality of parenting affects children's well-being (Laible & Thompson, 2008). Well-being is partly related to conflict levels within the family and partly to the mother's psychological health. One notion is that children are better monitored if they live in two-parent families. There is no evidence, however, that the degree of supervision is related to children's well-being, apart from the relationship quality (Amato, 2005). Because of the lack of an established social script, non-biological parents may have difficulties with disciplining stepchildren.

Issues concerning the relationship of children with biological and non-biological parents have been studied most thoroughly in adoptive families. Because adoptive parents are perceived as somehow not as genuine as birth parents, they may have difficulty believing that they are entitled to be parents to their adopted child. Some are strict and authoritarian because they try to be extra-good parents. Others are permissive or sometimes inconsistent because they fear losing their child's love (Ward, 1979). Thus, they are vulnerable to blackmail by their child.

Studies have shown that children of divorced parents are at a disadvantage. Divorced parents tend to spend less time with their children. They also tend to have fewer rules but use harsher discipline than parents who stay married. In addition, when mothers confide their worry about financial problems and complain about their ex-husbands, children have more difficulties (Amato, 2000; Koerner et al., 2000; Simons et al., 1999). Nevertheless, some research suggests that parenting does not change dramatically after divorce (Strohschein, 2007).

The history of the current relationship affects children's development. Is this the first family the child has known? The second? Is the parents' relationship stable? Have there been repeated separations and continuing fights? When children become attached to parents and then have to move, they mourn the separation. Separation can also lead to acting-out behaviour. One study found that adolescents who were particularly satisfied with the relationship with their same-sex parent beforehand were likelier to become delinquent after that parent moved out (Videon, 2002). Lack of contact with non-residential parents can also result in problems (Juby et al., 2007). Separation and lack of contact with the same-sex parent affects boys more than girls because custody is more often granted the mother. If there are many separations, children may fear becoming attached again—a problem with repeated moves in foster care and adoption (Shapiro & Shapiro, 2006). The impermanence of relationships can also affect children who belong to one stepfamily after another.

Although not as well studied as risk factors, other factors protect children from the disadvantages of non-traditional families and family disruption. Home and school environments with warmth and clear rules help children flourish. So does a parenting style that is warm and structured while allowing for the child's individuality. In inner-city public housing, stringent parental monitoring is one strategy to buffer youth against the socially toxic conditions that surround youth (Baptiste et al., 2007). Peer support is also important when children are experiencing family crises (Williams-Washington et al., 2008).

Day-to-Day Interaction

Symbolic interactionists focus on how daily interactions between family members help shape a child. Parents use different parenting styles, and this helps shape the overall family atmosphere.

Parenting Style

The day-to-day treatment of a child has long-term effects on the child's development. Diana Baumrind (1980, 1996) described three parenting styles: authoritarian, permissive, and authoritative. A fourth, the uninvolved parent, was added by later theorists (Simons & Conger, 2007). The four parenting styles are measured along two dimensions—demandingness and responsiveness. Table 6.2 illustrates each parenting style.

authoritarian: a parenting style that requires unquestioning obedience

Authoritarian parents are demanding but unresponsive to their children. Families headed by authoritarian parents are strong on obligations and responsibilities, but weak on recognizing children's individuality or their need to learn to make decisions. Often, authoritarian parents rely on a punitive discipline style where they scold, yell at, or physically punish children. Punitive discipline leads to children's aggressive behaviour (Thomas, 2004). Such parents also tend to believe that misbehaviour comes from their children's nature (Coplan et al., 2002). Children growing up in such families tend to become submissive and unable to make decisions for themselves, or defiant and rebellious (Hastings et al., 2008). A vicious cycle can arise in some families whereby children are defiant, parents become punitive, children hang out with a delinquent, and parents become harsher (Simons et al., 2001). It is difficult to know which came first—defiance or discipline. As always, context matters. For adolescents living in poor, urban, ethnic neighbourhoods, authoritarian parenting may not be as bad as it has been shown to be for their middle-class, suburban, white counterparts (Steinberg et al., 2006).

permissive: a parenting style that allows children to make their own decisions without providing firm guidelines

Permissive parents are at the other end of the scale. They respond readily to their children, but demand little from them. They recognize children's individuality and right to make decisions, but they do not set limits or assign responsibilities. Sometimes this is the result of low confidence; parents are afraid of the child. They often act more like friends than like parents. Children from these families are likelier to exhibit problem behaviour and not perform well in school (Xu, 2007). Although they often have high self-esteem, they may not recognize the rights of others or develop self-discipline. As a result, they may live aimless and disappointing adult lives.

authoritative: a parenting style that sets expectations for children, but adjusts them to the individual

Authoritative parents take a middle position. They have high expectations of their children, but they are also aware of their children's needs and are willing to adjust their

---

TABLE 6.2   Dimensions of Parenting Styles

		Demandingness	
		Low	High
Responsiveness	Low	Uninvolved	Authoritarian
	High	Permissive	Authoritative

Sources: Adapted from: D. Baumrind, "Effects of authoritative parental control on child behaviour," *Child Development*, Vol. 37 (4), Pg. 887–907; Eleanor E. Maccoby, "The role of parents in the socialization of children: A historical overview," *Developmental Psychology*, Vol. 28 (6), Pg. 1006–1017.

demands. Children from these families are often described as achievers and as competent and friendly (Baumrind, 1980). Several studies have found that adolescents who are raised in authoritative homes perform better in school (Steinberg & Lamborn, 1992). Positive interaction between parents and children, combined with consistent parenting—the hallmarks of the authoritative parent—improve children's social relationships. This finding is especially true for children subject to risk factors—poverty, lone-parent families, and divorce among them (Kelly & Emery, 2003). Regardless of family structure, high standards for behaviour and monitoring of children's activities, combined with warm supportiveness and avoidance of harsh punishment, result in the most positive child well-being (Amato & Fowler, 2002). Indeed, when parents switch from punitive to non-punitive parenting, children become less aggressive (Thomas, 2004). One authoritative parent can compensate for less effective parenting by the other parent (Simons & Conger, 2007). Nevertheless, authoritative parenting is not the only style that leads to children's social success. In certain societies, Asian for example, authoritarian parenting, combined with high levels of interest and encouragement, is the norm, and parents in such cultures who use this style raise children who do well (Rothbaum & Trommsdorff, 2008; Williams-Washington et al., 2008).

Uninvolved parents are low in both responsiveness and the demands they place on their children. They are cold and distant and often hostile to a child's need for attention (Simons & Conger, 2007). In extreme cases, this style may take the form of neglect. Because the parents are uncaring, these children may be socially aggressive. Sometimes, uninvolved parenting is the result of the parent's personality, but it may result from life situations. A family where both parents work long hours, or a single parent holds one or more jobs to make ends meet, may find involvement more difficult. Children with uninvolved parents are most likely to have poor academic performance and weak social skills. They also have the most behavioural problems (Xu, 2007).

uninvolved: a parenting style low in both responsiveness and demands placed on the children

Spanking

Spanking continues to be an issue drawing attention and criticism. In Ontario, at least one parent who spanked a child in public was at risk of being charged with child abuse. On the other hand, some popular authors advocate spanking, often based on strict religious beliefs. Spanking is probably less effective in changing children's behaviour than nonviolent forms of discipline. As part of a punitive parenting style, spanking can increase behavioural problems (Gromoski & McGuire-Jack, 2012; Straus, 2007). In addition, it teaches children that hitting is how to solve problems. At its worst, spanking can escalate into child abuse (Zolotor et al., 2008). This topic is discussed in more detail in Chapter 14.

Family Atmosphere

The general atmosphere in families vitally affects child development and socialization. Most studies have looked at levels of conflict in the family. The amount of conflict between parents and teenagers is related to parents' warmth and supportiveness. If they are hostile and authoritarian, the conflict tends to escalate. If parents are supportive, family relations improve over the teen years (Hillaker et al., 2008; Rueter & Conger, 1995).

Part of the family atmosphere is created by the parents' own relationship. Conflict between parents, especially when it concerns how children should be raised, increases the risk that children will have adjustment problems in several ways. Parents' use of destructive tactics, such as yelling, name-calling, threatening, and withdrawal, distresses children. Children in families that engage in such tactics may feel more threatened by disagreements and are more likely to blame themselves for their parents' problems than those whose parents use more constructive tactics. In addition, parents with high conflict levels are more likely to use harsh discipline; they are also less likely to be involved with their children, for example through reading or play (Buehler & Gerrard, 2002; Cummings et al., 2003; Feinberg et al., 2007; Grych et al., 2003). One Canadian study found that children from two-parent families with high levels of conflict were more at risk of parental psychological violence than children from separated families (Gagné et al., 2007). Parents who discuss issues calmly and show support and affection for each other can increase their children's sense of security. The risk of behaviour problems is therefore reduced (Cummings et al., 2003). Parents' conflict style seems to affect children both through parents' actual behaviour and children's perceptions of that behaviour (Buehler et al., 1994).

Family Routines, Rituals, and Traditions

Socialization comes from both everyday aspects of living and special occasions. Routines usually involve little conscious thought and often occur daily (Laible & Thompson, 2008). Families can use dinnertime, for example, as an opportunity for teaching social behaviour such as manners. Democratic values, to some degree, can also be demonstrated as children and parents talk about their experiences during the day (Fiese & Schwartz, 2008; Larson, 2008). Families that have extremely limited space, use electronic media or television during family meals, or are so involved in outside activities that members are rarely all home at once have a different view of proper mealtime behaviour. Increased use of the Internet also reduces face-to-face family communication (Kraut et al., 1998).

Rituals are events that tell families, "This is who we are." They can be individual family events, like sitting down together for Sunday dinner. Rituals that occur less frequently around some particular event, such as Hanukkah or Thanksgiving, are called traditions. Both rituals and traditions can weave families and kin together (Kirkwood & Engelbrecht, 2002; Laible & Thompson, 2008). Unfortunately, because they have so much meaning for families, traditions can also be the source of conflict between generations or between ex-partners.

Family story traditions also shape children. Events that are remembered and retold often encourage family values by emphasizing heroes or villains (Howard, 2007; Sidwell, 2007). Sometimes themes are repeated. For instance, one family repeatedly told a story about young men who ran away from home to make their fortunes in another country. This tradition gave permission to youth in later generations to move away from home yet keep their family identity.

The development of routines and rituals depends on time shared between parents and children. Although sociologists fear that family time is decreasing, new research has found that routine childcare has not declined and that activities such as playing and teaching have increased. Despite an increase in time spent at work, families where both parents are present but working full time still spend as much time parenting (Zukewich, 2003). Single mothers are most likely to feel a time crunch (Bianchi et al., 2006).

Time to Review

1. Which parental characteristics can influence the socialization of children?
2. What are some of the factors that account for the differences in child well-being?
3. What are the different parenting styles?

Diversity in Parenting

In a culturally diverse society such as Canada, anyone who works with families will inevitably encounter many different parenting styles. Issues concerning parent–child and other family relationships of immigrants and minority groups have been discussed elsewhere (see Chapter 2 and other sections of this chapter) and will be expanded here.

How Different Are English Canadians and French Canadians from One Another?

Few studies have compared the way English Canadians and French Canadians raise children, and most of these are outdated. One group of researchers looked at families of both cultural groups in Montreal (Smith & Grenier, 1975; Taylor et al., 1978), and found that English-speaking Montrealers encouraged their children to be more independent in solving problems than French-speaking Montrealers. Anglophones also tended to restrict their children's contact with friends and to treat children more harshly. French Canadians encouraged ties with their own social and family group, and tried to develop their children's reliance on the extended family. Since these studies are more than 35 years old, however, they do not reflect the strength of the nationalist movement in Quebec and any effect it may have on family relationships.

Another study looked at the language children learned at home when parents had different mother tongues. Outside Quebec, 79 percent of children with English- and French-speaking parents learned English first. In Quebec, 49 percent with French- and English-speaking parents learned French first, 34 percent learned English first, and 17 percent learned both. Thus, both the language spoken by parents and the language used in the community affected children's learning (Turcotte, 1993).

A 2004 survey by the research company Ipsos Reid, with CTV and *The Globe and Mail*, found that Quebec parents are less likely to spank their children than parents elsewhere (25 percent in Quebec versus 60 percent in Alberta). About 60 to 70 percent of parents in most of Canada believe using flashcards will make their babies smarter, while only 25 percent of Quebec parents agree (Anderssen & McIlroy, 2004; Ipsos Reid, 2004).

Aboriginal Families

When we speak of Aboriginal families in Canada, we are talking about a large and diverse group representing more than 50 different language groups and cultures. Yet they share a common value: they strongly emphasize interdependence and have a strong sense of spirituality. Traditional Aboriginal societies recognize the basic family unit of parents and children living together. But family also includes a broad network of grandparents, aunts, uncles, and cousins. Children are valued members of these societies. They are seen as gifts from the spirit world. In talking circles, every member of the community, including children, is allowed to speak (Blackstock, 2006–07).

From the 1890s to the 1970s, Aboriginal children were removed from their families and placed in residential schools. Those forced into this system have consistently stated that the hunger and other abuses suffered in residential schools was made worse by policies that aimed at erasing their Aboriginal language and culture (Castellano, 2006–07). Welfare dependency became the only way of survival for many families. The loss of their children to non-Aboriginal families and institutions added to their despair. Alcohol became a way of temporarily escaping the hopeless situation; in turn, however, alcohol made matters worse.

In April 2006, the federal government declared it would compensate an estimated 80 000 survivors of residential schools; however, the disruption of families and traditions has been blamed for many problems that still continue. In January 2011, $20 million was distributed to former students, their families, and their communities to acknowledge their experiences and the impacts of the residential school system (Aboriginal Affairs and Northern Development Canada, 2012). The growth of a new Aboriginal awareness is helping to re-create family health (Sinclair, 2007).

Immigrant Families

As we discussed in Chapter 2, children in immigrant families may be pulled between two cultural ideals, with their attitudes raising concern among their families. North American society encourages independence and spontaneity, while many other cultures, such as Chinese and South Asian, expect children to be more focused on their families and respectful of their elders. Some parents may respond to apparent influences of the new culture with exaggerated control. Immigrant communities tend to be tight-knit. Parents may wonder, "What will people say?"

Canada is a multicultural society. In urban areas where most immigrants settle, children of immigrants are exposed to multiple cultures at school. For them, this range of cultures seems normal, but many of their parents grew up in mono-cultural societies and may be less aware and tolerant of cultural diversity. For immigrant parents, preserving their cultural heritage and language and passing it on through their children is important. Children of immigrants are four times more likely to feel parental influence regarding language and traditions than children of Canadian-born parents (Helm & Warren, 1998).

Immigrant parents typically hold different expectations of their children than Canadian-born parents do. They often have more physical contact with young children, carrying them and sharing sleeping quarters, than their Canadian-born counterparts do. On the other hand, they tend to be authoritarian with their older children. Among Chinese and South Asian teenagers, 1 in 4 says that the parents want to choose his or her career, compared to 1 in 12 for children of Canadian-born parents, while 89 percent of Chinese parents expect their children to go to university, compared to 45 percent of Canadian-born parents (Helm & Warren, 1998).

In comparison to Euro-American parents, Chinese parents tend to have a more authoritarian parenting style. But some interesting research has found that whereas this more controlling and demanding parenting style is typically associated with negative outcomes for Euro-American children, it actually has positive outcomes in Chinese children. One possible explanation is that while Chinese parents are more likely to focus on negative traits, they also emphasize that these can be improved upon through work and effort (Mah & Johnston, 2012).

The Wider Family Circle

Parents have considerable control over children's relationships with other family members. For example, parents decide how many children to have. They influence how often children see grandparents and other relatives. This control is greater for younger than for older children.

Brothers and Sisters—Friends, Foes, and Teachers

Canadian families are getting smaller. Children are less likely to have siblings, or they have fewer siblings. In 2011, 45 percent of families with children had just one child living at home, 38 percent had two children, and 16 percent had more than three children (Statistics Canada, 2012k). Until recently, sibling relationships were the least studied of nuclear family relationships (Dunn, 2008). Yet because they are unique, these relationships are important to children. Brothers and sisters are family members, but they do not have the authority parents have over younger children, unless they are much older or the parents have failed in the caregiving role through neglect, illness, substance abuse, or some other absence. In many ways, sibling relationships are similar to peer relationships because they are more egalitarian than those between parents and children. Many siblings spend more time with each other than with their parents or even with their peers. There are, of course, wider age spans in sibling relationships than among most friends. Unlike peer relationships, the sibling relationship is ascribed; that is, it is not optional (Dunn, 2008). For practical purposes, the sibling relationship can be broken only by death or by leaving the family and cutting off contact.

Birth-Order Effects

The number of siblings, their age, and their sex affect the socialization of a child. An only child, for example, does not have the same experiences as the middle child among nine. Families with all boys differ from families with all girls or from those with a mix. One aspect of sibling relationships that has captured imaginations is the effect of birth order on personality development. For example, the eldest child is described as a conscientious person and an achiever; the middle child as a hellion or mediator; and the youngest as a charmer (McGoldrick et al., 1999). If there are more than three children in the family, the roles may become quite specialized (Bossard, 1975). The roles we assume in our families as children can affect how we deal with life as adults.

Many studies have found significant differences between firstborn and later-born children in outcomes such as educational achievement and income. Typically, the firstborn in the family is advantaged. Later-born children receive less quality time with their parents than do firstborns. Older siblings may partly replace the parents in providing some of this quality time, which benefits the firstborns because they have the opportunity to be teachers from an early age (Gugl & Welling, 2010).

Only children have many of the characteristics of firstborns with siblings. For example, they tend to have high academic achievement. They also complete about three additional years of schooling, achieve higher occupational prestige, and earn more money than firstborn children with siblings. However, only children miss the experiences of sibling relationships and of having to share their parents with brothers and sisters (Sailor, 2004).

Birth-order effects are not inevitable. They are modified by many factors. In large families, for instance, older and younger children have different relationships with parents. An oldest child is an only child for a time; so, often, is the youngest when older siblings move out. If death, divorce, and financial hardship hit a family,

Source: Close to Home/Universal Uclick.

middle ones may suffer most. A parent's favouritism may make one child feel secure and valued but undermine the self-confidence of another. The sex of a child also matters. An oldest daughter may be expected to assume household responsibilities when her mother is incapable or absent. Her brother may be favoured, for example, in a Japanese family (Conley, 2004; Dunn, 2008; Hines et al., 1999; Shanahan et al., 2008).

Siblings as Socializers

Older brothers and sisters socialize younger ones in many ways. They act as role models (Whiteman & Christiansen, 2008). Many children have learned the use of makeup, how to smoke or drink, or how best to get around parents from siblings. Older siblings teach skills. In the past, they often taught younger brothers and sisters how to swim or ride a bike. Now they are more likely to teach younger ones how to text, tweet, or use their smartphone or tablet. Older brothers and sisters can shape the attitudes of younger ones. For example, when siblings have a good relationship, they influence attitudes toward safe sex, especially for girls with older sisters (Kowal & Blinn-Pike, 2004). Role models are not always positive, though. One example of negative modelling occurs in delinquency. Younger brothers who copy older ones may also become delinquent. When the older sibling is hostile and bossy, both brothers and sisters may commit delinquent acts (Dunn, 2008; Slomkowski et al., 2001).

The early writings on sibling relationships tended to stress rivalry. Yet even conflict has a positive side: given that sibling relationships are obligatory, brothers and sisters must learn how to resolve conflict issues. One study found that older siblings try to control younger ones. Younger ones are more likely to use nonconfrontational methods such as submission or negotiation. If siblings are close, they are more likely to try to work out a solution that benefits both (Killoren et al., 2008). Siblings learn the importance of social context. Junior may hit little sister to get a toy if mother is out of the room, but not when she is there. They also learn bargaining skills—for example, "If you let me use your iPad, I won't tell Dad you came in drunk." Sibling relationships can affect relationships with friends as children put to use the social skills they learned with brothers and sisters (McCoy et al., 1994; Downey & Condron, 2004). A warm relationship with an older sister can help girls with difficult temperaments learn to avoid discord in friendships (McCoy et al., 2002).

Later investigators have pointed out that there can also be great warmth and affection between brothers and sisters. The closeness differs, however, across cultural groups. The sibling relationship can be one of the most enduring in a person's life; for example, elderly women who live with someone other than a husband are most likely to live with a sibling, usually a sister. Siblings have a store of memories in common and have been socialized in similar ways (Harwood, 2007; McGoldrick et al., 1999).

Affection between brothers and sisters depends on access. Siblings in rural areas may spend more time together than city children because nearby peers are few (Brody & Murry, 2001). Access can be limited if the children are widely separated in age because their interests are too different. Children from large families also say that younger ones do not really know older ones, since they did not share the house for long. Access also depends on parents. If they feel it important that their children know and like one another, they will encourage such relationships.

Sometimes, when parents abdicate authority and the children have access to one another, siblings may develop extreme loyalty to one another. Children may try to make up for the lack of parenting. One of the oldest may become a "parentified" child, trying to fill a role for which he, or more often she, is unequipped. In such a case, the younger children are often parented inadequately and the parental child fails to achieve a normal adulthood. Once the younger children are no longer dependent on the older child, that child may feel lost and depressed (Conley, 2004; Jurkovic, 1997). Social workers often see these characteristics in siblings from neglected or abused families, or in children who have moved together among foster homes.

Family Size

The number of siblings also affects development. As family size increases, resources must be spread among more people. These resources include money and parents' time and attention. A Canadian study found that mothers had less positive interaction with older children after they had a baby but became more consistent in enforcing rules (Strohschein et al., 2008). Parents of smaller families can spend more time interacting with each child and monitoring activities. They are also more likely to know their children's friends and their families, thus creating an interconnected social network. In general, children from smaller families do better academically and socially.

In part, positive effects associated with smaller families may be the result of residing in a particular neighbourhood. Larger families may not have the finances to live in an area with excellent schools or recreational facilities. On average, First Nations, Métis, and Inuit parents have larger families. The involvement of extended family members in child socialization, as in many Aboriginal families, may compensate for reduced attention from parents (Statistics Canada, 2008a).

Other researchers were surprised that even in smaller families, the timing and number of children affect both behaviour and learning. Having either a number of older siblings or closely spaced younger ones reduces a child's school performance. This effect on learning is long term (Conley, 2004; Parcel & Dufur, 2001; Parcel & Menaghan, 1994).

Impact of Parents on Sibling Relationships

Parents influence relationships among their children. Negative effects have been studied more than positive ones. Siblings often emphasize their differences to reduce conflict. If parents treat them as a single group, however, without individual qualities (e.g., "the kids"), children engage in more rivalry and conflict (Feinberg et al., 2003). On the other hand, favouritism also creates problems (Shanahan et al., 2008). Parents, especially when under stress, were found to treat children differently as to the degree of warmth and conflict shown and time spent (Tucker et al., 2002). The greater the differences in how a mother treats her children, the greater the children's maladjustment, especially if she subjects one child to more anger, harshness, and disapproval than the others. In such families, all children tend to be aggressive and disruptive (Boyle et al., 2004). Children who regard parents as distant and unaccepting, especially if favouritism is involved, may try to undermine a sibling's relationships with others (Updegraff et al., 2005).

Parents have yet another impact on children's relationships. Since families are becoming smaller, the present generation of children will have only one or two, if any, brothers or sisters to help socialize them. Some sociologists speculate that in the future, peers may become more influential in socialization than they already are because they will fill some of the vacuum in sibling relationships (McGoldrick et al., 1999).

Extended Family Members

The extended family consists of relatives such as grandparents, aunts, uncles, and cousins. Families vary in the number of extended family members they keep in contact with and in their level of contact. Most is known about grandparent–grandchild relationships.

How important are relatives? More children probably know their grandparents now than in earlier generations because of the increased life span. According to estimates, less than one-fourth of children born in 1900 had four living grandparents. A growing proportion of children are sharing a household with a grandparent. In 2011, 4.8 percent of all children under 14 years old lived with at least one grandparent, up from 3.3 percent in 2001. Most multigenerational households consist of children, their parents, and at least one grandparent. A smaller proportion of children, 0.5 percent, live in a **skip-generation family**; that is, with one or both grandparents where no parents were present (Statistics Canada, 2012l). In Chapter 8, we will take a closer look at grandparents raising grandchildren.

skip-generation family: a family in which children live with one or both grandparents where no parents are present

The closeness of the grandchild–grandparent relationship depends on a number of factors. Grandparents are usually closer to preteen children, especially those who live nearby and who visit and phone more often. Grandmothers and granddaughters on the mother's side of the family tend to have warmer relationships, especially when parents and grandparents get along. Grandparents can reduce the impact on children of parents' problems, such as mental health issues or family breakup (Silverstein & Ruiz, 2006). Children in stepfamilies, firstborn children, and children in one-child families are also closer to their grandparents. Often, one grandchild is considered special (Centre for Research on Families and Relationships, 2005; Harwood, 2007; Silverstein & Ruiz, 2006). There are also cultural differences. For example, Aboriginal cultures in Canada have assigned an important role to the extended family in child-rearing. Aboriginal children are more likely than others to be living with a grandparent. Most also have frequent contact with other extended family members (Statistics Canada, 2008a).

Grandparenting styles range from companionship without parenting, involvement with parent-like responsibilities, and remoteness, or combinations of the three styles (Connidis, 2010). Young adults describe grandparents' roles in four ways: as a friend and confidant, as an influential figure, as an indulgent caregiver, and as an intergenerational kin keeper. Traditional respect for elders seems to have been replaced by a more equal relationship (Brown, 2003).

A particular point of contact between generations is the observance of rituals and traditions. Christenings, bar mitzvahs, birthdays, first communions, and many other events bring families together. Grandparents are often involved in teaching cultural history and values. Shared traditions both increase family solidarity and transmit family and cultural values.

Physically or Mentally Challenged Children

Having a brother or sister with exceptionalities also affects socialization. Children may have to adjust to changes in family rhythms as parents and other family members pay attention to the special needs of the exceptional child. Children also need information about the exceptionality, especially if they fear they might "catch" it. Brothers or especially sisters may be expected to help with childcare and may be asked to include the sibling in social activities. Some youngsters feel they must make up for what the sibling cannot achieve. Often, parents impose a double standard on their children, expecting less from the exceptional child because of his or her limitations. Sometimes, these standards are unreasonable, for example expecting a higher standard of consideration from the "normal" child than from the one who is exceptional in some way.

Shared stress can improve family communication and closeness. Nearly half of parents report that their child's condition had little or no effect on their relationship, while nearly 1 in 5 report becoming closer with their partner due to the child's condition. However, 31 percent reported that the child's disability caused problems in the relationship. More than 3 in 4 parents report that their child's disability led to their separation or divorce (Statistics Canada, 2008m). The current trend away from the institutionalization of people with disabilities has created a situation where caregiving for these people by family members can span four or five decades (Weeks et al., 2009).

Time to Review

1. How do cultural groups differ in their parenting styles?
2. How do other members of the family influence the socialization of a child?
3. What are some of the challenges specific to families with a physically or mentally challenged child?

Society at Large

Parents and other family members are not the only people who affect the socialization of children. Society as a whole is involved. As children move out of the home, parents retain some control over their environment. This control is, however, limited and decreases as children become older.

Childcare

The choices parents make about childcare when they are at work affect a child's development. According to one estimate, young children in full-time childcare typically spend nine hours a day, 250 days a year there. They thus spend more waking hours with substitute caregivers than with parents (Doherty, 1996). The quality of the care they receive is therefore important. The atmosphere in a grand-parent's home is different from that in homes where one woman may care for three or four children, and different still from a daycare centre or a babysitter coming into the child's home. Moving frequently from one childcare arrangement to another can result in behaviour problems (Morrissey, 2009). According to one study, about half of Canadian children cared for by non-relatives received informal home care (Bushnik, 2006). Because many home care arrangements are informal and not supervised by government, it is difficult to measure their impact on children; however, this is not the case for daycare centres. The number of children in daycare centres has increased, especially in Quebec, where the cost is lower than in the rest of Canada (Bushnik, 2006; Kohen et al., 2008). Each province and territory regulates its own system. All regulated services are financed through user fees, although subsidies exist for low-income families, and through some direct funding (Childcare Resource and Research Unit, 2007). Such centres differ in their effects on children, with quality of care being critical.

Quality childcare goes beyond merely protecting a child's health and safety. It also helps the child's physical, emotional, language, and intellectual development. Centres that do this have caregivers who are sensitive to children's needs and understand child development. Each caregiver is responsible for a limited number of children, and the whole group is relatively small. In addition, children are less anxious when their caregivers do not change. Caregivers are more likely to be warm and supportive if they are satisfied with their jobs. Children in high-quality care are readier for school and have better social skills. This is especially true for children of mothers with low levels of education. Being placed in childcare attenuates the gap in academic readiness and achievement between children with and without the social disadvantage of a poorly educated mother (Geoffroy et al., 2010).

The School

Once a child has reached the age of four or five, large blocks of time are turned over to the school, which assumes much of the socialization process. At school, children learn to interact with new authority figures and with children their own age. Because children spend so much time there, policies introduced at the school level can have far-reaching effects (see Box 6.1). Children are introduced to many new ideas, and these may agree or conflict with the values they have already absorbed in the family.

Children learn best in situations where the material is culturally relevant. Minority families, for example immigrant or First Nations families, can enrich school experiences and help tie them to their culture. For example, Greek immigrant parents can use a lesson on Greek history to remind their children of their heritage. Students also need to feel they are part of the school community. The sense of belonging is undermined by prejudice among students and school staff (Bradley & McKelvey, 2007).

The first school years are important to children's self-esteem. Many children begin school feeling they are worthwhile individuals. Studies have shown, however, that within a few years, self-esteem can drop. In part, this drop is related to the amount of negative feedback children receive from teachers, in particular in the form of criticism, comparison with other children, and poor marks. Often, teachers expect less of children from low-income and minority-group families than from children belonging to white middle-class families. This phenomenon is known as the **teacher expectancy effect** (Rosenthal & Jacobson, 1968). Since youngsters are aware of differences in treatment, these expectations result in both lower achievement and lower self-esteem. On the other hand, warm and supportive teachers can partly make up for deficiencies in the home environment, such as neglect and lack of stimulation (Wentzel & Looney, 2008).

In school, children learn about other families through their peers, through books and stories, and through teachers' attitudes. One class assignment criticized by some parents is constructing a family tree. Children in divorced, stepparent, foster, and adoptive families, and in some created through reproductive technologies, may have difficulty placing family members in a conventional family tree (Shreck, 2001). In addition, some children may still be experiencing some of the trauma of separation, so this assignment is painful for them.

teacher expectancy effect: the impact of a teacher's expectations on a student's academic performance

BOX 6.1

Supportive School Environments—Students Fight Back

By Mary Crea-Arsenio, University of Guelph

Globally and in Canada, there is a childhood obesity epidemic. On a global level, it was estimated that in 2010, over 42 million children under the age of 5 were overweight (World Health Organization, 2013a). In May 2004, the World Health Organization (WHO) developed the Global Strategy on Diet, Physical Activity and Health (DPAS). Under the DPAS, the following recommendation was made to member states: "School policies and programmes should support the adoption of healthy diets and physical activity" (World Health Organization, 2013b). The WHO's *School Policy Framework: Implementation of the Global Strategy on Diet, Physical Activity and Health* was developed as a tool to help guide national policy around supporting healthy eating and physical activity in the school setting through changes in environment, behaviour, and education.

The reasons for childhood obesity are societal. According to the WHO, "Children and adolescents cannot choose the environment in which they live or the food they eat. They also have a limited ability to understand the long-term consequences of their behaviour. They therefore require special attention when fighting the obesity epidemic" (World Health Organization, 2013c).

Do you agree with this statement? What impact can policy have on changing the behaviours of children and teens?

In Canada, it is estimated that more than 1 in 4 children and youth are overweight or obese (Roberts et al., 2012). In September 2010, the federal, provincial, and territorial ministers of health agreed to focus efforts on promoting healthy weights for children by endorsing *Curbing Childhood Obesity: A Federal, Provincial and Territorial Framework for Action to Promote Healthy Weights.* Three key policy priorities were identified, including

1. Supportive environments: focusing on the environments within which children live, learn and play to ensure they support physical activity and healthy eating;
2. Early action: identifying at-risk children and youth and working to prevent obesity; and
3. Nutritious foods: identifying strategies that increase availability and accessibility of nutritious foods (Public Health Agency of Canada, 2012b).

A main focus for supportive environments is the school setting. Provincial and territorial policies have been developed that aim to reduce the incidence of childhood obesity through a focus on the school system. In Ontario, for example, the *Healthy Food for Healthy Schools Act* was introduced in 2008 to promote healthy eating in schools, including prohibiting trans fats from food and beverages sold in schools and creating mandatory nutrition standards for food and beverages sold in schools (Ministry of Education, 2013). In May 2012, two Toronto teens decided to fight back and argue for their right to choose the foods they eat. The following is an excerpt from a news article about the teens' protest: "We are not saying we don't want a healthy lifestyle. We are saying keep the healthy alternatives. But to say we can't have gum, Gatorade and cupcakes is going too far . . . I am 18. I can vote now, I can join the army and I can drive, but I can't choose what to eat."

Read more at http://toronto.ctvnews.ca/youtube-stars-say-ontario-cafeterias-need-junk-food-cash-1.823790#ixzz2T7zRKoXt

Points to consider:

1. How effective is policy in affecting teen behaviour?
2. What are the consequences of developing a policy at a macro level?
3. On a micro level, what is the possible outcome on individuals?

Minority Children in School

The interplay between family, school, and society as a whole is perhaps the most obvious with minority–group children. In general, children tend to be more successful in school if their parents are well educated and they do not live in poverty. Two groups more likely than others to be poor are recent immigrants and Aboriginal peoples. Their school experiences differ, however.

As with other groups, Aboriginal parents' level of education and income, especially for non-reserve families, is related to greater school success (Richards, 2008; Turcotte & Zhao, 2004). Many families live in rural and remote areas. Reliance on the extended family provides assistance for the individual and also the obligation to help others. Because there may be no high schools or colleges nearby, students must leave home and live in what is, for many, an alien environment. Being separated from their communities deprives them of social support and limits their ability to fulfill their own family responsibilities. Negative labels applied to Aboriginal peoples, such as "lazy" or "unreliable," mean that their school experience may be marred by prejudice (National Council of Welfare, 2007a; Richards, 2008). Now, larger numbers of Aboriginal peoples are graduating from high school and undertaking postsecondary studies, although their rates still lag behind the general population. Those who live in cities are most likely to earn a university degree (Tait, 1999; Turcotte & Zhao, 2004) (see Figure 5.2). Many recent immigrants, on the other hand, tend to be well educated, one factor in favour of their being granted admission to Canada. Poverty is often new for them, and a state they regard as temporary. Education, they feel, is the way for their children to succeed socially and economically. Children without English or French as a mother tongue begin school at a disadvantage but catch up by age 11 or 12. Those who speak an official language catch up much faster (Abada at al., 2008; Beiser et al., 1998).

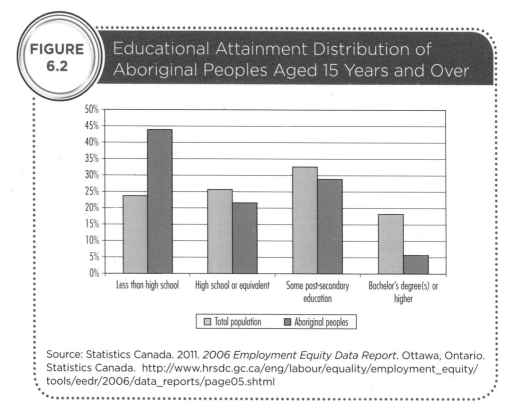

FIGURE 6.2

Educational Attainment Distribution of Aboriginal Peoples Aged 15 Years and Over

Legend: □ Total population   ■ Aboriginal peoples

Source: Statistics Canada. 2011. *2006 Employment Equity Data Report*. Ottawa, Ontario. Statistics Canada. http://www.hrsdc.gc.ca/eng/labour/equality/employment_equity/tools/eedr/2006/data_reports/page05.shtml

Peers

Once children start daycare or school, peers take on increased importance. When children are young, parents have some power over children's peers. This control grows less, however, as children become older and move more freely around the neighbourhood. Often, parents think of the peer relationship as negative and blame friends for being bad influences. For example, children tend to try alcohol or drugs, or engage in delinquent behaviour when with friends. Friends also influence children as consumers—what the leader of a group has, everyone wants, even if it conflicts with family standards. Children gravitate toward those with similar interests, such as photography or vandalism, and may move through several peer groups before adulthood. In the process, they learn to conform to group cultures. When children are rejected or ridiculed by peers, they may become isolated or antisocial (Bukowski et al., 2008).

Of course, friendship has good aspects. Peers can make up for some of a child's negative experiences at home. Through friends, children come to recognize that instead of being unique, they have interests and desires in common with others. The relationship is far more cooperative than that with parents and allows a different kind of development (Bukowski et al., 2008; Youniss, 1980).

Even as children mature, parents influence peer relationships. They select a neighbourhood in which to live. The degree to which they supervise their children also helps shape their children's peer network (Barnes et al., 2006; Knoester et al., 2006). For example, mothers tend to know their daughters' friends and to be involved in their children's activities, perhaps as coaches (Updegraff et al., 2001). When parents are supportive of teenagers, the teens, in turn, are supportive of friends, thus developing close ties (Cui et al., 2002). On the negative side, ineffective parenting is linked with a teen's choice of deviant peers and delinquent behaviour (Buehler, 2006; Knoester et al., 2006). It is not clear, however, which comes first—parenting quality or defiance (Simons et al., 2001). Adolescent groups come in two general types: socialized and oppositional. Socialized groups tend to accept positive values, such as training for a job. Oppositional ones choose dangerous activities, such as drug use and sexual promiscuity (Goddard et al., 2002). Parents may be able to influence socialized teens but have little control over oppositional ones.

As children become older, the peer group becomes more important. Most adolescents, for example, rely more on friends than on parents. Yet the growing independence of young people from their parents does not begin in adolescence; rather, it is a long process that starts early in life. It is the peer group that provides much of the opportunity for this gradual separation from the family of origin.

The Media

The media are important socializing agents. Indeed, one study remarks that "youth are awash in electronic media. What began as a media stream half a century ago has become a torrent whose strength continues to increase" (Roberts & Foehr, 2008, p. 12). The list is long: television, video games, computers, and other technologies, such as cellphones and hand-held Internet devices. New capabilities are constantly added. Media multi-tasking, the use of multiple media such as computer and cellphone at the same time, has become commonplace and complicates the estimation of media use. When we look at how the media affect socialization, we must examine the content—the messages that are being sent and received. But we must also look at how media are being used. How much time do family members spend using various media? How does this affect communication and interaction between family members?

Many young people devote more time to media than to any other activity except sleep. The current generation of children has more access to electronic media than those of any previous generation. As many as 90 percent of parents report that their children under two years old watch some form of electronic media. Parents may view television as a peacekeeper and a safe activity for their children while they are busy preparing dinner, getting ready for work, or doing household chores (American Academy of Pediatrics, 2011). The Internet has also become an integral part of our lives, and children benefit from becoming familiar with it. Not surprisingly, young people are more likely to use the Internet than older people. In 2012, 95 percent of those under 55 had Internet access and 47 percent had mobile access. In comparison, among those aged 55 and over, 68 percent had Internet access and just 16 percent had mobile access (Ipsos Reid, 2012). Internet users tend to spend less time than non-users socializing with family members and friends, having meals together, or playing with children, and are more likely to spend time alone (Vanier Institute of the Family, 2010). High levels of media use have been associated with obesity, sleep issues, aggressive behaviours, and attention issues in preschool and school-aged children (American Academy of Pediatrics, 2011).

The explosion of social media sites is both increasing connections among people and reducing privacy. Young people, university-educated, and urban Canadians, as well as recent immigrants, are most likely to use the Internet for staying connected to family and friends (Vanier Institute of the Family, 2010). Texting and emails keep family members connected and allow working parents to monitor their children's after-school activities. In addition, "tech-talk" can help build relationships between parents and children (Lanigan et al., 2009; Veenhof, 2006).

Large doses of screen violence seem to increase aggression, especially in boys (Dubow et al., 2008). Since 1997, sexual content on television has increased, both in conversation and behaviour, and only passing references to risk and individual responsibility are made (Kirkorian, et al., 2008). Listening to degrading sexual lyrics in music is linked to increased sexual activity, especially among heavy listeners (Martino et al., 2006; Primack et al., 2009). And, of course, unless controlled by parents, the Internet allows unrestricted access to all kinds of sexual content. Heavy television viewing and Internet use can also interfere with school performance, especially reading, because they take the place of homework and reading for pleasure (Roberts & Foehr, 2008). There is also the problem of stereotyping. Studies of American media, much of which are available in Canada, have looked at the images of men, women, and minorities presented. Since 1999, prime-time shows have increased the number of minority characters, especially African Americans and Latinos. White people tend to have high-status jobs, while Latinos are more often shown as doing lower-status work and Asians and people from the Middle East are more likely than others to appear as criminals. Men outnumber women in high-status careers such as physician, lawyer, or elected official. Meanwhile, women out-number men as domestic workers, nurses, and homemakers. Cultural diversity is not fully reflected in prime-time television. Thus, young people from minority groups see few positive role models (Children Now, 2004).

Some shows present variations in family structure, but these are usually unrealistic because the constraints of programming demand resolution of problems in either half an hour or an hour. Life, of course, does not work this way. The exceptions to the instant solution are the daytime drama and nighttime soaps, whose characters are shown with continuing problems, and the sensationalism of some "reality" shows. Although daytime talk shows discuss many family variations, some of the situations presented are bizarre. Few programs reflect ordinary, humdrum existence.

Whether media have a good or bad influence on children depends greatly on their age and their families. The way children handle what they see depends on their stage of development. By the age of eight, they understand that what they see on television or the Internet or in video games is not the real world. In addition, the more children think and talk critically about what they see, the less it affects them (Josephson, 1995). As already indicated, media use is related to a child's age, with a peak during ages 11 to 14. Infants and toddlers are often exposed to the media their parents use, but they learn better from real-life experiences. Older children and teens who do well in school have lower recreational media use. Less contented ones and sensation seekers spend more time with media and are more likely to multi-task. There is also a gender difference: boys are more likely to play online games and girls are more likely to multi-task (Kirkorian et al., 2008; Roberts & Foehr, 2008).

Parents have an important role in enabling and monitoring their children's use of media. There is a "digital divide" among families with higher and lower access. This divide is partly related to income. Parents with more money more often provide multiple electronic devices. The household media environment is also a factor. In some families, television is on all day, even when no one is watching. In these families, media exposure of all kinds is high. Exposure is less when parents set and enforce rules. Some use electronic controls to monitor media use (Roberts & Foehr, 2008; Subrahmanyam & Greenfield, 2008).

Parents and older siblings can help youngsters learn from and about media through their explanations and comments. Unfortunately, many parents do not make the time to do this (Kirkorian et al., 2008; Wilson, 2008). In general, parents are not as knowledgeable about the Internet and other media as their children. For example, many do not know what their teens have included in their personal online profiles. Also, some media, such as cellphones, are difficult to monitor. Most parents do not believe that computers interfere with family time. Conflict over media use may, however, arise, especially when authoritarian parents set out strict rules. In addition, heavy media use, especially when contacting friends through texting, can reduce communication within families (Lanigan et al., 2009; Subrahmanyam & Greenfield, 2008).

Okay, honey, which button do I push now?

Source: Barry Maguire.

Gender Socialization

No single influence shapes children's socialization. Rather, there is an interplay among the influences of parents, school, media, peers, and other people and institutions (Rudman & Glick, 2008). As an example, let us look at various ways children learn about gender roles.

Parents

Parents play a key part in gender socialization. Often, they model traditional gender roles within their families. Boys tend to receive more attention from parents than girls, both negative, such as punishment, and probably also positive, such as praise. When parents interact with sons, they stress achievement, independence, and the cognitive aspects of their activity. With daughters, they emphasize interpersonal closeness through encouragement and support. Boys are also more pressured than girls not to behave in ways seen as inappropriate for their sex. Sons, more than daughters, are encouraged to excel in sports (Golombok & Fivush, 1994; Leaper & Friedman, 2008). As adults, children of non-traditional parents are more likely than others to have non-traditional attitudes about gender roles (Cunningham, 2001).

Objects that surround children also affect socialization. Girls' toys, such as dolls and dishes, encourage caring and serving behaviours, while boys' toys, such as cars, are more active and complex, and help develop abilities like spatial relations. In addition, it is usually more acceptable for girls to play with toys that are designed for boys than vice versa (Raag & Rackliff, 1998). Sex-typing is related more to fathers' attitudes than to mothers'. In these ways, girls are encouraged to conform to the stereotype of women as passive, dependent, and nurturing. Boys, on the other hand, are encouraged to be more independent, active, and aggressive (Leaper & Friedman, 2008). Children who grow up in homes with single mothers or same-sex parents follow gender-typing as much as children with parents of opposite sexes (Stevens et al., 2003).

Schools

In the past, education was strongly related to gender stereotypes. For example, woodworking classes were for boys only and home economics for girls only. Boys traditionally have done better in mathematics and science, and girls have done better in language skills. Although attempts have been made to desegregate subjects and encourage girls to continue math and science into the higher grades, success has been somewhat limited. Studies of schools have shown that role models in these subjects, such as science teachers, are primarily men. Science also tends to be taught using examples from typical male interests, such as competitive sports, an example of earlier gender socialization. In addition, many teachers give more attention to boys than girls in the classroom (Golombok & Fivush, 1994; Leaper & Friedman, 2008).

Peers

Starting in daycare, children are aware of girls' and boys' play materials, and some boys already refuse to play with girls' toys (Raag & Rackliff, 1998). By middle childhood, children tend to play in groups of their own sex. Boys and girls develop contrasting peer cultures, with boys more active in large groups and girls quieter in pairs or small groups. Sex-typing is stronger in boys' time with peers. Girls' activities are more evenly divided between "masculine" and "feminine" activities. Boys gain more prestige for sports excellence than girls do (Leaper & Friedman, 2008; McHale et al., 2004).

The Media

As we have already seen, the media tend to stereotype male and female behaviour. In television programs, for example, males are more active and aggressive than females, and are focused on jobs or on sports. Women, though also shown in the workplace, are portrayed more than men as providing care to others. Female characters are more concerned with relationships than males. Advertisements show toys as appropriate for boys or for girls. Even children's books labelled "non-sexist" tend to contain gender stereotypes (Children Now, 2004; Leaper & Friedman, 2008).

Age Cohorts

Given that society changes, every age group grows up in a different world. These age groups are called **cohorts** (see Box 6.2). One cohort receiving a great deal of

cohort: a group of people, roughly the same age, living in the same historical time

attention is the baby boom generation, those born between about 1946 and 1964. Their experiences growing up differ markedly from those of both earlier and later cohorts. In fact, the baby boom is really made up of two groups whose experiences differ from each other. The older group formed the cutting edge of change, and the younger were born once change had already taken place (Stewart & Torges, 2006). And French Canadian youth had different issues from English Canadians (Owram, 1996).

A number of factors affected the socialization of the baby boom generation. First, the country was in prosperous times and the general affluence led people to expect that life would be easy. Second, technology mushroomed. Third, institutions were weakened and a loss of respect for authority resulted—the early baby boomers produced social protests and the hippie movement that rejected parents' values. Fourth, parents made Dr. Spock's *Baby and Child Care* a bestseller. He advised a more permissive care than recommended in earlier years. An example about the use of pacifiers appears at the beginning of this chapter. Some parents took his advice to the extreme and provided little structure for their children. Fifth, the effect of being born into a large family meant that more socialization was carried on by children and that teamwork and social skills were emphasized. These children also experienced more family instability because of an increasing number of divorces. Sixth, this is the first generation that never knew what it was like to live without television. Seventh, the period after World War II saw a migration from farm to town to city. Small towns tend to enforce standards more than cities, but they are also more supportive to families. Finally, advances in medicine meant a drop in infant and child mortality and a reduction of physical suffering (Hicks & Hicks, 1999; Kettle, 1980; Stewart & Torges, 2006).

There are problems with generalizations such as these, though. The baby boom generation encompasses a wide age group, and it is rash to equate infants with older teenagers. In addition, such statements ignore the many variations in life experience.

The size of the baby boom generation presented challenges to the worlds of education and work. As the big generation moved through the school system, they were subjected to crowding and a number of young, hastily trained teachers (Eggebeen & Sturgeon, 2006). Young people stayed in school longer, partly because they could not find jobs and partly because the jobs available required a higher level of technical skill. A number of experimental plans were introduced to cope with the many more students who did not plan to go to university. For this generation, the community college system was developed.

In contrast to the baby boomers, Generation X, which includes those born between 1965 and 1979, is much smaller. This cohort grew up in more difficult financial times than the baby boomers. Parents responded by having fewer children. The children were also less likely to be raised in traditional families. The divorce rate of their parents increased dramatically, and X-ers are the first generation to grow up with many mothers in the workforce.

A combination of factors has blocked X-ers' careers but encouraged them to value family. The economy made jobs harder to find. When positions matching their qualifications came up, baby boomers, who had been in the workplace longer, snapped them up. Many X-ers have shifted from job to job or become self-employed. As a result, they have become flexible and self-reliant. Although described as "job hoppers," most want job security, interesting work, and integrity in the workplace (Hicks & Hicks, 1999). Many put family needs above job demands. Their focus on relationships is also expressed in their definition of family, which includes those providing emotional commitment and support, regardless of their legal relationship. The attack on the World Trade Center in New York on September 11, 2001, has increased their focus on family as well (Clack, 2004; Hicks & Hicks, 1999). This cohort is now raising children.

Generation Y members (born between about 1982 and 1994) have baby boomers as parents. Their numbers are larger than Generation X (the baby bust) because of the large size of their parents' generation (Statistics Canada, 2007c). Many were born to older parents and are only children or have just one sibling. A large proportion experienced their parents' divorce and grew up with lone parents and in stepfamilies. Generation Y is the first generation to grow up with computers, cellphones, text messaging, and social media sites. They tend to think globally. There are two likely factors involved. Because of the Internet, they are connected to people worldwide. In addition, 9/11 demonstrated the far reach of terrorism. As a result of immigration trends, many have grown up in a socially diverse environment. They are more likely than older Canadians to approve of multiracial dating and of same-sex marriage (Huntley, 2006; Pew Research Center, 2007). In Chapter 7, we will look at Generation Y as emerging adults.

The latest age cohort comprises those born after 1995, and these people have been labelled Generation Z. They are the first generation to be born into a digital world. What distinguishes them from every other generation is that they are the most electronically connected generation in history. This connectivity allows them to communicate and collaborate in real time wherever they are. Perhaps because of both their young age and the overload of information, they also tend to not be very capable at critically evaluating resources (Geck, 2006).

BOX 6.2 Age Cohorts

How are age cohorts determined? People may disagree on the range of birth years that define a cohort, and people who bridge two generations may show characteristics of both generations However, the following cohorts, and some of their generational characteristics, have been identified:

Baby Boomers, born between 1946 and 1964

Most are team-oriented and driven individuals who work hard to further their career, raise a family and care for aging parents.

Generation X, born between 1965 and 1979

Often labelled as skeptical, they are independent and, unlike boomers, are not afraid to switch jobs or careers several times in an effort to continue gaining experience and knowledge.

Generation Y (also known as the **Millennials**), born between 1982 and 1994

They are just beginning to enter the workforce. They are expert multi-taskers and are always looking to balance hobbies and volunteer activities with work.

Generation Z, born after 1995·

Not yet in the workforce, they are used to customized information and entertainment such as text messaging, YouTube, and instant access to people.

Sources: Adapted from: D. Baumrind, "Effects of authoritative parental control on child behaviour," *Child Development*, Vol. 37 (4), Pg. 887–907; E. E. Maccoby, "The role of parents in the socialization of children: An historical overview," *Developmental Psychology*, Vol. 28, Pg. 1006–1017.

Some Issues

Concern is growing over the amount of control that parents have lost in the socialization process. With both parents working, non-family socializers, including babysitters and daycare staff members, influence children at a younger age than in the past. Children are also introduced earlier to the influence of peers not chosen by their parents. There is some controversy over whether this lower level of control is neutral or harmful for children.

Older children have less supervision now. Once they are beyond the age at which they legally require a babysitter, many are left to fend for themselves; these children have been popularized as "latchkey kids." Some are without adult control for several hours between the end of the school day and parents' return from work. Some adolescents are also unsupervised. There are concerns over the influence of the media on such children and their opportunities for experimentation with drugs or for sexual activity.

Another concern is over the reduced interaction between parents and children when both parents have jobs. Research results have been mixed, with some studies showing that children who are in daycare full time during their first year experience insecure attachment, higher levels of aggression, and lower school performance. Other findings suggest that children suffer no ill effects. The results appear to depend on the quality of the care children receive (Cleveland & Krashinsky, 2003).

helicopter parents: parents who are obsessively concerned about their children's safety and success

Although some parents worry that commitments limit the time they have to spend with their kids, others become **helicopter parents**. These parents constantly hover around their children. They are obsessively concerned about their children's safety and success. They arrange structured "playdates" with approved friends, confront teachers over a poor grade, and have even chastised work supervisors who give a less-than-glowing performance review to their child.

The recognition of physical and emotional abuse of children raises another issue. Should parenting education be compulsory? In the past, women learned how to raise children from their mothers and other female relatives. Systems theorists point out that this practice may result in the repetition of harmful patterns of interaction from one generation to the next. If parenting education is considered essential, who should be entrusted with it? Should it be a compulsory school subject? Will child protection agencies be able to step in to ensure that parents are adequately trained before they can raise their children?

Since socialization helps produce new members of society, it is a target for any group that feels the family or society is threatened. Anyone who feels that the present society is unjust looks to change the way children are raised. Socialization thus provides a focus for conflicts over many social issues.

Time to Review

1. How do various social institutions (childcare, schools, media) affect the socialization of children?
2. What are age cohorts? Describe the different cohorts.
3. What are some of the issues regarding socialization?

Parents and the Shaping of a Child

In this chapter, we have seen how parents, the larger family, and social institutions all have an impact on the socialization of a child. Each of the sociological perspectives focuses on certain factors in the socialization process. A more complete understanding comes with being able to look at any issue from various perspectives. As you read the sad story of Caleb, think about the different factors that are having an impact on him.

Caleb had several strikes against him when he was born. His parents weren't married and had an on-again, off-again relationship. The pregnancy was diagnosed late, only two months before his due date, and was an unwelcome surprise.

He weighed just 2.5 kg when he was delivered three weeks early. Right away, medical staff detected problems. He sucked poorly and showed no persistence in feeding. Even months later, he snacked frequently rather than settling down to a regular schedule of meals. He was more irritable than most newborns. His nose and ears looked a little odd. These were clear signs he had been hurt by his mother's binge drinking during her pregnancy. His development would probably be filled with problems, including learning and behavioural difficulties.

The local child protective services were called. They allowed Caleb to go home with his parents on condition that his mother stop drinking. Before long, however, a surprise visit caught her with alcohol on her breath—Caleb was taken to a foster home. Though he was soon back home again, within a few months his parents' relationship fell apart and Caleb was once more in foster care.

The search for a home with relatives was futile. His grandmother felt she was too old: she would be in her 80s before he was adult. Caleb's aunt, with a baby just a month older than Caleb, felt she couldn't care for her own daughter and a child needing special care. Finally, the family court terminated the rights of Caleb's parents and child welfare services found an adoptive family who could meet his needs and would be willing to care for him despite his uncertain future.

1. Which characteristics of Caleb's parents are important to his socialization?
2. In what ways has the wider social context had an impact on Caleb?
3. If you were a relative, what would you do?
4. If you worked for the local child protection services, what would you do?

Summary

What Is the Place of Socialization in the Family Life Cycle?

Socialization is the process of passing on to new members a culture's ways of thinking and acting. It occurs mainly in childhood, and by the time they are adults, people are expected to share the values and norms of society. The socialization of children often begins with parents and soon includes other family members. While every society socializes its members, how they are socialized can be quite different.

Through socialization, individuals develop a sense of their identity, status, and roles in society. Socialization does not take place in a vacuum. The child participates actively in the process. The levels of physical maturation, intellectual development, and social experiences help determine whether a child can understand and comply with socially approved behaviour. Children also make choices about their behaviour. These factors help explain why children from the same family can turn out so differently. How we socialize children reflects what we expect of their future and the value we place on them.

What Role Do Parents Play in the Socialization of Children?

Parents are the single most powerful influence on children. The number, marital status, gender, sexual orientation, education, and age of a child's parent figures help shape the child. Parenting styles (authoritarian, authoritative, permissive, or uninvolved) are important in day-to-day interaction. Families also affect the development of children through their routines and traditions.

In What Ways Do Cultural Groups Differ in Parenting Styles?

There are some differences between English Canadians and French Canadians. One study found that English-speaking Montrealers encouraged their children to be more independent in solving problems than French-speaking Montrealers. Aboriginal families strongly emphasize the interdependence of all life and have a strong sense of spirituality. Traditional Aboriginal societies recognize the basic family unit of parents and children living together, but family also includes a broad network of grandparents, aunts, uncles, and cousins. From the 1890s to the 1970s, many Aboriginal children were removed from their families and placed in residential schools. Children in immigrant families may be pulled between two cultural ideals, with their attitudes raising concern among their families. North American society encourages independence and spontaneity, while many other cultures, such as Chinese and South Asian, expect children to be more focused on their families and respectful of their elders. Immigrant parents typically hold different expectations of their children than Canadian-born parents do.

In What Ways Do Other Family Members Influence the Socialization of Children?

Other relatives also affect the socialization of children. Brothers and sisters affect socialization in many ways. The number, ages, and birth order influence development. Siblings also provide role models, give information about peer values and interaction, provide opportunities to practise solving conflicts, and offer affection and support. Having a sibling with special needs also affects development. Extended family members can provide affection and teach the child family traditions. The extended family is important among Aboriginal peoples, but its prestige has been damaged by the influence of white society.

How Do Society and the Family Interact in Socialization?

Children are also socialized by institutions and individuals who are not related to them. Babysitters and daycare personnel provide a variety of environments. In school, children learn the dominant social values about families, which help shape their self-concept. Peers are a source both of individual development and of potential conflict with families. The media provide models of gender roles and present popular ideas about families. It is also important to examine how media are used. The impact of the media on socialization is influenced by family factors such as supervision.

What Is Gender Socialization?

No single influence shapes children's socialization. Rather, there is an interplay among the influences of parents, school, media, peers, and other people and institutions. Parents play a key part in gender socialization. Objects that surround children also affect socialization. In the past, education was strongly related to gender stereotypes. Boys and girls develop contrasting peer cultures, with boys generally more active in large groups and girls quieter, in pairs or small groups. The media, however, tend to stereotype male and female behaviour.

What Are Age Cohorts?

Age cohorts also affect socialization; for example, cohort size can affect opportunities and expectations about education and employment.

Class Assignments

1. Some parents have difficulty letting go of their children. Discuss some of the reasons this might be so. What might be done to avoid this difficulty?
2. Look at five recent books written for preschool children that show family interaction in some way. What messages does each give about family and gender roles? Do these messages reflect the reality of present-day family life?
3. Do you think there should be a law that requires people to take a parenting course before having children? What do you see as the advantages and disadvantages of such legislation?

Personal Assignments

The following questions are designed to help you look at your own family experience and its influence on your life:

1. How have brothers and sisters affected your socialization? Consider their age, sex, number, and personalities. If you have no siblings, what effect has this had on you? Why?
2. What family stories were you told? What messages did they give you? How did these affect your development?

PART 4

THE MIDDLE YEARS OF THE FAMILY

Chapter 7

The Middle Years of the Family and the Not-So-Empty Nest

Goodluz/Shutterstock

LEARNING OBJECTIVES

Why are the middle years of a family described as a time of transition?

Why is midlife a time for assessment and what areas of their lives do individuals typically assess?

What developmental tasks do adolescents and emerging adults face?

How do the continuing dependency of children and the needs of elderly relatives affect family life?

When I was in my 20s, 40 seemed ridiculously far off—a venerable middle age at which I envisioned myself taking a crash course in bridge and migrating south to avoid the cold. Now, having rocketed to that age zone with astonishing speed, it seems the archetypal middle age about which I was so patronizing isn't quite so venerable after all.

For one thing, the much-hyped decline of the body, while not exactly welcome, is neither devastating nor inevitable. Sure, I've had to make the acquaintance of the colour technician at the hairdresser and I sport some lines on my face that surprise me every time I pass a mirror. But the overall physical plant is holding up just fine. Good genes may play a part here, but they don't tell the whole story. A better explanation is that I'm representative of the "new middle age," a generation that has radically changed what the 40s look and feel like. I exercise—something I never did in my 20s or even 30s—I eat sensibly and slather on the sunscreen. Happily, I can report that all these efforts really pay off. Without question, I'm in better shape now than I've ever been before.

> **Source:** Lesley Barsky, "40 Something: The New Exciting Middle Age?" *Chatelaine*, Jan. 1990. Pg. 34. Reprinted by permission of the author.

During the middle years of a family, parents and children are usually living at home. Midlife for parents—considered the years between the ages of 40 or 45 and 64—is a period of re-evaluation of their life course so far. Some set off in a new direction in work or in family relationships. Children in the family may range from toddlers to emerging adults. By the end of the middle years, many members of the younger generation are independent or are planning to leave their parents' home. In this chapter, we will focus on parents and their adolescent and emerging adult children.

Where Do I Fit In?

How do you see yourself 20 years from now?
   Think about your own family . . .
  1. Which age group are your parents in?
  2. What age group do you fit into?
  3. Do you experience conflicts between your parents' expectations and your own plans?

The Parent Generation at Midlife

Our notion of middle age is a fairly recent idea. In the past, for example, Robert and Ann Miller, who lived in the Niagara Peninsula in the 1800s, had 14 children. The oldest was born when Ann was 20, the youngest when she was 45. By the time her youngest daughter was married, Ann Miller was in her 60s. Child-rearing consumed about 45 years of her life. A busy middle age of sorts came for the Miller parents somewhere between the last birth and their children's independence.

With their smaller nuclear families, today's parents do not devote as long to active child-rearing. They have more years either before or afterward for individual and couple pursuits. They also expect many more years of life than earlier generations. Lesley Barsky's (1990) comments on turning 40 reflect these new values.

The current midlife generation consists of the baby boomers—the largest group in the population. In 2011, they were between 45 and 64 years of age. The working population is rapidly growing older. Those aged 55 to 64 increased the most between 2006 and 2011. At nearly 4.39 million, they outnumber those in the age group, 15 to 24 (4.37 million), when individuals typically enter the workforce. Never have so many people been close to retirement (Statistics Canada, 2012m). The median age of the population is 39.9 years; that is, half of Canadians are older and half younger than 39.9. The median is expected to rise to 44 as baby boomers age. Table 7.1 shows the numbers of two age groups and the proportion of each group in the Canadian population over a 30-year period. The number of Canadians aged 45 to 64 will nearly double between 1991 and 2021. This group already accounted for over one-quarter of all Canadians in 2011 (Bélanger et al., 2005; Statistics Canada, 2012n). As they have been doing since they were born, this large cohort will have a profound effect on Canadian society at this phase of their life.

The middle years of adulthood have now joined child-rearing as the longest stages in life. The midlife group is diverse. Since their ages span 20 to 25 years, group members may include first-time parents as well as great-grandparents (Blieszner & Roberto, 2006). At the beginning of the midlife period, many are approaching the peak of their careers, while others are nearing retirement. Many women in this group had jobs throughout their adult lives. Others are entering the workforce for the first time, or re-entering the workforce after an interval devoted to child-rearing. Therefore, any generalizations about this group will fit only parts

TABLE 7.1

Population by Selected Age Groups—1991, 2001, 2011, 2021

	1991	2001	2011	2021
Total Population (millions)	27.3	30.0	34.5	36.6
Age Group 35-44 (millions)	4.37	5.10	4.68	5.11
(proportion)	16.0%	17.0%	13.6%	14.0%
Age Group 45-64 (millions)	5.37	7.29	9.31	10.01
(proportion)	19.7%	24.3%	27.0%	27.3%

Note: Data for 2021 are estimated.

Sources: Adapted from: Statistics Canada. 2002. *Profile of the Canadian Population by Age and Sex: Canada Ages.* Statistics Canada Catalogue no. 96F0030XIE2001002. Ottawa, Ontario. Analysis Series, 2001 Census. http://www12 .statcan.ca/english/census01/Products/Analytic/Index.cfm (accessed Nov. 17, 2013); A. Bélanger, L. Martel, and É. Caron-Malenfant. Statistics Canada. 2010. *Population Projections for Canada, Provinces and Territories 2005-2031.* Catalogue No. 91-520-XIE. Ottawa, Ontario. Dec. 2005. Pg. 149, Table 10-1.

of the population. For example, until quite recently, few studies focused on gay, lesbian, and bisexual individuals in midlife (Hunter, 2005; Wight et al.,).

These years of the family life cycle are transitional. For many with children, there is a shift from active child-rearing at the beginning of this stage to the post-child family at the end. This period often marks the splitting of one family into two or more as children leave their families of origin and form their own nuclear families of procreation. The process involves a major readjustment of the family system. New boundaries must be drawn as to who is a family member. Relationships need to be worked out between the family of origin and the new families of procreation. New roles need to be established to reflect these changes.

Like all major life changes, family adaptation in the middle years contains a series of stressors. A **stressor** is a life event that can produce change in the family system (Boss, 2002). Examples are parenthood and death. Losing family members, gaining family members, and acquiring new responsibilities can all act as stressors. Early and late boomers report similar levels of stress. For older individuals, the main concerns are focused on another person, for example their parents' health or their children's ability to be successful in life. Younger boomers report more interpersonal tensions, such as arguments about finances. Having children at home means more interpersonal tensions (Almeida et al., 2006). Canadian middle-aged individuals have reported the most negative stressors involve their own health, the death of a loved one, and financial problems. American studies of gay men and lesbians have found that belonging to a sexual minority is an additional stressor (Barker et al., 2006; Wight et al., 2012).

The most important resource for meeting these challenges is family, followed by close friends and professionals (Keown, 2009). Beyond that, individuals at midlife are at the height of coping. They have high levels of practical knowledge and are more skilled in reducing stress (Aldwin, 2007). The coping patterns families have already established usually continue (Price et al., 2010).

Midlife: A Time for Evaluation

During midlife, individuals typically consider whether their lives have been fulfilling. Such an evaluation involves examining themselves as individuals and their work and family lives. Some changes are easier for younger individuals. New career paths, for example, are easier to explore in one's early 40s than in one's late 50s (Stewart & Torges, 2006). Daniel Levinson and his colleagues, who studied middle-aged men, describe this period as one of the major transitions in life, occurring at about 40 to 45 years of age (see Figure 7.1 on page 195). Midlife occurs at about the same time their children are going through the transition to independence and their parents are entering the transition to retirement (Levinson, 1978). Erik Erikson (1982) stated that the key issue in middle age (35 to 65 years) is **generativity**, or having children and passing on something of value to younger generations.

This long age span has since been divided into two periods. The first is midlife evaluation and transition, typically occurring in the early 40s to the late 50s. The second is a time of liberation, experimentation, and innovation that usually occurs

stressor: a life event that can produce change in the family system

generativity: a focus on one's legacy

FIGURE 7.1 — Levinson's Developmental Stages of Adulthood

AGE	SEASON (PHASE)	CHARACTERISTICS
18–20 years	Early adult transition	Seeks independence by separating from family
21–27 years	Entrance into the adult world	Experiments with different careers and lifestyles
28–32 years	Transition	Makes lifestyle adjustments
33–39 years	Settling down	Experiences greater stability
45–65	Pay-off years	Is self-directed and engages in self-evaluation

Source: Adapted from: D. Levinson, *The Seasons of a Man's Life*. New York: Knopf. 1978.

during the late 50s to early 70s. The recent popularity of "bucket lists" (things I want to do before I kick the bucket) reflects the growing number of individuals this age. The **midlife crisis**, a time of extreme strain during the period of evaluation (which is credited with the acquisition of sports cars and a new, younger wife) is quite rare. Rather, most adults enter a quest for meaning in life. Midlife re-evaluation leads more often to a sense of personal discovery than to a crisis (Cohen, 2005).

midlife crisis: extreme strain as a person re-evaluates his or her life in middle age

Assessing Oneself

Generativity, already mentioned, involves creating one's legacy and can take place within the family or in the wider society. An obvious strategy is having and raising children to adulthood. Generativity, however, can take various forms, such as mentoring a relative or another young person through an organization like Big Brothers or Big Sisters. The creation of artistic works is another form. So is working to better the community through advocacy or involvement in service organizations. Family leisure time is often used to teach young people skills and knowledge, as well as transmit family history and values (Hebblethwaite & Norris, 2011).

In the past, most research attention was focused on men's experience. Career and public life were seen as the most important forms of generativity. It was assumed that women expressed generativity primarily through the less esteemed function of having and raising children. Besides reflecting a sexist bias, such an assumption overlooks the many contributions women have made to society, for example in advocating for the right of women to vote. As men's and women's social roles become more similar, women will experience routes to generativity more closely resembling men's (Masciadrelli & Oswald, 2005; Milardo, 2005; Oswald & Masciadrelli, 2008).

empty nest syndrome:
the depression and sense of
uselessness some women
experience when the last
child leaves home

Homemaker mothers are sometimes described as suffering the **empty nest syndrome**, depression and a sense of uselessness when the last child leaves home. From a developmental perspective, emptying the nest is a significant and necessary task. For parents, it means allowing young adult children to develop their identities and independence, and redefining their marriage without dependent children. The empty nest often brings the couple increased happiness and marital satisfaction (Johnson & Wilkinson, 1995).

A second area of evaluation is identity. The search for personal meaning is important in midlife. This part of self-examination has long been recognized among men. The baby boom generation is perhaps the first where the majority of women have been encouraged to develop their separate identities. This trend has become more important both because of the many women in the workforce and because of high levels of divorce (Jones et al., 2006; Stewart & Torges, 2006).

A third area is the development of a sense of confidence and competence. At this age, women are particularly likely to have a sense of power in their jobs and organizations. Men, on the other hand, may be able to relax from demands that they perform at a high level (Moses, 2006; Stewart & Torges, 2006).

A final area is a growing sense of mortality. A number of factors are involved. The death of parents and people their own age reminds midlife adults that they won't live forever. They are now moving up one generation. This fact is emphasized if they become grandparents. If their parents die, they are the senior generation. They are obviously aging physically, something underlined by the fact that a number of men die in these years. So men begin realizing that their lives, too, will end, and that day may not be far off. For gay men, the sense of coming death may be sharpened by the death of friends from AIDS. In contrast, in spite of some minor complaints, most still feel vigorous though they face signs of aging: the appearance of grey hair and wrinkles, and the loss of some physical power. Women go through menopause, but most do not regard it as a major crisis. The current youth culture stigmatizes signs of aging, especially among women. Boomers with money call on medicine and fashion to maintain their youthful image; however, both men and women are more likely to worry about health than physical appearance, especially when over 50 (AARP, 2005a; Avis & Crawford, 2006; Jones et al., 2006; Moses, 2006; Stewart & Torges, 2006).

Assessing One's Career

Both men and women need goals to give them direction. According to Levinson (1978), a young man forms a dream of what he wishes to accomplish in life. By midlife, it should be apparent whether that dream is attainable. If he has not achieved it, he must alter his plans to fit reality. If he has achieved it, he needs to find another goal to give his life direction. Women in the workforce face similar decisions. Nearly as many women as men have paid employment. In 2009, 77.1 percent of women and 83.8 percent of men aged 25 to 44 were employed. For those aged 45 to 54, 77.3 percent of women and 82.9 percent of men had jobs, and for those aged 55 to 69, 53.1 percent of women and 62.3 percent of men had jobs (Ferrao, 2010).

Midlife is a time for stock-taking. Have values and circumstances changed? Does one want to continue this life for another 20 years? At midlife, many individuals want something different. They experience both a push toward excitement and a pull toward security. Women hoping to return to a career they had before children or to follow a new one may experience problems, partly because of age bias, partly because of the "mommy track" they followed, and partly because of their lack of current experience (Moses, 2006). For example, it is difficult for women to return to a law firm after an absence, but other available legal jobs can provide a satisfying alternative (Macdonald, 2009). Beyond stock-taking, a career crisis can be triggered by a disturbing life-changing event, such as a death in the family or a marriage breakup. People may also drift into career distress without noticing warning signs. A sizable minority of middle-aged adults do not reach their goals in their financial or work lives (AARP, 2005a).

Looking at Close Relationships

A final realm for re-evaluation is close relationships. Most baby boomers are involved in relationships with children and parents at the same time. A growing number are raising grandchildren; many are not prepared for a second parenthood. Greater life expectancy thus makes relationships more complex. People also have romantic relationships, friendships, and sibling ties (Blieszner & Roberto, 2006; Connidis, 2010). Boomers say that relationships with family and friends are among the most satisfying parts of life (AARP, 2005a).

Individuals often become grandparents around the age of 50. Because of smaller families, they have fewer grandchildren, on average, than their parents and grandparents did. Frequently, the number includes step-grandchildren. Sometimes, these generation-rich families are referred to as "beanpole families" (Blieszner & Roberto, 2006; Connidis, 2010).

Marriage and Sexuality

With the trends in cohabitation, marriage, divorce, remarriage, never-married, and same-sex relationships, romantic ties have become more diverse (Blieszner & Roberto, 2006; Hunter, 2005). Individuals are often faced with the prospect of spending the rest of their lives with their partners without children as a buffer. In addition, partners are also growing older and remind them of their own age. Some conclude that this relationship is not rewarding and separate. A number find new partners, often choosing someone who suits their new self-image. Others opt to remain in their relationship.

Often, as they adjust to the childless household, men and women find that their roles shift toward greater androgyny, or a balance between the masculine and feminine characteristics. Men often become more concerned with relationships, and the masculine trait of competitiveness may recede in them. Women, on the other hand, become more interested in achievement. Couples who modify their relationship usually experience increased marital satisfaction (Blacker, 1999).

A few other factors influence midlife couple happiness. Those who had warm and trusting relationships with their parents during adolescence are usually happy with their partner in midlife. Those with secure attachment to their partners have more stable relationships than those with anxious attachment (Blieszner & Roberto, 2006; Hollist & Miller, 2005). The little research on same-sex couples in midlife has found that the quality of their relationships was similar to that of heterosexual partners (Hunter, 2005).

Middle-aged parents with teens at home are more likely to be depressed than those with older children. Puberty in a firstborn child is linked to distress in the parents' relationship (Kiecolt et al., 2011). Both parents report lower marital satisfaction. Mothers of girls and fathers of boys report more conflict. Fathers tend to adjust by the time a second child reaches puberty, but mothers still experience problems. It may be that teens have become skilled at manipulating parents (Whiteman et al., 2007). In any case, increases in marital conflict over raising adolescent children are associated with decreases in marital satisfaction (Cui & Donnellan, 2009).

Once children have left home, the marriage relationship becomes more central. Couples who stay together may have to renegotiate some aspects of their relationship. For example, the husband may want to change the relationship to fit his new values, and his wife may be excited about her new job. Many couples report that they are more satisfied with their marriages in midlife. For women, at least, this improvement comes just after the last child leaves home. A longitudinal study that followed women from their 40s to 60s found that they were more relaxed with their spouse and enjoyed their time together more. They were also satisfied with having raised successful children (Gorchoff et al., 2008). When children continue living at home or return after moving out, arguments between couples increase, especially about money and chores (Turcotte, 2006a). The presence of a child cuts into couple time (Ward & Spitze, 2004).

The sexual relationship of the couple may change. For some couples, interest in sex increases. Now that children are grown, more private time is available with fewer interruptions. After menopause, there is no need to fear pregnancy. Men's slowed response time allows a more relaxed approach and often more pleasure for the woman (Blacker, 1999). On the other hand, interest may drop off through boredom. One couple who swore off sex spoke of how "the habit of sex" interfered with the companionship they both enjoyed in their marriage (Amiel, 1987). Some couples accept the stereotype that older people are asexual beings (Greenberg et al., 2002). This belief goes hand in hand with the idea that sex is intended only for procreation. According to this notion, once a woman has passed menopause, there is no reason for continuing sexual relations. Unfortunately, aging and sexuality are experienced differently by men and women in North America. A male's sexual attractiveness is often linked to success and financial stability, factors that often increase with age. For women, sexual attractiveness is usually based on a youthful physical appearance, which tends to decline with age (Barnes, 2010).

There is greater acceptance now of sexuality and less opposition to sex for unmarried people. For many people aged 45 and older, sexual activity is an important part of their relationship. This reality is hardly surprising, given that this generation ushered in the sexual revolution in the 1960s. Those with regular sexual partners are more satisfied sexually and generally more positive about life than the non-partnered. Men are more likely than women to try a variety of sex-related activities, and gay men are the most likely to be sexually active. In general, satisfaction with sex is related to the health both of oneself and of one's partner. Recently, the use of medicines and hormones has increased tremendously. About two-thirds of those who have used them report increased satisfaction with their sex life (AARP, 2010; Barnes, 2010; Hunter, 2005).

When adults over 50 look for a new partner, they increasingly turn to Internet dating sites, where they are the fastest-growing group of clients. According to a small interview study, men want committed relationships, while women look for companionship without the prospect of heavy caregiving. In their profiles, both sexes stress their youthfulness either in their appearance or their activities (McWilliams & Barrett, 2012).

Time to Review

1. Why is midlife described as transitional?
2. Identify three areas in which midlife adults assess their lives.
3. What kinds of changes might midlife adults make in their lives?

Adolescence and the Approach of Adulthood

The middle family years are also a time of change for children. In their first 12 or so years, children who develop normally move away from total dependence on adults. They gain in physical strength and agility. They grasp the language or languages around them. They understand the rules of their families and of society. They have formed relationships with family members and with people outside the family. The end of middle childhood is a period for consolidating the gains they have made and preparing for puberty.

During the next 12 years or more, they will physically mature, finish their education, move away from their parents' home, get a job, find a romantic and sexual partner, and perhaps have a child (Clark, 2007). The main criteria for adulthood are accepting responsibility for oneself, making independent decisions, and becoming financially self-supporting. Those of Asian origin also include the ability to take care of one's parents (Arnett, 2007). They develop the physical, intellectual, and social qualities that enable them to take on adult roles. During this period, a person forms identities around sexual behaviour, vocational direction, and the values and ideals that will guide his or her life.

Unlike some societies, in North America there are no specific rites of passage to mark the start of adulthood. Rather, there is a gradual shift from one status to the other, beginning in adolescence. In the past, graduation from high school was often a social event that marked the transition to adulthood. Nowadays, because of the complex needs of society, education takes longer and independence is delayed (Marcia, n.d., 1966, 1983). Researchers are now suggesting that there is a stage after adolescence that they call "emerging adulthood" (Tanner & Arnett, 2009). In this phase, individuals are still developing their own values and learning relationship skills and roles. Many are not independent of parents.

The Preliminaries—Preadolescence and the Earlier Teen Years

In spite of popular notions, adolescence need not be a period of *Sturm und Drang* (storm and stress) (Maccoby, 2007). It is often marked by bickering and disagreements over issues such as chores and curfews as teens and parents work out new roles (Blieszner & Roberto, 2006). It is a period of disorganization for the whole family, its members faced with the adolescents' changing bodies and the social significance of these changes. Adolescents become sexually developed. Teens also improve the ability to think abstractly. As a result, they can argue, sometimes interminably, and they usually develop their own values separate from their parents' (Cline & Fay, 2006; Marcia, 1984). Their peer groups also change because of differences in maturation.

The main task of adolescence is to turn these changes into an individual identity. To do so, adolescents' most basic need is confidence that their parents support them (Marcia, 1984). The need for a secure base from which to explore was identified in infants by Mary Ainsworth (Bretherton, 2003). It is still needed by adolescents.

Adolescents take many risks. According to one stereotype, teens believe that, although bad things happen to others, they will not happen to them. In fact, most know and understand risks but do not weigh consequences rationally. Following puberty, a young person experiences swings in emotion and also wants excitement. As a result, teens may do something they immediately recognize as stupid. Learning to manage impulses depends on experience and on brain maturation (Steinberg, 2005, 2007). A small minority believe they will die before they are 35 years old. They often use alcohol and drugs and have risky sex. Unfortunately, their behaviour makes it more likely that they will die early (Borowski et al., 2009).

Parents often blame the influence of peers for their children's problem behaviour. As teens distance themselves from their parents, peers do become increasingly important and exert pressure on early teens. Most young people, however, select friends who resemble them (Arnett, 2007). Risky or antisocial behaviour usually results from group culture or excitement, rather than simple persuasion. Resistance to peer pressure grows between the ages of 14 and 18. By the end of their teens, most are more concerned with romantic relationships and forming their own identity than with conforming to peers (Steinberg & Monahan, 2007). Studies of Canadian teens have found that taking part in extracurricular activities enhances their development. This is especially true when they stay with an activity they enjoy over time (Busseri & Rose-Krasnor, 2008; Busseri et al., 2009).

Many parents face the prospect of their children's adolescence with trepidation. A child's growth spurt is a visible reminder of what is coming. One study found that mothers felt separation anxiety as they anticipated the growing independence of a teenager. There was more anxiety when the youngster was a girl or the first-born. In addition, the mother's expectations affected her attitude (Richardson, 2005). One study looked at the satisfaction adults in the Vancouver area felt with their role as parents. A positive attitude was related to parents' perception of how their children turned out. Most were happy in their roles, especially if they were emotionally close to the child and had adequate finances and good health. Parents from Chinese and South Asian backgrounds were not as satisfied, probably because of cultural clash with their children (Mitchell, 2010).

Adolescents have better outcomes, researchers have found, when they come from families with emotionally close and involved parents. In these families, parents provide healthy role models. They also monitor their teens' activities. Well-adjusted teens tend to share information about their lives, especially when parents set clear rules for reporting what they are doing (Crosnoe & Kavanagh, 2010; Moore et al., 2009; Myers et al., 2012). When dual-career parents work non-standard shifts, adolescents say they are as close to their mothers as those whose parents work regular shifts, but they are more distant from their fathers (Davis et al., 2006). Parents' job dissatisfaction, however, can result in teens' exhibiting problem behaviour because of parents' unhappiness (Buehler et al., 2012). Most parents report that they feel close to their adolescent children, are able to talk about important matters with them, and know most of their children's friends. Parents believe that their involvement declines only somewhat as children become older (Bandy & Moore, 2008). However, parent and teen perspectives on their relationship can differ, something that may flag adolescent problems (Bogenschneider & Pallock, 2008).

When there is positive communication and a supportive relationship, compromises can be worked out. However, if parents react badly to a child's disclosure—for example, by becoming accusatory—they may set a vicious cycle in action. The young person becomes more secretive and defiant, and parents become more suspicious and controlling (Maccoby, 2007). Even relatively low levels of angry exchanges between parent and adolescent may test parents' patience and make teens less manageable (Buehler, 2006). Some teens become involved in parents' conflicts. As a result, their feelings of trust and security with their parents are undermined (Fosco & Grych, 2010). When parents treat their children with respect and try to understand them, teens tend to have fewer difficulties (Bogenschneider & Pallock, 2008). When teens think their parents know what they are talking about, they are more likely to accept parents' opinions and guidance (Guilamo-Ramos et al., 2006).

Later Adolescence and Emerging Adulthood
Later Adolescence
A major task for young people moving into adulthood is the development of a sense of identity, a sense of who they are based on their past and who they imagine

they will be in the future (Marcia, n.d.). Erik Erikson referred to the search for identity as a crisis. By this, he meant that it was a necessary turning point in a person's life. At this time, an individual develops mature attachment, independence, initiative, and employment. If there is no resolution, the individual suffers identity confusion. With the recent trend to more years of education, the young person matures in some ways but delays in others. Later adolescence is a period of moratorium, or a postponement of commitment (Erikson, 1982).

James Marcia expanded Erikson's ideas, adding exploration to commitment; the combination results in four possible types of identity. First, in identity achievement, there is both exploration and commitment leading to a preliminary life course. Second, when there is exploration and no commitment, the young person is in moratorium. Third, foreclosure involves making a commitment without looking at alternatives. For example, a person considering university may decide to be a lawyer because that is the family occupation, not because law really interests her. Finally, there is identity diffusion, where there has been neither exploration nor commitment (Marcia, n.d., 1966).

These types appear related to parenting styles. Authoritative parents are most likely to have children who have achieved identity. Permissive parents tend to have children in moratorium; authoritarian parents, children with identity foreclosure; and neglectful parents, children with identity diffusion (Ross & Benson, 2005). Some people worry that teenagers are overscheduled. The majority of 15- to 19-year-olds who are living with parents attend school. In 2005, they spent an average of 9.2 hours on school days doing schoolwork, homework, paid work, and housework, and 3.5 hours on weekends. Their 50-hour workweek resembles that of 20- to 64-year-olds. Those who did paid work for more than 20 hours a week did less homework and were more stressed than others (Marshall, 2007). In 2011, 27 percent of teens were in school and also held jobs (Marshall, 2012). Participation in organized after-school activities provides constructive activities. The benefit is less when these consume over 20 hours a week (Mahoney et al., 2008).

Emerging Adulthood

Emerging adulthood, roughly spanning the years from 18 to 25 or even later, has been identified as a new developmental stage between adolescence and young adulthood (Tanner & Arnett, 2009). Levinson (1978) dubbed this period the early adult transition (see Figure 7.1 on page 195). In less than half a century, these years changed from a time of entering marriage, parenthood, and long-term work to a period of self-development and building foundations for adult life. Emerging adulthood is a period of relative freedom and many possibilities. This stage is culturally based and occurs most often in developed countries. Three factors underlie the development of this stage. First, the change from an industrial to an information-based society requires specialized education. Second, women have greater educational and career opportunities. Finally, the acceptance of premarital sex and cohabitation means sex need not be postponed until marriage. As a result of these factors, the responsibilities of work, marriage, and child-rearing are postponed

(Arnett, 2011; Tanner & Arnett, 2009). Emerging adulthood can be a period of instability as the young person works through the choices open to him or her.

Scripts laying out the life course are no longer standardized (Arnett, 2011). In the Miller family, introduced earlier in the chapter, scripts were clear. Children were expected to help on the farm or in the house until they formed their own families. Women's and men's traditional roles offered some, but not many, choices. In contrast, emerging adults nowadays have the most freedom they will ever have to decide their lifestyle. Transitions to adult roles are delayed longer than in the past (Tanner & Arnett, 2009). Young adults report the greatest number of changes in their work and financial situations, and most view the changes as positive (Keown, 2009). By the time they are 25, not all young people are independent. Most are not married and do not have children, though many hope for both marriage and children in the future (Arnett, 2011). In 2011, a study of Canadian youth aged 15 to 29 years found that 13.3 percent were not in school and did not have a job. Among those aged 20 to 24 years, 15 percent were neither in school nor employed (Marshall, 2012).

STONE SOUP   **BY JAN ELIOT**

Source: Stone Soup/Universal Uclick.

Relationships change. Parents need to develop more flexibility in dealing with emerging adults' growing independence. An increasing number of young people live with their parents or return home after initially moving out (Beaupré et al., 2006a, 2006b; Clark, 2007). Okimoto and Stegall (1987) called them **boomerang kids**. When children live with parents, issues around physical and emotional privacy and parental intrusiveness become points of conflict. Typically, however, their relationships with parents are more harmonious than those of adolescents. Parents express fewer mixed feelings about their children as they move from adolescence into young adulthood (Arnett, 2007; Kiecolt et al., 2011).

Parents who understand and encourage their children's desire for independence foster healthy development. Some, however, demand a child's independence, making it a duty rather than the choice of the young person; they look upon their children as immature because they have asked for help (Soenen et al., 2009). Others, known

boomerang kids: children who return to their parents' home after moving out

as helicopter parents, have invested so much effort in raising their children that they are reluctant to let go and are ready to rescue their children from the possibility of failure (Social Technologies, 2007). Helicopter parents have received bad press, but they are not all bad. One study found that younger emerging adults and parents often communicate several times a day. Parents offer financial help and advice. When both parents and children feel that the level of help is appropriate, emerging adults develop more confidence (Fingerman et al., 2012).

Peers become less important during emerging adulthood than they were in earlier years. Emerging adults spend more time alone or with a romantic partner. The friends they have tend to be closer and to communicate on matters of personal importance. Once they marry, young men reduce risky behaviour and tend to follow social standards of adulthood (Arnett, 2011).

Time to Review

1. What are the characteristic features of adolescence?
2. How does emerging adulthood differ from adolescence?
3. How does children's growing maturity affect their relationship with their parents?

The Not-So-Empty Nest

Young adulthood used to be almost synonymous with living on your own. The situation has changed in the past 30 years. From 1981 to 2011, the number of unattached young adults aged 20 to 24 who lived with their parents increased from 41.5 percent to 59.5 percent. Among those aged 25 to 29, the increase was from 11.3 percent to 25.2 percent. More men than women were likely to be living at home (Statistics Canada, 2012o) (see Figure 7.2).

Transitions to independent living are occurring later and taking longer (Tanner & Arnett, 2009). Young people are now cohabiting or getting married later. More single young adults are choosing to continue to live with their parents or return home after being on their own. As a result, the transitional period from child-rearing to the empty nest is longer. More young adults are now in full-time post-secondary education than was the case in the mid-1970s. Finding and keeping a job that pays enough to allow independent living has been harder to do, both because of slow economic growth and the recession that began in Canada in 2008. Although the economy has recovered, the number of full-time jobs still lag behind pre-recession levels (Cross, 2011). Young people are most seriously affected (Marshall, 2011). In addition, the cost of establishing a separate household can be high, especially in urban areas such as Toronto, Vancouver, and Montreal.

Factors beyond money-related ones influence the delay in independent living. Children are more likely to live at home when parents were born in Asia or Latin America. Parents who own houses are more likely to have children at home (Turcotte, 2006a). Different life courses may produce similar effects. For instance,

FIGURE 7.2

Percentage of Young Adults Aged 20 to 24 and 25 to 29 Living in the Parental Home, Canada, 1981–2011

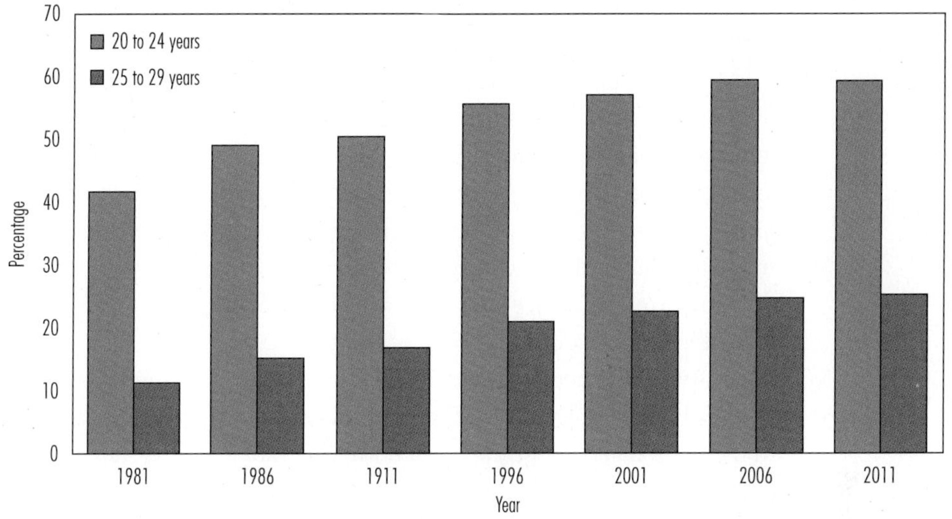

Source: Statistics Canada. 2012. *Living arrangements of young adults aged 20 to 29* (figure 1). "Census in Brief Series," Catalogue no. 98-312-x-2011003. Ottawa, Ontario. Statistics Canada. http://www12 .statcan.gc.ca/census-recensement/2011/as-sa/98-312-x/2011003/fig/fig3_3-1-eng.cfm

higher education and early pregnancy can both delay independence (Clark, 2007; Kliman & Madsen, 1999).

Some young people move away from home and come back repeatedly, a phenomenon that has been called the **revolving door**. They are more likely to return if they left to go to school or if they live in a large city. Children from stepfamilies and large families are less likely to return, as are those who were raised in Quebec (Beaupré et al., 2006a).

Both adult children and the parents they live with can benefit. The young person has the opportunity to complete an education or to find a job that will allow him or her to live independently. The parent can benefit from having someone to share both the work and the expenses of the household (Parker, 2012; Statistics Canada, 2012o). The financial and housework contributions of children tend to be quite modest, however. Children tend to do more housework in one-parent than in two-parent households. In most cases, though, the arrangement is designed to help children rather than parents (Connidis, 2010). An American study found that parents and young adult children differed over the amount of financial help the younger generation should receive. Children expected more assistance than parents felt they should give (Goldscheider et al., 2001).

Living with parents has become increasingly acceptable, but it does produce stresses. Having children at home or returning home as young adults can be stressful for parents and means an adjustment of roles, since the old parent–child ones may now be inappropriate. This situation may interfere with parents' own plans or place

revolving door: young people's repeated moving in and out of their parents' home

extra strains on their marriage. Nevertheless, many Canadian parents are quite satisfied with both the living situation and their marriages. Parents' expectations for their children's independence are important. Parents who are unhappiest with their own marriages have children who left and returned three or more times (Mitchell & Gee, 1996; Turcotte, 2006a). Most children report that the relationship with their parents has either remained the same or improved (Parker, 2012).

Many practical issues arise when parents and adult children live together: privacy for parents and children, the use of the family car, family rules and regulations, the sharing of expenses, and the use of the home for parties and other forms of socializing. The whole situation is ambiguous. On the one hand, parents feel the need to maintain control of their home. On the other, the adult "children" have a need to control their own lives. The revolving door has become so common that information and advice on living with boomerang children and parents are readily available (e.g., Jacob, 2012; Nance-Nash, 2012).

In some instances, midlife children return to their parents' home. This situation is usually the result of employment loss, relationship breakup, or poor health. In the case of marriage breakdown, both the child and any grandchildren may move in, and the grandparents are often faced with renewed childcare responsibilities to allow their adult child to enter the workforce (Brandon et al., 2007; Milan et al., 2007; Ward & Spitze, 1996).

The Sandwich Generation

At the same time as middle-aged individuals are experiencing pressure from their in-and-out children, they may also be trying to cope with the fact that their parents are aging and need assistance. As we shall see in the next chapter, the conflict between the need for help on the part of infirm elderly parents and their desire for independence is similar in some ways to adolescent–parent conflicts. Thus, the middle generation, often called the **sandwich generation**, is under stress from both the younger and older generations. The term "club sandwich" has been coined to describe midlife individuals caring for their parents, adult children, and grandchildren (Duxbury, n.d.).

The number of "sandwiched" Canadians at any one time is quite low, though numbers are hard to come by, partly because there is no single definition used in studies (Duxbury, n.d.). One study in 2004 estimated that 9.7 percent of the Canadian population aged 45 to 64 had children at home and provided care for elderly relatives. About four-fifths of these were also employed (Williams, 2004).

A number of factors contribute to "sandwiching." Parents are now older when they have children and family size is decreasing. Thus, there are fewer helpers available. Older children are living at home longer. Some have returned along with their young children. And one of the fastest-growing groups in Canada is the fragile elderly, for whom there are in many cases inadequate community supports. Although most elderly people live by themselves or with a spouse, they tend to live near relatives. As they age, they become more dependent on their children for assistance.

The burden of caring for elderly parents tends to fall more on women than on men. Middle-aged and older women provide most of the home health care.

sandwich generation: middle-aged adults who experience the stress of the continuing dependency of their children and the increasing disability of their parents

In contrast to earlier generations, many of these women have jobs. Women also provide part-time health care to aged relatives living elsewhere. In addition, many families provide assistance such as shopping, home maintenance, and home care. Even when adult children do not provide the services, they may be involved in the time-consuming and often frustrating task of locating required help. Caring for both children and elderly relatives can be stressful, especially for those with several children or those looking after more than one older person. Sandwiched workers may feel stressed, but 95 percent are satisfied with life in general (Connidis, 2010; Duxbury, n.d.; Williams, 2004).

The Social Time Clock

In our society, many aspects of life are governed by age. For example, there are minimum ages at which one can begin school, drive, drink alcohol, or vote. Marriage and family life are also affected by legal restrictions. Individuals wishing to marry without their parents' consent must be a certain age. People wishing to adopt usually have to be over a given age.

There are also social norms for the timing of life events. People say things like "I was young when I had my first baby" or "She was widowed very early." These statements indicate that we expect certain events to occur at particular times in life. This socially approved timetable has been called the social time clock, as we saw in Chapter 1.

Young people are taking longer to move out on their own, as we have seen. Cohabitation, marriage, and child-bearing are occurring later. Older people increasingly remain healthy and active even after retirement. Distinctions between life periods have become blurred (Neugarten & Neugarten, 1986). It is difficult, for example, to define when middle age begins or when old age takes over. Yet people are more likely to experience a crisis if life events occur "off time" (McGoldrick et al., 2008; Peterson et al., 2010). There are social scripts, or expected patterns of behaviour, for events such as an "empty nest." People can anticipate and plan for them. If, however, children do not leave home at the expected time, both parents and adult children may experience stress. Widowhood at age 38 is more of a crisis than at 65 (see Box 7.1.). Becoming a grandmother at 27 may be a crisis, but becoming one at 60 may be impatiently anticipated (Stark, 1986).

BOX 7.1   A Death Too Soon

Kari died on her way to work one morning. The car crash left Darren a widower at 38. His 17-year-old stepson, Killian, and his 12-year-old daughter, Alyssa, lost their mother.

Many studies have explored how survivors adjust to the loss of a spouse, but little attention has been paid to young widows and widowers or to those with dependent children. If a loss is predictable, such as the death of an elderly spouse, there is time for preparation and scripts to help the survivor. When a death is sudden and off-time, such as Kari's, there is no preparation and few scripts.

Darren has many stresses to handle. Beyond dealing with the loss of his wife, he must help the children with their grief. There are also practical issues to address. The family has lost Kari's income. Darren has a good income as a consultant, but his province-wide contracts require frequent trips. He needs to balance the demands of his work with providing a supportive home for his children. In addition, Killian may want to go to live with his biological father, whom he often sees. If he does so, Darren and Alyssa will lose another family member.

Families that have experienced the early loss of a parent and spouse face both the death and, sometimes with only limited support, the uncertainty about how to deal with the death. Some early deaths occur in the military. There, formal supports are available to bereaved families, but these may be short term. Some deaths, like Kari's, occur through accidents; some occur through sudden illness, occasionally through murder or suicide. In such instances, some families need longer-term support when a young parent and spouse dies. Part of the gap is covered by local and online support groups for young widows and widowers. Many individuals rely on family members, though these, too, may be grieving.

Sources: Boss, 2006; Hazelton, 2004; Murray, Toth, Larsen, & Moulton, 2010.

The Middle Years—A Time of Changes

The middle family years find both parents and children in flux. Families experience transitions at times more varied than their ancestors knew. The social time clock has recently become much less rigid. Emerging adults and middle-aged parents alike are assessing their lives and working out their identities. The child generation is establishing the basis of adult life; members of the parent generation are reassessing who they are as a result of changes in their families and workplaces. Midlife adults also think about how they can contribute to the welfare of those to come. Children, parents, and grandparents are all involved with decisions about work. Emerging adults are laying their foundations through education and early work experiences. Those in midlife assess their initial goals and readjust them to fit both the reality of their workplace and new values they have developed. Although they are not usually part of the middle-year families, decisions made by the grandparent generation can affect their younger children and grandchildren if they need financial or other practical assistance.

Relationships undergo change as well. Adolescents and emerging adults are establishing the basis of future intimate partnerships. They are also negotiating independence from their parents. Midlife adults need to rework their relationships with children and parents to reflect newly adjusted generational boundaries. In addition, partners assess existing relationships and either end or refresh them.

The middle years are a time of numerous changes within families—they are also opportunities for growth.

Time to Review

1. Explain why more young adults live with parents now than in previous years.
2. What are the characteristics of the sandwich generation?
3. What is meant by the social time clock?

Moving Back Home

Anneliese and Erik are 54 and 56 years old. They had been looking forward to spending time travelling, maybe moving from their comfortable house to a condo downtown. Their plans were put on hold eight months ago. Their son, Allen, was laid off when his company downsized. So he moved back home until he could find a new job. With him came his live-in girlfriend, Deirdre, who had just graduated from college. Both young people spend time on their computers in their job search; they go for the occasional interview. Between times, they are out with friends or using social media.

Anneliese liked Deirdre and secretly hoped that she and Allen would get married. Now she isn't sure she can share the house with the pair any more. Even though Anneliese held a job while her three children were growing up, she was proud that her house was always tidy and sparkling. It isn't tidy or even very clean any longer. She wasn't prepared at all for Deirdre's untidiness. It is bad enough that the room she and Allen share has piles of clothes on the furniture—dirty or clean Anneliese can't tell—but Deirdre's clothes and shoes are also scattered around the family room. Allen and Deirdre rarely tell his parents where they are going and when they'll be back. Anneliese doesn't know whether to expect them for meals. When they cook, they leave the kitchen counter piled with dirty saucepans and utensils. Neither Deirdre nor Allen offer very often to help with cleaning or even the dishes. Anneliese doesn't feel that the house is her own any more. And Allen complains that she treats them like children.

1. Explain the conflict between parent and children in terms of their role expectations.
2. What could this family have done before Allen and Deirdre moved in to make sharing the house more harmonious?
3. If you were a counsellor, what steps would you say the family might take to solve their problems?

Summary

Why Are the Middle Years of a Family Described as a Time of Transition?

The middle years of a family are a time of change and transition for both parents and their adolescent and emerging adult children. Children become independent following various timetables. Midlife adults adapt to changes in their own lives.

Why Is Midlife a Time for Assessment and What Areas of Their Lives Do Individuals Typically Assess?

Midlife is a time for evaluation. Individuals look at themselves to see if they have made a difference to society through various forms of generativity. They may need to build a new identity if there has been a major life change. The sense that they will die catches up with midlife adults as a result of personal aging and of deaths among relatives and friends. Midlife is a time for assessing work goals and for altering them. Close relationships are also evaluated. Many change their existing relationship, often finding increased satisfaction, especially after children leave home. Sex life remains important for most individuals, who consider it vital in a relationship.

What Developmental Tasks Do Adolescents and Emerging Adults Face?

Adolescence brings physical, emotional, and social change. Teens often take risks because they haven't learned to control their impulses. Peer pressure can be important, especially for younger teenagers. The understanding, support, and monitoring of parents encourage healthy development. Older teens and emerging adults need to develop a sense of identity that will guide them in choosing careers and developing relationships. Independence is delayed as emerging adults complete their education and otherwise build a foundation for adult life. Many continue to live with their parents. Emerging adults have the greatest freedom to decide present actions and future life course. Parents who encourage their children's desire for independence foster healthy development.

How Do the Continuing Dependency of Children and the Needs of Elderly Relatives Affect Family Life?

There are obstacles preventing the younger generation from living independently, such as the social trend for delayed cohabitation and marriage, employment difficulties, single parenthood, and marriage breakdown. A number of young people move back home after living on their own. In general, these arrangements are acceptable to both parents and children. Middle-aged adults may become caught between the continuing dependency of their children and the increasing disability of their parents. The pressure may be increased by off-time events, such as early widowhood or the pregnancy of an adolescent daughter. The burden of providing care for both young and old tends to fall disproportionately on women.

Class Assignments

1. Explore the opportunities for education and retraining available in your community for women in their 40s and 50s. How likely are they to find employment? In what fields? Explain.
2. How is midlife different for people who have children in their late 30s or 40s? Think about couples with "afterthought children," remarried couples wanting a child of the second marriage, and single parents who become pregnant or adopt.
3. Suggest markers of adulthood other than living alone and supporting oneself. What are the benefits and drawbacks of using such markers?

Personal Assignments

The following assignments are designed to help you look at your own family experiences:

1. Thinking about your experience or that of someone you know, explain both the advantages and disadvantages of the "revolving door"—of children moving in and out of their parents' home.
2. Who looks after older relatives in your family? Describe both the frustrations and the rewards.
3. Which midlife individuals do you admire? Give reasons for your answer.

Chapter 8
Grey Power and the Sunset Years

LEARNING OBJECTIVES

What are some of the dimensions of aging?

What can happen to lifestyles and family relationships as people age?

How do illness and death affect families?

How do different cultural groups deal with aging and death?

How do social policies affect families with older members?

LOCK UP YOUR MOMS!

Get used to the idea: one day your widowed mom might knock on your door arm-in-arm with a man you've never seen before. They'll both have a tan. And she'll say:

"Hey, kid, meet your new dad."

It's happening all the time. As women outlive their husbands, a whole generation of Canadians face the possibility of "re-patriation," usually by way of Florida . . .

They're stealing our women. And not just any of our women. They're stealing our moms!

Florida is where it's all happening for Canada's "rocker, walker and shawl" set. And it may be where your future "father" is living right now, at least for six months of the year.

Source: Jeff Mahoney, "Lock Up Your Moms," *The Hamilton Spectator*, Sept. 30, 2000. Pg. W2. Reprinted with permission of The Hamilton Spectator.

What Is Old?

Most societies have what is called a social time clock (Neugarten & Neugarten, 1986), or a sense of the age range in which certain life events are *supposed* to happen. As a result, life events that occur "on time" seem less traumatic than those that come too early or too late. When events such as retirement and grandparent-hood come at expected ages, they can be prepared for and are more acceptable. The time clock for becoming old is not that clear-cut, but it still exists.

In this chapter, we will look at how individuals and their families face aging. Growing older is a physical inevitability, but the social context has an important influence on how individuals and their families experience aging. From a macro perspective, we will look at how various cultural norms and values as well as government policies have an impact on older Canadians. From the micro perspective, we will look at how interactions between family members may change as people age. As a whole, the population is getting older. We will look at this trend and predict what kinds of changes it will bring to Canadian society.

Where Do I Fit In?

1. How might you react if you were the "kid" in the opening vignette?
2. Think about the older members in your family. What is the nature of your relationship to them? How often do you see them? What do you do together?
3. Think about how older people are portrayed in the media. Examine magazine ads, TV programs, or movies that show older people. What are they doing? How are they treated?

Dimensions of Aging

Old age is being redefined. Rather than one group of old people, most experts now see three: the "young-old" (65–74), the "old" (75–84), and the "old-old" (85 and over). While each group is different, many of the variations among individuals have more to do with physical and psychological functioning than with chronological age (LaPierre & Hughes, 2009). Decisions and events that occur earlier in life can also play a role. For example, a man who has a first child at the age of 25 may well be a grandfather, and possibly even a great grandfather, at 65. On the other hand, a man who has a child in his 50s will have parenting responsibilities that will continue into his old age.

Society recognizes several aspects of becoming old: chronological, physical, psychological, and social (Baker, 1988). All are connected to our notions of the social time clock.

Chronological Age

chronological age: the number of years a person has lived

Chronological age is the number of years a person has lived. In Canada, "seniors" are typically defined as all men and women age 65 and over (Healthy Aging and Wellness Working Group, 2006). Certain privileges and responsibilities go along with age, such as receiving a pension or having to take an annual driving test. Many people consider that old age begins at 65, but that is a relatively new standard. Does old age begin at retirement? If so, does that mean we now become old sooner than we did in the past? (See Box 8.1.)

BOX 8.1 · Aging Canadians Are Challenging the Concept of "Old"

Ask Alan Wilson to define "old" and he answers with a hearty chuckle. "It's just a number, it's how you feel," said Wilson, a spry 82-year-old who teaches line dancing classes at a seniors recreation centre in Peterborough, Ontario. "I had a heart attack 10 years ago and that didn't hold me back at all." To Wilson and many of his friends, being old is a state of mind—one that Canada's increasingly active senior set is choosing to ignore as the leading edge of the baby boom reaches the traditional retirement age of 65. So-called "elderly" Canadians are living longer, lingering on the job, and resisting the rocking chair. And as Canada gets ready to run on grey power, the very concept of age is in flux, experts say.

Source: The Canadian Press, "Aging Canadians are challenging the concept of 'old.'" Found at: http://www.cbc.ca/news/canada/story/2012/05/29/census-defining-old.html

Physical Age

Physical age refers to the physical changes that occur with age. White hair, wrinkles, and slower movement are just some of the inevitable changes. They affect how we perceive ourselves and how others treat us; as a result, they also affect our self-esteem.

Some social scientists suggest that old age begins when physical disability sets in. If we used this standard, we would have to exclude many people in their 70s or even 80s because they still remain vigorous. While much research on aging tends to focus on loss of ability and decline, Rowe and Kahn (1997) identified three components of successful aging: low probability of disease and disease-related disability, high cognitive and physical functional capacity, and active engagement with life. Another important feature of the Rowe and Kahn model is their emphasis on lifestyle factors as having a significant effect on the physical aging process.

physical age: the physical changes that occur with age

Psychological Age

Psychological age is a frame of mind and may be shown through "old" behaviour such as Granny sitting in a rocking chair, knitting. Attitude differences between the elderly and the young can be explained in part, of course, by the experience the former have gained by moving through the life cycle. Some characteristics are cohort effects (Baker, 1988; Karasik, 2005); that is, they are most likely the results of being raised during particular historical events, such as the social movements of the 1960s or the Cold War, and of being influenced by the values prevalent during their early lives. Yet it is difficult to find qualities that are characteristic of most elderly people. They show more differences than similarities, as do younger people.

psychological age: a frame of mind and behaviours associated with one's age

Social Age

Aging also has a social aspect. **Social age** is based on cultural norms that specify how we should act when we are a certain age and how we should interact with people older and younger than ourselves (Baker, 1988). The boundaries between periods of life are, however, becoming blurred. The timing of marker events, such as grandparenthood, widowhood, and retirement, are changing. Women born during the 1800s could expect to be widows in their late 50s; the corresponding age today is almost 70 (Gee, 1987; Neugarten & Neugarten, 1986). With these changes, our expectations of appropriate behaviour are also shifting. Retirement has lost its link with physical frailty and a sedentary lifestyle. Granny is probably not in her rocking chair; she is more likely to be playing golf or tennis. Attitudes toward changes in timing are not unanimous. While many people see earlier retirement as a desirable goal, others oppose mandatory retirement at a specific age.

There are sex and class differences in how aging is regarded. Men in professional positions are considered to have greater knowledge based on experience; grey hair is thus a mark of distinction. On the other hand, men who do manual labour see physical aging as a sign of failing ability. Aging can be an even greater crisis for

social age: expectations of how we should act when we are a certain age and how we should interact with people older and younger than ourselves

women, especially if they have depended on physical attractiveness to fill esteem needs (Baker, 1988; Karasik, 2005).

Developmental Tasks of Old Age

The key task for older people is accepting the shift of roles to allow the next generation to take over leadership in various areas of private and public life. This task involves a number of smaller changes. When people retire, they make room for younger employees to take over their jobs. Grandparents have a vital role in providing both moral support and practical help. The older generation must also adapt to their own physical decline. They may have to deal with the loss of spouse, brothers and sisters, and friends and acquaintances. Ultimately, they must prepare for their own death (Carter & McGoldrick, 1999b; Pitrou, 2006).

Erik Erikson (1982) describes the psychosocial task of old age as integrity versus despair. As individuals look back on their lives, they look for order and meaning. Every society has its own definition of what makes a good life; thus, the kind of meaning a person finds in his or her life may differ from one society to another. The attempt to find meaning, however, is common to all. Without a sense that life has had meaning and purpose, an individual sinks into a final despair. Time is now too short to start another life. With a sense that life has had meaning, on the other hand, a person need not fear death.

Erikson's stages were later divided into two phases. As one approaches 70, there is the desire to review one's life and give back to society. This time is prime for recording memoirs. In the late 70s to the end of life, individuals experience an "encore" phase of reflection and celebration of their lives (Cohen, 2005).

There are few differences in adjustment to old age between homosexual and heterosexual men and women (Maylor et al., 2007). They face many of the same issues around shifts in their relationships as they retire and as their health deteriorates. Relatively little is yet known about how gay men and lesbians age because many older individuals have remained in the closet, likely because when they were young, there were high levels of stigma against homosexual individuals (Connidis, 2010).

Three Key Issues

There are three key areas of conflict for older people and their family members: independence versus dependence, connectedness versus separateness, and openness versus privateness.

Independence versus Dependence

Most older Canadians (over 90 percent) live independently in the community and want to remain there (Healthy Aging and Wellness Working Group, 2006). Older people's satisfaction is related to the degree to which they can control their own lives. Stress may come from two sources: frustration at not being able to do accustomed tasks and a shift in their social roles.

The ability to remain independent is related to both the financial status and the physical and mental condition of the older individual. These factors work alone or in combination. For example, older people who cannot manage to do repairs to a house or clean an apartment can still live on their own if they have enough money to pay someone to do these things for them (Turcotte & Schellenberg, 2007). A number of older people move to smaller houses or apartments that require less care. Some maintain independence by modifying their homes or finding housing with special aids, such as bathroom modifications or a lift. Homeownership often allows seniors to maintain their independence, and homeowners are significantly less likely to be institutionalized than those who rent (Strohschein, 2011). Government services can help keep older people in their own homes, for example through the provision of grants to help finance renovations to make homes accessible to disabled persons and through the provision of homemaker and home nursing services that reduce the need for institutionalization.

The more assistance a person needs, the more independence and decision-making power are given up (Connidis, 2010). Women, who are more likely to be widowed, receive assistance from their daughters, followed by friends and neighbours, then from extended family members (Connidis, 2010; Maurier & Northcott, 2000; Turcotte & Schellenberg, 2007). Increasing disability can change the husband–wife relationship, especially when one partner must make decisions for the other.

Perhaps the most difficult adjustment comes when a partner needs to enter a nursing home. The institutionalized spouse is often angry, resentful, and depressed, while the other feels both relief and guilt (Machir, 2003). Of course, living in a seniors' residence or a nursing home greatly reduces independence. Due to rules and routines, there can also be problems practising the traditions and rituals of one's cultural background, which tend to become more important as one ages (Maurier & Northcott, 2000). In fact, however, relatively few older people live in an institution. In 2012, there were 2136 residences for the aged, which housed over 200 000 people (Statistics Canada, 2011d).

Dependence can also be related to the social perception of older people. The general public may treat them rather like children. Even more serious are the attitudes of relatives or nursing-home staff. If they see a person's condition as being worse than it is, and think that he or she is incompetent, they will try to make decisions for the older person and discourage any independence he or she might show. As a result, the older person is taught to be helpless (Fingerman & Pitzer, 2007; Harwood, 2007).

Connectedness versus Separateness

The struggle for independence often reflects tension between the desire for connectedness and separateness. In many ways this conflict between adult child and older parent is reminiscent of adolescent–parent conflicts. Older people value their relationships with their children and grandchildren, yet they also wish to maintain their own lifestyle (see Box 8.2 on page 218). As parents become older and frailer, their children may worry about them and try to limit their independence unnecessarily. For example, some children will be afraid that a parent will fall or become ill and lie helpless for hours, or even days, without being able to call for help. As a result, they will urge their parent to move in with them or to move to an institution where they can be supervised more closely, rather than working to arrange a checkup system or a method of summoning help. Since many older people resist being managed to this degree, the result is family conflict (Brosi, 2005; Kingsmill & Schlesinger, 1998).

BOX 8.2 | Not a Teasing Matter

Aunt Martha began acting strangely a year ago, after her husband's death following a long illness. Not only would she refuse invitations to go out but was very reluctant to allow us to visit any more. While she was downstairs, I saw she had replaced her twin bedroom set with a gigantic king-size bed!

I teased her about it: "What is a 74-year-old widow doing with a new king-size bed?" She got very angry and said she didn't think it was any of my business. She was sick and tired of the family's moral judgments, which she had endured all her life! Then she calmed down and told me. The man next door, a retired physician whose wife had died several years before, had begun "calling" on her. She felt so good about it. "I was a loyal wife for 53 years and it wasn't no picnic, believe me, especially when Andy got sick. Now I'm having some fun for a change."

Source: *Family Role and the Negotiation of Change for the Aged.* National Advisory Council on Aging, 1983. Reproduced with permission from the Minister of Health, 2013.

Openness versus Privateness

We all appreciate our privacy. In some cases, the older person, like Aunt Martha, may fear family members' disapproval of new ways of behaving and become secretive. Individuals with personal health problems, such as incontinence, may be embarrassed or humiliated to talk about their difficulties. Some have ostomies (openings made to allow the drainage of waste products, often into a bag). Some may find it preferable to obtain care from a stranger rather than a family member. If someone is cared for by a relative or is living in a nursing home, a private life is virtually impossible. Shared rooms and bathrooms make it difficult to discuss confidential topics or even to be private about matters such as elimination (Kuba, 2006; National Advisory Council on Aging, 2005d). For another example, husbands and wives sometimes do not share the same room in a nursing home. Even if they do, it is difficult for them to engage in any sexual activity without fear of interruption, or even in safety, if they are not provided a double bed (Connidis, 2010). The situation is even more difficult for couples who meet at the home.

Time to Review

1. What are some of the different dimensions of aging?
2. What are the developmental tasks of old age?
3. Explain three key issues that may lead to conflict between older people and their family members.

The Aging of Canada

In spite of some vagueness as to when old age really begins, one fact is clear: the population of Canada is aging. This reality represents the combined effect of several factors. As we have seen, people are living longer. The oldest members of the baby boom bulge are starting to retire and will swell the number of seniors. According to Statistics Canada, seniors aged 65 and older accounted for a record high of 14.8 percent of the population in Canada in 2011, up from 13.7 percent five years earlier (see Table 8.1 below), and the 2011 Census counted 5825 people aged 100 years and older, up from 4635 in 2006 and 3795 in 2001 (Statistics Canada, 2012m). Of the nearly five million seniors aged 65 and over in 2011, over half (56.4 percent) were part of couples, 24.6 percent lived alone, and 11 percent had other arrangements, such as living with relatives. The remaining 7.9 percent lived in nursing homes or residences for senior citizens. Between 2001 and 2011, the proportion of senior women who lived alone declined while the proportion of senior men living alone remained relatively stable (Statistics Canada, 2012j).

Since the birth rate is down, there are fewer young Canadians to offset the increase among the elderly. This imbalance will have far-reaching effects on our social and political institutions. Nevertheless, these effects are not felt equally by all parts of the country. Certain areas have an unusually high proportion of older people. The proportion of seniors was the highest in the Atlantic provinces, Quebec, and British Columbia. Alberta had the lowest proportion of seniors, with just 11.1 percent. In 2011, 7 of the 10 municipalities with the highest proportion of seniors were in British Columbia and seniors accounted for nearly 1 out of every 2 people in Qualicum Beach, B.C. (Statistics Canada, 2012m).

Economic Factors

Most Canadians will at some point retire from a long period of paid employment. Since they will continue to have expenses, they must have sufficient savings or alternative sources of income (or both) to pay the bills. In the past, pensions were often not available. If employers offered contributory plans, they were often optional. Under such circumstances, men and employed women continued to work as long as they were able. If they had a large enough income, they were able to put aside money for retirement. Otherwise, they were dependent on the support of their children or, at the extreme, of the community.

The Canadian retirement income system is made up of three pillars (MacDonald et al., 2011). The first pillar includes the government public pension

TABLE 8.1	Proportion of Persons Aged 65 and Over in the Canadian Population, 1956–2056

Year	Percentage
1956	7.7%
1961	7.6%
1966	7.7%
1971	8.1%
1976	8.7%
1981	9.7%
1986	10.7%
1991	11.6%
1996	12.2%
2001	13.0%
2006	13.7%
2011	14.8%
2031	23.0% to 25.0% (estimate)
2056	25.0% to 30.0% (estimate)

Sources: Adapted from: Statistics Canada. 2006. *Proportion of persons aged 65 years and over in the Canadian population, 1956 to 2006* (figure). "2006 Census: Portrait of the Canadian Population in 2006, by Age and Sex." Catalogue 97-551-XIE. Ottawa, Ontario. Statistics Canada. http://www12.statcan.ca/census-recensement/2006/as-sa/97-551/figures/c2-eng.cfm; Statistics Canada. 2005. *Population Projections for Canada, Provinces and Territories 2005–2031.* Catalogue 91-520-XIE. Ottawa, Ontario. Statistics Canada; Statistics Canada. 2012. *The Canadian Population in 2011: Age and Sex.* Catalogue no. 98-311-X2011001. Ottawa, Ontario. Statistics Canada. http://www12.statcan.gc.ca/census-recensement/2011/as-sa/98-311-x/98-311-x2011001-eng.pdf

programs. In 1951, the *Old Age Security Act* provided pensions for all Canadians aged at least 70. In 1966, the age was lowered to 65. Employment history is not a factor, and the applicant does not even need to be retired. However, this pension is taxable, so if the person has other sources of income or continues to work, they may have to pay back some or all of the OAS. However, if an individual has little or no other retirement income, they are also eligible for the Guaranteed Income Supplement (GIS). The government pension system is a pay-as-you-go system. This means that the present retirees are being paid from future contributions of later generations (Service Canada, 2012a).

The second pillar of the system is the Canada Pension Plan/Quebec Pension Plan (CPP/QPP). In 1966, Parliament passed legislation creating the Canada Pension Plan, a national social insurance plan funded by the contributions of employers, employees, and the self-employed. The CPP operates in all provinces and territories except Quebec, which established its own Quebec Pension Plan. The CPP/QPP was designed to provide workers and their families with a modest pension upon retirement. Payments are based on how much an individual contributed over his or lifetime of working (Service Canada, 2012b).

The third pillar consists of private pensions and savings. This includes company pensions and Registered Retirement Savings Plans (RRSPs). These plans have become increasingly popular, and it has become economically feasible for larger numbers of the population to enjoy travel and other leisure activities following retirement. In fact, these retirees are sometimes referred to as "Woopies"—well-off older people (Royal Bank, 1989).

Many inequities in pensions persist, and it is women who are often disadvantaged. Most pensions are related to the individual's lifetime earnings. Women are more likely to work part time. They usually do not work as many years as men, and they may take time off to care for children (McDonald, 2006). Many retire at the same time as their older husbands (Szinovacz, 2006). More women than men work in service occupations where there are no pensions. Women often earn less when they do work. Pensions reflect the inequities in pay. The Old Age Security pension and its accompanying income supplement were never designed to be the sole source of income in old age. Yet many women live at about the poverty line because the government pension is insufficient. However, the proportion of senior women receiving income from the CPP/QPP is increasing as a result of their increased participation in the labour force (National Seniors Council, 2011).

Median retirement age has changed due to a number of reasons. Throughout the 1970s and early 1980s, the median retirement age was around 65. In 1987, the government lowered the minimum age at which one could draw benefits from the Canada Pension Plan from 65 to 60. As a result, the median age at retirement declined (Gower, 1997), and in 2005, it was 61 years. Economic cutbacks and layoffs, illness, or caring for a family member may force older workers out of the workforce. Involuntary retirements make up about one-quarter of total retirements. The change can also be attributed to more generous private pension plans and the growing popularity of RRSPs, which make it financially possible for people to retire younger. However, the trend may be changing. Canadians aged 50 and over are working later and delaying retirement (Statistics Canada, 2012p). In June 2012, the eligibility age for the OAS and the GIS increased from 65 to 67 years old (Service Canada, 2012c).

Activities and Interests

Retirement usually marks a major change in activities, something that can be a problem for people who define their value as individuals by their occupations (Connidis, 2010). Most retirees, however, are happy and busy. They substitute active recreation, time with friends, caring for others, and volunteer work for paid work. They also take more time to rest and sleep (Stobert et al., 2006). Working women may not feel as much displacement as men, since many of them continue homemaking just as they did during their working years.

Health and Self-Care

Physical activity is an important determinant of successful aging (Gauvin et al., 2012). Health is an important factor in the amount of activity people undertake, and most of the young-old are still in good health. The older man who feels reasonably healthy is more likely to be satisfied with life. Women tend to put more value on the relationship with their children; if it is satisfying, then life is satisfying. People who perceive their friends and family members as supportive have a stronger sense of meaning in their lives. Those with strong social networks also report greater emotional well-being in day-to-day life as well as when they experience stressful life events (Charles & Carstensen, 2009).

As people grow older, physical well-being and concern about possible or actual illness become more important. Those over 75 are more likely to have a chronic health problem or disability. Most common are vision, mobility, and memory problems. Physical and mental deterioration can be made worse if an individual becomes depressed, feels helpless, and fears losing control over his or her life (Turcotte & Schellenberg, 2007). Individuals with lower incomes are at greater risk for illness and death than those with higher incomes (Strohschein, 2011). The healthcare system becomes increasingly important not only to seniors but to their families as well (see Box 8.3 on page 223).

The vast majority of seniors live in private households, where they may be cared for by others. Only about 8 percent live in nursing homes and hospitals, and most of these are over 85. Elderly people who live in senior residences or nursing homes may first have lived with other family members. Often overlooked are the seniors caring for others—a spouse, a friend, a neighbour, or grandchildren (Cranswick & Dosman, 2008). The caregiving often ends when the mental or physical health of the older person makes it impossible for the family to cope any longer. Some aspects of chronic illness can be extremely difficult to live with. For example, taking care of a person who has sleep disturbance and roams the house during the night, is incontinent, makes delusional statements, or behaves aggressively is very stressful. When an elder enters an institution, it does not mean that family contacts are cut off. Some family members go to the nursing home every day to feed or provide other care for a parent (Connidis, 2010; Stobert & Cranswick, 2004).

Whether seniors live in their own homes, with a child, or in an institution, family members, especially daughters, feel a duty to provide care, even if they have other responsibilities such as children or a job. Very mixed feelings can result. There can be conflict between responsibility to parents and to one's own family (Wilken, 2005). Disagreement among family members can add to the stress of caregiving (Scharlach et al., 2006). Some women are afraid they are neglecting their husbands or children, but feel they can never do quite enough to satisfy their elderly relative. They may become overprotective and interfere unnecessarily with their parent's independence.

In spite of the difficulties, many caregivers find looking after an older relative rewarding. Adult children who provide the most demanding care have reported that it is stressful and emotionally satisfying at the same time. Caregivers are most likely to see the rewards if they have enough practical help and financial aid

BOX 8.3 Healthy Aging: What Is the Government Doing?

By Mary Crea-Arsenio, University of Guelph

In Canada, the administration and delivery of healthcare is the responsibility of the provinces and territories, which are charged with the task of developing and implementing policies that aid in the care of seniors to ensure they are living healthier longer. The different policies created by governments to support the elderly can have profound effects on families, so it is important to understand how government action not only differs across the country but also how it impacts on families. Below are policy examples from three provinces, Ontario, Quebec, and British Columbia.

Ontario

In 2007, the Ontario government created the Aging at Home Strategy, a $1-billion investment in community-based services for seniors to live independently in their homes. The impetus for this initiative was the lengthy waiting lists for long-term care beds, which resulted in a drive toward better community supports for seniors to live independently longer. According to the Ministry of Health and Long-Term Care (2012), Aging at Home provided seniors and their caregivers with the appropriate local support services. In so doing, premature admission to long-term care homes or hospitals can be avoided.

Source: Ministry of Health and Long-Term Care, 2012.

Quebec

In Quebec, the Growing Old at Home Policy was developed in 2011 to support seniors to live longer and healthier in their homes. The investment is $2.7 billion over five years in community-based projects, housing, tax assistance, and adapted health services to support seniors. Some of the areas of focus include providing funding to over 5000 households composed of seniors for home adaptation, offering tax credits to more than 20 000 seniors for the purchase of equipment to help them live independently in their own homes, and providing respite to more than 15 000 spouses acting as informal caregivers.

Source: Gouvernement du Québec, 2012b.

British Columbia

British Columbia has come under recent attack for the lack of funding to support seniors to live independently in their homes. According to a study released by the Canadian Centre for Policy Alternatives (CCPA), cuts to residential care and home support for seniors has resulted in significant decreases in access to home and community care (Cohen, 2012). Cohen argues that "over a decade underfunding and restructuring has led to a home and community care system that is fragmented, confusing to navigate, and unable to meet seniors' needs" (p. 5). The impact of this lack of support for seniors has led to overcrowding in hospitals and increased wait times for long-term care home placements in the province.

Source: Cohen, 2012.

Considering the three provinces and what they are doing to support seniors in their home, answer the following questions:

1. What impact does policy have on family caregivers?
2. Do you think keeping seniors in their homes longer is the best approach to keeping seniors healthy?
3. Are there other strategies that can be developed and implemented at a government level to support seniors and their families?
4. What would you do if you were a policymaker?

(Connidis, 2010; Stobert & Cranswick, 2004). We will take another look at the stresses on caregivers in Chapter 12.

Death of Family Members

With medical advances and increased life expectancy, death is now regarded as belonging mainly to old age. As life expectancy has increased, so has the incidence of long and debilitating illnesses, such as cancer and Alzheimer's disease (Wilkins, 2006). As a result, when we talk about death, we need to distinguish between the actual death and the events leading up to it. Both have a profound but different impact on families (Rolland, 2003).

Terminal Illness

Terminal illness can be very stressful for families. First, both the dying person and his or her relatives must face the deterioration of physical or mental powers. Elderly people tend to fear prolonged illness and dependency more than death itself (Hill, 2005). This fear is related to the desire for independence, and in extreme cases may be expressed by refusing treatment. With degenerative illnesses, like Alzheimer's, the couple relationship is destroyed. The caregiving spouse becomes widowed for all practical purposes long before the partner dies (Connidis, 2010). Part of the stress involved in terminal illness comes from the changes in lifestyle needed to deal with the illness. A key stress factor for relatives is the time needed for the physical care of the dying person or for repeated hospital visits (Zarit, 2004). While the time and emotional commitment involved in caring for a terminally ill relative can be enormous, many feel that it is preferable to seeing the loved one institutionalized. This choice results in substantial savings to the government healthcare system and highlights the importance of family caregivers in Canadian society (Bainbridge et al., 2009).

Second, the family has to prepare for the death and for the changes that must occur in lifestyle and relationships. Individuals who know they are dying have the opportunity to look over their lives, to make plans for their families, and to say final goodbyes and make peace with people (Rolland, 2003). The ability to prepare for a partner's death does not, however, mean a smoother transition to widowhood.

Widows whose husbands die suddenly and those who expected the death suffered different reactions but felt the same loss. Preparation does not appear to ease the loss of so central a relationship (Fingerman & Pitzer, 2007).

The ability to prepare for death is affected by the information the family is given and by their degree of openness in talking about it. By the 1980s, most doctors treating patients with a terminal illness told the patient that he or she was dying. Some patients, however, may not be ready to accept the prognosis. Concerns over patient privacy may also limit how much medical staff will tell other family members (Giboney, 2001; Kuba, 2006). Even though family members know how serious the illness is, they may not give up hope until the moment of death. Ultimately, dying is something we all must face. Dr. Elisabeth Kübler-Ross has identified five psychological stages that many dying people go through if given enough time before death (see Box 8.4 on page 226).

Death and Its Aftermath

Funerals are family times. Even more than weddings, they are occasions when all the relatives gather together. Until the funeral is over, family members often forget their differences and offer assistance to one another (Baker, 1988). A funeral is also the occasion for formal leave-taking of the person who has died. As such, it is an important aspect of mourning.

During a serious or terminal illness, a homosexual partner may not be recognized as a family member by relatives. When a partner dies, grieving heterosexual spouses suffer deep grief. The understanding and support they receive helps them move through the grieving process. Before the legalization of same-sex marriage, lesbians and gay men were often denied this recognition and support, especially by medical personnel (Whipple, 2006). Negative social perceptions of gay men can complicate grief by imposing a "double stigma" on the bereaved (Hornjatkevyc & Alderson, 2011).

Adjustment to Widowhood

Widowhood initially involves a sense of loss, disorientation, and loneliness. The same responses are true for cohabiting and same-sex couples. The discussion here will focus on married couples because these are the most common.

Women who have centred their lives on their husbands and families often feel a loss of identity. They may also feel a loss of status. Over the years, the couple has built up a family identity with shared customs and habits. As married people, they have a recognized status within society. With the death of the spouse, all that is gone. Those who have looked after their partner during a long illness may feel they have lost their purpose in life. For some, however, the death comes as a relief, for example when one's partner has suffered for a long time or the relationship has been unhappy or abusive.

Women tend to manage better than men after the death of a spouse. That's probably because they depend on children and friends for social and emotional support. Men fare worse because they have usually depended on their wives for emotional support. In the crisis of death, they are often left isolated. Especially in the first year following the death of a spouse, men more than women suffer an increase in death and suicide rates (Connidis, 2010; Kuba, 2006).

Widowed people must grieve over the loss and then commit to their own continuing life. Typically, they go through three stages. First, they need to loosen their bonds to their spouse and accept the fact he or she is dead. Second, they must pay attention to day-to-day living, such as job and household management. Finally, they shift to new activities and interest in others. During this period, family relationships must be reworked to create a new balance. For example, a widow may now tell her worries to a daughter when in the past she confided in her husband. The process of mourning and adaptation to the new life is variable, but typically takes two to four years (Connidis, 2010). Some older people may experience a series of bereavements and thus go through extreme grief. They may also have limited time and energy to form new attachments (Berardo, 2001).

BOX 8.4

Kübler-Ross's Five Stages of Psychological Reactions to Death

From years of interacting with patients and their families going through the dying process, Dr. Elisabeth Kübler-Ross identified five stages the dying person goes through if given enough time before death. These stages are not gone through sequentially but rather experienced in a random order, depending on what the dying person is struggling with to go on living.

1. Denial: Rejecting the news of impending death so as to pursue life.
2. Anger: The emotions, ranging from envy, anger, rage, and resentment, about the reality that death is approaching.
3. Bargaining: An attempt to postpone death by making some kind of promise in exchange for more time to live.
4. Depression: When death can no longer be denied and the realization of what lies ahead is acknowledged.
5. Acceptance: Feelings have been expressed, bargaining is over, denial no longer offers the opportunity to pursue life, so the dying person comes to a quiet resolve that the struggle is over and life is coming to an end. The dying person begins to detach from relationships and seeks quiet solitude while waiting for her or his life to end.

Source: S. Blevins, "A Personal Journey through the Grief and Healing Process with Virginia Satir, Dr. E. Kubler-Ross, and J. William Worden," *Satir Journal,* 2 (2), 89–105, 2008.

The Economics of Death

Often, the death of a spouse means a drop in family income. This situation is especially true when an employed partner dies. Long-term hardships tend to be greater for women, since they often have limited financial resources, such as pensions, and are less likely to find a new partner. For women aged 65 years and over, the standard of living generally declines continuously for those who became widowed, while it remains relatively constant for their married counterparts (Li, 2004).

There are also the costs surrounding death itself. There may be a drop in income during the final illness because the sick person cannot work and the partner may need to take a leave of absence from a job. Funeral expenses may run high because the family wants to show their love and respect to the deceased by making elaborate arrangements. Add to these the cost of a cemetery plot and grave marker, and the total expenses can be significant.

A period of uncertainty often follows death as financial affairs are sorted out. If one partner has handled all the finances, the survivor may not even know what resources are available. A widow may not know for some time what income she is entitled to. Some survivors' pensions, for example, are based on the widow's age. If a person dies intestate—that is, without making a will—there is much greater delay and confusion. Common-law partners may be shocked to find they are not entitled to inheritance rights they expected. The growing diversity of family forms complicates the legal issues when somebody dies. The official definitions of relationships and inheritance rights may not always reflect the family dynamic. As a result, survivors may experience continuing distress until financial affairs are settled.

Time to Review

1. Describe the demographic changes that are happening in Canada.
2. What are some of the lifestyle changes that typically occur with old age?
3. What are some of the impacts of terminal illness and death on family members?

Family Relationships

We have seen how structural factors such as institutional care facilities and pensions have an effect on how Canadians experience aging. Symbolic interactionists focus on the relationships between individuals and how these are defined and perceived.

For the young-old, family relationships often undergo transformation. Most of them remain with their spouse or partner, but the relationship may change when one or both retire. Relationships with siblings usually stay the same but may become closer during a crisis such as the death or illness of a parent. The relationship with adult children often becomes more equally balanced. A new role of grandparent may be gained and needs to be defined. Sometimes, that role is actually parenting, a second time around.

Couple Relationships

The majority of older people live with a family member, especially a spouse. More men than women over the age of 65 are married, mainly because women live longer. An increasing number of older women are divorced. For a variety of reasons, more widowed and divorced men than women remarry. One key factor is that more eligible women than men are available because men tend to die earlier

ELDERBERRIES   **BY PHIL FRANK & JOE TROISE**

Source: Elderberries by Phil Frank & Joe Troise/Universal Uclick.

(Connidis, 2010). Homosexual individuals are affected like other aging adults by the imbalance between males and females, but in an unexpected way. One researcher reports, "A common complaint for older gay men is that they are vigorously pursued by older heterosexual women who are looking for mates and husbands" (Quam, 1993, para. 15).

Most couples are generally satisfied with each other. Those who were happy previously continue to be happy; the unhappy become less satisfied (Chalmers & Milan, 2005; Szinovacz, 2006). Successful marriages that last a long time involve mutual trust, support, shared philosophy of life, and commitment. The same holds true of same-sex relationships (Connidis, 2010).

Men are more likely to enter a new marriage following divorce or the death of a spouse (Connidis, 2010). Adult children may actively discourage remarriage because they see it as disloyalty to the deceased parent or because they are worried about their inheritance (Connidis, 2010; Kalish, 2005). Nevertheless, with the increasing popularity of websites such as Facebook, the number of rekindled romances among older adults is growing. First loves, for some, have endured over many years apart, and often through successful marriages to others. These renewed relationships are often successful (Kalish, 2005). A small but growing percentage of seniors are cohabiting, though it is not clear whether this choice is an alternative to marriage or to living alone (King & Scott, 2005).

Like other life transitions, retirement can have positive effects on relationships. When both partners are retired, they report better-quality relationships. In part, this improvement comes about because they are free from work-related stresses and have increased opportunity for companionship and shared activities. Couples also tend to be happier if no adult children are at home. The home atmosphere becomes more relaxed, and sharing of housework may become more equal.

Retirement, however, also presents drawbacks to relationships. Women who are still working tend to be less happy if their partner is retired. Homemakers may resent having a partner around all the time. Some men become critical of their wives' housekeeping or try to take over. These women feel they have lost personal freedom and have too many demands on their time. Conflict can occur when one partner depends on the other to fill all emotional and social needs. Some couples need to find a "good distance"; that is, a balance between togetherness and separation (Chalmers & Milan, 2005; Connidis, 2010; Szinovacz, 2006).

Sexual relationships remain important in old age. Among those who are sexually active, frequency of sex does not decrease much among those under 74 in spite of some bothersome sexual problems. Older men are more likely than older women to have a sexual partner and are more likely to regard sex as important. Sexuality is closely linked to health, especially at older ages. A good relationship, however, is more important to a majority of older people than good sex (AARP, 2010; Connidis, 2010; Lindau et al., 2007).

Relationships with Siblings

Sibling ties among older adults have received little attention until recently. Most young-old people have at least one living brother or sister. As the baby boom ages, a greater proportion will have several living siblings. This tie lasts longer than that between partners or between parents and children. The quality of sibling relationships does not usually undergo dramatic changes as people age. If they were friendly earlier, they remain on good terms. If they were bitter rivals, they remain distant (Connidis, 2010; Van Volkom, 2006). However, there are often changes in the level of contact and the kind of support among siblings as they age. During earlier adulthood and midlife, the demands of work and family life lead to a decline in the frequency of contact and closeness. With retirement and an empty nest, siblings often increase contact. In general, sisters are closest, followed by brother–sister pairs. Brothers are the most distant, although their relationships have been only slightly studied. Those who have never married and the childless widowed depend most on their siblings. The relationships of gay and lesbian siblings may depend on the degree to which they are out and the level of acceptance by their siblings. Brothers' and sisters' experience of growing up in the same family often draws them together. The illness and death of a parent can have one of two effects: siblings can become closer as they cope with the crisis, or existing enmities and jealousies can become worse. As Generation X (the baby bust) ages, they may have no brother or sister, or just one (Connidis, 2010; Kang, 2002; Van Volkom, 2006).

Relationships with Children

Most older people (80–90 percent) have at least one living child with whom they are in touch. Usually at least one of these children lives quite close to the parents, so most older people see one of their children about once a week. Contact is most often by telephone, followed in frequency by personal visits. Electronic communication is becoming increasingly common. Those who live nearby have shorter but more frequent visits than those who live at a distance. Frequent contact is not necessary, however, for a good relationship. The closest relationship is usually between mothers and daughters, partly because women are seen as "kin-keepers," those who are responsible for keeping up contacts with relatives (Connidis, 2010).

Married children are not as close to their parents as the divorced or separated and especially the never married (Sarkisian & Gerstel, 2008). Childless older people may have active social networks that take the place of children (Connidis, 2010).

When a partner is absent or unable to provide help, children often provide support (Stuifbergen et al., 2008). Distance appears to be one of the most influential factors in the risk of experiencing financial consequences. Caregivers living farther from the assisted parent were more likely to have extra expenses. They were also more likely to miss full days of work. The responsibility of providing long-distance care resulted in more work-related consequences for women than for men (Statistics Canada, 2011d).

However, the parent–child relationship is not one-sided. Almost two-thirds of older parents both give and receive support. Adult children may provide practical assistance in house and yard maintenance, and when adult children have crises such as divorce, widowhood, or the birth of a child with health problems, parents are key providers of support. Financial aid can flow in either direction (Connidis, 2010).

Like most other relationships, ties between older parents and their adult children are complex (Connidis, 2010). Troubled parent–child relationships may continue into old age. For example, parents may try to control adult children (Aronson & Weiner, 2007). The more adult children an individual has, the more likely there will be both positive and negative relationships (Ward et al., 2009). Adult children are aware of their parents' favouritism, although they and their parents may not agree on who is favoured (Suitor et al., 2006). Interactions with children-in-law are often ambivalent; that is, they have both positive and negative aspects (Connidis, 2010). A better relationship with in-laws improves the relationship with children and grandchildren. The opposite is true of a poor one (Connidis, 2010; Turner et al., 2006). When children have problems, both the parents' sense of well-being and the parent–child relationship suffer (Greenfield & Marks, 2006). The quality of communication is central to any relationship (Harwood, 2007). The fact that people are surviving longer now can create problems over who is eligible to fill certain age-related roles. One study of five-generation families found that there was confusion as to who had the rights and privileges of old age (Hagestad, 1986). Was it the very oldest, who were in their 80s and 90s? If so, where did it leave their children, who were in their 60s and 70s, an age often considered "old"? In these five-generation families, elderly people were looking out for still more elderly parents and were missing out on the benefits that can come with old age.

Relationships with Grandchildren

Family relationships across several generations are becoming increasingly important. As the population ages, there are more years of shared lives. It is becoming more and more common for grandparents, great-grandparents, grandchildren, and great-grandchildren to know one another. Grandparents often fulfill functions, like childcare, usually regarded as the responsibility of the nuclear family (Bengston, 2001; Connidis, 2010; Sheehan & Petrovic, 2005). More than three-quarters of those aged 65 or over have at least one grandchild and, on average, they have nearly five (Turcotte & Schellenberg, 2007).

The relationship between grandparents and grandchildren is often considered special because it is not complicated by parental responsibilities. Unlike the relationship with grown children, the emotional closeness is affected by how near grandchildren live to grandparents and how often they see one another. It is also influenced by the relationship between parents and grandparents. In general, grandchildren are close to grandparents with whom their parents have a good relationship. They are not as close when their parents and grandparents are not emotionally close (Monserud, 2008). Other factors, such as physical distance, are also involved. Seniors are now using email to keep in touch with widespread family members (Veenhof & Timusk, 2009). Most seniors see a grandchild at least once a month.

Having grandparents has been reported as being of particular significance to young adult grandchildren, who regard grandparents as important sources of emotional gratification and conveyers of family histories and traditions (Thiele & Whelan, 2008). Grandfathers tend to have less contact with grandchildren compared to grandmothers, but one study found no gender differences in overall role satisfaction (Stelle et al., 2010).

Being grandparents or great-grandparents can give the elderly a new lease on life. They see a part of themselves that will survive. Having grandchildren is also an opportunity to come to terms with both the satisfactions and disappointments of raising one's own children. It provides grandparents with the pleasure of seeing their children experience the fulfillment of being parents (Connidis, 2010; Walsh, 1999).

Grandparents can have a positive influence on their grandchildren. They can provide financial help, unconditional love, and emotional support. They also act as role models, encourage hard work, share family history, and teach religious and moral values. When grandparents are more involved, grandchildren have fewer emotional problems and more pro-social behaviour. In some cases, grandchildren are also better prepared for school values (Schlesinger & Schlesinger, 2005).

The impact of divorce on grandparents has now received some recognition. The relationship between grandparents and their adult children is important because the latter control access to the grandchildren. This connection is doubly important if the ex-spouse has custody of the grandchildren. Grandparents can provide support and a haven for grandchildren when problems at home are too difficult to live with (Connidis, 2010). The expectation that they be a resource for the family but at the same time not interfere can be a burden for some seniors. Often, family counselling ignores grandparents, although they may play a vital role in family interactions. The provinces vary in the rights given grandparents for access to a grandchild. The best interest of the child is often the criterion used, but the way this is applied can differ (Goldberg, 2003). If access is cut off, both grandparents and grandchildren may lose an important emotional resource. With the increase in remarriages of both older divorced parents and divorced adult children, the number of step-grandparents is growing. In some cases, these relationships are close (Connidis, 2010).

Grandparents Caring for Grandchildren

Many grandparents provide part-time or full-time care for their grandchildren. When parents are unable to care for a child, grandparents are the most likely family members to take on a surrogate parenting role (Gladstone et al., 2009). One grandmother, for example, heard a knock on her door at 3 a.m. She found her two-month-old grandson in a basket on her doorstep. "What choice did I have?" she said, "My daughter was back on the street" (Kornhaber, 1996, p. 133). Some grandparents take in their grandchildren because they feel guilt over how their own children turned out (Zimmerman, 2005). Grandchildren may need care because of their parents' death, divorce, mental illness, or incarceration (Connidis, 2010; Coyle, 2005; Zimmerman, 2005). Grandparents, especially grandmothers, are an important childcare resource for working parents, either for the whole day or before and after school. By one estimate, 1 in 5 children receives such care. Grandparents may provide full-time care for a limited period during family crises. They may also act as co-parents in a multi-generation household. Or they may be in "skipped generation" families with no middle generation in the home (Connidis, 2010). There are benefits to grandparental care. Siblings can be kept together and family and cultural ties maintained (Fuller-Thomson, 2005b; Levin et al., 2006). In 2011, nearly 5 percent of children aged 14 years and less lived in households that contained at least one grandparent. Of these, 0.5 percent lived in skipped-generation families; that is, with grandparents and not with their parents (Statistics Canada, 2012j).

When it is apparent that grandchildren need care, grandparents draw on their personal resources to meet the challenge. Once the immediate crisis is dealt with, the children's continuing needs call for a re-evaluation of the grandparents' abilities and resources. Some grandparents find that parenting grandchildren is more enjoyable than parenting their own children was. They feel they have more wisdom and experience, are more relaxed, and have more time and attention to give than they had for their own children (Dolbin-MacNab, 2006). In time, skipped-generation families settle into a new "life-as-usual" mode (Callahan et al., 2005).

Researchers have paid more attention to difficulties that caregiving grandparents face. On the practical side, grandparents need to reorganize space in the home and adjust their use of time and activities (including work) to accommodate a child in the household (Callahan et al., 2005). Financial needs also require consideration; some families face poverty when grandchildren move in (Wang & Marcotte, 2007).

Children coming into their grandparents' care have suffered family breakup and bring emotional baggage with them (Zimmerman, 2005). Many caregivers report that children, especially those over 10, have behaviour problems and are difficult to discipline. They may long for their parents, no matter how neglectful or abusive they have been, and resist changes and the unfamiliar rules and standards of their grandparents' home (Callahan et al., 2005; Levin et al., 2006).

Grandparents may wonder how well equipped to parent they are. Older ones especially may no longer have the energy they desire to care for children. They may be in poorer health and have physical limitations associated with aging (Coyle, 2005; Dolbin-MacNab, 2006; Wang & Marcotte, 2007; Zimmerman, 2005). They also face challenges over changing family roles. For example, if a grandfather has died, his widow may be a single parent for the first time and may worry about the lack of a male role model. Beyond the stress of parenting someone else's child, the grandparent is trying to be a parent and grandparent at the same time

(Dolbin-MacNab, 2006). If the grandparent is employed or is caring for an elderly relative, there is the possibility of role overload (Fuller-Thomson, 2005b).

Grandparents face handicaps in looking after their grandchildren. The Canadian government does not automatically recognize grandparents as legal custodians of their grandchildren unless a formal adoption takes place. As a result, full-time care-giver grandparents cannot identify their live-in grandchildren as dependants on their income tax. They also cannot have them covered on their private medical or dental insurance plans (Gladstone et al., 2009). Grandparents may have difficulty enrolling a grandchild in daycare or school or in accessing medical care if they do not have custody. Guardianship can provide security and protect the family from parents' threats to remove the child (Levin et al., 2006; Zimmerman, 2005); however, the cost of getting guardianship, especially if the parents contest it, may be prohibitive (Callahan et al., 2006).

Caregiving grandparents have both practical and information needs. When asked about their needs, grandparents listed housing repairs; clothing, dental and optometry services; and educational support, such as tutoring, for the children (Levin et al., 2006). Caregiving grandparents need to be made aware of services available to all families. They also need information about the growing number of groups for grandparents in their situation (Callahan et al., 2005; Zimmerman, 2005).

In spite of the difficulties these families experience, grandchildren raised by grandparents do not differ much from children raised by both parents in terms of their relationships and general well-being. The only major difference is that they tend to do less well in school. Grandchildren, in turn, can help their grandparents around the house and provide emotional support in crises (Connidis, 2010).

Minority Groups and Aging

Immigrants

Cultures differ greatly in their views on how to care for the elderly. Certain ethnic groups have strong beliefs about not "abandoning" relatives to nursing homes. Older people may feel isolated and shamed both because they are away from family and community and because elders are traditionally cared for within the family. Immigrants whose parents remain in the "old" country may feel strong conflicts between cultural expectations and responsibilities to their spouses and children (Coleman et al., 2006). Families that arrived earlier are more likely to consider seniors' residences and care homes. Nursing homes designed for a specific ethnic group help reduce the feeling of being cut off from one's culture. The waiting lists may, however, be very long (Maurier & Northcott, 2000; National Advisory Council on Aging, 2005b, 2005c).

Recent immigrants are more likely to live in three-generation households than those born in Canada, especially if they came from Asia or Latin America (Glick & Van Hook, 2002; Turcotte & Schellenberg, 2007). Black Canadians are also overrepresented in skipped-generation homes, especially among families of Caribbean origin, who have strong cultural norms favouring family care (Fuller-Thomson, 2005a, 2005b; Statistics

Canada, 2008a). Such households are most common in British Columbia and Ontario, where there are areas with high concentrations of newcomers.

Elderly immigrants living and aging in Canada face many challenges. The major challenges in their daily lives include language barriers, the disappearance of traditional social networks, and inability to access economic resources, including pensions and social benefits (Zhou, 2012). If they do not have other financial resources, they may have no choice where to live. One study found that nearly half (48 percent) of recent immigrants aged 65 and older lived with relatives, compared with only 5 percent of the Canadian-born (Thomas, 2001). The more recent the immigration, the more likely elders are to live with family members (Turcotte & Schellenberg, 2007). Many seniors of ethnic minority groups experience cultural barriers to accessing service, and this may lead to lower levels of care and greater health disparities (Chau & Lai, 2011). When they join their children in Canada, elders leave behind familiar attitudes toward seniors and customary ways of life. Their children may have adopted mainstream cultural norms. Thus, older immigrants may feel further displaced. They therefore become more dependent on other family members (Zhou, 2012).

There are also ethnic and class differences in the way people deal with death. North American culture tends to minimize everything that has to do with death. This tendency is reflected in the preference for a hospital as the place for dying, in the funeral industry's control of the ceremonies, and in the short time allowed for bereavement leave from work. Such practices make it difficult for some cultural groups to retain their traditional customs. For some ethnic groups, to die away from one's home and family compounds the tragedy. The presence of extended family members influences where a person wishes to die and have his or her remains kept (Usita, 2007).

In coming years, the numbers of immigrant elders will certainly increase, and they will need appropriate services.

Aboriginal Peoples

The Aboriginal population in Canada is much younger than the non-Aboriginal, although it too is aging and the number of Aboriginal seniors is growing more rapidly than the non-Aboriginal senior population. Statistics Canada projects that by 2017, seniors will make up 6.5 percent of the total Aboriginal population. Most Aboriginal seniors live in communities where the majority of the residents are Aboriginal. Relatively few live in urban centres. Many still retain their Aboriginal languages (Turcotte & Schellenberg, 2007).

Traditionally, among Aboriginal peoples in North America, the grandparent generation was responsible for socializing the children. Members had both practical knowledge and a wealth of cultural information they could pass on. In return, their grandchildren had the honoured responsibility of helping them remain independent. If elders had no grandchildren, they became informal grandparents to other children, who filled the grandchild role (Vanderburgh, 1987). Currently, Aboriginal children under the age of six are more likely to be living with grandparents than non-Aboriginal children.

The Elder role was eroded through the coming of Christian missions, with their accompanying residential schools, which removed children from their homes and cultures. In addition, during the 1960s and 1970s, many children were apprehended by child welfare authorities and placed with non-Aboriginal foster and adoptive families. As a result, Elders were no longer vital members of society: the socialization of children had passed to other people. Since children were no longer available to provide practical assistance, it also became more difficult for older people to retain their independence. Now the role of the family is being taken on by the community through services such as home support for the elderly and on-reserve nursing homes (Castellano, 2002; Vanderburgh, 1987).

In recent years, there has been a renewal of interest in traditional Aboriginal ways (see Box 8.5 below). Elders are once again valued as transmitters of culture. In the Far North, attempts are being made to reinstate the role of Elders as advisers (Brunes, 2004). A 2001 survey found that about half of Aboriginal children living off-reserve who could understand or speak an Aboriginal language had received help learning it from grandparents (Turcotte & Schellenberg, 2007).

Elders may, however, be filling a role somewhat different from the traditional one. They no longer act only within the confines of their family, but also in the context of voluntary groups such as Elders' circles (Statistics Canada, 2008a). Elders are included in school and college programs across the country, both to provide encouragement for education and to strengthen ties to Aboriginal traditions (Sinclaire & Storm, 2006). The Aboriginal Elder/Outreach Program was established in Saskatchewan in 1999 (Saskatchewan Education, 2001). The Ontario Arts Council supports the Aboriginal Artists in Schools program (Ontario Arts Council, n.d.). Valuable life experience has been redefined to include how to deal with schools, social service agencies, healthcare facilities, and the legal system. Indeed, such knowledge may be just as important for survival as traditional methods of hunting, fishing, or agriculture. In addition, elders are seen as custodians of the traditional culture, from which the younger generations have been alienated (Turcotte & Schellenberg, 2007; Vanderburgh, 1987).

Aboriginal seniors often lack socioeconomic supports, which places greater pressure on their health. Compared to non-Aboriginal seniors, Aboriginal seniors are more likely to reside in a home in need of significant repairs or in one that is overcrowded. An additional challenge is that Aboriginal seniors, like many immigrant seniors, face education and literacy barriers (Beatty & Berdahl, 2011).

BOX 8.5   Elders in the Past

There is no single definition of Elder. Traditionally, in First Nations, Inuit, and most ethnocultural minority cultures, Elders are those people, usually older, who are recognized by the community as possessing great wisdom and are called upon as an authority to advise or act on important family and community matters. The term "Elder" in some cultures referred to and may still refer to any older person to indicate respect, honour, and special status, as aging in many cultures is associated with experience, wisdom, the transmission of cultural heritage and language, leadership roles in the community, and, in some cases, spiritual knowledge. The term "Elder" has come to mean many different things to Elders themselves. It may mean frail elderly or it may signify wisdom and experience and/or spiritual knowledge; it may define a state of being to achieve or it may just mean old.

Source: Susan Judith Ship. *Our Nations Elders Speak.* 1997. Found at: http://www .niichro.com/Elders/Elders7.html (accessed Dec. 5, 2012).

Social Policies and Seniors

The greater number of elderly people in the population will call for changes and may create conflicts in society. Many of our myths about aging and the elderly will be challenged. Older people are remaining vigorous and independent much longer as a result of healthcare advances (National Advisory Council on Aging, 2006). Because of improved pensions, fewer elderly people are now living in poverty. In fact, the number of poor seniors has declined even as the total numbers of elderly people have risen sharply. Thus, we can expect an increase in "grey power" that is already reflected economically in the increasing number of television commercials aimed at older people. We can also expect pressure on governments to maintain, or even improve, services such as pensions and healthcare.

For the young-old, governments may encourage longer working lives by making it easier for workers to gradually transition from full-time work to full retirement. In an economy where more jobs are knowledge-based, it is possible and even desirable for employers to keep older workers. Older workers will be able to support themselves financially while still paying taxes to support social services. New tax, pension, employment and workplace policies that make it possible to combine work and retirement in any number of ways may be required from governments.

For the 75–84 age group, policies should help ensure healthy lifestyles and provide individuals with flexibility and knowledge to arrange their financial affairs. For instance, a network of community-based services to provide financial advice to the elderly could be implemented (Klassen, 2012). Hospital closures and the centralization of health services may have profound impacts on seniors who do not have access to a vehicle and may live in locations with limited transportation services (Ryser & Halseth, 2011). One study found that seniors who lived closer to resources and amenities such as banks, grocery stores, or places of worship were more likely to walk than those who lived further away (Gauvin et al., 2012).

Historically, family caregiving has been regarded as a private responsibility in Canada, not an area for public policy development. For the old-old, some suggest that governments should actively help individuals remain in their own homes. We have seen that many seniors prefer this option. However, there is a growing recognition that this may have unintended negative consequences for the family members who care for seniors. These include worse personal health, injury, depression, anxiety, fatigue, financial problems, and loss of employment. Researchers and practitioners in the field are currently implementing practices to better support caregivers, and many of these initiatives are being evaluated (Lilly et al., 2012). Various provincial and federal policies play a part in reducing the caregiver's burden, for example federal tax benefits for informal caregivers. Some provinces also support informal caregivers. For example, Ontario has the Family Medical Leave, which provides job security and up to 8 weeks of unpaid leave within a 26-week period so that employees can care for a family member (Williams et al., 2011). Since many of the old-old are women, gender considerations are essential (Klassen, 2012).

Can Canada continue to provide services at the present level or even improve them? It depends who you ask. Some think the solution rests with seniors and point to the taxes seniors will pay on their pensions and retirement savings. Others suggest that immigration can make up for the dwindling workforce.

Along with such pressure, there have been repeated alarms over the ability of coming generations to shoulder the tax burden for services to the elderly. In recent years, governments have increasingly shifted costs for present and future care to individuals. Every three years, the Canada Pension Plan is reviewed to determine whether the benefits and contribution rates should be changed to ensure that it remains fair and sustainable and that it responds to the evolving needs of Canada's aging population and to changes in the economy and labour market (Human Resources and Skills Development Canada, 2012d).

Others consider that lower expenses in other service areas will help cover the costs of services for seniors. For example, the dwindling number of younger people means lower expenses for education and correctional services, which will offset some of the costs for seniors (Bannerjee & Robson, 2009; Infrastructure Canada, 2008).

Still, mythical and stereotypical portraits of persons, such as the ones in Box 8.6, aggravate the tension between generations. Although they are likely to come under challenge, they persist as an integral part of the general images younger people have of older ones and have given rise to the popular concept of a "generation gap."

BOX 8.6 Myths versus Facts About Older People

Myth: Older people are all the same.
Fact: Each generation of older people brings its unique historical and cultural experiences with it as its members age. As in the rest of society, older people have different backgrounds and beliefs. They like to be treated as individuals.

Myth: Older people are a burden to society.

Fact: Older people contribute in many positive ways. In 2004, nearly 22 percent of people aged 65–69 took an active part in the labour force. Older people also play active roles in their communities: 10 percent of people aged 65 and over contribute time as volunteers, and, on average, they volunteer for more hours than younger people. Research has shown that they are more likely to provide financial and practical assistance to their families than they are to receive it. Many older people also care for children or ill relatives and friends.

Myth: Older people need looking after.

Fact: Contrary to popular stereotypes, most senior older adults live in their own homes and enjoy a measure of independence. Many older adults remain active and independent through hobbies, travel, volunteer activities, and meaningful relationships with family and friends.

Myth: All older people eventually become "senile."

Fact: The majority of older people do not experience significant memory loss. Alzheimer's disease and other dementias affect less than 2 percent of people aged 65 and older, and less than 4 percent of people aged 75 and older.

Source: Susan Reid, *Myths Vs. Facts About Older People*, Centre for Research on Youth at Risk, St. Thomas University. Found at: http://www.stthomasu.ca/research/youth/manual/myths.htm

One major concern in providing services to older people is "generational equity"; that is, each generation getting a fair share of resources. One fact remains: our society will be faced with major adjustments as we adapt to the increasing number of older people. Legislators and service providers will need to come up with innovative plans if the needs of all citizens are to be met (Infrastructure Canada, 2008; Maurier & Northcott, 2000).

Time to Review

1. Describe the various relationship changes that occur with aging.
2. How do Canadian seniors in minority groups experience aging?
3. Which social policies in particular will have an impact on seniors and all Canadians?

What to Do with Mother

In this chapter, we have seen how aging brings about changes that affect not only the person getting older but also those around her or him. As the Canadian population is getting older, more and more people will have to face situations involving aging relatives, and for many, this will include their parents. As you read the following case, think of how cultural norms and social policies have an impact on people's decisions about how to care for aging parents.

Mother fell again today. At least this time she didn't break anything, but I had to leave the daycare where I work and lost a whole afternoon of pay. My husband, Frank, and I are having enough problems financially, and I really need all the hours I can get. I have suggested to Mother that we look into a nursing home, but she refuses to talk about it. "In our culture, daughters take care of their mothers," she tells me, "they don't send them away to strangers." It's not like she couldn't afford it. My father worked for CN for nearly 40 years, and Mother still gets his pension every month. It would be enough to pay for a modest but comfortable retirement home with full care.

I asked them at the daycare for a paid leave to take more care of Mother, but I was told that they don't have anything like that. If I was pregnant, that would be something else. . . Frank tells me that I shouldn't worry about it so much. If the best solution is to put her in a home, then I should just do it. That's what he did with his mother after she got Alzheimer's. I reminded him that his two sisters were the ones who actually looked for the home and that they still went to visit her every day.

1. What are some of the social factors that are having an impact in this story?
2. Do you think the decision about how to care for an aging parent is entirely personal?
3. If you were the woman in this story, what would you do?

Summary

What Are Some of the Dimensions of Aging?

The population of Canada is growing older as a result of the aging baby boom generation and a low birth rate. Chronological age is the number of years a person has lived. Physical age refers to the physical changes that occur with age. Psychological age is a frame of mind and may be shown through "old" behaviour. Social age is based on cultural norms that specify how we should act when we are a certain age and how we should interact with people older and younger than ourselves. There are sex and class differences in how aging is regarded. The key developmental task for older people is accepting the shift of roles to allow the next generation to take over leadership in various areas of private and public life. There are three key areas of conflict involving older people and their family members: independence versus dependence, connectedness versus separateness, and openness versus privateness.

What Can Happen to Lifestyles and Family Relationships as People Age?

According to Statistics Canada, seniors aged 65 and older accounted for a record high of 14.8 percent of the population in Canada in 2011. The Canadian retirement income system is made up of three pillars: the government public pension programs—the old age security pension OAS), the Guaranteed Income Supplement (GIS), and Canada Pension Plan/Quebec Pension Plan (CPP/QPP)—and private pensions and savings. Median retirement age has changed for a number of reasons. Health is an important factor in the amount of activity people undertake, and most of the young-old are still in good health. The vast majority of seniors live in private households, where they may be cared for by others.

The majority of older people live with a family member, especially a spouse. Older couples are generally satisfied with each other. Successful marriages that last a long time involve mutual trust, support, shared philosophy of life, and commitment. The same holds true of same-sex relationships. Like other life transitions, retirement can have positive effects on relationships. Sexual relationships remain important in old age. Most young-old people have at least one living brother or sister. With retirement and an empty nest, siblings often increase contact. Most older people have at least one living child with whom they are in touch. When a partner is absent or unable to provide help, children often provide support. Family relationships across several generations are becoming increasingly important. The relationship between grandparents and grandchildren is often considered special. In general, grandchildren are close to grandparents with whom their parents have a good relationship. Being grandparents or great-grandparents can give the elderly a new lease on life. Many grandparents provide part-time or full-time care for their grandchildren. Grandparents face handicaps in looking after their grandchildren. The Canadian government does not automatically recognize grandparents as legal custodians of their grandchildren unless a formal adoption takes place. In spite of the difficulties these families experience, grandchildren raised by grandparents do not differ much from children raised by both parents, in terms of their relationships and general well-being.

How Do Illness and Death Affect Families?

Terminal illness can be very stressful for families. Widowed people must grieve over the loss and then commit to their own continuing life. Typically, they go through five stages. Often, the death of a spouse means a drop in family income.

How Do Different Cultural Groups Deal with Aging and Death?

Cultural groups differ greatly in their attitudes toward the elderly. Immigrants are more likely than other Canadians to live in three-generation families. Elderly immigrants living and aging in Canada face many challenges. The major challenges in their daily lives include language barriers, disappearance of traditional social networks, and inability to access economic resources, including pensions and social benefits.

Among Aboriginal peoples in the past, Elders held an important role in transmitting cultural values to the young; however, this role was eroded. In recent years, there has been a renewal of interest in traditional Aboriginal ways. Elders are once again valued as transmitters of culture. Aboriginal seniors often lack socioeconomic supports, which places greater pressure on their health. An additional challenge is that Aboriginal seniors face education and literacy barriers.

How Do Social Policies Affect Families with Older Members?

The greater number of elderly people in the population will call for changes and may create conflicts in society. Many of our myths about aging and the elderly will be challenged. For the young-old, governments may encourage longer working lives by making it easier for workers to gradually transition from full-time work to full retirement. For the 75–84 age group, policies should help ensure healthy lifestyles and provide individuals with flexibility and knowledge to arrange their financial affairs. For the old-old, some suggest that governments should actively help individuals remain in their own homes. However, there is a growing recognition that this may have unintended negative consequences for the family members who care for seniors. These include worse personal health, injury, depression, anxiety, fatigue, financial problems. and loss of employment. Various provincial and federal policies play a part in reducing the caregiver's burden. One major concern in providing services to older people is "generational equity"; that is, each generation getting a fair share of resources. Our society will be faced with major adjustments as we adapt to the increasing number of older people.

Class Assignments

1. Discover what facilities and services are available in your community for senior citizens. What are the difficulties in acquiring needed services?
2. Three options for the care of frail elderly people are going to an institution, living with relatives, and receiving services in their own homes. Describe the advantages and disadvantages of each of these options for older people and their relatives.

Personal Assignments

The following assignments are designed to help you explore your own family experiences and your expectations for the future:

1. Among the people you know, who do you think of as old? What characteristics, in your opinion, distinguish old and not old? Why?
2. Even though it seems far in the future, describe what you feel would make life worthwhile once you are retired. Be realistic. What steps can you take beforehand to make these plans attainable?

PART 5

CHANGES IN THE FAMILY

Chapter 9
The Lone-Parent Family—The Future Majority?

Orange Line Media/Shutterstock

LEARNING OBJECTIVES

What are the trends in lone-parent families?

What are the various paths to single parenthood?

What is the place of single parenthood in the family life cycle?

What is the quality of life of single-parent families (such as their economic and social welfare), including that of the children?

What is different about the very young single mother and the single father?

Rose is an accountant and an executive in her firm. When she was 37 and still single, she decided not to put off motherhood any longer. She considered adoption, but learned she would probably receive an older child, not the baby she wanted. So she decided to become pregnant through artificial insemination. Eighteen-month-old Alec spends days with a nanny and evenings with his mother.

After living with Jason for nearly a year, Suzanne, now aged 35, became pregnant. In spite of their stormy relationship, they married. After 10 years, she and the children left—Jason had assaulted her. As long as she's careful, she can make ends meet with her salary and the child support Jason pays. She's grateful her three children can go to their grandmother's before and after school. She doesn't know how she'd manage without her mother's help.

Cassie, 24 years old, has moved from one live-in relationship to another since she dropped out of school at the age of 17. She has held many jobs as a store clerk or waitress, but hasn't held any for long. She has two sons, aged five and three. She hopes her new baby will be a girl. All her children have different fathers. Her latest boyfriend is threatening to leave. He doesn't want a child and resents spending money on Cassie's boys. She has applied to welfare for help.

Andrew thought that he would be married forever. But he became a single parent at 44 years old when his wife died of cancer. He now lives with his two teenage children. Because he has a steady job, he is able to make ends meet. Since the children are older, they are somewhat more independent, but time is still often at a premium.

● ● ● ● ○

As a whole, North American society expects adults in the family to come in pairs, one of each sex—husband and wife, mother and father. Single parents offend against what Dr. Ben Schlesinger (1990) calls the "Noah's ark syndrome": they don't come two by two. Even many single mothers seem to accept the two-parent family as the ideal (Nelson, 2006b). (See Box 9.1 on page 244).

Yet for many years, the single-parent family has been among the fastest-growing family types in Canada. More children are experiencing single-parent families, and at younger ages. By the age of 16, 1 in 5 children born in the early 1960s had lived in a single-parent home. This "milestone" occurred by age 12 among children born in the early 1970s, by age 8 among those born in the early 1980s, and by age 5 for those born in the 1990s. According to the National Longitudinal Survey of Children and Youth, instituted in 1993–94, all signs indicate the trend is for more children to experience living in a lone-parent family at even earlier ages.

In this chapter, we will look at lone parenthood as an increasingly common experience. This trend is the result of several social factors, which we will examine in detail. We also recognize that within the category of lone-parent families, there is much diversity, often as a result of the different paths to lone parenthood. We will also look at how the lone-parent form can affect the parent and children in these families. Social policies and the wider cultural context also have an impact on the experiences of those living within this family form.

Where Do I Fit In?

1. What did you think as you read the stories in the opening vignette?
2. What is your experience with lone-parent families, either directly or indirectly through other family members or friends?
3. For many years, the single-parent family has been among the fastest-growing types in Canada. Why do you think this is happening?

BOX 9.1 — A Note on Terminology

In the past, and even now, some sociologists, social workers, and other concerned individuals refer to some families as "broken" or "not intact." Even Statistics Canada defines an "intact" family as "a family in which all children in the household are the biological and/or adopted children of both members of the couple" (Statistics Canada, 2012q, p. 17). Generally, a broken family is one that does not conform to the standard North American family model—married, opposite-sex parents and their children. Lone-parent, step-, skipped-generation, and blended families are all collectively grouped under the title "broken."

Of course, the use of the term "broken" implies that these families are somehow incomplete and dysfunctional. But consider two families. The first is a married couple with their three biological children, but the parents are verbally and physically abusive toward each other and their children. The second is a divorced single mother with her two children, and she uses an authoritative parenting style and there is no abuse. Which family do you think is more broken?

As we have seen, Canadian families are incredibly diverse. This is the reality, and each of the many family forms has its own advantages and challenges. The sociological perspective begins with the understanding that individuals make decisions and act in a context of powerful social forces that directly and indirectly affect them. If society characterises certain family types as "broken," this then becomes an additional challenge for people in these families. Teachers, healthcare workers, counsellors, and other social service providers can make the situation worse if they presume that some family forms are "broken." In this book, we have avoided the value-laden terms "intact" and "broken" when referring to family structures. Instead, we use more neutral descriptive terms, such as "lone-parent" or "single-parent" family.

Trends in Lone-Parent Families

Statistics Canada's definition of a **lone-parent family** is "a mother or a father, with no spouse or common-law partner present, living in a dwelling with one or more children" (Statistics Canada, 2009d). The share of lone-parent families increased slightly from 15.7 percent in 2001 to 16.3 percent of all census families in 2011. About 8 in 10 lone-parent families are headed by a woman, accounting for 12.8 percent of all census families, while male lone-parent families represent 3.5 percent of all census families. However, the proportion of lone-parent families headed by a male is growing (Statistics Canada, 2012q).

It is important to read statistics carefully. The actual proportion of Canadian families who have ever experienced lone parenthood is much higher than the number reported in any single year. Lone parenthood is often temporary. Many families spend some time as one-parent families before, after, or between two-parent episodes. Numbers can be deceptive in other ways too. Many single-parent families are that in name only. There may be live-in partners and others who act as parents, although they are not officially considered as parents (Ambert, 2006).

In 2011, the proportion of lone-parent families was higher than the national average in the territories—Nunavut (28.2 percent), Northwest Territories (21.3 percent), and Yukon (20.5 percent)—and provincially was highest in Nova Scotia (17.3 percent). Close to 20 percent of children aged 14 and under lived with lone parents in 2011, up slightly from 18.0 percent in 2001. Of these, 82.3 percent lived with a female lone parent (Statistics Canada, 2012l).

lone-parent family: a mother or a father, with no spouse or common-law partner present, living in a dwelling with one or more children

TABLE 9.1 — Lone-Parent Families in Canada, 1991–2011

Year	Total Lone-Parent Families		Male Parent		Female Parent	
	No.	%	No.	%	No.	%
1991	953 640	12.9	165 240	17.3	788 395	82.7
1996	1 137 510	14.5	192 275	16.9	945 230	83.1
2001	1 311 190	15.7	245 825	18.7	1 065 360	81.3
2006	1 414 100	15.9	281 406	19.9	1 132 694	80.1
2011	1 527 840	16.3	327 545	21.4	1 200 295	78.6

Note: Numbers may not add up due to rounding.

Sources: Adapted from: Canadian Council on Social Development, *A Profile of Canadian Families*, 2006, Pg. 3; Statistics Canada, A. Milan, M. Vézina and C. Wells, *Family Portrait: Continuity and Change in Canadian Families and Household in 2006, 2006 Census*, Catalogue No. 97-553-XIE, Pg. 15; Statistics Canada, *Portrait of Families and Living Arrangements in Canada, 2011.*

Lone-parent families are more frequent among visible minorities than among non-visible minorities, both for foreign-born and Canadian-born populations. In the 2006 Census, lone parenthood was most common among individuals reporting Somali, Jamaican, and Haitian ancestries. Lone parenthood was most rare among Chinese and South Asian, as well as most European groups (Mata, 2011). Most immigrants come to Canada as single individuals or as married families; comparatively few come as lone parents. How many become lone parents after their arrival is unknown.

Aboriginal families are more likely than others to have just one parent. In 2011, 34.4 percent of Aboriginal children lived in single-parent homes, the majority headed by a lone mother, compared with 17.4 percent of all Canadian children (Statistics Canada, 2012u). By group, 37.1 percent of First Nations children, 29.8 percent of Métis children, and 25.8 percent of Inuit children lived in lone-parent families (Statistics Canada, 2012u).

The Path of Single Parenthood

As we can see in the stories of Rose, Suzanne, Cassie, and Andrew with which this chapter opened, there is no one road leading to single parenthood. In 1961, the majority of lone parents (61.5 percent) were widowed. The number of widows was higher at this time partly because many men died during World War II. Less advanced medical technology and poorer health conditions also contributed to early deaths. A small proportion (2.7 percent) reported never having been married, and the remaining 35.8 percent were divorced or separated. Over time, the proportion of widowed lone parents has declined steadily. By 2011, the most common legal marital status for lone parents was divorced or separated (50.8 percent), followed by never married (31.5 percent), while 17.7 percent of all lone parents were widowed (Statistics Canada, 2012r).

Several factors are involved in the changing paths toward single parenthood. One is the increase in unmarried mothers. Although both the pregnancy and the birth rates among teens are considerably lower now than they were 30 or 40 years ago, fewer of today's teen mothers are married and fewer place their babies for adoption. So despite the lower rate of teen pregnancy, the overall result is an increase in the number of single teen mothers. In 1931, less than half of 1 percent of lone-parent families were the result of births to unmarried women, in contrast to 22 percent in 1996 (Milan, 2000).

More recently, divorces have increased due to changes in the law in 1981 and 1986 that made them easier to obtain and more acceptable. A mother who is divorced and has custody of her children would be considered a lone parent, even if the children regularly visit their father. Cohabitation has also increased, and statistically these relationships are not as stable as marriages. Underlying all these factors is the waning of the emphasis on the traditional nuclear family and the growing acceptability of variations in the forms families take.

Society has also come to regard children as separate from marriage (Ambert, 2006; Cherlin, 2009; Milan et al., 2007). North American culture now emphasizes individualism and self-gratification rather than responsibility. Working mothers have become commonplace, and family benefits are available to help them support their children; therefore, many more unmarried mothers choose to raise their children alone.

There is evidence that people have grudgingly accepted single parenthood after divorce as a reality, but they fail to see the situation as ideal. Although non-marital sex is increasingly accepted, child-bearing outside marriage still receives little social support. In one study, the author conducted a content analysis of American social science and popular literature of almost the entire 20th century. The results showed a substantial decline in negative depictions of divorce. However, this tentative acceptance of divorce did not extend to increased acceptance of non-marital child-bearing (Usdansky, 2009).

The life patterns of never-married, divorced, and widowed lone parents vary in a number of ways and may have less in common than is usually imagined. Because the majority of lone parents are women, most of the discussion will focus on their experiences. They include poor, never-married women with several children, like Cassie; older professional women who have chosen to be lone parents, like Rose; widowed women and men, like Andrew; and a growing number of the divorced, like Suzanne (Ambert, 2009; Anderson, 2003). These differences in life patterns include the age at which the person became a single parent, the likelihood of marriage and remarriage, current life circumstances, and the impact of the life-cycle stage when single parenthood began. Many of these factors are interrelated, though current living circumstances vary. The lone parent can live without the presence of another adult; have a live-in friend, either male or female, with or without a sexual relationship; have a live-in weekend friend; have an out-of-house heterosexual or homosexual relationship; or live with relatives (Anderson, 2003).

How Long Does It Last?

Lone parenthood can end for various reasons—remarriage, cohabitation, change of custody, or independence of children—but several patterns are noticeable in the length of lone parenthood and the exit from it.

Many young women who were teen mothers marry, about half before the age of 30. They usually wait a year or more after their baby's birth. Nearly half (46 percent) enter common-law relationships. They are more likely than older mothers to remain single, separate, divorce, and marry more than once (Luong, 2008).

Experiences of lone parenthood vary between formerly married and common-law couples. Among formerly married parents, about half of divorced and 60 percent of the separated had children, and they were usually older than those of common-law parents. For most of these families, this was the first experience of a union's dissolution. More than half of divorced Canadians, especially women, do not plan to remarry, especially if they have children. Many are choosing common-law unions instead. Divorced women with young children are the least likely to enter a union (Statistics Canada, 2012l). The continuing involvement of fathers with their young children following divorce likely deters the development of any new relationship.

As a group, widows are the oldest when they become single parents and remain lone parents the longest. They are least likely to remarry. A few women have more than one lone-parent period. The likelihood of remarriage depends on how desirable individuals think marriage is, how eligible they themselves are, what barriers such as children or religion exist, and how many eligible partners are available (Wu, 1994).

Less is known about men's experience as lone parents than women's. We do know that there are far fewer male lone parents and they are typically lone parents for shorter periods.

Single Parenthood and the Life Cycle

Differences in people's experiences are related to life-cycle issues. Women who have never married or cohabited begin their families through parenthood. Others start a lone-parent family after the couple relationship ends.

Age is important to the experience of single parenthood. Pregnancy during adolescence comes when most young women are struggling with the issues of independence from their family of origin. They often do not have realistic plans for future employment and have not finished their education. For young fathers, many of the same factors are true. Those who are younger are less likely to be able to make meaningful financial and social contributions to the rearing of their children (Ambert, 2006; Luong, 2008). We will look at teenage mothers in greater detail later in this chapter.

The age factor also affects older women. They are more likely to have completed their education and established careers. They are often better able to support themselves and their children. Older single women tend to have high ideals for marriage and an unwillingness to settle for anything less. Some women seek out a man to father a child or make use of artificial insemination. In this case, pregnancy is not accidental but the result of a woman's wish to become a parent (Hertz, 2006). Despite the revisions to the *Assisted Human Reproduction Act* in 2012, the federal principles enshrined in it still remain. Children born of assisted reproductive technology, as well as their parents, are eligible for the same social recognition and assistance as children who are born through conventional conception or are legally adopted (Assisted Human Reproduction Canada, 2012).

The divorced and widowed must both deal with the pain and anger that surrounds the end of a marriage. For such individuals, age is once again a significant factor in the single-parenting experience. How soon after marriage did the breakup occur? What were partners' roles within the marriage? Long-term homemakers may not have job skills necessary to match the standard of living in their marriage. Divorced couples can share family assets (Cochrane, 2007), but early in the family life cycle, there may be more debts than assets. Widows have the greatest chance of being financially stable. They do not share resources with an ex-spouse, and the family has generally had more time to acquire assets.

The situation for the formerly married or partnered is complicated by the age of the child at the time single parenthood begins. The impact of single parenthood varies according to whether the child is a new baby, a school-aged child, a teenager, or a young person on the brink of leaving home. Since children's needs and developmental tasks correspond to the different stages, they will make different emotional and financial demands on their parents (Anderson, 2003).

The Quality of Life

To better understand how the many single-parent families in Canada—most of which are headed by females—manage, it is important to look at their economic circumstances, housing, and social life.

Single Parents and Economic Survival

In the past, the one-parent family that needed financial aid was seen as being personally responsible for their economic problems and was regarded with some suspicion by social workers and other officials. The original Ontario legislation establishing the Mother's Allowance in 1920 strictly defined who was eligible for financial help. It followed similar legislation in Manitoba (passed in 1916) providing for payments to morally upright women with dependent children (Lessa, 2003). The Canada Assistance Plan was introduced in 1966 to share the costs of social assistance between federal and provincial governments. Under this plan, lone parents were classified as "unemployable" until their youngest child reached 18 years. But in the 1980s and 1990s, provinces increasingly made women, including those with young children, subject to the same work-related requirements as men. While this policy change was intended to reduce the dependency of lone parents, without flexible working arrangements and available and affordable childcare, these changes had a negative impact on single mothers (Cooke, 2009). In 1998, the federal government increased support to low-income families with children through the National Child Benefit. The goals of this benefit were to reduce child poverty, reduce overlap in social assistance programs, and encourage parents to find jobs. Currently, the Canada Child Tax Benefit is a tax-free monthly payment made to eligible families to help them with the cost of raising children under 18 years old. In addition, the National Child Benefit Supplement (NCBS) is paid monthly to low-income families with children under 18 (Canada Revenue Agency, 2013a).

As a group, lone-parent families have the lowest average total incomes. In 2008, female lone-parent families had the lowest average total income of all family types, $42 300, or 70 percent of the $60 400 earned by male lone-parent families (Williams, 2010). Nearly half lived below the poverty line. In 2009, lone-parent families headed by a female had the lowest median net worth of any family type in Canada at $17 000. In comparison, lone-parent fathers had a median net worth of $80 000 (Statistics Canada, 2011e). This reality was especially true for families with lone mothers below the age of 25, like Cassie, who had not graduated from high school and had more and younger children. Many of these were dependent on family benefits or welfare. As one would expect, higher education and more work experience are consistently found to increase the rate at which women leave social assistance. Also, the presence of children, particularly young ones, can make leaving social assistance more difficult (Cooke, 2009). This suggests that policies that support single parents getting more education and finding better jobs would help them break the dependency on social assistance.

The employment and income of lone mothers in Canada increased between 1980 and 2000. Much of the increase was among single mothers aged 40 and older, and was related to their higher level of education. An increase in employment among younger mothers appeared related more to changes in policies around social assistance. The trend toward greater employment among single mothers is unlikely to continue because so many are already employed (Myles et al., 2008). A mother in a common-law relationship who separates from her partner is at greater risk of poverty because the law provides her less protection than it does divorced mothers.

A study of incentives to help long-term welfare recipients become self-sufficient found that childcare and transportation problems, as well as physical and emotional disabilities, were barriers to employment (Michalopoulos et al., 2002). Lone mothers are over-represented among the chronically unemployed (Brooks, 2005). Many lone mothers are discouraged from working by the lack of available and affordable childcare. In 2010, regulated childcare spaces could accommodate only 19.9 percent of Canadian children 0–12 years old (Early Childhood Development, 2012). An international survey by the OECD (Organisation for Economic Co-operation and Development) ranked Canada last among developed countries as to access to childcare. Canadian families also pay among the highest childcare fees in the world (Canadian Centre for Policy Alternatives, 2009).

Where the mother is employed or studying, 50 to 60 percent use regulated daycare, with higher rates in Quebec, which has promoted childcare in regulated centres (Cleveland et al., 2008). In 1997, Quebec introduced $5-per-day regulated childcare for four-year-old children. In 2003, the price was increased to $7 per day, but all children aged 12 years and under were eligible for care. Quebec has the highest proportion of children 0–12 years old for whom there is a regulated childcare space (37.4 percent) compared to the rest of Canada (19.9 percent) (Early Childhood Development, 2012).

According to one study, working lone mothers experienced a great deal of tension in juggling work, family, and daycare. They do more combined paid and unpaid work than married mothers or men (Sauvé, 2009b). They feel more tired and overloaded, and have more trouble balancing the demands of home and work. In addition, single mothers worry more that their childcare plans will fall through. During classroom discussions, college students, many of whom are single parents, complain about problems in finding childcare during school breaks.

Lone parents face long-term challenges too. They feel they have fewer opportunities for promotion because their family responsibilities prevent them travelling in their jobs or working long hours. They are affected by inflexible working hours, long commutes, and, in some communities, lack of daycare. Many single mothers have dead-end jobs with low pay and little possibility for promotion. Lone parents, especially younger women, are at risk of income instability. That is, they are less likely to have a steady income. Loss of a job often means instant poverty (Ambert, 2006; Morissette & Ostrovsky, 2006).

In spite of its drawbacks, government assistance is often the only reasonable alternative for single parents, especially when their children are young. Lone mothers make up the largest category of people on social assistance (Pollack, 2009). It does not, however, provide an adequate standard of living, since benefits fall below the poverty line (National Council of Welfare, 2011). Furthermore, a stigma is attached to receiving benefits. Recipients are often regarded as freeloaders. They are open to invasion of privacy and judgments by professionals who administer the welfare system. Some places have established "snitch lines" where callers can report suspected welfare cheaters anonymously. All in all, there is growing pressure on mothers to seek employment, especially when governments are cutting social welfare spending.

Housing

Housing is the single largest expense for most single mothers. Low- and moderate-cost housing can be difficult to find because of cuts in funding for building new units and the conversion of older, cheaper areas into luxury apartments and condominiums. Lone-mother families, including Aboriginal ones, are more likely than others to spend over 30 percent of their income for sometimes inadequate housing. Even more would do so if they did not receive housing subsidies (Rea et al., 2008; Statistics Canada, 2008a; Will Dunning, Inc., 2007). Poor single women depend on public transportation to reach jobs and services beyond walking distance. Thus, employment and housing choices may be limited. Single mothers are likelier than others to live in low-income areas for longer periods of time (Frenette et al., 2004).

Most lone-parent families cannot buy a home and tend to live in apartments or co-op housing. Such accommodations, especially where rent is geared to income, contain large groups of female-headed single-parent families (Ambert, 2006). One proposal is to build multi-family housing units. These can ease the heavy demands placed on a single mother by allowing her friendship, shared childcare opportunities, and a level of safety not available in a single-family detached house or condo (Blackstock, 2006).

Some families who live in low-rent housing complexes face prejudice. For example, children may be stereotyped as troublemakers and other youngsters forbidden to play with them. Nevertheless, a nucleus of longer-term residents can provide lone-parent families with a social life and practical help (Boyce, 2006).

Social Life

According to an older survey of social services agency staff, many parents lack emotional support and social activities. Most single parents, however, reported adequate contact with others, although a few were lonely. Half were involved in leisure activities at least once a week. When asked what problems they encountered regarding leisure activities, they cited lack of money. Some found that timing was inconvenient. There can be scheduling conflicts with a job or with the need for after-school care for (City of Calgary, 1985). Relatives and neighbours provide social activities, especially in stable communities (Boyce, 2006).

Social support refers to two areas: (1) the supportiveness of society as a whole, and (2) the immediate sources of emotional and practical help. Most single mothers have informal networks made up of relatives, neighbours, and friends who provide information and practical assistance, support them emotionally, and bolster their self-esteem. Most support comes from other females. A few single parents find members of their networks so critical or demanding that they add to their stress levels. Both lone fathers and lone mothers have higher rates of mood disorders and substance abuse disorders than their married counterparts. Social support significantly reduces the likelihood of these disorders and is more of a protective factor for lone fathers than lone mothers (Wade et al., 2011). Parents with poor support systems may not be able to cope with emergencies or long-term stress. As a result, they may become clients of social service agencies to get the backup they need. There has been an explosion of Internet websites devoted to lone parents. These offer everything from dating sites for single parents to suggestions about raising children alone to how to make money from home (Anderson, 2003; Edin & Kefalas, 2005; Hansen, 2005; Nelson, 2006b).

Source: Barry Maguire.

Are Children in Lone-Parent Families at Risk?

In view of the difficulties many single mothers face, an important question is the effect on children of growing up in such a family. Studies have focused on children's problems rather than their strengths, such as resilience. Nevertheless, findings are anything but definite. Children raised in lone-parent families are stereotyped as being more likely to become emotionally disturbed or delinquent. There is some truth in this, but the facts are much more complex. Although children in lone-parent families are at risk for problems, most do not have unusual difficulties (Amato, 2005; Ambert, 2006; Chapple, 2009). It is also important to remember that many negative results, including academic and behavioural problems, have multiple hidden causes. For example, a girl who is living with her single mother might need to work 30 hours a week to help pay expenses. When she does not do well in school, we cannot tell if her marks result from living with a single mother or from working so many hours. We will look at three aspects of adjustment: school achievement and employment, family life, and personal adjustment.

School Achievement and Employment

Children from lone-parent families where the parent has divorced or never married do not, on average, do as well in school as children in stable two-parent families. By their early 20s, they are more likely to have dropped out of school and less likely to have technical qualifications or be pursuing postsecondary education. Those who spend less time in a single-parent family and have fewer brothers and sisters are more likely to stay in school. So are those who have only one parent because the other one has died. The development of children whose mothers have a good income is similar to children with married mothers (Amato, 2005; Amber, 2006). Dropping out of school affects other aspects of life. Employment prospects are, of course, affected by education. Generally, adults who grew up in a single-parent family have a lower income, are more likely to have received welfare, and are less likely to own their home. Those from divorced homes are likely to start work earlier than those from a two-parent family or with a widowed mother (Amato, 2005; Ambert, 2006; Luong, 2008).

Family Life

Two aspects of family life are affected by lone parenthood: relationships within the single-parent family and relationships within families formed by adult children of single parents.

In lone-parent families, parents and children may not be as close as in stable two-parent ones. Some problems may arise because of stress, both from time demands on the parent and the result of a breakup (Cooper et al., 2009). Single parents, especially young mothers, are less likely to be emotionally supportive of their children; they use harsher discipline and are often more inconsistent—that is, they do not use an authoritative parenting style (Amato, 2005; Barnett et al., 2008). Single mothers have worse mental and physical health than partnered parents and the population in general (Cooper et al., 2007), a problem that affects the quality of their parenting. Children who were unwanted at birth have lower levels of psychological well-being (Logan et al., 2007). Three-year-olds whose mothers had changed partners were likelier than others to be aggressive or anxious. The more partner changes, the worse the outcomes for the child (Osborn & McLanahan, 2007). When mothers use a hostile parenting style, children have more difficulties in school and in relationships (Ross et al., 1998; Thomas, 2004). Children raised in lone-parent families often receive less parental supervision, and especially that which might be provided by fathers (Kerr & Michalski, 2007). On the other hand, single parents may also comment that as a result of their having had to grow up a little faster, their children appear to them to be more mature than children of the same age living in two-parent households (Weiss, 1979).

Individuals who grew up in lone-parent families because their parents had divorced are more likely to enter partnerships at an early age. They are also more likely to have a child as teens. Young women also tend to leave home earlier, especially if their parents have remarried (Anderson, 2003). Once they have married, they are more likely to divorce. Besides growing up in a lone-parent family, other influences are early marriage and cohabitation before marriage, both of which are tied to higher divorce rates (Ambert, 2006).

Personal Adjustment

Young adults whose parents separated before they were five are more likely than others to have long-term emotional difficulties, to have committed a serious crime, or to have had a child outside marriage. They are more disruptive and unhappy, and seem more worried as teenagers than those whose parents did not divorce. Many, however, showed similar behaviour before their parents' separation. It is difficult to know how much has been caused by divorce and how much by factors like family conflict (Ambert, 2006).

Explanations for Difficulties

Several explanations are offered to account for the differences between children from one-parent and stable two-parent families. First, some may be explained by economic hardship. Many children from lone-parent families resemble others who grew up in poverty. Second, the quality of parenting provided by single parents may contribute. Young mothers may be immature. Some use an uninvolved style; others are harsh. Mothers who are depressed, which is common after family dissolution, are less sensitive to their children's needs. Third, stress can include a parent's change of partner, loss of contact with a non-residential parent, and any move away from friends and family. Fourth, conflict between parents and between parents and children can lead to emotional and behavioural problems. Finally, there may be a genetic factor: some personality characteristics, such as aggressiveness, may be partly biologically influenced (Amato, 2005; Ambert, 2006).

The problem with these explanations is that they do not apply to all families. At best, they provide only partial answers. Lone-parent families, as we have seen, are a varied group with quite different histories. There may also be cohort effects. Young people are more likely today to live, at least for a time, with a single parent. These explanations also fail to account for the influence, for good or ill, of extended family members and friends.

Time to Review

1. What are some of the economic characteristics and challenges of lone-parent families?
2. What are some of the housing and social life challenges facing single parents?
3. What are some of the potential risks facing children in lone-parent families?

A Special Worry—The Teen Mother

Teenage mothers are women who have their first birth under the age of 20. Many have expressed grave concern over the so-called "epidemic" of adolescent mothers. There are fears that they are doomed to live on welfare and that their children will be troubled and possibly abused (Lessa, 2003). The real story is more complex.

First, there is no epidemic of teen births. Even in the United States and Britain, where the rates of teen pregnancies are double those in Canada, numbers have fallen since 1990 (McKay, 2006). During 2010, the proportion of births to Canadian women under 20 was quite low, at just over 4 percent of all births. Only 102 babies were born to girls under 15 (Statistics Canada, 2012s). Of the rest, most were born to women of 18 and 19, an age when individuals are often considered adults. Fewer teens are giving birth now than in the 1970s, partly because more turn to abortion and partly because fewer become pregnant. What has changed, however, is that most teen mothers are now single mothers (McKay, 2006; Statistics Canada, 2012s). Teen births, especially second and third ones, are much more common among Aboriginal peoples than among the rest of the Canadian population. In 2009, 20 percent of births in Nunavut were to 15- to 19-year-olds (Guèvremont & Kohen, 2012).

The concern over teen births is focused on the fewer younger ones rather than the older ones, who are in the majority. These younger mothers have not finished growing physically and have just begun the developmental tasks of adolescence. They have the least education and seem likeliest to spend most of their lives in poverty. They are also more often known to social service agencies than older mothers. Most of the following discussion will therefore focus on younger teens.

Why do teenagers have children? There is no simple answer. Factors related to early motherhood include poverty, membership in a lone-parent or stepfamily, poor school performance, and a family history of teenage child-bearing (Amato, 2005; Ambert, 2006; Luong, 2008). Few plan to have a baby. Those who really do not want to have a child are more likely to use contraceptives and, should pregnancy occur, resort to abortion. Many pregnant teens do not see strong reasons against having the baby, even if they do not really want to be mothers. Often, they feel that their life prospects are unpromising. Many have school difficulties even before they become pregnant. When young mothers have suffered emotional deprivation, a baby may promise emotional closeness. For some, having a child marks the beginning of adulthood. Cultural factors may also be involved. For Inuit children, a teenage mother might not be associated with negative health outcomes. In these communities, teenage pregnancy may be perceived differently than it is in non-Inuit communities (Guèvremont & Kohen, 2012).

Teen child-bearing has an impact on the parents of the teens. Often the youngest teen mothers live at home. Financial resources are stretched by the needs of the young mother and her child (Ambert, 2006). Young parents, married or not, are more likely to be poor than older ones as a result of lower education and less work experience (National Council of Welfare, 2011). Although many fathers in their teens and early 20s care about their children, they may be hard put to support

teenage mother: a woman who has her first birth under the age of 20

a family. Once the baby is born, the teen mother may have difficulty returning to school, especially if she has dropped out before becoming pregnant (Bissell, 2000; Luong, 2008). Even when teen mothers marry, they rarely improve their financial status greatly because of their husbands' poor prospects (Gillmore et al., 2008; Luong, 2008). Those who become mothers as teenagers are likely to have a lower educational level (Luong, 2008).

Teen mothers face unique stresses. It is difficult to be both an adolescent and a parent. Responsibilities to a baby make a normal dating life difficult. Some teen mothers bring casual sexual partners home without regard to the effect on their children. They also experience more than the usual number of stressful life events—illness, death of a baby, or loss to the child welfare system (Ambert, 2006).

Children of teen mothers face problems that other children do not. Low birth weights, usually the result of prematurity, are most common among girls under 15 or women over 44 years. Low birth weight results in more deaths among newborns, and higher levels of physical and learning problems (Garriguet, 2005; Rotermann, 2007b). Very young mothers often know less about how to look after a child and how a child develops. Teen mothers are somewhat more likely to abuse or neglect their babies than others (Ambert, 2006).

The kind of support the young teen receives from her own parents and other relatives may prove crucial for her future, for example allowing her to complete her education or hold a job. The younger the teen, the more likely grandparents (the teen's parents) will help with baby care and financial support. Mothers receiving such help usually have better mental health and are thus better parents (Anderson, 2003).

Yet support can bring conflicts. Disagreements may arise over how children should be raised or over who is responsible for what. In the worst cases, the child is used as a weapon in the parent–grandparent relationship. For example, if the grandmother complains about her daughter's irresponsibility, the daughter might threaten to move out and cut off any contact between grandmother and grandchild.

These problems are symptoms of boundary and role confusion. When three generations live together, confusion about who should fill parent and child roles may result because of an unclear division of responsibilities. Is the single mother an adult or is she a child? Ordinarily, the individual has established her own adult identity before becoming a parent. Since she has not separated from her parents, she is still filling the role of a child in the family. Her motherhood, however, marks her as an adult. Who should act as the child's parents?

The well-being of adolescent mothers and their children depends both on the characteristics of the mother and on the family and community of which she is a part. If she wants an education, has support from her family, and lives in a safe community, she and her child are more likely to overcome the disadvantages of her early parenthood.

The Single Father

The proportion of lone-parent fathers is growing. In 2011, 21.4 percent (nearly 1 in 5) of single parents were men, mainly because mothers are less frequently being awarded sole custody of children following the breakdown of a union. Men tend to become single parents in the middle and late years of the life cycle—few are lone parents in their teens or 20s. The children of lone-parent fathers tend to be older. Men are lone parents for shorter periods than women because they are more likely to marry or cohabit (Beaupré et al., 2010).

Single fathers, like single mothers, are expected to be solo primary caregivers and primary breadwinners. However, single fathers, more so than single mothers, are expected to be the sole economic support for their families (Hook & Chalasani, 2008). Single fathers tend to spend less time in caring for young children than single mothers do. Single fathers spend approximately 14 more minutes on childcare per day than married fathers, 12 minutes less than single mothers, and 46 minutes less than married mothers. The difference between mothers and fathers narrows as children get older (Hook & Chalasani, 2008).

When we compare lone mothers and lone fathers, we find more similarities than differences because fathers experience many of the same stresses and frustrations as mothers (Pruett, 2000). Both men and women face economic problems following separation or divorce. Mothers, however, experience greater financial disadvantages because they tend to be less educated and earn less pay.

What of the Future?

All forecasts suggest that single-parent families will increase, especially as the result of divorce. Many young people will spend part or all of their childhood in such families. This fact raises a number of issues for all of us.

First, the level of poverty is high among single parents. As we shall see in more detail in Chapter 15, poverty has far-reaching effects on children's physical and intellectual development. In addition, children from low-income families tend not to stay in school. They are therefore more likely to end up in lower-paying jobs, with the prospect of raising poor families. Ultimately, this cycle will affect all of us through the cost of providing the income support programs or other services many of these families will need. Social policies, such as more available and affordable childcare so that single parents can work, may go a long way toward improving the lives of children in single-parent families. In the long run, such investments will have many benefits, both for individuals and for society.

Second, fathers are important to children's development. We need to look at ways to encourage the greater involvement of fathers with children in female-headed single-parent families. Doing so will include looking at the appropriateness of contact with particular fathers, for example a violent individual. In addition, there may be some need to overcome the resistance of mothers who fear losing custody.

Third, many single parents receive much emotional and practical support from their extended families. It is important for agency personnel to encourage this support. Too often, they devalue or undermine it (Anderson, 2003). The future well-being of the family depends in part on the continuing involvement of relatives and friends.

Finally, it is important, especially for the sake of the children, to eliminate the stigma against single-parent families that remains in society. If society as a whole recognizes that single parents are, for the most part, as concerned and competent as the majority of other parents, we will have come a long way toward that goal.

Time to Review

1. What are some of the characteristics of teenage mothers?
2. What are some of the characteristics of single fathers?
3. What is the likely future of single-parent families?

A New Situation

This chapter opened with four stories of single parents who each had a different path to single parenthood. We have seen that lone parents are a fast-growing proportion of Canadian families and that these families face many challenges. As you read the following case, think of how the wider social context is having an impact on the individual family members.

Sofia was living with Allan when she became pregnant in her mid-20s. When she refused to have an abortion or place the baby for adoption, Allan left her. He never provided any child support. On one occasion, he reported her to provincial child welfare authorities for throwing drunken parties and neglecting baby Graham. Investigation found the allegations groundless.

While Graham was a preschooler, Sofia received welfare. She attended a family support centre that helped her navigate government red tape and provided advice on childcare and child development. Once Graham was in school, however, she was pressured by the government to find a job. She has worked in a restaurant kitchen at a low wage since then. She has made ends meet by sharing her apartment with her sister and later with a friend. When her son was young, Sofia arranged to work an early shift and her friend made sure Graham got to school. Sofia picked him up after school. She has focused her life on Graham and has supervised him closely. Even as a young teenager, he checks to learn her opinion about his activities, clothes, and even his food.

She has had numerous financial crises. One apartment mate moved out and left her footing the entire rent for the month. Following an injury, she needed money to pay physiotherapist's fees not covered by provincial insurance. Another time, Graham needed expensive shoes because of difficulty fitting his feet. When a crisis arose, she phoned her parents, who lived in another province, and they pitched in financially. Sofia has done her best to be a good mother.

Recently, Sofia found a boyfriend, Will. They have many similarities in their backgrounds and Will has a steady job. Sofia hopes that he will be there for her as Allan was not.

1. What factors have helped Sofia cope with the pressures of single parenthood?
2. What problems do you think may arise in the future? Why?
3. What advice would you give Sofia as she faces the future?

Summary

What Are Some of the Trends in Lone-Parent Families?

For many years, the lone-parent family has been one of the fastest-growing types in Canada. Lone parents and their children now experience less stigma than in the past, although some remains. Children in single-parent families are often expected to have emotional or behavioural problems. They tend to leave school earlier and have lower paying jobs than individuals raised in two-parent families. Their families of procreation may be less stable. Many of their difficulties, however, can be explained by financial hardship, family conflict, and quality of parenting rather than by the number of parents in the household.

What Are the Various Paths to Single Parenthood?

Life patterns vary among the never married, divorced, and widowed as to the duration of lone parenthood and the likelihood of marriage. Differences in people's experiences are also related to life-cycle issues. Individuals who become lone parents during adolescence have quite different experiences from those whose lone parenthood begins in middle age. The ages and needs of the children also affect the parents.

What Is the Quality of Life of Single-Parent Families (Such as Their Economic and Social Welfare), Including That of the Children?

Many lone parents have limited emotional support and social activities, partly because of the cost of entertainment and partly because of the lack of time. Most single parents receive emotional support and practical help from relatives and neighbours. A few must depend on social agencies. Many female lone parents, especially young ones, live below the poverty line. Those who are employed often have dead-end jobs or face barriers such as childcare difficulties. The quality of housing is related to income levels.

What Is Different About the Very Young Single Mother and the Single Father?

Teen mothers experience conflict between being an adolescent and the needs of their children. Many live below the poverty line, since they have limited education and job skills. Babies of younger mothers may be at greater risk for health and psychological problems. Mothers who receive support from relatives are more likely to complete school and enter employment. Such support, however, can result in conflict between the generations.

The proportion of lone-parent fathers is increasing, mainly because mothers are less frequently being awarded sole custody of children following a union breakdown. Single fathers, more so than single mothers, are expected to be the sole economic support for their families. Although their circumstances vary, single fathers are usually older than single mothers and are more likely to be employed, to have more education, and to earn more income.

Class Assignments

1. Some individuals believe that being a single parent is a handicap in our society. Others point out that it has its advantages. What arguments can be made for each side?
2. A large percentage of single-parent families headed by women live below the poverty line. What effects might this have on the development of children raised in such families? Consider both short- and long-term physical, psychological, and social aspects.
3. How does single parenthood differ for men and women? Consider work, childcare, school, extended family relationships, and any other aspects that seem relevant.

Personal Assignments

The following assignments are designed to help you think about your own family experience:

1. Do you think it is ethical for a woman to choose to become pregnant if she is not married? What factors affected your answer? Does it make any difference if a single person who chooses to adopt a child is male or female?
2. On the basis of your own experience or that of someone you know, what practical suggestions can you make for developing a satisfying family life for both the single parent and his or her children? Consider relationships within the family and between the family and the rest of society.
3. Do you think that society should help single parents and their children? In what ways? Which support programs do you think would be most effective?

Chapter 10
Coming Apart—The Divorce Experience

LEARNING OBJECTIVES

What has been the history of divorce in Canada?

What are some of the causes of divorce?

What are the developmental stages of divorce?

What are the three crises of divorce?

How might divorce affect children?

What are some of the issues around the custody of children?

Public Announcement

John and Jane Smith announce an amicable divorce.

Their friends and relatives are asked not to take sides and to please keep in touch with both.

For the time being they are both still at home:

1234 14th Street,

Western City,

Prairie Province, Canada

> *Source:* Statistics Canada. 1982. *Divorce: Law and Family in Canada*. Catalogue No. 89-502. Ottawa, Ontario. Statistics Canada. Pg. 159.

● ● ● ● ○

A separation occurs when a couple's relationship breaks down and they decide to live apart. Couples who separate may be married to each other, or they may be unmarried but living together in a common-law relationship. A **divorce** is the legal dissolution of a marriage, so only married couples can divorce (Department of Justice Canada, 2012c).

divorce: the legal dissolution of a marriage

Divorce is the most common deviation from the traditional family life cycle. It is becoming so common, in fact, that it may in time come to be considered a "normal" family event. Divorced families add two or three phases to the life cycle: separation, perhaps remarriage, and, finally, stabilization in a new family pattern.

It is an oversimplification to view divorce as a uniform event. Every couple who decides to divorce does so for different reasons and in practice the divorce experience is quite diverse. The divorcing couple and their families may face different challenges, have access to a wide range of social and emotional support, and deal with the divorce in vastly different ways.

The symbolic interactionist perspective looks at the individual reasons for divorce, for example the nature of the relationship and how each partner perceives the relationship. The macro perspectives focus on the wider social context and how these create trends in the divorce rate.

In this chapter, we will look at the historical trends in divorce in Canada and recognize that social forces have a powerful effect on each couple's decision to divorce. We will pursue this issue further when we look at reasons why people divorce. Many researchers have identified several phases in the divorce cycle. The divorce experience also typically results in three crises—emotional, economic, and parenting. We will look at how each of these is manifested and the different strategies people use to resolve them. When children are involved, divorce becomes more complicated, and we will look at some of the issues around the effect of divorce on children.

Where Do I Fit In?

1. What do you think about the "public divorce announcement" in the opening vignette?
2. What is your experience with divorce, either directly or indirectly through other family members or friends?
3. Why do you think some couples get divorced? What factors would make you come to this decision yourself?

A Short History

For much of history, marriage was considered a way of uniting families and providing stability for society. Divorce was seen as an exception to be undertaken for only grave reasons. (See Box 10.1 below.) When biological descent for inheritance of property or titles was important, illegitimacy was considered a threat; therefore, adultery by a wife once carried much social stigma and was grounds for divorce. Cruelty, on the other hand, was considered part of family life and usually was not seen as a reason for breaking up the marriage.

Before Confederation, marriage was controlled by the Church of England in Upper Canada (now Ontario) and by the Roman Catholic Church in Lower Canada (now Quebec). Since neither church recognized divorce, no divorce law existed. New Brunswick allowed divorce in 1758 on the grounds of adultery and desertion. In 1787, Nova Scotia allowed divorce on the grounds of adultery. There is little indication, however, of how many divorces were granted.

With Confederation in 1867, the federal Parliament gained exclusive authority in matters of divorce, but simply allowed existing provincial laws to stand or to change. Anyone living in a province without a divorce court could submit a private member's bill to Parliament; when it passed, the person was granted a divorce. The process was long and expensive, and the rules differed depending on the petitioner. Men had to prove adultery on the part of their wives. Women, on the other hand, also had to prove either desertion for two years or longer, or extreme physical or mental cruelty. Deserting your family (often called "the poor man's divorce") was easier than going through a legal divorce (Douglas, 2001). From 1925 on, women could sue for divorce on the same grounds as men. They had only to prove adultery, not adultery and another cause. By 1968, all provinces except Quebec and Newfoundland had divorce laws, with adultery basically the sole grounds for divorce (Douglas, 2001).

BOX 10.1 — Other Times, Other Customs

In the early 20th century, Harriet McGill of Churchbridge, Saskatchewan, wrote to the Minister of Justice in Ottawa seeking help in resolving her marital situation.

Dear Sir:-
I was married to Angus McGill on Dec 16th 1914. We were only married 6 days when he was called up for the war. While in Yorkton, Sask. he came to see me every week or so. . . . My baby girl was born April 21 1915. He wrote me regular until Sept 6th 1916 then stopped until June 6 1917 when he wrote a letter saying our marriage was all a mistake. He stopped my allowance for three months in 1917 but I got that alright after I wrote to Ottawa. . . . He came back from overseas on March 1st 1919,

but he never came back to me. Now what I want to know is this: is it possible for me to get this marriage annulled so I could marry again. . . . Now I have no money for a divorce . . . I have no home nor no money and times are very hard alone. I have been with this other young man for two years now . . . my mother says for us to get married and we were advised in Winnipeg to get married so please do what you can to make us happy.

The Justice Department replied that, while it could not advise her in legal matters, she could not legally remarry without a divorce that would cost "considerable expense." Harriet wrote back asking for "a written permission" to remarry. There is no record of a reply.

Source: James G. Snell, *In the Shadow of the Law: Divorce in Canada, 1900-1939.* Toronto: University of Toronto Press. 1991. Pg. 4.

divorce rate: a measure that predicts the proportion of couples that can be expected to divorce before their 30th wedding anniversary, based on current patterns of divorce

The **divorce rate** is a measure that predicts the proportion of couples that can be expected to divorce before their 30th wedding anniversary, based on current patterns of divorce (Vanier Institute of the Family, 2010). Immediately after World War II, the divorce rate in Canada jumped. During the war, many women replaced men in the workforce, since the latter were in the military. The freedom and financial independence these women experienced undoubtedly encouraged some divorces, as did hasty wartime marriages and prolonged separations.

Soon, however, the divorce rate dropped off. In the stability following the war, people married in increasing numbers, and the idea of family was attractive to many. Neither the Roman Catholic nor the Anglican Church recognized divorce or remarriage, and the United Church opposed any broadening of the grounds for divorce. The few divorce-related bills that were introduced in the House of Commons or the Senate in the 1940s did not pass (McKie et al., 1983).

In 1960, a divorce cost $2500, which meant that only the very wealthy could afford it (Niren, 2009). Parliament was still handling divorces for Quebec and Newfoundland. Two senators blocked all divorce bills coming before Parliament in order to force a change in the law. In 1966, a Special Joint Committee of the Senate and House of Commons on Divorce held many hearings on the subject. By this time, the churches had changed their position. The Roman Catholic Church stated that its members could vote according to their conscience, and the Catholic Women's League stated that Roman Catholics should not make other Canadians live by their beliefs. Both the Anglican Church and the United Church briefs included marriage breakdown as an acceptable cause for divorce.

Bill C-187 proposed wider grounds for divorce. Most significantly, it introduced the no-fault principle of marriage breakdown as a legitimate ground for divorce while retaining the traditional fault-based grounds, such as adultery and cruelty. Both fault and no-fault grounds were equally available to husbands and wives. The bill also transferred jurisdiction for all divorces to the courts (Douglas, 2001). On July 2, 1968, the new divorce law received royal assent (McKie et al., 1983). The divorce rate increased dramatically as a result of the wider grounds for divorce. (See Figure 10.1).

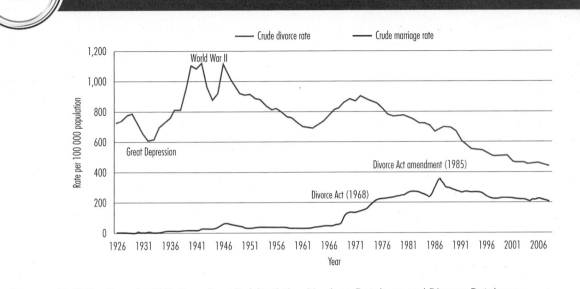

FIGURE 10.1 — Crude Marriage and Divorce Rates, Canada, 1926–2008

Sources: Statistics Canada. 2011. Canadian Vital Statistics, Marriage Database and Divorce Database; Statistics Canada Demography Division, demographic estimates.

In 1985, amendments to the law led to another jump in the divorce rate. The amendments reduced the waiting period for divorce on the grounds of marriage breakdown to one year. For the first time, partners could petition jointly for divorce (Douglas, 2001). The number of divorces reached their peak, at 96 200, in 1987 but dropped to 67 408 in 1997. Since then, the annual number of divorces has remained stable. The decrease in divorces since 1987 may be partly due to marrying at an older age and the greater number of people who choose to cohabit (Statistics Canada, 2008j). The total of relationship dissolutions is much higher than the number of divorces alone, however. The separations of cohabitors are not included in divorce statistics and are probably more common (Osborne et al., 2007).

Divorce is now increasingly common at midlife and among couples 65 years old and older. These "silver separations" usually occur after the children have left the family home and couples have the chance to reassess their marriages (Nguyen, 2012). Many of these divorces are initiated by women. Although frightened about being on their own financially, most feel relief at leaving an unfulfilling relationship. Divorce can be difficult for a homemaker wife who is suddenly faced with finding a job when she has been out of the workforce for many years. Other women see divorce as a personal failure because they did not make their marriages work (Blacker, 1999).

Why People Divorce

There are two ways of looking at why people divorce: we can examine either the stated reasons for divorce or the social causes underlying these reasons.

TABLE 10.1 — 30-Year Total Divorce Rate per 100 Marriages, Canada, Provinces, and Territories, 1998–2008

Province or Territory	30-Year Total Divorce Rate[1]					
	1998	2000	2002	2004	2006	2008
Canada	36.1	37.6	37.6	37.9	41.9	40.7
Newfoundland and Labrador	23.2	22.9	21.8	21.6	22.3	25.0
Prince Edward Island	26.4	26.9	25.2	29.1	28.4	31.7
Nova Scotia	28.2	30.4	30.4	30.2	33.7	31.1
New Brunswick	26.9	31.9	27.2	26.9	30.0	29.7
Quebec	45.2	47.4	47.6	48.4	48.0	47.4
Ontario	33.0	34.6	34.9	35.5	44.1	42.1
Manitoba	30.1	30.3	30.3	30.6	29.9	31.5
Saskatchewan	31.5	31.4	28.7	27.6	30.7	30.3
Alberta	39.0	41.5	41.9	41.9	42.1	46.0
British Columbia	40.0	40.6	41.0	40.8	42.3	37.1
Yukon	55.2	33.6	43.4	34.8	44.8	59.7
Northwest Territories and Nunavut[2]	37.5	40.7	31.2	35.5	30.8	35.1

1. The 30-year total divorce rate (TDR-30) represents the proportion of married couples who are expected to divorce before their 30th wedding anniversary. For example, a TDR-30 of 40.7 per 100 marriages for Canada in 2008 indicates that 40.7% of marriages are expected to end in divorce before the 30th year of marriage (if the duration-specific divorce rates calculated for 2008 remain stable).
2. Northwest Territories and Nunavut are combined to calculate the rates in this table because marriage and divorce data are not available for these territories separately for the 30- and 50-year periods required for the calculation of the total divorce rates.

Sources: Statistics Canada. 2011. Canadian Vital Statistics, Marriage Database and Divorce Database; Statistics Canada Health Statistics Division.

The *Divorce Act* recognizes three legal grounds for divorce: cruelty, adultery, or being separated for one year. The main ground for divorce used in Canada is separation for a year, because proving cruelty or adultery can be very time-consuming and expensive (Canadian Divorce Laws, 2012b). In a study of Canadians' attitudes to divorce, researchers have identified three kinds of reasons: fundamental issues, such as infidelity and abuse; experiential issues, such as disagreements and unsatisfactory sex life; and fertility issues, such as infertility and deciding whether or not to have children. (See Table 10.2 on page 267.) Almost all Canadians feel that divorce is justified when one partner abuses the other, fails to show respect, or is unfaithful. Experiential issues and fertility issues rated lower. Interestingly, older people (aged 50 and over) have the most lenient attitude about divorce, something that may reflect their greater experience of married life (Frederick & Hamel, 1998).

TABLE 10.2	Older Canadians More Likely than Younger Canadians to Agree with Reasons to Divorce			
	Gen-Xers	**Boomers**	**Older People**	**Total**
Fundamental Issues				
Abusive behaviour from the partner	95%	95%	94%	95%
Unfaithful behaviour from the partner	89%	85%	89%	88%
Lack of love and respect from the partner	86%	87%	87%	88%
Partner drinks too much	68%	73%	80%	74%
Experiential Issues				
Constant disagreement about how family finances should be handled	28%	40%	49%	40%
Unsatisfactory sexual relationship with partner	21%	37%	45%	35%
Unsatisfactory division of household tasks with partner	12%	16%	21%	17%
Conflict about how the children are raised	14%	17%	21%	17%
Fertility Issues				
Inability to have children with the partner	8%	12%	17%	13%
Disagreement about the number of children to have	3%	6%	11%	7%
Would stay for the children	44%	39%	52%	43%

Source: Adapted from: Statistics Canada. "Elders More Likely Than Younger Canadians to Agree With Reasons to Divorce," *Canadian Social Trends*. Catalogue 11-008. Ottawa, Ontario. Statistics Canada. Spring 1998. Pg. 8.

John Gottman (1994) has researched married and divorced couples for many years and identified various signs that predict a couple is more likely to divorce. According to Gottman, there are four types of negative interaction so lethal to a marriage that he has labelled them the "Four Horsemen of Apocalypse." The first is criticism, though Gottman distinguishes between criticism and complaint. A complaint focuses on a specific behaviour, while a criticism attacks the character of the person. The second horseman, contempt, often follows criticism. When one partner uses contempt, the other partner often reacts with defensiveness, which is the third horseman. The escalating conflict finally leads to one partner tuning out the other, and this is called stonewalling. While each of these four horsemen can predict divorce by themselves, typically they are found together in an unhappy marriage.

While each divorce is ultimately the result of the personal dynamics of a couple, researchers have also catalogued social risk factors. For first marriages, age is important. Those who marry before 20 are much more likely to separate than those who marry in their later 20s and 30s. Another risk factor is having less than a high school education. There is a strong association between education and income, and lower socioeconomic status is related to higher divorce rates. Many studies have found that when financial resources are limited, stress and worry arise; these, in turn, have a negative impact on the harmony in the marriage, causing more marital conflict and increasing the likelihood of divorce. Cohabitation before marriage increases the likelihood of divorce, perhaps because of a lower level of commitment or a lesser value placed on marriage. When one partner is imprisoned, there is also an increased likelihood of divorce. Those who go to church infrequently are at risk. Statistically, interracial marriages are less stable than inracial ones. Because same-sex marriages have been legal in Canada only since 2005, we are just starting to get statistics on same-sex couples who divorce. Spouses whose parents have divorced are more likely to do so as well. When a couple has been together a longer time and they have children, they are less likely to divorce (Ambert, 2009; Hewitt & de Vaus, 2009; Zhang & Van Hook, 2009).

Second or later marriages are subject to different risk factors. Premarital cohabitation is less of a risk factor in second marriages. Remarriages at a young age are more likely to be dissolved than those of partners who remarry in their 30s or 40s. Especially those entering third or more marriages are less likely to claim that being married is important to their happiness. When women, but not men, bring children into a remarriage, there is an increased likelihood of disruption (Clark & Crompton, 2006; Teachman, 2008).

The structural functionalist view looks at how an institution like the family is affected by wider social changes. In the traditional family, men provided economic support and women provided personal care. The basis for this "contract" has changed over the past 50 years. Culturally, the concept of marriage has also changed. It is now commonly regarded as a matter for individual choice and satisfaction rather than a social responsibility and a covenant before God. When marriage does not meet expectations for personal fulfillment, individuals have become readier to separate. The liberalization of laws has made divorce more common and reduced stigma (Ambert, 2009; Cherlin, 2009; Coontz, 2007). Meanwhile, other social institutions, such as daycare, have taken over some family functions. This development further undermines the family's role and makes divorce more likely.

The exchange perspective considers the costs and benefits of divorce. When there are many costs, divorce is less likely than when there are fewer. Such costs can be both economic (e.g., a drop in disposable income) and social (e.g., stigma). Divorce is more likely if possible new partners are available, as when a wife has many male colleagues (Ambert, 2009; Fine et al., 2010). Because of changes in the law and the greater social acceptability of divorce, the costs of divorce have become lower. More women have greater economic independence; thus, they are better able to support themselves. When they earn about half the family income, the dependence of one partner on the other for support is less and divorce is likelier (Ambert, 2009; Previti & Amato, 2003; Rogers, 2004). The presence of children reduces the likelihood of divorce because it increases the costs to the parents, though these costs may be different for fathers and mothers. For a mother, having young children at home may mean that she is not working and is therefore economically dependent. For a father, divorce usually results in custody being given to the mother, so for him the higher cost is that he will see less of his children (Kalmijn & Poortman, 2006).

According to feminists, traditional marriage supports the unequal division of power between husbands and wives. Now that women have more opportunities, they no longer need to depend on men to support them and can leave oppressive relationships. This freedom is especially relevant if they are victims of abuse (Ambert, 2009; Rogers, 2004).

Symbolic interactionist theorists focus on the patterns of interchange between husband and wife. Individuals' expectations affect their behaviour. There has been a shift in emphasis from finding security in marriage to reaching one's highest potential. Thus, an unhappy spouse feels justified in leaving an unsatisfying marriage and searching for fulfillment elsewhere (Ambert, 2009; Coontz, 2007).

Divorce has a different impact at different stages of the family life cycle. The least disruption occurs with the newly married couple with no children. Fewer people are involved, and fewer family traditions need to be dropped. Since each partner has been single fairly recently, they are able to slip back into single roles and lifestyle more easily than those married for a long time. As more people are added to the family and the family has a longer history together, divorce becomes more difficult. Many plans and hopes—vacation, new house, children—have to be cancelled. Traditions build up through years of interaction. With a long-time marriage, part of the dislocation of divorce is the loss of these rituals (Ahrons, 1999).

None of these factors is by itself sufficient to explain the changes in divorce rates; together, however, they go a long way.

Time to Review

1. What has been the history of divorce in Canada?
2. What are some of the factors involved in a couple's decision to divorce?
3. How do the different sociological perspectives see divorce?

The Road to Divorce

Divorce is rarely a sudden event; the process takes place in several phases that involve both rational and emotional aspects.

The Decision to Divorce

The decision to divorce follows many steps. In the first step, one or both individuals come to realize that something is wrong with their marriage, though a period of denial often precedes this (Ahrons, 1999). Many couples who divorce appear to follow what Gottman (1994) calls the "divorce cascade." First, there is increasing conflict, then serious consideration of divorce, then separation, and finally divorce. The further along husband and wife are in this sequence, the harder it is to avoid divorce. It is as if they are caught in a strong river current that sweeps them into the rapids and over the waterfall of divorce. Not all couples who have conflicts take the same route, though. Many work out their problems and have satisfying relationships.

People may delay separation until a time they consider suitable. Women may find a job or go back to school. Often, the couple will decide to delay the divorce until the children leave home. During this period, they may become involved in activities outside the family, in a kind of emotional withdrawal. For some families, this period is one of great uncertainty and stress. The old husband and wife roles are disappearing and new ones, for example those of divorced co-parents, have not yet been developed. Eventually, the couple needs to move past the tendency to blame each other; they must accept the fact that the marriage cannot be saved and that both individuals have played a part in its failure (Ahrons, 1999; Carter & McGoldrick, 1999a).

Some minority groups emphasize family ties and responsibilities above personal satisfaction. Recent immigrants from these cultures are less likely to approve of divorce. The longer they live in Canada, however, the more likely they are to adopt the values of the majority (Sherif Trask & Koivunen, 2007).

Planning the Breakup

custody: the legal right and responsibility to care for a child in one's own home

In the second stage, the couple must plan the breakup of the family system. They need to work cooperatively to settle issues such as **custody** of children, visitation, and finances. They also need to tell extended family members and deal with their reactions. The planning process often does not run smoothly. Many couples separate and reconcile again, sometimes repeatedly. During these temporary separations, the family can be under much stress because its members do not know whether the separation will become permanent and there is uncertainty about who belongs in the family and whether roles should be reorganized. This kind of stress is called "boundary ambiguity." At this stage, the family may also face the reality of what a divorce will mean economically (Ahrons, 1999; Boss, 2006; Carter & McGoldrick, 1999a).

Separation and Family Reorganization

The third phase is the separation prior to divorce. Separation changes the relationship between husbands and wives. If only one partner wishes to separate, boundaries may be particularly uncertain, something that frequently leads to conflict and is perhaps centred on the children. The conflict may be an attempt to punish, to maintain contact with, or simply to get a rise from the former partner (Cochrane, 2007).

The couple now needs to restructure the family by separating the marital and parental relationships (Amato et al., 2009; Hardesty et al., 2008). Restructuring may be orderly or disorderly and marked by conflict. Parents need to work out new rules for the continuing relationship between the child and each of them. They also need to decide how they will coordinate their responsibilities as co-parents.

An important aspect of the separation is deciding custody arrangements for children. Many people feel that **joint custody** is best for children, with both parents sharing responsibility and decision making. Others question their ability to share decision making if they cannot get along well enough to live together. One of the keys is the parents' maturity and their ability to put the child's needs ahead of their own disagreements. Couples also need to work out their relationships with the extended family, including the spouse's relatives, so that the children do not lose touch with them. Professional mediators, such as social workers and family lawyers, can help parents resolve custody and access issues (Ahrons, 1999; Brownstone, 2009; Carter & McGoldrick, 1999a).

When the parent without custody fades out of the picture, we have a true one-parent family. When both parents are involved, the children act as links between two connected households. Both parents continue to be part of the child's family in an arrangement sometimes referred to as a **binuclear family**. This arrangement can reduce the stress of divorce for children because they do not lose either parent. Occasionally, the parents remain good friends; more often, they are able to focus only on the children's welfare without open conflict (Ahrons, 1999).

joint custody: the legal right and responsibility of both parents to make decisions and care for their child

binuclear family: an arrangement where both father and mother act as parents to their child(ren) following divorce but maintain separate homes

The Crises of Divorce

The breakdown of a marriage or cohabitation brings with it three crises: the emotional crisis, the economic crisis, and the parenting crisis. A bitter court battle makes all of these crises worse (Payne, 1986). Divorce produces what is called a **transitional state**; that is, it creates a temporary imbalance as a result of the changes in relationships, routines, assumptions, and roles. New patterns of behaviour are needed. Since separation and divorce interrupt the usual family developmental tasks, they require a series of adjustments that throw all family members off balance. This **disequilibrium** usually lasts for one to three years. Many factors influence each individual's reaction to divorce: the circumstances of the separation, the quality of life after separation, the person's sex, the length of the marriage, the family's life-cycle stage, the acceptance of the person's ethnic or religious group, and past experience with stress (Ahrons, 1999; Allen, 2007; Hetherington, 2003). One area needing more research is how same-sex couples adjust to breakup.

transitional state: a state of temporary imbalance resulting from changes in relationships, routines, assumptions, and roles

disequilibrium: a lack of balance in the family system

The Emotional Crisis

During and after the separation process, individuals suffer the loss of an important relationship. Often, it has served as a centre for their lives, whether it was seen as satisfactory or unsatisfactory. The breakup is more painful for a person who does not expect or want it, and easier if the two partners have made the decision together (Ahrons, 1999). The emotional loss felt in divorce is akin to that felt on the death of a loved one, except that the ex-partner is still around (Cochrane, 2007). This continuing presence can lead to a recurring sense of loss, as well as renewed bitterness or anger. Some have expressed these negative emotions on Facebook for all, including their children, to see (Luscombe, 2009). Both men and women are likely to experience depression, even if they are leaving a difficult relationship (Kalmijn & Monden, 2006; Rotermann, 2007a). Often, it takes considerable time for an individual to become emotionally divorced from a partner. Yearning for the lost relationship and anger over the breakup are signs that this emotional divorce has not occurred. When children are involved, total emotional separation is usually impossible because the former partners must deal with each other as parents or grandparents of their children and grandchildren (Ahrons, 1999). Friendship is healthy; preoccupation with the lost marital relationship is not (Madden-Derdich & Arditti, 1999).

Separation and divorce usually mean that individuals have to redefine themselves as people, sometimes with help. The roles they have filled within the marriage are now lost, and to lose a role is to lose part of oneself. Women with young children suffer more at divorce than those without children. Researchers suggest that they experience more stressors, such as money problems. In addition, younger people may not have developed the coping resources older parents have (Williams & Dunne-Bryant, 2006). With the growing number of divorced people, new social scripts are being developed. However, taking on a new role is still difficult. More social services are becoming available. Over three-quarters of people who divorce take advantage of legal services, mediators, and family law information centres. People leaving a common-law union who use such services constitute one-third of the overall proportion (Beaupré & Cloutier, 2007).

Divorced and separated individuals, men more than women, are often socially isolated at first. The relationship with extended family members changes. Although they may maintain a connection, they are no longer legally related to their ex-spouse's relatives. And they may have limited support from their own relatives. Families that have dealt with divorce before are often more comfortable in dealing with the issues that arise. Some individuals cut themselves off from the extended family and friends to avoid criticism. By doing this, they isolate themselves further. For individuals with strong religious beliefs, divorce may be considered a sacred loss or desecration. As a result, they may experience spiritual struggles as they come to terms with it. Women from minority groups that do not condone divorce may also face shunning by extended family members and their ethnic community (Anderson et al., 1990; Krumrel et al., 2009; Rotermann, 2007a).

Divorced women may find social life limited by their lack of identity as a single. Many isolate themselves because they feel overloaded with tasks; others do so because they feel the sense of failure common after divorce. There is often a sharp decline in support for women from married friends. Divorced men often have an easier time socially than divorced women do. Although they usually do not have the circle of intimate friends that women have, they often have a social network at their place of employment. Men tend to remarry sooner than women, often to partners much younger than themselves (Brinig, 1999).

By about two years post-divorce, many people are adapting. Within six years, most have built a reasonably satisfying life. There are six patterns of adjustment (see Table 10.3). "Enhancers" blossom. They become more competent and fulfilled. Through their work or by continuing their education, this predominantly female group finds a higher quality of life. The "goodenoughs," the largest group, manage quite well. About six years post-divorce, their lives are similar to what they were pre-divorce. "Seekers" are anxious for a new mate and may not be careful in their choice. One woman said, "I wanted a man so badly, anyone looked good." "Swingers" dress youthfully, go to singles bars, use more alcohol and drugs, and are involved in more casual sex—and they tend to be men rather than women. There are also "competent loners," similar to "enhancers" but not wanting a long-term partner. Finally, the "defeated" are mired in despair long after the divorce. Some had problems before divorce; others could not escape poverty (Hetherington, 2003).

There are three aspects of the emotional crisis of divorce. First, the ex-spouses must accept the loss of the marriage and mourn its passing. Second, they must deal with identity issues. Third, they must build new social networks as single people to replace those that supported the marriage. In successfully accomplishing these tasks, they will find that divorce can provide an opportunity for growth.

TABLE 10.3

Patterns of Adjustment to Divorce

Pattern	Characteristics
Enhancers	Predominantly female, this group finds a higher quality of life through work or by continuing their education
Goodenoughs	The largest group, they manage quite well; about six years after the divorce, their lives are similar to what they were pre-divorce
Seekers	Are anxious for a new mate and may not be careful in their choice
Swingers	Tend to be male; they dress youthfully, go to singles bars, use more alcohol and drugs, and are involved in more casual sex
Competent loners	Similar to enhancers but not seeking a new partner
Defeated	Are still mired in despair long after the divorce

Source: E. M. Hetherington, "Intimate pathways: Changing patterns in close personal relationships across time," *Family Relations*, Vol. 52, Issue 4. 2003, Pg. 318–331.

The Economic Crisis

custodial parent: an individual who has custody of his or her child

Divorce is called "the most expensive life event" (Investors Group, 2004). It usually means a drop in the standard of living, especially for the **custodial parent**, the parent who has custody of any children. Since women are usually granted custody of children, their financial needs following divorce are greater than their husbands'. Yet, as we have seen, they often do not have the ability to earn as much as men (Ambert, 2009; Fine et al., 2010; Rotermann, 2007a). Cohabiting partners who separate suffer similar difficulties (Avellar & Smock, 2005).

noncustodial parent: the parent who does not have custody of the child

Both parents are responsible for the support of their children. In the past, amounts paid by the **noncustodial parent** varied widely. In 1997, the federal government passed the Federal Child Support Guidelines, which take into account the costs of raising a child, the parents' income, and the number of children. The custodial parent is assumed to pay a similar percentage of his or her income. Opting out of the federal child support system is possible, but the judge will ensure that the agreement will meet the child's needs (Cochrane, 2007). If the noncustodial parent, usually the father, does not have a steady job or has disappeared and the support order cannot be enforced, the family may be reduced to living on welfare (Statistics Canada, 2009b). This misfortune is most likely if the mother has few or no marketable skills (Brownstone, 2009; Marcil-Gratton et al., 2000). Chapter 15 looks in more detail at the serious implications of poverty for the development of children.

In Canada, the federal government has authority over marriage and divorce, but the provinces deal with the division of property. Generally, any property or other assets acquired during the course of the marriage, by either spouse, is deemed to be the property of both spouses. A married couple may wish to have an alternative division of property, and this can be arranged with a legal domestic contract (Department of Justice Canada, 2012d). Unfortunately, many common-law couples mistakenly believe that the property division laws govern their relationships as well. In 2002, the Supreme Court of Canada made it quite clear that this is not the case.

The Supreme Court became involved because living in a common-law relationship became a rights debate based on the *Charter of Rights and Freedoms*. Many common-law couples argue that it is their fundamental right to be distinct from married couples and that the same laws should not automatically apply to them (Feldstein Family Law Group, 2012). While some provinces have provisions for spousal support, under Quebec laws, partners do not owe each other anything when a common-law union ends. In January 2013, The Supreme Court of Canada upheld that Quebec does not have to give common-law spouses the same rights as married couples (CTV News, 2013).

The issue of spousal support is governed by the federal *Divorce Act*. Spousal support is granted on certain principles. One of these is that a spouse should not suffer economic hardship as a result of divorce. Another recognizes that in a marriage, the spouses may have agreed on a division of tasks that may put one partner at a disadvantage. For example, a woman who has spent many years as a homemaker has forfeited work experience and skills. She may be compensated both for her contribution to the family and for giving up employment benefits.

The federal Department of Justice has drafted spousal support guidelines in an effort to help judges and courts determine the amount and length of spousal support (Department of Justice, 2009f).

The Parenting Crisis

When a family separates, new boundaries must be drawn. Much of the confusion and stress during the separation process arise from an absence of clear boundaries. The old family, with its old rules and rituals, no longer exists, but new ones have not yet taken their place. This vacuum is especially true for parenting. Both authority and responsibility concerning the children need to be renegotiated. To do this successfully, parents need to separate spousal roles from parental roles— only the former are ended by divorce. They also need to establish new rules. For example, who does the child ask for money or help with homework? How much participation is expected of a noncustodial parent?

Each parent needs to establish a relationship with the children separate from the other parent. How much authority will she or he have over the children? If joint custody is decided upon, how will the responsibility for the children be shared? Parents' communication is an important factor as to whether each parent will allow the other to relate to the child without prejudice or interference. If there is no clear understanding of the new rules of the relationship, the child is likely to become the victim of conflicts between the parents (Ahrons, 1999; Brownstone, 2009). Children can manipulate parents who do not communicate with each other (Manning, 2003). Many divorcing parents use counselling and legal services to help them work out an agreement (Beaupré & Cloutier, 2007).

Divorcing parents may be unable to respond to their children's emotional needs. There are several reasons for this. The initial sense of shock may paralyze them. Later on, parents may be too absorbed in their own crisis to be aware of how the divorce is affecting their children. They may also feel that very young children cannot understand what is going on and may ignore their distress. Often, a parent becomes depressed, and one aspect of depression is that the individual becomes less sensitive to the feelings of others. For all these reasons, children may be emotionally neglected at a time when they need special care (Ambert, 2009; Meadows et al., 2007).

Time to Review

1. What steps typically follow the decision to divorce?
2. What are the three crises that arise in a divorce situation?
3. What are the patterns of adjustment to divorce?

Children and Divorce

Parents' divorce transforms children's lives forever. It affects where they live, how they interact with parents, and if and how they can continue relationships with friends. Some come through the experience and flourish. Others do not (Ambert, 2009; Wallerstein, 2007). Health Canada has a publication called *Because Life Goes On . . . Helping Children and Youth Live with Separation and Divorce* that is intended to reach out to Canadian families in need of information and resources to help their children to live through the process of separation and divorce (Health Canada, 2012). Because same-sex marriage has been legal in Canada only since 2005, research on the effects of divorce on same-sex couples has just started, because of course some same-sex marriages also end in divorce. Even less is known about the effects of divorce on the children of same-sex couples.

Few children want their parents to divorce, no matter how much tension there has been in the marriage. For them, it means changing the relationship with each parent. Many children cling to a fantasy that their parents will be reunited and the family will be whole again (Stahl, 2007; Thompson, 2000). They may also believe that they have the power to bring parents back together. Sometimes, they feel responsible for the family breakup (Ambert, 2009).

Children from divorced families are at greater risk of developing problems than children from stable two-parent families. Most, however, do not (Ambert, 2009). Around the time of separation, children may suffer a short-term drop in their marks. As a result, their long-term educational and occupational opportunities may be reduced (Frisco et al., 2007; Sun & Li, 2008). In addition, they tend to move out from parents' homes earlier, making it harder financially to undertake postsecondary education (Ambert, 2009). For many children, emotional adjustments take up to two years. When children experience several transitions, such as change of custody, remarriage of a parent, and a move away from relatives and friends, their adjustment tends to be poorer (Braver et al., 2003; Fine et al., 2010).

A Canadian study found a connection between divorce and antisocial behaviour. Children whose parents later divorced already had higher levels of anxiety, depression, and antisocial behaviour. Following divorce, their anxiety and depression increased, but not their antisocial behaviour. In fact, when very dysfunctional marriages dissolved, antisocial behaviour decreased (Strohschein, 2005). Other researchers have found that children from divorced families are more likely to be hyperactive and aggressive, to engage in fighting, and to become young offenders. When they become older, children of divorce are more prone to become unmarried teen parents. They are also more likely to be divorced themselves. Some have lingering problems trusting their partners (Ambert, 2009; M. Baker, 2007; Wallerstein, 2007).

The impact of divorce on children depends on a number of factors, the first of which is the age of the child. Very young children are less likely to be affected long term by divorce if they receive good parenting. Children over 10 years old are able to understand divorce in a realistic way, though they do not need to hear all the details of the breakup.

Divorce affects adolescent children differently. Some may feel relieved at the end of continuing conflict (Ahrons, 1999; Strohschein, 2005). Others experiment with sex or drugs and may separate prematurely from their family (Ambert, 2009). Many children of divorce are less attached to their parents than those from two-parent families. Recent research suggests that, regardless of age, children who have warm relationships with parents prior to the divorce do as well as children from intact families.

If parenting is upset by the divorce, then adolescents have problems. If a parent turns to them for support, or if they feel the need to look after a devastated parent, they may have difficulty getting on with their own lives. This problem is especially true in a high-conflict divorce when the child is expected to take sides. Teens and young adults may show similar reactions if they have lived for years in an angry family. Researchers describe what they call a **sleeper effect**, in which a problem emerges only long after the event. Young adults whose parents divorced when they were children may display a fear of intimacy or betrayal that will interfere with any attempts to form intimate relationships. Serious problems are, however, the exception (Ambert, 2009; Wallerstein, 2007).

sleeper effect: a problem that emerges only long after an event such as divorce

The second factor relating to impact is that divorce may affect boys and girls differently. Since the mother usually has primary custody of the children, boys will lack the presence of their primary male role model. Girls tend to adapt better than boys, but not necessarily to their mother's remarriage. Among teenagers, girls whose parents have divorced are more likely than boys to become depressed. Most studies, however, have found that effects are similar for both boys and girls (Ambert, 2009; Leon, 2003).

The third factor, the level of parental conflict both before and after separation, probably has more impact on children's post-divorce adjustment than the absence of a parent. Children openly exposed to conflict do less well, especially if violence is involved or if children feel caught in the middle. At its worst, such conflict can result in alienation from one parent as a result of pressure from the other (Ambert, 2009; A. J. L. Baker, 2007; Brownstone, 2009).

The fourth factor, life changes after divorce, is also important. The number and degree of changes affect the children's ability to adapt. For example, a child who moves from a house to a small apartment in a new neighbourhood and experiences a dramatic lowering of his or her standard of living will probably have more difficulties adapting than a child who stays in the family home and still goes to the same school with his or her friends. The absence of the father, as we have already discussed, is related directly to economic instability. Divorce will also affect the children's relationship with other relatives, especially grandparents. The children may have limited access to the extended family members of the nonresidential parent if that parent is not taking an active role. Parents may also form one or more new relationships. If these are disrupted, children have multiple losses and adjustments. It is suspected that the connection between divorce and greater rates of delinquency, underachievement, and promiscuity in children depends more on stress-inducing changes, including changes in the relationship with parents, than on the divorce itself (Braver et al., 2003; Butler et al., 2003).

Finally, the nature of the new parenting arrangements is important to the children's adjustment—children want and need an ongoing relationship with both parents.

Most of the research deals with nonresidential father–child relationships because mothers more often have custody. Fathers tend to be more involved with their children if they pay child support regularly (DeGarmo et al., 2008; Huang, 2009). If fathers establish a pattern of parenting before entering a new relationship, visits will not become less frequent once they have a new partner or another child. Visits may become fewer, however, if the mother remarries. Cooperative parenting results in more frequent father–child contact, a better relationship, and more responsive fathering. Some abusive ex-partners can form co-parenting relationships if they are able to separate their spouse and parent roles. When children have close relationships with their fathers before separation, a good mother–child relationship can prevent the father–child link from deteriorating. Fathers who receive support for their parenting from relatives and new partners are more likely to encourage their children's social development.

It is best for children to have strong ties to both parents. If, however, children have a good relationship with only one parent, they will have fewer problems than if they are distant from both (DeGarmo et al., 2008; Hardesty et al., 2008; King & Sobolewski, 2006).

Social supports are important for children, just as they are for adults. Grandparents, friends, teachers, and others may provide the emotional and practical help children need to help them cope with the emotional fallout of divorce. Children need accurate information about the separation and custody arrangements (Stahl, 2007). Grandparents can soften some of the stresses of divorce. Since the grandparent–grandchild relationship can remain stable when the parent–child relationship is undergoing structural changes, it teaches children that not all relationships are temporary and unhappy. To provide effective support to children, grandparents must show their concern and involvement without interfering or taking sides (Connidis, 2010). A Department of Justice publication for children ages 9 to 12 offers support as well. It explains family law and helps children understand it's normal to have an emotional response to their parents' separation or divorce (Department of Justice Canada, 2009g).

A useful way of looking at the impact of divorce on children is to consider both stressors and protective factors (see Figure 10.2). Stressors include the actual separation, conflict between parents before and after separation, poorer quality of parenting after divorce, loss of important relationships (including friends), and financial hardship (Kelly & Emery, 2003). Protective factors include effective parenting by both parents and reduced conflict after divorce. Those with serious problems tend to have more stressor factors and few protective ones. Those with more protective factors often cannot be distinguished from other children (Kelly & Emery, 2003).

Custody and Parenting

Who Gets Custody?

As we have already seen in the chapter on single parents, mothers are usually granted custody after divorce. This was not always so. In English common law, fathers had automatic right to custody of their children. Mothers had few legal

FIGURE 10.2

Stressors and Protective Factors for the Child during Divorce

During a divorce, a child will experience certain stressors. The effect of these stressors can be reduced by a child's protective factors. In the image below, stressors are indicated in red and protective factors in green.

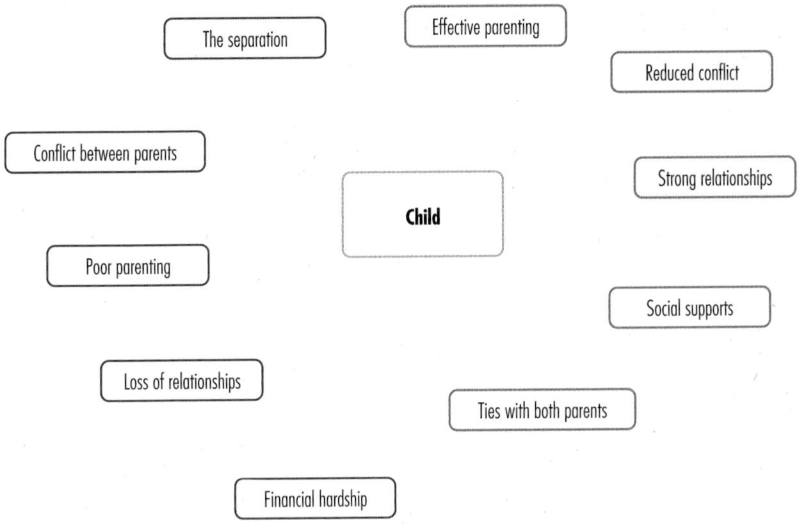

The separation

Effective parenting

Reduced conflict

Conflict between parents

Strong relationships

Child

Poor parenting

Social supports

Loss of relationships

Ties with both parents

Financial hardship

Source: Created by authors.

rights. During the 19th century, changes began to take place. Mothers were gradually given custody, first of young children, then of older children. This shift was partly the result of the Industrial Revolution, during which the workplace and the home became separated. Men had to be free to earn an income, and women were expected to stay home and raise their children. Power passed from the father to the family court judge, who could decide if the mother deserved to have custody of her children. Custody could be denied her if she was considered at fault in the divorce by committing adultery or by leaving the home (Arnup, 1989; McKie et al., 1983).

There are four types of child custody in Canada. The first is sole custody, whereby one parent alone has custody of the child. A second is joint custody, where both parents equally have custody and time with the child. A third type is shared custody. In this arrangement, both parents have joint custody of the child and each spends at least 40% of the time with their child. A final type is split custody. This takes place when one parent has custody over some of the children, while the other parent has custody over the others. Courts are quite hesitant to award custody in this manner, as they don't want to split up siblings (Canadian Divorce Laws, 2012c).

The current standard is the best interests of the child. This being the case, mothers are still usually granted custody. There used to be some reluctance to grant custody to a lesbian mother, especially if she was open in her lifestyle or was a gay activist, on the grounds that living with her might be harmful for the child (Arnup, 1989). This has changed, and presently many openly lesbian mothers and couples have full or shared custody of their children. When parents agree on custody and visiting arrangements, nonresidential parents see their children more often and also provide support more regularly (Marcil-Gratton et al., 2000).

Although the numbers are still relatively small, more fathers are now gaining custody of their children following divorce. Most often, fathers gain custody when the mother consents. Some mothers believe that the father can offer the children more stability immediately after the divorce. Others want to avoid the emotional stress for themselves, and especially for their children, that comes with a contested custody case. Men obtain custody for a number of reasons. They may seek it out of a strong sense of family or a belief that they parent better than the mother, or out of revenge. They may also obtain it against their will because they have been deserted by their wives.

Source: Barry Maguire.

Custodial fathers who do best have certain characteristics in common. They tend to have higher incomes. They are those who wanted custody and were involved with child-rearing before the marriage breakup. They do not place the entire blame for the failure of the marriage on either partner. They allow their ex-wives to be involved with the children on a regular basis, so that they do not carry the full burden of parenting (Edwards, 1989; Greif, 1985).

There is a growing move to joint or shared custody following divorce. The principle of shared parenting is, in theory, beneficial because both parents take part in decision making and care; however, key questions arise. Joint custody works best if the parents can lay aside their personal disagreements to act together in the best interests of their child. Unfortunately, they do not always do this. Children can and do become pawns in the angry fighting between parents (A. J. L. Baker, 2007; Brownstone, 2009). One study found that adolescents with dual residence were especially likely to feel caught between parents when conflict levels were high. When conflict levels were low, however, they felt close to both parents (Buchanan et al., 1991; Greene et al., 2003). Although research findings are still scarce, it appears that children do adjust to moving back and forth between homes. Some object to the terms "custody" and "access" altogether because these words imply a winner parent and a loser parent. Whatever terms are used, when parents sincerely do what is best for their children, the negative effects of divorce are much less.

Problem Areas

Some parents fail to pay child support and must be made to do so. A parent may choose not to pay if he or she thinks the settlement was unjust or custody arrangements unfair. Sometimes, not paying is a method of harassing an ex-partner or trying to exert control over decisions affecting children. Provinces are responsible for enforcing child support orders. Each provincial enforcement agency has a variety of powers to find parents who haven't paid support and make them pay. Wages and salaries, bank accounts, pensions, employment insurance payments, and income tax refunds can be garnished. Some jurisdictions can also suspend driver's licences, fishing and hunting licences, and even passports (Brownstone, 2009). Some parents try to prevent visits if support is not paid (Brownstone, 2009). This breach of the terms of custody can backfire, though. The noncustodial parent can request change of custody because access has been denied.

Occasionally, a noncustodial parent kidnaps the child, maybe even taking the child out of the country. Abductions are usually discovered when the parent does not return the child after a visit. One of the most urgent steps in abduction cases is locating the child, especially if there is a danger that she or he will be taken out of the country. The *Hague Convention on the Civil Aspects of International Child Abduction,* which has been accepted by many countries, tries to ensure that an abducted child is returned promptly to the custodial parent. It also attempts to ensure that one country's rights of custody and access are respected by other countries. When the child is taken to a country that does not recognize the convention, especially one where fathers normally get custody and mothers have few rights, getting the child back is much more difficult. In such cases, parents can spend large sums on detectives and foreign lawyers in attempts to find and reclaim their children. Long-term abductions can be particularly damaging to children (Chiancone et al., 2001; Foreign Affairs and International Trade Canada, 2009).

In noncompliance with child support orders and kidnapping cases, the main victim is usually the child. Regardless of the parents' intentions, the child suffers in these cases through poverty, deprivation of a parent, being uprooted from a home, and being forced to live on the run.

Parents without Custody

Most noncustodial parents are men. For them, divorce often means the loss of a sense of home and family. Women traditionally have been expected to provide for the emotional needs of their families. When the marriage is broken, men are sometimes at a loss as to how to manage the father–child relationship on their own. Visits are seen as playtime, with little discipline involved. Sometimes, the father will increase his time at his parents' home, especially if it is conveniently located. Visits tend to become fewer and further apart if the ex-spouses are hostile toward each other or if the father does not make support payments regularly. Those who receive support for keeping up the relationship with their children are more likely to stay close to them (DeGarmo et al., 2008; Greene et al., 2003; Scott et al., 2007).

Society puts much pressure on mothers to assume custody of their children following the breakup of a marriage, but circumstances don't always permit it. The title of the Harriet Edwards book, *How Could You?* (1989) reflects the stigma experienced by mothers who do not have custody. These mothers, however, often feel that it is in their children's best interests to stay with their father because he can provide a more stable home at a time when they cannot. Regardless of their motives, noncustodial mothers are often deemed "unnatural" by society. In a few cases, courts have awarded custody to the father against the mother's wishes after she has left the children with him temporarily until she can establish her own home. By the time she can take them, the ex-husband can argue that it would be better if the children were not uprooted. Some mothers feel a custody battle would be too damaging for their children. Many women have no choice in the custody matter; they simply cannot afford to raise the children because their earning power is so much less than that of their former husbands (Edwards, 1989; Eicher-Catt, 2004).

The Future

Divorce shows no signs of going away. In fact, there are predictions that in the future, at least half of all marriages will be dissolved. As a society, this phenomenon presents us with a crucial issue: how best to ensure the healthy development of children living in divorced families.

Children tend to do best when they have continuity in their relationships. Unless there are overriding reasons, such as serious abuse, to deny it, they need regular contact with both parents. They also need contact with both extended families. For this to occur, all the adults involved must cooperate. Children also need to be assured of adequate financial support. Achieving this demands the serious commitment of both parents to the welfare of the children. It also requires effective enforcement laws as backup. For this to happen, the courts, and society at large, must take the matter seriously. Finally, children's interests are best served if their parents receive adequate backup from their extended families and society as a whole. If single parents are left to do everything alone—earn a living and raise children—without any assistance, the phenomenon of single-parent burnout will continue to occur. In the end, it means that society at large must be concerned about the well-being of these families.

Time to Review

1. How does divorce affect children?
2. What are the stressors and protective factors for children in a divorce situation?
3. Describe the different custody arrangements following a divorce.

Paul's Experience of Divorce

Maria and Francis married when they were both in their mid-20s. Francis worked as an engineer for a large automotive company and Maria was a financial consultant with a growing list of clients. Both focused on their careers during the first years. Much to their joy, Paul was born 10 years after their marriage.

By the time Paul was seven years old, Maria and Francis were hardly talking to each other except to argue about Paul. Francis was much more permissive than Maria, who said she needed Paul to be quiet and well-behaved so she could work from home. When Paul was eight, the couple separated and the divorce was finalized shortly after. The judge granted their request for shared custody. Maria stayed in the family home and Francis moved to an apartment half an hour away. Paul spent one week with Maria and the next with Francis. In the weeks with Francis, Paul stayed at the daycare after school until Francis picked him up. When he was with Maria, Paul often walked home with a friend.

From the start, Paul had been a "problem child" at school, calling other children names and occasionally bullying them. After his parents' separation, he began acting more aggressively. He gave a classmate a black eye when he was taunted for being a baby who had to go to daycare. Because the school had a no-violence policy, he was suspended for a week. He swore at the principal and accused her of unfairness. Maria and Francis had several meetings at the school with the principal, Paul's teacher, and a counsellor. On the advice of school staff, Paul started to see a psychologist. Both Francis and Maria were included in the first two sessions.

Five years after the divorce, Paul is much calmer and he is doing well academically at his junior high. He is a star on the soccer and basketball teams at school.

1. What are some of the social factors that have affected Paul and his family?
2. What do you think has caused Paul's difficulties? Identify his stressors and his protective factors.
3. Imagine you were one of the people in this story. What would you do differently?

Summary

What Has Been the History of Divorce in Canada?

Divorce is the most common deviation from the traditional family life cycle. Before Confederation, no divorce law existed in Canada. New Brunswick and Nova Scotia were the earliest provinces to have a divorce law, with very limited grounds. With Confederation in 1867, the federal Parliament gained exclusive authority in matters of divorce but simply allowed existing provincial laws to stand or to change. By 1968, all provinces except Quebec and

Newfoundland had divorce laws, with adultery basically the sole grounds. In 1968, Bill C-187 proposed wider grounds for divorce, including the no-fault principle. In 1985, the federal *Divorce Act* allowed for no-fault divorce and a shorter waiting period. Following each legal change, the number of divorces increased dramatically.

What Are Some of the Causes of Divorce?

The *Divorce Act* recognizes three legal grounds for divorce—cruelty, adultery, or being separated for one year. Almost all Canadians feel that divorce is justified when one partner abuses the other, fails to show respect, or is unfaithful. There are two ways of looking at why people divorce: we can examine either the stated reasons for divorce or the social causes underlying these reasons. Gottman identified four types of negative interaction so lethal to a marriage that he has labelled them the "Four Horsemen of Apocalypse." While each divorce is ultimately the result of the personal dynamics of a couple, researchers have catalogued social risk factors for divorce. Age is important, as is having less than a high-school education. Cohabitation before marriage increases the likelihood of divorce. Those who go to church infrequently are at risk. Statistically, interracial marriages are less stable than inracial ones. Spouses whose parents have divorced are more likely to divorce. When a couple has been together a longer time, and if they have children, they are less likely to divorce. Fewer people believe in the traditional idea of marriage and its responsibilities. Women's employment enables them to leave oppressive relationships. Costs of divorce are no longer as high, both socially and economically, as in the past. People now value individual happiness over family duty.

What Are the Developmental Stages of Divorce?

There are several phases in a divorce. The decision to divorce comes with the realization that the marriage cannot be saved. Often, it follows continuing conflict and temporary separation. Couples then must plan the breakup: they need to settle custody and financial issues. Finally, following separation, the family must reorganize. They need to separate marital and parental roles in order to allow the children to be part of the families of both parents.

What Are the Three Crises of Divorce?

The three crises of divorce are the emotional, the economic, and the parental. In the emotional crisis, the ex-spouses need to mourn the loss of their marriage, establish new identities as single persons, and form new social networks. If these tasks are accomplished, opportunities for personal growth will result. Economically, a divorce usually means a drop in the standard of living, especially for the parent with custody of the children. Legally, both parents are responsible for supporting the children. Any unfairness this might cause is tempered by the fact that property is divided equally and through child support and spousal support arrangements.

In addition, the parents need to work out new guidelines for authority over and responsibility for the children.

How Might Divorce Affect Children?

Children from divorced families are at greater risk of developing problems than those from stable two-parent families. As adults, they are more likely to have lower educational and employment achievement. They are also more likely to divorce. Most, however, do not have serious problems. In a divorce situation, children have stressors and protective factors. Ongoing conflict between parents, especially if children are drawn into it, means children are more likely to have serious problems. Children do best if their parents cooperate to provide them stable lives and if they keep up regular contact. Social support is also important. The fewer the transitions, such as moves or changes in custody, the better children fare. Regular child support payments help reduce poverty.

What Are Some of the Issues Around the Custody of Children?

Mothers were usually granted custody in the past. Now joint custody is the most common form and father custody is increasing. There are two major problem areas regarding custody. One is the failure to comply with support orders; provinces now have support enforcement programs in place. A second problem area is the failure to comply with custody and visiting provisions. If the custodial parent will not allow court-ordered visits with the other parent, this refusal may be grounds for a change in custody. The main victim in support, visitation, and custody violations is the child. Many parents without custody lose the sense of home and family. In these cases, visiting and support may taper off. Mothers who give up custody of their children often face stigma, even if they feel they are acting in the best interests of the children.

Class Assignments

1. In some communities, mediation is available for couples seeking divorce. How does mediation differ from using the court to solve differences over custody and support? Explain the factors that make mediation most effective. Find out if mediation services are available in your community.
2. Imagine a family with a seven-year-old boy. The parents are planning to divorce and would like joint custody of their son. Working in pairs, draw up a plan for co-parenting. Take into account schooling, residence, holidays, transportation, and any other factor you think is relevant.
3. Collect references to divorce in the media: movies, TV shows, magazines, books, newspapers, online, etc. Organize these references as positive, negative, or neutral toward divorce. Summarize what you found and present to the class how the media portray divorce.

Personal Assignments

The following assignments are designed to help you think about your own experience and opinions:

1. Following some divorces, custody of children is split: one child will stay with the mother and another with the father. What are the advantages and disadvantages of this arrangement? Do you think that it is all right for siblings to be separated in this way or do you think they should be kept together? Explain.

2. Do you think that grandparents should be given the legal right to have access to their grandchildren or either sole or joint custody following the divorce of the parents? Why or why not?

3. What do you think are legitimate reasons for a couple to divorce? How does this compare with Canada's divorce law?

Chapter 11
The Second Time Around

LEARNING OBJECTIVES

What are the trends in remarriage in Canada?

What are some of the issues in forming a stepfamily?

Which are some of the factors that lead to success and failure in stepfamily relationships?

What is the relationship between the stepfamily and society at large?

Once upon a time there lived a man with a wife and a beautiful daughter. While his child was still young, the man's wife died. The man was at his wit's end trying to make a home for his child.

"I must find a wife," he told himself. "Then we will have a proper home."

So he did as he said, and found a widow with two daughters. They were soon married. His new wife happily moved in, along with her children.

Soon, however, both she and her daughters had turned his child into a servant. The girl had to do all the heavy cleaning, and was at their beck and call all day and all night. Sometimes she crept into the fireplace to rest from the demands of her stepmother and stepsisters, so she was always covered in ashes.

"You're just a cinder girl," they taunted her.

And that is how she came to be called Cinderella.

While most people intend their marriage to last forever, the reality is that some marriages do not and end in divorce or the death of one spouse. However, a large proportion of people who experience divorce or widowhood will at some point try again to form a couple. If children are involved, this becomes a stepfamily. Although they are increasingly common, in our society there is still a great deal of confusion and ambiguity about how to form, maintain, and deal with stepfamilies.

In this chapter, we will look at the trends in remarriage and stepfamily formation in Canada. While stepfamilies may look like other two-parent families, there are many significant differences. Each stepfamily must negotiate new boundaries and roles for its members. We will examine the different stages of forming the new family system and some of the factors that can help or hinder its success. The wider society can also give support or create challenges to families as they undergo this process.

Where Do I Fit In?

1. Do you think that Cinderella is just a fairy tale, or do you know any real Cinderellas?
2. What is your experience with stepfamilies, either directly or indirectly through other family members or friends?
3. What are the differences between stepfamilies and non-stepfamilies?

Remarriage and Stepfamiles

remarriage: a marriage that takes place after a previous marriage has ended

Remarriage is a marriage that takes place after a previous marriage has ended. As we have seen, the divorce rate is increasing, so remarriages are also increasing. The 2011 census counted stepfamilies for the first time and they represented about 1 in 8 couple families with children. The census also for the first time counted the number of children living in stepfamilies, and 1 out of every 10 children aged 14 and under lived in a stepfamily in 2011 (Statistics Canada, 2012t). **Stepfamily** refers to a family where the children are related to one parent but not the other. If the current married spouse or common-law partner has adopted the child or children of the other married spouse or common-law partner, then it is no longer a stepfamily.

The 2011 census counted 464 335 stepfamilies, which represented 12.6 percent of couple families with children. More than half were **simple stepfamilies**; that is, those in which all children are the biological or adopted children of one and only one married spouse or common-law partner in the couple and whose birth or adoption preceded the current relationship. The rest were **complex stepfamilies**, also called blended families. A complex stepfamily is a couple family that contains children from:

- each married spouse or common-law partner and no other children
- one married spouse or common-law partner and at least one other biological or adopted child of the couple
- each married spouse or common-law partner and at least one other biological or adopted child of the couple (Statistics Canada, 2012t)

While the proportion of stepfamilies has remained fairly stable, the predominant type of stepfamily is changing. Over the past 15 years, the proportion of simple stepfamilies has declined while the proportion of complex stepfamilies has grown (see Figure 11.1). The growth in the proportion of complex stepfamilies is primarily due to an increase in the number in which the parents have a child together (Vézina, 2012).

stepfamily: a family where the children are related to one parent but not the other

simple stepfamily: a family in which all children are the biological or adopted children of one and only one married spouse or common-law partner in the couple

complex (blended) stepfamily: variations of the stepfamily form

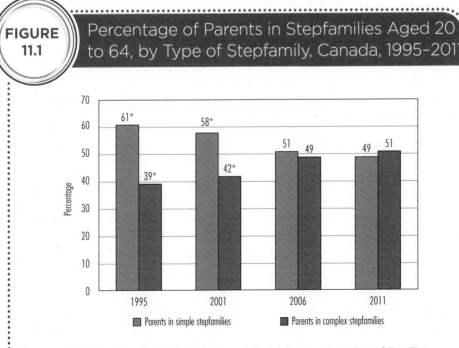

FIGURE 11.1

Percentage of Parents in Stepfamilies Aged 20 to 64, by Type of Stepfamily, Canada, 1995–2011

Source: Statistics Canada. 2012. *2011 General Social Survey: Overview of Families in Canada*. Catalogue No. 89-650-XWE. Ottawa, Ontario. Statistics Canada. http://www5.statcan.gc.ca/bsolc/olc-cel/olc-cel?catno=89-650-XIE&lang=eng#formatdisp

Until the end of World War II, most remarriages followed the death of a spouse. Now they are likelier to follow divorce. Complex factors lie behind the shift from remarriage after widowhood to remarriage after divorce. First, life expectancy has increased, so there is less likelihood people will be widowed at a young age, when remarriage is more likely. Second, following changes in the law in 1968 and 1985, divorces have increased enormously, a pattern most evident in younger rather than older people. Other factors that may affect remarriage rates are improved pensions, which permit older people to choose to live independently, and greater acceptance of common-law unions and single living.

Over the past 25 years, the trend has been that fewer people who are divorced intend to remarry. Between 1990 and 2006, the proportion of divorced people stating that they intended to remarry decreased from 26 percent to 22 percent. Put another way, more than 6 out of 10 divorced Canadians stated that they did not wish to remarry (Beaupré, 2008). When looking at these statistics, there are two things to consider. First, these data are based on asking people what they intend to do, which may be quite different from what they actually do. Second, this question is only about people's intentions to remarry. However, people may form common-law relationships without remarrying. In 2006, the last year that data were available, 26 percent of women and 37 percent of men had entered into a new conjugal relationship (married or common-law) within three years of divorce. For the five-year period following divorce, these proportions rose to 36 percent of women and 51 percent of men, and within 20 years, 69 percent of women and 82 percent of men had formed new unions (Vanier Institute of the Family, 2010).

Certain factors can influence the choice to remarry. Fewer divorced parents with children plan to rewed, and the intention to remarry decreases with age. Also, people who have divorced multiple times are less likely to want to remarry. (See Table 11.1.) If divorced Canadians plan to remarry less often today than in the past, it is partly because many are choosing common-law unions rather that marriage when starting a new relationship (Beaupré, 2008).

Parents in stepfamilies differ from those who are not in stepfamilies. First, they tend to be older. This is not surprising, because a stepfamily is often not the first family formed by the parents. Second, stepfamily parents are more than three times more likely to be in a common-law union than to be married. About 48 percent of parents in stepfamilies were living common-law in 2011, compared with 14 percent among parents in non-stepfamilies. Third, nearly twice as many parents in stepfamilies identified financial concerns as the main source of stress in their daily lives compared to non-stepfamily parents (Vézina, 2012).

There are also some notable similarities. There is no significant difference between the family income of parents in stepfamilies and those in non-stepfamilies. Parents in stepfamilies are slightly more active in the labour force, but the difference is minor. Roughly 6 in 10 parents in both stepfamilies and non-stepfamilies reported that they have delayed payments when they were unable to meet a financial deadline (Statistics Canada, 2012t).

The experience of being in a stepfamily is more common than most statistics show. For example, we must consider the probability of living in a stepfamily

TABLE 11.1

Proportion of People Who Intend to Marry or Remarry by Marital Status and Region of Residence, Canada, 2011

Region	Marriage Intentions (persons never married)			Remarriage Intentions (persons who have already been married)				Total
	Single	Common-law	Total	Common-law	Divorced	Widowed	Total	
Canada								
Yes	62%	39%	56%	24%	10%	2%	10%	44%
No	20%	38%	24%	50%	66%	89%	71%	37%
Uncertain	17%	22%	18%	25%	23%	8%	18%	18%
Atlantic								
Yes	62%	56%	61%	34%	10%	n/a	10%	46%
No	22%	25%	23%	36%	68%	89%	71%	37%
Uncertain	15%	17%	16%	32%	22%	10%	18%	16%
Quebec								
Yes	44%	30%	38%	14%	6%	n/a	7%	30%
No	33%	46%	39%	66%	74%	91%	77%	48%
Uncertain	22%	24%	23%	19%	19%	7%	15%	21%
Ontario								
Yes	69%	44%	65%	27%	11%	1%	10%	51%
No	16%	30%	18%	43%	61%	88%	70%	31%
Uncertain	14%	23%	16%	29%	26%	8%	18%	16%
Prairies								
Yes	67%	53%	64%	31%	13%	2%	13%	51%
No	16%	26%	17%	38%	64%	85%	66%	30%
Uncertain	17%	20%	17%	27%	22%	11%	19%	18%
British Columbia								
Yes	64%	51%	62%	34%	11%	n/a	11%	48%
No	16%	34%	19%	38%	62%	90%	69%	33%
Uncertain	19%	14%	18%	26%	26%	9%	19%	19%

Notes: Percentages may not add to 100%. Totals include the "don't know" and "refused to answer" categories, which are not shown in the table.

In each region, respondents were asked about their intention to marry or remarry. For example, in Canada, 62 percent of people who are currently single said they intend to marry, and 39 percent of people who have never married and are currently living common-law said they intend to marry. Among those who were once married but no longer are, 56 percent of those who are currently living common-law said they intend to remarry. Among those who are currently divorced, 10 percent said they intend to remarry, and among those who are currently widowed, just 2 percent intend to remarry.

Source: Statistics Canada. 2012. *Distribution of people who intend to marry or remarry by de facto marital status and region of residence, Canada, 2011* (table). "2011 General Social Survey: Overview of Families in Canada." Catalogue No. 89-650-XWE. Ottawa, Ontario. Statistics Canada. http://www.statcan.gc.ca/pub/89-650-x/2012001/tbl/tbl01-eng.htm

over a lifetime. In addition, most statistics are based on the residential family unit. Children can have step-relatives they see regularly, but only those with whom they usually live enter the statistics (Juby, 2003–04). Stepfamilies are also formed through first marriages of single mothers and through cohabitation. A small proportion of stepfamilies result when a gay or lesbian partner brings along a child. They face the same problems as heterosexual couples, as well as stigma over their sexual orientation (Pann & Crosbie-Burnett, 2005).

Time to Review

1. What are the different types of stepfamilies?
2. What are the trends in remarriage and stepfamily formation in Canada?
3. How do parents in stepfamilies differ from those who are not in stepfamilies?

Forming a New Family System

Unlike nuclear families, remarriage families have few social norms to guide them. They do not fit the expected patterns set for first-marriage families.

Stages of Remarriage—Family Formation

There are three distinct stages in establishing a second marriage: entering the new relationship, planning the new marriage and family, and forming the remarriage family (Carter & McGoldrick, 1999a). These stages are similar to creating a first-marriage family, but the presence of children and ex-partners adds complications.

First, people must achieve an emotional divorce from their earlier union (Recker, 2002). If a great deal of anger toward the ex-spouse continues, there will be no emotional divorce because anger provides a powerful link. The new couple must also commit themselves to the new family with all its complications. When children are present, the new relationship also involves becoming a stepparent as well as a romantic partner. Some couples move cautiously before making a commitment. Others rush into a new relationship, often ignoring its impact on their children (Marsiglio, 2004).

The second phase involves planning the new marriage. Open and honest communication is important. The couple must accept that difficulties will not be solved overnight. They need to maintain relationships with others outside the household, for example with the ex-spouse over co-parenting and financial support. Extended family members must establish relationships with the new spouse and his or her children. Children need to stay connected with the extended families of both ex-spouses. Throughout this phase, partners must accept their own and others' anxieties.

Finally, the new family is formed. Doing so involves renegotiating boundaries and roles, and letting children maintain their relationship with their other biological parent and other relatives. Members may find the cultures, customs, and even forms of communication that individuals bring from prior families unfamiliar. The new family now has to develop its own rituals to promote a sense of identity. Expanding the co-parenting team to include the stepparent is critical. The responsibilities of each adult, therefore, need to be negotiated (Marsiglio, 2004; Pasley & Lee, 2010; Whiteside, 2006).

Boundaries

One of the main differences between first marriages and later ones involves family boundaries. As we saw in Chapter 1, boundaries mark out who belongs to the family. They must be open enough to allow interaction with others, yet clear enough that the family feels some unity. Establishing traditions, for example with holidays and events like birthdays, helps build family solidarity (Kelley, 2003–04; Visher et al., 2003).

In first-marriage families, boundaries are relatively well defined. Members live in the same place and are supported by household adults. Authority and responsibility rest with the married couple, who are also the parents of the children (Kaufman, 1993). Remarriage families do not fit this pattern. First, parents and children do not all live together. Custody arrangements determine where children live, how they visit, and whether siblings live together. If both adults have children, the custody and visiting arrangements of the second set complicate the situation. The number of people in the home can vary from week to week.

Second, partners often keep finances separate, partly because of the needs of children from earlier unions. Money management is a source of stress for many families (Pasley & Lee, 2010). Financial support for children is often partly provided by non-household members. The parent paying may have little control over the use of money.

Third, authority over the children and responsibility for them rest in two households, often with varying rules. Family members may have individual definitions of family membership. There may also be ambiguity when stepparents cohabit rather than marry (Sarkisian, 2006; Visher et al., 2003). Having children with more than one partner expands kin networks. However, the resulting boundary ambiguity may reduce the financial and childcare support available (Harknett & Knab, 2007).

Some families respond to boundary ambiguity by attempting to become like a first-marriage family, but doing so is not realistic. Families may, for example, try to draw a tight boundary of loyalties around the remarriage family and cut off contact with the nonresidential parent. Demands to belong exclusively to one parent's family can throw children into a conflict of loyalties. In fact, keeping boundaries permeable, or open, is usually the most workable option. The new family needs to allow members, including visiting children, to move in and out and yet establish a stable lifestyle. It also needs to allow for contact between households of current and former spouses with respect to the children. Permeable boundaries also permit children to move back and forth between households with the least amount of strain (Church, 2004; McGoldrick & Carter, 1999; Visher et al., 2003).

Roles

Confusion over roles goes along with boundary ambiguity. Role strain occurs if there is a misfit between individuals and the roles they are expected to fill, or if there is no recognized role. For example, stepmothers at present have only two social scripts to follow—the adoring biological mother and the stereotypically wicked stepmother—neither of which fits most families.

One of the main difficulties in remarriage families is that too many candidates exist for available roles. This fact affects stepparents in particular. The children already have two biological parents and are not usually interested in replacing them. If the new spouse tries to assume the role of the parent of the same sex, children will be resistant and resentful. North American culture has no terms to identify these new relationships other than adding "step" before "mother," "brother," and so on. The lack of appropriate terms makes it difficult, especially for children, to understand these relationships (Kellas et al., 2008). Loyalty issues are involved. Conflict can break out over many issues, from unfamiliar rituals to discipline.

A key time for discomfort is any event involving the child. At graduations, for example, families have the potentially awkward task of including an extra parent figure. Such issues emphasize that the stepparent is not the "real" parent (Kaufman, 1993). Similarly, there are "extra" grandparents and other kin (see Box 11.1 on page 296). It is important for remarried adults to be realistic and remain flexible (Recker, 2002).

Traditional gender roles (in which women are expected to take responsibility for the emotional well-being of the family and men are expected to manage finances) work against stepfamilies. These roles are unrealistic when some children are virtual strangers to the wife and some of the family's income and expenditure is outside the husband's control. Stepparents need to work out an appropriate role. Often, in successful remarriage families, they serve as adult friends rather than as parents to the stepchildren (Schmeeckle, 2007; Visher et al., 2003).

A difficulty facing some children is the loss of accustomed roles, something that can occur in at least three ways. One way is that when the new family includes stepsiblings, one oldest child loses his or her position, and so does one youngest child. Another way is that if the child has been the only boy or girl and gains a same-sex stepsibling, the child forfeits that special status. A third way is that if the child has been a confidant of a single parent, that role is usually taken by the new partner (Kelley, 2003–04; Pann & Crosbie-Burnett, 2006).

Renegotiating family boundaries and roles may take place over an extended period. Even when the family achieves a comfortable working arrangement, it will need continuing adjustment as children mature and visiting and custody agreements are altered. Role ambiguity may continue throughout life. Young adults often perceive current and former stepparents as not quite family members. Stepparents tend to be regarded as family if they are currently married to, not simply cohabiting with, parents (Schmeeckle et al., 2006). Adults also feel less responsibility to support aging stepparents than they do biological parents (Coleman et al., 2006; Sherman, 2006).

The Couple Relationship

As in any other marriage, partners in remarriages have the task of commitment, because a strong couple bond is the foundation for the new family. Commitment may be considered the combination of the benefits that come from a partnership (love, trust) and the barriers that can make it difficult to leave the relationship (children, financial need). How partners view commitment reflects their desire to maintain the relationship and is an important predictor of other positive aspects (Ehrenberg et al., 2012). Establishing boundaries around the couple relationship helps define social roles, but this task is made more difficult by the many pulls on it, the presence of children and the influence of previous partners among them. Couples also need to realign relationships with their children, ex-spouses, extended family, and friends.

Often, couples in second marriages are less romantic but more realistic and honest about difficulties in the marriage. After an earlier breakup, remarried couples may be particularly sensitive to conflict. This sensitivity can result in more open communication and greater awareness of the partner's feelings. Some couples, however, are so afraid that disagreements will lead to another divorce that they avoid them, but this approach can lead to deep-rooted difficulties in their relationship (Allen et al., 2001; Coleman et al., 2000).

The fact that the parent–child bond began before the marriage, not following it, can create difficulties in the new spousal relationship. Stepparents may compete with stepchildren for the attention of the spouse/parent. In addition, privacy and time alone for the couple may be scarce. Frequently, couple time cuts into children's time when the latter feel left out and confused following the remarriage (Visher et al., 2003).

The ex-spouse can also affect the new marriage. The fact that he or she has a continuing relationship with the children means there is also a continuing relationship with the ex-partner. Some contacts are necessary to arrange visits and deal with the children's welfare. What happens in one household, such as how bedwetting is handled, affects what happens in the other (Whiteside, 2006). Ann Crytser (1990) has coined the expression "wife-in-law" to refer to the relationship between current and ex-wives. This relationship is usually unchosen, unwanted, and without rules or traditions.

The influence of ex-spouses can vary widely. Last-minute cancellations or requests for visits can disrupt a couple's plans or deprive them of privacy. The ex-spouse may apply for a custody change. Failure to meet support obligations on time or requests for additional money can wreak havoc with financial planning. Occasionally, an individual expects an ex-partner to solve problems, such as household repairs and day-to-day discipline; a new spouse can resent such intrusions. Some difficulties involve boundaries and appropriate roles, and need to be resolved during system reorganization. Others are a necessary point of contact for the children's well-being. Often, current and ex-spouses must interact in public places, for instance at times of crisis (funerals) or celebration (graduations and weddings); such situations add to the stress (Church, 2004; Pann & Crosbie-Burnett, 2005).

BOX 11.1 | Do Grandparents Have Rights?

The story is sad but too common. When Mattie and Brad divorced, Mattie was granted primary custody of their two children. Brad had visiting rights. On his weekends, he brought the children to his parents' home. After three years, Brad was transferred out of province. About the same time, Mattie remarried. She now refuses to let Brad's parents visit their grandchildren. She believes that visits should take place on Brad's time. Besides, she says his parents are critical of her and her new husband, and believes their attitude will harm her relationship with her children. Brad's parents consider suing for visiting rights.

Following divorce, grandparents tend to be cut off from grandchildren in two situations. In the first, their former child-in-law has custody and their own child has little contact with the children. In the second, there is conflict between grandparents and their former child-in-law's new partner. The father's parents are at particularly high risk of losing contact if the mother has custody. Some grandparents try extra hard to get along with the custodial parent. Others lose touch with grandchildren. A few go to court.

Provinces vary in rights granted grandparents. Quebec is most far-reaching in its Civil Code. A father or mother cannot interfere with grandchild–grandparent relationships unless there is a grave reason. When there is a dispute, the court decides. In other provinces, a relative can apply for access. Some, such as Alberta, specifically mention grandparents in their laws.

Courts in most provinces rely on the child's best interests in making a decision. In Quebec, parents need to show that contact will harm the child. In most other provinces, grandparents need to prove that having contact will benefit the child. It is presumed, unless proven otherwise, that parents will make the best choices for their children. Courts tend to place more weight on grandparents' claims if they have lived with their grandchild or have had a great deal of contact; for instance, by providing daycare. If there is a high level of conflict between parents and grandparents, then courts usually decide that cutting off visits is better for the child's family and thus for the child.

In some cases, the conflict is settled with the help of a mediator. That is how Mattie and Brad's parents reached a resolution. The grandparents can have six visits a year. Mattie will decide the time and place.

Sources: Connidis, 2010; Department of Justice, 2004; Goldberg, 2003; Kruk, 1995.

The most common difficulty between spouses, however, is conflict over children. When a partner wants the romantic relationship but not the children, the relationship is often doomed. Since the stepparent role is not clearly defined, parents, stepparents, and children alike may have contradictory expectations.

Conflict may develop out of parents' different approaches to discipline, or out of children's attempts to manipulate or to appeal to the birth parent's loyalty. In families where there are teens or young adults, conflict may occur if the biological parent becomes jealous of affection between stepparent and stepchild, especially if it is interpreted in sexual terms (Bray & Kelly, 1998; Marsiglio, 2004; McGoldrick & Carter, 1999). Results from studies are mixed. Some find that the presence of children is a prime factor in remarriage failure. Others report that their presence contributes to marital satisfaction. Partners usually become aware of insurmountable difficulties early in the remarriage; thus, most divorces occur quickly. If the marriage survives longer, it is likely to be as stable as any first marriage (McGoldrick & Carter, 1999).

Residential Parent–Child Relationships

The parent–child relationship often suffers in the early post-divorce period. Given that the residential parent is restructuring his or her life, often little emotional or physical energy is available for the child. The child, who is also having difficulty, often takes bad feelings out on the parent through defiance or other forms of obnoxious behaviour (Greene et al., 2003).

Some children face the parent's restructuring after a breakup by becoming a parentified child—a child who accepts an unusually high degree of the parent's responsibilities of care and nurturing. Often, the single parent and child close ranks and become dependent on each other. The child may become a confidant(e), especially if parent and child are mother and daughter. (In general, there is more information about residential mothers than residential fathers.) When the parent remarries, the child must give up some responsibility and closeness to the new adult in the family. Naturally, the child feels loss and resentment. As a result, the child may become more demanding toward the birth parent or become depressed and withdrawn (Kaufman, 1993; Kelley, 2003–04). Often, the residential parent, especially the mother, continues to take the main responsibility for the child (Visher et al., 2003). Biological fathers tend to spend more time with children than stepfathers do (Whiteside, 2006).

Nonresidential Parent–Child Relationships

The relationship between the child and the nonresidential parent varies a great deal among families. Some parents have little or no contact with their children. Others are very involved in decisions about children and in their physical care. Variations are related to the type of custody, the distance between homes, the length of time since the divorce, the age of the child, and the amount of support paid. If the parent is depressed or feels guilty, visits may be avoided because they aggravate unpleasant feelings. Higher income and education and reasonably friendly relations with the ex-spouse usually mean more frequent contact. Nonresidential mothers are more likely to maintain regular visits. If either parent remarries, visits with the nonresidential parent tend to drop off (Greene et al., 2003). The level of contact is also tied to regular payment of child support.

About one-fourth of American adolescents who have both a residential stepfather and a nonresidential biological father say they have a close relationship with both. They also tend to be closer to their mothers, especially when the new union is happy. If they are close to neither father, on average, they experience more problems. About 16 percent are close to their nonresidential father but not their stepfather (King, 2006). Even those who have limited contact with biological fathers tend to increase contact in adulthood (Schmeeckle, 2007).

Often, children's contact with nonresidential parents involves social and fun activities such as games or trips, while the residential parent is involved in day-to-day activities, including homework and discipline. Thus, noncustodial parents are seen as the source of pleasure but are cut off from daily living. Custodial parents, however, may become resentful at being forced to be the disciplinarian and "bad guy."

Even though the residential parent may have negative feelings about visits, contact between the children and nonresidential parent is valuable for children's well-being. Yet keeping up connections may be a source of conflict. Children in stepfather families see more conflict between parents than other children do. It is not that there is unusually high disagreement at home or between their biological parents; rather, the two types of conflict added together produce the higher levels (Hanson et al., 1996).

The Stepparent–Stepchild Relationship

The relationship between stepparent and stepchild is important for two reasons. First, many marriages founder because problems in this relationship eventually destroy the marriage. Second, adolescents in stepfamilies are at risk of developing behavioural problems.

Successful stepparents accomplish two tasks: they develop an appropriately affectionate relationship with the child, and they establish themselves as legitimate parental authorities. Unfortunately, the tasks are somewhat contradictory and many families fall short of these goals. But one factor works in favour of stepfamilies: most children prefer to live in a two-parent family.

Developing a Relationship

How well stepparents develop relationships with children depends somewhat on the children's age and sex. Stepparents tend to be more successful with younger children, who may become attached more readily. Both stepfathers and stepmothers also report more positive relationships with boys than girls. The stepmother–stepdaughter relationship brings the most severe problems. Often, daughters feel responsible for family emotional relationships. Since stepmothers also feel responsible, stepdaughters either feel displaced or resist sharing this role (McGoldrick & Carter, 1999; Whiteside, 2006).

The acceptance of stepfamily members is often affected by loyalty issues. The child may see the stepparent as an intruder trying to take the "real" parent's place. If attachment does begin to grow, the child may feel disloyal to the same-sex

Victim Impact
Statement cards,
for Wicked
Stepmother's Day.

Source: Cornered by Baldwin/Universal Uclick.

biological parent. In either case, the child may be anxious and resentful enough to ward off the new parent: he or she may try to drive a wedge into the marriage (Pann &Crosbie-Burnett, 2005; Whiteside, 2006). Stepparents may also feel disloyal if they become attached to their stepchildren. Men who left their children in the custody of their ex-wife do not relate as well to stepchildren as do men who were bachelors. Part of the reason, some believe, results from the father's guilt over leaving his own children (Bray & Kelly, 1998).

Another complication between some opposite-sex stepparents and stepchildren arises because there is no explicit incest taboo surrounding this relationship. Stepfathers may find it easier to express affection verbally or through granting special privileges than physically. Sometimes, conflict is used to keep a safe distance, since showing fondness may arouse sexual feelings (Bray & Kelly, 1998; Pann & Crosbie-Burnett, 2005).

Stepparenting is not one-way. It is affected by the stepparent's attitudes toward family life and by previous experiences with children. It is also shaped by the residential parent's relationship with the children and her or his comfort at supporting the stepparent's efforts at parenting. The children themselves take an active role in shaping the relationship. They may be compliant with new rules or defy them (Marsiglio, 2004; Pann & Crosbie-Burnett, 2005). Sometimes. stepparents withdraw from stepchildren to reduce conflict. Disagreement can be healthier than disengagement, however, because at least it is a sign of stepparent involvement.

Discipline

Discipline is another potential area of conflict. Stepparents are not seen as "real" parents because they are not the children's birth parents. Only "real" parents, in the minds of many, are entitled to be disciplinarians. The issue can be complicated by differences in child-rearing styles and strategies or by the failure of the residential birth parent to be a disciplinarian. The most successful stepparents are those who first develop a friendly relationship with the child and then assert their authority. Adolescents tend to do best when stepparents are supportive and not very controlling. The secret to success lies with the birth parent. He or she must legitimate the role and authority of the stepparent (Coleman et al., 2000; Whiteside, 2006).

Relationships between Stepbrothers and Stepsisters

A marriage between divorced parents creates stepsiblings. Many stepsiblings do not live together, since it is most common for children to live with their mothers. Unless visits are arranged so only one set of children is in the house at once, there is periodic interaction between resident and visiting children. With more fathers being granted custody, the likelihood of two sibling groups living together has increased. For children in these blended families, adjustments have to be made on a more permanent basis.

Children expect their birth parents to consider them special and to side with them in conflicts. Any differences in treatment are usually interpreted by children as favouritism. A key ingredient in this mix is a sense of loss and jealousy when birth parents spend more time with stepchildren and less with their own. Yet stepparents tend to respond less to affection from stepchildren than from biological children (Kaufman, 1993; Kelley, 2003–04). There may also be problems when only some children receive expensive gifts from relatives (Kelley, 2003–04).

If one set of children visits or moves into the family home, problems may arise over turf. When children are expected to share space and toys, opportunities for friction increase greatly. The conflict is made worse if the two sets of children differ in such aspects of daily life as tidiness or use of others' property (Kelley, 2003–04; Visher et al., 2003).

Children's roles in families may conflict. Two only children, for example, may have difficulty getting used to having another child around, especially if they are the same age and sex. Adjusting to the fact that there can be only one oldest and one youngest in a family may also be hard. Parents often discount a child's sense of loss if he or she has to give up an important role (Kelley, 2003–2004; Pann & Crosbie-Burnett, 2005).

When there are adolescents of both sexes in a family, conflict may be adopted as a way of maintaining a safe distance. The incest taboo between stepsiblings ranges from weak to nonexistent, and conflict provides a buffer against sexual attraction (Kaufman, 1993).

On the positive side, stepsiblings can provide one another with emotional support, for example if visits with the nonresidential parent fall through. Since they have all had similar experiences of losing their original family and having to adjust to living in a new blended family, they can form a mutual self-help group (Kaufman, 1993).

The Child Born into a Stepfamily

About half of stepfamilies have a child born to them. This event is most common with younger mothers. Such children change the family because they are related to everyone biologically. Having a baby is related to stepfamily stability, either because the baby strengthens relationships or because couples having a child are likelier to have a strong bond (Juby, 2003–04; Martin & Le Bourdais, 2009). The mutual child may symbolize family peace and harmony because the birth demonstrates the love and commitment of the couple. Such a position may make it harder for the child to separate from the family as a teen or young adult (Whiteside, 2006). There have, however, been only a few studies of relationships in these families or of the effect on both stepchildren and children of the remarriage.

The birth of a new child may reduce the attention given other children in the family. However, this shift occurs regardless of family type, and is not specific to stepfamilies (Stewart, 2005).

One study compared shared children in blended families to those in non-stepfamilies. Both have the same relationship with their biological parents and generally live in stable families. The shared adolescent in a blended family, however, fares worse. Shared and stepchildren are similar in the way they turn out. The researchers speculate that these findings come from family system effects, where events in one part have an impact on the whole system (Halpern-Meekin & Tach, 2008).

FIGURE 11.2

Stepfamilies Are Different

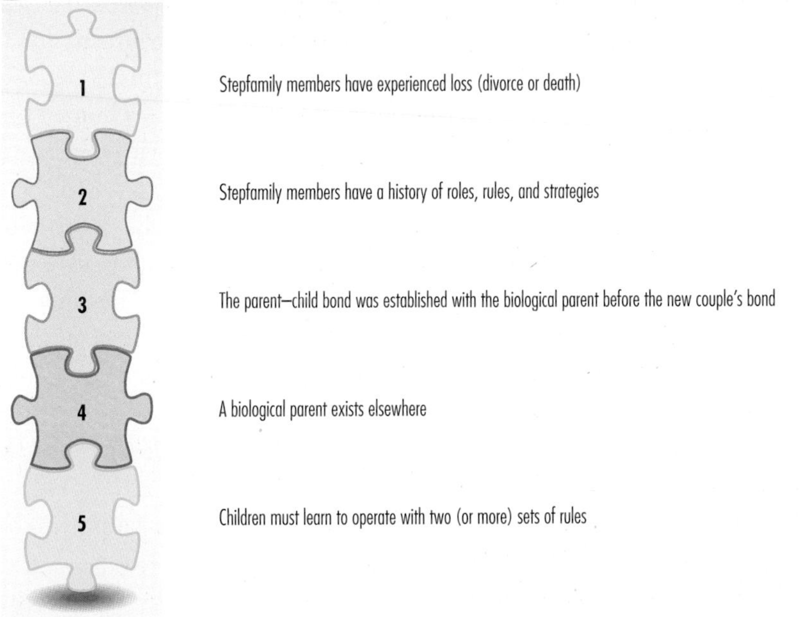

1. Stepfamily members have experienced loss (divorce or death)

2. Stepfamily members have a history of roles, rules, and strategies

3. The parent–child bond was established with the biological parent before the new couple's bond

4. A biological parent exists elsewhere

5. Children must learn to operate with two (or more) sets of rules

Source: PointaDesign/Shutterstock.

Effects of Stepfamily Living on Children

Researchers have studied the effects on children of living in a stepfamily. Stepchildren fare much like children raised by single mothers. They have more educational, emotional, and behavioural difficulties than children growing up in their original nuclear families. As always, though, we need to separate statistics from individuals. Many studies have found that children in stepfamilies are at greater risk for maladjustment and lower self-esteem; on the other hand, many stepchildren do as well as those living with both biological parents (Coleman et al., 2000).

One way to explain why some stepchildren do better than others is to look beyond blaming the stepfamily as the primary cause of problems. The number and nature of stressors a child experiences during the parents' divorce and remarriage, as well as the resources the child has to deal with them, help identify children at greater risk of negative effects.

As suggested earlier, some children in stepfamilies may be at greater risk because they have undergone several family transitions. The more life changes children experience, the more stress they have. The social capital model suggests that the time and energy these new relationships require can place a burden on the family's social capital—the time parents have for interacting with their children.

In our culture, stepfamilies are full of ambiguous roles that must be negotiated. The lack of readily available social scripts leads to further conflict. Negative social stereotypes of stepfamilies may directly affect a child's self-esteem. They may also create general family stress that trickles down to the children (Doyle et al., 2002). Parenting may differ in stepfamilies when stepparents show less affection and supervise children less. However, the parenting styles—authoritative, authoritarian, permissive, and uninvolved—have similar results whether used by biological parents or stepparents.

Finally, stepchildren's problems may reach back before the new family was formed, for example from parents' psychological problems or from poverty. None of the explanations succeed in fully accounting for stepchildren's disadvantages (Coleman et al., 2000; Pann & Crosbie-Burnett, 2005; Whiteside, 2006).

Remarriage and the Family Life Cycle

The experience of remarriage differs according to the life-cycle stage of each partner. If they are in the same phase, they share common problems. Their greatest strain involves responsibilities to their children, especially if they are adolescents. For example, the family's need to form attachments often conflicts with the adolescent's normal need to separate from the family. Difficulties also arise out of the teen's ability to manipulate parents and out of adolescent sexuality. In later life-cycle stages, grown children may be reluctant to shift their "normal" image of parents and/or grandparents to include a stepparent. Particular problems arise if one spouse is considerably older than the other and their life-cycle stages differ. Some men, for instance, marry women roughly the same age as their children. In general, the greater the difference in life-cycle stage, the harder it is to adapt because husband and wife are dealing with different life-cycle issues (McGoldrick & Carter, 1999; Pann & Crosbie-Burnett, 2005; Visher et al., 2003; Whiteside, 2006).

Family Adaptation

After a 10-year longitudinal study, James Bray identified three types of stepfamily forms. These are described in Table 11.2.

TABLE 11.2 — James Bray's Stepfamily Types

Type	Characteristics
Romantic	The couple romanticizes the new family and expects that feelings of love, closeness, and harmony will arise immediately. Probably as a result of unrealistic expectations, this type is least likely to succeed.
Matriarchal	As the name suggests, the female parent has a dominant function. She often has a powerful personality and is comfortable taking the leadership role. This type can succeed if the male parent has compatible values.
Neotraditional	This type comes closest to the idealized image of the loving and functional stepfamily. The couple has a realistic understanding of the issues and challenges of forming a stepfamily and develops effective strategies for dealing with them. This type of stepfamily is the most successful.

Source: James H. Bray & John Kell, *Stepfamilies: Love, Marriage and Parenting in the First Decade*. New York: Broadway Books. 1998.

A useful way of looking at how remarriage families adapt is by considering the stressors they face, the resources they use, and the meaning they place on their experiences. All these factors are in play in early and later stages of forming new family relationships. Stressors include boundary and role ambiguity, unresolved emotional issues from earlier relationships, and the need to adjust to different family cultures. Negative social attitudes can add to the stress. When stressors outweigh strengths, the family can enter crisis mode.

Successful stepfamilies have certain strengths in common. Flexibility, respect, patience, communication, and a sense of humour are characteristic within the family group (Michaels, 2006). Other strengths include realistic expectations and the ability to cooperate with one another. Support for the new relationship among the extended family and within the community may also help.

How family members view the remarriage affects their adaptation. Family members may regard the new union as a second chance or an intrusion into the parent–child relationship. Some may expect the new family to be exactly like an intact family. Others consider it a flexible family form that can be shaped to meet members' needs. All these perspectives affect family adaptation (Pann & Crosbie-Burnett, 2005).

The Stepfamily and the Wider Society

The relationship of the stepfamily to society is somewhat confused. In some ways, stepfamilies are indistinguishable from first-marriage families because two parents are living with their children. Yet the fact that they seem the same leads to the expectation that they will be like other families. Some of the differences seem almost petty, yet they can create problems. For example, school officials may not send duplicate school notices to each parent (Olsen, 1997).

Stepfamilies also experience role ambiguity. They do not receive clear messages from society about norms for dealing with the complex relationships in their families. The stepfamily is sometimes called an "incomplete institution" because it does not come with the kind of ready-made norms and roles surrounding first-marriage families (Marsiglio, 2004). On the one hand, they are expected to have something wrong with them. For example, an analysis of films showing stepfamilies found that most portrayals are negative or mixed in tone (Leon & Angst, 2005). In part, this presentation is realistic, since many children in these families do display problems; yet expecting problems often becomes a self-fulfilling prophecy. On the other hand, society may expect the stepfamily to act like "one big happy family."

Important examples of the split attitude toward stepfamilies involve the issues of parental rights and financial support. Society resists formally recognizing non-traditional caregivers such as grandparents or stepparents, regardless of their importance in a child's life. Yet most provincial and territorial governments obligate someone who has acted like a parent to support children financially. This obligation applies to both married and cohabiting stepparents. An exception is Quebec, which requires no support from a cohabiting stepparent. The reverse does not hold. Individuals have no obligation to support a stepparent like a biological parent (Leckey, 2009; Malia, 2005).

Given the number of children involved, it is important for all of us to develop a model of stepfamily health rather than stepfamily disturbance. With such a model, we will be able to support parents in creating a stable and nurturing environment.

Time to Review

1. What are some of the effects of stepfamily living on children?
2. What are the three types of adaptation in stepfamilies?
3. How does society view and deal with stepfamilies?

A Matter of Gifts

Caitlyn and Carlos have been married for two years. Theirs is a complex stepfamily. Caitlyn was a never-married mother whose daughter, Emma, is seven. Carlos's first wife left him for another man and moved across the country. Carlos has custody of his two sons, Marco and Andres, aged nine and six, and they see their mother two or three times a year. The couple is considering having a baby to cement family relationships.

Although the couple had high hopes for their marriage, they have recently been quarreling over the attitude of Carlos's parents to the children. For Christmas, birthdays, and other occasions, they give expensive gifts to Marco and Andres but none to Emma. The boys delight in showing off their new tablets and smartphones. Carlos is the only son and his parents value carrying on the family name. In fact, the boys are named for their grandfather and great-grandfather. Caitlyn is part of a large extended family whose motto seems to be "the more the merrier." They have accepted her stepsons as part of the clan, just as they accepted the children of a young woman they informally fostered. All the youngsters are treated equally at Christmas and on birthdays. Emma is asking why her step-grandparents hate her.

In the most recent crisis, Carlos's parents are planning a big party for Marco's 10th birthday next month. They have told Carlos that it will be a "family only" party and that Caitlyn and Emma won't be welcome, especially since the boys' birth mother will be there. Caitlyn feels hurt and angry to be excluded. Carlos has been making excuses for his parents.

1. What social norms are contributing to the conflict in this family?
2. What factors within the stepfamily might be making the situation worse?
3. How do you think Caitlyn and Carlos could reduce the conflict?
4. Do you think that having a child together would improve relationships in the family? Explain your answer.

Summary

What Are the Trends in Remarriage in Canada?

Remarriage is a marriage that takes place after a previous marriage has ended. A stepfamily is a family where the children are related to one parent but not the other. In simple stepfamilies, all the children are from just one spouse. Complex stepfamilies are those with other variations. The proportion of simple stepfamilies has declined, while the proportion of complex stepfamilies has grown. In the past, most remarriages followed the death of a spouse. Now they are likelier to follow divorce. Parents in stepfamilies differ from those who are not in stepfamilies.

What Are Some of the Issues in Forming a Stepfamily?

Forming a stepfamily occurs in several stages. First, the couple needs to recover from the loss of their first marriages and commit themselves to their new one. Second, anxiety about remarrying and arrangements for children's continued contact with the other parent and his or her relatives need to be worked out. Third, boundaries and roles need to be renegotiated. Since the children belong in two households, boundaries need to be flexible enough to allow their coming and going. Financial support and parental authority are divided. There is often lack of clarity over roles in stepfamilies, in particular, over the stepparent role.

What Are Some of the Factors That Lead to Success and Failure in Stepfamily Relationships?

Members of stepfamilies must work out relationships with old and new family members. Partners need to commit to the new union. Roles are complicated by pressures from children and previous partners. When the parent remarries, the child must give up some responsibility and closeness to the new adult in the family. Previous partners can affect the new couple through child support and visitation arrangements. Continuing contact, in most cases, improves children's well-being. Stepparents need to develop an appropriately affectionate relationship with the child and to establish themselves as legitimate disciplinarians. Children often resist becoming attached to their stepparent because of loyalty to the same-sex birth parent. Discipline is another area of conflict because children may not accept the stepparent's authority. Often, stepsiblings do not live in the same household but have contact during periodic visits. Whether they visit or share a home, there may be conflict over space, possessions, rules, and attention from parents. Having a child born into a stepfamily tends to increase family stability.

Children in stepfamilies have, on average, more problems than children living with both biological parents. Explanations include increased stress levels resulting from the many transitions, ambiguous roles, negative social stereotypes of stepfamilies, stepparents' parenting styles, and problems from the past.

As in divorce, the impact of remarriage depends partly on the life-cycle stage of the new partners. For example, the age of the children has an effect on family life. Additional pressures may exist if the new partners are in different life-cycle stages.

James Bray identified three types of stepfamily adaptation: romantic, matriarchal, and neotraditional. The success of stepfamilies depends on several factors: the stressors they encounter, the family strengths and support systems, and the meaning members find in their experience. Adaptation is helped by flexibility, respect, patience, communication, and a sense of humour.

What Is the Relationship between the Stepfamily and Society at Large?

Since stepfamilies superficially resemble first-marriage families, they are often expected to be like them. On the other hand, they are also expected to have something wrong with them. Society still needs to develop positive models of stepfamily roles.

Class Assignments

1. Many of the problems of remarriage families centre on power issues. Identify areas where power or control might be a problem. What difficulties can these issues cause, and how might they be avoided?
2. One issue that sometimes arises is the possibility of a stepparent adopting a stepchild. What is the law in this regard? Explain the advantages and disadvantages of stepparent adoptions.
3. Schools often ask for parental permission for various activities. Should stepparents be allowed to sign these forms? Why or why not? Identify other contexts in which society is unclear about how to deal with stepfamilies.

Personal Assignments

The following questions are designed to help you reflect on your own experience:

1. In stepfamilies you are acquainted with, what factors made for relatively harmonious relationships? Explain why. How do you think such relationships can be encouraged in other families?
2. Often, little things, or hassles, are a major source of friction in families. Identify some of these apparently small difficulties you feel can cause serious problems in stepfamilies. Explain your answer.

Chapter 12
The Family and the World of Work

LEARNING OBJECTIVES

What is the current situation for families and the world of work?

In what ways do work and family life interact?

What kinds of care are available for dependent family members?

What are some of the effects of unemployment on the family?

What kinds of family-friendly work arrangements are available?

© Photos.com

"Billy, where on earth are your mittens?"

"Rick, can you make me a sandwich for lunch—I'll eat it on the way to pick up Felicia for her orthodontist appointment. Don't forget I have to stay late tonight since I'll be gone most of the afternoon. You'll have to pick up Billy from the daycare . . ."

"Mom, did you sign the form I have to bring to school?"

"It's in your schoolbag, Felicia."

"Honey, did you forget that I need to meet a client at 4:30? There's no way I can be at the daycare before they close at 5:00."

"Damn, I remember you told me last week. But you really need to remind me of these things, Rick. I can't take care of everything."

"Mom, you forgot to sign the other paper too . . ."

"What other paper! That crazy school, all I do is sign their papers—here, give it to me. Give me a pen from your pencil case. Okay, there, now is there anything else to sign?"

"So, darling, what are you going to do about Billy and the daycare?"

"What am *I* going to do about it—*I* will call my mother on the way in and *I* will ask her if she can pick up Billy, and if she can't, *I* really don't know what *I* will do . . ."

"Billy, where on earth are your mittens?"

● ● ● ● ○

This scene, or one like it, is played out in Canadian homes every day. More and more families are affected by the interplay between work and family responsibilities. Between 1987 and 2011, the average workweek for individuals decreased from 37.5 to 36 hours (Statistics Canada, 2013). But while this may suggest more personal time on an individual level, in fact overall family work hours have increased because the number of dual-earner families has increased (Marshall, 2009).

We saw in Chapter 1 that economic support is one of the fundamental functions of the family. How families provide economic support for all members has an impact on the family dynamics. In this chapter, we will look at the current situation for families and the world of work—perhaps the most prevalent and influential relationship between families and other social institutions. In most families, some members, usually the parents, work outside the home to earn wages that support all family members. We will look at what kinds of care are available for dependent family members while the caregivers are at work. We will also look at the complex interactions between work and family life, and what happens when an economic provider becomes unemployed. Finally, we will look at some of the innovative family-friendly work arrangements that have been created.

> ## Where Do I Fit In?
>
> 1. Who do you sympathize with most in the opening vignette?
> 2. Who in your family works outside the home?
> 3. How does work affect your family life?
> 4. How are the dependent (non-working) members of your family cared for?

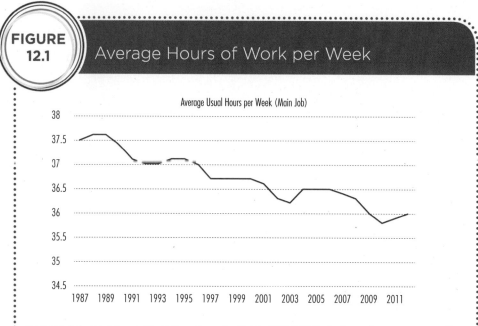

FIGURE 12.1

Average Hours of Work per Week

Average Usual Hours per Week (Main Job)

Source: Adapted from: Statistics Canada. *Table 282-0023—Labour force survey estimates (LFS), by usual hours worked, class of worker, National Occupational Classification for Statistics (NOC-S) and sex, unadjusted for seasonality, monthly (persons unless otherwise noted)*, CANSIM (database). (Accessed Nov. 17, 2013.)

One Family, Two Incomes—The New Reality

A significant trend in our society is the increase in the number of women employed outside the home. In 1976, less than half of all women aged 15 and over were in the paid labour force, but this had increased to 63 percent in 2009. Women in their "prime" working years (aged 25 to 54 years) experienced the greatest shift, with 82 percent now in the paid labour force, compared to 52 percent in 1976. This age group also represents women most likely to have children at home. In contrast, the labour force participation rate among men aged 15 and over has been declining slowly over the past three decades (see Table 12.1).

In 2009, over two-thirds of mothers (69.7 percent) with children aged three to five were in the paid labour force, including 64.4 percent with children under three. This is nearly double the proportion in 1976 (see Table 12.2).

Increasing involvement in paid work has profoundly changed the economic status of women and family incomes. In 2008, three-quarters of all couples with dependent children had both parents working. The total weekly employment hours of couples increased from an average of 57.6 in 1976 to 64.8 in 2008—a 13 percent increase and the equivalent of just under one full day of paid work (7.2 hours) per week. As a result of converging labour force participation rates, the division of labour within families and the relationship between families and the workplace continues to change (Vanier Institute of the Family, 2010).

TABLE 12.1

Employment Trends of Women and Men Aged 15 and Over, 1976–2009

Year	Women Aged 15 Years and Older	Men Aged 15 Years and Older	Women as a Percentage of Total Employment
1976	41.9%	72.7%	37.1%
1981	47.7%	72.8%	40.3%
1986	50.3%	69.6%	42.8%
1991	52.8%	66.9%	45%
1996	52.1%	65%	45.4%
2001	55.6%	66.8%	46.2%
2006	58.3%	67.7%	47.1%
2007	59.1%	68%	47.3%
2008	59.3%	68.1%	47.3%
2009	58.3%	65.2%	47.9%

Source: Statistics Canada. 2011. *Employment trends of women and men aged 15 and over, 1976 to 2009* (table 5.1). "Women in Canada: A Gender-based Statistical Report." Catalogue No. 89-503-X. Ottawa, Ontario. Statistics Canada. http://www.statcan.gc.ca/pub/89-503-x/89-503-x2010001-eng.pdf

TABLE 12.2

Employment Rate of Women with Children by Age of Youngest Child, 1976–2009

Year	Youngest Child Less Than 3	Youngest Child 3 to 5	Youngest Child Less Than 6	Youngest Child 6 to 15	Youngest Child Less Than 16
1976	27.6%	36.8%	31.4%	46.4%	39.1%
1981	39.3%	46.7%	42.1%	56.2%	49.3%
1986	49.4%	54.5%	51.4%	61.9%	56.7%
1991	54.4%	60.1%	56.5%	69%	62.8%
1996	57.8%	60.5%	58.9%	69.8%	64.5%
2001	61.3%	67%	63.7%	75.3%	70.1%
2006	64.3%	69.4%	66.4%	78.2%	72.9%
2007	65.1%	72.6%	68.1%	79.4%	74.3%
2008	64.6%	70.3%	66.8%	80%	73.8%
2009	64.4%	69.7%	66.5%	78.5%	72.9%

Source: Statistics Canada. 2011. *Employment rate of women with children by age of youngest child, 1976 to 2009* (table 5). "Women in Canada: A Gender-based Statistical Report." Catalogue No. 89-503-X. Ottawa, Ontario. Statistics Canada.

The proportion of dual-earner couple families rose steadily from 40 percent in the 1970s to a bit over 60 percent in the 1990s, when it began to level off (Marshall, 2009). While the proportion of dual-earner families has remained constant over the decade from 2000 to 2010, the median income of these families increased more than any other family type (see Table 12.3).

As work and home responsibilities change, families must balance the time and commitment demands of their various roles. When the expectations make one or more of the roles difficult to manage, then individuals experience work–life conflict. Work demands can influence the family and vice versa, either negatively or positively. The relationship between work and family involves a number of facets: changing roles, household responsibilities, use of time, relationships with partners, role spillover and role overload, care of family members, unemployment, and stress and burnout.

Changing Roles

Marital and partner roles have changed since the first half of the last century. Most married women now work outside the home. As a result, couples have new issues they need to settle in their marriages.

Role Choices

According to studies by Kathleen Gerson (1987), women follow one of four different life paths. The first group choose homemaking. These women tend to have a

TABLE 12.3

Family Characteristics, Single-Earner and Dual-Earner Families

Family Type	2000	2002	2004	2006	2008	2010
Proportion of Families						
Single-earner-male couple families	17.8%	17.3%	16.7%	16.5%	16.5%	17.3%
Single-earner-female couple families	6.5%	6.6%	6.6%	6.9%	7.1%	7.9%
Dual-earner couple families	62.9%	62.4%	63%	63.6%	63.8%	62.6%
Lone-parent families	12.9%	13.7%	13.7%	13%	12.6%	12.3%
Median Income						
Single-earner-male couple families	$30 100	$30 100	$30 000	$30 700	$30 600	$29 800
Single-earner-female couple families	$16 900	$17 900	$18 000	$19 100	$19 820	$21 190
Dual-earner couple families	$62 500	$66 000	$69 700	$74 900	$80 330	$81 960
Lone-parent families	$20 800	$22 400	$23 900	$26 100	$28 470	$29 320

Source: Statistics Canada. *Table 111-0020—Family characteristics, single-earner and dual-earner families, by number of children, annual (dollars unless otherwise noted)*, CANSIM (database). (Accessed: Nov. 17, 2013.)

stable marriage and are neither pushed into the workplace by economic necessity nor pulled into it by enticing opportunities. In contrast, a second group of women plan a traditional marriage but end up in the paid workforce. They are more likely to be influenced by unstable relationships, economic problems, and job opportunities. A third group have always wanted to have careers and are reluctant to become mothers and homemakers. Finally, some women planned to have careers, but circumstances have prevented this. The paths chosen seem to depend on the stability of the marriage, on job opportunities, on the ability of a woman's partner to earn enough so that she can stay home, and on how rewarding she considers homemaking. Similarly, men are also susceptible to workplace opportunities and experiences with their partners and children that influence their career and domestic decisions (Gerson, 1993).

Household Responsibilities

Housework is not the hard labour it once was. Much of the physical labour of housework has been reduced through the introduction of utilities such as electricity and running water. Advances in household technology, it is said, have made it possible for women to enter the workforce in ever-increasing numbers (Cowan, 1992). The fact is, however, that technology has made household work different rather than less. Appliances have made tasks like doing laundry quicker and easier. Some work may be easier, but the quantity has increased. One reason is that standards of cleanliness have increased. To take an everyday example, people usually change their underwear more often now than in the 1900s. Families have also taken over tasks that used to be sent out—laundry, for instance. Technology has caused an acceleration in all domains, including work, leisure, and private life. The result is that speed and efficiency have become cultural values. Technology creates a new kind of impatience. We feel more stressed by time. And, ironically, all this technology may mean that we spend less time together.

How much time is spent on household work is related to such factors as hours spent in paid work, income levels, age and quality of the housing, and personal standards for meal preparation and cleanliness. Older houses and apartments usually require more effort in cleaning, as do crowded quarters and those with inadequate storage. Not everyone can afford modern appliances. Those with low income levels must spend more time in planning and in finding bargains to make ends meet (Armstrong & Armstrong, 1987; DeVault, 1991).

Someone needs to do household work, and, in many cases, the "someone" is a woman. The shift from wage-earner husbands to dual-earner families has not meant an equal shift in household responsibilities. Rather, it has led to conflicts over just how household work and childcare should be divided.

Since men traditionally have not had to concern themselves with family care, some view housekeeping chores as unmasculine. They feel demeaned if they do traditional "women's work." Men do take on more responsibility when their wives are employed, but often choose more enjoyable tasks, such as playing with children (Luxton, 1998). Fathers are more likely to care for children if they work different hours than their wives do, especially if they have preschoolers. Most often this happens when men work afternoon or evening shifts (Brayfield, 1995). Husbands tend to do the highest share of housework (about 35 percent) when partners' earnings are equal (Greenstein, 2000).

Both married men and women do more household work than single people. The most serious time crunch comes, however, when children are present. Both parents assume more household work; mothers gain about two hours a day, compared with fathers' one hour. To allow for childcare and housework, mothers cut back on paid work, leisure, and personal care, while fathers reduce leisure activities (Baxter et al., 2008; Fast & Frederick, 2004) (See Table 4.3, page 101.) In general, couples do not need a 50-50 division of paid and unpaid work to be happy. They do, however, need to regard that division as fair (Stevens et al., 2001).

Parents have increased their workday by nearly an hour since 1986 by cutting back on personal care and leisure. Mothers, rather than fathers, reduce paid work to care for children. The difference has narrowed, however, as mothers spend more time in paid work (Fast et al., 2001; Maume, 2006; Pronovost, 2007; Sauvé, 2009b). Although quality time is generally seen to be more important than the number of hours spent with a child, it is difficult to both define quality time and make it happen on schedule (Daly, 2001).

Role Expectations

One of the major stressors in dual-income families is the expectations of family members. For instance, women complain that if they stay home, they are seen as failing to live up to their potential. If they work outside the home, they fear being criticized for neglecting their children. Expectations about traditional roles can also affect a couple's relationship. When a wife's pay catches up to or passes her husband's, men who value themselves as providers may see their marriage as less satisfying (Pappenheim & Graves, 2005). Income does not have the same effect on women, though they report happier marriages if husbands assume more childcare (Brennan et al., 2001).

Couples more often favour the husband's career, but this trend is not as strong as in the past (Pixley & Moen, 2003). Whose career is favoured may depend on who has the higher income or better possibilities for advancement. Couples realize that in many occupations, individuals are expected to be highly committed if they are to gain promotion. People who take time off to raise a child are often not considered to be serious about work. Some companies need an employee who is willing to relocate to be promoted; others require a person to stay in one place to get established.

Some couples address the career issue by choosing a commuter marriage, where they live in different cities or even different countries. This arrangement is often a temporary solution for competing career opportunities. A drawback is that maintaining a relationship can become more difficult. In general, couples who have been together longer and have no children at home manage commuter relationships better (Holmes, 2009; Rhodes, 2002).

Sometimes, a job demands that one partner be away a great deal. For instance, a sales representative who is responsible for a large territory may often be out of town. Difficulties with communication and sharing can result. If one spouse is often out of town or works long hours, the other can find it difficult to develop a career, especially if they have young children.

In addition to pressure from social expectations, individuals are affected by their own expectations. Some, for example, are perfectionists who place themselves under unnecessary stress because they want to do everything well. Traditional ideals of family togetherness and quality time with children may also lead to dissatisfaction with the balance of work and family responsibilities. Such ideals cannot be easily met by dual-earner parents (Daly, 2001; Guendouzi, 2006; Moen, 2006).

The expectations of employers and co-workers may be anti-family. According to the "career mystique," people find happiness in jobs that require them to devote all their time and energy to their career advancement (Moen, 2006). Thus, employers may expect employees to work more than eight hours a day and five days a week, especially if they want to move ahead in their careers. Job transfers disrupt relationships with relatives and friends. If a spouse refuses to move, he or she may be blamed for holding the partner back (Duxbury et al., 2003).

Some researchers suggest that shift work creates problems for marriages. Others think that this type of stress is related to expectations. If relatives and friends work shifts, this work pattern may appear normal (Elquist & Hilton, 2003).

The Working Couple and Their Social Network

Given the many demands on their time, dual-earner couples often spend relatively little time with friends and extended family, and the proportion has declined over time (Turcotte, 2007). This situation places a greater demand on the nuclear family to meet all the social and emotional needs of its members. When social networks are limited, families may experience lower levels of social support, and thus may feel higher levels of stress. Support systems assume that give and take occurs. One person cannot expect to be helped all the time without helping in return (La Gaipa, 1981). If the relationship remains one-sided for too long, the social support may be cut off. When this occurs, families may become isolated.

Work and Marital Happiness

One study that looked at working mothers found there was little connection between the fact that mothers had jobs and the marital satisfaction they and their husbands felt. When fathers were more involved with their children, both spouses tended to rate their marriages as happier. The only exception was husbands in dual-earner families with traditional ideas about gender roles (Hoffman & Youngblade, 1999). If both partners are happy, women's work status has no effect on marital disruption. If either partner is dissatisfied with the marriage, the couple is more likely to separate if the wife is employed (MacDermid, 2006). When men work long hours and have high levels of job-related stress, relationships with their wives and children suffer (Crouter et al., 2001; Fraenkel, 2003).

Another study looked at partners' work schedules. Researchers found that when individuals worked night or rotating shifts, their marriages were at greater risk for separation. The researcher suggests that those working after midnight are prone to both physical and social stresses. One spouse needs to sleep during the day. When there are children, that parent may go short on sleep. In addition, people in some of the occupations requiring night-shift work—for example, nurses, emergency personnel, police, and on-call workers—are subject to high levels of stress. In 1995, in 40 percent of families with children, at least one parent had an atypical schedule (Le Bourdais et al., 2003). Weekend workers experience lower levels of stress (Davis et al., 2005). In contrast, a study of blue collar workers found that shift work was not related to marital happiness. Rather, women's perception that they carried unfair household responsibility in addition to their jobs was connected with marital dissatisfaction (Elquist & Hilton, 2003). As we move toward 24-hour businesses operating seven days a week, more workers will probably have night and rotating shifts.

Time to Review

1. Describe the trends in Canada between paid work and families.
2. What are some of the new role choices for working Canadians?
3. How can household responsibilities be divided when both partners work?

Work and Family Conflict

Families and work are interrelated in many ways. The tensions from paid work can carry over to the home, and family issues may affect the job. Work–family conflict is defined as a form of conflict in which work and family demands are mutually incompatible, so that meeting demands in one domain makes it difficult to meet demands in the other (Higgins et al., 2008). Work–family conflicts have progressively worsened. The percentage of parents who have a hard time juggling work and family has steadily risen since 1996 and now sits between 46 percent and 61 percent. Some studies suggest that this situation will likely continue to deteriorate (Barrette, 2009). We will look at four categories of conflict between work and family.

Role Spillover and Role Overload

Individuals must now fill more roles than was expected of them in the past, since a clear-cut separation of men's and women's domains in family life no longer exists. Often, they need to juggle a career, children, a marriage, and household responsibilities. The individual, family, and work worlds overlap, and one may interfere with the others.

Many individuals have problems balancing the demands of work and family. There are only 24 hours to allocate to all activities in a day; thus, priorities must be set. There never seems to be enough time and energy for individuals to accomplish all they wish to in either their work or family roles. This problem may result in short-term difficulties in getting day-to-day work completed, or it can result in failure to achieve overall goals. There can also be difficulties over scheduling of time. For some workers, shift work may allow partners to juggle job and family demands (Elquist & Hilton, 2003). Frequent travel and long hours at work may mean that family members spend little time with one another. The situation is made worse when people believe that everything can be solved through more efficient time management rather than through compromises between ideals and real life (Daly, 2001; Fraenkel, 2003).

Role spillover describes a situation where family and work roles or time demands interfere with each other. However, an individual's perception of being stressed or overwhelmed by the pressures of multiple family and work roles can be more serious than those coming from the lack of time. This condition is known as **role overload.**

One method of dealing with overload is to stagger the periods of stress at work and in the family. Just as families go through a life cycle, so do careers have a cycle. The most stressful stages in the family cycle are often considered to be child-rearing and adolescence. In the career cycle, getting established in a job or changing jobs are the most demanding periods. Couples may also set different priorities at different times of life. For example, some couples try to establish their careers before they have children in order to avoid having high levels of stress both at home and at work. The theory may break down in practice, however. Once both partners are employed, it may be difficult for one to leave the workforce if they have accumulated debts and other obligations based on their higher income; for example, they may have bought a house or an expensive car (Hertz, 1987).

The most time-crunched are dual-earner couples, especially those with young children. In such families, women are under more stress than men because women traditionally have been the caregivers in our society (Sauvé, 2009b). Often, they are expected—and they themselves expect—to be responsible for the physical and emotional well-being of the family. Men tend to reduce the amount of housework time when they begin to live with a woman, while women increase theirs when living with a man (Coontz, 2005). When a child enters the family, women increase the time spent on housework more than men do (Baxter et al., 2008). Sometimes, women find that the demands of paid work and family care conflict. If they go to work when a child is ill, for instance, they may feel guilty no matter what quality of care they have arranged. If no one else can care for a sick family member, women are usually expected to stay home. On the other hand, if a woman stays home from work because she has a sick child, she feels guilty for not attending to work responsibilities.

In families with children under five, 30 percent of women are severely time-crunched, in contrast to less than 26 percent of men. One explanation for this difference is that, even in dual-earner families, women are still mainly responsible for children and the household. It is women who most often shop for groceries, take children to doctors' appointments, arrange for daycare, and see to all the many

role spillover: a situation where family and work roles or time demands interfere with each other

role overload: the perception of being stressed or overwhelmed by the pressures of multiple family and work roles

other responsibilities of a family. To make matters worse, women usually have less flexibility at work than men. It is more difficult for them to come in late or leave early (Duncana & Pettigrew, 2012).

Couples need to relieve the stress from role overload. Many use extra money to buy timesaving products such as permanent-press fabrics or microwaves, or they pay for household aids, such as takeout food, housecleaning, or childcare. When wives make a larger share of the income, the family is more likely to hire outside help (Marshall, 2006; Treas & de Ruijter, 2008).

Work-to-Family Interference

This type of role conflict occurs when work demands and responsibilities make it more difficult to fulfill family-role responsibilities. Most workers report negative work-to-family effects, although positive influences are possible (Duxbury & Higgins, 2003; Neal & Hammer, 2007). The influence is circular. Stresses at work can lead to less time and emotional energy for home. The worker's partner may then feel overburdened and resentful, leading to marital upset. In turn, the individual may be distracted from his or her work, thereby increasing work-related stress (Barrette, 2009).

Many businesses have a culture where a person must work long hours to succeed. Budgets, not people, count. Such attitudes worsen work-to-family spillover. Managers may also forget that workers have partners with careers when they schedule travel and meetings (Higgins & Duxbury, 2005). Downsizing and greater demands placed on the remaining staff, especially managers, increase work hours and multiply work-related demands (Higgins & Duxbury, 2005; Pronovost, 2007). Perceptions also matter. Workaholics and the time-crunched believe they do not have enough time to accomplish daily tasks. Others, equally busy, do not feel a similar time stress (Keown, 2007; Pronovost, 2007).

A large study of Canadians working for big companies, governments, or institutions found that work-to-family interference is a serious problem for 1 in 4 employees. As we have seen, the percentage of parents who have a hard time juggling work and family has steadily risen. Nevertheless, many people still feel that they can separate work and family and that work does not affect family life.

Negative work-to-family spillover occurs most often when individuals have heavy workloads and little control at work. It is also common among women, parents of young children, and single parents (Duxbury & Higgins, 2003; Sauvé, 2009b; Voydanoff, 2004). One occupation with high levels of spillover is police work. Stressors include shift work, long hours, unpredictability, and public scrutiny (Kirschman, 2007). One study found that among couples in which the husband was a police officer, his stress at work was related to separation and divorce, while exhaustion did not appear to be (Roberts & Levenson, 2001). Unfortunately, the researchers did not look at the effects of a female officer's workplace stress on her family.

Family-to-Work Interference

Men and women respond differently to the pressures of their work and family roles. Men generally allow work to intrude on family activities. Some bring work home. Others develop a sense of camaraderie with men at work, and their social activities after work hours can cut into family time. Women, on the other hand, are more likely to let family responsibilities interfere with work. About one-tenth of workers aged 45 to 54 caring for elderly relatives lost income because of family responsibilities. About 2 percent quit paid work (Cranswick, 2003). One study estimated that men in unhappy marriages lost about 38 days a year of work time. Their absenteeism was higher than happier men, partly because of stress-related illnesses. They also did not accomplish as much when they were at work (Forthofer et al., 1996). Some studies have found that the more family-friendly the workplace, the less strain parents undergo in juggling work and family roles. Their strain level was especially low if the supervisor was flexible about work scheduling. If parents could take phone calls at work from or about children, if they could come in late or leave early to keep appointments, or take occasional days off without pay, they could manage both family and work responsibilities.

Care for Family Members

The care of children and disabled and elderly people makes demands on working family members. **Caregiver strain** is a term used to describe the burdens in the caregivers' day-to-day lives that can be attributed to the need to provide care or assistance to someone else. Relatively little consideration has been given to the interplay between family and work responsibilities and the care of aging family members. Much more attention has been paid to childcare. Both aspects depend on individuals' choices, workplace flexibility, programs such as subsidies, tax policies, and community and other social resources (Cleveland et al., 2008).

caregiver strain: a term used to describe the burdens in the caregivers' day-to-day lives that can be attributed to the need to provide care or assistance to someone else

Childcare

Childcare in Canada is closely tied to social attitudes toward women's work. There has long been the assumption that children are best off at home, looked after by their mothers. (See Table 12.2 on page 311, which summarizes how an increasing number of women with children under age 16 are working outside the home.) Daycare centres were established only when it was seen to benefit society, either from the desire for better supervision of children or from the need for the mothers to join the workforce.

The first daycare centres were established in response to problems experienced by lone mothers. Most were developed by religious organizations, such as the earliest day nurseries in Montreal, or by volunteer women's organizations in Ontario. These services were always seen as a means to fulfill the needs of society. As a form of welfare, they allowed mothers to work to support themselves and their children. Children in these centres received training to turn them into productive members of society. There was a continuing sense, however, that such care was second-rate, lagging far behind care at home (Schulz, 1978).

Childcare can be unregulated or regulated (see Figure 12.2 below). Unregulated care is provided by someone other than the parents or immediate family members. It may be in the child's home or in the caregiver's home. This kind of care is not required to meet provincial standards and is not formally monitored unless there is a complaint. Regulated care is usually centre-based (community centres, schools, and other public facilities), where service is provided by college-trained early childhood educators. These centres are required to meet provincial health and safety standards. Some regulated childcare services are provided in family homes, but these are less likely to have trained early childhood educators. Some analysts also include kindergarten as a type of formal daycare (Anderson, 2012).

In the past decade, there has been a modest increase in the number of regulated spaces Canada-wide and the proportion of children for whom a regulated space is available has increased somewhat. Nevertheless, childcare in Canada is far from covering all children, with spaces available for just 20 percent of 0- to 12-year-olds in 2010. Of these spaces, 50 percent were centre-based (full- and part-day) for children under school age (generally up to age six), 15 percent were in regulated family childcare, and 35 percent were for school-age children (Friendly & Beach, 2013).

FIGURE 12.2

Childcare in Canada

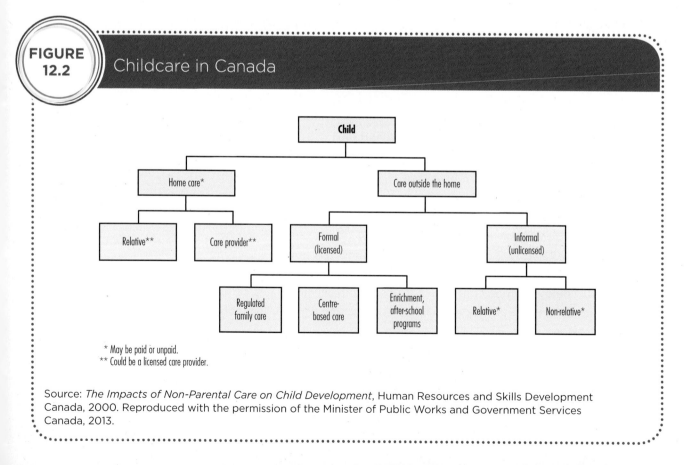

* May be paid or unpaid.
** Could be a licensed care provider.

Source: *The Impacts of Non-Parental Care on Child Development*, Human Resources and Skills Development Canada, 2000. Reproduced with the permission of the Minister of Public Works and Government Services Canada, 2013.

The Four Pillars of Childcare

Childcare in Canada has been described as resting on four "pillars"(Cleveland et al., 2008). The first pillar is government funding. From the 1960s to the 1990s, regulated child care was funded through the Canada Assistance Plan. This was a cost-sharing agreement between the federal government and the provinces and territories, but only for low-income families or children considered to be dis- advantaged. The eligibility rules were set by each province and varied across the country. The Canada Assistance Plan was eliminated in 1996 and tax money trans- ferred from Ottawa to the provinces and territories was combined into a single grant: the Canada Health and Social Transfer. The federal government reduced its ability to shape social programs and provinces moved in different directions. In Ontario, there were cuts to childcare funding, while Quebec instituted its universal childcare system with low daily fees.

The second pillar of childcare policy is income tax relief for families. The Child Care Expense Deduction (CCED) allows the lowest earner in a family to deduct the cost of childcare (in 2012, up to a limit of $7000 per child under seven years of age) from their taxable income (Canada Revenue Agency, 2013b). Some examples of eligible childcare expenses are nursery schools and daycare centres, day camps and sports camps where the primary goal of the camp is to care for children, and boarding schools or overnight camps where lodging is involved. The Universal Child Care Benefit (UCCB) provides direct financial assistance to all Canadian families with young children, regardless of family income. Parents receive $100 a month for each child under six (Canada Revenue Agency, 2013c).

The third pillar of childcare policy is maternity and parental leave and benefits paid through the federal Employment Insurance fund. Eligible parents are paid a proportion of their income to permit them to stay at home with a newborn child for up to one year. The first 17 weeks of leave are reserved for the mother of the newborn, but the next 35 weeks can be split between the two parents as desired. While parental leave allows parents to spend time away from work caring for their newborn child, by providing a job guarantee it also encourages new parents to return to the workforce once the leave is over.

The fourth pillar of childcare policy is universal and free kindergarten. This is provided through the school system and is voluntary, although nearly all families use it. Across the country, kindergarten is provided for children who are five years of age and, in Ontario, half-day kindergarten is available for children from four years of age.

Variations in Childcare

There are different levels and types of childcare in Canada. There are several reasons for such differences.

First, there is no national policy regarding childcare because it is a provin- cial responsibility. From the 1960s on, federal governments have promised to contribute funding for childcare, but little money has materialized. For the first time, in 1995 the federal government announced spending cuts. The growth and continuing existence of childcare programs depends on available money—any reduction in federal funding reduces the ability of provinces to pay for social programs.

Quebec is an exception. The provincial government shifted money from other social programs to subsidize new childcare spaces in its Early Childhood Education and Care Policy. The program was implemented in stages; in the fall of 2000, all children up to age 12 were eligible. The province reduced the cost to $5 per day per child (raised to $7 in 2003). Parents who cannot find a $7 spot can claim a Quebec income tax credit for childcare. In addition, children from low-income families may be subsidized. Following the establishment of this policy, there was a substantial increase in the employment of women from two-parent families (Baker et al., 2008; Cleveland et al., 2008; Lefebvre & Merrigan, 2008). Some studies have found that higher-income families are more likely to use the subsidized childcare program. Families with annual income over $60 000 were three times more likely to have children in $7 childcare than families making less than $40 000. Part of the explanation may be that families with higher income are more likely to have working mothers (Richards & Brzozowski, 2006).

Another reason for the wide variety of childcare choices is that social and political attitudes toward such care are still mixed. Some point out that

TABLE 12.4

Median Reported Parent Monthly Fees, 2012

	INFANT	TODDLER	PRE-SCHOOL
Newfoundland and Labrador	NA	$773	$783
Prince Edward Island	$696	$566	$544
Nova Scotia	$825	$694	$685
New Brunswick	$740	$653	$620
Québec	$152	$152	$152
Ontario	$1152	$925	$835
Manitoba	$631	$431	$431
Saskatchewan	$650	$561	$535
Alberta	$900	$825	$790
British Columbia	$1047	$907	$761

Note: Due to the very few infant programs in Newfoundland and Labrador, the median reported fees for infants has not been included. The territories are not included due to small sample size.

Source: Child Care Human Resources Sector Council. *You Bet We Still Care! A Survey of Centre-Based Early Childhood Education and Care in Canada*. Pg. 15. 2013. Found at: http://www.ccsc-cssge.ca/sites/default/files/uploads/Projects-Pubs-Docs/EN%20Pub%20Chart/YouBetSurveyReport_Final.pdf

high-quality childcare should be a right granted to all working parents and their children. On the other hand, childcare can be seen as a legitimate expense that should be paid by parents, especially mothers, who take on the "indulgence" of a job (Cleveland et al., 2008; Friendly & Prentice, 2009). For those who think that families should take on full responsibility for raising their children, subsidized childcare should be an exception rather than something all families should have.

Childcare in Canada is primarily a user-pay service. In most parts of Canada, with the exception of Quebec, many families have difficulty with its cost. Fees have increased, and for most families, the type of childcare used is based on the cost of care compared with the family income (Bushnik, 2006). Families choose the best care they can afford. For those with low income, this may mean unpaid or low-cost caregivers without training. The care parents use may not be their preferred choice. In one study, more than half who preferred a daycare centre or a babysitter in their own home were using other forms of care (Beaujot, 2000).

Finding care that meets family needs is complicated by the fact that nearly half of employed parents do not work from 9 to 5. Many work weekends, late afternoons, evenings, or irregular hours. Schedules like these are the result of the growing number of jobs in service occupations. Unfortunately, most daycare is still based on the 9 to 5 schedule (Friendly & Prentice, 2009).

Because so many parents of young children work, they need to have backup plans if children are ill or if something out of the ordinary, like a family emergency or school holiday, happens. In the Ottawa area, for example, many parents have access to emergency care through the National Capital Region Emergency Child Care Consortium. This service is supported by employers, unions, and other groups (Vanier Institute, 2007).

Other factors influence the type of childcare children receive. The age of the child matters. According to a Statistics Canada study, children under one year are the most likely to be cared for outside the home by a relative. Those aged two to four were the most likely to be in a daycare centre, and five-year-olds to be in preschool or before- and after-school care. Location is also important. Most children in Quebec are in daycare centres, and over half of children in Saskatchewan are cared for outside their home by a non-relative. Urban children are more likely to be in a daycare centre. Children from families below the low-income cutoff, often children of single mothers, are also primarily in daycare centres. Among parents born outside Canada, their children are more likely to be cared for in their home by a relative who lives there as well (Bushnik, 2006).

Changes in availability and cost of daycare affect women more than men because they are still expected to provide the bulk of care. As parents, women may have to choose between full-time or part-time employment. If they do have paid work, they may have less choice in the childcare they can afford. Working mothers are more likely to be under stress if they have less confidence in the care their children receive.

Source: Darko Zeljkovic/Shutterstock.

Source: © Jeff Gilbert / Alamy.

If you were a parent, which childcare would you choose?

Eldercare

As the baby boom ages, there will be a growing need for eldercare services in Canada (Chaykowski, 2006). After more than a decade of concerted effort by policymakers to encourage older adults to age at home, there is now growing recognition that the aging-in-place movement has had unintended negative consequences for family members who care for seniors (Lilly et al., 2012). In recent decades, there has been a 100 percent increase in days taken off work for personal and family reasons. Over one-third of this increase is spent caring for an elderly relative.

Just over 1 in 5 employed Canadians has responsibility for the care of elderly relatives. Only rarely does the elderly dependant live with them, which makes providing care even more difficult (Duxbury et al., 2009). While it is often assumed that older adults are the ones who provide care to even older dependants, a recent survey found that nearly a quarter of respondents providing eldercare were employees aged 15 to 34 (Marcellus, 2012). Women bear the brunt of this care. Although roughly the same proportion of men and women aged 45 to 64 give care to seniors, women are more likely to put in more hours. They also provide more personal care than men, who tend to focus more on transportation and outside chores. Taking elderly people for medical appointments and dealing with social service agencies can be time-consuming and frustrating, and usually must occur during work hours. Women are more likely than men to miss work-related social events and lose out on promotions as a result of eldercare responsibilities. In 2007, about 15 percent of women caregivers aged 45 to 54 cut back on work hours. Some even quit. Financial costs include reduced wages, savings, and pension contributions. Another 26.3 percent missed full days of work to provide eldercare (Cranswick & Dosman, 2008).

When demands for senior care are high, many care providers are assisted by relatives and friends. Caregivers can receive Employment Insurance Compassionate Care Benefits for up to six weeks when they are looking after a family member at risk of dying within six months (Service Canada, 2012d). Regulations for other personal emergency leave situations vary from province to province (Workershelp.ca, 2013).

Time to Review

1. How are family and work interrelated?
2. What are the important issues regarding childcare in Canada?
3. Why is eldercare becoming a more important issue for Canadian families?

Losing a Job—The Effects of Unemployment

A different kind of work-related stress comes with unemployment. Of course, whether expected or sudden and unpredicted, unemployment has a financial impact on the family. This impact is most noticeable if the family has only one income. If a family lives in an area with one major industry that drastically reduces its workforce or even closes, there may be widespread layoffs or business closures

(Boss, 2002). Other jobs may be difficult to find, forcing the worker to relocate.

A study of fishery workers in Newfoundland describes the effect of widespread unemployment. Fishing has long been part of the cultural identity of the province. When people lose a fishing job, they also lose a traditional way of life. In addition, many people, especially young ones, move away from outport communities to find work. Thus, they lose both social and emotional support (Borgen et al., 2002).

Family well-being depends on the way family members think about unemployment and the strategies they use to deal with both practical and emotional needs (Bartholomae & Fox, 2010). Government policies such as Employment Insurance may soften some of the financial stress caused by loss of a job.

Most people go through a series of reactions to job loss. The first stage is usually shock and denial, especially if the layoff is unexpected. (See Box 12.1 on page 328.) Often, they feel anger next, followed by worry and anxiety. When they start a job search, they frequently feel a sense of anticipation. Depending on its success, the person may go through a yo-yo of emotions—fear, anger, frustration. If the job search is unsuccessful for a long time, an individual can give up. Families also bear the brunt of the emotional roller coaster because the feelings and behaviour of the unemployed member become unpredictable (CMHA, n.d.).

Work serves many functions beyond the financial. It structures time—sleeping and eating times, weekdays and weekends, work and vacation. With unemployment, this framework suddenly disappears, not only for the unemployed individual but also for the rest of the family. Deprivation of time structures is connected with psychological distress (Waters & Moore, 2001). Work also provides for regular contact outside the family. Often, one of the first ways families cut back financially is to limit recreation, thus reducing social contact still further (Waters & Muller, 2003). Finally, work provides a person with status and identity. For young people, in particular, having a job means being counted as an adult (CMHA, n.d.).

Unemployment often undermines an individual's sense of self-esteem (Waters & Moore, 2001). If a man or his family holds the traditional value that a man provides financially for the family, losing a job means that he has failed as a person (Waters & Moore, 2002). The individual whose personal identity depends on his or her profession (a police officer or a surgeon, for example) may also feel a deep sense of loss.

A common response to the need for income is for the spouse of the unemployed individual to find a job or increase work hours. This strategy is less feasible now because so many women already work full time. Among families with no children of working age, women's income increased following husbands' layoffs. Five years later, however, their earnings made up for only about 22 percent of their husbands' lost earnings (Morissette & Ostrovsky, 2008). One or both partners may relocate, sometimes to another province or even country, for a job opportunity (Mattioli, 2009).

Families may have problems in coping with the practical aspects of unemployment. Sometimes their difficulties are psychological and social. They may make costly decisions out of panic. In families where a professional husband loses his job or has to take a lower-paying position, the partners often try to carry on almost as if nothing has changed. At times, this approach can lead to serious credit card and other debt (Bartholomae & Fox, 2010). Eventually the family can no longer hide what has happened. Loss of the family car, for instance, limits the activities in which children can participate. If the family has to sell their home, there is usually some financial relief, but the money is probably earmarked for debt payment. Sometimes, older children help out; however, there is usually little increase in the earnings of youth following their father's job loss (Morissette & Ostrovsky, 2008).

Work–Family Balance

Work–family balance is a self-defined state of well-being that recognizes the inter-relatedness of work life and life apart from work. Work–family balance consists of three components:

1. *Time balance* refers to equal time being given to both work and family roles
2. *Involvement balance* refers to equal levels of psychological involvement in both work and family roles
3. *Satisfaction balance* refers to equal levels of satisfaction in both work and family roles (European Agency for Safety and Health at Work, 2012)*

Those who have balance are satisfied with their work and home lives; are able to fulfill their multiple responsibilities at home, at work, and in the community without guilt or regret; are healthy physically, emotionally, and socially; have a sense of control over their life; and feel that the decisions they make are informed choices as opposed to forced sacrifices.

Although many families manage to juggle work and family responsibilities, others find the task extremely stressful. One danger is the possibility of **burnout**. Burnout is a state that occurs when a person experiences prolonged stress without learning how to cope with it. Women, especially those in management and professional positions, and those with heavy caregiving responsibilities, are more likely than men to experience burnout (Duxbury & Higgins, 2003).

Burnout produces physical and emotional exhaustion because of the excessive demands placed on the individual. People may impose extremely high standards on themselves, or their families, employers, friends, and society itself may impose high expectations. Perceived or actual conflicts with co-workers and clients, as well as lack of respect from managers, increase the likelihood of burnout (Poncet et al., 2007; Ramarajan et al., 2008). For example, if an employed woman with young children is a perfectionist at work, and her husband expects her to keep the house spotless and take the children to numerous activities, she may be a candidate for burnout. Her first response will probably be to try harder, but she will find that she cannot keep up with the many demands on her time and energy. She is likely to become exhausted and depressed, and much less able to respond to the emotional needs of her husband and children or to be productive at work (Center for Mental Health in Schools at UCLA, 2008; Pines, 1996).

work–family balance: a self-defined state of well-being that recognizes the inter-relatedness of work life and life apart from work

burnout: a state that occurs when a person experiences prolonged stress without learning how to cope with it

---

* H. J. Greenhaus, M. K. Collins, & D. J. Shaw, "The relation between work-family balance and quality of life," *Journal of Vocational Behaviour*, Vol. 63, 2003, Pg. 510-531.

Job stress has more severe effects on families than exhaustion does. For example, in police families, both exhaustion and job stress are damaging to family life, but stress has worse effects (Roberts & Levenson, 2001). Among Protestant clergy, the pastor's well-being is tied to how demanding he or she perceives the congregation to be. The stress effect may, however, be worse if the spouse and children are resentful of the unpredictability and time demands of the pastor's work (Lee & Iverson-Gilbert, 2003). In addition, a clergy partner may experience high levels of stress when the congregation believes it has hired not only a minister, but a clergy couple (Roberts, 2004)

Indirect Effects

Burnout can have an indirect impact on the family. Often, emotional exhaustion goes hand in hand with physical exhaustion. As a result, the individual becomes susceptible to illness. Stress is a direct factor in some illnesses, such as heart disease and ulcers. The individual may also suffer psychologically. The reduced sense of accomplishment and lower self-esteem that go with burnout and the loss of one's zest for life are the main characteristics of depression. In attempts to deal with the emotional effects of burnout, the individual may take to alcohol or drugs. Physical and emotional disorders, such as outlined above, affect the family if the burned-out member normally cannot take part in family life (American Psychological Association, 1997; Center for Mental Health in Schools at UCLA, 2008). If the individual chooses the extreme response of suicide, then the family will be completely deprived of one of its members.

BOX 12.1   Sudden Stress

Ralph Brown was numb, barely able to comprehend that after 10 years he was suddenly indefinitely laid off from his job. Sure, he had heard rumours of impending layoffs, but he had reasoned that certainly 10 years of seniority would prevent him from being affected. Soon he would have to face his family with the word. What would happen to all of their plans—the addition he was going to build on the house, skis for his daughter, camp for his son, the new freezer for his wife? How could he explain that he had no job, no plans for getting one, and no knowledge as to whether or when he would be called back to his old job? What would they think? What would they say? Of course, they knew times were tough. Several friends and neighbours had already been laid off. But that was different. What would happen to him, his family? What if his wife were laid off too?

Source: "Underemployment . . . Stress and the Family." 1983 Adaptation by Patricia Voydanoff in *Stress and the Family, Vol. II: Coping with Catastrophe*, 1983, Pg. 90, Charles R. Figley and Hamilton I. McCubbin, eds. (New York: Brunner/Mazel). Reproduced with permission. All rights reserved.

Direct Effects

Burnout also directly affects the family. In an effort to reduce stress, the individual may treat others like objects (Center for Mental Health in Schools at UCLA, 2008). The overstressed individual may be irritated with and angry at family members. When emotionally drained, individuals cannot calmly handle everyday hassles at home. They want to be left in peace and are less able and willing to spend time with family members. Or they may demand extra attention and understanding by the family and then feel ashamed of needing such attention. If other family members expect someone to interact as in the past, the burned-out person may withdraw out of a sense of hurt and neglect. This reaction may lead, in turn, to injured feelings on the part of a spouse or children. Sometimes, the desire for a hassle-free home leads to pressure on other family members to be perfect (Pines, 1996; Texas Medical Association, 2001).

Burnout may reduce individuals' ability to cope with stress. Some are resistant to therapy. This reaction seems to occur especially among doctors and mental-health workers who do not want to admit to the same kinds of problems their patients and clients display. Often, they are too tired to make active efforts, such as exercising, to reduce stress, especially if their schedules require them to work long hours. Many are unable to open up emotionally to their spouses. Some may worry that doing so is a breach of professional confidentiality. Others wish to protect their family from the grim realities of the job. They may also be trying to protect themselves (Maslach, 1982; Texas Medical Association, 2001).

As we saw in our discussion of family systems, a change in the behaviour of one member affects the rest of a family's members. The burnout victim's increased irritability and lower levels of patience and tolerance may lead to squabbling and bickering that escalate into serious marital and family conflict. The resulting separation or divorce may be blamed on problems in the marital relationship rather than on job stress, the real cause.

Burnout may also be contagious. Some partners may be nurturers and will respond to the obvious distress of their spouse by increased nurturing. In spite of this, the burned-out person does not feel better, so the partner tries harder. But the burnout victim's apathy and unwillingness to communicate eventually tend to make the spouse feel rejected. If the situation does not change after a while, the partner may burn out too (Pines, 1996).

Flexible Work Arrangements

One way employers and families have tried to address the problem of competing work and family demands is by setting up alternative work arrangements. There are benefits for both parties (Hill et al., 2001). Alternative arrangements take three forms: flexible time, flexible workplace, and reduced hours of work. In addition, some large firms provide daycare and eldercare services. These options may not be available to all employees. Flextime and flexible workplace arrangements are more common in small to medium-sized businesses (Comfort et al., 2003; Ferrer & Gagné, 2006; Pohlman & Dulipovici, 2004).

Flexible Time Arrangements

flextime: a system of working a set number of hours with the starting and finishing times chosen within agreed limits by the employee

A number of employers have established alternatives to the traditional eight-hour workday, **flextime** being one arrangement. In one variation, all employees are expected to be at work during a core period in the middle of the day but may decide for themselves when they will arrive or leave, provided they work the usual number of hours (Ferrer & Gagné, 2006). Theoretically, this arrangement allows parents to better meet family needs as well as workplace responsibilities. Indeed, women with flexible work schedules feel less stressed by family responsibilities than those with more rigid schedules (Hill et al., 2001). Workers who use this benefit tend to have school-aged children (Ferrer & Gagné, 2006).

compressed workweek: a work schedule based on working longer shifts over fewer days

Some people prefer longer periods off work. Their needs may be met by a **compressed workweek**, in which they work 10- or 12-hour shifts for three or four days and then have three or four days off. The long hours can, however, contribute to exhaustion and burnout. In addition, the hours may make it more difficult to look after family needs on working days (Gottlieb, 1999; Saskatchewan Women's Secretariat, n.d.).

Flexible Workplace

telecommuting: a work arrangement in which the employee works outside the office, often from home

Computers and communications technology make it possible for people to work outside the office, an option sometimes referred to as **telecommuting** or the virtual office. This type of arrangement appeals to people who commute long distances every day, who do not want their children to spend 10 hours or more a day in childcare, and who want flexibility to schedule their daily work. Telecommuting is not a magic solution, however, for work–family problems. Some do find the flexibility helpful because having a parent at home solves daycare problems. But laptops, tablets, and smartphones also make it easy for work to intrude on family life. The need to be constantly connected means that we are never really off the job. Increased cellphone use, but not computer use, is linked to lower family satisfaction. Overall, the use of technology is blurring work and family boundaries (Chesley, 2005; Ferrer & Gagné, 2006; Fraenkel, 2003). Some companies, however, are pulling back from telecommuting arrangements. For example, Yahoo! executives have ruled that employees can no longer work from home (Suddath, 2013).

Reduced Hours of Work

job sharing: a work arrangement in which two employees share one full-time job, with prorated salaries and benefits

Part-time work allows individuals to fulfill care responsibilities for children or older relatives. It may, however, be feasible only for those whose partners earn a good income (Hill et al., 2004). Women, more than men, choose to work fewer hours (Ferrer & Gagné, 2006). Labour unions are also concerned with the trend to converting full-time jobs into part-time jobs without benefits. Cutting back on hours can hurt a career. Part-time workers tend to be paid less and to be passed over for promotion (Comfort et al., 2003). Protected part-time work occurs when salaries and benefits are prorated according to the hours worked. The arrangement can be either permanent or temporary. Another plan is **job sharing**, in which two employees share one full-time job, with prorated salaries and benefits. Reduced work hours do not appeal to everyone, since few can afford to live on less than a full-time salary (Lowe, 2005; Ontario Women's Directorate, 1991).

Who Uses Family-Friendly Work Arrangements?

Full-time workers in two-parent families with children under 16 have most access to family-friendly benefits. Low-income families, including lone parents, do not have as much flexibility in their work (Boots et al., 2008). Flextime and telecommuting are used more by men than women. Managers and those in professions are more likely to be offered flexible work arrangements. Women are more likely to work part time. Some jobs don't lend themselves to telecommuting: these include manufacturing and nursing (Comfort et al., 2003; Ferrer & Gagné, 2006). An American study suggested that those who most need family-friendly benefits are the least likely to get them (Holcomb, 2003).

The Family, Work, and Society

Some of the tensions between family and the workplace can be better under-stood using the ecological model of interacting systems (discussed in Chapter 1). In the macrosystem, we find conflicting values. For example, some believe that women should find their greatest fulfillment as wives and mothers. Others con-sider that women can best achieve their potential through careers. No matter what choice women make, someone will tell them that they are wrong. Another source of tension in families is the unequal value placed on men's and women's work. This imbalance can be seen in levels of pay and in the concern over the effect of working mothers, but not working fathers, on their children's development.

In the exosystem, institutions such as the workplace and daycare centres also seem to present conflicting values. On the one hand, women are encouraged to find employment. On the other, many employers are unfriendly toward families. Daycare centres are planned as a service for working parents, yet it is difficult to find one with hours that will accommodate shift work.

Some of these conflicts are played out in the mesosystem. Teachers, for example, may feel that children's failure to do homework arises from inadequate supervision when two parents are employed out of the home. Parents, for their part, may feel that the school's expectations are unrealistic. All these pressures work together to produce stress in the family microsystem over such matters as childcare and house-hold chores. In turn, the marital and parental subsystems are also affected.

Many individuals feel that the only real answer to some of these problems is a shift in values in our society. There are signs that norms are changing to accommo-date the needs of two-earner families.

Time to review

1. How does unemployment affect families?
2. What factors contribute to work–family balance?
3. What kinds of flexible work arrangements are available for Canadians?

To Go or Not to Go

Lisette doesn't know what to do. To cut costs, the company she works for is centralizing its operations. It will be closing the local office, where she is the manager. She has been offered a promotion in the head office, 200 kilometres away. As well as receiving a substantial pay raise, she will keep supplementary health, life insurance, and pension benefits. If Lisette refuses to move, she will need to find a new job, probably at a lower salary.

If Lisette were single, she would accept the promotion without hesitation, but she needs to consider her family's needs too. She and her husband, André, have a daughter aged 12 and a son, 9, who are honours students in their schools. The children have a circle of friends they have grown up with. André has a successful business as an electrical contractor. He depends on the local contacts he has built up over the years. On the other hand, the family has relied on Lisette's salary and fringe benefits to help maintain their comfortable lifestyle.

André and Lisette cannot decide what is best. Should Lisette move to the new city for the job and commute home on weekends? This decision would place a greater responsibility on André for parenting. Should Lisette refuse the promotion? Her income with a new job will likely be lower and may not come with the supplementary benefits the family has enjoyed. Should the whole family move to the new city? André would need to find a job until he can build up his own business again. The children will have to adjust to new schools and find new friends.

1. What other issues might be involved in the decision about Lisette's promotion? Consider both financial and social factors.
2. Explain how social expectations might affect the family's decision.

Summary

What Is the Current Situation for Families and the World of Work?

The proportion of dual-earner couple families rose steadily from 40 percent in the 1970s to a bit over 60 percent in the 1990s, when it began to level off. Currently, 82 percent of women in their "prime" working years (aged 25 to 54 years) are in the paid labour force, compared to 52 percent in 1976. In 2008, over two-thirds of mothers (69.47 percent) with children aged three to five were in the paid labour force. As a result, couples have new issues they need to settle in their marriages. According to studies by Kathleen Gerson, women follow one of four different life paths. The shift from wage-earner husbands to dual-earner families has not meant an equal shift in household responsibilities. Couples more often favour the husband's career, but this trend is not as strong as in the past. Given the many demands on their time, dual-earner couples often spend relatively little time with friends and extended family, and the proportion has declined over time.

In What Ways Do Work and Family Life Interact?

Work and family conflicts have progressively worsened. Individuals must now fill more roles than was expected of them in the past, since a clear-cut separation of men's and women's domains in family life no longer exists. Role spillover describes a situation where family and work roles or time demands interfere with each other. Role overload is an individual's perception of being stressed or overwhelmed by the pressures of multiple family and work roles. The most time-crunched are dual-earner couples, especially those with young children. Stresses at work can lead to less time and emotional energy for home. Women are more likely more likely to let family responsibilities interfere with work. Burnout, the result of extreme stress, is often job related. It results in physical and emotional exhaustion, poor job performance, and a reduced ability to deal with the demands of others. Accordingly, it has serious effects on the family. Indirectly, an individual's stress-related illness or substance abuse creates additional stress for the family. Directly, individuals may withdraw from family life or be much less tolerant of family-related stressors.

What Kinds of Care Are Available for Dependent Family Members?

The care of children and disabled and elderly people makes demands on working family members. Caregiver strain is a term used to describe the burdens in the caregivers' day-to-day lives that can be attributed to the need to provide care or assistance to someone else. Childcare in Canada is closely tied to social attitudes toward women's work. Childcare can be unregulated or regulated. Childcare in Canada is far from covering all children, with spaces available for just 20 percent of 0 to 12-year-olds in 2010. Childcare in Canada has been described as resting on four "pillars." There are different levels and types of childcare in Canada because there is no national policy regarding childcare, because it is a provincial responsibility, and because social and political attitudes toward such care are still mixed. Childcare in Canada is primarily a user-pay service. Fees have increased, and for most families, the type of childcare used is based on the cost of care compared with the family income. Finding care that meets family needs is complicated by the fact that nearly half of employed parents do not work from 9 to 5. Other factors influence the type of childcare children receive. The age of the child matters. Urban children are more likely to be in a daycare centre. Among parents born outside Canada, their children are more likely to be cared for in their home by a relative who lives there as well. As the baby boom ages, there will be a growing need for eldercare services in Canada. Just over 1 in 4 employed Canadians has responsibility for the care of elderly relatives. Women bear the brunt of eldercare.

When demands for senior care are high, many care providers are assisted by relatives and friends.

What Are Some of the Effects of Unemployment on the Family?

Unemployment affects families not only through loss of income, but also through changes in time management and family roles, which may affect the unemployed individual's self-esteem.

What Kinds of Family-Friendly Work Arrangements Are Available?

One solution for the conflict between family and employment is adapting work hours so that they meet family needs. These alternative arrangements include flexible work hours, a compressed workweek, telecommuting, and job sharing. Full-time workers in two-parent families with children under 16 have most access to family-friendly benefits. Low-income families, including lone parents, do not have as much flexibility in their work.

Class Assignments

1. Explore in more detail different work options, such as flextime and job sharing, that might help individuals manage both family and work responsibilities. What are the advantages and disadvantages of each?
2. What are the various daycare options available in your community or at your school? Who offers them? How are they supervised? What are the potential problems?
3. Interview one or more couples in which both partners work. Ask them what conflicts they face between work and family life. What strategies do they use to control these conflicts?

Personal Assignments

The following assignments are designed to help you reflect on your own experience:

1. Students often experience high levels of stress, especially if they have family responsibilities. What do you consider the main sources of these kinds of stress? Describe the effect they have on families. What suggestions can you offer for reducing such stress?
2. Select an occupation in which you are interested. What do you feel may be the main sources of stress in this occupation? How might these particular stressors affect a family?
3. In your family, who are the older members who need, or may need, care? Who is primarily responsible for their care?

PART 6

SOCIAL PROBLEMS IN THE FAMILY

Chapter 13
The Family Beleaguered—When Problems Come

Shchipkova Elena/Shutterstock

LEARNING OBJECTIVES

What is the definition of a problem within the family context?

How does the ABCX model help us describe the response of the family system to problems?

What is the seven strengths model of resilience?

How can the ABCX model be used to understand two family problems (chronic illness and alcoholism)?

What part does communication play in problem solving?

When the police charged my son and his friend with break, enter, and theft, we were angry but didn't realize how difficult the whole experience would be for us. Since he was a young offender, at least one parent was expected in court. And it wasn't just the one time. There was a preliminary interview with the lawyer. There were repeated returns to court over the next several months because there was a second charge pending and it would be to his benefit to have both tried together.

It got pretty awkward after a while to explain why I kept asking for time off work. My husband could just as easily have taken time off, but he argued that he would lose more pay than I would, so I was the one who went.

It was a real worry when our son broke the conditions of his probation, including the curfew that was imposed. When it appeared he was dealing drugs out of the house, we asked him to move out. After all, we were worried about the effect on our other children if we overlooked his behaviour. He quit school—a further violation of his probation. I can't understand why his probation officer never called him to task.

In all those months, we didn't talk about the situation with our friends or relatives. It was embarrassing, to say the least. We also felt some guilt. After all, parents are supposed to control their children, aren't they?

● ● ● ● ○

Families have problems. While each family's situation may be unique, family problems also have a social dimension. Because the family is a fundamental social institution, problems that affect families become social problems.

What exactly is a social problem? A useful definition is that "a social problem exists when a significant number of people believe that a certain condition is in fact a problem" (Coleman & Kerbo, 2002, p. 4). Yet this definition raises a number of issues. When there are competing views, who decides what is a problem? For whom is it a problem? How do social problems affect families? Anyone planning to work in a social service field must recognize that they will often work with families quite different from the one they were raised in. In this chapter, we will look at some of the problems faced by families and how they deal with them. It is important to recognize the diversity of family experiences, and to understand the range of strategies that families and their individual members use, either successfully or ineffectively, to deal with problems when they arise. It is also important to recognize that the social context plays an important role in helping or hindering families deal with problems. In fact, sometimes the social context may be the source of the problem. As always, looking at the communication and interaction between family members is also important for understanding how they deal with problems.

Where Do I Fit In?

1. To what extent do you think the parents in the opening vignette are responsible for what their son did?

2. What kinds of problems have you had to deal with in your family?
3. What do you think helped, or hindered, your family in dealing with this problem?

Who Decides When a Problem Is a Problem?

The simplest answer is that the public decides when a problem is a problem. Public opinion does not always remain the same, however. For example, harsh physical discipline of children has at times been encouraged so that they may grow into law-abiding adults. Sayings like "Spare the rod and spoil the child" (which many people wrongly assume is a quotation from the Bible) are used to justify such practices (Greven, 1990). In contrast, a major concern nowadays is the possible damage to children as a result of corporal punishment (Gershoff, 2002).

Similarly, over the years, homosexuality has been seen as a sin, a crime, a mental illness, or simply a variation on family living. Originally, homosexuality was a church rather than a criminal matter. In 1535, England passed a law making male sodomy (anal intercourse between men) a crime. By the 20th century, homosexuals were often referred to psychiatrists for what was considered a psychological disorder. Early researchers also suspected that "self-abuse," in other words, masturbation, could produce homosexuality (Kinsman, 1987). In 1967, Pierre Trudeau introduced an Omnibus Bill in the House of Commons. Among other changes, the bill proposed decriminalization of "homosexual acts" performed in private. In a famous statement, Trudeau told reporters that "there's no place for the state in the bedrooms of the nation" (CBC, 2003). Even though gay men and lesbians argue that homosexual couples are a legitimate form of family, many people believe that such relationships are abnormal (Laird, 2003). Since 2005, same-sex marriages have been legal in Canada. Does this mean that homosexual couples are no longer a social problem?

Obviously, a problem is undesirable in some way. Behaviour that tends to cause physical harm to oneself and, more importantly, to others is almost always seen as a problem. Yet some individuals are not given as much protection as others.

According to the conflict perspective, society consists of many groups that often have competing interests. One or more groups in society are always more successful than others. They are the dominant group, and are said to have **vested interests** because they have a stake in keeping society as it is. These powerful groups tend to have the greatest influence in defining problems. Since they are usually among the wealthiest and benefit from the current system, they may be concerned with the cost of problems to society. As taxpayers, they may wish to reduce problems to curtail the cost (Bogenschneider, 2002; Coleman & Kerbo, 2002). For example, child abuse can be very expensive. Victims can become a continuing financial burden on society. They may need repeated medical treatment. If they are severely damaged, they may need lifelong care. Adults who were abused as

vested interests: interests of a group of people who have a stake in keeping society as it is

children may require psychiatric services or welfare assistance because of emotional damage that prevents them from becoming productive. They may also harm their own children, thus extending the cost to another generation (Barnett et al., 2005).

gatekeepers: individuals recognized as having special expertise in identifying problems and who control access to important people or services

Gatekeepers control access to important people or services. In the case of social problems, they are individuals recognized as having expertise in identifying problems and often have the authority to label individuals or groups as being the source of a problem. Some of the gatekeepers in Canadian society are doctors, police officers, judges and juries, and social workers. For example, doctors decide whether an individual's mental condition is dangerous enough to require confinement. They decide whether a person is sick or injured enough to be admitted to a hospital. The actions and decisions of police officers, judges, and juries determine whether to label an individual a criminal. Child welfare workers are entrusted with deciding whether children are in sufficient danger to remove them from their homes. All these people work within laws, regulations, and guidelines that they are responsible for following, even if they personally disagree with them. They thus support the power of the dominant group.

Not everyone in society defines problems in the same way. Two groups may see a particular situation as being a problem, but they may differ drastically as to just what the problem is (Coleman & Kerbo, 2002). In the case of homosexuality, for instance, many in society, such as conservative religious groups, see homosexual behaviour as bad or sick. On the other hand, gay rights activists see the problem in the intolerance of society. Groups that advocate rights for gays, for people who are physically or mentally challenged, or for fathers to have custody of their children are called special-interest groups. Often, they want regulations or laws supported by vested interests to be changed. When the special interests of two groups are similar, they may work together to force change. For example, although they disagree on some issues, such as trapping fur-bearing animals, conservationists and Aboriginal peoples have cooperated to protect old-growth forests in Northern Ontario.

The ABCX Model

When society decides a situation is a problem, individuals and families are affected. The social definition of a problem can create internal problems for the family. For example, when the breadwinner father in a family loses his job, this may affect his relationship with his spouse and children.

ABCX model: a model that explains how families respond to stressors based on the resources they have and how they perceive the stressor

stressor: an event that is so significant it causes changes in the family

Dealing with a New Problem

Families differ in the way they respond to a stressful situation. Some seem to handle far more than their share of misfortune and still keep a positive outlook. Others seem to fall apart at the slightest difficulty.

Reuben Hill (1958) proposed what he called the **ABCX model** of response. He developed this model after extensively observing families who survived the Great Depression of the 1930s. In his model, "A" refers to the **stressor** event, the breadwinner losing his job, for example (Price et al., 2010). The model also describes how the stressor event is influenced by the family's resources and their perception of the event. These determine the family's adaptation. (See Figure 13.1 below.)

The impact of the stressor is affected by resources that exist within the individual, within the family system, and within the community—the "B" factor (Schock-Giordano, 2013). What skills does the breadwinner have that will help him or her find another job? Does the family have money saved for day-to-day living? Can the extended family provide support? Is Employment Insurance available? A family will usually try to solve problems in ways that have worked before. Some families may have more experience in job searching or in applying for EI support; thus, they have some practical know-how other families do not.

The response of the family is also affected by the way the family members perceive the stressor event—the "C" factor (Price et al., 2010). Perceptions are critical in determining the impact of the stressor because they determine how the family assesses the magnitude of a stressor, and also how the family assesses the availability and utility of internal and external resources (Schock-Giordano, 2013). For instance, is the breadwinner discouraged and demoralized by the loss of his job, or does he see this as an opportunity to try something new? Does his spouse see him as a victim, or does she blame him? The children may consider their father's job loss as a source of shame, or they may not be concerned.

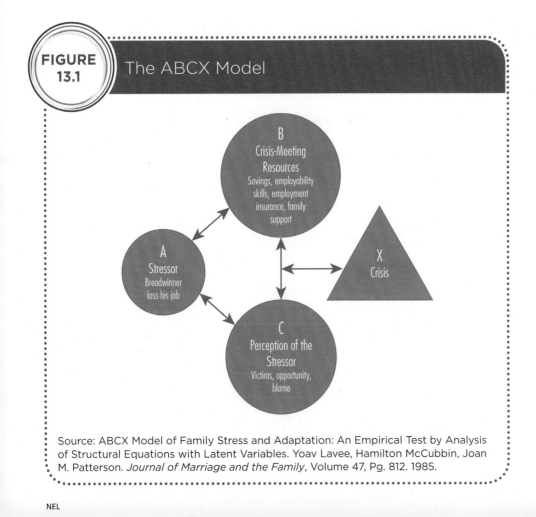

FIGURE 13.1

The ABCX Model

Source: ABCX Model of Family Stress and Adaptation: An Empirical Test by Analysis of Structural Equations with Latent Variables. Yoav Lavee, Hamilton McCubbin, Joan M. Patterson. *Journal of Marriage and the Family*, Volume 47, Pg. 812. 1985.

crisis: an imbalance in the demands placed on an individual or the family by a stressor and their ability to meet the demands

These three factors interact to produce the "X" factor—the **crisis.** When a family is in crisis, it means that there is an imbalance in the demands placed on the family and their ability to meet the demands. Once the familiar problem-solving methods fail, the family boundaries are loosened enough to allow for new information, rules and roles become confused, and tension between family members increases. At such times, the family is open to try new solutions. These solutions may be functional or dysfunctional; that is, they may increase the family's ability to solve new problems (functional) or they may temporarily reduce family tensions but create problems in the future (dysfunctional) (Price et al., 2010). Functional solutions might involve a stay-at-home spouse finding a job; someone in the family discovering sources of practical help, such as social assistance services; or the unemployed breadwinner developing new employability skills. Dysfunctional solutions may involve blaming the husband and father for all the family's difficulties or depleting all the family's savings.

The Double ABCX Model

double ABCX model: an elaboration of the original ABCX model that includes post-crisis factors as well

Usually, a family does not experience a problem as a single "bolt from the blue" stressor. Family crises evolve over time, and pressures from various sources accumulate. The ABCX model describes only pre-crisis factors, such as the existing resources available to the family. But following a longitudinal study of families dealing with crises, McCubbin and Patterson expanded the original ABCX model and proposed the **double ABCX model** (see Figure 13.2 below), which begins with the ABCX variables but includes post-crisis factors as well (McCubbin & Patterson, 1983).

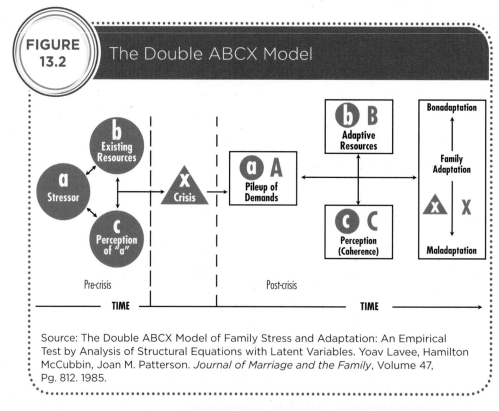

FIGURE 13.2 The Double ABCX Model

Source: The Double ABCX Model of Family Stress and Adaptation: An Empirical Test by Analysis of Structural Equations with Latent Variables. Yoav Lavee, Hamilton McCubbin, Joan M. Patterson. *Journal of Marriage and the Family*, Volume 47, Pg. 812. 1985.

According to this expanded model, five general types of stressors can pile up. First, there is the initial stressor and its hardships: for example, a breadwinner in the family loses her or his job. Second, the family experiences normative stresses, or the expected changes that most families go through. The growing independence of an adolescent or young adult is one of these "ordinary" stressors. Timing may be important. If stressful events occur at the same time as other important life events, then stress may be greater. If the job loss occurs just as a child is about to go to university, the strain may be more acute. Third, families may also experience strains that began before the particular stressor. Perhaps the family does not have much money saved. Perhaps the spouse has few employable skills. Fourth, there are the efforts of the family to cope. If they deny the problem, for example, they may cut themselves off from outside help or be unable to come up with a concrete plan of action. Fifth, there may be ambiguity. In other words, the situation within the family or within society may not be clear. Ambiguity can also be the result of not knowing how long the problem—for instance, how long the breadwinner will be unemployed—will last. All these stressors work together to cause pileup—the "aA" factor (Boss, 2006; Price et al., 2010).

The resources that help the family adapt to the situation make up the "bB" factor. Adaptive resources refer both to existing resources and to new resources that are developed in response to the demands posed by the stressor event (Lavee et al., 1985). These can include personal resources of individual family members, such as education, health, and money. If the unemployed breadwinner retrains, this may make him more employable. As well, the "B" factor encompasses the resources of the family system, such as flexible role relationships and the ability to share power. If the family breadwinner loses his job, can the spouse find a job to support the family? Finally, it includes social support, which can provide practical help and emotional support and foster a sense of self-esteem in family members. As time goes on, the resources available may change as some are used up and new sources of help are found (Price et al., 2010).

The meaning a family finds in an event affects how members cope with it. First, they may see it as having nothing to do with them, as favourable, or as threatening. Second, they evaluate what might be done and how likely a strategy is to work. Third, their perception of the event may change as a result of new information.

Families may also have snag points, or areas of difficulty, that interfere with constructive efforts to cope with problems (Patterson, 2002; Walsh, 2003b). Some families may have rules about open communication; for example, talking about the loss of the job may be avoided. Another snag point may be related to the level of intimacy in the family. In some families, members are so distant that no one feels involved in anyone else's life. Thus, family members might not support each other. In other families, members are so enmeshed in one another's lives that it is unclear who really has the problem. In such families, all members feel as disgraced as if they themselves had lost a job. When families are rigid about roles—for example, men's and women's duties—there may be a crisis when someone cannot fulfill the role. Sometimes, a family's unrealistic values fail to allow for changed circumstances and therefore interfere with problem-solving ability.

Some of these snag points are also related to the "cC" factor, which is the family's appraisal of the situation and the meaning they find in it (Patterson, 2002; Walsh, 2003b). For example, goals and values are reflected in the assessment of the situation. Some families feel it is a disaster if they cannot achieve a goal. Others give the crisis a special meaning. A healthy attitude does not, however, deny the reality of the situation or minimize what needs to be done to meet the situation.

All these factors combine to create the "xX" factor, the family's adaptation to the problem (Patterson, 2002). Family efforts need to be coordinated so that members can develop a lifestyle to suit the changed circumstances. Strategies may include attempts to change the situation. Some coping strategies control the meaning of the problem, for instance by saying this is an opportunity to learn new skills and find a new job or for the spouse to start working outside the home. Positive results are called bonadaptation, while negative results are called maladaptation.

Resilience

Recently, researchers have focused on family resilience, the ability to do well in the face of adversity. For example, some families break apart after the birth of a child with a disability. After the initial shock, others go on to manage the difficulties well. Resilience does not, however, mean making the best of a bad situation. Rather, it involves change, sometimes drastic, to produce a stronger and healthier adaptation (Boss, 2006; Patterson, 2002; Walsh, 2003b).

Individuals who find themselves in difficult family situations are inevitably affected by these challenges. Yet for many years, mental health professionals and other gatekeepers tended to focus almost exclusively on the negative effects of family trauma by reconstructing the life histories of individuals with persistent behaviour disorders or serious emotional problems. This created the impression that a poor developmental outcome is inevitable if a child is exposed to trauma, parental mental illness, alcoholism, or chronic family discord, since it examined only the lives of the "casualties," not the lives of the successful "survivors" (Regional Research Institute for Human Services, 2005). In a notable reversal of this tendency, Wolin and Wolin (2010) have described how some people can rise above adversity by developing skills and focusing on the positive. **Resiliencies** are the strengths that are developed in the struggle with family challenges, and the seven resiliencies they identified provide a framework for talking about these strengths. They are:

resiliencies: the strengths that are developed in the struggle with family challenges

Insight: asking tough questions and giving honest answers.
Independence: distancing oneself emotionally and physically from the sources of trouble in one's life.
Relationships: making fulfilling connections to other people.
Initiative: taking charge of problems.
Creativity: using imagination and expressing oneself in art forms.
Humour: finding the comic in the tragic.
Morality: acting on the basis of conscience rather than self-interest or practical considerations (Wolin & Wolin, 2010).

The seven resiliencies are tools to be used by teachers, counsellors, and other social service workers. They can serve as a guide to help professionals know where to look for strengths rather than harms.

Time to Review

1. How is a social problem defined?
2. What is the ABCX model?
3. What is the double ABCX model?
4. What are the seven resiliencies?

Two Specific Family Problems

The double ABCX model describes the way families respond to many crises and ongoing problems. In this section, we will look at two situations that both society and families define as problems.

Chronic Illness and Disability

Many people experience chronic illness or a disability. In 2006, 14.3 percent of Canadians had some sort of disability. The numbers ranged from about 3.7 percent of children under 15 to 56.5 percent of adults over 74 years of age (Statistics Canada, 2009h). An earlier survey found that developmental delays were most common among young children, and mobility and memory problems among older adults (Cossette & Duclos, 2002).

Chronic illness or disability may occur suddenly or develop over a period of time. Although in many ways the effect on the family is similar in the two situations, there are also differences.

The Initial Shock

The illness or disability may be the result of an accident, be detected in a prenatal diagnosis, or be the result of the birth of a child with obvious problems (Seligman & Darling, 2007). One parent described the birth of such a child as learning she had arrived in Holland when she had planned a wonderful trip to Italy (Kingsley, 2002). For some people, the way they are given the news is a problem, especially when information is slow in coming. Most prefer to be told sooner rather than later and to be given the facts fully and clearly, thus reducing the stress of ambiguity (Seligman & Darling, 2007). After the initial shock, the first concern may be with the affected individual's survival. Soon, energy increases, shown by visiting the family member in hospital, taking him or her for tests, providing the new care that is necessary, or taking over the responsibilities the ill member used to look after. The "A" factor includes the acute illness, the diagnosis, the first attempts at medical treatment, and the energy rush needed to meet the immediate demands on the family (Walsh, 2006).

Later, a period of assessment will determine the likely level of functioning. Sometimes, the assessment cannot occur until there has been time for healing or testing. During this process, the problem may become chronic, extending over a period of time.

During the initial phase of illness, the needs of other family members are often ignored (Williams, 2006). Meals may become "catch as catch can." Laundry may pile up. Children may receive little attention and supervision. If the illness lasts more than a few days, one or more family members may burn out and no longer have the energy to respond to physical and emotional demands. As a result, they become irritable and tend to withdraw from others. They may become ill. The family system starts to break down as family members can no longer meet the demands of illness. The family goes into crisis (Price et al., 2010).

In other cases, the onset of illness is gradual. Little by little, the family or others come to believe that something is wrong (Seligman & Darling, 2007). Gradual discovery may take place when an older member is showing memory loss and personality changes, or a baby is not meeting developmental stages. At the point when the disorder is diagnosed as chronic—for example, Alzheimer's disease, a chromosomal disorder leading to physical and mental delays in development, or AIDS—the family faces a crisis similar to the acute onset of an illness. In addition, these families have already undergone long periods of worry and fear that will have created other stressors as members have tried to cope.

In both cases, the meaning the family attaches to the illness is important and is affected by a variety of factors. What is their script for what family relationships should be like? Do they have experience with a similar disorder? If so, do they feel their experience has given them the power to cope, or do they dread the problem? Do they feel that an individual can live a rewarding life if he or she is confined to a wheelchair or is facing death? Or do they fear the process? Do they blame themselves because they were not more careful, or do they see an accident or a genetic disorder as occurring in spite of all their precautions? Do they blame the sufferer? (Coleman & Kerbo, 2002; Power & Dell Orto, 2004).

The Long Haul

As an illness becomes chronic, stressors on the family pile up (Price et al., 2010). These can come from many sources. The illness itself is a continuing stress, especially if there are unpredictable episodes or it is progressive (Okazaki & Yorgason, 2006). If the prognosis is uncertain, ambiguity produces further stress (Boss, 2002). The stress of ambiguity may make it difficult for parents to accept their child's disability. Some may hesitate to become attached to a child who may die soon. When a child has a severe disability, she or he may be physically present but psychologically absent. How does such a child fit into the family system? What is the family role of a child who is institutionalized? In such circumstances, parents are at increased risk of depression and anxiety (Berge & Holm, 2007; O'Brien, 2007; Roper & Jackson, 2007).

Within the family, members may approach burnout and no longer be able to handle everyday hassles. Relationships with other family members can become strained. Chronic illness or disability can place enormous stress on the marital subsystem (Seligman & Darling, 2007). In fact, a disproportionate number of children with disabilities live with women, especially with single parents (Cohen & Petrescu-Prahova, 2006). There may also be resentment over the demands of the ill member and often a feeling of guilt about one's impatience (Okazaki & Yorgason, 2006). Sometimes, the needs of well family members are felt to be a burden. Overall, tension and conflict may increase.

Family activities and goals may be subject to change. For example, women whose firstborn is disabled are less likely to have another if their child has extensive needs (MacInnes, 2008). Changes in plans may result from financial limitations, as a direct result of either the needs of the patient or the impact the illness has on other members' employment. If an illness is unpredictable, for example asthma, it may be difficult to count on family rituals and customs because they may be interrupted by the individual's medical needs. When a parent is emotionally disturbed, the family environment may also be unpredictable. Sometimes, members fill their roles well. At other times, the family is thrown into chaos when the parent's disorder flares up. In a progressive illness, such as multiple sclerosis, the family has the strain of repeatedly adjusting to new care and role demands (Okazaki & Yorgason, 2006). Planning for the future may be difficult if the prognosis is uncertain (Aldwin, 2007). Will the patient recover? If not, when is death likely to occur—tomorrow or five years from now?

Social activities may also change, for example if the behaviour of the person with a chronic illness or disability is unpredictable, or if the illness demands much time from the caregiver. Sometimes the family may become socially isolated just when they need other people most.

Added to all these stressors are **normative family changes**—the changes expected as part of the family life cycle. These include puberty, the growing independence of young people, finding a mate, having children, and retiring (Boss, 2006). Chronic illness can have a different effect, depending on the stage of the family life cycle of either parents or children. For instance, chronic illness or disability may influence a young person's decision (or even opportunity) to marry and perhaps to have children. Illness can also interfere with the growing independence of a young person. If the adolescent or young adult is ill, he or she may remain dependent on the family of origin long past the time most young people are living on their own (Seligman & Darling, 2007). If a parent is ill, the young person may feel duty bound to stay home and help with care. In later life, the illness of a partner can disrupt plans for activities, such as travel after retirement. Middle-aged children can also feel trapped by their parents' need for care on the one hand and their dependent children's needs for care on the other hand (see Chapter 7).

As already mentioned, the resources an individual can call on affect the ability to cope. Some resources create their own demands and difficulties. Dealing with the medical system, especially if it is not sensitive to family members' needs, can add stress (Neufeld et al., 2003). Supplementary health insurance can help relieve the financial burden of chronic illness. At times, however, it is unclear how many costs the plan will cover, thus increasing anxiety (Jacobs, 1991). Similarly, friends and relatives can play a key role in protecting children from the periodic neglect

normative family changes: changes that are expected as part of the family life cycle

of a mentally ill parent. If, however, they take responsibility when the parent can still manage, they may undermine the individual's position in the family (Walsh, 2006). On the other side, the care receiver can provide support for the caregiver by encouraging a discussion of frustrations and by being appreciative (Wright & Aquilino, 1998).

Over time, families may change their perception of the illness. (See Box 13.1 below.) For example, one family with a child with severe physical challenges started by blaming one another. Eventually, they saw him as a force pulling them together because he depended on them for survival. Some couples who have had a child with mental or physical challenges, or who nurse a chronically ill child, have adopted other children with similar problems because they feel that the skills gained in dealing with their birth child should be used for others' welfare (Sandness, 1983).

BOX 13.1   Doing Pretty Well

She's not the woman I remember. My competent, dependable mother is gone. She can't manage her own money, even if she could see to sign a cheque. She's surprised every time she's wished "Happy Birthday," and asks her age over and over, then queries, "How did I get so old?"

My father looked after her as long as he could. He lived with her endless repetitions and her need to have everything explained again and again. And he did it with patience well beyond mine. He tried to allow her the dignity of shaping her routines, even past her ability to decide if she needed a bath or change of clothes. Finally he could cope no longer, and they entered a home together.

My mother still has memories. Some are false. For a time, she imagined my father died from a wild animal attack, though he slipped away in his sleep. She does recall childhood places and events. She remembers her children's names and recognizes the ones who visit most often. But she doesn't remember the stroke that consigned her to a wheelchair some months ago.

And yet her old humour and spunk still sparkle through her dimness. She informed one grandson, "My, how you've grown—in both directions!" And recently she announced, "I'm doing pretty well for a 94-year-old."

How society in general perceives an illness or disability also has a significant impact. First, the social perceptions of an illness may increase the stress burden. This increase is most likely to happen when the illness or disability is stigmatized, as in the case of AIDS or a mental disorder (Schock-Giordani & Gavazzi, 2010). Second, when the perception is more favourable, it is more likely that social support services will be available. These can help reduce the stress burden on the family.

As a result of the interplay of these factors, family coping patterns emerge. Dysfunctional coping can include overprotection of the ill or disabled member, denial of the reality of the illness, and anger and resentment toward the ill person or others. Often, the family feels out of control and victimized. Functional coping, on the other hand, helps the family feel in control. They try to understand the medical situation through communicating with others like themselves and with medical personnel. They work at keeping the family together and emphasize cooperation. They do not cut themselves off from social support. Because they have a sense of control, their self-esteem is high and they remain psychologically stable.

Counselling and support, while often given only at the time of diagnosis, can help families cope. In the case of a disabled child, parents may not have the energy to deal with psychological issues at first. In addition, if the problem is diagnosed when the child is an infant, the "differences" the parents have to deal with may not be obvious until the child enters school. It is at this point that parents may benefit most from counselling (Patterson, 2002; Power & Dell Orto, 2004; Seligman & Darling, 2007).

With Internet use now nearly universal, nurses and other health care workers must be prepared to discuss the availability of online social support. The emergence of online communities and social support networks has become a significant factor in assistance and sustenance of people seeking healthcare, as well as for caregivers, who have their own life, health, and professional concerns. The effect of age does not appear to be important; chronically ill seniors who have online access to health information have been shown to use services an average of 37 minutes per day. Men are more likely to look for support about their own condition, whereas women seek support for themselves and on behalf of parents and other relatives (LaCoursiere, 2001).

The Alcoholic Family System

Like other problems, alcohol and other substance abuse is defined by society. The acceptance of alcohol use varies among cultures. Alcohol was not a problem for Aboriginal Canadians, for example, until the British brought rum and the French brought brandy from Europe (Hudak et al., 1999; Stewart & Wall, 2004).

In 2009, 76.5 percent of Canadians reported drinking in the past 12 months (Canadian Centre on Substance Abuse, 2010). The economic impact of alcohol-related harm in Canada is estimated to be $14.6 billion per year (Canadian Centre on Substance Abuse, 2013). The personal and social costs of alcohol abuse include illness, inability to fulfill family and work responsibilities, and premature death (Rehm et al., 2006). Heavy use of alcohol by pregnant women can cause fetal alcohol syndrome in the child (Stewart & Wall, 2004).

Why do we refer to an alcoholic family system rather than to a family with an alcoholic member? One of the difficulties with alcohol abuse, as we shall see, is the fact that so much of family life focuses on the alcohol abuse that the entire family system is involved with alcoholism (Boss, 2006).

Alcoholism has a number of factors similar to chronic illness. The alcoholic member may not fill his or her usual family roles and responsibilities; others, therefore, have to adjust their behaviour. Alcohol abuse adds stresses in terms of changed behaviour; physical states, such as alcohol–related illness; income difficulties, if drinking interferes with work; and social isolation (Rehm et al., 2006; Stewart & Wall, 2004). As with chronic disease, further stresses are created by developmental demands on the family and society's attitudes. (See Figure 13.3 below.)

But alcoholism and chronic illness differ in important ways. Unlike many chronic illnesses, alcoholism does not start suddenly; rather, it develops over time. Society considers it discreditable and the alcoholic as morally weak (Hudak et al., 1999). The family, along with the alcoholic member, often goes to great lengths to avoid acknowledging the problem. As a result, family members often assume

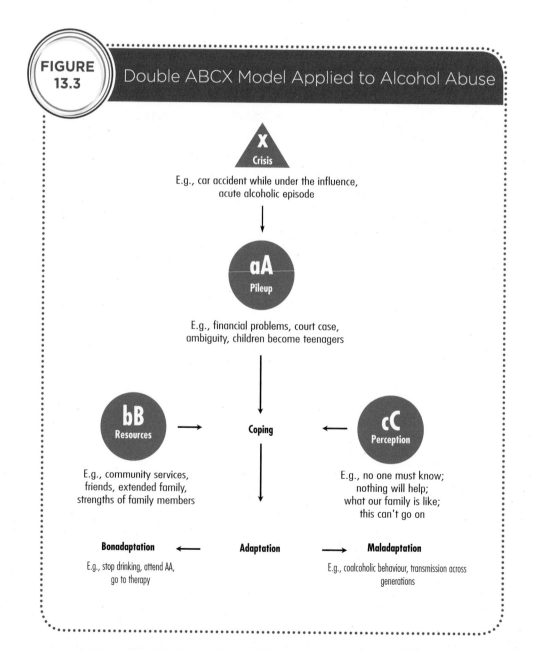

FIGURE 13.3

Double ABCX Model Applied to Alcohol Abuse

X
Crisis

E.g., car accident while under the influence,
acute alcoholic episode

aA
Pileup

E.g., financial problems, court case,
ambiguity, children become teenagers

bB
Resources

E.g., community services,
friends, extended family,
strengths of family members

Coping

cC
Perception

E.g., no one must know;
nothing will help;
what our family is like;
this can't go on

Bonadaptation ← **Adaptation** → **Maladaptation**

E.g., stop drinking, attend AA,
go to therapy

E.g., coalcoholic behaviour, transmission across
generations

stereotyped roles. One or more may be enablers. **Enablers** are persons whose behaviour allows another to act in a certain way; in the case of alcoholic families, the behaviour allows the individual to continue drinking without suffering the most extreme consequences (Copans, 1989; Roberts & McCrady, 2003). For example, a wife may phone her husband's workplace to say that he is sick, or young children may look after their hung-over mother.

The concept of a "drinking partnership" is useful in understanding the dynamic. Both members work out norms about alcohol use for their household. Each shapes the other's beliefs and behaviours about drinking (Roberts, 2005). The partner or child of an alcoholic may be a **codependent**. Codependence (the tendency for nonalcoholic members of an alcoholic family to display a variety of psychological symptoms as a result of the alcoholic member's behaviour) is one effect of the drinking partnership. Originally, it was viewed only as it affected the alcoholic. Now, however, it is recognized as a psychological problem in its own right.

Symptoms of codependence are quite characteristic. The individual has little sense of self-worth and needs continuing approval from others. This need has several results. First, the codependent person does not have clear personal boundaries and takes on the drinker's problems. The entire life of the family may revolve around the alcoholic member. Second, the codependent finds meaning and worth in caretaking. By becoming indispensable, she or he makes it easier for the alcoholic to become and remain dependent. Third, the codependent believes that he or she is responsible for whatever happens to the significant other. Thus, as the situation becomes more chaotic, the individual tries to exert more control, perhaps by watching every move of the drinking partner. Fourth, as pressures increase, the codependent partner is at risk of developing stress-related illnesses, such as ulcers and high blood pressure. All these characteristics are not signs of a personality disorder. Rather, they are an individual's way of coping with continuing stress (Boss, 2006; Hudak et al., 1999; Schaeff, 1986).

Alcoholism can have a profound effect on the marriage relationship, in addition to the development of codependence. Communication may be affected. Alcoholics have a reduced ability to read nonverbal facial cues to emotions (Marinkovic et al., 2009). Irritability during drinking bouts may alternate with excessive kindness during sober spells. The kindness, however, feels unnatural, as if the alcoholic is exaggerating the role of the good spouse and parent. The husband or wife of the drinker may, however, use sober periods to express festering anger by being cold, sarcastic, and complaining. Sometimes, anger escalates into violence. Conversation can disappear if husbands refuse to talk during periods of heavy drinking. Meals may be missed and recreation spoiled by embarrassing behaviour. Sex may disappear. Sometimes the nondrinking partner will refuse sexual relations as punishment (Hudak et al., 1999; Roberts & McCrady, 2003).

Members of alcoholic families learn a number of lessons about family life (Copans, 1989). In such families, individuals spend their time worrying about the alcoholic member's behaviour and the attitudes of others. The first lesson, then, is that alcohol is the centre of family life (Boss, 2006; Schaeff, 1986; Wiseman, 1991). A second lesson is that alcohol can make things better. In some cases, the alcoholic

enabler: a person whose behaviour allows another to act in a certain way; often used in reference to nonalcoholic members of alcoholic families

codependent: often the partner or child of an alcoholic and who also displays a variety of psychological symptoms as a result of living with an alcoholic

member is more loving and warm while drinking than while sober. Drinking more alcohol can reduce the unpleasant withdrawal symptoms. A third lesson is that alcohol abuse is a family secret to be covered up.

This pattern of coping has its costs. It may lead to a variety of symptoms in the nonalcoholic members, including anxiety, depression, shame, and anger. Children of alcoholic parents, especially if the parents have antisocial behaviour, are more likely to display behaviour problems themselves. For example, they may have more difficulty than others in regulating their behaviour in terms of problem solving and emotional control (Schroeder & Kelley, 2008). In part, problems occur because the nonalcoholic parent may use coercive or other ineffective parenting methods (Loukas et al., 2001). Keeping up family rituals and routines protects children from psychological problems (Haugland, 2005).

On the positive side, some adult children of alcoholics enter the helping professions, where they can care for others in a socially approved manner. Yet they may have difficulty with particular clients or patients as a result of their early experiences. For example, one psychiatrist who as a teenager was sent to bring his alcoholic father home found that he was impatient and ineffective when he tried to treat alcoholic patients.

Often, the alcoholism is not admitted until a decisive event, such as criminal charges for drunk driving, makes denial impossible (Brown & Lewis, 1999). This event may differ for the alcoholic and family members. For example, the alcoholic may not experience drinking as a problem until his wife leaves him. Obviously, an earlier series of events created a crisis for her.

When the alcoholic member stops drinking, however, there may be a "crisis" of sobriety. The family still has its old patterns and has to learn new ones. The period of adjustment typically lasts from six months to two years. All family members may need counselling or involvement in mutual support groups, such as Alcoholics Anonymous, Al-Anon, and Alateen. The irresponsible family member needs to learn to take responsibility for his or her behaviour, and overly responsible members need to learn to stop assuming responsibility that is not theirs. Both lessons may be extremely difficult because they involve creating a completely different family pattern (Brown & Lewis, 1999; Hudak et al., 1999).

Communication and Problem Solving

As families encounter problems, they must find solutions if they are to cope. As we have seen, communication can help couples and families find solutions. In families where positive communication is less, there are lower levels of adaptability and less change than in families with more balanced communication (Olson, 1990). Families who can talk openly about their feelings adapt relatively well to chronic illnesses and other disabilities. By doing so, they provide valuable emotional and practical support to each other (Walsh, 2006).

Families with more effective problem-solving skills usually communicate clearly, both in words and through a wide range of interpersonal messages. When they encounter a problem, they try out various patterns of interaction that have worked in the past. If they are unable to solve the problem right away, they do not feel helpless. Instead, they look for new solutions. On the other hand, families that are less effective in solving problems often have more limited interpersonal communication and seem to talk at cross-purposes. Since they also attempt to keep things the same and resist change, they cannot adapt to new circumstances (Walsh, 2006).

The Long View

All families are changed by the problems they experience. The way they change is shaped by what they themselves, and society as a whole, believe about the situation. Old patterns of problem solving, the resources available, and other pressures all contribute to striking a new balance. Some families break under the stress; others develop strengths they never dreamed possible.

Time to Review

1. What are some of the stressors that may start to pile up in a family with a member who has a chronic illness or a disability?
2. What are some of the symptoms of codependence?
3. Why is communication important in families facing problems?

New in Canada

Maricel sometimes wondered if it was all worth it. Coming to Canada with the Live-in Caregiver Program had been hard work. Her sister, Alma, had urged her to apply because it was a quick way to become an immigrant and employment prospects were better in Canada than in the Philippines. She had already completed two years of college before her marriage to Efren and the birth of their daughter, Estrella. To qualify, she needed to complete a course in caregiving, find a job that met the program requirements, pass an English exam, and produce a contract from her employer. Efren and Estrella were still in the Philippines, living with his relatives. As soon as Maricel had worked as a live-in caregiver for two years, she could apply for permanent residence and bring her family to Canada. Alma was already a permanent resident and now worked as an office manager for an accountant. Maricel had taken over Alma's first job, caring for her employer's elderly father in Flin Flon.

Things had been hard. Although Maricel knew English, she found it difficult to catch jokes or understand local expressions. At least she'd stopped looking for tricks with hats during hockey games. Canadian customs like Halloween were strange. She didn't like the unfamiliar foods at the store; she'd rather buy eggs, chickens, and vegetables from neighbours. The old man she cared for was sometimes difficult. He didn't always know where he was and at times resisted being bathed. Some days, he'd refuse to take his daily handful of pills. On bad days, he called her unpleasant names. Winter weather made things worse. Maricel found the short days, long nights, and bitter cold oppressive, especially when it hit minus 40. She missed the warmth and sun of home. Most of all she missed Efren and Estrella.

There had been good things, too. Her employer, a former mine supervisor, was generous and grateful for her help. Maricel saw Alma at least once a week and they savoured familiar food like lumpia and noodles as they chatted in their familiar Tagalog. Alma had taught her so much about Canadian ways that Maricel didn't know how she would have managed without her sister's help. Once a week, she spoke over the Internet with her family in the Philippines.

Maricel had come to like Canada and the lakes and forests around Flin Flon. She saw opportunities for employment or even for starting a childcare business. Perhaps they'd move to Winnipeg or Calgary. Alma had introduced her to the local Filipino community so that she didn't feel so alone. And soon Efren and Estrella would join her. She wanted her child to have a good education, a good future.

1. Using the double ABCX model, identify the stressors and pileup (A and Aa) factors Maricel has experienced.
2. What resources can Maricel draw upon to help her adapt? (B and Bb factors)
3. How do her perceptions of the situation affect her adaptation? (C and Cc factors)

Summary

What Is the Definition of a Problem within the Family Context?

A social problem exists when a significant number of people believe it is a problem. What is considered a problem has changed over the years. For example, homosexuality has been described at different times as a sin, a crime, a mental disorder, and an alternative lifestyle. Often, the dominant group in society has the greatest influence in deciding what a problem is.

How Does the ABCX Model Help Us Describe the Response of the Family System to Problems?

The way families respond to a problem depends on the stressor ("A" factor), the family's resources ("B" factor), and their interpretation of the situation ("C" factor). These factors work together to produce a crisis ("X" factor), which calls for new ways of solving problems. If the problem is long term, stressors can pile up. Again, family resources and interpretation affect the outcome—the eventual adaptation of the family to the problem. This second pattern has been called the double ABCX model.

What Is the Seven Strengths Model of Resilience?

For many years, mental health professionals and other gatekeepers tended to focus almost exclusively on the negative effects of family trauma by reconstructing the life histories of individuals with persistent behaviour disorders or serious emotional problems. Resiliencies are the strengths that are developed in the struggle with family challenges. The seven resiliencies are tools to be used by teachers, counsellors, and other social service workers to help these individuals.

How Can the ABCX Model Be Used to Understand Two Family Problems (Chronic Illness and Alcoholism)?

Chronic illness can occur suddenly or gradually. In either case, the illness and the diagnosis create stress, which is affected by both the coping resources of the family and the meaning they attach to the illness. Often, members respond to the crisis with high levels of activity. When the illness is prolonged, other stressors, such as changes in family lifestyle and ordinary life-cycle changes, come into play. Different resources may be required to cope in the long term, and the family's interpretation of the situation may change over time. These combine to produce new coping patterns.

Like chronic illness, alcohol abuse is a family stressor. As in chronic illness, the family's coping resources and the meaning members place on alcohol abuse will affect the severity of the crisis. Various attempts at coping may combine with other stressors to produce a pileup. Eventually, the family may adapt by making alcohol abuse part of the family pattern through enabling behaviours. The husband or wife of an alcoholic may become codependent. Often, the marriage suffers. If the alcoholic member stops drinking, the family may go through a further crisis because the old coping patterns are no longer appropriate.

What Part Does Communication Play in Problem Solving?

Positive communication is important for helping families change in a positive way. Often, those who are less effective at solving problems have limited or negative patterns of communication.

Class Assignments

1. By reading newspapers, watching television, and/or using the Internet, explore two current issues that present the family with problems. Explain what stresses they place on the family and solutions that have been proposed. What are the advantages and disadvantages of these solutions?
2. Explain why an individual in a helping profession (such as a nurse, teacher, or social worker) would find the double ABCX model useful. Illustrate your answer by applying the model to a specific problem.

3. As a group, find out more about the Alcoholics Anonymous, Al-Anon, or Alateen programs in your community. Prepare a presentation about what you learn.

Personal Assignments

The following assignments are designed to help you think about your own experience:

1. What problems has your family experienced? How have they affected family relationships and roles? Did they change the day-to-day organization of family life? Explain.
2. When you have personally experienced problems, what methods have you used to try to resolve them? Did these methods work? Why or why not? What other means might you have used?

Chapter 14

Home Dangerous Home— Violence in the Family

LEARNING OBJECTIVES

What is family violence?

What kinds of violence and abuse occur in families and intimate relationships?

Why do people abuse family members?

What are the different theories about abuse and violence within families?

How can family violence be prevented?

Daniel Korzeniewski/Shutterstock

Jannie, I'll call her, was my neighbour—a pretty, thirtyish woman. I was young and naive when we met. Within a month, she started telling me the troubles of her marriage. She provided the main family income as a secretary and struggled to keep on top of their debts. When her husband worked, he made good pay, but soon after taking up a new job, he would find some grievance against his boss and quit. They'd moved often as he looked for more opportunities. He enjoyed fine things. He had the latest in stereo and television equipment, all charged to credit cards. Jannie found out about the bills when the cards were cancelled. When she dared challenge him, he beat her. This wasn't the first time, either. It had been much worse during her two pregnancies. In between, he told her how stupid, how ugly she was. Jannie feared for their children. Her husband flew into a rage if they touched any of his electronics. I wondered why she stayed with him. She said she couldn't leave. After all, she had made her marriage vows. He threatened to keep the children if she left. Besides, he treated her like a princess afterwards to make up for beating her. Why didn't she get her parents to help? Her family had warned her she shouldn't marry him. All they'd say was, "I told you so." What about her priest or the police? They'd tell her it was her job to make the marriage work—she should try harder to please her husband. There was nowhere else for her to go anyway. Her husband usually commandeered her paycheque and she couldn't afford her own apartment. Why, you ask, didn't she go to a shelter, call an abuse hotline? This was 1958, long before wife abuse was publicly acknowledged. You either rescued yourself or made do—or told your neighbour your woes.

● ● ● ● ○

"A haven in a heartless world" (Lasch, 1979) is how the family is often described. Home is the one place where we should feel protected and safe. Yet for too many people, the family home is the most dangerous of places.

In this chapter, we will examine the issue of abuse and violence in the family. As we saw in Chapter 13, the public decides when a problem is a problem, and the definition of what is considered violence within families has been evolving. Although family violence has been around for a long time, concern about it is relatively recent. Historically, the first type of abuse to catch public attention was child abuse, followed by wife beating and elder battering. Trying to understand why some people abuse other family members is a complex undertaking. We will look at various theories about abuse within families. Finally, we will look at some of the social strategies for preventing abuse. Over the past few decades, victims have become more aware of their rights and the resources available to them. No one should be subjected to violence within their family, and hopefully, with greater understanding of the underlying causes of abuse and social support for survivors, we can reduce, if not eliminate, this terrible situation.

Where Do I Fit In?

Authors' note: The topic of this chapter is one that may arouse powerful feelings. The truth is that some of you have experienced first-hand the kinds of abuse described here. It is important to know that you are not alone. There are many resources available, and we strongly encourage you to seek them out.

1. If you were Jannie's neighbour, what advice would you give her? What else might you do?
2. What do you consider abuse within a family?
3. Why do you think family violence occurs?

What Is Family Violence?

Family violence wears many faces. It is the baby who is battered, the child who is sexually assaulted, the woman who is punched and kicked by her husband, the elderly man who is exploited by his children. We recognize all these individuals as abused.

Yet the issue of family violence suffers from confusing definitions. In defining family violence, two elements must be considered: the forms of abuse to be included and the types of family relationships. In Canada, the term **family violence** is used to refer to "a range of abusive behaviours that occur within relationships based on kinship, intimacy, dependency or trust" (Sinha, 2012, p. 9). Violence refers to many actions, ranging from throwing things, to shoving and punching, to using a knife or a gun. Although not usually recognized as violence, verbal abuse—yelling, screaming, swearing—may be equally intimidating. The same act may have an entirely different effect depending on who does it and against whom it is directed. For example, a small woman may shove a large man without hurting him, but a strong man's shove may send a child slamming into a wall (Barnett et al., 2005).

Abuse refers to a situation in which a person takes advantage of a less powerful person. Thus, it encompasses neglect, sexual and emotional abuse, and financial exploitation, as well as physical violence. In this chapter, we will use the term "family violence" to refer to any form of abuse, mistreatment, or neglect that children or adults experience from other members of their family.

Definitions are important. Levels of reporting depend on what we consider abuse. Do we count explicit sexual language or walking around naked in front of a child as a form of sexual abuse? Does slapping a child rate as child abuse? Is belittling a person a form of abuse? Definitions determine who is counted as abused and who is eligible for services. They also decide the type of help offered and how well it stops the abuse.

Two main sources of information are used to measure the incidence of family violence in Canada. The first is police-reported information from the Uniform Crime Reporting Survey (UCR). The second is self-reported victimization data

family violence: any form of abuse, mistreatment or neglect that children or adults experience from other members of their family

abuse: a situation in which a person takes advantage of a less powerful person

from the General Social Survey on Victimization, which does not report violence against children. According to police-reported data, in 2010 there were almost 99 000 victims of family violence. Half of these victims were spouses and the other half were other family members, such as children, parents, siblings or extended family members. Females were twice as likely as males to be be a victim of police-reported family violence (Sinha, 2012).

In the following sections, we will look at three kinds of abuse that occur in families—child abuse, abuse between partners, and elder abuse.

Child Abuse

History of Child Abuse

For centuries, children were considered the property of their parents, especially of their fathers. The saying "Spare the rod and spoil the child" was often quoted. This belief is even reflected in nursery rhymes. The old woman who lived in a shoe with her many children "whipped them all soundly and sent them to bed." Children were seen as basically bad. Through punishment, they could be transformed into God-fearing individuals (Frankel-Howard, 1989; Tower, 1989). The result was that many children were not only whipped but also physically injured, all in the name of turning out good citizens.

Sexual exploitation of children was also common. In the past, fathers often arranged the marriages of their young daughters. These marriages were sometimes consummated before the girls reached puberty. In spite of laws and social criticism of the sort found in Charles Dickens's novels (e.g., *Oliver Twist*), most abuse of children was overlooked. A man's home was his castle. Outsiders had no business poking their noses into what went on in the privacy of his four walls.

In Canada, attention was first given to the idea of child abuse through the formation of the Children's Aid Society in Toronto in 1891. *An Act for the Prevention of Cruelty to and Better Protection of Children* was passed in Ontario two years later. The initial concern of reforms were centred on child employment and substitute caregivers rather than on neglect and abuse by parents, although the latter was covered by the legislation. For many years, Canadian legislation changed little. For example, British Columbia kept most of the wording of its 1893 act into the 1970s (Kieran, 1986; Wachtel, 1989).

As attention to abuse grew, definitions became broader and more inclusive. All definitions assume that appropriate standards of behaviour for parents exist. The problem is that these standards vary over time, for example those concerning appropriate discipline. They also vary across cultures and between social groups. What is seen as abusive or neglectful by one group may be considered responsible parenting by another (Malley-Morrison & Hines, 2004).

Following popularization of the term "battered child syndrome," coined by C. Henry Kempe in the early 1960s, mandatory reporting laws were passed. By the late 1970s, 9 of the 12 provincial and territorial jurisdictions had passed such laws and the remainder had set up monitoring programs (Wachtel, 1989). In December

1991, Canada signed and ratified the UN *Convention on the Rights of the Child*. This international agreement protects the economic, social, and cultural rights of children (Unicef Canada, 2013).

What Is Child Abuse?

Child abuse includes physical, sexual, and emotional abuse. It also includes neglect, and any violence that children see or hear in their families (Department of Justice, 2013). The abuse may occur in a child's home or in other places, such as other people's homes, schools, or community centres. In Canada, there are federal, provincial, and territorial laws to protect children from abuse.

Physical Abuse

Physical abuse is the intentional use of physical force against a child that results in injury or causes bodily harm. There is an ongoing debate about how to distinguish physical abuse from corporal punishment (see Box 14.1). **Corporal punishment** is any form of physical force that is used to inflict pain and that serves as a punishment for an offence or to discourage inappropriate behaviour. Most laws allow parents to use "reasonable force" against their children. The *Criminal Code of Canada*, for example, allows for the physical discipline of children. "Every schoolteacher, parent or person standing in the place of a parent is justified in using force by way of correction toward a pupil or child, as the case may be, who is under his care, if the force does not exceed what is reasonable in the circumstances" (Department of Justice, 2009e). When does force stop being reasonable and become abusive?

physical abuse: the intentional use of physical force against a child resulting in injury or causing bodily harm

corporal punishment: any kind of physical force used to inflict pain and which serves as a punishment for an offence or to discourage inappropriate behaviour

---

BOX 14.1 | Is Spanking Child Abuse?

In 2010, a father in New Brunswick was sentenced to 45 days in jail for spanking his six-year-old son. The judge who sentenced the man said that while she does not believe that corporal punishment should always result in incarceration, it was appropriate in this case (CBC, 2010). Researchers state that most parents spank their children, if only occasionally. An American study found that younger, less well-educated mothers tended to spank children more often than fathers and older, better-educated mothers. Spanking tapered off as children became older. The researchers suggest that mothers have most responsibility for day-to-day care of children. As youngsters get older, they are easier to reason with. In addition, older mothers have probably learned a wider range of ways to manage children's behaviour (Day et al., 1998).

The use of spanking, or corporal punishment, has roots in literal interpretations of biblical passages, but the issue provokes strong opinions. Those who argue that spanking is not abuse might state that their parents spanked them and it did them no harm. On the opposite side, child development experts point out that parents who spank often tend to spank a lot and that the severity usually increases. Children disciplined this way are at risk, when they are adults, of becoming abusers (Gershoff, 2008; Straus, 2007). Taking a more moderate view, some suggest that occasional, mild spanking does no harm, but they point out that other forms of discipline are more effective. One challenge is that the definitions of physical punishment and physical abuse have to be clearly distinguished. It is also difficult to determine whether any negative effects resulting from physical punishment are attributable to the punishment itself or to other factors.

Sources: American College of Pediatricians, 2007; Barnett, 2008; Baumrind, 1996.

Sexual Abuse

sexual abuse: any form of sexual conduct directed at a child, with or without physical contact

Sexual abuse includes any form of sexual conduct directed at a child, with or without physical contact. Sexual abuse usually involves fondling and may include inviting a child to touch or be touched sexually. Other forms of sexual abuse include sexual intercourse, juvenile prostitution, and sexual exploitation through child pornography. Sexual abuse is also emotionally abusive and is often accompanied by other forms of mistreatment. Like all forms of child abuse, it is a betrayal of trust and an abuse of power over the child (Public Health Agency of Canada, 2009).

Emotional Abuse

emotional abuse: any situation in which a child is seriously or repeatedly subjected to behaviour that could cause harm to the child

Emotional abuse occurs in any situation in which a child is seriously or repeatedly subjected to behaviour that could cause harm to the child. Verbal attacks or demeaning actions that have an impact on a child's self-esteem and sense of self-worth are considered emotional abuse. Other behaviours include indifference, denigration, emotional rejection, isolation, threats, exploitation, and exposure to partner or domestic violence (Batshaw Youth and Family Centres, 2008).

Neglect

neglect: failure to give appropriate attention or care to a child, resulting in serious emotional or physical harm

Neglect is the failure to give appropriate attention or care to a child, resulting in serious emotional or physical harm. It is important to distinguish between short-term and chronic neglect; the latter has far more serious effects. Neglected children tend to live in families under stress. Often, they have single parents and/or parents who depend on welfare. Children in larger families are also more likely to be neglected. They are endangered by their parents' failure to provide for them or protect them.

Child Witnesses of Domestic Violence

Children are seriously affected by violence directed at other family members, both by what they see and by what they hear. All are terrified. Some become withdrawn and anxious; others act out through aggression and delinquency. Children may come to understand that violence is part of a close relationship between adults (Bancroft & Silverman, 2002; Harris, 2007; Hotton, 2003).

How Many Parents Abuse or Neglect Their Children?

The actual extent of child abuse is unknown, but when comparing statistics on the subject, it is important to remember that changes may be a result of several factors. First, changes in public and professional awareness of the problem can affect reporting rates. Second, changes in legislation and definitions can also affect reporting rates. Of course, there may also be actual variation in the rate of child abuse (Public Health Agency of Canada, 2010). Currently, all the provinces and territories have mandatory reporting laws requiring professionals working with children and other members of the general public to report suspected cases of child abuse to authorities, either the police or child welfare agencies. But unlike for older victims, where surveys such as the General Social Survey on Victimization are able to provide data based on self-reported victimization, there is no equivalent national survey for children and youth (Sinha, 2012). And because some forms of abuse are difficult to detect or prove, they may not be included in official definitions. Emotional abuse, psychological aggression, and neglect can be just as damaging to a child as physical abuse. Yet it is difficult for an outsider to prove that a parent is rejecting or cold enough to be abusive; as a result, few cases of emotional abuse are reported (Straus & Field, 2003).

We do know that the reporting of all kinds of abuse has increased since the 1970s (Pottie Bunge & Locke, 2000). Since children are the most vulnerable members of society, they often depend on others to report the abuse for them. As shown in Table 14.1, schools and police account for the largest number of reported incidents. There are many variations in estimates of abuse (Cabrera, 1995). In the area of sexual abuse, for example, estimates vary widely. A figure commonly cited comes from the 1984 Badgley Report on the sexual abuse of children (Trocmé et al., 2001): 1 in 2 girls and 1 in 3 boys under 18 reported unwanted sexual acts. These numbers are the result of a wide definition of sexual abuse, ranging from indecent exposure to forced intercourse. Reanalysis of the Badgley Report data suggests that 1 in 5 girls and 1 in 10 boys are victims of sexual abuse (Wachtel, 1999). More recent studies have found that for every 1000 children, sexual abuse was confirmed or strongly suspected for 1.2 children, a much lower rate than suggested by the Badgley Report. More than four times as many girls as boys are victims. In both Canada and the United States, reports of sexual abuse have declined in recent years (Brzozowski, 2004; Jones & Finkelhor, 2001; Nemr, 2009).

Usually, only the most extreme cases of abuse are reported to police or child protection agencies. There are various explanations for low reporting and recognition rates. First, since child abuse is frowned on by society, it may be hidden. Second, children may be too afraid or too young to disclose abuse. Third, professionals who see signs of abuse may not report the incident. They may not understand their responsibility to report abuse, or they may not admit to themselves that abuse is really happening. Fourth, a parent's or caregiver's explanation for injuries may seem plausible, so that no one becomes suspicious. Fifth, people may feel it isn't their business and therefore fail to report an abuse they know about. They

TABLE 14.1

Referral Sources in Child Abuse Investigations in Canada, 2008

Referral Source	Number of Investigations	Rate per 1000 Children	Percent of Referrals
Non-professional			
Custodial or non-custodial parent	26 612	4.42	11%
Child (subject of referral)	3 608	0.6	2%
Relative	16 463	2.73	7%
Neighbour/friend	16 508	2.74	7%
Professional			
Community health or social services	27 683	4.6	12%
Hospital (any personnel)	11 812	1.96	5%
School	56 255	9.34	24%
Other child welfare service	13 855	2.3	6%
Daycare centre	2 489	0.41	1%
Police	52 792	8.77	22%
Anonymous/other			
Anonymous	11 414	1.9	5%
Other	8 046	1.34	3%
Total investigations	235 842	39.16	100%

Note: Because there may be more than one referral source, percentages do not add to 100.

Source: *Canadian Incidence Study of Reported Child Abuse and Neglect 2008: Major Findings*, Pg. 26, Table 3-4b, Public Health Agency of Canada, 2010. Reproduced with the permission of the Minister of Public Works and Government Services Canada, 2013.

may think that reporting will not solve the problem or that it is not in the child's best interests (Department of Justice, 2009d; Hay, 1997).

The most common type of child maltreatment investigated by child welfare authorities is exposure to intimate partner violence, followed by neglect (Public Health Agency of Canada, 2010).

Which Children Are at Risk of Abuse or Neglect?

Children at risk of being abused include unwanted children (see Box 14.1 on page 359), children living with a lone parent, those born prematurely, those with

TABLE 14.2	Primary Category of Child Abuse Investigations in Canada, 2008		
Primary Category of Abuse	**Number of Investigations**	**Rate per 1000 Children**	**Percent in this Category**
Physical abuse	17 212	2.86	20%
Sexual abuse	2 607	0.43	3%
Neglect	28 939	1.23	34%
Emotional maltreatment	7 423	1.23	9%
Exposure to intimate partner violence	29 259	4.86	34%
Total Investigations	85 440	14.19	100%

Source: *Canadian Incidence Study of Reported Child Abuse and Neglect 2008: Major Findings*, Pg. 4, Fig. 5 – pg. 41. Public Health Agency of Canada, 2010. Reproduced with the permission of the Minister of Public Works and Government Services Canada, 2013.

"When Daddy gets angry, I feel scared and I want to cry"

Children are the most vulnerable members of society and they depend on others to report abuse for them.

Source: Kellie L. Folkerts/Shutterstock.

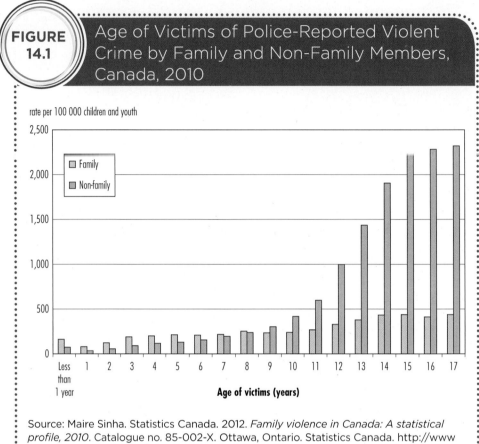

FIGURE 14.1

Age of Victims of Police-Reported Violent Crime by Family and Non-Family Members, Canada, 2010

rate per 100 000 children and youth

Age of victims (years)

Source: Maire Sinha. Statistics Canada. 2012. *Family violence in Canada: A statistical profile, 2010*. Catalogue no. 85-002-X. Ottawa, Ontario. Statistics Canada. http://www.statcan.gc.ca/pub/85-002-x/2012001/article/11643-eng.pdf

physical or mental challenges, or those in poor health. According to one report, being a stepchild is the single most important risk factor for severe child abuse (Daly & Wilson, 1996). Young children are more likely to be abused by a family member. As they get older, children are more likely to be abused by a non-family member (see Figure 14.1). In 2008, the rate of child abuse was four times higher in Aboriginal populations than in non-Aboriginal populations (49.69 per 1000 Aboriginal children versus 11.85 per 1000 non-Aboriginal children) (Public Health Agency of Canada, 2010).

Overall, girls are more likely than boys to be the victims of abuse committed by family members. This increased risk grows with age. While the rates of family violence against boys and girls are similar until three years of age, after this the rates begin to diverge and the difference continues to widen until adolescence. By 12 to 17 years of age, the rate of abuse against girls is nearly double the rate for boys (Sinha, 2012). Girls are more at risk of sexual abuse. Children who are particularly vulnerable to sexual abuse are often emotionally deprived and socially isolated. They usually know and trust the adult who abuses them and have a special fondness for this person, usually a male. Sometimes, the abuser is the only person who shows the child affection and is often someone who is expected to be protective. Girls are most often sexually abused by family members (Barnett et al., 2005; Nemr, 2009; Spitalnick et al., 2008).

What Kinds of People Abuse or Neglect Their Children?

Early studies produced a stereotype of the abusive parent. Particular groups that were identified were the young (under 20 years) and the unmarried (Bert et al., 2009). A mother whose parents separated before she was 15 years old, or who lived in a foster home because she or her siblings were neglected or abused, was considered to be at particular risk of being an abuser herself (Frankel-Howard, 1989).

Originally it was thought that abusers were mainly from the lower socioeconomic level of society. This view, however, was probably based on the fact that people who are on welfare, who come in contact with social agencies, and who live in apartments rather than houses are more open to observation and are thus more likely to be reported. If this is so, many middle- and upper-class abusers are probably not identified (Maidman, 1984).

Social interaction models recognize that abuse always takes place in a certain context. The social environment, which can be explained in terms of the ABCX

TABLE 14.3	Caregiver Risk Factors in Canada, 2008		
Caregiver Risk Factors	**Number of Investigations**	**Rate per 1000 Children**	**Percent in This Category**
No primary caregiver risk factors	19 158	3.18	22%
Type of Risk Factor			
Alcohol abuse	18 346	3.05	21%
Drug/solvent abuse	14 355	2.38	17%
Cognitive impairment	5 543	0.92	6%
Mental health issues	22 991	3.82	27%
Physical health issues	8 387	1.39	10%
Few social supports	33 235	5.52	39%
Victim of domestic violence	39 624	6.58	46%
Perpetrator of domestic violence	11 156	1.85	13%
History of foster care/group home	6 713	1.11	12%
Total investigations	85 440	14.19	100%

Note: Because there may be more than one risk factor, percentages do not add to 100.

Source: *Canadian Incidence Study of Reported Child Abuse and Neglect 2008: Major Findings*, Pg. 41, Table 5-6, Public Health Agency of Canada, 2010. Reproduced with the permission of the Minister of Public Works and Government Services Canada, 2013.

model (discussed in Chapter 13), may make it more likely that some parents will become abusive. These parents are often under high levels of stress. The stressors may be of many kinds—problems in the marriage, unemployment, and illness or disability of a family member. Often, the coping resources of abusive parents are poor. Those at particular risk of abusing children are felt to have poor self-esteem. Others lack financial resources. Abusive parents often perceive parenting as stressful. For instance, they may believe they have little control over the situation. Many abusive families are isolated from relatives and have few close friends. Some live in areas with little community feeling. They may view their neighbours or relatives as unsupportive and are less involved in social activities. They are also more likely to have had earlier involvement with child welfare services and to have mental health and/or substance abuse problems (Barnett et al., 2005; Mersky et al., 2009; Tonmyr et al., 2006). Such parents also have difficulty seeing the relationship from the children's point of view; that is, they are not aware of age-appropriate emotional states and needs. When there is a crisis, they give first claim to their own needs, with the children's needs sometimes not considered at all. Many believe that their children deliberately set out to defy them. They often set standards for children's behaviour well beyond their developmental level. These attitudes help feed the parents' feelings of stress and loss of control, and thus act as a trigger for aggression (Acton & During, 1990; Barnett et al., 2005; Schatz & Lounds, 2007).

Sexually abusive parents have two features in common: they are sexually aroused by children, and they are likely to act on that arousal. When these pre-conditions are in place, other factors increase the likelihood of abuse. Often, these families are isolated. They have little relief from a poor marital relationship and relatively few opportunities for extramarital sexual activity, such as having an affair or going to a prostitute. The marital relationship is often emotionally and sexually unsatisfying. Frequently, the wife is not interested in sex or is ill, disabled, or absent.

The oldest daughter is often at risk, especially if she has become a parentified child. Her father may regard her as a partner in a sexual as well as a parental sense. Often, abusive fathers interpret young daughters' normal attachment to them and their curiosity about physical differences in an inappropriate sexual way. Many believe they are promoting their children's welfare rather than hurting them. Yet the love and caring such fathers express for their children is contradicted by their lack of concern for the effect the incest will have on the victims (Barnett et al., 2005; Gilgun, 1995; Waterman, 1986).

Contrary to popular notions, women also sexually abuse both boys and girls. In 2007, 4 percent of sexual assaults on children by family members were committed by females, half of them by mothers (Nemr, 2009). Greater stigma is attached to mother–child incest than father–child. Women do not initiate this abuse in all cases. Sometimes they do so to go along with their male partner, or they comply because they fear being abused themselves. Child sexual abuse by women has many long-term effects similar to abuse by men (Jennings, 1994; Ogilvie, 2004).

BOX 14.2   Jonathan's Story

The day my son received his black graduation cap and diploma from pre-school was one of the happiest days of my life. It was more than a mile-stone for Jonathan, it was a celebration of his life and our togetherness, despite our experience with domestic violence. As I watched him, my eyes welled with tears. There was my Jonathan; he had made it out alive.

From the moment Jonathan was conceived, his biological father sub-jected Jonathan and I to physical and emotional abuse. Throughout my very difficult pregnancy, the father pushed, shoved, slapped, and kicked me, hoping I would miscarry the child he publicly crowed about.

When Jonathan was an infant his so-called "father" yelled and threw things at him. On Jonathan's first birthday, his father threw an electric typewriter at him. At two and a half, his father slashed Jonathan's pet cat Caley with a knife, while hissing, "That's what I'd like to do to your mother."

This little boy saw his father beat and rape me. He heard my screams and couldn't do anything about it. Those screams will stay with him for the rest of his life. Later, during a court-ordered access visit, this man managed to slam Jonathan's foot in a door, spraining his ankle—an "accident" of course. The incidents of abuse go on and on. You cannot imagine the tor-ture I felt seeing my little boy being hurt like that.

Jonathan was fortunate in connecting with two great counsellors, people who believed him and supported him through this ordeal. The pre-school Jonathan attended took the time to listen. They showed him it was okay to talk about the abuse. The teachers knew the violent pictures he drew were his way of dealing with his anger and fear; they did not tell him the pictures were unacceptable. The teachers also made me feel better and they did not blame me or think that I was crazy.

Other things could have made it easier for Jonathan. It would have helped if the police had been better trained to work with children. The police felt Jonathan was not able to tell the difference between truth and fiction, even though our lawyer felt otherwise. Judges also need to be trained about domestic violence. Even with the evidence of extreme abuse, Jonathan's father was granted supervised access. (If it had been me up on the abuse charges, Jonathan would have been taken away from me.) There were times I couldn't take Jonathan with me to my various appointments with police or court personnel, because they didn't have any place for him to play. It would also have helped Jonathan to have a support group to join. He would have realized that he was not alone, that other children are also abused.

Yes, Jonathan has survived the experience, but at what cost to his young life? As they called his name at his preschool graduation, I smiled. In spite of everything, we are the lucky ones. At least we are together here tonight, and we have each other.

Source: *Vis-à-Vis.* Volume 13, Number 4, Pg. 12, © 1996. Reprinted with permission from The Canadian Council on Social Development (www.ccsd.ca).

Children and Adolescents as Abusers

Only recently has attention turned to children and adolescents as abusers. While researchers have taken some notice of adolescent sexual offenders, abuse by children in the family has been largely ignored.

Sibling Abuse

Violence between siblings is often considered part of the normal experience of growing up. As Pagelow says, "Violence by children is seen, but it is not seen as violence" (1984, p. 341). She suggests this perception is the reason little research is done on either its incidence (or percentage of the population affected) or its after-effects. Another reason for the lack of research can be found in society's generally complacent attitude about sibling rivalry in general and boys' aggression in particular (Caffaro & Conn-Caffaro, 2005).

   Natural and healthy sexual exploration between children of similar age, size, and developmental stage is not sibling abuse. Sexual play that is mutual, voluntary, and not coercive is also not sibling abuse (Family Services of Greater Vancouver, 2008). Sibling abuse can be distinguished from non-abusive sibling interaction using the following questions. Is there a marked difference in power between the siblings? How often and for how long does the behaviour take place? How much pressure and how much secrecy are involved? How harmful are the interactions? Does

Source: Toles/Universal Uclick.

the behaviour fall outside levels of typical sibling rivalry or normal sex play? Do parents stop the behaviour appropriately? (Barnett et al., 2005; Caffaro & Conn-Caffaro, 2005). Sibling sexual abuse, or incest, can involve a brother and sister, two sisters, or two brothers, but abuse by an older brother against a younger sister is the most common form (Family Services of Greater Vancouver, 2008).

Parent Abuse

Even less is known about parent abuse than sibling abuse. Only recently have Canadian statistics begun to be recorded. Parent abuse is not an argument or disagreement. It occurs when a teen or young adult tries to have control and power over their parent or parents. They control and manipulate and try to intimidate. This abuse is ongoing and is not an occasional or one-time event. Abused parents have lost the ability to parent their teens or young adults and need support to regain a leadership role in their families (Envision Counselling And Support Centre, 2012). Often, parents do not admit such abuse except in extreme cases. Estimates suggest that 7 to 13 percent of children attack their parents. Of parent abusers reported to the police in 2005, 53 percent were aged 18 and over; the remainder were under 18. Most still depend on their parents for financial support, and 6 out of 10 were living at home in 2005. Mothers were victims in 7 out of 10 violent episodes. Most of those accused of physical or verbal abuse were male (Beauchamp, 2007).

Of known cases, older children tend to be more violent toward parents than younger ones, with a peak in the late teens (Beauchamp, 2007). Yet abusers are not necessarily the largest or strongest. Parent abusers often have little interest in school and are already involved with the police or child welfare authorities. They are likely to have friends who are delinquent and may also assault their parents. Substance abuse is common. Some researchers suggest that parent abuse may be retaliation for earlier abuse by a parent, though such aggression may be aimed at the less powerful parent rather than the one who was the abuser (Cottrell, 2003; Denham & Gillespie, 1999).

Effects of Abuse on Children

All abuse is harmful to children, though the actual effects may vary by type of abuse. Some effects are long term. Physical difficulties often occur in physical and sexual abuse and neglect. These include broken bones, genital bleeding, and failure to thrive. In extreme cases, the child dies. Children suffering any form of abuse may have learning problems as the result of either physical or emotional damage. Problem behaviours are common. These include physical aggression and delinquency, seductive behaviour among the sexually abused, apathy and withdrawal, and substance abuse. As a result, many have difficulty getting along with other children and forming satisfying relationships as adults. Often, they find it hard to trust others. In addition, victims may suffer from serious depression and, among the physically and sexually abused, from post-traumatic stress disorder. Not all abused children, fortunately, suffer serious or long-term effects from maltreatment. The frequency and severity of abuse or neglect has been found to be more important than the specific type of maltreatment in explaining subsequent psychological problems (Barnett et al., 2005; Higgins, 2004; Maholmes et al., 2007; Weaver & Akai, 2007).

Official Responses to Child Abuse

Child protection laws are in place at both the national and provincial levels. These require cases of child abuse to be reported. Problems arise, however, because there is no standard definition of child abuse. If the abuse is severe, the abuser is prosecuted; in less severe cases, social service agencies, such as a Children's Aid Society or provincial child welfare department, deal with the matter. They may remove the child permanently or temporarily until the home can be made safe. They may provide counselling and treatment to the various family members, teaching them proper parenting methods or ways of dealing with the after-effects of abuse (Cabrera, 1995).

There are contradictory pressures on protection agencies. On the one hand, they are expected to prevent abuse from recurring. If a child is returned home and then is severely abused or killed, the public is outraged. On the other hand, these agencies may be accused of child snatching and intruding on family life. It is impossible to predict whether the child will be safe at home. Children who are removed from their homes may be damaged further by the system designed to protect them. Many children are moved repeatedly while they are in foster care. Many are further physically or sexually abused, either by caregivers or by other children in the same placement (Cabrera, 1995; Plant & Siegel, 2008).

Child welfare policies have also been insensitive to cultural differences and destructive to minority families (McDonald & Skopp, 2007). This criticism is particularly true in the case of Aboriginal children and their families. The current thrust to establish Aboriginal-run child welfare agencies and services underlines the importance of providing culturally appropriate services to all minority families (Malley-Morrison & Hines, 2004). An approach that gathers together extended family members to propose a plan for safeguarding the child draws on traditional Aboriginal ways of problem solving (Pennell & Burford, 2008).

Many programs for abusive families emphasize re-educating abusive parents so that children can be raised safely at home. These programs focus on the social aspect as well—the parents' isolation and the development of social competence and self-esteem. Counselling, education, and support services reduce repeat child-neglect referrals (Jonson-Reid et al., 2009). Often, the focus of such programs is on mothers. Including fathers, both residential and non-residential, can add support for the mother and another layer of protection for the child (Pruett et al., 2009).

Time to Review

1. What is family violence?
2. Identify the different kinds of child abuse.
3. Why is it difficult to accurately measure child abuse?
4. Which children are most at risk?
5. Who are the child abusers in Canada?
6. What are sibling abuse and parent abuse?
7. How do we respond to child abuse in Canada?

Abuse Between Partners

Intimate partner violence refers to violence committed by legally married, separated, divorced, or common-law partners, current or previous dating partners, and other intimate partners (Northcott, 2012; Sinha, 2012). The focus of research and service provision, however, has primarily been on violence against women by their male partners.

This kind of abuse can take many forms, often in combination—physical assault (hitting, punching, kicking), psychological abuse (belittling, threatening, destroying possessions), restriction of movement (locking in or out of the dwelling), economic deprivation, sexual abuse, and homicide (Bala, 1999)—but a number of factors distinguish intimate partner violence from violence against friends, acquaintances, or strangers. First, the ongoing relationship, potential economic dependence, and emotional attachment of intimate partner victims to their abusers make this type of violence unique. Second, intimate partner violence may also involve the safety and well-being of children. Third, the violence often involves multiple incidents over a period of time, rather than single, isolated events. Together, these particular victim–offender relationship factors, as well as the ongoing nature of the violence, make intimate partner violence a distinct form of violence (Sinha, 2012).

Like child abuse, female partner abuse is rooted in history. Women have long been seen as possessions of men. In England, women and children were considered the property of the husband and father, who had the obligation to control and discipline them. A man was allowed to beat his wife as long as the stick he used was no thicker than his thumb (from which we get the phrase "rule of thumb"). This law was not repealed until 1820. From 1909 to 1960, the Canadian *Criminal Code* included the separate offence of wife battering, in which the victim had to demonstrate a greater degree of bodily harm than was required in cases of assault by a stranger. Abused children received protection under the law earlier than did abused wives, who had to wait for the women's movement to publicize their plight. In the 1970s, homicide against an intimate partner was treated more leniently than against an acquaintance or stranger. Under Canadian law, before 1983, a man could not be charged with raping his wife. Since then, procedures and programs have become more sensitive to the needs of the victims of abuse (Ad Hoc Federal-Provincial-Territorial Working Group, 2003; Dawson, 2004; MacLeod, 1989). Yet spousal violence still does not appear as a specific offence under the *Criminal Code* (Taylor-Butts, 2009).

intimate partner violence: violence committed by legally married, separated, divorced, or common-law partners, current or previous dating partners, and other intimate partners.

How Many Partners Are Assaulted?

Since violence against wives was considered a private family matter and was tolerated for centuries, it has largely been a hidden crime. Figures are usually based on estimates and, as in child abuse, vary according to the definition used. In the following discussion, there is usually no distinction made between married and cohabiting couples, since violence in these relationships is similar. The statistics also include violence against dating partners.

In 2011, about 78 000 incidents of violence against women by current or previous intimate partners were reported to police. The overall rate of intimate partner violence against women was 542 per 100 000 women, almost four times higher than the rate for men. The General Social Survey on Victimization found a decline in the percentage of women who reported experiencing spousal violence between 1999 and 2009, from 8 percent to 6 percent. This change is attributed to a decline in violence involving former spouses (Statistics Canada, 2013c). Men and women aged 25 to 34 years had the highest risk of intimate partner violence, followed closely by those aged 15 to 24 years. Rates generally decline with age (Sinha, 2012).

Women are more likely to be killed by a partner than by a stranger on the street; the reverse is true for men. However, there has been concern about husband abuse and how severe a problem it is. The debate began in the United States, where the rates of spousal homicide by women and men are nearly equal; only slightly more women than men are murdered by their partners. That some wives strike their husbands meaning to injure them is not disputed. But is husband abuse as serious a problem as wife abuse? Several studies have suggested that women attack men at least as often as men attack women. One problem with these studies is that they often do not indicate whether women use violence mainly as a means of self-defence. If they do, they are still the principal victims of marital violence (Loseke & Kurz, 2005; Straus, 2005). However, between the ages of 55 and 64, the rate of dating violence where the male was the victim was virtually equal to the female rate. By age 65, the rate of dating violence against males surpassed the rate against females. Starting at age 55, men's risk of being killed by their dating partner was higher than women's, according to homicide data collected between 2001 and 2011 (Sinha, 2012).

Those who believe that abuse of females is more serious than abuse of males point to the following facts. First, women are likelier to suffer more serious injuries than men. Men are, on the average, stronger than women. They are not as likely to be injured by a blow from their partners (Gelles, 2010). Second, many men kill their wives after prolonged periods of escalating physical violence. Women are more likely to be afraid of violence by a male partner than vice versa. Third, men are more apt to hunt down and kill partners who left them or who were unfaithful. Fourth, men far more often kill their children along with their spouses. Finally, women who kill partners often do so as a "defensive" action following years of physical and sexual abuse. Usually, they can see no other way out (Anderson, 2002; Holtzman-Munroe, 2005; LaViolette & Barnett, 2000; Loseke & Kurz, 2005; Ogrodnik, 2007b; Straus, 2005).

Dating Violence

Until recently, not much was known about dating violence. Often, it was not included in discussions of family violence. However, we now know that dating violence shares many similarities with spousal violence. For example, research has found that the characteristics of police-reported dating violence generally mirror those of spousal violence. In addition, understanding the characteristics of violence in dating relationships is important to the development of effective prevention programs. Other studies have found that experiencing violence in early dating relationships can have an impact on future patterns of violence for both victims and abusers (Sinha, 2012). In 2011, however, both women and men were at greater risk of violence by dating partners than by spouses. Among women, rates of dating violence were 60 percent higher than the rate of spousal violence (Statistics Canada, 2013c).

Dating violence is most often initiated by the male. Many male college and university students who abused their partners believed male–female relationships should be patriarchal; that is, that the male should be dominant. Often, they had been drinking at the time of the abuse. Many had experienced violence in their families of origin. When women resort to violence, often it is in self-defence (Davis, 2008; Department of Justice Canada, 2003; O'Keefe, 2005).

Some studies have found that dating violence is common among adolescents and young adults. Types of violence include physical and sexual assault, sexual coercion, and emotional abuse. Estimates vary from 20 to 67 percent of couples, depending on whether emotional and verbal types of abuse are included. Young males are more likely to use physical violence to control their girlfriends. Young girls are more likely than males to suffer serious injuries. Girls who have experienced severe violence with injuries have especially low self-esteem and more signs of psychological disturbance (Collin-Vézina et al., 2006).

Women at Special Risk

According to the 2009 General Social Survey on Victimization, nearly 13 percent of Aboriginal women aged 15 or older reported that they had been the victim of one or more violent crimes in the 12 months prior to the survey (Statistics Canada, 2011h). Aboriginal peoples point to the destruction of traditional cultures by colonialism. The removal of Aboriginal children from their homes exposed them to abuse in institutions and meant that they were not taught about normal family life. They were thus more likely to become abusers (Hart, 1997; LaRoque, 1994).

Women in new partnerships are abused more often. These numbers may reflect the fact that many soon leave. They may also be related to the fact that younger people tend to be more violent. Cohabiting women are assaulted more often than those who are married. When women leave abusive partners, they are particularly at risk of more violence (Aston, 2007; Hart & Jamieson, 2002; Statistics Canada, 2006a).

Other problems add to the likelihood of abuse, although they do not cause it. Abuse occurs more often among poor people, not because they are poor but because poverty creates stress. More Aboriginal people live in poverty than any other group. The Aboriginal population is also younger than the general population of Canada and more likely to be in common-law relationships. Alcohol and substance abuse is tied to violence; using drugs can loosen usual controls over a person's behaviour. The fact that abuse continues from one generation to the next suggests that violent role models teach this behaviour (Statistics Canada, 2006a).

Three other groups of women are at particular risk of being victims of partner abuse. The first consists of those who live in rural or isolated areas, where they may have difficulty getting to a shelter, even if there is one in the area. Few shelters for abused women serve villages and rural areas. Since everyone knows everyone in a small community, it may be hard for the woman to ask for help. She may find this especially so if the doctor or police officer is a friend of her husband's. Safe homes have been set up in some communities, but here, too, lack of anonymity may be a problem (Burns & Taylor-Butts, 2009; Jiwani et al., 1998).

Immigrant women, the second group, report slightly lower rates of violence than the general public—but fewer reported incidents do not necessarily mean less abuse (Smith, 2004; Statistics Canada, 2006a). Several factors put immigrant women at special risk. They may not speak English or French, so they may not be able to successfully call 911 or even report the abuse. They may not know their rights in Canada or how the law enforcement and court systems work. Many of them fear being deported if they talk about abuse. Women are further isolated if they are cut off from their original ethnocultural community. They may not have any relatives nearby. In addition, they may risk more severe poverty than other women if they leave an abusive situation. There is also a shortage of culturally appropriate services (Smith, 2004).

Women with physical challenges make up the third group of those at particular risk. They are twice as likely to be physically and sexually assaulted as able-bodied women are. They also experience more severe forms of violence. Yet women with physical challenges have many difficulties in reporting abuse. Those who go for help may find that they cannot even enter the building because it lacks wheelchair access or that they are not believed, especially if they report sexual abuse (Denham & Gillespie, 1999; Hart & Jamieson, 2002; Perreault, 2009). In 2008, only three-quarters of shelters had a wheelchair accessible entrance. Two-thirds had wheelchair accessible bedrooms and bathrooms. Only a few provided special services for people who were hearing and visually impaired. Since they are largely dependent on their caregivers, these women may be institutionalized if they complain of abuse (Burns & Taylor-Butts, 2009).

Abuse in Gay and Lesbian Relationships

Abuse in gay and lesbian relationships is a latecomer to the field of family violence. There are several reasons for the oversight. First, partner violence (in addition to spousal violence) has received attention only in the past 35 to 40 years. Second, stereotypes of gay and lesbian relationships interfere with recognizing abuse. Lesbians, for example, are regarded as warm and supportive and thus non-abusive. When a gay man assaults his partner, the situation may be regarded as a fair fight between equals, an extension of "boys will be boys." Third, some individuals fear that admitting problems in same-sex relationships will only increase stigma against them. Finally, victims doubt that police and other professionals will regard such abuse as a serious issue (Kirkland, 2004; Ristock & Timbang, 2005).

According to 2008 police-reported data, approximately 10 percent of male victims and 1 percent of female victims of dating violence involved same-sex relationships (Mahony, 2010). Levels appear to be similar to those of heterosexual couples, or somewhat higher. Lesbian women probably experience less violence than those in a heterosexual relationship, while gay men are subject to higher levels. There are virtually no numbers concerning abuse involving bisexual and transgender individuals (Ristock & Timbang, 2005). Regardless of the numbers and types of abuse, gay men and lesbians are affected in the same way as victims in heterosexual couples.

Abused gay men and lesbians encounter further difficulties akin to other groups at special risk. They may face social isolation if they live in rural areas or small towns, especially if they wish to remain closeted. If one partner has a chronic illness, such as AIDS, he or she may need the partner as a caregiver. There are no shelters for battered men. There may also be barriers to accessing services because of stereotypes or homophobia. However, an opinion survey found that members of the public felt that intimate violence against lesbian women and gay males should be reported (Kirkland, 2004; Ristock & Timbang, 2005; Sorenson & Thomas, 2009).

Who Abuses Their Partners?

Research on perpetrators has focused on men in heterosexual relationships. The following social and psychological characteristics are fairly common among these men.

They tend to accept fully the traditional male and female roles and to draw strict lines between what is masculine and feminine. Part of their image of the "ideal" man is someone who is in control of all aspects of his life, including his wife and children. They use violence as a way of solving problems and controlling others. They have difficulty dealing with emotions. They appear to believe that "real men" do not express soft emotions such as tenderness or fear. These men have trouble trusting others, including their partners. They have poor self-images, but a sense of being in control of the people around them makes them feel more adequate. They do not take responsibility for their actions. Instead, they blame stress, an alcohol problem, or their partners for the violence (Bancroft & Silverman, 2002).

A few schools of thought distinguish between types of abusers. One school divides partner violence according to levels of control. Intimate terrorism is characterized by a high level of control and is more likely to result in injury—violent resistance is a response to intimate terrorism. Situational couple violence results from the escalation of a specific conflict or series of conflicts (Johnson, 2005). Control, even without violence, can have severe emotional effects. The type and frequency of violence are important factors (Anderson, 2008). Others separate abusers by personality types, for example by level of control of their emotions and their degree of impulsiveness (Dutton, 2007). The discussion around types of abusers is continuing. Later in the chapter, we will look more generally at the roots of violence.

Why Do Partners Stay?

Leaving an abusive relationship occurs in stages. First, victims recognize the abuse as a problem and weigh the pros and cons of leaving. In the next step, they intend to change the situation. They develop a plan and actively make changes to stop the abuse, such as seeking counselling or going to a shelter. Finally, they take steps to leave. Some victims move through these stages in order. Others go directly from admitting a problem to leaving. Still others waver; they leave and return, often repeatedly. This type of wavering is common in decision making, especially if the relationship has been long (Khaw & Hardesty, 2007, 2009).

There are three basic reasons women stay. First, they are committed to the caretaker role. Second, they are afraid of the consequences of leaving. Third, they have learned to feel powerless and guilty (Barnett et al., 2005). Relatively little is known about why men stay in or return to abusive relationships.

Commitment to the Caretaker Role

Many women in abusive relationships have fully accepted traditional male and female roles. Some believe they have married "for better or for worse" and must keep their vows. They were taught that it is a woman's responsibility to make an intimate relationship work and to keep family peace. Therefore, asking for help means admitting that they have failed in their main task in life. In dating relationships, the young woman may want to rescue the abuser. Older women may return to an abusive partner because there is no one else to look after him. Some women also feel that a mother should sacrifice herself for her children and that a single-parent home would harm them. Often, the last straw before leaving is a physical attack on the children.

Women in abusive relationships experience conflicting attitudes. Since they are ashamed, they may cut themselves off from family and friends to keep the violence secret. Doing this makes it easier for the attacker to continue the abuse. If attacks occur only once in a while and are followed by apologies and promises that they will never happen again, many women hope the violence will stop. It rarely does. In addition, many women love the "nice" side of their partners, even if it is fleeting (Few & Rosen, 2005; Hart & Jamieson, 2002; Weitzman, 2000).

Fear of the Consequences of Leaving

Abused women fear many things. Some men threaten to severely injure or even kill their partners if they leave. Indeed, abuse often escalates when the victim threatens to leave or moves out. A woman may fear poverty and isolation. Often, abused women have been homemakers and have been out of the workforce for some time; they feel it is impossible to support themselves or their children on the low wages they can earn, if they can even find a job. Many fear going on welfare. If an abused woman has been working, her partner is likely to have controlled the finances. If so, she has no resources and yet is not eligible for social assistance. Immigrant women may fear deportation if they leave their partner (Barnett et al., 2005; Hart & Jamieson, 2002; Khaw & Hardesty, 2009).

Some men and women try to control their partners through their children. They may make threats in regard to the children—either of injury or of custody suits. Some try to alienate the children from the other parent. Tactics include grilling the children for information, undermining the children's respect through name-calling, blaming the other parent for the family breakup, or saying that the other parent does not love the children. This campaign to alienate the children from the other parent has been described as a form of emotional abuse (A. J. L. Baker, 2007; Brownstone, 2009).

Feeling Powerless

Many abused women feel helpless. After years of emotional and physical abuse, their self-esteem may be so low that they no longer believe they can be successful at anything (Few & Rosen, 2005). When they find that all their attempts to escape violence are unsuccessful, they not only stop trying but also give up all hope of their circumstances changing.

Helplessness may, in fact, be a reality. Many women find no source of help. Controlling men may cut the abused spouse off from friends, neighbours, and even family. Some men physically prevent their partners from seeking help by locking them in the house or removing telephones. The victims of abuse might not get social assistance until they have their own address, and they cannot get an address without money. If no shelter is nearby or if it is full, they may have nowhere to go. Some women do not want to leave their familiar neighbourhood. Some stay with or return to an abusive husband because they cannot find affordable housing or the means to provide the necessities of life for themselves and their children (Denham & Gillespie, 1999; Hart & Jamieson, 2002; Khaw & Hardesty, 2007, 2009).

There is sometimes further victimization by the people the abused woman turns to for help. Clergy, family members, or friends may assume it is her fault if the relationship is not working and may urge her to go home and try harder. The woman then feels guilty for somehow having failed. She may also feel guilty for her natural anger and frustration. The insensitivity of those around her fuels her sense of helplessness (Weitzman, 2000). With education efforts concerning partner abuse in recent years, such blaming is less likely.

How Does Society Respond to Spousal Abuse?

In the past, our society was not very responsive to wife abuse, tending to regard it as a private family matter. Since the late 1970s, however, the demand for spousal assault to be taken as seriously as any other form of violence has increased.

An abused woman's first need is for protection, something that initially depends on reporting. Protection can be provided through the police and courts, and through places of safety such as shelters. Most victims reported an incident to police to stop the violence or receive protection.

In the past, police have not always laid charges in cases of spousal abuse. Three factors for this failure have been suggested: (1) the belief that what happens in the home is private, (2) the belief that couples should try to reconcile rather than expose their problems in court, and (3) the fear that the victim will refuse to testify. Police viewed their task as one of quieting down the situation so that there would be no more violence that day (Bala, 1999).

Since 1982, all provincial and territorial governments have issued directives to police and Crown attorneys that encourage a more careful investigation and prosecution of spousal assault cases. This emphasis means that it is not up to the victim to ask that charges be laid; it is the responsibility of the police to do so. The growing concern about partner abuse has resulted in improved training throughout the justice system. Larger police forces have established special units to respond to family violence (Ad Hoc Federal-Provincial-Territorial Working Group Reviewing Spousal Abuse Policies and Legislation, 2003). In 2007, charges were laid by police in 78 percent of cases reported to them. Charges were somewhat more likely to be laid in cases involving female rather than male victims (Taylor-Butts, 2009). Nearly 60 percent of all victims reported that the violence decreased after police intervention. This finding suggests that the new legislation and treatment of partner abuse as a public concern have made a difference (Public Health Agency of Canada, 2007b).

battered woman syndrome: a pattern of signs and symptoms appearing in women who are physically and mentally abused over an extended period by an intimate partner; a legal defence used by a woman accused of killing her abusive partner

Battered woman syndrome is a pattern of signs and symptoms appearing in women who are physically and mentally abused over an extended period by an intimate partner (Walker, 2009). In 1990, the Supreme Court of Canada accepted that this syndrome was an acceptable legal defence by a woman accused of killing her abusive partner. This decision was hailed by some as a victory. The legal system finally recognized that years of abuse may cause a woman to believe that her life is in danger and killing her partner is an act of self-defence. But others cautioned that such a defence is yet another example of a patriarchal justice system that perceives women as frail and somehow incompetent. They worry that the battered woman syndrome defence may prove detrimental to women. For example, an abused wife who kills her husband may receive a lighter sentence if she uses the battered woman syndrome defence; however, the court may also pronounce her irrational and unfit to care for her children, and they may be taken from her (Shaffer, 1997).

Often, a pressing need for abused women is safe housing. The immediate need is met by transition and safe houses, but their numbers fall far short of need. There are variations in services provided in the provinces and territories. **Second-stage housing** provides longer-term accommodation lasting usually from three months to one year. With it, too, in great demand, loans are available to upgrade current emergency and second-stage shelters and, in some cases, to provide new ones (Canada Mortgage and Housing Corporation, n.d.). Women who use extended services often have endured serious abuse and need continuing safety.

second-stage housing: longer-term housing for abused women

Shelters provide more than just safety for abused women. Transition houses offer information, emotional support, and practical resources so that women can plan for their future. Some shelters have expanded services to include follow-up programs, life-skills training, drop-in centres, and support groups for women and children. Funds for these services come largely from provincial ministries, other government sources, and donations (Burns & Taylor-Butts, 2009).

Economic cutbacks by federal and provincial governments have, however, affected the services offered abused women and their children. Whole sections of the safety net no longer receive public funding. Services must therefore often rely on donations. Burnout among those working with abuse victims has always been high. Experienced staff members often leave this field of work because of job cuts, overwork, safety concerns, and poor pay. More volunteers are used to fill the gap, but program funders take little account of the time and money needed to train, advise, and emotionally support them. As a result of these factors, fewer services are available (Denham & Gillespie, 1999).

In many large centres, treatment is available for all family members. Women suffer emotional as well as physical damage when they are abused. Children from violent families may be anxious, even terrified. They may also have problems managing their anger. Therapy is offered to abusive men. This focuses on the way they victimize and control their partners in an atttempt to stop their violent behaviour. Members of minorities such as gay men and lesbians and recent immigrants, however, may have difficulty finding appropriate help (Dutton, 2007; Kirkland, 2004; Pepler et al., 2000).

Time to Review

1. What is intimate partner violence?
2. How prevalent is this kind of violence?
3. What is dating violence?
4. Who is most at risk?
5. To what extent does partner abuse occur in same-sex relationships?
6. Why do many victims of partner abuse stay?
7. How does Canadian society respond to partner abuse?

Abuse of Older Adults

Abuse of older adults is the most recent kind of family violence to be recognized. With the aging of the population and the associated caregiving demands, a parallel rise in all forms of elder abuse is expected (Walsh & Yon, 2012). In addition, there has been a shift away from institutional care, which places additional demands on family members and thus may provoke more abuse (Kinnon, 2001; Lai, 2008).

There is still no standard definition of elder abuse. The World Health Organization defines elder abuse as "a single, or repeated act, or lack of appropriate action, occurring within any relationship where there is an expectation of trust which causes harm or distress to an older person" (Walsh & Yon, 2012). Most professionals agree on three basic kinds—neglect (which includes isolation, abandonment, and social exclusion); the violation of human, legal, and medical rights; and the deprivation of choices, decisions, status, finances, and respect. Most studies of elder abuse include physical abuse, psychological or emotional abuse, sexual abuse, and financial abuse as well as neglect. Spiritual abuse is an attack on a person's cultural or religious beliefs and is usually associated with Aboriginal and ethnic groups (Walsh & Yon, 2012). Financial abuse involves the theft of money or objects of value. It occurs most commonly by cashing pension or Old Age Security cheques and not giving the senior the money or by misusing a power of attorney. Neglect can be classified as active or passive, depending on whether failure to provide is intentional or unintentional. Some service providers also add abandonment as a form of abuse (Kinnon, 2001; Lai, 2008). There is disagreement about whether elder abuse should include abuse that began prior to old age, such as spousal violence or abuse by children that started years earlier.

The risk of being the victim of a violent crime in Canada generally decreases with age. In 2010, seniors had the lowest rates of police-reported violent crime, regardless of whether this violence was perpetrated by a family member or a stranger. The rate of family violence was about 7.5 times lower than that of the most at-risk age group, 25- to 34-year-olds, and half the rate of the second-oldest age cohort, 55- to 64-year-olds (Sinha, 2012).

These occurrences are probably under-reported. Many older people feel stigma in reporting a child who mistreats them (Kinnon, 2001). In addition, a telephone survey like the General Social Survey (GSS) cannot reach individuals who are confined to their rooms without a phone or who have conditions like dementia. The most recent GSS confirmed that older adults are less likely to experience spousal violence than younger ones.

Other surveys also established patterns in elder abuse. Older adults were less likely to report emotional or financial abuse by a spouse in the previous five years (Department of Justice Canada, 2009a). Some had been cut off from family and friends. Men were more likely than women to report being victims of emotional or financial abuse, as were divorced or separated elders (Pottie Bunge & Locke, 2000). Women were more likely than men to be victims of family violence. The fact that women suffer from spousal violence more than men largely accounts for the difference in rates. Seniors were usually victimized by someone they knew, most often adult children, spouses, or ex-spouses (Sinha, 2012).

Who Is at Risk?

Researchers and people working with elderly people suggest a number of risk factors. First, many abusers have a history of psychiatric illness and problems with drugs and alcohol. Second, abusers may have experienced family violence as children. Third, older adults who depend on others for care may become too heavy a burden and then be abused—or the opposite may be true. The abuser is dependent on the victim and strikes out in words or actions because he or she feels powerless. Fourth, stress can lead to violence. This appears to occur most often when an older person suffers from some form of dementia, such as Alzheimer's disease, and when the caregiver is clinically depressed. Abusive caregivers tend to have provided care for more years and for more hours a day to a more difficult relative than had non-abusive caregivers. Fifth, society tends to hold negative stereotypes of older people. As a result, the elderly may be seen as less human and are thus more susceptible to abuse (Department of Justice Canada, 2009a; Kinnon, 2001; Pillemer, 2005; Steinmetz, 2005).

Elder Abuse and Society

Many service providers offer training sessions on recognizing elder abuse and helping its victims (McDonald & Collins, 2000). Nevertheless, some professionals may not believe complaints of abuse. Disbelief may be the result of ageism; for example, some individuals cannot imagine an old person being attractive enough to be sexually assaulted. They may also see an older person's symptoms as part of the aging process rather than abuse (Kinnon, 2001).

Some individuals feel that reporting of elder abuse should be mandatory, just as it is for child abuse. Many provinces have special adult protection laws and require everyone, including members of the helping professions, to report abuse and neglect (Canadian Network for the Prevention of Elder Abuse, n.d.; Department of Justice Canada, 2009c). Mandatory reporting, however, has drawbacks. First, it may violate the rights of the elderly under the *Charter of Rights and Freedoms*. Second, if their caregivers have been abusive, elderly people may end up in a nursing home or institution against their will. Third, in some cases, abuse escalates once it has been reported (Brandl, 2005; Canadian Network for the Prevention of Elder Abuse, n.d.; McDonald & Collins, 2000).

Why Do People Abuse Family Members?

Characteristics of Abusers

Most of the theories about violence and abuse focus on individuals and families, and less often on society as a whole. Much of the research is based on cross-sectional methods, such as surveys. Thus, it ignores how relationships develop and change over time (McDonald & Collins, 2000).

According to Dr. Jane Gilgun, who has interviewed many men who murdered family members, perpetrators want the same things from life as most people: a sense of safety and security, the ability to affect their personal world, and a sense of identity. The problem lies in how they go about satisfying these desires (Gilgun, 1999).

Perpetrators come in several different types.

Reactors, the first type, use violence as a means of feeling competent and in control. After the violent act, they often feel guilt and remorse. Soon, however, they start feeling inadequate and powerless again. Tension builds. They then become violent. Often, there is some trigger event that releases the assault (Dutton, 2007; Gilgun, 1999). The victim is frequently blamed for "causing" the violence when all she or he did was unwittingly provide a trigger—one abusive incident occurred because the victim cut carrots the wrong way (Island & Letellier, 1991). The sequence of violent event, remorse, building tension, and another violent act is referred to as the "violence-relaxation cycle" (Women's Issues and Social Empowerment, 1998). Often, reactors have unrealistic expectations of relationships. There may be role reversal, where parents expect their children to provide them with the kind of love, approval, and sense of importance they should really provide to their children. When the child does not do this, the parent reacts with abuse.

Abusers of another type, the entitled, are quite different. They are not driven by the emotional cycle experienced by reactors. They feel no remorse or shame. Rather, they act out of a long-term sense of being entitled to what they want. They use violence because they have learned it works, for example extorting money from an elderly relative to buy drugs. This kind of abuser may rape a partner if he is refused sex. Unlike the reactors, the entitled do not need a trigger event to set them off (Dutton, 2007; Gilgun, 1999).

There are several other types of abusers. A third type is impulsive. These individuals have high levels of chronic anger, fearful attachment style, and low behavioural control (Dutton, 2007). A fourth type is overwhelmed by events. Often, the violence occurs once only. For example, a woman who has been abused for many

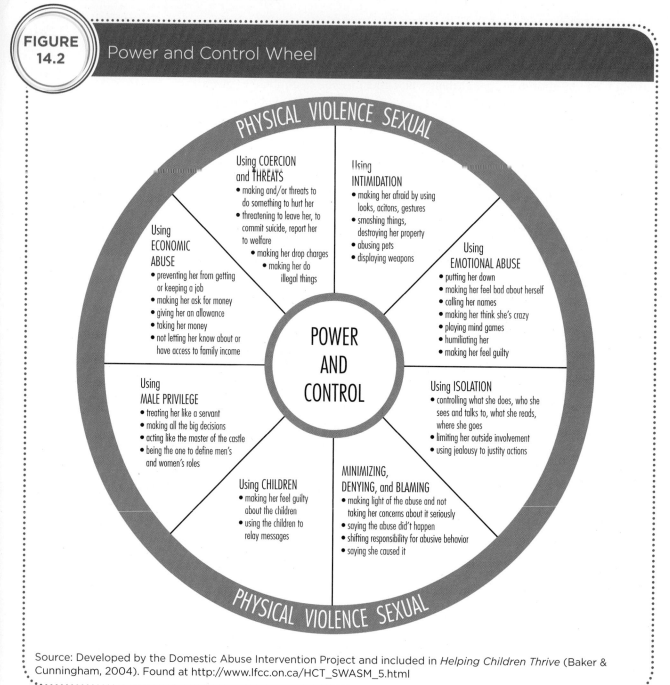

Source: Developed by the Domestic Abuse Intervention Project and included in *Helping Children Thrive* (Baker & Cunningham, 2004). Found at http://www.lfcc.on.ca/HCT_SWASM_5.html

years may lash out just once and kill her batterer. Finally, a few abusers are neurologically or psychologically ill (Gilgun, 1999). A rare example is the schizophrenic individual who has delusions that family members are trying to harm him or her (Arboleda–Flórez et al., 1996). Attempts to find genetic or biological causes for abuse have, however, been largely unsuccessful.

The power and control wheel (see Figure 14.2) can help us understand the complex pattern of abusive and violent behaviours used by a batterer to establish and maintain control over his partner. Violence is often accompanied by an array of these other types of abuse. This model helps women put names to the behaviour of an abusive partner.

Theories of Abuse and Neglect

Situational Theory

The situational, or stress, theory suggests that abuse occurs when the abuser is under stress. Such situations include a physically frail or mentally incompetent adult or a hard-to-care-for child. This explanation, however, comes dangerously close to blaming the victim. In addition to difficulties inside the family, stressors can also include work problems, poverty, and other environmental factors. The situational theory fails to account for the facts that not all abusers are under high levels of stress and that many people who experience high levels of stress are not abusive (McDonald & Collins, 2000). By taking account of individual and family resources and the meanings other family members find in the situation, the ABCX model (Chapter 13) provides a fuller explanation than a purely stress theory model.

Social Exchange Theory

The social exchange theory states that social interaction involves rewards and penalties between people. The abuser will use violence as long as it is rewarding or if the rewards outweigh the costs. Calling the police may tip the balance so that the violence is no longer rewarding. We saw above that new legislation that allows police to lay charges in cases of partner abuse has made a difference. Victims will stay as long as the satisfaction of their needs outweighs the costs of abuse. Because some people hold more power, they expect more rewards. Those with less power expect fewer rewards. This theory may explain some abuse. It fails, however, in instances where the abuser is dependent on his or her victim, as in parent abuse by a teenager (Barnett et al., 2005; Gelles, 2010; McDonald & Collins, 2000). It also does not apply in the case of child abuse, where a child cannot leave even if needs are not met.

Symbolic Interactionist Theory

The symbolic interactionist theory focuses on the interaction between the abuser and abused. It emphasizes both the behaviour and the meanings both people find in this behaviour. One example is the abuser who believes that men should rule in their homes and the victim who believes her responsibility is to keep the family happy. Symbolic interactionist theory also includes social learning, or modelling one's behaviour on another's. Thus, children learn to be violent by observing their parents (Barnett et al., 2005; McDonald & Collins, 2000). One study, for example, found that both males and females who abused children were more likely to have seen one parent hit another and to have been hit by an adult themselves (Heyman & Smith Slep, 2002).

Family Systems Theory

According to family systems theory, we learn patterns of interaction within families. These patterns include roles, which are expected patterns of behaviour for family members. These roles become so ingrained that they are difficult to change. Families with an abusive member include violence in the father and husband roles, for example, and victimization in the child and wife roles. Thus, when abused children grow up, males may become batterers, living out roles they learned from their fathers, and females become battered women, following their mothers' roles. Some research supports this view (Gelles, 2010; Heyman & Smith Slep, 2002; Widom & Maxfield, 2001). This pattern is sometimes referred to as the "cycle of violence" but is also called *intergenerational transmission* of abuse. In a follow-up study of more than 1500 victims of child abuse and neglect, it was found that 18 percent had been arrested for violent crimes, in contrast to 14 percent in a non-abused group. Not all these crimes involved family violence (National Institute of Justice, 1996). Thus, although their rates of violence are slightly higher than for those who were not abused, the majority of child victims do not become abusive adults. In addition, most abusers do not have violent families of origin (Duffy & Momirov, 1997).

Feminist Theories

Feminist theories consider that violence is the result of a patriarchal social system. Patriarchy allows men more power than women and asserts that it is right for them to have this power. This imbalance leaves women vulnerable to abuse. In an extension, parents, especially fathers, have power over children, making children vulnerable. The strict feminist view fails to account for abuse in gay and lesbian relationships or for women's violence against men. The real issue may involve a power imbalance between abuser and abused rather than gender itself (Barnett et al., 2005; Gelles, 2010; McDonald & Collins, 2000).

Societal Perspectives

Many identified abusers are from lower socioeconomic classes. Violence may be a response to the stress of social factors such as poverty, unemployment, poor and crowded housing, and a sense of powerlessness. In addition, as we can see any day of the week on our media screens, our society is violent and thus provides a model for violent behaviour (Barnett et al., 2005; Gelles, 2010; Josephson, 1995). Some theorists have used an ecological perspective to explain family maltreatment. For example, there may be a mismatch between the family and the community. A family needing help may live in an area with few resources. Yet many abusers are well educated and financially comfortable.

All these theories about violence in our society are helpful. Although there is evidence to support most of them to some degree, no one theory fully accounts for violence; there is no simple explanation. Rather, violence is probably the result of a complex interaction of many factors: the individual characteristics of the abuser, the stresses resulting from both family relationships and society, and the manner in which people are socialized to accept the values and norms of society.

Preventing Family Violence

Despite the various forms of family violence, there are three basic approaches to prevention.

One approach, *primary prevention*, aims to keep abuse from ever occurring. Its principal method is education. Many programs are school based. For example, some try to reduce aggression in children. A 2002 study found that an online educational program helped family physicians become more confident and effective in dealing with cases of domestic violence (Harris et al., 2002). Marriage preparation and prenatal and parent education courses can include discussion of abuse. Home visits made to new parents are key in child abuse prevention because visitors can spot early signs of abuse or refer stressed parents to educational and support programs. Awareness campaigns in the media have also become important in teaching

---

FIGURE 14.3

Services to Support Victims of Abuse

Use Justice System $

- family court
- assessments
- criminal court
- legal aid
- victim/witness programs
- probation services
- parole services
- incarceration
- criminal injuries compensation
- men's counselling programs

Contact Police $

- police surveillance/response
- police investigation
- access to reports

Seek Medical Help $

- ambulance service
- emergency medical care
- hospital stays
- X-rays, lab work
- doctors' appointments
- dental treatments
- drug and alcohol centres
- chiropractors
- prescription drugs
- eating disorder clinics
- psychiatric institutions
- community health clinics
- services for children labelled as having attention deficit disorder

Struggle with Employment $

- time off work
- loss of productivity
- retraining programs
- lost tax revenues due to death, injury, or incarceration

Find Housing $

- transition houses
- second-stage shelters
- rent-to-income housing
- volunteer programs
- YMCA
- emergency housing

Seek Educational Support $

- special education
- violence prevention programs
- tutor services
- social work services

Contact Social Agencies $

- counselling programs
- mental health services
- sexual assault centres
- child welfare services
- foster care
- youth services
- education and prevention programs
- volunteer programs
- Kids Help Line
- Aboriginal women's centres
- immigrant and visible minority women's services
- disabled women's services
- daycare

Seek Income Assistance $

- welfare
- mother's allowance
- employment insurance
- enforcement of child support payments

Source: *Vis-à-Vis*, Volume 13, Number 4, Pg. 12, © 1996. Reprinted with permission from the Canadian Council on Social Development (www.ccsd.ca).

the public about abusive situations and sources of help (Chamberlain, 2008; Tremblay et al., 2008; Wolfe & Jaffe, 2001).

Secondary prevention programs involve working with groups considered to be at risk for abuse. Some that are aimed at preventing child abuse are prenatal nutrition programs, fetal alcohol syndrome support programs, and remedial schooling. A community program in Vancouver is specifically directed at families from the South Asian community (Borkowski et al., 2007; Chamberlain, 2008; Wolfe & Jaffe, 2001). There are also programs to teach seniors how to avoid financial exploitation (McDonald & Collins, 2000).

The third and most common approach is referred to as *tertiary prevention*. This is treatment or some other intervention to keep abuse from recurring and minimize its effects. It includes services to battered women that empower them to leave an abusive situation: these include shelters, second-stage housing, and skills training. It can also include treatment of perpetrators. Legislative changes are part of tertiary prevention strategies too. Some programs teach parenting skills to abusive parents, provide group therapy for violent husbands, and treat behaviour problems, such as aggression, in children from abusive homes. (See Figure 14.3 on page 385.) These services can be very expensive and some treatments show only limited success (Chamberlain, 2008; Cukier, 2008; Wolfe & Jaffe, 2001).

Because primary and secondary prevention efforts are broadly based, they provide the best hope for making the family home a place where members are protected and safe. However, there is a lack of knowledge about their effectiveness. We also cannot predict accurately who is likely to abuse a family member, so many education or community-based programs may be unfocused. All the same, primary and secondary prevention efforts hold promise because they reach so many people. In addition, resilience—the process that allows us to adjust and adapt in a healthy way after adverse events—can be fostered. Given the right resources and support, survivors can learn to successfully cope and minimize the consequences of abuse and maltreatment (Public Health Agency of Canada, 2012c).

Time to Review

1. What are some of the different kinds of elder abuse?
2. Who is most at risk of elder abuse?
3. What are the social responses to elder abuse?
4. Why do people abuse family members?
5. How can we prevent family violence?

Finding the Courage to Break Free

It is an unfortunate reality that the most intimate relationships can be tainted by abuse. In 2010, police reported more than 54 000 victims of dating violence (Sinha, 2012). Alyssa's account of abuse follows. Although Alyssa herself is fictional, her experiences happen all too often to other young people.

Brandon was my older brother's pal. When he wanted to be my boyfriend, it seemed like a dream come true. He was a basketball star in our high school, tall, of course, and good-looking. My parents liked him and thought he had a great future ahead of him. The other girls envied me.

At first, he treated me like a princess. But soon things changed. The first time I wanted to watch a video with him instead of going to the football game, he told me I was no-good, grabbed my arm, and twisted it until I agreed to go. Every time he didn't get his way, he'd call me names. Often, he hurt me. At first, the abuse was "mild," like being pushed or slapped. Bit by bit, the abuse increased. Over the year and a half I was with him, I received many scrapes and bruises. The worst was when he threw me against a wall and broke my collarbone. I came to feel worthless and believe all the names Brandon called me.

I told no one about the incidents. I didn't think my parents or brother would believe me because they liked Brandon so much and he never showed his mean side to them. Besides, after each time he hurt me, he would be remorseful and promise never to harm me again. He'd make me feel like a princess once more. Each time I believed him and each time he broke his promise. He told me that he couldn't live without me and that he'd kill himself if ever I left him. Or else he'd threaten to do something to my family.

All this time, Brandon came to the house, watching sports with my brother and dad. They'd joke about he-men and make rude remarks about girls.

Then one day, a neighbour saw Brandon trip and kick me on the street and then blame me for clumsiness. She told my parents. When my mother challenged Brandon, he said that I'd tripped and he was just trying to catch me. The kick was accidental. My father and brother just continued to watch the hockey game on TV. No one seemed to believe that he'd deliberately hurt me. I never felt as close to my parents and brother afterwards.

When my family didn't seem to care what happened to me, I decided I'd have to help myself. I broke off with Brandon. He didn't kill himself or do anything to hurt my family. He still came around to the house, but I made sure I was never alone with him. He did start a rumour campaign about me on Facebook and Twitter. I decided to go to college in another province to escape the rumours if I could.

1. What resources are available in your college and/or community to help victims of dating violence?
2. If you were a friend or a co-worker, how would you react?
3. Do teachers or other service providers who work with teens have an obligation to report it if they hear about dating violence?

Summary

What Is Family Violence?

The issue of family violence and abuse suffers from confusing definitions. In Canada, the term "family violence" is used to refer to "a range of abusive behaviours that occur within relationships based on kinship, intimacy, dependency, or trust." Abuse refers to a situation in which a person takes advantage of a less powerful person. Due to problems with definitions and reporting, actual levels of abuse are unknown.

What Kinds of Violence and Abuse Occur in Families and Intimate Relationships?

Child abuse has probably always occurred, although it has only recently been recognized as a problem. In Canada, the first laws against it were passed in the late 1800s. Child abuse includes physical, sexual, and emotional abuse. It also includes neglect and any violence that children see or hear in their families. In Canada, there are federal, provincial, and territorial laws to protect children from abuse. Abused children are often young, unwanted, and physically or mentally disadvantaged. While sibling abuse is common, little is known about it. Not much is known about children who abuse parents. Victims of child abuse can display a variety of problems both in the short term and as adults. When abuse is reported, the perpetrator may be charged, the child may be removed from the home, and the family may receive therapy.

Violence between partners became a social concern more recently than did child abuse. Partner violence can begin before marriage, and it occurs more commonly among married and cohabiting couples than in more casual relationships. Victims of spousal abuse do not fit a single description. Perpetrators tend to accept traditional gender roles and use violence as a method of control. Some women spend many years in an abusive relationship. They may be committed to the caregiving role; they may also fear the consequences of leaving. In addition, they may feel powerless, and this feeling can be reinforced by society. Groups at particular risk include Aboriginal, immigrant, physically challenged, and isolated women. Abuse in gay and lesbian relationships appears to be similar to other forms of partner abuse. In the past, spousal assault was often considered a private matter. Now police are directed to charge abusers when there are reasonable grounds to do so. Although shelters do not meet the demand, some are available for abused women and their children.

Elder abuse has only recently received much attention. In addition to neglect, physical, psychological, and sexual abuse, it also includes financial exploitation. Both partners and children may be perpetrators. In some families, elder abuse is part of a long-standing pattern of violence. In others, it may result from frustration with the needs of the older person, and the lack of resources and support to help the caregiver meet these needs. There is controversy over whether reporting elder abuse should be mandatory or infringes on the rights of the older person.

Why Do People Abuse Family Members?

Abusers come from every class in society. Often, they are under high levels of stress, are isolated socially or physically, and perceive parenting as stressful. Sexual abusers, in addition, tend to have unsatisfactory marital relations. Abusers have the same desires as other people but use violent means to fulfill them. Five types of individuals using violence can be described as the reactors, the entitled, the impulsive, the overwhelmed, and, occasionally, the psychiatrically impaired.

What Are the Different Theories about Abuse and Violence within Families?

No single theory of abuse and neglect can fully explain family violence. The situational theory points to stress; social exchange theory to costs and benefits; symbolic interactionist theory to the meaning given to events; family systems theory to intergenerational transmission of violence; feminists to imbalance of power between the sexes; and societal theorists to cultural attitudes.

How Can Family Violence Be Prevented?

There are three basic approaches to prevention. The first is to prevent violence through education or by encouraging society to be supportive to families. The second is to provide services to groups thought to be at risk. The third is to treat abusers or separate them from their victims to keep the violence from happening again.

Class Assignments

1. What facilities assist victims of abuse in your community? Are they adequate? Why or why not? Are there gaps in the services available? Explain.
2. State the arguments for and against using battered woman syndrome as a defence when a woman kills her partner. Be sure to identify possible effects on their children.
3. There are two basic approaches to dealing with families that abuse children. One is to leave the children in the home while the family receives treatment. The second is to remove the children from the home. Outline the advantages and disadvantages of each approach.

Personal Assignments

The following assignments are designed to help you think about your own experience:

1. Do you know anyone who is (was) abused? What effect has the abuse had on the individual, either in the short or the long term? How could the abuse have been prevented or stopped earlier?

2. If you plan to have children, what discipline methods will you use? Do you think that spanking, or corporal punishment, can be effective? Why or why not?

3. Do you believe that reporting abuse of the elderly should be compulsory? Why do you think it should or should not be?

Chapter 15
Poverty and the Family

LEARNING OBJECTIVES

How is poverty defined in Canada?

Who is poor in Canada?

What can poverty do to children?

What can be done to reduce poverty in Canada?

Dave and Alana married after high school and had two children, now ages 6 and 8. The couple worked in upholstery plants in the Cambridge, Ontario, area, Dave full time as a supervisor and Alana part time in quality control. Both were laid off in March 2008 with severance packages of 4 percent for each year worked.

At the time of the layoffs they had two cars—a 2003 Chevy Cobalt and a 2001 Taurus. They had saved $20 000 in RRSPs (Registered Retirement Savings Plans), which they planned to use as a down payment on a house.

In the months following the layoffs, Dave went into a serious depression. By March 2009, the marriage had dissolved under the strain. Dave moved in with his parents. He is undergoing treatment for clinical depression and attending an anger management course.

Alana has been struggling to pay off credit card debt and the higher-than-expected income taxes caused by the severance payment. She is pursuing support from Dave, and although he wants to pay, he still has not secured a job. Both have exhausted their EI (Employment Insurance) and severance money.

When Alana finally sold the family piano for $3000, she realized she had to look into going on welfare temporarily—just until she could get back on her feet. During her first interview with Ontario Works, she discovered she had too much money to qualify for social assistance—the $3000 from the piano and the RRSPs. The caseworker advised her to return when the RRSP money is exhausted and her bank balance falls below $2050.

Dave agreed to cash out the RRSPs, which were in mutual funds. Unfortunately, because of the stock market crash in the fall of 2008, their value was only $12 000. After Alana had exhausted this money, she reapplied for welfare.

This time, she qualified.

So Alana was on welfare, but she hadn't hit bottom yet. In February 2010, Alana found out that she owed a lot of tax on the RRSPs she had cashed in. Since she couldn't pay the taxes, Canada Revenue Agency suggested that she accept a reduction in her Canada Child Tax Benefit. Alana agreed.

The tax problems affected Alana's credit rating, which had been deteriorating for two years. In May 2010, Alana received a letter from her credit card company which told her that her credit rating had been reassessed. The company was going to cancel her last remaining card. To top things off, in June of 2010, Alana's landlord increased the rent by 2 percent—an increase that social assistance did not cover.

Now, Alana has no life savings to draw from. She has almost nothing in the bank. She has no credit. She has no money for gas or clothes to look for work.

Alana may be on welfare a lot longer than she planned.

Source: John Stapleton, *Why Don't We Want the Poor to Own Anything? Our Relentless Social Policy Journey Towards Destitution for the 900,000 Poorest People in Ontario*. Metcalf Foundation. Oct. 2009. Pg. 4–5.

● ● ● ● ○

Most poor people in Canada do not become homeless or starve. Yet they may have serious difficulties, like Dave and Alana, in making ends meet. In general, poverty is defined almost entirely in terms of income. Yet financial levels alone do not accurately reflect the ability of some people to manage better than others with the money available to them. For example, some are able to grow or gather food to supplement what they can buy. Others have developed shrewd management skills. But families require a certain minimum level of income to create satisfying lives in our society.

In this chapter, we will look at poverty in Canada. The most striking fact is that poverty is not evenly spread. Certain groups are much more likely than others to be poor. There are different ways to look at poverty, and it is ultimately a social issue, but how we define poverty will affect who gets labelled as poor. It also affects the number and the types of programs we develop to address the problem of poverty. If we understand the root causes of poverty, we can be much more effective in designing programs that will successfully help people improve their situation.

Where Do I Fit In?

1. How did you feel when you read the opening vignette about Dave and Alana?
2. Would you consider your family (or yourself) rich, middle-income, or poor?
3. Why do you think that in a country as prosperous as Canada, we still have people who are poor?
4. What, if anything, should governments or other organizations be doing to help poor people?

Helping the "Worthy" Poor

In the early years of European settlement in Canada, the poor depended almost entirely on their families or on other private individuals for help. Public assistance was provided by local governments or charities on an emergency basis only. Most of the help involved the provision of groceries, secondhand clothing, and vouchers for fuel. Little cash was provided, partly because poverty was believed to result from bad budgeting (along with a variety of vices, such as drinking). It was also generally felt that help should be at a level lower than the earnings of the most poorly paid labourer. Handouts were barely enough to survive on. The notion that asking for help should be so unpleasant that a person who did not need it would not ask also prevailed. For example, homeless elderly people were kept in local jails on charges of vagrancy because there was no other place for them. Some places demanded that people receiving assistance live in a workhouse (Guest, 1985).

When Canada became a nation in 1867, social programs were primarily the responsibility of provincial and local governments. Gradually, what is called the **social safety net** developed. An early form of social assistance was financial aid provided for workers and their families during periods of disability. Mothers' pensions (later called Mothers' Allowance) were set up to help needy children. Eligibility depended on the mother and the criteria varied from province to province. In British Columbia, for example, mothers were eligible if their husbands

social safety net: basic social security programs needed to support family life

means test: a method of screening applicants to ensure that only those who need financial assistance receive it

were in a tuberculosis sanatorium, mental hospital, or prison or if they themselves were chronically ill, disabled, or widowed. Applicants had to be of good character (even having to provide letters of reference); they also had to pass a strict **means test** to prove they needed help. Once they received the allowance, mothers were subject to intrusion into their personal lives—no man except a close relative could live in the house, and permission was needed to move from city to country or vice versa. In 1927, old age pensions were established for the needy, again subject to a strict means test (Guest, 1985). During the Great Depression of the 1930s, the federal government assumed a growing role as a provider of basic financial support to the many destitute families.

Since World War II, the pace of this involvement has increased. In 1942, a nation-wide program of unemployment insurance was introduced, funded through employer and employee contributions. In 1944, the federal government introduced family allowances for each child up to 16 years of age. In 1952, the federal government introduced Old Age Security, and unemployment assistance was introduced in 1956. In 1966, the Canada and Quebec pension plans provided pensions for workers 65 and over, based on contributions. In 1972, a new *Unemployment Insurance Act* was introduced, with universal coverage and benefits; now, maternity and illness were covered. In 1974, the federal *Family Allowance Act* was introduced to provide for an increased benefit per child, subject to taxation. Through the Employment Insurance program, maternity and parental benefits became available to new parents. Since 2006, the Universal Child Care Benefit program has provided a taxable $100 per month to families for each child younger than six to help cover childcare costs (Robinson, 2008; Service Canada, 2012e).

Poverty, Officially Defined

absolute poverty: lacking the minimum basic requirements necessary for physical survival

There are two basic ways of defining poverty. **Absolute poverty** is a reflection of the minimum basic requirements necessary for physical survival. These include a diet that sustains life, clothing that protects from the elements, and appropriate shelter. Yet even this measure reflects what is considered appropriate and "decent" in one's society (Sarlo, 2008). Another approach to defining poverty considers poverty a relative concept based on social well-being in addition to physical survival. Individuals or families are identified as poor by comparing them to others in the population. Most measures of poverty in Canada, such as Statistics Canada's low-income cutoffs, are definitions of **relative poverty** (Ross et al., 2000; Statistics Canada, 2009f).

relative poverty: a definition of poverty based on comparing individuals or families to others in the population

In Canada, there are a few measures that define absolute poverty. According to Prof. Chris Sarlo of Nipissing University, "The basic needs poverty line is the cost of a list of basic needs required for long-term physical well-being. Those needs include nutritious food purchased at a grocery store fulfilling all Canada Food Guide requirements, rental accommodation, clothing purchased new at major department stores, household furnishings, supplies, personal hygiene items, laundry, insurance, out-of-pocket health costs such as medications, dental, and vision care, and so on" (Sarlo, 2008, p. 3).

Another attempt to define absolute poverty in Canada is provided by the Market Basket Measure (MBM). The MBM is the cost of a basket of goods that includes food, shelter, clothing, and other basic needs. This measure accounts for regional variations. For example, in 2010, the MBM for a family of two adults and two children in Regina was $29 875, in Ottawa $32 155, and in Halifax $32 303 (Statistics Canada, 2012v).

Currently, poverty is considered in relation to the income of the "average" Canadian. One of the most commonly used definitions is the Statistics Canada low-income cutoff (LICO), which is updated annually. This measure takes into account family size up to seven members and community size. The poverty lines are set at a level where a family needs to spend more than 70 percent of its income on food, clothing, and shelter (see Table 15.1 below). Statistics Canada has clearly and consistently emphasized that the LICOs are not measures of poverty (Statistics Canada, 2013h). Furthermore, these cutoff points are arbitrary and artificial (Sarlo, 2008). A family with an income 10 percent above the poverty line could afford only a couple of extra bus tickets or cups of coffee per day more than those at the poverty line.

Three factors that influence the impact of poverty on families are its depth, its breadth, and its duration. Depth of poverty refers to the amount a family or individual income is below the poverty line. The further below, the more difficult it is to provide the basic needs. Breadth refers to other aspects associated with poverty, such as illiteracy, poor health, and physical insecurity. Duration or persistence refers to how long the poverty lasts. Short-term low income is easier to weather than prolonged periods because individuals usually have some resources to help tide them over a bad period. When poverty is prolonged, however, all accumulated

TABLE 15.1 Low-Income Cut-offs (1992 Base), 2011 after Tax

Community Size	Rural Areas	Less than 30 000	30 000–99 999	100 000–499 999	500 000+
1 person	$12 629	$14 454	$16 124	$16 328	$19 307
2 persons	15 371	17 592	19 625	19 872	23 498
3 persons	19 141	21 905	24 437	24 745	29 260
4 persons	23 879	27 329	30 487	30 871	36 504
5 persons	27 192	31 120	34 717	35 154	41 567
6 persons	30 156	34 513	38 502	38 986	46 099
7 or more persons	33 121	37 906	42 286	42 819	50 631

Source: Statistics Canada. *Low income cut-offs (1992 base) after tax* (table). "Income Research Paper Series." Catalogue No. 75F0002MWE. Ottawa, Ontario. Statistics Canada. http://www.statcan.gc.ca/pub/75f0002m/2012002/tbl/tbl01-eng.htm

resources, such as savings, are eventually depleted and need to be renewed. For example, income could initially be used almost entirely for living expenses. Eventually, it must stretch to cover replacement costs for clothing and for household supplies, such as furniture and bedding. The longer poverty lasts, the harder it is to make ends meet (Clark & Hulme, 2005; Ross et al., 2000).

Who Is Poor in Canada?

For several reasons, determining the number of poor people in Canada is difficult. First, the total depends on the definition used. Second, the poorest of the poor are almost impossible to count because they include the homeless.

Poverty rates have varied with fluctuations in the economy. In the mid- to late 1970s, they began to fall and reached a low point in 1978. Then 1981 saw the beginning of a recession and poverty levels rose in the next years; with economic improvement, the rates dropped again to the 1981 levels. Following yet another recession, the economy picked up once more by 1997. Nevertheless, poverty levels remained above those in 1981 and 1989. By 2007, the poverty rate was at a record low of 9.2 percent.

The recession that started in late 2008 has resulted in increased poverty (National Council of Welfare, 2009; Yalnizyan, 2009). In 2010, 9.4 percent of Canadians had low income. However, the rate of low income has declined since 1996, when more than 15 percent of Canadians were experiencing low income (HRSDC, 2013). Poverty rates are lowest for families with two or more earners. They are also relatively low for married or common-law couples. The rate rises, however, for two-parent families with one earner. Single-adult households are even more likely to be poor. Lone parents, especially mothers, have the lowest incomes of any families with two or more members, including elderly couples. Unattached women and women in lone-parent families are more likely than others to remain poor for an extended time. Men in single-adult households also experience long-term poverty, but not to the same extent as women (Morissette & Picot, 2005; Senate of Canada, 2009; Townson, 2009).

As far as numbers are concerned, five groups stand out—unattached individuals aged 45 to 64, people with disabilities, off-reserve Aboriginal people, recent immigrants, and lone parents (of whom 4 out of 5 are lone mothers). In every working-age group, those most likely to be poor are younger, have lower levels of education, and are less likely to hold full-time jobs. Women, especially young women, are likelier than men to remain poor longer. Those who do move out of poverty tend to go from a one-adult to a two-adult, two-earner household. Conversely, those who move from a two-adult to a one-adult household risk becoming poor (Feng et al., 2007; Ross et al., 2000; Townson, 2009).

There has been a decrease in poverty among elderly people as a result of improved pensions and government benefits. The majority receive most of their income from public programs. Old Age Security is paid to all seniors, although it is subject to clawback at higher income levels. If the individual was employed, the Canada or Quebec Pension Plan provides additional income. For those with low

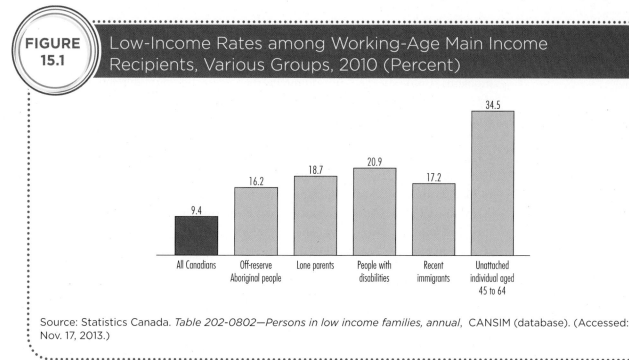

FIGURE 15.1 Low-Income Rates among Working-Age Main Income Recipients, Various Groups, 2010 (Percent)

Source: Statistics Canada. *Table 202-0802—Persons in low income families, annual,* CANSIM (database). (Accessed: Nov. 17, 2013.)

incomes, benefits are also provided through the Guaranteed Income Supplement. The combination of these income sources has moved many older people above the poverty line. A large number, however, are among the near-poor. Many of the elderly poor are women. They are less likely to have contributed to the Canada or Quebec Pension Plan and are more dependent on the Guaranteed Income Supplement. Some retirees benefit from workplace pensions and personal retirement savings. Because personal plans suffer during a recession, more seniors may live in or near poverty in the future (National Advisory Council on Aging, 2005a; Prince, 2009).

Minority Groups and Poverty

In 2006, the median income for Aboriginal people was $18 962—30 percent lower than the $27 097 median income for the rest of Canadians (Wilson & Macdonald, 2010). A number of factors contribute to their low income—lower levels of education, fewer jobs, greater health problems, and more lone-parent families (Noël & Larocque, 2009).

Recent immigrants (those who arrived in Canada after 2000) have a greater risk of poverty (17.2 percent in 2010), especially in large cities (Human Resources and Skills Development Canada, 2013). Rates were highest among those who had been in Canada for one to two years. Entry-level jobs, which many immigrants must take, are usually low-paying. In addition, there has been a swing toward self-employment, which is difficult for newcomers without connections. Those who come from countries with language and customs very different from Canada's may have the most difficulty finding well-paying jobs. And refugees are even more likely than other immigrants to live in poverty (Picot et al., 2007).

In 2010, 20.9 percent of those with a disability lived in poverty, compared with 9.4 percent of individuals without a disability (Human Resources and Skills Development Canada, 2013). Poverty rates were particularly high for those with problems communicating or with intellectual or psychological difficulties. Often, their costs of living are higher than average because of their special needs. Their employment levels, on the other hand, are lower than for other Canadians. People with longer-term disabilities are more likely than others to have low income (Galarneau & Radulescu, 2009). Members of the deaf community, for example, have difficulty finding employment. Between 60 and 70 percent of deaf people in Canada are functionally illiterate, or unable to read or write everyday materials (Griffiths & Cruise, 1999). Because of lower educational levels, they are streamed into jobs with low wages, few benefits, and little opportunity for a better position (Canadian Hearing Society, 2002).

What Is Beyond the Numbers?

One of the most striking facts about poverty in Canada is that many people who live in poverty have jobs. In 2010, 3.2 percent of all individuals living in households where the main income recipient had at least 910 hours of paid work had a low income (Human Resources and Skills Development Canada, 2013). Female lone parents fared worst, with 28.2 percent in poverty (Sauvé, 2009a). In 2007, 13.5 percent of those using Canadian food banks received their primary income from employment (Senate of Canada, 2008).

Who is the typical working-poor family? They most likely live in a city in Ontario; they have not had as much schooling as others; they have more children (even the family with one or two children is twice as likely to be poor as a childless couple); the parents are aged 25 to 44; and they have only one employed family member. Families that are not poor are far more likely to have two or more adult earners. In poor families with one child, even if both parents work full time at the minimum wage, the family will still fall below the poverty line. Obviously, single parents are at an even greater disadvantage (see Box 15.1) (Canadian Council on Social Development, n.d.; Fleury, 2008; Hay, 2009; Morissette & Picot, 2005).

Market poverty—that is, poverty based on wages alone—has grown. There are several reasons. First, many jobs do not pay well enough to allow even full-time workers, especially women, to support families. In 2010, women earned just 68 percent of the average wages earned by men and were likelier to have low-wage jobs (Statistics Canada, 2012x). Self-employment and part-time work also contribute to lower income.

Second, unemployment has increased since the recession that began in 2008. Layoffs turned double-income families into single-income families with a double-income debt load (Sauvé, 2009a). The official numbers do not count those who became discouraged or those finding part-time instead of full-time employment. In 1997, it took longer to find a job than in 1981—an average of 22.3 weeks instead of 15.1 weeks. The current job outlook does not appear more promising. Changes to Employment Insurance since the 1990s have reduced benefit levels from 75 percent to 55 percent of earnings.

Third, some individuals experience special barriers in finding and holding jobs. For many parents, especially women, it costs less to stay home with children once childcare, transportation, and other employment-related costs are paid. Many people with disabilities are able and willing to work, but the lack of affordable transportation and unwillingness of employers to redesign jobs or provide flexible hours set up barriers. A growing number of older workers aged 55 to 64 are retired or "involuntarily idle." They may, however, have little choice over early retirement. Others have been laid off. These older people have problems finding employment because they compete against younger workers (Campaign 2000, 2009; Hay, 2009; Ross et al., 2000; Schellenberg & Silver, 2004; Townson, 2009).

When families do not have jobs and are not eligible for employment insurance, they turn to social assistance. Welfare rates in all provinces are well below the low-income cutoff, with two exceptions. A lone parent with one child receives benefits at or slightly above the poverty line in Quebec and Newfoundland and Labrador (National Council of Welfare, 2011). For some families, add-ons, notably drug and dental care, make welfare preferable to low-paying jobs without such benefits (Sayeed, 1999). There is increasing pressure on welfare recipients, even parents with young children, to find employment (Gazso, 2007; Klein & Pulkingham, 2008). However, when welfare recipients do find work, they may lose benefits such as subsidized housing and become worse off financially (Stapleton, 2007).

Income often does not cover families' living costs. Many food bank users in the Toronto area did not have a telephone, walked rather than using a bus, relied on charities, borrowed money, and were given money and food by others. Most stated they went hungry at least once a month, and half said their children did too (Michalski, 2003).

BOX 15.1   Making Ends Meet

An American study of single mothers surviving on welfare and low-wage work describes several strategies they used for making ends meet. First choice was financial help from the child's father or a live-in boyfriend. Second choice was asking relatives for help. Third choice was to take a job under the counter—illegally—or a "real" job using false ID. In both cases, their pay was not reported so that their welfare would not be cut. Going to an agency for help was near the bottom of the list. The last strategy was selling sex, drugs, or stolen goods. Many women moved between the various strategies, using a new option when another dried up (Edin & Lein, 1997). Although no study of the same scope has taken place in Canada, people cut off from welfare in British Columbia reported staying with friends, using soup kitchens, stealing, and engaging in survival sex. A number of women returned to abusive relationships (Klein & Pulkingham, 2008).

Some people have temporary difficulties in obtaining affordable housing. For others, it is a chronic problem. Finding affordable housing is a challenge for many Canadian households. Those with the most problems were adults living alone, lone parents, people with disabilities, recent immigrants, and Aboriginal people. More than 50 percent of their income was spent on housing (Senate of Canada, 2008). Cheaper housing near city cores is being "gentrified"; that is, renovated into stylish and expensive homes costing far more than earlier residents could afford. Less subsidized housing is being built. Most is available to families and seniors, with a small number reserved for those with disabilities. Usually, young unattached individuals are not eligible. Some people double up to save money. Many of the poor, however, must depend on the "for-profit" rental market (Caragata, 2003; Federation of Canadian Municipalities, 2000; Senate of Canada, 2008; Swanton, 2009).

Since housing is so expensive, people with low incomes have to cut back in other ways. One area is food. "Food insecurity" is the term used to describe the uncertainty that people can buy enough nutritious food or the actual inability to do so. Rates are highest in Nunavut and the Northwest Territories (Ledrou & Gervais, 2005). When food runs short, mothers tend to eat less or miss meals altogether so they can feed their children. To fill the need, families turn to food banks, soup kitchens, and friends and relatives for help. Food banks and soup kitchens are especially common in Ontario, where they seem to be social institutions (McIntyre et al., 1998). Unfortunately, supplies at food banks are often limited because they depend on donations. Users also have little choice. Sometimes, people are even turned away when quantities run low. Hunger occurs much less often than food insecurity.

Time to Review

1. What is the history of dealing with poverty in Canada?
2. How is poverty defined in Canada?
3. Who is poor in Canada?
4. How does poverty affect families in Canada?

Homelessness

Despite its prosperity, Canada has failed to help the homeless people of unknown number in its midst. There are no exact figures for the number of homeless people in Canada, partly because of the difficulty in counting them. In addition, the homeless population changes from day to day, and so do definitions of homelessness. A head count of people staying in shelters was conducted on January 22, 1987 (the Year of the Homeless), in which 305 shelters participated. Using the average of these agencies, it was estimated that 10 672 people spent that night in a shelter. Of course, this figure did not include homeless people still on the street (McLaughlin, 1987). In 2006 and 2007, Canada West Foundation researchers studied street-level social problems in western cities. Absolute homelessness was a serious problem in Vancouver, Calgary, and Edmonton, where both street dwellers and shelter users were increasing. Beyond that, the invisible homeless, or those who live temporarily with family and friends ("couch surfers"), as well as those at serious risk of becoming homeless, were thought to be more numerous than the absolute homeless (Wilkie & Berdahl, 2007).

Who are the homeless? Homeless people include two-parent families, single parents and their children, single women, older persons, and young people. Among them are psychiatric patients and individuals with disabilities. Many receive social assistance; some have low-paying jobs (Salvation Army, 2009; Schindler & Coley, 2005; Senate of Canada; 2008; Wilkie & Berdahl, 2007). There appear to be three different groups among the homeless: those who are chronically homeless and often have substance abuse problems; those who are cyclically homeless because of job loss, family violence, or release from prison, and may be repeaters; and those who are temporarily homeless because of marital separation or a disaster such as a fire (Begin et al., 1999).

About 30 percent of homeless people are women. Mother-headed lone-parent families appear at greatest risk, especially when they have few backup resources. They are usually less noticeable than men, partly because they fear child protection services will take their children. Many remain homeless for shorter periods because they exchange sex or housekeeping for accommodation. Such women are often separated or escaping abuse.

Some groups are overrepresented among the homeless. The number of young homeless people is increasing. Among them are those living in shelters with a parent and runaways, many of whom are escaping abuse—living on the streets, however, is also violent. The number of families needing emergency shelter appears to be growing. Members of minorities, especially Aboriginal people in Prairie cities, are overrepresented among the homeless. Immigrants may also experience problems in finding housing (Begin et al., 1999; Caragata, 2003; Wingard et al., 2003; Senate of Canada, 2008; Wilkie & Berdahl, 2007).

Most reasons given for the increase in homelessness are based on educated guesses. The shortage of affordable and secure housing in every city in Canada is a key reason, but it fails to explain the whole phenomenon. Changes in employment patterns mean that many men now using shelters found casual and seasonal labour in the past. Some people point to the policy of releasing psychiatric patients from long-term care—"deinstitutionalization"—without adequate community resources. Still others suggest drug and alcohol abuse are factors. Most recently, changes in the eligibility for and levels of welfare are blamed (Wilkie & Berdahl, 2007; Senate of Canada, 2009).

Conditions in shelters do not favour family living. Men's shelters are generally worse than women's. Many of the latter are designed to house abused women. Some men's shelters are in old buildings, including former warehouses and factories. There is little privacy because beds are in dormitories. Lice, dirt, and illness are common. Often, shelters lack privacy, and other residents and staff members may interfere with parenting strategies (Anderson & Koblinsky, 1995; Caragata, 2003; Novac et al., 1996).

Currently, much of our strategy in dealing with homelessness in Canada is to provide emergency services such as shelters and food banks. However, much research has shown that investing in homelessness prevention costs less than it does to provide for someone who is already homeless (National Council on Welfare, 2011). If we shifted the focus to prevention and provision of housing, we would not only be responding appropriately and compassionately to a problem that harms individuals, families, and communities, but we would also be saving money (Gaetz, 2012).

Source: Barry Maguire.

What Can Poverty Do to Children?

Children are the largest single group of poor people in Canada. In 1989, the federal government resolved to eliminate child poverty by the year 2000. It has not done so. In 2010, 979 000, or 14.5 percent, of children in Canada lived in poverty, whereas in 1989 the number was 912 000, or 13.7 percent. The Canada Child Tax Benefit and the National Child Benefit Supplement, a joint federal, provincial, and territorial initiative, were introduced in 1998. These have been important in reducing child and family poverty but still leave the poorest families below the poverty line. Although most poor children are members of two-parent families, a growing proportion of poor families are headed by single mothers. Child poverty in Canada is higher than in most Western European countries, though not as high as in the United States (Campaign 2000, 2009; Conference Board of Canada, 2009; Fleury, 2008).

Poverty affects the family, and poor children are twice as likely as others to have poorly functioning families. Parents are often depressed and carry emotional scars from their own parents' divorce, substance abuse, or violence. Under chronic stress, poor parents are more apt to be distracted or hostile in their parenting than are those who are not poor. Families often move because of marriage breakup or as a result of job loss or change. They may also look for better or more affordable housing. Poor children are twice as likely as others to live in substandard housing. Apartments are often crowded and uninviting for play or study (Jones et al., 2002; Pinderhughes, Nix et al., 2001; Ross & Roberts, 1999; Statistics Canada, 2005c). The community is also important. Children interact with peers and adults, learning values and forming social networks. Poor children are more likely than others to live in neighbourhoods with at least one serious problem. Drug use and dealing, public drinking, burglaries, delinquency, unrest from racial or religious prejudice, and littering of garbage and glass are among the problems. Twice as many poor parents as those who are not poor consider their neighbourhood unsafe and do not allow children out alone to play. The children are thus limited in their ability to form relationships and learn social skills (Kohen et al., 2008; Leventhal & Brooks-Gunn, 2008; Ross & Roberts, 1999; Swisher, 2008).

Children's behaviour, health, school learning, and recreational activities are all affected by income levels. Behaviour, as we saw in Chapter 6, is shaped by children's temperaments and by the people with whom they interact. Poor children are more likely to be considered troublemakers, to have emotional problems, to be hyperactive and inattentive in school, to engage in delinquency (cheating, stealing, vandalizing), and to hang around with other children in trouble with the law (Ross & Roberts, 1999).

Children in low-income families also tend to have poorer health. When money is tight, the food budget often suffers and with it the health of the mother and the unborn child. Babies with low birth weight are more commonly born to mothers in low-income families than in more affluent ones. Low birth weight is associated with a greater number of birth defects and higher infant mortality (McIntyre et al., 1998; Urquia et al., 2007). The effects of poverty continue into school age. Poor children suffer a wide range of health problems. Often, they have inadequate nutrition, lacking essential vitamins (See Box 15.2). If a family lives in substandard housing, children may be more exposed to illnesses they are less able to resist because of their diet. Children in poor families have more problems with hearing, vision, speech, and physical mobility and dexterity (Malat et al., 2005; Séguin et al., 2007; Ross & Roberts, 1999).

BOX 15.2 — Hunger and Its Impact on Children

By Mary Crea-Arsenio, University of Guelph

In terms of child poverty, Canada ranks a humiliating 24th among 35 of the wealthiest OECD countries worldwide (Campaign 2000, 2012). Among one of the greatest impacts of living in poverty is child hunger. Hunger is defined as a need or desire for food and the physiological state of weakness as result of a need for food (Meal Exchange, 2006). The term "food insecurity" refers to not knowing where your next meal will come from or not having enough resources to prepare a sufficient and nutritious meal for your family (Government of Canada, 1998). In Canada, 7.7 percent of households. or 1.92 million Canadians. are considered "food insecure" (Statistics Canada, 2010d).

What are policymakers doing to ensure food security among Canadian families?

Canada's Action Plan for Food Security is the government's response to the issue of food insecurity. It outlines the highest priorities of action to ensure food security in the country. According to the plan, food security means access to adequate and sufficient food supplies. The plan identified the following nine priorities:

Priority 1: The right to food

Priority 2: The reduction of poverty

Priority 3: Promotion of access to safe and nutritious food

Priority 4: Food safety

Priority 5: Traditional food acquisition methods of Aboriginal and coastal communities (e.g., hunting, fishing)

Priority 6: Food production

Priority 7: Emphasis on environmentally sustainable practices

Priority 8: Fair trade

Priority 9: Acknowledgment of peace as a precursor to food security

Many organizations exist in Canada to help combat issues related to child poverty and its impact on diet and nutrition. For example, the Breakfast Club of Canada is a charitable organization formed in 1994 to ensure children at risk are receiving a nutritious breakfast at school. In the 2011–12 school year, over 118 000 Canadian children in 1170 schools were given a healthy start to their school day (Breakfast Club of Canada, 2013). In addition, Meal Exchange, a national youth-driven charity, focuses on engaging, educating, and mobilizing youth to work with their communities to eradicate hunger and achieve food security. The programs have been run in over 100 communities across Canada and generated over $3 million worth of food. The Food Banks of Canada is a group of charitable organizations that work to alleviate hunger across the country. It is estimated that 93 000 people each month access a food bank for the first time and 38 percent of those turning to food banks are children and youth (Food Banks of Canada, 2012).

Source: *Canada's Action Plan for Food Security.* Found at: http://www.agr.gc.ca/misb/ fsec-seca/pdf/action_e.pdf. Agriculture and Agri-Food Canada, 1998. Reproduced with the permission of the Minister of Public Works and Government Services Canada, 2013.

School poses many challenges for poor children. They are often not as ready for school as others because of limited experiences, as well as physical and health problems. Their disadvantage shows up in vocabulary development in preschoolers, reading difficulties, and the need for special education. More poor children repeat grades and drop out without completing high school. Few go on to postsecondary education. Since they are ill more frequently, poor children miss more time from school and may have trouble catching up. If they go to school hungry, they may have difficulty concentrating in class. Crowded homes may mean they lack a suitable place for homework. When housing is substandard, poor families tend to move more often. As a result, children must adapt to new schools and different curriculums. They may be stigmatized if they cannot pay for school activities or if they wear unfashionable clothes. For many children, schooling is so unpleasant that dropping out is a relief. As a result, 1 in 6 teens from low-income families is neither in school nor employed. Such teens are at much greater risk of committing delinquent acts, abusing alcohol and drugs, and becoming poor adults (Frenette, 2007; Moore et al., 2009; Ross & Roberts, 1999).

Both income and community recreational facilities affect how much children are involved in sports and cultural activities. The cost of sports equipment and fees, musical instruments and lessons, for example, limit their participation. If there are no free or cheap, well-run play or sports facilities nearby, there are further barriers. Fewer children in low-income families play unorganized sports—for example, pickup hockey. The lower levels are due in part to a lack of safe play spaces. Children in low-income families thus miss out on learning skills and social competence (Frenette, 2007; Ross & Roberts, 1999).

At the bottom end of the poverty scale are homeless children. American studies have found that health, psychological, behavioural, and educational effects are similar to those of other poor children but more extreme. Many of these children see life as temporary. People, places, and schools come and go. So do families. Many homeless children are separated from parents and/or brothers and sisters. With impermanence a fact of life, there is no urge to complete school projects. Homeless children have not developed a sense of their space or possessions. Many lack the experiences with toys and places that would help develop knowledge of size, colour, and spatial relationships. Nevertheless, some of these children succeed in spite of adversity (Gewirtzman & Fodor, 1987; Lindsey & Sanchez, 2010).

What Can Be Done?

The main cause of poverty in Canada is simple: low wages (Canada Without Poverty, 2013). Thus, providing people with adequate income is clearly the answer.

In 2009, the Canadian Senate published a report on poverty in Canada. Their first recommendation was "to adopt as a core [goal] poverty eradication, that programs dealing with poverty and homelessness [be] designed to lift Canadians out of poverty rather than make living within poverty more manageable" (Senate of Canada, 2009, p. 7). The question is how this goal should be achieved. In April 2013, the House of Commons conducted a study on income inequality in Canada. A panel of academics, policy experts, and organizations gave suggestions as to how the federal government could best address inequality and poverty in Canada (Lewchuk, 2013). Here, we will look at various suggestions.

1. *Create jobs.* The best form of social security is to have a job and support oneself. The downturn in the economy beginning in 2008 made job creation both more important and more difficult. In an attempt to be globally competitive, companies are using foreign labour, providing employment for only limited periods (e.g., contract work), or both. Many Canadians are unemployed even though they want to work. No amount of retraining will get them work if jobs are not there. Job creation has been a goal adopted by both federal and provincial governments. Many of the new jobs that have been created, however, pay low wages, are often part time or temporary, and offer no benefits such as health plans or pensions.

2. *Raise wages.* Raising the minimum wage would also reduce poverty. In its report, the Senate proposed $10 per hour, while Campaign 2000 proposed $11 per hour. To succeed, job training and employment assistance need to be long term and geared to occupations needing workers (Campaign 2000, 2009; Senate of Canada, 2009; Torjman, 2008). There should be national wage standards to ensure that no fully employed individual lives below the poverty line (Lewchuk, 2013).

3. *Increase social assistance.* Some people wish to provide an adequate income through direct grants. This approach has been rejected by provincial governments. British Columbia, for example, made it harder to qualify for welfare and has imposed a time limit (Michael & Reitsma-Street, 2002). A change in focus toward social assistance has occurred. In 1998, the federal government, using funds from other programs, set up the National Child Benefit Supplement. All families with incomes less than a specified amount are eligible for the benefit, whether this income comes from welfare or employment. Some provinces deduct the amount from welfare payments to fund programs for families, for example extra money to families moving from welfare into the workforce. Others provide noncash services, such as school nutrition and "head start" education for preschoolers. It is too early, however, to tell how much this program will reduce family poverty. There will always be individuals who are disabled or otherwise disadvantaged, and they will need longer-term support—they should receive better levels of benefits (Torjman, 2008). We should also invest in programs that help youth with disabilities transition from school to work and fund more research to determine why more and more people with disabilities are relying on social assistance programs (Lewchuk, 2013).

4. *Support families with children.* A child benefit of $5400, coupled with a higher minimum wage, can lift families out of poverty (Campaign 2000, 2009;

Lewchuk, 2013). One suggestion is to increase federal spending on early child-hood education and care (ECEC) by providing $1.3 billion in new provincial transfer payments for ECEC services, as well as ensuring that federal spending on ECEC reaches at least 1 percent of GDP by 2023 (Lewchuk, 2013).

No simple strategy will achieve the goal. Government programs often work at cross-purposes. Moving from dependence on social assistance to reliance on paid employment creates obstacles and barriers to improving life. Families can lose bene-fits tied to income levels, such as subsidized housing, when they move from welfare to paid employment. These benefit losses may reduce the family's living standard below the one it had on welfare. There needs to be an overarching policy that sup-ports individuals who cannot work and provides adequate services, such as childcare assistance, longer-term training, and financial assistance, during the transition from welfare to work with a living wage. Changes will probably need to be made to current programs to achieve these goals (Hay, 2009; National Council of Welfare, 2007b; Senate of Canada, 2009; Stapleton, 2007; Torjman, 2009). Whatever solution or combination of solutions is chosen, moving families out of poverty is a complex and difficult task. Yet it must be tackled, especially for the benefit of children.

Time to Review

1. Who are the homeless in Canada?
2. Why are there homeless people in Canada?
3. What can poverty do to children?
3. How can we reduce poverty in Canada?

The Money Pinch

Peter and Brianne are young, just 24. They married shortly before the birth of their first child, Matthew, now three. Their daughter, Sofie, is eight months. Matthew was born with spina bifida, a defect where the spine doesn't close around the spinal cord. When he was only a month old, surgery closed the spinal defect, but he has only limited use of his legs. He has since been admitted to hospital several times. Fortunately, Sofie is developing normally.

Peter works as a clerk at the grocery store in their small town in southern Manitoba. On his days off, he helps out on his uncle's dairy farm. Brianne spends her days caring for the children, including providing therapy for Matthew to help him develop the use of his legs. She has been unable to hold a job since his birth but hopes to find employment once the children are in school.

The couple has only limited income, well below the official low-income cutoff. They have used several strategies to help them survive financially. Brianne's aunt has provided them with an apartment above her store at low rent. Peter walks to his job and gets a ride to his uncle's farm. Relatives and friends have driven the family to Winnipeg for Matthew's medical care. Most of their furniture came from

Peter's grandmother in Winnipeg when she moved to an assisted living facility. The children's used stroller and cribs came from a cousin. Their clothes are mostly hand-me-downs and thrift store buys. To cut food costs, Peter brings home cheap soon-to-expire items from the store and buys staples in bulk. Brianne has cajoled leftover turkey carcasses from church dinners so she can make soup. They also receive produce from neighbours and family members. Brianne's mother and sister provide respite care once a week. For entertainment, the couple takes the children to the playground, with a special ice cream treat afterwards. They also visit extended family members.

Although they manage financially on a daily basis, they have no reserve funds to meet emergencies. The frame of Brianne's glasses broke a month ago but remains taped together because they cannot afford a replacement. They're not sure how they'll manage accommodation costs if Matthew needs further medical care in Winnipeg, because they can no longer stay with Peter's grandmother.

Peter and Brianne are thinking about moving to Winnipeg to be closer to the hospital, but they don't know how they would cope financially in the city.

1. What social supports allow Peter and Brianne to cope with their limited income?
2. How well are their strategies likely to work if they move to Winnipeg?
3. What other services might they receive in the city?
4. Apply the double ABCX model from Chapter 13 to this family.

Summary

How Is Poverty Defined in Canada?

Two ways have commonly been used to define poverty. The first measures absolute poverty and uses as a standard the minimum amount of money required to ensure physical survival. The second is a relative measure and is based on the standard of social well-being. In North America, the focus was initially on providing the barest essentials to "deserving" poor. Often, charitable groups gave this aid. Gradually, the government provided more income support services, and today the definition of poverty is closer to the well-being standard. One of the most used definitions is the Statistics Canada low-income cutoff (LICO).

Who Is Poor in Canada?

There are five principal groups of poor people: unattached individuals aged 45 to 64 years old, people with disabilities, off-reserve Aboriginal people, recent immigrants, and lone parents. Older women have often not been employed and are solely dependent on their government pension. Young adults aged 16 to 24 are affected by the shift of employment from well-paying industries to poorer-paying consumer services. Often, these jobs are part time. Young working couples make up a third group. These tend to be single-earner families with several children. The hardest hit are female-headed single-parent families, especially young mothers. Those with low educational levels tend to be the worst off. Those supported by welfare or low-paying jobs use various strategies: help from family and friends, unreported work, and, occasionally, illegal activities. The situation of poor people is made worse by the lack of affordable housing. With much of their income going for shelter, individuals have little left for food and other essentials. During the past several years, use of food banks has increased. Estimates of the number of homeless people vary widely. Shelter residents are a diverse population. Shelter conditions do not favour family living, both because of the lack of privacy and because some residents have problems that disturb others. Shelters are often a last resort after several moves.

What Can Poverty Do to Children?

Children are the largest single group of poor people. Poverty affects both health and education. Since so much of family income goes for shelter, nutrition may be inadequate and resistance to illness low. Substandard and crowded housing may expose children to more illnesses. Many children from low-income families do poorly in school, a tendency that may be linked to both health and living conditions. Many who drop out of school have poor job prospects and continue poverty into a new generation. Children in shelters suffer more severe health, educational, and emotional difficulties than other poor children.

What Can Be Done to Reduce Poverty in Canada?

A number of remedies that address parts of the problem have been suggested. These include job creation, targeting of social assistance to special groups, and supporting families with children. Government bodies and agencies need to better coordinate their regulations to foster the financial well-being of families. The goal should be to help Canadians get out of poverty rather than to live more comfortably in poverty.

Class Assignments

1. Many students live in poverty. What strategies do they use to make money go further? Would these strategies work for a family over a long time? Explain.

2. What is the minimum wage in your province? If a person works 40 hours per week, what will the take-home pay be after Employment Insurance, Canada (or Quebec) Pension Plan, and taxes (if any) are deducted? How much will have to go for rent (a) for a single person and (b) for a single parent with one child? Draw up a budget to cover other costs, such as food, clothing, transportation, and childcare. What occasional expenses may occur? How will they be met?

3. Find out what services are available to help poor individuals and families in your community. Prepare a report or presentation that shows the different services and strategies that are used.

Personal Assignments

The following assignments are designed to help you think about your own experience:

1. On the basis of your own experience or that of people you know, explain the differences between those living on a low income who manage reasonably well financially and those who have extreme financial difficulties.

2. Describe the effects of poverty on the parent–child relationship. Explain your answer.

3. If you were to suddenly be on your own financially, what changes would you have to make? If you are already in this position, how do you make ends meet?

PART 7

THE FUTURE OF CANADIAN FAMILIES

Chapter 16

The Crystal Ball—Predicting the Future of the Family

LEARNING OBJECTIVES

What are the implications of an aging population for the future?

What forms will families likely take in the future and what changes in roles will follow?

How does technology affect on the family?

How do government policies affect families?

Will the family survive?

Zurijeta/Shutterstock

"On all sides concern has been expressed over an ever increasing divorce rate. The institution of the family, we are told, is endangered. One out of every five or six marriages now existing is likely to end in the divorce court. Divorce certainly has increased—this no one can deny. Our divorce rate is far greater than that of any country in the western world. . . ."

Source: Albert C. Jacob, *Marriage Laws*. National Council on Family Relations. 1939.

"The number of divorces has increased fifteen-fold. One out of every seven marriages ended in divorce, and there was no reason to think that the trend toward more and more frequent divorce would reverse itself."

Source: Christopher Lasch. *Haven in a Heartless World: The Family Besieged*. New York: W. W. Norton. 1995. Pg. 8.

"The family, in its old sense, is disappearing from our land, and not only are our institutions threatened, but the very existence of our society is endangered."

Source: Barbara A. Mitchell, *The Boomerang Age: Transitions to Adulthood in Families*. New Jersey: Aldine Transaction, 2005. Pg. 31.

You may think that each of the above quotations reflects concern about the demise of the family in the 21st century. In fact, the first is from an article written in 1939, the second refers to the period between 1870 and 1920, and the third, though quoted in a recent book, was published in the *Boston Quarterly Review* at the end of the 19th century. As these excerpts show, concern about the future of the family is not new. Perhaps every generation has looked to the future with some trepidation. What will the Canadian family look like in 10 years? In 30 years? Will we be able to recognize it as a family? Will families even exist at the beginning of the next century? Or will the forms we already know survive?

We can make educated guesses about the future of the family by looking at several factors: in particular, statistical trends, recent government policies, and activist issues. Predictions are more likely to be accurate one or two years down the road than for 10, 30, or 40 years. We can attempt to explain what trends may mean in terms of family experiences, but this is shakier ground. There are so many unknowns in the situation that in 20 years, predictions made today may seem absolute foolishness. In spite of that risk, let's look into the crystal ball to try to ascertain the future of the family.

Where Do I Fit In?

When you read the opening vignette, did you think that each statement was about families in Canada today?

Think about your own extended family . . .

1. How many different family arrangements are there?
2. Why do you think there are so many different family forms in Canada today?

An Aging Population

Canadians can expect the population as a whole to become older. Three trends are working together to push up the average age of Canadians: the aging of the baby boom generation, the low birth rate, and advances in medical technology (Infrastructure Canada, 2008; Sauvé, 2006; Statistics Canada, 2013i). In the past 50 years, there have been large swings in the birth rate. From the end of World War II until the early 1960s, the rate was high—the baby boom. The older members of this generation have now moved out of child-bearing age. By 2026, they will be aged 60 to 80 and many will have retired. The baby boom was followed by a "baby bust." The birth rate has now dropped below the level necessary to replace the population. Meanwhile, advances in medical technology have had their impact at both ends of life. The development of relatively easy-to-use, safe contraceptives has made it easier to avoid having children. More women now have children later in life, have fewer than in the past, or have none at all. At the other end of life, people are living longer. The oldest old, those over 85, make up the fastest-growing age group. The increased life span will magnify the effects of the dropping birth rate (Statistics Canada, 2013i).

What Does an Old Population Mean?

The aging of the population will have a number of consequences in the future. Several practical questions arise. Who will support the growing number of seniors? What new or expanded services will be needed? How much will the costs of medical care increase as seniors age? How will such costs be covered? In sum, who will care for the elderly as they become frailer, and how will this care be paid for?

One way of looking at the cost of providing services to an aging population is through a **dependency ratio**—the ratio of the combined youth (0 to 19 years) and senior population (65 or older) to the working-age population (20 to 64 years), expressed as the number of dependants for every 100 workers (Statistics Canada, 2010e). In the 1950s and 1960s, Canada had high dependency ratios because of the large number of children born during the baby boom. As this cohort entered the workforce, the ratio fell. Between 1971 and 2006, the dependency ratio fell from 89 to 60 dependants per 100 workers. It is rising again as the boomers retire and should increase in the following years; however, the ratios are unlikely to be as high as in the 1960s.

dependency ratio: the ratio of the combined youth and senior population to the working-age population, expressed as the number of dependants for every 100 workers

What is different is that it is seniors more than youth who are the dependants, so the need for age-related services will increase. The cost will be partly offset by reduced spending in areas such as education because of the smaller percentage of children in the population (Infrastructure Canada, 2008). Some suggest that modifying immigration policies to attract younger workers can also ease the elderly dependency ratio. Such a policy, however, will make only a small difference unless immigration increases dramatically (Bannerjee & Robson, 2009).

Private pensions have improved, both in availability and level of benefits. Seniors are also covered by the Canada or Quebec Pension Plan. Many have saved additional money. Thus, many people, especially the "young-old," are paying much of their own way. There is no guarantee, however, that this situation will continue. Meanwhile, the job market for young people is insecure. Service jobs, such as caring for the elderly, have increased but do not pay well. Because many have only temporary or part-time work and others are self-employed, pensions may be low or nonexistent. Taxes pay for other benefits—medical care, Old Age Security, and the Guaranteed Income Supplement. But the taxes seniors pay on their incomes only partially cover the costs of pensions and medical care, especially as they become frailer. Thus, the tax burden will fall increasingly on the smaller working population who can less readily afford the cost (Infrastructure Canada, 2008).

In the past, care was provided primarily by families. It still is, although there has been growing reliance on seniors' residences and nursing homes. As the population ages, the demand for housing and residential care for the elderly will increase. Staffing shortages and the need for increased funding may become problems. There has been a move away from institutional care. Should more facilities be built? The need will be temporary, as was the need for more and larger schools while the baby boom passed through the educational system. Should more services be offered to keep seniors living in the community and assist family members in their care? With more women—traditionally, the caregivers—in the workforce, family members may not be able to provide needed care without changing their work patterns. Employers may have to scramble to replace both retiring workers and those who care for older relatives (Infrastructure Canada, 2008; Maxwell, 2007).

The aging of the population has had an unexpected benefit for families. More generations coexist now than at any other time in history. Children nowadays are more likely to know their grandparents and great-grandparents than ever before (Connidis, 2010). The multi-generation extended family provides continuity by passing on traditions and family history, but it may also place more demands on younger relatives.

Different Types of Families

The "traditional" family—husband, wife, and their biological children—has been considered the norm in Canadian society, although there have always been variations on the theme, for instance never-married individuals living alone or with relatives, widowed parents and their children, and childless couples. Since the late 1960s, however, the numbers of these "different" family forms have shown a marked increase, a trend that is expected to continue into the future.

More people live alone now than in the past. The increase has been greatest among older women. Those aged 65 and over in 2011 were nearly twice as likely to live alone—31.5 percent compared to 16 percent of men. This relates in part to the lower life expectancy of males, and women are outliving their husbands in greater numbers (Statistics Canada, 2012y). Widows are better able to live alone rather than with family members because most of these women have worked outside the home and have their own savings or pensions. This trend will probably continue.

At the other end, younger people are finding it harder to establish themselves financially. Thus, they will probably continue to delay marriage and may continue living with their parents. Or they may return following a job loss or divorce. The tendency among young adults aged 20 to 29 to live with their parents appears to have levelled off. In 2011, 42.3 percent lived in the parental home, either because they had never left it or because they returned home after living elsewhere. This proportion was relatively unchanged from 2006, although it was well above the share of 32.1 percent in 1991 and 26.9 percent in 1981 (Statistics Canada, 2012j).

Marriage patterns are changing. Unmarried cohabitation, including relationships between same-sex individuals, has increased. Although cohabitation is often a prelude to marriage, many of these relationships are temporary. The very meaning of marriage appears to be changing. In the past, it marked the union of one man and one woman, with the purpose (among others) of having and raising children. Bearing children outside marriage has become increasingly common (Le Bourdais & Lapierre-Adamcyk, 2004). Divorce and remarriage have increased. Gay and lesbian groups successfully pressured the government to legalize same-sex marriages (Hurley, 2005). The ban against polygamy has been questioned (Shelly, 2009). In 2011, for the first time, stepfamilies were counted in the census (Statistics Canada, 2012j). Despite the many challenges, though, the norm in our society of one relationship at a time (serial monogamy) remains constant.

Children's living situations have also changed. Most children are born to married couples, although marriages are occurring later in life. As a result, children have older parents and fewer siblings. They are also likely to have more living grandparents. Many children live with just one parent, either because their parents never married or because they have separated or divorced. The situation has changed from the 1950s, when most single parents were widowed. More children now live in stepfamilies than in the past (Statistics Canada, 2012j). While it is true that many widowed parents in the past remarried, the children in such families were not faced with the conflicting loyalties of having a parent outside the stepfamily. Most children also have both parents in the workforce and are socialized by a variety of caregivers.

"I guess we'd be considered a family. We're living together, we love each other, and we haven't eaten the children yet."

Source: Sam Gross/The Cartoon Bank.

Since the late 1960s, immigration patterns have changed. The number of individuals coming from Europe has dropped, while the number coming from countries in Asia, South Asia, Africa, the Caribbean, and Latin America has increased (Statistics Canada, 2013d). Immigrants bring different traditions with them, including those involving the family. Some rely more strongly on the extended family for social life and for practical and moral support. A number of traditions encourage arranged marriages. The increase in multiracial unions and the adoption of children from developing countries are also contributing to family diversity.

Changes in Family Roles

A young person can no longer count on going through the "traditional" family life cycle, which includes marriage, having and raising children, the empty nest, and shared retirement and old age, with appropriate roles established for each phase. New stages are added as individuals cohabit, marry, separate, divorce, and recouple. With second and third marriages, the social time clock is becoming more and more blurred. Parents may have two sets of children widely separated in age. New social scripts that specify behaviour appropriate for the new life stages are already emerging (Walsh, 2003a). Since 2004, the *Assisted Human Reproduction Act* has specified and regulated the legal issues pertaining to assisted human reproduction. In the future, we can expect new laws or court cases to clarify grey areas surrounding lone parenthood, remarriage, and stepfamilies. Societal pressure to respect the differences in families of racial, ethnic, and sexual minorities will continue. There will also be demands for social institutions such as schools and the legal system to be more sensitive to these differences.

There is increasing role flexibility between the sexes. The breadwinner husband and homemaker wife have become a minority as more and more women are working outside the home. The increase in the cost of living, as well as high levels of unemployment, often demand at least two wage earners if the family is to avoid poverty. With high levels of separation and divorce, women can no longer depend on a spouse for lifelong financial support. Having a job provides a certain level of financial insurance. The responsibilities of earning a living and looking after the home and children are shared by both spouses, although often not equally. Advocates call for greater equality both in women's pay and in men's participation in homemaking. There is also pressure for more daycare and a greater variety in the forms it takes to better meet the needs of working parents and their children (Daly, 2004a; Friendly & Prentice, 2009; Marshall, 2003, 2009).

Children will have more parent figures in the coming years. These will, of course, include the biological parents, but parents' lovers, partners, surrogate mothers, stepparents, babysitters, and daycare personnel may be added. As a result, the socialization of children may be less directly under their parents' control, even though they may choose many of the providers. Experts disagree over the effect this trend will have on children.

Although the two forms exist side by side, there seems to be a basic shift in society from a **patrilineal** to a **matrilineal** family organization (Segalen, 1986);

matrilineal: counting descent through one's mother

patrilineal: counting descent through one's father

in other words, kinship is being counted through the mother rather than the father. In "traditional" families, patrilineal descent is reflected in the wife's taking the husband's name at marriage and in the desire to give birth to a son "to carry on the family name." When a couple divorces, custody of the children is usually awarded to the mother. The number of mothers with custody is swelled by the number of never-married mothers. When mothers remarry, children acquire a new father figure with a new set of relatives; they may even take his name. Through all the family changes the children experience, the connection with the mother's extended family is the most enduring. This trend may be lessened through the growing number of fathers gaining sole or shared custody of their children.

Technology and Family Life

In the 1940s and 1950s, forecasters predicted a robot in every 21st-century home to look after all the drudgery—dishes, meals, cleaning, laundry. In spite of the influx of dishwashers, automatic washers and dryers, central and robotic vacuums, and microwaves, this prediction has not been fulfilled. As we have seen, technology, including contraceptives, reproductive technologies, and other medical breakthroughs, has had and will continue to have a great impact on families. For example, researchers are uncovering an increasing number of markers for genetic disorders. There are reports of advances in genetic engineering that may provide cures for currently untreatable diseases. Yet these advances raise questions about who should know about the likelihood of hereditary disorders, as well as the ethics of cloning and experimentation on human embryos (Galvin, 2006; Glover, 2006).

One of the most profound influences on families is in the area of communications technology. We have already discussed how electronic media have made it possible for people to work from home and how children are affected by these media. But there is concern over the effect of these technologies on family relationships. Some individuals spend long hours surfing the Internet or engaging in discussions, some quite intimate, in online chat rooms and social media. Virtual dating offers many "perks" that real-life dating cannot, such as sexual encounters without fear of disease or pregnancy, anonymity, and, for some, a chance to cheat on a partner without ever leaving home(Jones, 2010). When this occurs, family relationships may suffer and fade through lack of interaction. Some individuals worry that the growth in the use of computers, smartphones, and social media may undermine parents' authority because many children have more expertise than their parents (Bold, 2001). This situation is similar to that of immigrant families where children interpret the new language for their parents.

Yet communications technology can also help families keep in touch. Busy working parents use cellphones and tablets so that they can always be available if their children need them and to check up on their children's activities. Text messaging, email, and social media sites, such as Facebook and Twitter, keep distant family members in contact. There are even reports of virtual family dinners taking place through videoconferencing (Babwin, 2006). Because of its growth, communications technology will continue to affect families into the future. What that effect will be depends on the people who use it and how they choose to use it.

The Family in Society

While we often think of the family as a personal and special kind of relationship, it is also a fundamental social institution. Families influence society and are influenced by social changes. For example, when the divorce law was revised to make divorce easier, there was an immediate and dramatic increase in the number of divorces. People have pressured governments to provide Employment Insurance, free education, and subsidized childcare. We will look at the impact of governments on changing definitions of the family and on the rights and responsibilities of family members. We will also consider other areas where we can expect government influence.

The Supreme Court ruling that same-sex marriage is legal followed a growing number of provincial court decisions that banning such marriage violates the *Charter of Rights and Freedoms* ("Supreme Court Approves," 2004). The legislation came into effect on July 20, 2005 (Department of Justice, 2009b). Many laws affecting families are based on a "traditional" marriage model. As the above ruling suggests, though, this standard no longer fits many close relationships among adults. Some benefits, such as the dependent spouse deduction for income tax, have been revised to include the new definition of spouse and also to include common-law partners (Revenue Canada, 2010).

Governments at all levels have changed regulations to increase the self-sufficiency of individuals, for example through changes in eligibility for Employment Insurance and welfare and through the establishment of workfare programs. The term "welfare wall" refers to barriers that discourage the transition from dependence on social assistance to independent work (Starkey, 2006). Recent governments have moved away from universal benefits and shifted funds to help selected groups of people, such as poor families with children. Two examples are the clawback that reclaims part of the Old Age Security pension from more affluent individuals and the shift from a family allowance paid for each child to the Child Tax Credit, which provides larger sums to poorer families. There is also increased emphasis on financial responsibility for family members.

Parents are still expected to be financially responsible for their children. To be eligible for social assistance, even single parents are considered to be employable and required to actively seek and accept reasonable employment (Human Resources and Skills Development Canada, 2006). The responsibility does not end with family breakup. After a divorce, regardless of which parent has custody, both parents are legally responsible for the financial support of their children, in keeping with their means (Divorce in Canada, 2009). As family forms become more diverse, issues such as these will become more commonplace. The government and the legal system will need to respond with clear policies. Changes in the family thus drive changes in legislation and social policy.

The efforts of federal and provincial governments to reduce deficits are placing more responsibility on family members for the physical care of relatives. Since most adults are employed, this need conflicts with workplace demands. Quebec has offered universal childcare subsidies since 1997, and the federal government introduced the Universal Child Care Benefit in 2006 (Government of Canada, 2009; Lefebvre, 2004). But with an aging population, the concern might shift from childcare to eldercare. If families are to cope, they will need more community services for the elderly, such as home nursing and relief help (Neysmith, 2003). A Senate committee found that the cost of home care is significantly less than the cost of care in a facility (Senate of Canada, 2002). However, there is no national program to support caregivers. New policies will be needed to provide financial and other kinds of support for those who care for older family members (Keefe et al., 2007).

We can expect more official control in other areas too. First, in spite of the *Assisted Human Reproduction Act*, grey areas in assisted human reproduction will continue to arise. Changes in laws will undoubtedly be recommended to deal with these issues. Second, we can expect society to be more involved in regulating particular family relationships. Increasingly, homes are developing "see-through walls." Children are cared for by non-family members either in or out of the children's homes. Social services are available to seniors in their own homes. Concern that many children and adults alike are receiving substandard care from family members or other caregivers is growing. In October 2008, the federal government launched a national public awareness campaign to raise awareness and change the attitudes of Canadians about elder abuse (National Seniors Council, 2009).

Time to Review

1. What are the implications of an aging population for the future?
2. What forms will families likely take in the future and what changes in roles will follow?
3. How does technology affect the family?
4. How do government policies affect families?

The Unknowns

Any predictions made so far have been based on statistical trends in Canadian society, on current social activism, and on recent laws and budgetary policies. These do not take into account many unknown influences that can also produce profound changes. These include global factors such as widespread economic recessions, wars, or natural disasters (including epidemics such as AIDS and new strains of influenza and antibiotic-resistant TB). Political action within Canada has already affected families and will do so in the future. The direction of these changes is difficult to predict many years ahead. Immigration policies have influenced the age, family composition, origin, and occupation of various segments of the population, and will continue to do so. Social and economic policies at the federal, provincial, and municipal levels determine what services are available to families and who can benefit from them. Taxation and income distribution programs, such as tax benefits and clawbacks, will also affect the disposable income of families. Finally, it is impossible to predict the decisions of individuals and their families. Such decisions can have an enormous influence on society.

Will the Family Survive?

Rather than worrying about whether the family will disappear, it is far more productive to understand how and why the family is changing. Families are becoming more diverse in response to changing social circumstances. The "traditional" nuclear family system of parents and their dependent children has been the predominant family form in Western societies only since the Industrial Revolution. As we enter a new era, we can expect further changes to this kind of family.

In Chapter 1, we saw that the family fulfills five functions—reproduction, socialization, social placement, economic support, and emotional support. Yet over time and across cultures, there is change and movement in how these functions are met. Signs of the movement in current Canadian society are numerous. One is the growth of secular individualism, whereby people gradually abandon religious beliefs and put an emphasis on self-fulfillment. There is a focus on the individual couple rather than on the wider family and community (Popenoe, 2007). For many, there has been a movement away from marriage (a public event that includes the community) toward a pact between individuals (a private event) that does not require legal or religious sanction.

In keeping with this shift, fewer families provide the services that were seen as their responsibility in the past: the care of sick, elderly, disabled, and mentally ill members. This sense of responsibility has never totally disappeared, perhaps because of a shortage of services and specific government policies. But more and more, even the functions the family has kept, such as the socialization of children or the financial support of family members, are shared with people and institutions outside the family. Childcare centres, babysitters, and schools all share the responsibilities of raising children; governments provide pensions and family benefits. However, as the government and other institutions take over many of the functions of the family, some have started to ask, "Who needs the family?" (Canada Free Press, 2013).

Will the family survive? The answer depends on how we define the family. If we consider the traditional patriarchal family, the answer may well be no. However, its disappearance is by no means certain. As we saw in the opening quotations, at the end of the 19th century the American press looked with alarm at the state of the family. The concerns sound familiar: the divorce rate was rising; middle-class women were having fewer children; women's social position was changing as they attended university and demanded the vote; and morals were declining (Lasch, 1979). Yet following World War II, there was a blossoming of "traditional" family values (Dumas & Peron, 1992). Indeed, most people still hold this traditional family as their ideal, though they may not attain it (Bibby, 2004–05; Daly, 2004b). Families are reshaped during periods of major social and economic change. We are now living through a transition to a global society that is undoing the breadwinner–homemaker model of the family. Such a transition is stressful both to individuals and to society itself. In time, there will be some sort of compromise where we reach a balance between old and new values (Skolnick, 2006).

Throughout history, the family has taken many forms, but it has never disappeared. The family thus far has been the most efficient way of meeting many individual and social needs. Individual needs include economic needs and the need for intimate relationships; social needs encompass producing the next generation and socializing all members. As long as we have groups of people who perform these functions, we will have families. How we carry out these functions will reflect the incredible creativity of the human spirit.

Dr. Kerry Daly, of the University of Guelph, suggests that we are caught up in negative stories—that the family is fragile and declining. He encourages us to think of the positive. First, families are a force for justice, for example openness in adoption and the growing rights of gay and lesbian couples and their children. Second, families act as an anchor of care. Whether they provide the care themselves or arrange for others to do so, members rely on and take responsibility for each other (Daly, 2004b). The family has proven itself highly adaptable. Its varying forms enable us to meet the challenges of a constantly changing society (Erera, 2002). Remember Adela and Sara from the opening of Chapter 1? Adela described to Sara how her own family has changed, adapted, and diversified in ways she probably never would have imagined. One day, Sara will probably be sitting with her own granddaughter and describing similar changes. There is no case study for this final chapter—it is yet to be lived and written by you, the reader.

Although the family of the future may be quite different from what we have known to date—yes, the family will survive.

SUMMARY

What Are the Implications of an Aging Population for the Future?

We can expect an older population as the result of demographic changes such as the aging baby boom generation and a reduced birth rate. Medical advances also result in more people living longer. There may, however, be a financial crisis in providing care and support for the elderly.

What Forms Will Families Likely Take in the Future and What Changes in Roles Will Follow?

Family types will probably become more varied in the future. More people will live alone. Unmarried cohabitation will likely continue to delay marriage and child-bearing. Children will live in various family settings. Given the number of immigrants from non-European countries, new traditions will be brought to Canada. Family roles will change to accommodate family variety. There will be greater role flexibility between the sexes as both husband and wife work outside the home. Children will have more parent figures. Due to the high divorce rate and the number of single parents, there appears to be a basic shift from a patrilineal to a matrilineal society.

How Does Technology Affect the Family?

The explosion in communication technologies will loosen relationships or keep family members in closer touch, depending on how they are used.

How Do Government Policies Affect Families?

Governments will be more involved in the family by defining rights and responsibilities, regulating reproductive technologies, and supervising family relationships. Government programs and support will arise in response to changes in the family. Government policies can sometimes have significant and unintended impacts on families. Finally, unpredictable factors, such as economic trends, wars, or natural disasters, may also deeply affect the family. Government actions that affect immigration and income distribution policies are difficult to forecast.

Will the Family Survive?

Although the traditional nuclear family may not survive, the family will adapt to meet new challenges.

Class Assignments

1. What solutions are available to increase the proportion of young people in the Canadian population? Explain the benefits and drawbacks of each of the choices.
2. What is meant by "a shift from a patrilineal to a matrilineal society"? Describe the possible impact of this shift on institutions such as schools, daycare centres, and the workplace.
3. Choose a communications technology such as Facebook or Skype. Research how this technology has affected family relationships and present your findings.

Personal Assignments

The following assignments are designed to help you explore your own feelings and opinions:

1. In the year 2035, what do you expect your family situation will be? Give reasons for your answer.
2. Do you think that the family will disappear? Give reasons for your answer.
3. What do you (or others you know) think of electronic media? Do you believe it helps or harms the family? Explain.

Major Sociological Perspectives

Different Perspectives

A theory is a systematic way of seeing the world. It should be logical, consistent with empirical data, generalizable, and practical. A theoretical perspective refers to a general way of understanding and interpreting social reality. In sociology, there are four major theoretical perspectives. In recent years, new perspectives have also developed. Each makes different assumptions about the fundamental character of social life. No perspective is "better" or "right"; each should be used to look at society in a different way. In fact, each perspective has developed as a reflection of the social norms and values at the time and in the society from which it emerged.

One important distinction between the various perspectives lies in their level of analysis. Theories that focus on large-scale social forces are *macrosociological*; those that focus on the details of interaction between people are *microsociological*.

Auguste Comte (1798–1857) has been called the father of sociology. He coined the term "sociology" to refer to the study of social groups. He believed that, by using scientific means, the laws of society could be discovered. Ever since, sociologists have followed Comte's example and made sociology the scientific study of human social behaviour.

Currently, there are four major schools of sociology: (1) structural functionalism, (2) conflict theory, (3) symbolic interactionism, and (4) feminist theories. We will look at the main ideas of each of these theories and at some of the people who helped develop them. The descriptions are based on the writings of Brym,

:, Nelson, Guppy, and McCormick (2003); Henslin, Glenday, Pupo, and Duffy 010); Lindsay, Beach, and Ravelli (2009); and Macionis, Jansson, and Benoit 2008).

Structural Functionalism

Main Ideas

1. Structural functionalism is a macro-level perspective.
2. Society is a complex structure made up of many interrelated parts.
3. Each part of the structure has a function—it does something to help the system keep running.
4. All the parts are connected, so that changes in one part will affect the other parts.
5. Institutions exist and persist because they help society survive.
6. Societies require solidarity. Mechanical solidarity, typical of traditional, pre-industrial societies, is based on being alike. Organic solidarity, typical of modern industrial societies, is based on interdependence and specialization.
7. Lack of solidarity leads to anomie, a condition of instability where individuals do not feel connected to their society.
8. When looking at society from this perspective, ask, "What is the purpose?"

Critique: Structural functionalism overemphasizes stability. It is good at explaining why societies are the way they are, but not so good at explaining social change.

Structural Functionalist Sociologists

Émile Durkheim (1858–1917). Durkheim, a Frenchman, was the first professor of sociology. Through his efforts to develop research methods, sociology came to be accepted as a scientific discipline. He stated that sociology was the study of what he called *social facts*, or the structures, values, and norms found in any society. While they exist outside of any individual, they become internalized and govern a person's behaviour. In a landmark study, Durkheim showed that suicide is related to social facts. Rather than asking which individuals commit suicide, Durkheim identified certain groups whose members were more likely to commit suicide. For example, if you are male, Protestant, or unmarried, you are more likely to commit suicide than someone who is female, Roman Catholic, or married.

Robert K. Merton (1910–2003). Merton focused on the functions that institutions perform in society. He identified three functions that social structures may have. Manifest functions are the recognized and intended functions. Latent functions are often unrecognized and unintended. Dysfunctions disrupt the smooth operation of society. For example, one manifest function of nuclear families is to reproduce the next generation. A latent function of nuclear families is that they make mobility easier, so such families can move around more. Nuclear families may be dysfunctional when they discourage women from entering the workforce.

Conflict Theory

Main Ideas

1. Conflict theory is a macro-level perspective.
2. The economic organization of a society affects the class structure, institutions, and even the values and beliefs of that society.
3. Conflict and inequality originate from struggles for economic resources (property), power, or prestige, or a combination of these.
4. Groups in society are engaged in a continuous power struggle for scarce resources.
5. Social structures exist because they benefit a particular group. Inequality is built into the social structure.
6. Conflict is always present within and between social groups—this is the normal state of society. Change and tension are normal and inevitable.
7. Lack of control leads to alienation.
8. When looking at society from this perspective, ask, "Who benefits?"

Critique: Conflict theory ignores that there is often much consensus and cooperation in social behaviour.

Conflict Theory Sociologists

Karl Marx (1818–1883) and **Friedrich Engels** (1820–1895). Marx and Engels jointly wrote several books in which they outlined the conflict theory of society. Two of their most famous books are *The Communist Manifesto* and *Wage Labour and Capital.* Marx and Engels argued that class struggle is the key to understanding all human history and that social change occurs through conflict and struggle. In any society, one small group controls the means of production and exploits those who do not. Marx and Engels wanted people to understand their social world in order to gain control over that world. Friedrich Engels also wrote *The Origin of the Family, Private Property and the State,* in which he presented an explanation for the rise and popularity of the monogamous nuclear family.

   Ralf Dahrendorf (1929–2009). Dahrendorf adopted Marx's conflict perspective but enlarged its scope. While Marx and Engels focused on conflict in the economic sphere, Dahrendorf saw conflict as inherent in all relationships that involve hierarchy and authority.

Symbolic Interactionism

Main Ideas

1. Symbolic interactionism is a micro-level perspective.
2. It focuses on small groups and person-to-person interaction rather than on large-scale social structures.
3. Society is the sum of the interactions of individuals and groups, and how they make sense of these interactions; reality is socially constructed.

4. If we are to understand human behaviour, we must look at what it means to the individual. People define for themselves the meaning of each situation and interaction.

5. We each occupy certain social statuses. Roles are associated with each status, and we are judged by others according to how well we play our roles.

6. Symbols are the basis of communication. Through communication, we can have orderly social relationships.

7. An important aspect of the symbolic interactionist perspective is the Thomas theorem, which states, "Situations that are defined as real become real in their consequences."

8. When looking at society from this perspective, ask, "What does it mean?"

Critique: Symbolic interactionism often underestimates the influence of outside forces on the individual.

Symbolic Interactionist Sociologists

Charles Horton Cooley (1864–1933). Cooley is most famous for his concept of the looking-glass self, according to which we imagine how we appear to other people and imagine what they think of us. We react to these imaginings, for example with pride or embarrassment. What we do is governed by how we believe others see us. The self develops only as we interact with other people and with society as a whole.

George Herbert Mead (1863–1931). Mead's central idea was that human beings can adapt to their environment if they have symbols, such as language, in common. Through his interest in how a baby learned the rules of its society, he understood that learning takes place through interaction with others, especially through play and games. Because reality is created through people's interactions, it is always changing. People invent new roles and new meanings. We exist as ourselves only through interaction with others. Mead also explained that each individual is both "I" and "me," with the "I" being the private self who observes and thinks, and the "me" being the social self who is aware of being an object to other people.

Feminist Theories

Main Ideas

1. Feminist theories use both macro and micro perspectives.

2. Physical and biological differences between the sexes have resulted in different social roles for each sex.

3. While "sex" refers to the biological differences, "gender" refers to the different roles that members of each sex are expected to perform.

4. Gender roles are socially created and reinforced.

5. Social systems are almost always patriarchal (favourable to men). In the relationship between the sexes, masculine roles are dominant and valued, while feminine roles are subordinate and devalued.

6. Feminist theories first emerged as critiques of the traditional (male-dominated/androcentric) theories and methodologies. Research from the feminist perspective has brought the personal problems of women (violence, poverty, sexism) into the public forum.

7. There are several variations of feminist theories, including Marxist, liberal, and radical; however, they all share certain fundamental assumptions.
8. When looking at society from this perspective, ask, "How does this benefit men (and disadvantage women)?"

Critique: Feminist theories have been accused of being biased and overly simplistic—not all social relations are based on gender inequality.

Feminist Theories Sociologists

Harriet Martineau (1802–1876). Martineau has been called the first female sociologist. In 1853, she translated the writings of Comte into English, making them accessible to a whole new group of social thinkers. She wrote about slavery in the United States and the exploitation of factory workers; she also promoted the standing of women.

Margrit Eichler (1942–...) Eichler is one of the best-known Canadian sociologists. She has written on feminist methodology and family policy. Her writings have resulted in a redefinition of work to include unpaid housework.

Recent Theories

In recent years, new perspectives have emerged, and while none has yet replaced the major theories, they offer new and interesting insights into many social phenomena, including studies of the family.

Other Feminist Theories

Liberal Feminism

1. Liberal feminists focus on the laws and customs that are detrimental to women.
2. They seek reform through legitimate means to address the problems of inequality.

Radical Feminism

1. Radical feminists believe that the patriarchal system of society is the cause of gender inequality.
2. They propose more fundamental and revolutionary changes than those proposed by liberal feminists.

Marxist Feminism

1. Marxist feminists share the Marxist view that social class is important in explaining inequality.
2. They argue that revolutionary change in the capitalist system is the only way to address inequality of both women and men.

Postmodernist Theory

Main Ideas

1. Science does not lead to the "truth" about the social world; discovering an objective truth is impossible and unachievable.
2. Subjective knowledge is the dominant form of discourse and alters the relationship between the observer and the observed.
3. Uses both micro- and macro-level observation.
4. When looking at society from this perspective, ask, "How can we understand societies while rejecting the traditional theories and methods of the social sciences and our assumptions about human nature?"

Critical Race Theory

Main Ideas

1. Was developed in American law schools in the 1980s.
2. Racism is deeply engrained in the culture and systems of North American society.
3. These power structures are based on white privilege and white supremacy, which perpetuate the marginalization of people of colour.
4. When looking at society from this perspective, ask, "What would society look like if people of colour were more involved in decision making?

Queer Theory

Main Ideas

1. Emerged in the early 1990s, in part as a reaction to the feminist argument that women are a group with common characteristics and interests.
2. Challenges the idea of fixed identity and views sex, gender, and desire as a continuum.
3. The social system is not just patriarchal; it also reflects a heterosexual norm and a dichotomy of the sexes.
4. When looking at society from this perspective, ask, "How does this reflect the interests of heterosexual men?"

These theories have shaped much thinking about the family. For example, the ecological, family systems, and family development theories draw on the system aspect of structural functionalism. The exchange, family systems, and developmental theories make use of some of the concepts of symbolic interactionism. All are concerned about conflict within the family, although they have different ways of studying it. The family has long been a central topic of study for many feminist scholars, while more recent theories are leading us to examine issues within families from different perspectives.

REFERENCES

AARP. (2005a). *Boomers at midlife 2004: The AARP life stage study, wave 3: Executive summary.* Washington, DC: Author. Retrieved from http://assets.aarp.org/rgcenter/general/boomers_midlife_2004_1.pdf

AARP. (2005b). *Sexuality at midlife and beyond: 2004 update of attitudes and behaviors.* Washington, DC: Author. Retrieved from http://assets.aarp.org/rgcenter/general/2004_sexuality.pdf

AARP. (2010). *Sex, romance, and relationships: AARP survey of midlife and older adults.* Washington. DC: Author. Retrieved from http://assets.aarp.org/rgcenter/general/srr_09.pdf

Abada, T., Hou, F., & Ram, B. (2008). *Group differences in educational attainment among the children of immigrants* (Catalogue No. 11F0019M, no. 308). Ottawa: Statistics Canada.

Abbott, E. (1999). *A history of celibacy.* Toronto: Harper Perennial Canada.

Abell, E., Dorr, K., & Guarino, A. (2003, November). *The effects of different living arrangements on the parenting practices of adolescent mothers.* Poster presentation at the annual conference of National Council on Family Relations, Vancouver, BC.

Abma, J. C., & Martinez, G. M. (2006). Childlessness among older women in the United States: Trends and profiles. *Journal of Marriage and Family, 68,* 1045–1056.

Aboriginal Affairs and Northern Development Canada. (2012, March 28). *Indian residential schools—key milestones.* Ottawa: Author. Retrieved from http://www.aadnc-aandc.gc.ca/eng/1332939430258/1332939552554

AbortionInCanada.ca. (2008). *History of abortion in Canada.* Retrieved from http://www.abortionincanada.ca/history

Acton, R. G., & During, S. (1990). The treatment of aggressive parents: An outline of a group treatment program. *Canada's Mental Health, 38*(2/3), 2–6.

Adams, O. B., & Nagnur, D. N. (1988). *Marriage, divorce and mortality: A life table analysis for Canada and regions.* Ottawa: Statistics Canada.

Ad Hoc Federal-Provincial-Territorial Working Group Reviewing Spousal Abuse Policies and Legislation. (2003). *Final report.* Ottawa: Federal-Provincial-Territorial Ministers Responsible for Justice.

Adoption Council of Canada. (2005, May 27). *China leads adoption statistics for 2004.* Ottawa: Author. Retrieved from http://www.adoption.ca/news/050527stats04.htm

Adoption Council of Canada. (n.d.). *Myths and realities.* Ottawa: Author. Retrieved from http://www.adoption.ca/myths-and-realities

Adoptive Parents (n.d.). *Types of adoption.* Retrieved from http://adoptiveparents.ca/adopt101_typesofadoption4.shtml

Ahrons, C. R. (1999). Divorce: An unscheduled family transition.

In B. Carter & M. McGoldrick (Eds.), *The expanded family life cycle: Individual, family, and social perspectives* (3rd ed., pp. 381–398). Boston: Allyn & Bacon.

Air Canada. (2009). *Bereavement fares.* Retrieved from http://www.aircanada.com/en/travelinfo/before/bereavement.html

Aldous, J. (1996). *Family careers: Rethinking the developmental perspective.* Thousand Oaks, CA: Sage.

Aldwin, C. M. (2007). *Stress, coping, and development: An integrative perspective* (2nd ed.). New York: Guilford.

Allen, E. S., Baucom, D. H., Burnett, C. K., Epstein, N., & Rankin-Esquer, L. A. (2001). Decision-making power, autonomy, and communication in remarried spouses compared with first-married spouses. *Family Relations, 50,* 326–334.

Allen, K. R. (2007). Ambiguous loss after lesbian couples with children break up: A case for same-gender divorce. *Family Relations, 56,* 175–183.

Almeida, D. M., Serido, J., & McDonald, D. (2006). Daily life stressors of early and late baby boomers. In S. K. Whitbourne & S. L. Willis (Eds.), *The baby boomers grow up: Contemporary perspectives on midlife* (pp. 165–183). Mahwah, NJ: Lawrence Erlbaum.

Amato, P. R. (2000). The consequences of divorce for adults and children. *Journal of Marriage and the Family, 62,* 1269–1287.

Amato, P. R. (2005). The impact of family formation change on the cognitive, social, and emotional well-being of the next generation. *The Future of Children, 15*(2), 75–96. Retrieved from http://www.futureofchildren.org

Amato, P. R., Booth, A., Johnson, D. R., & Rogers, S. J. (2007). *Alone together: How marriage in America is changing.* Cambridge, MA: Harvard University Press.

Amato, P. R., & Fowler, F. (2002). Parenting practices, child adjustment, and family diversity. *Journal of Marriage and Family, 64,* 703–716.

Amato, P. R., & Hohmann-Marriott, B. (2007). A comparison of high- and low-distress marriages that end in divorce. *Journal of Marriage and Family, 69,* 621–638.

Amato, P. R., Meyers, C. E., & Emery, R. E. (2009). Changes in nonresident father–child contact from 1976 to 2002. *Family Relations, 58,* 41–53.

Ambert, A.-M. (2005a). *Cohabiting and marriage: How they are related.* Ottawa: Vanier Institute of the Family.

Ambert, A.-M. (2005b). *Same-sex couples and same-sex parent families: Relationships, parenting, and issues of marriage* (Rev.). Ottawa: Vanier Institute of the Family. Retrieved from http://www.vifamily.ca

Ambert, A.-M. (2006). *One parent families: Characteristics, causes, consequences, and issues.* Ottawa: Vanier Institute of the Family.

Ambert, A.-M, (2009). *Divorce: Facts, causes, and consequences* (3rd ed.). Ottawa: Vanier Institute of the Family. Retrieved from http://www.vifamily.ca/library/cft/divorce_09.pdf

American Academy of Pediatrics. (2011). Media use by children younger than 2 years. *Pediatrics, 128,* 1040–1045. doi:10.1542/peds.2011-1753

American Anthropological Association. (1998, May 17). *American Anthropological Association statement on "race."* Retrieved from http://www.aaanet.org/stmts/racepp.htm

American College of Pediatricians. (2007). *Corporal punishment: A scientific review of its use in discipline.* Retrieved from http://www.acpeds.org

American Psychological Association. (1997). *The road to burnout.* Retrieved from http://helping.apa.org/work/stress6.html

Ames, B. D., Brosi, W. A., & Damiano-Teixeira, K. M. (2006). "I'm just glad my three jobs could be during the day": Women and work in a rural community. *Family Relations, 55,* 119–131.

Amiel, B. (1987, June). No sex please, we're British. *Chatelaine,* 147–148.

Anderson, C. (2003). The diversity, strengths, and challenges of single-parent households. In F. Walsh (Ed.), *Normal family processes: Growing diversity and complexity* (3rd ed., pp. 121–152). New York: Guilford.

Anderson, E. A., & Koblinsky, S. A. (1995). Homeless policy: The need to speak to families. *Family Relations, 44,* 13–18.

Anderson, J. M., Waxler-Morrison, N., Richardson, E., Herbert, C., & Murphy, M. (1990). Conclusion: Delivering culturally sensitive health care. In N. Waxler-Morrison, J. M. Anderson, & E. Richardson (Eds.), *Cross-cultural caring: A handbook for health professionals* (pp. 245–267). Vancouver: UBC Press.

Anderson, K. L. (2002). Perpetrator or victim? Relationships between intimate partner violence and well-being. *Journal of Marriage and Family, 64,* 851–863.

Anderson, K. L. (2008). Is partner violence worse in the context of control? *Journal of Marriage and Family, 70,* 1157–1168.

Anderson, L. (2012, July). From rose-coloured glasses to reality. *Healthcare Quarterly, 15*(Special Issue), 18–25.

Anderssen, E. (2009, June 6). Salma's prom night. *Globe and Mail,* pp. A1, A10–A11.

Anderssen, E., & McIlroy, A. (2004, April 10). Quebec distinct in nursery too, poll finds. *Globe and Mail,* pp. A1, A5.

Andrews, L. B. (1999, March 28). The sperminator. *New York Times Magazine,* 62–65.

Appleblatt, A. (1976). *Saskatchewan and the Ku Klux Klan.* Retrieved from http://www.usask.ca/education/ideas/tplan/sslp/kkk.htm

Arboleda-Flórez, J., Holley, H. L., & Crisanti, A. (1996). *Mental illness and violence: Proof or stereotype?* Ottawa: Health Canada.

Archer, S. (1985). Career and/or family: The identity process for adolescent girls. *Youth and Society, 16,* 289–314.

Armstrong, P., & Armstrong, H. (1987). The conflicting demands of "work" and "home." *Family matters* (pp. 113–140). Toronto: Methuen.

Arnett, J. J. (2007). Socialization in emerging adulthood: From family to the wider world, from socialization to self-socialization. In J. E. Grusec & P. D. Hastings (Eds.), *Handbook of socialization: Theory and research* (pp. 208–231). New York: Guilford.

Arnett, J. J. (2011). Emerging adulthood(s): The cultural psychology of a new life stage. In L. A. Jensen (Ed.), *Bridging cultural and developmental approaches to psychology: New syntheses in theory, research, and policy* (pp. 255–275). New York: Oxford University Press.

Arnup, K. (1989). "Mothers just like others": Lesbians, divorce, and child custody in Canada. *Canadian Journal of Women and the Law, 3,* 18–32.

Aronson, M. K., & Weiner, M. B. (2007). *Aging parents, aging children: How to stay sane and survive.* Lanham, MD: Rowman and Littlefield.

Artis, J. E., & Pavalko, E. K. (2003). Explaining the decline in women's household labor: Individual change and cohort differences. *Journal of Marriage and Family, 65,* 746–761.

Assisted Human Reproduction Canada. (2009). *Legislation, regulations and guidelines.* Retrieved from http://www.ahrc-pac.gc.ca/index.php?lang=eng

Assisted Human Reproduction Canada. (2012, August 24). *Closure of Assisted Human Reproduction Canada.* Retrieved from http://www.ahrc-pac.gc.ca/v2/index-eng.php

Aston, C. (2007). Spousal homicide narratives, 1997–2005. In L. Ogrodnik (Ed.), *Family violence in Canada: A statistical profile 2007* (Catalogue No. 85-224-XIE, pp. 16–17). Ottawa: Statistics Canada. Retrieved from http://www.statscan.gc.ca

Atkins, D. C., & Kessell, D. E. (2008). Religiousness and infidelity: Attendance, but not faith and prayer, predict marital infidelity. *Journal of Marriage and Family, 70,* 407–418.

Atkinson, N., Ermter, A., & Velasco, A. (2003, August 14). The *fab* fairy wedding guide. *fab: The Gay Scene Magazine,* 13–15, 17–18, 21–22, 24, 26, 29–30.

Attar-Schwartz, S., Tan, J.-P., Buchanan, A., Flouri, E., & Griggs, J. (2009). Grandparenting and adolescent adjustment in two-parent biological, lone-parent, and step-families. *Journal of Family Psychology, 23,* 67–75.

Austin, L. (2004, Spring). Multiracial youth in care. *The Connection.* Retrieved from http://www.casanet.org/library/foster-care/multiracial-%5Bconnection-04%5D.htm

Average wedding cost (2005–2009). Retrieved from http://www.costofwedding.com

Avellar, S., & Smock, P. J. (2005). The economic consequences of the dissolution of cohabiting unions. *Journal of Marriage and Family, 67,* 315–327.

Avis, N. E., & Crawford, S. (2006). Menopause: Recent research findings. In S. K. Whitbourne & S. L. Willis (Eds.), *The baby boomers grow up: Contemporary perspectives on midlife* (pp. 75–109). Mahwah, NJ: Lawrence Erlbaum.

Azoulay, D. (2001, February/March). Only the lonely. *The Beaver,* 35–41.

Babbie, E., & Benaquisto, L. (2010). *Fundamentals of social research* (2nd Canadian ed.). Toronto: Nelson Education.

Babwin, D. (2006, December 24). Mom in Chicago can eat with son in Yuma via virtual family dinner. *Arizona Daily Star,* p. A9.

Baby bonus program works as Quebec birth rate increases. (1990, July 17). *Toronto Star,* p. A10.

Bailey, M. (2004, January). Regulation of cohabitation and marriage in Canada. *Law and Policy, 26*(1), 153–175. doi:10.1111/j.0265-8240.2004.00166.x

Bailey, M. (2007). Polygamy and plural marriage. *Les ateliers de l'éthique, 2*(1), 18–22. Retrieved from http://www.creum.umontreal.ca/IMG/pdf_04_Vol.2N1_Bailey.pdf

Bainbridge, D., Krueger, P., Lohfeld, L., & Brazil, K. (2009, July). Stress processes in caring for an end-of-life family member: Application of a theoretical model. *Aging & Mental Health 13*(4), 537–545.

Baines, B. (2007). Polygamy's challenge: Women, religion and the post-liberal state. *Les ateliers de l'éthique, 2*(1), 23–29. Retrieved from http://www.creum.umontreal.ca/IMG/pdf_04_Vol.2N1_Baines.pdf

Baker, A. J. L. (2007). *Adult children of parental alienation syndrome: Breaking the ties that bind.* New York: W. W. Norton.

Baker, M. (1988). *Aging in Canadian society: A survey.* Toronto: McGraw-Hill Ryerson.

Baker, M. (1995). *Canadian family policies: Cross-national comparisons.* Toronto: University of Toronto Press.

Baker, M. (2001). *Families: Labour and love.* Vancouver: UBC Press.

Baker, M. (2007). *Choices and constraints in family life.* Don Mills, ON: Oxford University Press.

Baker, M., Gruber, J., & Milligan, K. (2008, April). Universal child care, maternal labor supply and family well-being. *Journal of Political Economy, 118,* 709–745.

Bala, N. (1999). *Legal responses to domestic abuse.* Retrieved from http://www.familylawcentre.com/ccbaladomviolence.html

Bala, N. (2004). *Controversy over couples in Canada: The evolution of marriage & other interdependent relationships.* Retrieved from http://qsilver.queensu.ca/law/papers/evolutionapril.htm

Balakrishnan, T. R., Lapierre-Adamcyk, E., & Krotki, K. J. (1993). *Family and childbearing in Canada: A demographic analysis.* Toronto: University of Toronto Press.

Baltes, P. B., Reese, H. W., & Nesselroade, J. R. (1977). *Lifespan developmental psychology: Introduction to research methods.* Monterey, CA: Brooks/Cole.

Bancroft, L., & Silverman, J. G. (2002). *The batterer as parent: Addressing the impact of domestic violence on family dynamics.* Thousand Oaks, CA: Sage.

Bandy, T., & Moore, K. A. (2008, August). *The parent–child relationship: A family strength.* Retrieved from http://www.childtrends.org/Files//Child_Trends_2008_08_08_FS_ParentChild.pdf

Bannerjee, R., & Robson, W. B. P. (2009). *Faster, younger, richer? The fond hope and sobering reality of immigration's impact on Canada's demographic and economic future.* Toronto: C. D. Howe Institute. Retrieved from http://www.cdhowe.org/pdf/commentary_291.pdf

Baptiste, D. R., Tolou-Shams, M., Miller, S., Mcbride, C., & Paikoff, R. (2007). Determinants of parental monitoring and preadolescent sexual risk situations among African American families living in urban public housing. *Journal of Child and Family Studies, 16,* 261–274. doi:10.1007/s10826-006-9083-4

Barker, J. C., Herdt, G., & de Vries, B. (2006). Social support in the lives of lesbians and gay men at midlife and later. *Sexual Research & Social Policy, 3*(2), 1–23.

Barnes, G. M., Hoffman, J. H., Welte, J. W., Farrell, M. P., & Dintcheff, B. S. (2006). Effect of parental monitoring and peer deviance on substance abuse and delinquency. *Journal of Marriage and Family, 68,* 1084–1104.

Barrette, J. (2008). Work/family balance: What do we really know? Ottawa: University of Ottawa Telfer School of Management and the Vanier Institute of the Family.

Barnett, L. (2008). *The "spanking" law: Section 43 of the* Criminal Code. PRB 05-10E. Ottawa: Library of Parliament. Retrieved from http://www2.parl.gc.ca/Content/LOP/ResearchPublications/prb0510-e.pdf

Barnett, M. A., & The Family Life Project Key Investigators. (2008). Mother and grandmother parenting in low-income, three-generation rural households. *Journal of Marriage and Family, 70,* 1241–1257.

Barnett, O., Miller-Perrin, C. L., & Perrin, R. D. (2005). *Family violence across the lifespan: An introduction* (2nd ed.). Thousand Oaks, CA: Sage.

Barnes, S. F. (2010). *Sex at midlife and beyond.* Retrieved from http://calbooming.sdsu.edu/documents/SexatMidlife.pdf

Barnett, R. C., & Gareis, K. C. (2006). Parental after-school stress and psychological well-being. *Journal of Marriage and Family, 68,* 101–108.

Barraket, J., & Henry-Waring, M. S. (2008). Getting it on(line): Sociological perspectives on e-dating. *Journal of Sociology, 44*(2), 149–165.

Barret, R. L., & Robinson, B. E. (2000). *Gay fathers: Encouraging the hearts of gay dads and their families* (2nd ed.). San Francisco: Jossey-Bass.

Barrett, F. M. (1980). Sexual experience, birth control usage, and sex education of unmarried Canadian university students: Changes between 1968 and 1978. *Archives of Sexual Behavior, 9,* 367–390.

Barrette, J. (2009, January 14). *Work/family balance: What do we really know?* Ottawa: Vanier Institute of the Family.

Barsky, L. (1990, January). 40 something: The new exciting middle age? *Chatelaine,* 33–37.

Bartholomae, S., & Fox, J. (2010). Economic stress and families. In S. J. Price, C. A. Price, & P. C. McKenry (Eds.), *Families & change: Coping with stressful events and transitions* (4th ed., pp. 185–209). Los Angeles: Sage.

Basavarajappa, K. G. (1998). *Living arrangements and residential crowding: The situation of older immigrants in Canada, 1991.* Ottawa: Statistics Canada.

Bass, S., Shields, M. K., & Behrman, R. (2004). Children, families, and foster care: Analysis and recommendations. *The Future of Children, 14*(1), 5–29. Retrieved from http://www.futureofchildren.org

Bassett, B. (n.d.). *Adam @ home.* Retrieved from http://www.ucomics.com/adamathome

Batshaw Youth and Family Centres. (2008). *To report is to protect.* Retrieved from http://www.batshaw.qc.ca/sites/default/files/filling-report-with-dyp-08-838-01A.pdf

Batson, C. D., Qian, Z., & Lichter, D. T. (2006). Interracial and inracial patterns of mate selection among America's diverse Black populations. *Journal of Marriage and Family, 68,* 658–672.

Baucom, D. H., Notarius, C. I., Burnett, C. K., & Haefner, P. (1990). Gender differences and sex-role identity in marriage. In F. D. Fincham & T. N. Bradbury (Eds.), *The psychology of marriage: Basic issues and applications* (pp. 150–171). New York: Guilford.

Baudoin, C., & Blaikie, H. (2009). *Surrogacy in Quebec: First legal test.* Retrieved from http://www.cfasonline.ca/

Baumrind, D. (1966). Effects of authoritative parental control on child behavior. *Child Development, 37*(4), 887–907.

Baumrind, D. (1980). New directions in socialization research. *American Psychologist, 35,* 639–652.

Baumrind, D. (1996). The discipline controversy revisited. *Family Relations, 45,* 404–414.

Baylis, F. (2011). Supreme Court of Canada decision on the Assisted Human Reproduction Act creates urgent need for action. *Journal of Obstetrics and Gynaecology in Canada, 33*(4), 317–319.

Baxter, J., Hewitt, B., & Haynes, M. (2008). Life course transitions and housework: Marriage, parenthood, and time on housework. *Journal of Marriage and Family, 70,* 259–272.

B.C. men plead not guilty to polygamy (2009, May 23). *National Post.* Retrieved from http://www.nationalpost.com/story.html?id=1622102

Beaton, J. M., Norris, J. E., & Pratt, W. (2003). Unresolved issues in adult children's marital relationships involving intergenerational problems. *Family Relations, 52,* 143–153.

Beatty, B. B., & Berdahl, L. (2011, May 16). Health care and Aboriginal seniors in urban Canada: Helping a neglected class. *International Indigenous Policy Journal, 2*(1), 1–16.

Beauchamp, D. (2007). Parents victimized by their children. In L. Ogrodnik (Ed.), *Family violence in Canada: A statistical profile 2007* (Catalogue No. 85-224-XIE, pp. 24, 31). Ottawa: Statistics Canada. Retrieved from http://www.statscan.gc.ca

Beaujot, R. (2000). *Earning and caring in Canadian families.* Peterborough, ON: Broadview Press.

Beaujot, R. (2004). *Delayed life transitions: Trends and implications.* Ottawa: Vanier Institute of the Family.

Beaupré, P. (2008). *I do . . . take two? Changes in intentions to remarry among divorced Canadians during the past 20 years* (Catalogue No. 89-630-X). Ottawa: Statistics Canada. Retrieved from http://www.statcan.gc.ca/pub/89-630-x/2008001/article/10659-eng.pdf

Beaupré, P., & Cloutier, E. (2007). *Navigating family transitions: Evidence from the General Social Survey* (Catalogue No. 89-625-XIE, no. 2). Ottawa: Statistics Canada. Retrieved from http://www.statcan.gc.ca

Beaupré, P., Dryburgh, H., & Wendt, M. (2010, June 8). *Making fathers "count."* Retrieved from http://www.abdads.ca/sites/default/files/Making%20Fathers%20Count.pdf

Beaupré, P., Turcotte, P., & Milan, A. (2006a, Winter). Junior comes back home: Trends and predictors of returning to the parental home. *Canadian Social Trends* (Statistics Canada Catalogue No. 11-008), 28–34.

Beaupré, P., Turcotte, P., & Milan, A. (2006b, Winter). When is junior moving out? Transitions from the parental home to independence. *Canadian Social Trends* (Statistics Canada Catalogue No. 11-008), 9–15.

Béchard, M. (2007). *Family structure by region, 2006* (Rev.) (Catalogue No. 89-625-XIE-001). Ottawa: Statistics

Canada. Retrieved from http://www.statcan.gc.ca/pub/89-625-x/89-625-x2007001.eng.pdf

Becker, G., Butler, A., & Nachtigall, R. D. (2005). Resemblance talk: A challenge for parents whose children were conceived with donor gametes in the US. *Social Science & Medicine, 61,* 1300–1309.

Begin, P., Casavant, L., Chenier, N. M., & Dupuis, J. (1999). *Homelessness.* Ottawa: Library of Parliament. Retrieved from http://www.parl.gc.ca/information/library/prbpubs/prb991-e.htm

Beigel, H. G. (1951). Romantic love. *American Sociological Review, 16,* 326–334.

Beiser, M., Dion, R., Gotowiec, A., Hyman, I., & Vu, N. (1995). Immigrant and refugee children in Canada. *Canadian Journal of Psychiatry, 40,* 67–72.

Beiser, M., Hou, F., Hyman, I., & Tousignant, M. (1998). *Growing up Canadian—A study of new immigrant children.* Ottawa: Human Resources Development Canada.

Bélanger, A., & Gilbert, S. (2003). The fertility of immigrant women and their Canadian born daughters. In A. Bélanger (Ed.), *Report on the demographic situation in Canada 2002: Current demographic analysis* (Catalogue No. 91-209-XPE, pp. 127–151). Ottawa: Statistics Canada.

Bélanger, A., & Malenfant, É. C. (2005, Winter). Ethnocultural diversity in Canada: Prospects for 2017. *Canadian Social Trends* (Statistics Canada Catalogue No. 11-008), 18–21.

Bélanger, A., & Malenfant, É. C., with Martel, L., Carrière, Y., Hicks, C., & Rowe, G. (2005). *Population projections of visible minority groups, Canada, provinces and regions 2001–2017* (Catalogue No. 91-541-XIE). Ottawa: Statistics Canada.

Bélanger, A., Martel, L., & Caron-Malenfant, É. (2005). *Population projections for Canada, provinces and territories 2005–2031* (Catalogue No. 91-520-XIE). Ottawa: Statistics Canada.

Bélanger, A., & Ouellet, G. (2002). A comparative study of recent trends in Canadian and American fertility. In A. Bélanger (Ed.), *Report on the demographic situation in Canada 2001* (Catalogue No. 91-209-XPE, pp. 107–136). Ottawa: Statistics Canada.

Belsky, J., & Kelly, J. (1994). *The transition to parenthood: How a first child changes a marriage.* New York: Delacorte.

Belsky, J., Lowe Vandell, D., Burchinal, M., Clarke-Stewart, K. A., McCartney, K., & Tresch Owen, M. (2007). Are there long-term effects of early child care? *Child Development, 78,* 681–701.

Bengston, V. L. (2001). Beyond the nuclear family: The increasing importance of multigenerational bonds. *Journal of Marriage and Family, 63,* 1–16.

Benzies, K., Tough, S., Tofflemire, K., Faber, A., & Newburn-Cook, C. (2003, November). *Timing of motherhood: Factors influencing women's decisions to delay childbearing.* Poster presentation at the annual conference of National Council on Family Relations, Vancouver, BC.

Berardo, F. M. (2001, December). Elder grief. *Family Focus,* F23–F24.

Berge, J. M., & Holm, K. E. (2007). Boundary ambiguity in parents with chronically ill children: Integrating theory and research. *Family Relations, 56,* 123–134.

Berger, D. M. (1980). Infertility: A psychiatrist's perspective. *Canadian Journal of Psychiatry, 25,* 553–559.

Bernard, A., & Li, C. (2006, July). *Death of a spouse: The impact on income for senior men and women* (Catalogue No. 11-621-MIE2006046). Ottawa: Statistics Canada. Retrieved from http://www.statcan.ca

Berns, R. M. (2013). *Child, family, school, community: Socialization and support* (9th ed.). Belmont, CA: Wadsworth.

Berry, J. W. (2005). Acculturation: Living successfully in two cultures. *International Journal of Intercultural Relations, 29*(6), 697–712.

Bert, S. C., Guner, B. M., Lanzi, R. G., & Centers for Prevention of Child Neglect. (2009). The influence of maternal history of abuse on parenting knowledge and behavior. *Family Relations, 58,* 176–187.

Bettinger, M. (2006). Polyamory and gay men: A family systems approach. In J. J. Bigner (Ed.), *An introduction to GLBT family studies* (pp. 161–181). New York: Haworth.

Bianchi, S. M., Robinson, J. P., & Milkie, M. A. (2006). *Changing rhythms of American family life*. New York: Russell Sage Foundation.

Bibby, R. W. (2001). *Canada's teens: Today, yesterday, and tomorrow*. Don Mills, ON: Stoddart.

Bibby, R. W. (2004–05, Winter). Future families: Surveying our hopes, dreams, and realities. *Transition*, 3–14.

Biblarz, T. J., & Stacey, J. (2010, February). How does the gender of parents matter? *Journal of Marriage and Family, 72,* 3–22. doi:10.1111/j.1741-3737.2009.00678.x

Bigner, J. J. (2006). Introduction. In J. J. Bigner (Ed.), *An introduction to GLBT studies* (pp. 1–2). New York: Haworth.

Births. (2000, October 18). *Hamilton Spectator*, C1.

Bissell, M. (2000). Socio-economic outcomes of teen pregnancy and parenthood. *Canadian Journal of Human Sexuality, 9,* 181–190.

Blacker, L. (1999). The launching phase of the life cycle. In B. Carter & M. McGoldrick (Eds.), *The expanded family life cycle: Individual, family, and social perspectives* (3rd ed., pp. 287–306). Boston: Allyn & Bacon.

Blackstock, C. (2006–07, Winter). Building on the multi-generational strength of First Nations communities. *Transition*, 7–10.

Blackstock, C. (2009). The occasional evil of angels: Learning from the experience of Aboriginal peoples and social work. *First Peoples Child & Family Review, 4*(1), 28–37. Retrieved from http://www.fncfcs/pubs/vol14num1/Blackstock_pp28.pdf

Blackstock, G. (2006, Spring/Summer). Multi-family housing. *Women and Environments International Magazine*, 71–72.

Blevins, S. (2008). A personal journey through the grief and healing process with Virginia Satir, Dr. E. Kübler-Ross, and J. William Worden. *Satir Journal, 2*(2), 89–105.

Blieszner, R., & Roberto, K. A. (2006). Perspectives on close relationships among the baby boomers. In S. K. Whitbourne & S. L. Willis (Eds.), *The baby boomers grow up: Contemporary perspectives on midlife* (pp. 261–281). Mahwah, NJ: Lawrence Erlbaum.

Bloemraad, I. (2006). *Becoming a citizen: Incorporating immigrants and refugees in the United States and Canada*. Berkeley: University of California Press.

Blow, A. J., & Hartnett, K. (2005). Infidelity in committed relationships II: A substantive review. *Journal of Marital and Family Therapy, 31,* 217–233.

Boardman, J. D., & Saint Onge, J. M. (2005). Neighborhoods and adolescent development. *Children, Youth and Environments, 15*(1), 138–164. Retrieved from http://www.colorado.edu/journals/cye

Bogenschneider, K. (2002). *Family policy matters: How policymaking affects families and what professionals can do*. Mahwah, NJ: Lawrence Erlbaum.

Bogenschneider, K., & Pollock, L. (2008). Responsiveness in parent-adolescent relationships: Are influences conditional? Does the reporter matter? *Journal of Marriage and Family, 70,* 1015–1029.

Bogle, K. A. (2008). *Hooking up: Sex, dating, and relationships on campus*. New York: New York University Press.

Boivin, J., Rice, F., Hay, D., Harold, G., Lewis, A., van den Bree, M. M. B., et al. (2009). Associations between maternal older age, family environment and parent and child well-being in families using assisted reproductive techniques to conceive. *Social Science and Medicine, 68,* 1948–1955.

Bold, M. (2001, March). Impact of computer-mediated communication on families. *Family Focus*, F16–F17.

Bond, A., Madsen, B., Willoughby, B. (2012, October). *Links between reasons for cohabitation and relational outcomes*. Paper presented to National Council on Family Relations conference, Phoenix, AZ.

Boone, T. (2006, July 19). *Sex before competition*. Retrieved from http://boonethink.com

Boots, S. W., Macomber, J., & Danziger, A. (2008, July). *Family security: Supporting parents' employment and children's development*. Washington, DC: Urban Institute.

Borgen, W. A., Amundson, N. E., & McVicar, J. (2002). The experience of unemployment for fishery workers in Newfoundland: What helps and what hinders. *Journal of Employment Counseling, 39,* 117–126.

Borkowski, J. G., Farris, J. R., & Weed, K. (2007). Toward resilience: Developing effective prevention programs. In J. G. Borkowski, J. R. Farris, T. L. Whitman, S. S. Carothers, K. Weed, & D. A. Keogh (Eds.), *Risk and resilience: Adolescent mothers and their children grow up* (pp. 259–278). Mahwah, NJ: Lawrence Erlbaum.

Borowsky, I. W., Ireland, M., & Resnick, M. D. (2009). Health status and behavioral outcomes for youth who anticipate a high likelihood of early death. *Pediatrics, 124,* e81–e88. Retrieved from http://www.pediatrics.org/cgi/content/full/124/1/e81

Boss, P. (2002). *Family stress management: A contextual approach* (2nd ed.). Thousand Oaks, CA: Sage.

Boss, P. (2006). *Loss, trauma, and resilience: Therapeutic work with ambiguous loss*. New York: W. W. Norton.

Bossard, J. H. S., with Boll, E. S. (1975). *The large family system*. Westport, CT: Greenwood. (Originally published in 1956)

Bouchard, G., Lussier, Y., & Sabourin, S. (1999). Personality and marital adjustment: Utility of the five-factor model of personality. *Journal of Marriage and the Family, 61,* 651–660.

Boutwell, B. B., Beaver , K., & Barnes, J. (2012). More alike than different: Assortative mating and antisocial propensity in adulthood. *Criminal Justice and Behavior, 39*(9)1240–1264. doi:10.1177/0093854812445715

Bowal, P., & Campbell, C. (2007). The legalization of same-sex marriage in Canada. *American Journal of Family Law, 21*(2), 37–41.

Bowen, M. (1974, April). Alcoholism as viewed through family systems theory and family psychotherapy. *Annals of the New York Academy of Sciences, 233*, 115–122. doi: 10.1111/j.1749-6632.1974.tb40288.x

Boyce, I. (2006). Neighborliness and privacy on a low-income estate. *Sociological Research Online, 11*(3). Retrieved from http://www.socresonline.org.uk/11/3/boyce.html

Boyce, W., Doherty-Poirier, M., MacKinnon, D., Fortin, C., Saab, H., King, M., & Gallupe, O. (2006). Sexual health of Canadian youth, sexual health and HIV/AIDS study. *Canadian Journal of Human Sexuality, 15*, 59–67.

Boyd, M., & Li, A. (2003, Autumn). May–December: Canadians in age-discrepant relationships. *Canadian Social Trends* (Statistics Canada Catalogue no. 11-008), 2–6.

Boyle, M. H., Jenkins, J. M., Georgiades, K., Cairney, J., Duku, E., & Racine, Y. (2004). Differential-maternal parenting behaviour: Estimating within- and between-family effects on children. *Child Development, 75*, 1457–1476.

Bradbury, T. N., & Karney, B. R. (2004). Understanding and altering the longitudinal course of marriage. *Journal of Marriage and Family, 66*, 862–879.

Bradley, R. H., & McKelvey, L. (2007). Managing the differences within: Immigration and early education in the United States. In J. E. Lansford, K. Deater-Deckard, & M. H. Bornstein (Eds.), *Immigrant families in contemporary society* (pp. 157–176). New York: Guilford.

Bramham, D. (2008). *The secret lives of saints: Child brides and lost boys in Canada's polygamous Mormon sect.* Toronto: Random House Canada.

Brand, R. J., Markey. C. M., Mills, A., & Hodges, S. D. (2007). Sex differences in self-reported infidelity and its correlates. *Sex Roles, 57*, 101–109.

Branden, N. (2008). *The psychology of romantic love: Romantic love in an anti-romantic age* (Rev.). New York: Penguin.

Brandl, B. (2005). *Mandatory reporting of elder abuse: Implications for domestic violence advocates.* National Clearinghouse on Abuse in Later Life (NCALL)/Wisconsin Coalition Against Domestic Violence. Retrieved from http://www.ncall.us/docs/Mandatory_Reporting_EA.pdf

Brandon, P. D., Heyworth, C., & Griffen, L. (2007). *The rise of three-generation households among two-parent and single-parent families.* Retrieved from http://www.melbourneinstitute.com/hilda/conf/conf2007/

Bratter, J. L., & King, R. B. (2008). "But will it last?": Marital instability among interracial and same-race couples. *Family Relations, 57,* 160–171.

Braver, S. L., Ellman, I. M., & Fabricius, W. V. (2003). Relocation of children after divorce and children's best interests: New evidence and legal considerations. *Journal of Family Psychology, 17,* 206–219.

Bray, J. H., & Kelly, J. (1998). *Stepfamilies: Love, marriage, and parenting in the first decade.* New York: Broadway Books.

Brayfield, A. (1995). Juggling jobs and kids: The impact of employment schedules on fathers' caring for children. *Journal of Marriage and the Family, 57*, 321–332.

Breakfast Club of Canada. (2013). *History.* Retrieved from http://www.clubdejeuner.org/en/about-the-club/history

Brennan, R. T., Barnett, R. C., & Gareis, K. C. (2001). When she earns more than he does: A longitudinal study of dual-earner couples. *Journal of Marriage and Family, 63,* 168–182.

Brennan, S. (2012, May 28). *Youth court statistics in Canada, 2010–2011.* Ottawa: Statistics Canada. Retrieved from http://www.statcan.gc.ca/pub/85-002-x/2012001/article/11645-eng.htm

Bretherton, I. (2003). Mary Ainsworth: Insightful observer and courageous theoretician. In G. A. Kimble & M. Wertheimer (Eds.), *Portraits of pioneers in psychology* (Vol. 5). Washington, DC: American Psychological Association. Retrieved from http://www.psychology.sunysb.edu/attachment/pdf/mda_inge.pdf

Brinig, M. F. (1999). The effect of divorce on wives. In D. W. Allen & J. Richards (Eds.), *It takes two: The family in marriage and finance* (pp. 36–62). Toronto: C. D. Howe Institute.

Brinkerhoff, M. B., & Lupri, E. (1989). Power and authority in the family. In K. Ishwaran (Ed.), *Family and marriage: Cross-cultural perspectives* (pp. 213–236). Toronto: Wall & Thompson.

Brobeck, S., & Montalto, C. (2008). *The financial condition of women on their own.* Washington, DC: Consumer Federation of America. Retrieved from http://www.consumerfed.org/pdfs/Women_on_Their_Own_Report_12_2_08.pdf

Broderick, C. B. (1993). *Understanding family process: Basics of family systems theory.* Newbury Park, CA: Sage.

Brodribb, S. (1984). The traditional roles of native women in Canada and the impact of colonization. *Canadian Journal of Native Studies, 4*(1), 85–103.

Brody, G. H., & Murry, V. M. (2001). Sibling socialization in rural, single-parent African-American families. *Journal of Marriage and Family, 63*, 996–1008.

Bronfenbrenner, U. (1979). *The ecology of human development: Experiments by nature and design.* Cambridge, MA: Harvard University Press.

Bronfenbrenner, U. (1993). Ecological models of human development. In M. Gauvain, & M. Cole (Eds.), *Readings on the development of children, 2nd ed.* (pp. 37–43). New York: Freeman.

Bronfenbrenner, U. (2005). Ecological systems theory. In U. Bronfenbrenner (Ed.), *Making human beings human: Bioecological perspectives on human development* (pp. 106–173). Thousand Oaks, CA: Sage.

Brooks, B. (2005). *Chronic unemployment: A statistical profile* (Statistics Canada Catalogue No. 11-621-MIE-No. 031). Ottawa: Statistics Canada. Retrieved from http://www.statcan.gc.ca/pub/11-621-m/11-621m2005031-eng.pdf

Brosi, W. (2005, September). Integrating recipients into family care systems. *Family Focus, F*28–F29.

Brotherson, S. E., & Moen, D. A. (2011). Establishing a home: A study of practical dimensions in the transition to marriage. *Family Science Review, 16*(2), 59–74.

Brown, B., Moore, K., & Bzostek, S. (2003, October). *A portrait of well-being in early adulthood: A report to the William and Flora Hewlett Foundation.* Retrieved from http://www.childtrends.org

Brown, B. B. (2006). A few "course corrections" to Collins and van Dulmen's "the course of true love." In A. C. Crouter & A. Booth (Eds.), *Romance and sex in adolescence and emerging adulthood: Risks and opportunities* (pp. 113–123). Mahwah, NJ: Lawrence Erlbaum.

Brown, L. H. (2003, November). *Grandparent–grandchild role expectations as viewed by young adults.* Poster presentation at the annual conference of National Council on Family Relations, Vancouver, BC.

Brown, S., & Lewis, V. (1999). *The alcoholic family in recovery: A developmental model.* New York: Guilford.

Brown, S. K., & Bean, F. D. (2006, October 1). *Assimilation models, old and new: Explaining a long-term process.* Washington, DC: Migration Policy Institute. Retrieved from http://www.immigrationinformation.org/Feature/print.cfm?ID=442

Brownstone, H. (2009). *Tug of war: A judge's verdict on separation, custody battles, and the bitter realities of family court.* Toronto: ECW Press.

Brunes, L. (2004, Spring). The seniors of Canada's far north. *Expression,* 1–8.

Bryant, C. M., Conger, R. D., & Meehan, J. M. (2001). The influence of in-laws on change in marital success. *Journal of Marriage and Family, 63,* 614–626.

Brym, R. J., & Lenton, R. (2001, March 25). *Love online: A report on digital dating in Canada.* Retrieved from http://www.bestsoftworks.com/docs/loveonline.pdf

Brym, R. J., Lie, J., Nelson, A., Guppy, N., & McCormick, C. (2003). *Sociology: Your compass for a new world* (1st Canadian ed.). Toronto: Thomson Nelson Canada.

Brzozowski, J.-A., (Ed.). (2004). *Family violence in Canada: A statistical profile 2004* (Catalogue No. 85-224-XIE). Ottawa: Statistics Canada.

Buchanan, C. M., Maccoby, E. E., & Dornbusch, S. M. (1991). Caught between parents: Adolescents' experience in divorced homes. *Child Development, 62,* 1008–1029.

Buehler, C. (2006). Parents and peers in relation to early adolescent problem behavior. *Journal of Marriage and Family, 68,* 109–124.

Buehler, C., & Gerard, J. M. (2002). Marital conflict, ineffective parenting, and children's maladjustment. *Journal of Marriage and Family, 64,* 78–92.

Buehler, C., Krishnakumar, A., Anthony, C., Tittsworth, S., & Stone, G. (1994). Hostile interparental conflict and youth maladjustment. *Family Relations, 43,* 409–416.

Buehler, C., Weymouth, B., & Chia, E. (2012, November). *Work-family spillover: Parent and adolescent mental health outcomes.* Poster presentation at the annual conference of the National Council of Family Relations, Phoenix, AZ.

Bukowski, W. M., Brendgen, M., & Vitaro, F. (2008). Peers and socialization: Effects on externalizing and internalizing problems. In J. E. Grusec & P. D. Hastings (Eds.), *Handbook of socialization: Theory and research* (pp. 355–381). New York: Guilford.

Bullen, J. (1992). Hidden workers: Child labour and the family economy in late nineteenth-century urban Ontario. In B. Bradbury (Ed.), *Canadian family history: Selected readings* (pp. 199–219). Toronto: Copp Clark Pitman.

Burgess, E. W., & Locke, H. J. (1960). *The family: From institution to companionship* (2nd ed.). New York: American Book Company.

Burns, M., & Taylor-Butts, A. (2009). A profile of Canada's shelters for abused women. In Statistics Canada, *Family violence in Canada: A statistical profile 2009* (Catalogue No. 85-224-X, pp. 8–23). Ottawa: Statistics Canada. Retrieved from http://www.statcan.gc.ca/pub/85-224-x/85-224-x2009000.eng.pdf

Bush, K. R., Bohon, S. A., & Kim, H. K. (2010). Adaptation among immigrant families: Resources and barriers. In S. J. Price, C. A. Price, & P. C. McKenry (Eds.), *Families & change: Coping with stressful events and transitions* (4th ed., pp. 285–310). Los Angeles: Sage.

Bushnik, T. (2006, April). *Child care in Canada.* (Catalogue No. 89-599-XIE). Ottawa: Statistics Canada. Retrieved from http://www.statcan.gc.ca/pub/89-599-m/89-599-m2006003-eng.pdf#10

Bushnik, T., & Garner, R. (2008). *The children of older first-time mothers in Canada: Their health and development* (Catalogue No. 89-599-M, no. 005). Ottawa: Statistics Canada.

Busseri, M. A., & Rose-Krasnor, L. (2008, March). *A longitudinal, person-centered examination of activity involvement and successful adolescent development.* Poster presentation at the biennial meeting of the Society for Research on Adolescent Development, Chicago, IL.

Busseri, M. A., Rose-Krasnor, L., Centre for Excellence for Youth Engagement (Canada), & YMCA of Greater Toronto. (2009, April). *Activity involvement and positive youth development: Examining the roles of engagement and fixtures of the activity.* Poster presentation at the biennial meeting of the Society for Research in Child Development, Denver, CO.

Butler, A. C. (2002). Welfare, premarital childbearing, and the role of normative climate: 1968–1994. *Journal of Marriage and Family, 64,* 295–313.

Butler, I., Scanlan, L., Robinson, M., Douglas, G., & Murch, M. (2003). *Divorcing children: Children's experience of their parents' divorce.* London, England: Jessica Kingsley.

Buunk, A. P., Park, J., & Duncan, L. (2010, February). Cultural variation in parental influence on mate choice. *Cross-Cultural Research, 44*(1), 23–40. doi:10.1177/1069397109337711

Buxton, A. P. (2006). A family matter: When a spouse comes out as gay, lesbian, or bisexual. In J. J. Bigner (Ed.), *An introduction to GLBT family studies* (pp. 67–87). New York: Haworth.

C-36: An act to amend the Canada Pension Plan and the Old Age Security Act. (2006). Ottawa: Human Resources and Skills Development Canada. Retrieved from http://www.hrsdc.gc.ca/eng/isp/common/hrsdc/billc-36.shtml

Cabrera, N. J. (1995). Violence by and against children in Canada. In J. I. Ross (Ed.), *Violence in Canada: Sociopolitical perspectives* (pp. 126–152). Don Mills, ON: Oxford University Press.

Caffaro, J. V., & Conn-Caffaro, A. (2005). Treating sibling abuse families. *Aggression and Violent Behavior, 10,* 604–623.

Cahill, B. (1992). *Butterbox babies.* Toronto: McClelland-Bantam.

Cahill, L. (2005, April 25). His brain, her brain. *Scientific American*. Retrieved from http://www.sciam.com

Calgary Herald (May 24, 2008). *Canadians are lucky in love: Survey*. Retrieved from ProQuest database.

Callahan, M., Brown, L., MacKenzie, P., & Whittington, B. (2005, November). The underground child welfare system: Grandmothers raising grandchildren. *Perspectives* (Newsletter of BC Association of Social Workers), 27(5), 12–13. Retrieved from http://www.bcasw.org/Images/PDFs/Nov2005.pdf

Campbell, A. (2009, January 10). In the name of the mothers . . . *Globe and Mail*, p. A17.

Campaign 2000. (2009). *Report card on child and family poverty in Canada: 1989–2009*. Retrieved from http://www.campaign2000.ca/reportCards/national/2009EnglishC2000NationalReportCard.pdf

Campaign 2000. (2012). *Needed: A federal action plan to eradicate child and family poverty in Canada. 2012 report card on child and family poverty*. Family Service Toronto. Retrieved from http://www.campaign2000.ca/reportCards/national/C2000ReportCardNov2012.pdf

Canada Adopts. (2001). *Adopting in Canada*. Retrieved from http://www.canadaadopts.com/canada/overseas.shtml

Canada Free Press. (2013). Who needs the family? Retrieved from http://www.canadafreepress.com/index.php/article/53237?utm_source=CFP+Mailout&utm_campaign=66d5e43c2a-Call_to_Champions&utm_medium=email

Canada Mortgage and Housing Corporation. (n.d.). *Shelter enhancement program (SEP)*. Ottawa: Author. Retrieved from http://www.cmhc-schl.gc.ca/en/co/prfinas/prfinas_011.ctm

Canada Revenue Agency. (2013a). *Canada child benefits*. Ottawa: Author. Retrieved from http://www.cra-arc.gc.ca/E/pub/tg/t4114/t4114-12e.pdf

Canada Revenue Agency. (2013b, January 3). *Information about child care expenses*. Ottawa: Author. Retrieved from http://www.cra-arc.gc.ca/E/pbg/tf/t778/t778-12e.pdf

Canada Revenue Agency. (2013c, February 21). *Universal Child Care Benefit (UCCB)*. Ottawa: Author. Retrieved from http://www.cra-arc.gc.ca/bnfts/uccb-puge/menu-eng.html

Canada Without Poverty. (2013). *Child poverty worse now than it was 20 years ago*. Retrieved http://www.cwp-csp.ca/2012/11/child-poverty-worse-now-than-it-was-20-years-ago

Canadian Agency for Drugs and Technologies in Health. (2012). *Assisted reproductive technologies in Canada*. Retrieved from http://www.cadth.ca/products/environmental-scanning/health-technology-update/issue-10-september-2008/assisted-reproductive

Canadian Centre for Policy Alternatives (2009, September). *Women and poverty fact sheets*. Retrieved from http://www.policyalternatives.ca/~ASSETS/DOCUMENT/National_Office_Pubs/2009/Women_and_Poverty_Fact_Sheets.pdf

Canadian Centre on Substance Abuse. (2010, June 30). *Prevalence and patterns of use of alcohol*. Retrieved from http://www.hc-sc.gc.ca/hc-ps/drugs-drogues/stat/_2009/summary-sommaire-eng.php#alc

Canadian Centre on Substance Abuse. (2013). *National alcohol strategy: Reducing alcohol-related harm in Canada*. Retrieved from http://www.ccsa.ca/Eng/Statistics/Canada/GHAS/Pages/default.aspx

Canadian Conference of Catholic Bishops. (2006, December 8). *Debate on redefining marriage not over*. Retrieved from http://www.cccb.ca/site/eng/media-room/archives/public-statements/2006/2412-debate-on-redefining-marriage-not-over

Canadian Council of Natural Mothers. (n.d.). *Provincial search information*. Retrieved from http://www.ccnm-mothers.ca/English/ProvincialInfo.htm

Canadian Council on Social Development. (n.d.). *Economic security fact sheet #2: Poverty*. Ottawa: Author. Retrieved from http://www.ccsd.ca/factsheets/economic_security/poverty/index.htm

Canadian Council on Social Development. (2006). *A profile of Canadian families*. Retrieved from http://www.ccsd.ca/family/families.pdf

Canadian Divorce Laws. (2012a). *Common law marriage*. Retrieved from http://www.canadiandivorcelaws.com/common-law-marriage

Canadian Divorce Laws. (2012b). *Grounds for divorce*. Retrieved from http://www.canadiandivorcelaws.com/divorce

Canadian Divorce Laws. (2012c). *Child custody*. Retrieved from http://www.canadiandivorcelaws.com/child-custody

Canadian Hearing Society. (2002). *Employment and employability needs of the deaf community in Peel and Halton Regions*. Mississauga, ON: Canadian Hearing Society—Peel.

Canadian Institute for Health Information. (Annual). *Induced abortions performed in Canada*.

Canadian Network for the Prevention of Elder Abuse. (n.d.). *Mandatory reporting*. Retrieved from http://www.cnpea.ca/mandatory%20reporting_1.pdf

Canadian Press. (2010, January 20). Canada eases restrictions for Haitian adoptions. Retrieved from http://www.winnipegsun.com/news/haiti/2010/01/20/12540526.html

Canadian Press. (2012, May 29). Aging Canadians are challenging the concept of "old." Retrieved from http://www.cbc.ca/news/canada/story/2012/05/29/census-defining-old.html

Canadian Society of Muslims. (2005). *The Review of the Ontario Civil Justice System*. Retrieved from http://muslimcanada.org/submission.pdf

Canary, D. J., Stafford, L., & Semic, B. A. (2002). A panel study of the associations between maintenance strategies and relational characteristics. *Journal of Marriage and Family, 64*, 395–406.

Capizzano, J., Adelman, S., & Stagner, M. (2002). *What happens when the school year is over? The use and costs of child care for school-age children during the summer months*. Washington, DC: Urban Institute.

Caragata, L. (2003). Housing and homelessness. In A. Westhues (Ed.), *Canadian social policy: Issues and perspectives* (3rd ed., pp. 67–89). Waterloo, ON: Wilfrid Laurier University Press.

Carmalt, J. H., Cauley, J., Joyner, K., & Sobal, J. (2008). Body weight and matching with a physically attractive romantic partner. *Journal of Marriage and Family, 70*, 1287–1296.

Carr, D. (2004). The desire to date and remarry among older widows and widowers. *Journal of Marriage and Family, 66,* 1051–1068.

Carter, B., & McGoldrick, M. (Eds.) (1999). *The expanded family life cycle: Individual, family and social perspectives* (3rd ed). Boston: Allyn & Bacon.

Carter, B., & McGoldrick, M. (2005). The e*xpanded family life cycle: Individual, family and social perspectives* (4th ed.). Boston: Pearson Education.

Carvery. I. (2008, January 2). Africville: A community displaced. Ottawa: Library and Archives Canada. Retrieved from http://www.collectionscanada.gc.ca/northern-star/033005-2601-e.html

Castellano, M. B. (1989). Women in Huron and Ojibwa societies. *Canadian Woman Studies, 10*(2/3), 45–48.

Castellano, M. B. (2002). *Aboriginal family trends: Extended families, nuclear families, families of the heart.* Ottawa: Vanier Institute of the Family.

Castellano, M. B. (2006–07, Winter). Healing narratives: Recovery from residential school trauma. *Transition, 36*(4).

Castro-Martín, T., Domínguez-Folgueras, M., & Martín-García, T. (2008). Not truly partnerless: Non-residential partnerships and retreat from marriage in Spain. *Demographic Research, 18,* 443–468.

CBC. (1999). Montreal scientists clone goats. *CBC Digital Archives.* Retrieved from http://www.cbc.ca/archives/categories/science-technology/biotechnology/canada-enters-the-clone-age/montreal-scientists-clone-goats.html

CBC. (2003, August 14). "There's no place for the state in the bedrooms of the nation." *CBC Digital Archives.* Retrieved from http://archives.cbc.ca

CBC. (2007, January 3). Ontario court says boy can have dad, mom—and mom. Retrieved from http://www.cbc.ca/news/canada/toronto/story/2007/01/03/twomom-court.html

CBC. (2009). Abortion rights: Significant moments in Canadian history. Retrieved from http://www.cbc.ca/canada/story/2009/01/13/f-abortion-timeline.html

CBC. (2010, February 2). N.B. man jailed for spanking son. Retrieved from http://www.cbc.ca/canada/new-brunswick/story/2010/02/02/nb-spanking-sentencing.html

CBC. (2012, April 23). Assisted human reproduction and the law. Retrieved from http://www.cbc.ca/news/health/story/2012/04/20/f-regulation-fertility-assisted-human-reproduction.html

CBC. (2013, January 5). 9 questions about Idle No More. Retrieved from http://www.cbc.ca/news/canada/9-questions-about-idle-no-more-1.1301843

Center for Impact Research. (2000). *Domestic violence and birth control sabotage: A report from the teen parent project.* Chicago: Author.

Center for Mental Health in Schools at UCLA. (2008). *Understanding and minimizing staff burnout.* Los Angeles: Author. Retrieved from http://smhp.psych.ucla.edu

Centers for Disease Control and Prevention. (2008). *Assisted reproductive technology success rates: National summary and fertility clinic reports.* Atlanta: U. S. Department of Health and Human Services,

Centers for Disease Control and Prevention. Retrieved from http://www.cdc.gov/ART/ART2006

Centre for Children and Families in the Justice System. (2010). Power and Control Wheel. Retrieved from http://www.lfcc.on.ca/HCT_SWASM_5.html

Centre for Research on Families and Relationships. (2005, June). *Relationships between grandparents and teenage grandchildren: Research briefing 23.* Edinburgh: Centre for Research on Families and Relationships, University of Edinburgh. Retrieved from http://www.crfr.ac.uk/reports/rb23grand-parents.pdf

Chabot, J. M., & Ames, B. D. (2004). "It wasn't 'let's get pregnant and go do it'": Decision making in lesbian couples planning motherhood via donor insemination. *Family Relations, 53,* 348–356.

Chalmers, L., & Milan, A. (2005, Spring). Marital satisfaction during the retirement years. *Canadian Social Trends* (Statistics Canada Catalogue no. 11-008), 14–17.

Chamberlain, L. (2008, March). *A prevention primer for domestic violence: Terminology, tools, and the public health approach.* Harrisburg, PA: VAWnet, A Project of the National Resource Center on Domestic Violence/Pennsylvania Coalition Against Domestic Violence. Retrieved from http://www.vawnet.org

Chapple, S. (2009, March 23). *Child well-being and sole-parent family structure in the OECD: An analysis.* Paris: OECD, Directorate for Employment, Labour, and Social Affairs. Retrieved from http://www.olis.oecd.org/olis/2009doc.nsf/LinkTo/NT00000F32/$FILE/JT03261729.PDF

Charles, S. T., & Carstensen, L. L. (2009). Social and emotional aging. *Annual Review of Psychology, 61,* 383–409.

Chau, S., & Lai, D. W. (2011). The size of an ethno-cultural community as a social determinant of health for Chinese seniors. *Journal of Immigrant Minority Health, 13,* 1090–1098.

Chaussard, M., Gerecke, M., & Heymann, J. (2008). *The Work Equity Canada Index: Where the provinces and territories stand.* Montreal: McGill University, Institute for Health and Social Policy.

Chaykowski, R. P. (2006, June). Toward squaring the circle: Work–life balance and the implications for individuals, firms and public policy. *IRPP Choices, 12*(3). Retrieved from http://www.irpp.org

Che-Alford, J., & Hamm, B. (1999, Summer). Under one roof: Three generations living together. *Canadian Social Trends,* 6–9.

Cheal, D. (1991). *Family and the state of theory.* Toronto: University of Toronto Press.

Chen, X., French, D. C., & Schneider, B. H. (2006). *Peer relationships in cultural context.* New York: Cambridge University Press.

Cherlin, A. J. (2004). The deinstitutionalization of American marriage. *Journal of Marriage and Family, 66,* 848–861.

Cherlin, A. J. (2009). The origins of the ambivalent acceptance of divorce. *Journal of Marriage and Family, 71,* 226–229.

Chesley, N. (2005). Blurring boundaries? Linking technology use, spillover, individual distress, and family satisfaction. *Journal of Marriage and Family, 67,* 1237–1248.

Chiancone, J., Girdner, L., & Hoff, P. (2001, December). Issues in resolving cases of international child abduction by parents. *Juvenile Justice Bulletin.* Washington, DC: U.S. Department of Justice.

Child Care Human Resources Sector Council. (2013) *You bet we still care! A survey of centre-based early childhood education and care in Canada.* Ottawa: Author.

Childcare Resource and Research Unit (2007, December). *Trends & analysis 2007: Early childhood education and care in Canada 2006.* Retrieved from http://www.childcarecanada.org/pubs/other/TandA/Trends_Analysis07.pdf

Children Now. (2004). *Fall colors 2003–04: Prime time diversity report.* Retrieved from http://www.childrennow.org

Children's Aid Society of Toronto. (2009). *Celebrating Family Day in Canada.* Retrieved from http://www.torontocas.ca/main.php/?p=278

Christopher, F. S., Madura, M., & Weaver, L. (1998). Premarital sexual aggressors: A multivariate analysis of social, relational, and individual variables. *Journal of Marriage and the Family, 60,* 56–69.

Chui, T., Tran, K., & Flanders, J. (2005, Spring). Chinese Canadians: Enriching the cultural mosaic. *Canadian Social Trends* (Statistics Canada Catalogue no. 11-008), 24–32.

Chui, T., Tran, K., & Maheux, H. (2007). *Immigration in Canada: A portrait of the foreign-born population, 2006 Census* (Catalogue No. 97-557-XIE). Ottawa: Statistics Canada. Retrieved from http://www.statcan.gc.ca

Chung, L. (2006, June). Education and earnings. *Perspectives on Labour and Income* (Statistics Canada Catalogue no. 75-001-XIE), pp. 5–12.

Church, E. (2004). *Understanding stepmothers: Women share their struggles, successes, and insights.* Toronto: HarperCollins.

CIA. (2013). Country comparison: Infant mortality rate. *The World Factbook.* Retrieved from https://www.cia.gov/library/publications/the-world-factbook/rankorder/2091rank.html

Citizenship and Immigration Canada. (2008, October 24). *Policy and legislation concerning multiculturalism.* Retrieved from http://www.cic.gc.ca/multi/pol/framework-eng.asp

Citizenship and Immigration Canada. (2009a). *Marriage Fraud.* Retrieved from http://www.cic.gc.ca/english//information/protection/fraud/marriage.asp

Citizenship and Immigration Canada. (2009b, February 11). *News release: Canada to double number of Iraqi refugees.* Ottawa: Author. Retrieved from http://www.cic.gc.ca/english/department/media/releases/2009/2009-02-11.asp

Citizenship and Immigration Canada (2009c, May 12). *Sponsoring your family: Spouses and dependent children—who can apply.* Ottawa: Author. Retrieved from http://www.cic.gc.ca/english/immigrate/sponsor/spouse-apply-who.asp#spouse

Citizenship and Immigration Canada. (2010a, April 20). *New citizenship rules.* Ottawa: Author. Retrieved from http://www.cic.gc.ca/english/citizenship/rules-citizenship.asp

Citizenship and Immigration Canada. (2010b, October 19). *Programs and services for immigrants.* Ottawa: Author. Retrieved from http://www.cic.gc.ca/english/celebrate/menu-promotion.asp

Citizenship and Immigration Canada. (2012a, June 1). *Definition of family member.* Ottawa: Author. Retrieved from http://www.cic.gc.ca/english/information/applications/guides/5578ETOC.asp

Citizenship and Immigration Canada. (2012b, June 28). *IMDB 2008 immigration category profiles.* Ottawa: Author. Retrieved from http://www.cic.gc.ca/english/resources/research/imdb2008-cat-profiles.asp

Citizenship and Immigration Canada. (2012c, April 2). *Quebec.* Ottawa: Author. Retrieved from http://www.cic.gc.ca/english/newcomers/pt/qc.asp

Citizenship and Immigration Canada. (2012d, March 9). *Marriage fraud.* Ottawa: Author. Retrieved from http://www.cic.gc.ca/english/information/protection/fraud/marriage.asp

Citizenship and Immigration Canada. (2013, July 3). *Canada to resettle 1,300 Syrian refugees by end of 2014.* Retrieved from http://www.cic.gc.ca/english/department/media/releases/2013/2013-07-03.asp

City of Calgary. (1985). *A profile and needs assessment of Calgary's single-parents.* Calgary: City of Calgary, Social Services Department.

Clack, E. E. (Ed.). (2004, May 1). Study probes generation gap. *Children's Business.* Retrieved from http://www.reachadvisors.com/childrensbusinessarticle.html

Clapton, M. S. (2008). *Murdoch v. Murdoch:* The organizing narrative of matrimonial property law reform. *Canadian Journal of Women and the Law, 20,* 197–230.

Clark, D., & Hulme, D. (2005, May 16). *Towards a unified framework for understanding the depth, breadth and duration of poverty* (GPRG-WPS-020). Manchester, UK: Global Poverty and Research Group, University of Manchester. Retrieved from http://www.gprg.org/pubs/workingpapers/pdfs/gprg-wps-020.pdf

Clark, W. (2007, Winter). Delayed transitions of young adults. *Canadian Social Trends* (Statistics Canada Catalogue no. 11-008), 14–22.

Clark, W., & Crompton, S. (2006, Summer). Till death do us part? The risk of first and second marriage dissolution. *Canadian Social Trends* (Statistics Canada Catalogue no. 11-008), 23–33.

Clark-Ibañez, M., & Felmlee, D. (2004). Interethnic relationships: The role of social network diversity, *Journal of Marriage and Family, 66,* 293–305.

Cleveland, G., Forer, B., Hyatt, D., Japel, C., & Krashinsky, M. (2008). New evidence about child care in Canada: Use patterns, affordability and quality. *IRPP Choices, 14*(12).

Cleveland, G., & Krashinsky, M. (2003). *Fact and fantasy: Eight myths about early childhood education and care.* Toronto: University of Toronto, Childcare Resource and Research Unit.

Cline, F., & Fay, J. (2006). *Parenting teens with love and logic: Preparing adolescents for responsible adulthood* (2nd ed.). Colorado Springs, CO: NavPress.

CMHA (Canadian Mental Health Association, Newfoundland and Labrador Division). (n.d.). *Guide to coping with unemployment.* Retrieved from http://www.infonet.st-johns.nf.ca/cmha/resource/publications/gcwu/

Cochrane, M. G. (2007). *Surviving your divorce: A guide to Canadian family law* (4th ed.). Mississauga, ON: Wiley.

Cohen, G. D. (2005). *The mature mind: The positive power of the aging brain*. New York: Basic Books.

Cohen, M. (2012). Caring for BC's aging population improving health care for all. Vancouver: BC Health Coalition and CCPA–BC. Retrieved from http://www.policyalternatives.ca/newsroom/news-releases/continued-reductions-access-seniors-care-leads-hospital-overcrowding-longer-w

Cohen, P. N., & Petrescu-Prahova, M. (2006). Gendered living arrangements among children with disabilities. *Journal of Marriage and Family, 68*, 630–638.

Cohler, B. J. (2006). Life-course social science perspectives on the GLBT family. In J. J. Bigner (Ed.), *An introduction to GLBT family studies* (pp. 23–49). New York: Haworth.

Cole, E. S. (1984). Societal influences on adoption practice. In P. Sachdev (Ed.), *Adoption: Current issues and trends* (pp. 15–29). Toronto: Butterworths.

Coleman, J. W., & Kerbo, H. R., with Ramos, L. L. (2002). *Social problems* (8th ed.). Upper Saddle River, NJ: Prentice Hall.

Coleman, M., Ganong, L., & Fine, M. (2000). Reinvestigating remarriage: Another decade of progress. *Journal of Marriage and the Family, 62*, 1288–1307.

Coleman, M., Ganong, L. H., & Rothrauff, T. C. (2006). Racial and ethnic similarities and differences in beliefs about intergenerational assistance to older adults after divorce and remarriage. *Family Relations, 55*, 576–587.

Collin-Vézina, D., Hébert, M., Manseau, H., Blais, M., & Fernet, M. (2006). Self-concept and dating violence in 220 adolescent girls in the child protective system. *Child Youth Care Forum, 35*, 319–326.

Comfort, D., Johnson, K., & Wallace, D. (2003). *Part-time work and family-friendly practices in Canadian workplaces* (Catalogue No. 71-584-MIE, no. 6). Ottawa: Statistics Canada.

Common Law Relationships. (2013). Retrieved from http://www.commonlawrelationships.ca

Common Law Separation Canada. (2007). *Quebec common law property division*. Retrieved from http://www.common-law-separation-canada.com/quebec.htm

Concerned Christians Canada. (2012). *Standing for the biblical family*. Retrieved from http://www.concernedchristians.ca/component/content/category/115

Conference Board of Canada. (2009). *Child poverty*. Ottawa: Author. Retrieved from http://www.conferenceboard.ca/hcp/details/society/child-poverty.aspx

Conger, R. D., & Dogan, S. J. (2008), Social class and socialization in families. In J. E. Grusec & P. D. Hastings (Eds.), *Handbook of socialization: Theory and research* (pp. 433–460). New York: Guilford.

Conley, D. (2004). *The pecking order: A bold new look at how family and society determine who we become*. New York: Vintage.

Connidis, I. A. (2010). *Family ties and aging* (2nd ed.). Los Angeles: Pine Forge.

Connolly, C. M. (2006). The process of change: The intersection of the GLBT individual and his or her family of origin. In J. J. Bigner (Ed.), *An introduction to GLBT family studies* (pp. 5–21). New York: Haworth.

Conseil de la famille et de l'enfance. (2008). *La politique familiale au Québec: visée, portée, durée et rayonnement* (Rev.). Québec City: Conseil de la famille et de l'enfance, Gouvernement du Québec. Retrieved from http://www.cfe.gouv.qc.ca

Conservatives vow to toughen youth justice act. (2008, September 22). *CBC*. Retrieved from http://www.cbc.ca/news/canadavotes/story/2008/09/22/harper-elxn.html?ref=rss

Cook, T. E. (2003). *Separation, assimilation, or accommodation: Contrasting ethnic minority policies*. Westport, CT: Praeger.

Cooke, M. (2009). A welfare trap? The duration and dynamics of social assistance use among lone mothers in Canada. *Canadian Review of Sociology/Revue canadienne de sociologie, 46*(3), 179–206. doi:10.1111/j.1755-618X.2009.01211.x

Coontz, S. (2000). Historical perspectives on family studies. *Journal of Marriage and the Family, 62*, 283–297.

Coontz, S. (2005). *Marriage, a history: From obedience to intimacy or how love conquered marriage*. New York: Viking.

Coontz, S. (2007, December). Divorce and dissolution: Recognizing reality. *Family Focus*, F5–F6.

Cooper, C. E., McLanahan, S. S., Meadows, S. A., & Brooks-Gunn, J. (2009). Family structure transitions and parenting stress. *Journal of Marriage and Family, 71*, 558–574.

Cooper, C., et al. (2007). Depression and common mental disorders in lone parents: Results of the 2000 National Psychiatric Morbidity Survey. *Psychological Medicine, 38*, 335–342.

Copans, S. (1989). The invisible family member: Children in families with alcohol abuse. In L. Combrinck-Graham (Ed.), *Children in family contexts: Perspectives on treatment* (pp. 277–298). New York: Guilford.

Coplan, R. J., Hastings, P. D., Lagacé-Séguin, D. G., & Moulton, C. E. (2002). Authoritative and authoritarian mothers' parenting goals, attributions, and emotions across different childrearing contexts. *Parenting: Science and Practice, 2*, 1–26.

Cornelius, T. L., & Alessi, G. (2007). Behavioral and physiological components of communication training: Does the topic affect the outcome? *Journal of Marriage and Family, 69*, 608–620.

Correctional Service of Canada. (2011, December 20). *Private family visiting*. Retrieved from http://www.csc-scc.gc.ca/text/pblct/visit/index-eng.shtml

Cossette, L., & Duclos, E. (2002). *A profile of disability in Canada, 2001*. (Catalogue No. 89-577-XIE). Ottawa: Statistics Canada.

Cottrell, B. (2003). *Parent abuse: The abuse of parents by their teenage children* (Catalogue No. H72-22/25-2003E). Ottawa: National Clearinghouse on Family Violence.

Council of Canadians with Disabilities. (2009). *As a matter of fact: Poverty and disability in Canada*. Retrieved from http:www.ccdonline.ca/en/socialpolicy/poverty-citizenship/poverty-disability-canada

Court of Appeal for Ontario (Toronto). (2007, January 2). *A.A. v. B.B.*, 2007 ONCA2, 20070102, C39998.

Coutts, M. (2012, May 16). YouTube stars say Ontario cafeterias need junk food cash. *CTV News*. Retrieved from http://toronto.ctvnews.ca/youtube-stars-say-ontario-cafeterias-need-junk-food-cash-1.823790#ixzz2TOAmkGWs

Cowan, C. P., Cowan, P. A., Heming, G., Garrett, E., Coysh, W. S., Curtis-Boles, H., & Boles, A. J., III. (1985). Transitions to parenthood: His, hers, and theirs. *Journal of Family Issues, 6,* 451–481.

Cowan, D. B. (2003). Assisted reproductive technology and the fertility clinic. In J. Haynes & J. Miller (Eds.), *Inconceivable conceptions: Psychological aspects of infertility and reproductive technology* (pp. 11–16). New York: Brunner-Routledge.

Cowan, P. A., & Cowan, C. P. (2003). Normative family transitions, normal family process, and healthy child development. In F. Walsh (Ed.), *Normal family processes: Growing diversity and complexity* (3rd ed., pp. 424–459). New York: Guilford.

Cowan, R. S. (1992). Twentieth-century changes in household technology. In A. S. Skolnick & J. H. Skolnick (Eds.), *Family in transition: Rethinking marriage, sexuality, child rearing, and family organization* (7th ed., pp. 82–92). New York: HarperCollins.

Cowdery, R. S., & Knudson-Martin, C. (2005). The construction of motherhood: Tasks, relational connection, and gender equality. *Family Relations, 54,* 335–345.

Cox, M. J., Paley, B., Burchinal, M., & Payne, C. C. (1999). Marital perceptions and interactions across the transition to parenthood. *Journal of Marriage and the Family, 61,* 611–625.

Coyle, J. P. (2005, June). Raising the grandkids. *Family Focus,* F21–F22.

Craine, P. B. (2009, May 4). Prominent rabbi: AIDS, swine flu, economic crash–Spiritual cause and effect. *LifeSiteNews.com.* Retrieved from http://www.lifesitenews.com/ldn/printer-friendly.html?articleid=09050406

Cranswick, K. (2003). *General social survey cycle 16: Caring for an aging society* (Catalogue No. 89-582-XIE). Ottawa: Statistics Canada.

Cranswick, K., & Dosman, D. (2008, Winter). Eldercare: What we know today. *Canadian Social Trends* (Statistics Canada Catalogue no. 11-008), 49–57.

Crissey, S. R. (2005). Race/ethnic differences in the marital expectations of adolescents: The role of romantic relationships. *Journal of Marriage and Family, 67,* 697–709.

Crompton, S., & Keown, L.-A. (2009, October 27). Do parental benefits influence fertility decisions? *Canadian Social Trends* (Statistics Canada Catalogue No. 11-008), 45–52.

Crompton, S., & Vickers, M. (2000, Summer). One hundred years of labour force. *Canadian Social Trends* (Statistics Canada Catalogue No. 11-008), 2–13.

Crosnoe, R., & Cavanagh, S. E. (2010). Families with children and adolescents: A review, critique, and future agenda. *Journal of Marriage and Family, 72,* 594–611. doi:10.1111/j.1741-3737.2010.00720.x

Cross, P. (2011, January). How did the 2008–2010 recession and recovery compare with previous cycles? *Canadian Economic Observer* (Statistics Canada Catalogue No. 11-010-x). Retrieved from http://www.statcan.gc.ca/pub/11-010-x/2011001/part-partie3-eng.htm

Crouter, A. C., Bumpus, M. F., Head, M. R., & McHale, S. M. (2001). Implications of overwork and overload for the quality of men's family relationships. *Journal of Marriage and Family, 63,* 404–416.

Crytser, A. (1990). *The wife-in-law trap.* New York: Pocket Books.

CTV News. (2013, January 25). Common-law and married couples not due same rights in Quebec: Court. Retrieved from http://www.ctvnews.ca/canada/common-law-and-married-couples-not-due-same-rights-in-quebec-court-1.1129045

Cui, M., Conger, R. D., Bryant, C. M., & Elder, G. H., Jr. (2002). Parental behavior and the quality of adolescent friendships: A social-contextual perspective. *Journal of Marriage and Family, 64,* 676–689.

Cui, M., & Donellan, M. B. (2009). Trajectories of conflict over raising adolescent children and marital satisfaction. *Journal of Marriage and Family, 71,* 478–494.

Cukier, W. (2008). *Family violence: Background paper.* Retrieved from http://www.cacp.ca/media/library/download/383/family-violencewndy.pdf

Cultural "honour" killing brought to Canada. (2007, June 11). *Regina Leader-Post.* Retrieved from http://www.canada.com

Cummings, E. M., Goeke-Morey, M. C., & Papp, L. M. (2003). Children's responses to everyday marital conflict tactics in the home. *Child Development, 74,* 1918–1929.

Cunningham, J. D., & Antill, J. K. (1995). Current trends in nonmarital cohabitation: In search of the POSSLQ. In J. T. Wood and S. Duck (Eds.), *Under-studied relationships: Off the beaten track* (pp. 148–172). Thousand Oaks, CA: Sage.

Cunningham, M. (2001). The influence of parental attitudes and behaviors on children's attitudes toward gender and household labor in early adulthood. *Journal of Marriage and Family, 63,* 111–122.

Cunningham, M., & Thornton, A. (2005). The influence of union transitions on white adults' attitudes toward cohabitation. *Journal of Marriage and Family, 67,* 710–720.

Curtis, L.J. & Pennock, M. (2006, September/October). Social assistance, lone parents and health: What do we know, where do we go? *Canadian Journal of Public Health, 97* (Health Module), S4–S10.

Cutas, D. (2011). On triparenting. Is having three committed parents better than having only two? *Journal of Medical Ethics, 37,* 735–738. doi:10.1136/jme.2011.043745

Dad guilty of stabbing daughter. (2005, March 4). *CNEWS.* Retrieved from http://cnews.canoe.ca/CNEWS/Law/2005/03/4/pf950550.html

Daly, B. (2012, January 26). Honour killings on the rise in Canada: Study. *Toronto Sun.* Retrieved from http://www.torontosun.com/2012/01/26/honour-killings-on-the-rise-in-canada-study

Daly, K. J. (2001). Deconstructing family time: From ideology to lived experience. *Journal of Marriage and Family, 63,* 283–294.

Daly, K. (2003). Family theory versus the theories families live by. *Journal of Marriage and Family, 65,* 771–784.

Daly, K. (2004a). *The changing culture of parenting.* Ottawa: Vanier Institute of the Family.

Daly, K. (2004b, October 4). *Reframed family portraits.* 40th anniversary lecture presented at the meeting of the Vanier Institute of the Family, Ottawa.

Daly, K. (2007a). *Changing patterns of time in families.* Ottawa: Vanier Institute of the Family. Retrieved from http://www.vifamily.ca/library/cft/faster.html

Daly, K. J. (2007b). *Qualitative methods for family studies & human development*. Los Angeles: Sage.

Daly, M., & Wilson, M. I. (1996, June). Violence Against Stepchildren. *Current Directions In Psychological Science, 5*(3), 77–81. doi:10.1111/1467-8721.ep10772793

Daneshpour, M. (2009). Bridges crossed, paths traveled: Muslim intercultural couples. In T. A. Karis & K. D. Killian (Eds.), *Intercultural couples: Exploring diversity in intimate relationships* (pp. 207–228). New York: Routledge.

Dannefer, D., & Perlmutter, M. (1990). Development as a multidimensional process: Individual and social constituents. *Human Development, 33*, 108–137.

Das Gupta, T. (2000). Families of Native people, immigrants, and people of colour. In N. Mandell & A. Duffy (Eds.), *Canadian families: Diversity, conflict, and change* (2nd ed., pp. 146–187). Toronto: Harcourt Canada.

Davis, A. (2008, September). Interpersonal and physical dating violence among teens. *Focus: Views from the National Council on Crime and Delinquency*. Retrieved from http://www.nccd-crc.org/nccd/pubs/Dating%20Violence%20Among%20Teens.pdf

Davis, K. D., Crouter, A. C., & McHale, S. M. (2006). Implications of shift work for parent–adolescent relationships in dual-earner families. *Family Relations, 55*, 450–460.

Davis, K. D., Pirretti, A. E., Goodman, W. B., & Almeida, D. M. (2005, November). *Nonstandard work schedules: Implications for marital quality, work-family spillover, and daily stressors*. Poster presentation at the annual conference of National Council on Family Relations, Phoenix, AZ.

Davis-Kean, P. E. (2005). The influence of parent education and family income on child achievement: The indirect role of parental expectations and the home environment. *Journal of Family Psychology, 19*, 294–304.

Dawson, M. (2004, March 31). *Criminal justice outcomes in intimate and non-intimate partner homicide cases*. (Catalogue No. rr04-6e). Ottawa: Department of Justice Canada. Retrieved from http://www.justice.gc.ca/eng/pi/rs/rep-rap/2004/rr04_6/rr04_6.pdf

Day, C. F., Kirk, S. A., & Gallagher, J. J. (1985). *Educating exceptional children* (Canadian ed.). Scarborough, ON: Nelson Canada.

Day, R. D. (2005). Relationship stress in couples: Situations involving infidelity, infertility, and imprisonment. In P. C. McKenry & S. J. Price (Eds.), *Families & change: Coping with stressful events and transitions* (3rd ed., pp. 333–353). Thousand Oaks, CA: Sage.

Day, R. D., Peterson, G. W., & McCracken, C. (1998). Predicting spanking of younger and older children by mothers and fathers. *Journal of Marriage and the Family, 60*, 79–94.

Day, R. J. F. (2000). *Multiculturalism and the history of Canadian diversity*. Toronto: University of Toronto Press.

DeGarmo, D. S., Patras, J., & Eap, S. (2008). Social support for divorced fathers' parenting: Testing a stress-buffering model. *Family Relations, 57*, 35–48.

Degler, C. (1974). What ought to be and what was: Women's sexuality in the nineteenth century. *American Historical Review, 79*, 1467–1490.

de Jong Gierveld, J. (2004). Remarriage, cohabitation, living apart together: Partner relationships following bereavement or divorce. *Journal of Marriage and Family, 66*, 236–248.

DeKeseredy, W. S. (1993). *Four variations of family violence: A review of sociological research*. Ottawa: National Clearinghouse on Family Violence.

de Magalhães, J. P. (n.d.) *What is aging?*. Retrieved from http://www.senescence.info/definitions.html

Denham, D., & Gillespie, J. (1999). *Two steps forward … One step back: An overview of Canadian initiatives and resources to end woman abuse 1989–1997*. Ottawa: Health Canada. Retrieved from http://www.hc-sc.gc.ca/hppb/familyviolence/html/two_steps/english/

Department of Justice Canada. (2003). *Dating violence fact sheet*. Ottawa: Department of Justice Canada. Retrieved from http://canada.justice.gc.ca/eng/pi/fv-vf/facts-info/dati-freq.html

Department of Justice Canada. (2004). *Canadian custody and access provisions: Extended family custody and access*. Retrieved from http://canada.justice.gc.ca/en/ps/pad/reports/chart/chart1-4e.html

Department of Justice Canada. (2006). *Divorce law: Questions and answers* (Catalogue No. JUS C-777). Ottawa: Author. Retrieved from http://www.justice.gc.ca/en/ps/pad/resources/divorce

Department of Justice Canada. (2008). *Civil marriage and the recognition of same-sex unions*. Ottawa: Author. Retrieved from http://justice.gc.ca/eng/news-nouv/fs-fi/2004/doc_31108.html

Department of Justice Canada. (2009a). *Abuse of older adults: Department of Justice Canada overview paper*. Ottawa: Author. Retrieved from http://www.justice.gc.ca/eng/pi/fv-vf/facts-info/old-age/

Department of Justice. (2009b). *Bill C-38—The Civil Marriage Act—Receives royal assent*. Ottawa: Author. Retrieved from http://www.justice.gc.ca/eng/news-nouv/nr-cp/2005/doc_31578.html

Department of Justice Canada. (2009c). *Canadian laws on abuse and neglect*. Ottawa: Department of Justice Canada, Canadian Network for the Prevention of Elder Abuse. Retrieved from http://www.cnpea.ca/canadian_laws_on_abuse_and_negle.pdf

Department of Justice Canada. (2009d). *Child abuse: A fact sheet from the Department of Justice Canada*. Ottawa: Author. Retrieved from http://www.justice.gc.ca/eng/pi/fv-vf/facts-info/child-enf.pdf

Department of Justice Canada. (2009e). *Criminal Code*. Ottawa: Author. Retrieved from http://laws.justice.gc.ca/eng/C-46/index.html

Department of Justice Canada (2009f, August 26). *Spousal support advisory guidelines: A draft proposal*. Ottawa: Author. Retrieved from http://www.justice.gc.ca/eng/pi/fcy-fea/spo-epo/g-ld/ss-pae/proj/1.html

Department of Justice Canada (2009g, August 26). *The supporting families experiencing separation and divorce initiative*. Ottawa: Author. Retrieved from http://www.justice.gc.ca/eng/pi/fcy-fea/

Department of Justice. (2011, December 1). *Annotated bibliography on comparative and international law relating to forced marriage*. Ottawa: Author. Retrieved from http://www.justice.gc.ca/eng/pi/fcy-fea/lib-bib/rep-rap/2007/mar/chap1.html

Department of Justice. (2012a, August 3). *Polygyny and Canada's obligations under international human rights law.* Ottawa: Author. Retrieved from http://www.justice.gc.ca/eng/dept-min/pub/poly/chap1.html

Department of Justice Canada. (2012b, August 3). *Custody, access and child support: Findings from the National Longitudinal Survey of Children and Youth.* Ottawa: Author. Retrieved from http://www.justice.gc.ca/eng/pi/fcy-fea/lib-bib/rep-rap/1999/anlsc-elnej/p2_01.html

Department of Justice Canada. (2012c, August 3). *About separation and divorce.* Ottawa: Author. Retrieved from http://www.justice.gc.ca/eng/pi/fcy-fea/div/index.html

Department of Justice Canada. (2012d, August 3). *About division of property.* Ottawa: Author. Retrieved from http://www.justice.gc.ca/eng/pi/fcy-fea/prop/index.html

Department of Justice. (2013, March 7). *Family violence initiative.* Ottawa: Author. Retrieved from http://www.justice.gc.ca/eng/pi/fv-vf

Department of Justice Canada. (n.d.). *About parenting arrangements (custody and access).* Ottawa: Author. Retrieved from http://www.justice.gc.ca/eng/pi/fcy-fea/pa-ep/index.html

Department of Public Health, Toronto. (1922). *The care of the infant and young child.* Toronto: Author.

DePaulo, B. (2006). *Singled out: How singles are stereotyped, stigmatized, and ignored, and still live happily ever after.* New York: St. Martin's Press.

DeVault, M. L. (1991). *Feeding the family: The social organization of caring as gendered work.* Chicago: University of Chicago Press.

Dickson, F. C. (1995). The best is yet to be: Research on long-lasting marriages. In J. T. Wood & S. Duck (Eds.), *Under-studied relationships: Off the beaten track* (pp. 22–50). Thousand Oaks, CA: Sage.

Dijkstra, P., & Barelds, D. (2008). Do people know what they want: A similar or complementary partner? *Evolutionary Psychology, 6*(4), 595–602.

Dion, M. R. (2005). Healthy marriage programs: Learning what works. *The Future of Children, 15*(2), 139–156. Retrieved from http://www.futureofchildren.org

Directeur de l'état civil, Québec. (2007). *Change of name.* Québec: Directeur de l'état civil. Retrieved from http://www.etatcivil.gouv.qc.ca/en/change-name.html

Divorce in Canada (2009). *General information: Children and child support.* Retrieved from http://www.divorceincanada.ca/general2.htm#Child Support

Doherty, G. (1996). *The great child-care debate: The long-term effects of non-parental child care.* Toronto: University of Toronto, Childcare Resource and Research Unit. Retrieved from http://www.childcarecanada.org/resources/CRRUpubs/op7/7optoc.html

Doherty, G., Friendly, M., & Oloman, M. (1998). *Women's support, women's work: Child care in an era of deficit reduction, devolution, downsizing and deregulation.* Ottawa: Status of Women Canada.

Dolbin-MacNab, M. L. (2006). Just like raising your own? Grandmothers' perceptions of parenting a second time around. *Family Relations, 55,* 564–575.

Dolnick, S. (2007, December 31). Commercial surrogacy—some call it "wombs for rent"—booms in India. *Arizona Daily Star,* p. A5.

Donnelly, D. A., & Burgess, E. O. (2008). The decision to remain in an involuntarily celibate relationship. *Journal of Marriage and Family, 70,* 519–535.

Dorow, S. (2006). Racialized choices: Chinese adoption and the "white noise" of blackness. *Critical Sociology, 32*(2/3), 357–379. doi:10.1163/156916306777835277

Douglas, K. (2001). *Divorce law in Canada* (Rev. 96-3E). Ottawa: Government of Canada, Depository Services Program. Retrieved from http://dsp-psd.tpsgc.gc.ca/Collection-R/LoPBdP/CIR/963-e.htm

Douglas, S. J., & Michaels, M. W. (2004). *The mommy myth: The idealization of motherhood and how it has undermined women.* New York: Free Press.

Douthitt, R. A., & Fedyk, J. (1990). *The cost of raising children in Canada.* Toronto: Butterworths.

Downey, D. B., & Condron, D. J. (2004). Playing well with others in kindergarten: The benefit of siblings at home. *Journal of Marriage and Family, 66,* 333–350.

Doyle, K. W., Wolchik, S. A., & Dawson-McClure, S. (2002). Development of the stepfamily events profile. *Journal of Family Psychology, 16*(2), 128–143.

Dreby, J. (2007). Children and power in Mexican transnational families. *Journal of Marriage and Family, 69,* 1050–1064.

Driver, J., Tabares, A., Shapiro, A., Nahm, E. Y., & Gottman, J. M. (2003). Interactional patterns in marital success or failure: Gottman laboratory studies. In F. Walsh (Ed.), *Normal family processes: Growing diversity and complexity* (3rd ed., pp. 493–513). New York: Guilford.

Dryburgh, H. (2000). Teenage pregnancy. *Health Reports, 12*(1), 9–19.

Dubeau, D. (2002). *Portraits of fathers.* Ottawa: Vanier Institute of the Family.

Dubow, E. F., Huesmann, L. R., & Greenwood, D. (2008). Media and youth socialization: Underlying processes and moderators of effects. In J. E. Grusec & P. D. Hastings (Eds.), *Handbook of socialization: Theory and research* (pp. 404–460). New York: Guilford.

Duffy, A., & Momirov, J. (1997). *Family violence: A Canadian introduction.* Toronto: James Lorimer.

Duhaime, L. (2010). *Abortion law in Canada.* Retrieved from http://duhaime.org/LegalResources/FamilyLaw/LawArticle-27/Abortion-Law-in-Canada.aspx

Duhaime, L. (2011, October 31). *Adoption law in Canada.* Retrieved from http://www.duhaime.org/LegalResources/FamilyLaw/LawArticle-190/Adoption-Law-in-Canada.aspx

Duhaime, L. (2012). *About marriage in Canada.* Retrieved from http://www.duhaime.org/LegalResources/FamilyLaw/LawArticle-34/Marriage-in-Canada.aspx

Dumas, J. (1987). *Current demographic analysis: Report on the demographic situation in Canada 1986.* Ottawa: Statistics Canada.

Dumas, J., & Bélanger, A. (1996). *Report on the demographic situation in Canada 1995: Current demographic analysis.* Ottawa: Statistics Canada.

Dumas, J., & Peron, Y. (1992). *Marriage and conjugal life in Canada: Current demographic analysis.* Ottawa: Statistics Canada.

Dunifon, R., & Kowaleski-Jones, L. (2007). The influence of grandparents in single-mother families. *Journal of Marriage and Family, 69,* 465–481.

Dunn, J. (2008). Siblings and socialization. In J. E. Grusec & P. D. Hastings (Eds.), *Handbook of socialization: Theory and research* (pp. 309–327). New York: Guilford.

Duschesne, L. (2004). *La diffusion des naissances hors mariage, 1950–2003.* Retrieved from the Institut de la Statistique (Québec) website http://www.stat.gouv.qc.ca/publications/demograp/extraits/extrait_bilan2004.pdf

Dutton, D. G. (2007). *The abusive personality: Violence and control in intimate relationships* (2nd ed.). New York: Guilford.

Duvall, E. M., & Miller, B. C. (1985). *Marriage and family development* (6th ed.). New York: Harper & Row.

Duxbury, L. (n.d.). *Squeezed in the middle: The sandwich employee.* Retrieved November 30, 2012, from http://www.academicrelations.sfu.ca/documents/Duxbury.pdf

Duxbury, L., & Higgins, C. (2003). *Work–life conflict in Canada in the new millennium: A status report: Final report.* Ottawa: Health Canada.

Duxbury, L., Higgins, C., & Coghill, D. (2003). *Voices of Canadians: Seeking work–life balance.* Hull, QC: Human Resources Development Canada. Retrieved from http://labour-travail.hrdc-drhc.gc.ca/worklife/vcswlb-tcrctvp/tm.cfm

Duxbury, L., Higgins, C., & Schroeder, B. (2009, January). *Balancing paid work and caregiving responsibilities: A closer look at family caregivers in Canada.* Retrieved from http://www.cprn.org/documents/51061_EN.pdf

Early Childhood Development. (2012). *Public investments in early childhood education and care in Canada, 2010.* Retrieved from http://www.ecd-elcc.ca/eng/ecd/ececc/page18.shtml#tbl14bot

Edin, K., & Kefalas, M. (2005). *Promises I can keep: Why poor women put motherhood before marriage.* Berkeley: University of California Press.

Edin, K., & Lein, L. (1997). *Making ends meet: How single mothers survive welfare and low-wage work.* New York: Russell Sage Foundation.

Edin, K., & Reed, J. M. (2005). Why don't they just get married? Barriers to marriage among the disadvantaged. *The Future of Children, 15,* 117–137. Retrieved from http://www.futureofchildren.org

Edlund, J. E., Heider, J. D., Scherer, C. R., Farc, M.-M., & Sagarin, B. J. (2006). Sex differences in jealousy in response to actual infidelity. *Evolutionary Psychology, 4,* 462–470. Retrieved from http://www.epjournal.net

Edmonston, B., Lee, S. M., & Wu, Z. (2008). *Childless Canadian couples.* Victoria: University of Victoria, Department of Sociology and Population Research Group. Retrieved from http://www.policyresearch.gc.ca/

Edwards, H. (1989). *How could you? Mothers without custody of their children.* Freedom, CA: Crossing Press.

EGALE (Equality for Gays and Lesbians Everywhere). (1999a, May 20). *M. v. H: An EGALE backgrounder.* Retrieved from http://www.egale.ca/legal/backgrd3.htm

EGALE. (1999b, May 20). *Supreme court rules: Same-sex couples entitled to equality.* Retrieved from http://www.egale.ca/pressrel/990520.htm

EGALE. (n.d.). *Bill C23 and conjugal relationships.* Retrieved from http://www.egale.ca/documents/conjugality.htm

Eggebeen, D. J., & Sturgeon, S. (2006). Demography of the baby boomers. In S. K. Whitbourne & S. L. Willis (Eds.), *The baby boomers grow up: Contemporary perspectives on midlife* (pp. 3–21). Mahwah, NJ: Lawrence Erlbaum.

Ehrenberg, M. F., Robertson , M., & Pringle, J. (2012). Attachment style and marital commitment in the context of remarriage. *Journal of Divorce and Remarriage, 53*(3), 204–219.

Ehrensaft, D. (2005). *Mommies, daddies, donors, surrogates: Answering tough questions and building strong families.* New York: Guilford.

Eicher-Catt, D. (2004, March). Noncustodial mothers and mental health: When absence makes the heart break. *Family Focus,* F7–F8.

Eichler, M. (1983). *Families in Canada today: Recent changes and their policy consequences.* Toronto: Gage Educational.

Eichler, M. (1987). Family change and social policies. In *Family Matters.* Toronto: Methuen.

Eichler, M. (2012). Marriage and divorce. *Canadian Encyclodepia.* Retrieved from http://www.thecanadianencyclopedia.com/articles/marriage-and-divorce

Elliott, S. A., & Watson, J. P. (1985). Sex during pregnancy and the first prenatal year. *Journal of Psychosomatic Research, 29,* 541–548.

Ellison, M. M. (2004). *Same-sex marriage: A Christian ethical analysis.* Cleveland, OH: Pilgrim.

Elmore, J. (2003, Fall). Foster families working with birth families to help move children to timely permanency. *Permanency Planning Today,* pp. 8–11. Retrieved from http://www.hunter.curry.edu/socwork/nrcfcpp/downloads/ppt-fall-2003.pdf

Elquist, M. J., & Hilton, J. M. (2003, November). *Marital satisfaction and equity in work/family role responsibilities in dual earner shiftworkers.* Poster presentation at the annual conference of National Council on Family Relations, Vancouver, BC.

Engels, F. (1884/2004). *The origin of the family, private property and the state.* Chippendale: Resistance Books. Retrieved June 3, 2012, from http://readingfromtheleft.com/PDF/EngelsOrigin.pdf

English-Lueck, J. A. (2001, March). Technology and social change: The effects on family. *Family Focus,* F1–F3, F5.

Envision Counselling and Support Centre. (2012). *Parent abuse.* Retrieved from http://www.envisioncounsellingcentre.com/parent-abuse.html

Erera, P. I. (2002). *Family diversity: Continuity and change in the contemporary family.* Thousand Oaks, CA: Sage.

Erikson, E. H. (1982). *The life cycle completed: A review.* New York: W. W. Norton.

Escobar-Chavez, S. L., & Anderson, C. A. (2008, Spring). Media and risky behaviors. *The Future of Children, 18*(1), 147–180.

Ethics Committee of the American Society for Reproductive Medicine. (2004a). Child-rearing ability and the provision of fertility services. *Fertility and Sterility, 82,* 564–567.

Ethics Committee of the American Society for Reproductive Medicine. (2004b). Informing offspring of their conception by gamete donation. *Fertility and Sterility, 81*, 527–531.

Ethics Committee of the American Society for Reproductive Medicine. (2006). Access to fertility treatment by gays, lesbians, and unmarried persons. *Fertility and Sterility, 86*, 1333–1335.

European Agency for Safety and Health at Work. (2012). Family issues and work–life balance. Retrieved from https://osha.europa.eu/en/publications/e-facts/e-fact-57-family-issues-work-life-balance

Evan B. Donaldson Adoption Institute. (2003, March). *Unintended consequences: "Safe haven" laws are causing problems, not solving them.* New York: Author. Retrieved from http://www.adoptioninstitute.org/whowe/Last%20report.pdf

Evan B. Donaldson Adoption Institute. (2006, March). *Expanding resources for children: Is adoption for gays and lesbians part of the answer for boys and girls who need homes?* New York: Author. Retrieved from http://www.adoptioninstitute.org

Evan B. Donaldson Adoption Institute. (2009, February). *Old lessons for a new world: Applying adoption research and experience to assisted reproductive technology.* New York: Author. Retrieved from http://www.adoptioninstitute.org/

Family Services of Greater Vancouver. (2008). *Sibling sexual abuse: A guide for parents.* Retrieved from http://www.phac-aspc.gc.ca/ncfv-cnivf/pdfs/nfntsx-visac-sib_e.pdf

Fan, X., Miller, B. C., Christensen, M., Park, K.-E., Grotevant, H. D., van Dulmen, M., et al. (2002). Questionnaire and interview inconsistencies exaggerated differences between adopted and non-adopted adolescents in a national sample. *Adoption Quarterly, 6*(2), 7–27.

Farris-Manning, C., & Zandstra, M. (2003, March). *Children in care in Canada.* Retrieved from http://www.nationalchildrensalliance.com/nca/pubs/2003/Children_in_Care_March_2003.pdf

Fast, J. (2005, Summer). Caregiving: A fact of life. *Transition, 4*–9.

Fast, J., & Frederick, J. (2004). *The time of our lives: Juggling work and leisure over the life cycle* (Catalogue No. 89-584-MIE). Ottawa: Statistics Canada.

Fast, J., Frederick, J., Zukewich, N., & Franke, S. (2001, Winter). The time of our lives . . . *Canadian Social Trends* (Statistics Canada Catalogue no. 11-008), 20–23.

Fauth, R. C. (2004). The impacts of neighborhood poverty deconcentration efforts on low-income children's and adolescents' well-being. *Children, Youth and Environments, 14*(1), 1–55. Retrieved from http://www.coloradu.edu/journals/cye/

Fawcett, G., Ciceri, C., Tsoukalas, S., & Gibson-Kierstead, A. (2004). *Supports and services for adults and children aged 5-14 with disabilities in Canada: An analysis of data on needs and gaps.* Ottawa: Canadian Council on Social Development. Retrieved from http://socialunion.gc.ca/pwd/

Federation of Canadian Municipalities. (2000). *A national affordable housing strategy.* Ottawa: Author.

Feigelman, W. (2001). Comparing adolescents in diverging family structures: Investigating whether adoptees are more prone to problems than their non-adopted peers. *Adoption Quarterly, 5*(2), 5–27.

Feinberg, M. E., Kan, M. L., & Hetherington, E. M. (2007). The longitudinal influence of coparenting conflict on parental negativity and adolescent maladjustment. *Journal of Marriage and Family, 69*, 687–702.

Feinberg, M. E., McHale, S. M., Crouter, A., & Cumsille, P. (2003). Sibling differentiation: Sibling and parent relationship trajectories in adolescence. *Child Development, 74*, 1261–1274.

Feldstein Family Law Group. (2012). *Division of property and assets: An overview.* Retrieved from http://www.separation.ca/family-law/division-of-family-assets

Felson, R. B., & Paré, P.-P. (2005). The reporting of domestic violence and sexual assault by nonstrangers to the police. *Journal of Marriage and Family, 67*, 597–610.

Feng, Y., Dubey, S., & Brooks, B. (2007). *Persistence of low income among non-elderly unattached individuals* (Catalogue No. 75F002MIE, no. 005). Ottawa: Statistics Canada.

Ferrao, V. (2010). Paid work. *Women in Canada: A gender-based statistical report* (Catalogue No. 89-503-x). Ottawa: Statistics Canada. Retrieved from http://www.statcan.gc.ca/pub/89-503-x/2010001/article/11387-eng.pdf

Ferrer, A., & Gagné, L. (2006, September). *The use of family friendly workplace practices in Canada* (IRPP Working Paper Series No. 2006-02). Montreal: Institute for Research on Public Policy. Retrieved from http://www.irpp.org/wp/archive/wp2006-02.pdf

Few, A. L., & Rosen, K. H. (2005). Victims of chronic dating violence: How women's vulnerabilities link to their decisions to stay. *Family Relations, 54*, 265–279.

Fiese, B. H., & Schwartz, M. (2008). Reclaiming the family table: Mealtimes and child health and wellbeing. *Social Policy Report, 22*(4), 1, 3–15.

Financial Consumer Agency of Canada. (2012, March 14). *How prenuptial and cohabitation agreements affect your finances.* Retrieved from http://www.fcac-acfc.gc.ca/eng/consumers/lifeevents/couple/law/prenup-eng.asp

Fincham, F. D., Stanley, S. M., & Beach, S. R. H. (2007). Transformative processes in marriage: An analysis of emerging trends. *Journal of Marriage and Family, 69*, 275–292.

Fine, M. A., Ganong, L. H., & Demo, D. H. (2010). Divorce: A risk and resilience perspective. In S. J. Price, C. A. Price, & P. C. McKenry (Eds.), *Families & change: Coping with stressful life events and transitions* (4th ed., pp. 211–233). Los Angeles: Sage.

Fingerman, K. L., Cheng, Y.-P., Wesselmann, E. D., Zarit, S., Furstenberg, F., & Birditt, K. S. (2012). Helicopter parents and landing pad kids: Intense parental support of grown children. *Journal of Marriage and Family, 74*, 880–896. doi:10:10.1111/j.1741-3737.2012.00987.x

Fingerman, K. L., & Pitzer, L. (2007). Socialization in old age. In J. E. Grusec & P. D. Hastings (Eds.), *Handbook of socialization: Theory and research* (pp. 232–255). New York: Guilford.

Finkel, E. J., Eastwick , P., Karney, B., Reis, H., & Sprecher, S. (2012). Online dating: A critical analysis from the perspective of psychological science. *Psychological Science in the Public Interest, 13*(1), 3–66. doi:10.1177/1529100612436522

Fitzpatrick, J., Sharp, E. A., & Reifman, A. (2009). Midlife singles' willingness to date partners with heterogeneous characteristics. *Family Relations, 58*, 121–133.

Fleury, D. (2008, May). Low-income children. *Perspectives on Labour and Income* (Statistics Canada Catalogue No. 75-001-X), 14–23. Retrieved from http://www.statcan.gc.ca/pub/75-001-x/2008105/pdf/10578-eng.pdf

Food Banks of Canada (2012). *HungerCount 2012*. Retrieved from http://www.foodbankscanada.ca/Learn-About-Hunger/Publications/Research.aspx

Foreign Affairs and International Trade Canada. (2009). *International child abductions: A manual for parents* (Rev., Catalogue No. FR4-10/2005). Ottawa: Author. Retrieved from http://www.voyage.gc.ca/publications/int_child_abduct-en.pdf

Forthofer, M. S., Markman, H. J., Cox, M., Stanley, S., & Kessler, R. C. (1996). Associations between marital distress and work loss in a national sample. *Journal of Marriage and the Family, 58,* 597–605.

Fosco, G. M., & Grych, J. H. (2010). Adolescent triangulation into parental conflicts: Longitudinal implications for appraisals and adolescent-parent relations. *Journal of Marriage and Family, 72,* 254–266. doi:10.1111/j.1741-3737.2010.00697.x

Foulds, N. B. (2012). Quebec Act. *Canadian Encyclopedia.* Retrieved from http://www.thecanadianencyclopedia.com/articles/quebec-act#SUBLinks

Fox, G. (2006). Development in family contexts. In L. Combrick-Graham (Ed.), *Children in family contexts: Perspectives on treatment* (2nd ed., pp. 26–50). New York: Guilford.

Fox, G. L., & Murry, V. M. (2000). Gender and families: Feminist perspectives and family research. *Journal of Marriage and the Family, 62,* 1160–1172.

Fox, K. E. (2005). Are they really neglected? A look at worker perceptions of neglect through the eyes of a national data system. *First People's Child and Family Review, 1*(1), 73–82.

Fraenkel, P. (2003). Contemporary two-parent families: Navigating work and family challenges. In F. Walsh (Ed.), *Normal family processes: Growing diversity and complexity* (3rd ed., pp. 61–95). New York: Guilford.

Frankel-Howard, D. (1989). *Family violence: A review of theoretical and clinical literature.* Ottawa: Health and Welfare Canada.

Fraser, K. (2010, January 13). Polygamist sect leader sues B.C. government. *National Post.* Retrieved from http://www.nationalpost.com/news/story.html?id=2438556

Fravel, D. L., McRoy, R. G., & Grotevant, H. D. (2000). Birthmother perceptions of the psychologically present adopted child: Adoption openness and boundary ambiguity. *Family Relations, 49,* 425–433.

Frazer, J. G. (2010). *Totemism and exogamy* (Vol. III). New York: Cosimo.

Frederick, J. A., & Hamel, J. (1998, Spring). Canadian attitudes to divorce. *Canadian Social Trends* (Statistics Canada Catalogue no. 11-008-XPE), 6–11.

Freeman, T., Jadva, V., Kramer, W., & Golombok, S. (2009). Gamete donations: Parents' experiences of searching for their child's donor siblings and donor. *Human Reproduction, 24,* 505–516.

Frenette, M. (2007, February). *Why are youth from lower-income families less likely to attend university? Evidence from academic abilities, parental influences, and financial constraints* (Catalogue No. 11F0019MIE—No. 295). Ottawa: Statistics Canada. Retrieved from http://www.statcan.gc.ca

Frenette, M., & Picot, G. (2003). *Life after welfare: The economic well being of welfare leavers in Canada during the 1990s* (Catalogue No. 11F0019MIE—No. 192). Ottawa: Statistics Canada.

Frenette, M., Picot, G., & Sceviour, R. (2004). *How long do people live in low-income neighbourhoods? Evidence for Toronto, Montreal, and Vancouver* (Catalogue No. 11F0019MIE—No. 216). Ottawa: Statistics Canada.

Freundlich, M. (2000). *The market forces in adoption.* Washington, DC: Child Welfare League of America.

Freundlich, M. (2001). *Adoption and assisted reproduction.* Washington, DC: Child Welfare League of America.

Freundlich, M. (2007). *For the records: Restoring a legal right for adult adoptees.* New York: Evan B. Donaldson Adoption Institute. Retrieved from http://www.adoptioninstitute.org

Frideres, J. S. (2005, May 28). *Immigrants, integration and the intersection of identities.* Retrieved from http://canada.metropolis.net/events/diversity/immigration.pdf

Friedmann, M.-L. (2005, September). Couples taking care of each other: Does ethnicity matter? *Family Focus,* F27–F28.

Friendly, M., & Beach, J. (2013). *The state of early childhood education and care in Canada, 2010: Trends and analysis.* Retrieved from http://www.childcarecanada.org/sites/default/files/state_ecec_canada_2010_CRRU.pdf

Friendly, M., & Prentice, S. (2009). *About Canada: Childcare.* Halifax & Winnipeg: Fernwood.

Frisco, M. L., Muller, C., & Frank, K. (2007). Parents' union dissolution and adolescents' school performance: Comparing methodological approaches. *Journal of Marriage and Family, 69,* 721–741.

Fu, V. K. (2008). Interracial-interethnic unions and fertility in the United States. *Journal of Marriage and Family, 70,* 783–795.

Fuller-Thomson, E. (2005a). Canadian First Nations grandparents raising grandchildren: A portrait in resilience. *International Journal of Aging and Human development, 60,* 331–342.

Fuller-Thomson, E. (2005b, October). *Grandparents raising grandchildren in Canada: A profile of skipped-generation families* (SEDAP Research Paper No. 132). Hamilton, ON: SEDAP (Social and Economic Dimensions of an Aging Population).

Gaetz, S. (2012). *The real cost of homelessness: Can we save money by doing the right thing?* Retrieved from http://www.homelesshub.ca/ResourceFiles/costofhomelessness_paper21092012.pdf

Gaffield, C. (1982). Schooling, the economy, and rural society in nineteenth-century Ontario. In J. Parr (Ed.), *Childhood and family in Canadian history* (pp. 69–92). Toronto: McClelland & Stewart.

Gagné, M.-H., Drapeau, S., Melançon, C., Saint-Jacques, M.-C., & Lepine, R. (2007). Links between parental psychological violence, other family disturbances, and children's adjustment. *Family Process, 46*(4), 523–542. doi:10.1111/j.1545-5300.2007.00230.x

Galarneau, D., & Radulescu, M. (2009, May). Employment among the disabled. *Perspectives on Labour and Income* (Statistics Canada Catalogue no. 75-001-X). Retrieved from http://www.statcan.gc.ca

Galvin, K. M. (2006, December). Genetic health and family interaction: Who, what, when and how to tell. *Family Focus,* F10, F12.

Garbarino, J. (1992). *Children and families in the social environment* (2nd ed.). New York: Aldine de Gruyter.

Garcia, J. R., Reiber, C., Massey, S. G., & Merriwether, A. M. (2012). Sexual hookup culture: A review. *Review of General Psychology, 16*(2), 161–176. doi:10.1037/a0027911

Garcia, L. T. (2006). Perceptions of sexual experience and preferences for dating and marriage. *Canadian Journal of Human Sexuality, 15*, 85–94.

Garlick, S. (2011, August). A new sexual revolution? Critical theory, pornography, and the Internet. *Canadian Review of Sociology, 48*(3), 221–239.

Garriguet, D. (2005). Early sexual intercourse. *Health Reports* (Statistics Canada Catalogue no. 82-003), *16*(3), 9–18.

Gascon, C. S. (2009). The current recession: How bad is it? *Economic Synopses*. Retrieved from http://www.users.drew.edu/fmbiekop/Synopsis_recession.pdf

Gauvin, L., Richard, L., Kestens, Y., Shatenstein, B., Daniel, M., Moore, S., et al. (2012). Living in a well-serviced urban area is associated with maintenance of frequent walking among seniors in the VoisiNuAge study. *Journals of Gerontology, Series B: Psychological Sciences and Social Sciences, 67*(1), 76–88.

Gauvain, M., & Perez, S. M. (2008). The socialization of cognition. In J. E. Grusec & P. D. Hastings (Eds.), *Handbook of socialization: Theory and research* (pp. 588–613). New York: Guilford.

Gazso, A. (2007). Balancing expectations for employability and family responsibilities while on social assistance: Low-income mothers' experiences in three Canadian provinces. *Family Relations, 56*, 454–466.

Geck, C. (2006, February 19). The generation Z connection: Teaching information literacy to the newest Net generation. *Red Orbit*. Retrieved from http://www.redorbit.com/news/technology/397034/the_generation_z_connection_teaching_information_literacy_to_the_newest

Gee, E. M. (1987). Historical change in the family life course of Canadian men and women. In V. W. Marshall (Ed.), *Aging in Canada: Social perspectives* (2nd ed., pp. 265–287). Markham, ON: Fitzhenry & Whiteside.

Gelles, R. J. (2000). Controversies in family preservation programs. In R. A. Geffner, P. G. Jaffe, & M. Suderman (Eds.), *Children exposed to domestic violence: Current issues in research, intervention, prevention, and policy development* (pp. 239–252). New York: Haworth Maltreatment & Trauma Press.

Geoffroy, M.-C., Côté, S., Dionne, G., Zelazo, P., Tremblay, R., Giguère, C.-E., . . . Boivin, M. (2010). Closing the gap in academic readiness and achievement: The role of early childcare. *Journal of Child Psychology and Psychiatry, 51*(12), 1359–1367. doi:10.1111/j.1469-7610.2010.02316.x

Gelles, R. J. (2010). Violence, abuse, and neglect in families and intimate relationships. In S. J. Price, C. A. Price, & P. C. McKenry (Eds.), *Families & change: Coping with stressful events and transitions* (4th ed., pp. 119–139). Los Angeles: Sage.

Gershoff, E. T. (2002). Corporal punishment by parents and associated child behaviors and experiences: A meta-analytic and theoretical review. *Psychological Bulletin, 128*(4), 539–579.

Gershoff, E. T. (2008). *Report on physical punishment in the United States: What research tells us about its effects on children.* Columbus, OH: Center for Effective Discipline. Retrieved from http://www.phoenixchildrens.com/PDFs/principles_and_practices_of_effective_discipline.pdf

Gerson, K. (1987). *Hard choices: How women decide about work, career, and motherhood.* Berkeley, CA: University of California Press.

Gerson, K. (1993). *No man's land: Men's changing commitments to family and work.* New York: Basic Books.

Gewirtzman, R., & Fodor, I. (1987). The homeless child at school: From welfare hotel to classroom. *Child Welfare, 66*, 237–245.

Giboney, S. K. (2001, December). A visible death. *Family Focus*, F3, F7.

Gilbert, W. S. (1996). Trial by jury. In I. Bradley (Ed.), *The complete annotated Gilbert and Sullivan.* Oxford: Oxford University Press. (Originally published 1875.)

Gilgun, J. F. (1995). We shared something special: The moral discourse of incest perpetrators. *Journal of Marriage and the Family, 57*, 265–281.

Gilgun, J. F. (1999). *Brainstorming: A comprehensive theory of family violence.* Retrieved from http://www.mincava.umn.edu/documents/jgilgun/brainstorm.html

Gilmore, J. (2009, November). *The 2008 Canadian immigrant labour market: Analysis of quality of employment.* Statistics Canada. Retrieved from http://www.statcan.gc.ca/pub/71-606-x/71-606-x2009001-eng.pdf

Gillmore, M. R., Lee, J., Morrison, D. M., & Lindhorst, T. (2008). Marriage following adolescent parenthood: Relationship to adult well-being. *Journal of Marriage and Family, 70*, 1136–1144.

Gladstone, J. W., Brown, R. A., & Fitzgerald, K. J. (2009). Grandparents raising their grandchildren: Tensions, service needs, and involvement with child welfare agencies. *International Journal of Aging and Human Development, 69*(1), 55–78.

Gleason, M. (1999). *Normalizing the ideal: Psychology, schooling, and the family in postwar Canada.* Toronto: University of Toronto Press.

Glick, J. E., & Van Hook, J. (2002). Parents' coresidence with adult children: Can immigration explain racial and ethnic variation? *Journal of Marriage and Family, 64*, 240–253.

Glover, J. (2006). *Choosing children: Genes, disability, and design.* Oxford: Clarendon.

Goddard, H. W., Goff, B. G., Dennis, S. A., & Melancon, M. V. (2002, November). *Value differences in adolescent crowds.* Poster presentation at the annual conference of National Council on Family Relations, Houston, TX.

Goldberg, A. E., & Sayer, A. (2006). Lesbian couples' relationship quality across the transition to parenthood. *Journal of Marriage and Family, 68*, 87–100.

Goldberg, D. L. (2003). *Grandparent–grandchild access: A legal analysis.* Ottawa: Department of Justice Canada.

Goldberg, K. (1996, Fall). Corporal punishment of children: When family issues become public concerns. *Canada's Children.* Retrieved from http://www.cfc-efc.ca/docs/00000823.htm

Goldscheider, F., & Sassler, S. (2006). Creating stepfamilies: Integrating children into the study of union formation. *Journal of Marriage and Family, 68*, 275–291.

Goldscheider, F. K., Thornton, A., & Yang, L.-S. (2001). Helping out the kids: Expectations about parental support in young adulthood. *Journal of Marriage and Family, 63,* 727–740.

Golijan, R. (2012, September 7). Couple says "I do" ... via Twitter. Retrieved from http://digitallife.today.com/_news/2012/09/07/13733538-couple-says-i-do-via-twitter?lite

Golombok, S., & Fivush, R. (1994). *Gender development.* Cambridge: Cambridge University Press.

Goodwin, C. (2000, January 16). "Nobel sperm bank" babies ... and how they grew. *Toronto Star.* Retrieved from http://www.thestar.ca/thestar/editorial/life/20000116BOD016_BS-BRAINS.html

Goodwin, P.Y. (2003). African American and European American women's marital well-being. *Journal of Marriage and Family, 65,* 550–560.

Gorchoff, S. M., John, O. P., & Helson, R. (2008). Contextualizing change in marital satisfaction during middle age: An 18-year longitudinal study. *Psychological Science, 19,* 1194–1200.

Gorlick, C. A., & Pomfret, D. A. (1993). Hope and circumstance: Single mothers exiting social assistance. In J. Hudson & B. Galaway (Eds.), *Single parent families: Perspectives on research and policy* (pp. 253–270). Toronto: Thompson Educational Publishing.

Gosden, R. (1999). *Designing babies: The brave new world of reproductive technology.* New York: W. H. Freeman.

Gossman, I., Julien, D., Mathieu, M., & Chartrand, E. (2003). Determinants of sex initiation frequencies and sexual satisfaction in long-term couples' relationships. *Canadian Journal of Human Sexuality, 12,* 169–181.

Gotta, G., Green, R.-J., Rothblum, E., Solomon, S., Balsam, K., & Schwartz, P. (2011). Heterosexual, lesbian, and gay male relationships: A comparison of couples in 1975 and 2000. *Family Process, 50*(3), 353–376.

Gottlieb, B. H. (1999, July/August). Flexible work arrangements: The promise and the practice. *CFWW Research News.* Retrieved from http://www.uoguelph.ca/cfww/news_07_99.html

Gottman, J. M. (1991). Predicting the longitudinal course of marriages. *Journal of Marital and Family Therapy, 17,* 3–7.

Gottman, J. M. (1993). A theory of marital dissolution and stability. *Journal of Family Psychology, 7,* 57–75.

Gottman, J. M. (1994). *What predicts divorce? The relationship between marital processes and marital outcomes.* Hillsdale, NJ: Lawrence Erlbaum.

Gouvernement du Québec. (2008). *The legal framework of searches into origins.* Retrieved from http://www.adoption.gouv.qc.ca/site/index.php?en_antecedents_cadre_legislatif

Gouvernement du Québec. (2012a). *De facto separation.* Retrieved from http://www4.gouv.qc.ca/en/Portail/Citoyens/Evenements/separation-divorce/Pages/separation-fait.aspx#

Gouvernement du Québec (2012b, March). *Budget 2012-2013. Québec and its seniors: More support for growing old at home.* Retrieved from http://www.budget.finances.gouv.qc.ca/Budget/2012-2013/en/documents/seniors.pdf

Government of Canada. (2009). *Canada's universal child care plan.* Retrieved from http://www.universalchildcare.ca/eng/support/index.shtml

Government of Canada (1998). *Canada's Action Plan for Food Security.* Ottawa: Author. Retrieved from http://www.agr.gc.ca/misb/fsec-seca/pdf/action_e.pdf

Gower, D. (1997, Summer). *Measuring the age of retirement* (Statistics Canada Catalogue no. 75-001-XPE, pp. 11–17). Retrieved from http://www.statcan.gc.ca/studies-etudes/75-001/archive/e-pdf/3071-eng.pdf

Graham, E. (1996, May 4). Craving closer ties, strangers come together as family. *Wall Street Journal* (Eastern ed.), p. B1.

Grant, Tavia. (2011, July 20). Statistics Canada to stop tracking marriage and divorce rates. *Globe and Mail.* Retrieved from http://www.theglobeandmail.com/news/national/statistics-canada-to-stop-tracking-marriage-and-divorce-rates/article4192704

Granzow, K. (2007). De-constructing "choice": The social imperative and women's use of the birth control pill. *Culture, Health & Sexuality, 9*(1), 43–54.

Green, A. I. (2008). Health and sexual status in an urban gay enclave: An application of the stress process model. *Journal of Health and Social Behavior, 49,* 436–451.

Greenberg, J., Schimel, J., & Martens, A. (2002). Ageism: Denying the face of the future. In T. D. Nelson (Ed.), *Ageism: Stereotyping and prejudice against older persons* (pp. 27–48). Cambridge, MA: MIT Press.

Greene, S. M., Anderson, E. R., Hetherington, M. E., Forgatch, M. S., & DeGarmo, D. S. (2003). Risk and resilience after divorce. In F. Walsh (Ed.), *Normal family processes: Growing diversity and complexity* (3rd ed., pp. 96–120). New York: Guilford.

Greenfield, E. A., & Marks, N. F. (2006). Linked lives: Adult children's problems and their parents' psychological and relational well-being. *Journal of Marriage and Family, 68,* 442–454.

Greenstein, T. N. (2000). Economic dependence, gender, and the division of labor in the home: A replication and extension. *Journal of Marriage and the Family, 62,* 322–335.

Greenstein, T. N. (2006). *Methods of family research* (2nd ed.). Thousand Oaks, CA: Sage.

Greif, G. L. (1985). *Single fathers.* Lexington, MA: Lexington Books.

Greven, P. (1990). *Spare the child: The religious roots of punishment and the psychological impact of physical abuse.* New York: Vintage Books.

Grever, C., & Bowman, D. (2008). *When your spouse comes out: A straight mate's recovery manual.* New York: Haworth.

Griffiths, A., & Cruise, D. (1999). *Hear no evil.* 14th Annual Atkinson Fellowship in Public Policy. Toronto: Atkinson Charitable Foundation. Retrieved from http://atkinsonfdn.on.ca

Gromoski, A. N., & Maguire-Jack, K. (2012). Transactional and cascading relations between early spanking and children's social-emotional development. *Journal of Marriage and Family, 74,* 1054–1068. doi:10.1111/j.1741-3727.2012.01013.x.

Grotevant, H. D. (2008, September). Open adoption: What is it and how is it working? *Family Focus*, F1–F2, F17–F19.

Grusec, J. E., & Davidov, M. (2008). Socialization in the family: The roles of parents. In J. E. Grusec & P. D. Hastings (Eds.), *Handbook of socialization: Theory and research* (pp. 284–308). New York: Guilford.

Grych, J. H., Harold, G. T., & Miles, C. J. (2003). A prospective investigation of appraisals as mediators of the link between interparental conflict and child adjustment. *Child Development, 74*, 1176–1193.

Guendouzi, J. (2006). "The guilt thing". Balancing domestic and professional roles. *Journal of Marriage and Family, 68*, 901–909.

Guest, D. (1985). *The emergence of social security in Canada.* Vancouver: University of British Columbia Press.

Guèvremont, A., & Kohen, D. (2012, November 21). *The physical and mental health of Inuit children of teenage mothers.* Ottawa: Statistics Canada. Retrieved from http://www.statcan.gc.ca/pub/82-003-x/2012004/article/11741-eng.htm

Gugl, E., & Welling, L. (2010, July). The early bird gets the worm? Birth order effects in a dynamic family model. *Economic Inquiry, 48*(3), 690–703. doi:10.1111/j.1465-7295.2009.00214.x

Guilamo-Ramos, V., Jaccard, J., Dittus, P., & Bouris, A. M. (2006). Parental expertise, trustworthiness and accessibility: Parent–adolescent communication and adolescent risk behavior. *Journal of Marriage and Family, 68*, 1229–1246.

Gunby, J., Bissonnette, F., Librach, C., & Cowan, L. (2011). Assisted reproductive technologies (ART) in Canada: 2007 results from the Canadian ART Register. *Fertility and Sterility, 95*(2), 542–547.

Güngör, D. (2011, April 12). *Immigration and acculturation in adolescence.* Encyclopedia on Early Childhood Development. Retrieved from http://www.child-encyclopedia.com/documents/GungorANGxp1.pdf

Haddock, S. A., Zimmerman, T. S., & Lyness, K. P. (2003). Changing gender norms: Transitional dilemmas. In F. Walsh (Ed.), *Normal family processes: Growing diversity and complexity* (3rd ed., pp. 301–336). New York: Guilford.

Hagestad, G. O. (1986). The family: Women and grandparents as kin-keepers. In A. Pifer & L. Bronte (Eds.), *Our aging society: Paradox and promise* (pp. 141–160). New York: W. W. Norton.

Hague Conference on Private International Law. (2012). *Press release—Operation of the Hague Intercountry Adoption Convention.* Retrieved from http://www.hcch.net/upload/press20100624CSadoption-e.pdf

Hall, E. T. (1973). *The silent language.* Garden City, NY: Anchor Press/Doubleday.

Hall, S. S., & Adams, B. (2005, November). *"Is this what I expected?" A qualitative study of newlyweds' expectations.* Poster presentation at the annual conference of National Council on Family Relations, Phoenix, AZ.

Halpern-Meekin, S., & Tach, L. (2008). Heterogeneity in two-parent families and adolescent well-being. *Journal of Marriage and Family, 70*, 435–451.

Hamilton, J. (1971). *Progress.* Calgary: Calgary Power.

Hampton, M. R., Jeffrey, B., McWatters, B., & Smith, P. (2005).

Influence of teens' perceptions of parental disapproval and peer behaviour on their initiation of sexual intercourse. *Canadian Journal of Human Sexuality, 14*, 105–121.

A handy budget checklist to keep track of wedding cost. (n.d.). Retrieved from http://www.ataaa.com/budget.htm

Hans, J. D. (2009). Beliefs about child support modification following remarriage and subsequent childbirth. *Family Relations, 58*, 65–78.

Hansen, K. V. (2005). *Not-so-nuclear families: Class, gender, and networks of care.* New Brunswick, NJ: Rutgers University Press.

Hanson, T. L., McLanahan, S. S., & Thomson, E. (1996). Double jeopardy: Parental conflict and stepfamily outcomes for children. *Journal of Marriage and the Family, 58*, 141–154.

Hardesty, J. L., Khaw, L., Chung, G. H., & Martin, J. M. (2008). Coparenting relationships after divorce: Variations by type of marital violence and fathers' role differentiation. *Family Relations, 57*, 479–491.

Haring, M., Hewitt, P. L., & Flett, G. L. (2003). Perfectionism, coping, and quality of intimate relationships. *Journal of Marriage and Family, 65*, 143–158.

Harknett, K., & Knab, J. (2007). More kin, less support: Multipartnered fertility and perceived support among mothers. *Journal of Marriage and Family, 69*, 237–253.

Harris, H. L. (2003). Multiracial students: What school counselors need to know. *ERIC Digest* (ERIC Document Reproduction Service No. ED479354). Retrieved from http://www.ericdigests.org/2005-2/multiracial.htm

Harris, J. M., Kutob, R. M., Surprenant, Z. J., Maiuro, R. D., & Delate, T. A. (2002). Can Internet-based education improve physician confidence in dealing with domestic violence? *Family Medicine, 34*(4), 287–92. Retrieved from http://www.medicaldirectionsinc.com/PDFs/2002_fammed.pdf

Harris, J. R. (2009). *The nurture assumption: Why children turn out the way they do.* New York: Free Press.

Harris, M. S. (2007). Silent victims: Issues and interventions for children exposed to violence. *Protecting Children, 22*(3 & 4), 45–53.

Hart, D., Atkins, R., & Tursi, N. (2005, April). *The influence of neighborhood poverty on personality change.* Poster presentation at the annual meeting of Society for Research in Child Development, Atlanta, GA. Retrieved from http://hart.camden.rutgers.edu/personality%20and%20neighborhood%20poster.pdf

Hart, L., & Jamieson, W. (2002). *Woman abuse* (Rev., Catalogue No. H72-22/4-2002E). Ottawa: Health Canada.

Hart, R. (1997). *Beginning a long journey: A review of projects funded by the Family Violence Prevention Division, Health Canada, regarding violence in Aboriginal families.* Ottawa: Health Canada.

Harwood, J. (2007). *Understanding communication and aging: Developing knowledge and awareness.* Los Angeles: Sage.

Haskey, J. (2005, Winter). Living arrangements in contemporary Britain: Having a partner who usually lives elsewhere and living apart together (LAT). *Population Trends, 122*, 35–45.

Hastings, P. D., Utendale, W. T., & Sullivan, C. (2008). The socialization of prosocial development. In J. E. Grusec & P. D. Hastings (Eds.), *Handbook of socialization: Theory and research* (pp. 638–664). New York: Guilford.

Haugland, B. S. M. (2005). Recurrent disruptions of rituals and routines in families with paternal alcohol abuse. *Family Relations, 54*, 225–241.

Havighurst, R. J. (1952). *Developmental tasks and education* (2nd ed.). New York: Longman's Green.

Hay, D. I. (2009). *Poverty reduction policies and programs in Canada*. Ottawa: Canadian Council on Social Development. Retrieved from http://www.ccsd.ca/SDR2009/Reports/Canada_Report_FINAL.pdf

Hay, T. (1997). *Child abuse and neglect* (Rev. ed.). Ottawa: Health Canada.

Hazelton, D. (2004). *Letter from the founder*. Widows Too Young: A support site for widows and widowers under age 50. Retrieved from http://www.widowstooyoung.com/

Health Canada. (1999). *Reproductive and genetic technologies overview paper (1999)*. Ottawa: Author. Retrieved from http://www.hc-sc.gc.ca/english/rgt/overview.htm

Health Canada. (2009). *Canadian Alcohol and Drug Use Monitoring Survey: Summary of results for 2008*. Ottawa: Author. Retrieved from http://www.hc-sc.gc.ca/hc-ps/drugs-drogues/stat/_2008/summary-sommaire-eng.php

Health Canada. (2012, August 9). *Because life goes on . . . Helping children and youth live with separation and divorce*. Ottawa: Author. Retrieved from http://www.phac-aspc.gc.ca/publicat/mh-sm/divorce/index-eng.php

Health Canada. (n.d.). *Publication of proposed human reproduction regulations delayed until Supreme Court appeal is decided*. Ottawa: Author. Retrieved from http://www.hc-sc.gc.ca/hl-vs/reprod/hc-sc/legislation/delay-interruption-eng.php

Healthy Aging and Wellness Working Group. (2006). *Healthy aging in Canada: A new vision, a vital investment from evidence to action*. Retrieved from http://www.health.gov.nl.ca/health/publications/vision_rpt_e.pdf

Healthy Workplaces. (2003). *Boomerang kids: Strategies for the not-so-empty nest*. Retrieved from http://www.healthyworkplaces.com/images/boomerangkids.pdf

Hebblethwaite, S., & Norris, J. (2011). Expressions of generativity through family leisure: Experience of grandparents and adult grandchildren. *Family Relations, 60*, 121–133. doi:10.1111/j.1741-3729.2010.000637.x

Hébert, M., Chenier, N. M., & Norris, S. (2004). *Bill C-6: Assisted Human Reproduction Act*. Retrieved from http://www.parl.gc.ca/common/Bills_ls.asp?Parl=37&Ses=3&ls=C6

Hébert, M., Tourigny, M., Cyr, M., McDuff, P., & Joly, J. (2009). Prevalence of childhood sexual abuse and timing of disclosure in a representative sample of adults from Québec. *Canadian Journal of Psychiatry, 54*(9), 631–636.

Helm, B., & Warren, W. (1998, September). Teenagers talk about cultural heritage and family life. *Transition, 28*(3). Retrieved from http://www.vifamily.ca/library/transition/283/283.html

Henslin, J.M., Glenday, D., Pupo, N., & Duffy, A. (2010). *Sociology: A down-to-earth approach*. Toronto: Pearson Education Canada.

Herman, R. D. (1963). The "going steady" complex: A re-examination. In M. B. Sussman (Ed.), *Sourcebook in marriage and the family* (2nd ed., pp. 75–79). Boston: Houghton Mifflin.

Hertlein, K. M., & Piercy, F. P. (2006). Internet infidelity: A critical review of the literature. *The Family Journal, 14*, 366–371. Retrieved from http://tfj.sagepub.com/cgi/content/abstract/14/4/366

Hertz, R. (1987). Three careers: His, hers, and theirs. In N. Gerstel & H. E. Gross (Eds.), *Families and work*. Philadelphia: Temple University Press.

Hertz, R. (2006). *Single by chance, mothers by choice: How women are choosing parenthood without marriage and creating the new American family*. New York: Oxford University Press.

Hetherington, E. M. (2003). Intimate pathways: Changing patterns in close personal relationships across time. *Family Relations, 52*, 318–331.

Hewitt, B., & de Vaus, D. (2009). Change in the association between premarital cohabitation and separation, Australia 1945–2000. *Journal of Marriage and Family, 71*, 353–361.

Heyman, R. E., & Smith Slep, A. M. (2002). Do child abuse and interparental violence lead to adulthood family violence? *Journal of Marriage and Family, 64*, 864–870.

Hicks, R., & Hicks, K. (1999). *Boomers, Xers, and other strangers: Understanding the generational differences that divide us*. Wheaton, IL: Tyndale.

Higginbotham, B. J., Miller, J. J., & Niehuis, S. (2009). Remarriage preparation: Usage, perceived helpfulness, and dyadic adjustment. *Family Relations, 58*, 316–329.

Higgins, C., & Duxbury, L. (2005, July/August). Saying "no" in a culture of hours, money and non-support. *Ivey Business Journal*. (Reprint #9B05TD09). Retrieved from http://www.iveybusinessjournal.com

Higgins, C., Duxbury, L., & Lyons, S. (2007, October). *Reducing work–life conflict: What works? What doesn't?* Ottawa: Health Canada. Retrieved from http://www.hc-sc.gc.ca/ewh-semt/alt_formats/hecs-sesc/pdf/pubs/occup-travail/balancing-equilibre/full_report-rapport_complet-eng.pdf

Higgins, C., Duxbury, L., & Lyons, S. (2008, January). *Reducing work–life conflict: What works? What doesn't?* Ottawa: Health Canada. Retrieved from http://www.hc-sc.gc.ca/ewh-semt/alt_formats/hecs-sesc/pdf/pubs/occup-travail/balancing-equilibre/full_report-rapport_complet-eng.pdf

Higgins, D. (2004) Differentiating between child maltreatment experiences. *Family Matters, 69*, 50–55.

Hilborn, R. (2009, January 7). *China still Canadian favourite for intercountry adoption: 2007 statistics*. Retrieved from http://www.adoption.ca/Intl%Stats%200109

Hill, E. J., Hawkins, A. J., Ferris, M., & Weitzman, M. (2001). Finding an extra day a week: The positive influence of perceived job flexibility on work and family life balance. *Family Relations, 50*, 49–58.

Hill, E. J., Märtinson, V., & Ferris, M. (2004). New concept part-time employment as a work-family adaptive strategy for women professionals with small children. *Family Relations, 53*, 282–292.

Hill, L. (2007, February–March). Freedom bound. *The Beaver*, 17–23.

Hill, R. (1958). Generic features of families under stress. *Social Casework, 49*, 139–150.

Hill, R. D. (2005). *Positive aging: A guide for mental health professionals and consumers*. New York: W. W. Norton.

Hill, T. J. (2005, September). Structural factors related to grand-child and grandparent co-residence in 2000. *Family Focus*, F17, F19.

Hillaker, B. D., Brophy-Herb, H. E., Villaruel, F. A., & Haas, B. E. (2008). The contribution of parenting to social competencies and positive values in middle school youth: Positive family communication, maintaining standards, and supportive family relationships. *Family Relations, 57*, 591–601.

Hines, P. M., Preto, N. G., McGoldrick, M., Almeida, R., & Weltman, S. (1999). Culture and the family life cycle. In D. Carter & M. McGoldrick (Eds.), *The expanded family life cycle: Individual, family, and social perspectives* (3rd ed., pp. 69–87). Boston: Allyn & Bacon.

Hinman, L. M. (n.d.). *Reproductive technology and surrogacy: An introduction to the issues.* Retrieved from http://ethics.acusd.edu/Papers/Introduction%20Technologies.html

Hoffman, L. W., & Youngblade, L. M. (1999). *Mothers at work: Effects on children's well-being.* Cambridge: Cambridge University Press.

Hohmann-Marriott, B. (2006). Shared beliefs and union stability of married and cohabiting couples. *Journal of Marriage and Family, 68*, 1015–1028.

Holcomb, B. (2003). Friendly for whose family? In M. Coleman & L. Ganong (Eds.), *Points & counterpoints: Controversial relationship and family issues in the 21st century: An anthology* (pp. 167–169). Los Angeles: Roxbury.

Holland, B. (1998, March). "The long good-bye," *Smithsonian*, 91–92.

Hollinger, M. A. (2007). Ethical reflections for a globalized family curriculum: A developmental paradigm. In B. Sharif Trask & R. R. Hamon (Eds.), *Cultural diversity and families: Expanding perspectives* (pp. 244–278). Thousand Oaks, CA: Sage.

Hollist, C. S., & Miller, R. B. (2005). Perceptions of attachment style and marital quality in midlife marriage. *Family Relations, 54*, 46–7.

Holmes, M. (2009, April). Commuter couples and distance relationships: Living apart together. In S. Sweet & J. Casey (Eds.), *Work and family encyclopedia*. Chestnut Hill, MA: Sloan Work and Family Research Network. Retrieved from http://wfnetwork.bc.edu/encyclopedia_entry_php?id=15551&area=A11

Holtzman, M. (2005, June). The family definitions continuum. *Family Focus*, F1, F3.

Holtzworth-Munroe, A. (2005). Male versus female intimate partner violence: Putting controversial findings into context. *Journal of Marriage and Family, 67*, 1120–1125.

Home modifications and assistive devices. (2007, August 7). Retrieved from http://www.revolutionhealth.com/healthy-living/caring/daily-care/safety-mobility/

Hook, J. L., & Chalasani, S. (2008). Gendered expectations? Reconsidering single fathers' child-care time. *Journal of Marriage and Family, 70*, 978–990.

Hornjatkevyc, N., & Alderson, K. (2011, October). With and without: The bereavement experiences of gay men who have lost a partner to non-AIDS-related causes. *Death Studies, 35*(9), 801–823.

Hotton, T. (2003). *Childhood aggression and exposure to violence in the home* (Catalogue No. 85-561-MIE). Ottawa: Statistics Canada.

How much does a wedding cost? (n.d.) Retrieved from http://www.directweddings.co.uk/costs/

Howell, R. (n.d.). *Market Segmentation: The Importance of Age Cohorts.* Retrieved from http://www.neumann.edu/academics/divisions/business/journal/Review2012/Howell.pdf

Hou, F., & Myles, J. (2011, December 14). Interracial marriage and status-caste exchange in Canada and the United States. *Ethnic and Racial Studies*, pp. 1–22. doi:10.1080/01419870.2011.634505

Howard, B. (2007, Autumn). The stories we tell. *Transition*, 3–5.

Huang, C.-C. (2009). Mothers' reports of nonresident fathers' involvement with their children: Revisiting the relationship between child support payment and visitation. *Family Relations, 58*, 54–64.

Huck, B. (2001, February/March). Love in another world. *The Beaver*, 12–19.

Hudak, J., Krestan, J. A., & Bepko, C. (1999). Alcohol problems and the family life cycle. In B. Carter & M. McGoldrick (Eds.), *The expanded family life cycle: Individual, family, and social perspectives* (3rd ed., pp. 455–469). Boston: Allyn & Bacon.

Human Resources and Skills Development Canada. (2006). *Social assistance statistical report: 2005.* Retrieved from http://www.hrsdc.gc.ca/eng/cs/sp/sdc/socpol/publications/reports/sd10-3-2004e/page04.shtml

Human Resources and Skills Development Canada. (2009). *Low income in Canada: 2000–2007 using the market basket measure—August 2009.* Ottawa: Author. Retrieved from http://www.hrsdc.gc.ca/eng/publications_resources/research/categories/inclusion/2009/sp-909-07-09/page05.shtml

Human Resources and Skills Development Canada. (2012a, August 30). *Family life—marriage.* Ottawa: Author. Retrieved from http://www4.hrsdc.gc.ca/.3ndic.1t.4r@-eng.jsp?iid=78

Human Resources and Skills Development Canada. (2012b, September 23). *Canadians in context—population size and growth.* Ottawa: Author. Retrieved from http://www4.hrsdc.gc.ca/.3ndic.1t.4r@-eng.jsp?iid=35

Human Resources and Skills Development Canada. (2012c, July 17). *Intercountry adoption in Canada.* Ottawa: Author. Retrieved from http://www.hrsdc.gc.ca/eng/community_partnerships/international_adoption/index.shtml

Human Resources and Skills Development Canada. (2012d, January 23). *Amendments to the Canada Pension Plan.* Ottawa: Author. Retrieved from http://www.hrsdc.gc.ca/eng/oas-cpp/legislation/bill_c51/index.shtml

Human Resources and Skills Development Canada. (2013, May 23). *Financial Security —Low Income Incidence.* Ottawa: Author. Retrieved from http://www4.hrsdc.gc.ca/.3ndic.1t.4r@-eng.jsp?iid=23

Hunter, S. (2005). *Midlife and older LGBT adults: Knowledge and affirmative practice for the social services.* New York: Haworth.

Huntley, R. (2006). *The world according to Y: Inside the new adult generation.* Crows Nest, NSW, AU: Allen & Unwin.

Hurley, M. C. (2005, September). *Bill C-38: The Civil Marriage Act.* Ottawa: Library of Parliament. Retrieved from http://www2.parl.gc.ca/LOP/Legislative_Summaries

Huston, T. L. (2000). The social ecology of marriage and other intimate unions. *Journal of Marriage and the Family, 62*, 298–320.

Hymowitz, K. S. (2006). *Marriage and caste in America: Separate and unequal families in a post-marital age.* Chicago: Ivan R. Dee.

Imber-Black, E. (1989). Women's relationships with larger systems. In M. McGoldrick, C. M. Anderson, & F. Walsh (Eds.), *Women in families: A framework for family therapy* (pp. 451–469). New York: Norton.

Imber-Black, E. (1993). Secrets in families and family therapy: An overview. In E. Imber-Black (Ed.), *Secrets in families and family therapy* (pp. 3–28). New York: Norton.

Infidelity dissected: New research on why people cheat. (2008, September 13). *Science Daily.* Retrieved from http://www.sciencedaily.com/releases/2008/09/080908185238.htm

Infrastructure Canada. (2008). *Population aging and public infrastructure: A literature review of impacts in developed countries.* Ottawa: Author. Retrieved from http://www.infc.gc.ca/altformats/pdf/rs-rr-2008-02-eng.pdf

Ingoldsby, B., Smith, S. R., & Miller, J. E. (2004). *Exploring family theories.* Los Angeles: Roxbury.

Institute for Research on Public Policy. (2007). *Leisure time on the wane in Canada.* Retrieved from http://www.irpp.org/newsroom/archive/2007/020107e.pdf

Ipsos Reid. (2004, April 10). *Parents on parenting: How are Canada's children being raised? Part IV* [Press release]. Toronto: Author.

Ipsos Reid. (2012) *The Ipsos Canadian inter@ctive Reid report: 2012 fact guide.* Retrieved from http://www.ipsos.ca/common/dl/pdf/Ipsos_InteractiveReidReport_FactGuide_2012.pdf

Island, D., & Letellier, P. (1991). *Men who beat the men who love them: Battered gay men and domestic violence.* New York: Harrington Park.

Jacobs, A. (2012, June 18). 7 tips for boomerang kids. *Wise Bread Blog.* Retrieved from http://money.usnews.com/money/blogs/my-money/2012/06/18/7-tips-for-boomerang-kids

Jacobs, A. C. (1939). Marriage laws. *Living, 1*(1), 4–7.

Jacobs, J. S. (1991). Families with a medically ill member. In F. H. Brown (Ed.), *Reweaving the family tapestry: A multigenerational approach to families* (pp. 242–261). New York: W. W. Norton.

Jacobs, N. N., & O'Donohue, W. T. (2007). *Coping with infertility: Clinically proven ways of handling the emotional roller coaster.* New York: Routledge.

Jennings, K. T. (1994). Female sexual molesters: A review of the literature. In M. Elliott (Ed.), *Female sexual abuse of children* (pp. 219–234). New York: Guilford.

Jiwani, Y., Kachuk, P., & Moore, S. (1998, June). *Rural women and violence: A study of two communities in British Columbia.* The FREDA Centre for Research on Violence Against Women and Children. Retrieved from http://www.harbour.sfa.ca/freda/articles/rural00.htm

Johnson, M. P. (2005). Domestic violence: It's not about gender—or is it? *Journal of Marriage and Family, 67*, 1126–1130.

Johnson, P., & Wilkinson, W. K. (1995). The "re-nesting" effect: Implications for family development. *The Family Journal, 3*(2), 126–131.

Jones, A. G., & Ratterman, N. (2009, June 16). Mate choice and sexual selection: What have we learned since Darwin? *PNAS, 106*(1), 10001–10008. doi:10.1073pnas.0901129106

Jones, C. (2010). Lying, cheating, and virtual relationships. *Global Virtue Ethics Review, 6*(1), 3–12.

Jones, C., Clark, L., Grusec, J., Hart, R., Plickert, G., & Tepperman, L. (2002). *Poverty, social capital, parenting, and child outcomes in Canada* (Catalogue No. RH63-1/557-01-03E). Ottawa: Human Resources Development Canada. Retrieved from http://www11.sdc.gc.ca/en/cs/sp/arb/publications/research/2002–002357/

Jones, K. M., Whitbourne, S. K., & Skultety, K. M. (2006). Identity processes and the transition to midlife among baby boomers. In S. K. Whitbourne & S. L. Willis (Eds.), *The baby boomers grow up: Contemporary perspectives on midlife* (pp. 149–164). Mahwah, NJ: Lawrence Erlbaum.

Jones, L., & Finkelhor, D. (2001, January). The decline in child sexual abuse cases. *Juvenile Justice Bulletin.* Washington, DC: U.S. Department of Justice.

Jonson-Reid, M., Swarnes, A., Wilson, B., Stahlschmidt, M. J., & Drake, B. (2009). Building healthy families: An innovative approach to working with families affected by chronic neglect. *Protecting Children, 24*(1), 57–66.

Jose, A., O'Leary, K. D., & Moyer, A. (2010, February). Does premarital cohabitation predict subsequent marital stability and marital quality? A meta-analysis. *Journal of Marriage and Family, 72*, 105–116. doi:10.1111/j.1741-3737.2009.00686.x

Joseph, E. (1997). *Polygamy: The ultimate feminist lifestyle.* Retrieved from http://www.polygamy.com/Practical/Ultimate.htm

Josephson, W. L. (1995). *Television violence: A review of the effects on children of different ages.* Ottawa: Health Canada.

Juby, H. (2003–04, Winter). Yours, mine, and ours: New boundaries for the modern stepfamily. *Transition.* Retrieved from http://www.vifamily.ca/library/transition/334/334.html

Juby, H., Billette, J.-M., Laplante, B., & Le Bourdais, C. (2007). Nonresident fathers and children: Parents' new unions and frequency of contact. *Journal of Family Issues, 28*, 1220–1245. Retrieved from http://jfi.sagepub.com/cgi/reprint/28/9/1220

Juby, H., Marcil-Gratton, N., & Le Bourdais, C., with Huot, P.-M. (2001). A step further in family life: The emergence of the blended family. In A. Bélanger, Y. Carrière, & S. Gilbert, *Report on the demographic situation 2000: Current demographic analysis* (Catalogue No. 91-209-XPE, pp. 169–203). Ottawa: Statistics Canada.

Jurkovic, G. J. (1997). *Lost childhoods: The plight of the parentified child.* New York: Brunner/Mazel.

Justice Québec. (2003). *Marriage.* Québec: Justice Québec. Retrieved from http://www.justice.gouv.qc.ca/english/publications/generale/maria-a.htm

Justice Québec. (2008, May 8). *De facto unions.* Retrieved from http://www.justice.gouv.qc.ca/publications/generale/union-a.htm

Kale, R. (2012, March 6). "It's a girl!"— could be a death sentence. *Canadian Medical Association Journal, 184*(4), 387–388. doi:10.1503/cmaj.120021

Kalish, N. (2005, September). Rekindling romance: Seniors who find lost loves. *Family Focus,* F9–F11.

Kallen, E. (1989). *Label me human: Minority rights of stigmatized Canadians.* Toronto: University of Toronto Press.

Kallen E. (2003). *Ethnicity and human rights in Canada: A human rights perspective on ethnicity, racism, and systemic inequality* (3rd ed.). Don Mills, ON: Oxford University Press.

Kalmijn, M. (2004). Marriage rituals as role transitions: An analysis of weddings in the Netherlands. *Journal of Marriage and Family, 66*, 582–594.

Kalmijn, M., & Monden, C. W. S. (2006). Are the negative effects of divorce on well-being dependent on marital quality? *Journal of Marriage and Family, 68*, 1197–1213.

Kalmijn, M., & Poortman, A.R. (2006, April). His or her divorce? The gendered nature of divorce and its determinants. *European Sociological Review, 22*(2), 201–214.

Kamp Dush, C. M., Taylor, M. G., & Kroeger, R. A. (2008). Marital happiness and psychological well-being across the life course. *Family Relations, 57*, 211–226.

Kang, H.-A. (2002, September). *The nature of adult sibling relationship: Literature review.* University of Illinois at Urbana-Champaign, Children and Family Research Center. Retrieved from http://www.crfc.illinois.edu/LRpdfs/AdultsiblingRel.LR.pdf

Karasik, R. J. (2005, September). Aging: Everybody's doing it! *Family Focus,* F1, F3.

Karasik, R. J., & Hamon, R. R. (2007). Cultural diversity and aging families. In B. S. Trask & R. R. Hamon (Eds.), *Cultural diversity and families: Expanding perspectives* (pp. 136–153). Thousand Oaks, CA: Sage.

Kaufman, T. S. (1993). *The combined family: A guide to creating successful step-relationships.* New York: Plenum.

Kebede, R. (2009, April 23). *Recession linked to more abortions, vasectomies.* New York: Reuters. Retrieved from http://www.reuters.com/articlePrint?articleId=USTRE53L0S5200090423

Keefe, J., Légaré, J., & Carrière, Y., (2007). Developing new strategies to support future caregivers of older Canadians with disabilities: Projections of need and their policy implications. [Supplement]. *Canadian Public Policy, 33,* S65–S80. Retrieved from http://economics.ca/cgi/jab?journal=cpp&view=v33s1/CPPv33s1p065.pdf

Kellas, J.K., LeClair-Underberg, C., & Normand, E.L. (2008, October). Stepfamily address terms: "Sometimes they mean something and sometimes they don't." *Journal of Family Communication, 8*(2), 238–263.

Keller, J. (2010, April 28). Polygamy court case will proceed without Bountiful leader, says lawyer. *Canada East.* Retrieved from http://www.canadaeast.com/news/article/1032021

Kelley, P. (2003–04, Winter). Suddenly siblings: Helping children adapt to life in a stepfamily. *Transition.* Retrieved from http://www.vifamily.ca/library/transition/334/334.html

Kelly, J. B., & Emery, R. E. (2003). Children's adjustment following divorce. *Family Relations, 52*, 352–362.

Kelly, K. (n.d.). *Dating violence.* Ottawa: National Clearinghouse on Family Violence. Retrieved from http://www.phac-aspc.gc.ca/ncfv-cnivf/familyviolence/html/femdatfreq_e.html

Kelly, M., Zimmer-Gembeck, M., & Boislard, P, M.-A. (2012). Identity, intimacy, status and sex dating goals as correlates of goal-consistent behavior and satisfaction in Australian youth. *Journal of Adolescence, 35*(6), 1441–1454. doi:10.1016/j.adolescence.2012.03.002

Kempe, R. S., & Kempe, C. H. (1984). *The common secret: Sexual abuse of children and adolescents.* New York: W. H. Freeman.

Keown, L.-A. (2007, Summer). Time escapes me: Workaholics and time perception. *Canadian Social Trends* (Statistics Canada Catalogue no. 11-008), 30–3.

Keown, L.-A. (2009, June 26). Social networks help Canadians deal with change. *Canadian Social Trends* (Statistics Canada Catalogue no. 11-008). Retrieved from http://www.statcan.gc.ca/pub/11-008-x/2009002/article/10891-eng.pdf

Kerr, D., & Michalski, J. (2007). Family structure and children's hyperactivity problems: A longitudinal analysis. *Canadian Journal of Sociology/Cahiers canadiens de sociologie, 32*(1), 85–112.

Kershaw, S. (2009, April 23). Mr. Moms (by way of Fortune 500). *New York Times.* Retrieved from http://www/nytimes.com

Kettle, J. (1980). *The big generation.* Toronto: McClelland & Stewart.

Keung, N. (2008, May 23). "Rent-a-guest" schemes tipped off immigration. *The Star.* Retrieved from http://www.thestar.com/News/GTA/article/429199

Khaw, L., & Hardesty, J. L. (2007). Theorizing the process of leaving: Turning points and trajectories in the stages of change. *Family Relations, 56*, 413–425.

Khaw, L. B. L., & Hardesty, J. L. (2009). Leaving an abusive partner: Exploring boundary ambiguity using the stages of change model. *Journal of Family Theory & Review, 1*, 38–53.

Kiecolt, K. J. (2003). Satisfaction with work and family life: The evidence of a cultural reversal. *Journal of Marriage and Family, 65*, 23–35.

Kiecolt, K. J., Blieszner, R., & Savla, J. (2011). Long-term influences of intergenerational ambivalence on midlife parents' psychological well-being. *Journal of Marriage and Family, 73*, 360–382. doi:10.1111/j.1741-3737.00812.x

Kieran, S. (1986). *The family matters: Two centuries of family law and life in Ontario.* Toronto: Key Porter.

Killoren, S. E., Thayer, S. M., & Updegraff, K. E. (2008). Conflict resolution between Mexican origin adolescent siblings. *Journal of Marriage and Family, 70*, 1200–1212.

Kim, H. K., Laurent, H. K., Capaldi, D. M., & Feingold, A. (2008). Men's aggression toward women: A 10-year panel study. *Journal of Marriage and Family, 70*, 1169–1187.

Kim, J., & Fram, M. S. (2009). Profiles of choice: Parents' patterns of priority in child care decision-making. *Early Childhood Research Quarterly, 24*, 77–91.

Kim, J. R. (2009, Winter). Ambiguous loss haunts foster and adopted children. *Adoptalk,* 6–7.

Kim, S., & Woolfolk, T. (2007). Women, work, and families: Locating experiences in social contexts. In B. Sharif Trask & R. R. Hamon (Eds.), *Cultural diversity and families: Expanding perspectives* (pp. 100–117). Thousand Oaks, CA: Sage.

King, V. (2006). The antecedents and consequences of adolescents' relationships with stepfathers and nonresident fathers. *Journal of Marriage and Family, 68*, 910–928.

King, V., & Scott, M. E., (2005). A comparison of cohabiting relationships among older and younger adults. *Journal of Marriage and Family, 67,* 271–285.

King, V., & Sobolewski, J. M. (2006). Nonresident fathers' contributions to adolescent well-being. *Journal of Marriage and Family, 68,* 537–557.

Kingsley, E. P. (2002, Spring). Welcome to Holland. *Transition, 3.*

Kingsmill, S., & Schlesinger, B. (1998). *The family squeeze: Surviving the sandwich generation.* Toronto: University of Toronto Press.

Kingston, A. (2004). *The meaning of wife.* Toronto: HarperCollins.

Kinnon, D. (2001). *Community awareness and response: Abuse and neglect of older adults* (Catalogue No. H39-262/2001E, rev.). Ottawa: Health Canada, Family Violence Prevention Unit.

Kinsman, G. (1987). *The regulation of desire: Sexuality in Canada.* Montreal: Black Rose.

Kirk, H. D. (1984). *Shared fate: A theory and method of adoptive relationships* (2nd ed.). Port Angeles, WA: Ben-Simon.

Kirkland, K. (2004). *Abuse in gay male relationships: A discussion paper* (Catalogue No. H72-21/191-2004E). Ottawa: Public Health Agency of Canada, National Clearinghouse on Family Violence. Retrieved from http://www.phac-aspc.gc.ca/nc-cn

Kirkorian, H. L., Wartella, E. A., & Anderson, D. R. (2008, Spring). Media and young children's learning. *The Future of Children, 18*(1), 39–60.

Kirkwood, D., & Engelbrecht, J. (2002, November). *Family rituals, routines, and traditions: Building bridges and making memories.* Poster presentation at the annual conference of National Council on Family Relations, Houston, TX.

Kirschman, E. (2007). *I love a cop: What police families need to know* (Rev.). New York: Guilford.

Klassen, T. (2012, March 2). Don't pit young against old. *Globe and Mail.* Retrieved from http://www.theglobeandmail.com/commentary/dont-pit-young-against-old/article550235

Klein, S., & Pulkingham, J. (2008, April). *Living on welfare in BC: Experiences of longer-term "expected to work" recipients.* Vancouver: Canadian Centre for Policy Alternatives, BC Office. Retrieved from http://www.policyalternatives.ca

Kliman, J., & Madsen, W. (1999). Social class and the family life cycle. In B. Carter & M. McGoldrick (Eds.), *The expanded family life cycle: Individual, family, and social perspectives* (3rd ed., pp. 88–105). Boston: Allyn & Bacon.

Kline, S. L. E., Karel, A. I., & Chatterjee, K. (2006). Covering adoption: General depictions in broadcast news. *Family Relations, 55,* 487–498.

Kluwer, E. S., & Johnson, M. D. (2007). Conflict frequency and relationship quality across the transition to parenthood. *Journal of Marriage and Family, 69,* 1089–1106.

Knoester, C., Haynie, D. L., & Stephens, C. M. (2006). Parenting practices and adolescents' friendship networks. *Journal of Marriage and Family, 68,* 1247–1260.

Knoppers, B. M. (2000, April). DNA profiles put families to test. *Families & Health, 7.*

Knowles, V. (2000). *Forging our legacy: Canadian citizenship and immigration, 1900–1977* (Catalogue No. Ci51-93/2000E). Ottawa: Public Works and Government Services Canada. Retrieved from http://www.cic.gc.ca/english/department/legacy/

Koerner, S. S., Jacobs, S. L., & Raymond, M. (2000). When mothers turn to their adolescent daughters: Predicting daughters' vulnerability to negative adjustment outcomes. *Family Relations, 49,* 301–309.

Kohen, D., Dahinten, V. S., & Hertzmann, C. (2008). Child care in Quebec: Access to a universal program. *Canadian Journal of Public Health, 99,* 451–455.

Kohen, D. E., Leventhal, T., Dahinten, V. S., & McIntosh, C. N. (2008). Neighborhood disadvantage: Pathways of effects for young children. *Child Development, 79,* 156–169.

Kornhaber, A. (1996). *Contemporary grandparenting.* Thousand Oaks, CA: Sage.

Koropeckyj-Cox, T. (2002). Beyond parental status: Psychological well-being in middle and old age. *Journal of Marriage and Family, 64,* 957–971.

Koss-Feder, L. (2009, March 2). Bunking in with mom and dad. *Time,* 45–46.

Kowal, A. K., & Blinn-Pike, L. (2004). Sibling influences on adolescents' attitudes toward safe sex practices. *Family Relations, 53,* 377–384.

Kramar, K. J. (2005). *Unwilling mothers, unwanted babies: Infanticide in Canada.* Vancouver: UBC Press.

Kraut, R., Patterson, M., Lundmark, V., Kiesler, S., Mukopadhyay, T., & Scherlis, W. (1998, September). Internet paradox: A social technology that reduces social involvement and psychological well-being? *American Psychologist, 53*(9), 1017–1031. Retrieved from http://www.cs.cmu.edu/~kraut/RKraut.site.files/articles/kraut98-Internet Paradox.pdf

Kronby, M. C. (2006). *Canadian family law* (9th ed.). Mississauga, ON: Wiley.

Kruk, E. (1995). Grandparent–grandchild contact loss: Findings from a study of "grandparent rights" members. *Canadian Journal on Aging, 14,* 737–754.

Krumrel, E. J., Mahoney, A., & Pargament, K. J. (2009). Divorce and the divine: The role of spirituality in adjustment to divorce. *Journal of Marriage and Family, 71,* 373–383.

Kuba, C. A. (2006). *Navigating the journey of aging parents: What care receivers want.* New York: Routledge.

Kubey, R. W., Levins, M. J., & Barrows, J. R. (2001, June). Internet use and collegiate academic performance decrements: Early findings. *Journal of Communication, 51*(2), 366–382.

Kunkel, D., Eyal, K., Finnerty, K., Biely, E., & Donnerstein, E. (2005). *Sex on TV 2005.* Menlo Park, CA: Henry J. Kaiser Family Foundation.

Kurdek, L. A. (1995). Predicting change in marital satisfaction from husbands' and wives' conflict resolution styles. *Journal of Marriage and the Family, 57,* 153–164.

Kurdek, L. A. (2004). Are gay and lesbian cohabiting couples *really* different from heterosexual married couples? *Journal of Marriage and Family, 66,* 880–900.

Kurdek, L. A. (2005). What do we know about gay and lesbian couples? *Current Directions in Psychological Science, 14*(5), 251–254.

Kurdek, L. A. (2006). Differences between partners from heterosexual, gay, and lesbian cohabiting couples. *Journal of Marriage and Family, 68,* 509–528.

Lachance-Grzela, M., & Bouchard, G. (2009). La cohabitation et le mariage, deux mondes a part? Un examen des caractéristiques démographiques, individuelles et relationnelles. *Canadian Journal of Behavioural Science, 41*(1), 37–44. doi:10.1037/a0013407

LaCoursiere, S. P. (2001). A theory of online social support. *Advances in Nursing Science, 24*(1), 60–77.

La Gaipa, J. J. (1981). A systems approach to personal relationships. In S. Duck & R. Gilmour (Eds.), *Personal relationships I: Studying personal relationships* (pp. 67–89). London: Academic.

Lahey, K. A., & Alderson, K. (2004). *Same-sex marriage: The personal and the political.* Toronto: Insomniac.

Lai, S. (2008, March). *Elder abuse and policing issues: A review of the literature.* United Senior Citizens of Ontario. Retrieved from http://www.uscont.ca/pdf/elder_abuse_and_policing_issues.pdf

Laible, D., & Thompson, R. A. (2008). Early socialization: A relationship perspective. In J. E. Grusec & P. D. Hastings (Eds.), *Handbook of socialization: Theory and research* (pp. 181–207). New York: Guilford.

Laird, J. (2003). Lesbian and gay families. In F. Walsh (Ed.), *Normal family processes: Growing diversity and complexity* (3rd ed., pp. 176–209). New York: Guilford.

Lalonde, R. M., & Cameron, J. E. (1993). An intergroup perspective on immigrant acculturation with a focus on collective strategies. *International Journal of Psychology, 28*(1), 57–74.

Landry, Y. (1992). Gender imbalance, *les filles du roi,* and choice of spouse in New France. In B. Bradbury (Ed.), *Canadian family history: Selected readings* (pp. 14–32). Toronto: Copp Clark Pitman.

Lanigan, J. D., Bold, M., & Chenoweth, L. (2009). Computers in the family context: Perceived impact on family time and relationships. *Family Science Review.* Retrieved from http://www.familyscienceassociation.org

Lansford, J. E., Ceballo, R., Abbey, A., & Stewart, A. J. (2001). Does family structure matter? A comparison of adoptive, two-parent biological, single-mother, stepfather, and stepmother households. *Journal of Marriage and Family, 63,* 840–851.

Laplante, B. (2006). *The rise of cohabitation in Quebec: Power of religion and power over religion.* Retrieved from http://www.ucs.inrs.ca/Cours/laplante/LaplanteB_2006a.pdf

LaPierre, T. A., & Hughes, M. E. (2009). Population aging in Canada and the United States. In P. Uhlenberg (Ed.), *International Handbook of Population Aging* (pp. 191–230). Chapel Hill, NC: Springer.

LaRochelle-Côté, S., & Dionne, C. (2009, August). Family work patterns. *Perspectives on Labour and Income* (Statistics Canada Catalogue no. 75-001-X), 15–26. Retrieved from http://www.statcan.gc.ca/pub/75-001-x/2009108/pdf/10912-eng.pdf

LaRoque, E. D. (1994). *Violence in aboriginal communities.* Ottawa: Royal Commission on Aboriginal Peoples.

LaRossa, R. (2009). Single-parent family discourse in popular magazines and social science journals. *Journal of Marriage and Family, 71,* 235–239.

LaRossa, R., Jaret, C., Gadgil, M., & Wynn, G. R. (2000). The changing culture of fatherhood in comic-strip families: A six-decade analysis. *Journal of Marriage and the Family, 62,* 375–387.

Larson, R. (2008). Family mealtimes as a developmental context. *Social Policy Report, 22*(4), 18.

Lasch, C. (1979). *Haven in a heartless world: The family besieged.* New York: Basic Books.

Laszloffy, T. A. (2002a). *AAMFT consumer update: Multiracial families.* American Association for Marriage and Family Therapy. Retrieved from http://www.aamft.org/families/Consumer_Updates/Multiracial%20Families.asp

Laszloffy, T. A. (2002b). Rethinking family development theory: Teaching with the Systemic Family Development (SFD) Model. *Family Relations, 51,* 206–214.

Lavee, Y., McCubbin, H. I., & Patterson, J. M. (1985). The double ABCX model of family stress and management: An empirical test by analysis of structural equations with latent variable. *Journal of Marriage and Family, 47,* 811–825.

Lavee, Y., & Olson, D. H. (1993). Seven types of marriage: Empirical typology based on ENRICH. *Journal of Marital and Family Therapy, 19*(4), 325–340.

LaViolette, A. D., & Barnett, O. W. (2000). *It could happen to anyone: Why battered women stay* (2nd ed.). Thousand Oaks, CA: Sage.

Leaper, C., & Friedman, C. K. (2007). The socialization of gender. In J. E. Grusec & P. D. Hastings (Eds.), *Handbook of socialization: Theory and research* (pp. 561–587). New York: Guilford.

Le Bourdais, C., Desrosiers, H., & Laplante, B. (1995). Factors related to union formation among single mothers in Canada. *Journal of Marriage and the Family, 57,* 410–420.

Le Bourdais, C., & Juby, H. (2002). The impact of cohabitation on the family life course in contemporary North America: Insights from across the border. In A. Booth & A. C. Crouter (Eds.), *Just living together: Implications of cohabitation on families* (pp. 107–118). Mahwah, NJ: Lawrence Erlbaum.

Le Bourdais, C., & Lapierre-Adamcyk, É., with Pacaut, P. (2004). Changes in conjugal life in Canada: Is cohabitation progressively replacing marriage? *Journal of Marriage and Family, 66,* 929–942.

Le Bourdais, C., Marcil-Gratton, N., & Juby, H. (2003). Family life in a changing world: The evolution of the Canadian family in a context of marital and economic instability. In M. J. Kasoff & C. Drennan (Eds.), *16th Annual Reddin Symposium: Family, work, and health policy in Canada* (pp. 21–45). Bowling Green, OH: Bowling Green State University, Canadian Studies Center.

Le Bourdais, C., Seltzer, J. A., & Trost, J. (2003, November). *Cohabitation and marriage in western countries* [Videotape]. Panel presentation at the annual meeting of National Council on Family Relations, Vancouver.

Ledrou, I., & Gervais, J. (2005, May). Food insecurity. *Health Reports* (Statistics Canada Catalogue no. 83-003), 47–51. Retrieved from http://www.statcan.gc.ca/studies-etudes/82-003/archive/2005/7841-eng.pdf

Lee, C., & Iverson-Gilbert, J. (2003). Demand, support and perception in family-related stress among protestant clergy. *Family Relations, 52,* 249–257.

Lee, J. A. (1975). The romantic heresy. *Canadian Review of Sociology and Anthropology, 12,* 514–528.

Lefebvre, P. (2004). Quebec's 1998 early childhood education and care and its weaknesses. *Policy Options.* Retrieved from http://www.irpp.org/po/archive/mar04/lefebvre.pdf

Lefebvre, P., & Merrigan, P. (2008). Child-care policy and the labor supply of mothers with young children: A natural experiment from Canada. *Journal of Labor Economics, 26,* 519–548.

Leland, J. (2008, October 7). In "sweetie" and "dear," a hurt for the elderly. *New York Times.* Retrieved from http://www.nytimes.com/2008/10/17/us/

Lenhart, A. (2009, December 15). *Teens and sexting: How and why minor teens are sending sexually suggestive nude or nearly nude images via text messaging.* Washington, DC: Pew Research Center. Retrieved from http://www.pewinternet.org/~/media//Files/Reports/2009/PIP_Teens_and_Sexting.pdf

Leon, K. (2003). Risk and protective factors in young children's adjustment to parental divorce: A review of the research. *Family Relations, 52,* 258–270.

Leon, K., & Angst, E. (2005). Portrayals of stepfamilies in films: Using media images in remarriage education. *Family Relations, 54,* 3–23.

Lero, D., & Joseph, G. (2007, September). *A systematic review of the literature on combining work and eldercare in Canada.* Guelph, ON: University of Guelph, Centre for Families, Work, & Well-Being. Retrieved from http://www.cfww.uoguelph.ca/resources/documents/WorkandEldercarepaperSEPT19-FinalsenttoHomewood.doc

Lessa, I. (2003). Single motherhood in the Canadian landscape: Postcards from a subject. In A. Westhues (Ed.), *Canadian social policy: Issues and perspectives* (3rd ed., pp. 90–107). Waterloo, ON: Wilfrid Laurier University Press.

LeVay, S. (1993). *The sexual brain.* Cambridge, MA: MIT Press.

Leventhal, T., & Brooks-Gunn, J. (2008). Neighborhood residence and youth development. *The Prevention Researcher, 15*(2), 3–6.

Levin, E. (1987, October 19). Motherly love works a miracle. *People Weekly,* 39–43.

Levin R., Bahrmasel, W., Creekmur, A., Kalmes, L., Lessem, S., & McKean, L. (2006, April). *Help to keep going as long as they need me: A report on seniors raising children.* Center for Impact Research. Retrieved from http://www.impactresearch.org/documents/SeniorCaregiversReport.pdf

Levinson, D. J., et al. (1978). *The seasons of a man's life.* New York: Alfred A. Knopf.

Levitt, C., & Shaffer, W. (1987). *The riot at Christie Pits.* Toronto: Lester & Orpen Dennys.

Lewchuk, S. (2013, May 17). *Reducing income inequality in Canada: Federal finance committee commences study.* Retrieved from http://www.dignityforall.ca/en/reducing-income-inequality-canada-federal-finance-committee-commences-study

Li, C. (2004, July). *Widowhood: Consequences on income for senior women.* Ottawa: Statistics Canada. Retrieved from http://publications.gc.ca/collections/Collection/Statcan/11-621-M/11-621-MIE2004015.pdf

Li, N. P., Bailey, M., Kenrick, D., & Linsenmeier, J. (2002). The necessities and luxuries of mate preferences: Testing the tradeoffs. *Journal of Personality and Social Psychology, 82*(6), 947–1055. doi:10.1037//0022-3514.82.6.947

Li, P. S. (1998). *The Chinese in Canada* (2nd ed.). Toronto: Oxford University Press.

Lichter, D. T., & Qian, Z. (2008). Serial cohabitation and the marital life course. *Journal of Marriage and Family, 70,* 861–878.

Lilly, M. B., Robinson, C. A., Holtzman, S., & Bottorff, J. L. (2012). Can we move beyond burden and burnout to support the health and wellness of family caregivers to persons with dementia? Evidence from British Columbia, Canada. *Health and Social Care in the Community, 20*(1), 103–112.

Lin, J. (2005, Winter). The housing transitions of seniors. *Canadian Social Trends* (Statistics Canada Catalogue No. 11-008), 22–26.

Lindau, S. T., Schumm, L. P., Laumann, E. O., Levinson, W., O'Muircheartaigh, C. A., & Waite, L. J. (2007). A study of sexuality and health among older adults in the United States. *New England Journal of Medicine, 357,* 762–774. Retrieved from http://www.nejm.org

Lindsay, L. L., Beach, S., & Ravelli, B. (2009). *Core concepts in sociology* (2nd Canadian ed.). Toronto: Pearson Education Canada.

Lindsey, E. W., & Sanchez, C. A. (2010). Homeless families. In S. J. Price, C. A. Price, & P. C. McKenry (Eds.), *Families & change: Coping with stressful events and transitions* (4th ed., pp. 333–356). Los Angeles: Sage.

Lipman, M. (1984). Adoption in Canada: Two decades in review. In P. Sachdev (Ed.), *Adoption: Current issues and trends* (pp. 31–42). Toronto: Butterworths.

Lipman-Blumen, J. (1984). *Gender roles and power.* Englewood Cliffs, NJ: Prentice-Hall.

Living without enough to eat. (2007–2008, Winter). *Transition,* 13.

Lochhead, C. (2003, July). *The transition penalty: Unemployment among recent immigrants to Canada.* Canadian Labour and Business Centre. Retrieved from http://www.clbc.ca

Logan, C., Holcombe, E., Manlove, J., & Ryan, S. (2007, May). *The consequences of unintended childbearing: A white paper.* Washington, DC: Child Trends. Retrieved from http://www.childtrends.org/Files//Child_Trends_2007_01_FF_Consequences.pdf

Loseke, D. R., & Kurz, D. (2005). Men's violence toward women is the serious problem. In D. R. Loseke, R. J. Gelles, & M. M. Cavanaugh (Eds.), *Current controversies in family violence* (2nd ed., pp. 79–95). Thousand Oaks, CA: Sage.

Loukas, A., Piejak, L. A., Bingham, C. R., Fitzgerald, H. E., & Zucker, R. A. (2001). Parental distress as a mediator of problem behaviors in sons of alcohol-involved families. *Family Relations, 50,* 293–301.

Lowe, E. (2005, October). *Social innovations: Competitive advantage through flexibility: MDS Nordion.* Ottawa: Vanier Institute of the Family. Retrieved from http://www.vifamily.ca/library/social/

Lowe, E. (2006, Summer). Love without borders. *Transition,* 7.

Luker, K. (1996). *Dubious conceptions: The politics of teenage pregnancy.* Cambridge, MA: Harvard University Press.

Luong, M. (2008, May). Life after teenage motherhood. *Perspectives on Labour and Income* (Statistics Canada Catalogue no. 75-001-X), 5–45.

Lupri, E., & Frideres, J. (1981). The quality of marriage and the passage of time: Marital satisfaction over the family life cycle. *Canadian Journal of Sociology, 6,* 283–305.

Luscombe, B. (2009, June 22). Facebook and divorce. *Time*, 93–94.

Luscombe, B. (2012, July 23). I do, I do, I do, I do. *Time,* 44–47.

Luster, T., Bates, L., Fitzgerald, H., Vandenbelt, M., & Key, J. P. (2000). Factors related to successful outcomes among pre-school children born to low-income adolescent mothers. *Journal of Marriage and the Family, 61*, 178–187.

Luxton, M. (1998). Families and the labour market: Coping strategies from a sociological perspective. In D. Cheal, F. Woolley, & M. Luxton, *How families cope and why policymakers need to know* (pp. 57–73). Ottawa: Canadian Policy Research Networks.

Maccoby, E. E. (1992). The role of parents in the socialization of children: An historical overview. *Developmental Psychology, 28*, 1006–17.

Maccoby, E. E. (2003). The gender of child and parent as factors in family dynamics. In A. C. Crouter & A. Booth (Eds.), *Children's influence on family dynamics: The neglected side of family relationships* (pp. 191–206). Mahwah, NJ: Erlbaum.

Maccoby, E. E. (2007). Historical overview of socialization research and theory. In J. E. Grusec & P. D. Hastings (Eds.), *Handbook of socialization: Theory and research* (pp. 13–41). New York: Guilford.

MacDermid, S. (2006, June). Work-family research; Learning from the "best of the best." *Family Focus*, F15–F16.

MacDonald, B.-J., Moore, K. D., Chen, H., & Brown, R. L. (2011, February). The Canadian national retirement risk index: Employing Statistics Canada's LifePaths to measure the financial security of future Canadian seniors. *Canadian Public Policy, 37*(s1), 73–94.

Macdonald, C. (2009, Summer). Women in law. *U of T Magazine*, 11–12.

MacDonald, J. A. (1984). Canadian adoption legislation: An over-view. In P. Sachdev (Ed.), *Adoption: Current issues and trends* (pp. 43–61). Toronto: Butterworths.

Machir, J. (2003, September). The impact of spousal caregiving on the quality of marital relationships in later life. *Family Focus*, F11–F13.

MacInnes, M. D. (2008). One's enough for now: Children, dis-ability, and the subsequent childbearing of mothers. *Journal of Marriage and Family, 70*, 758–771.

Macionis, J. J., Jansson, S. M., & Benoit, C. M. (2008). *Society: The basics* (4th Canadian ed.). Toronto: Pearson Education Canada.

Macintosh, H., Reissing, E. D., & Andruff, H. (2010). Same-sex marriage in Canada: The impact of legal marriage on the first cohort of gay and lesbian Canadians to wed. *Canadian Journal of Human Sexuality, 19*(3), 79–90.

Mackey, R. A., Diemer, M. A., & O'Brien, B. A. (2004). Relational factors in understanding satisfaction in the lasting rela-tionships of same-sex and heterosexual couples. *Journal of Homosexuality, 47*(1), 111–136.

Mackrael, K. (2012, October 1). New debate looms over sex-selective abortion motion. *Globe and Mail*. Retrieved from http://www.theglobeandmail.com/news/politics/new-debate-looms-over-sex-selective-abortion-motion/article4581249

MacLeod, L. (1989). *Discussion paper: Wife battering and the web of hope: Progress, dilemmas and visions of prevention.* Ottawa: Health and Welfare Canada.

Madden-Derdich, D. A., & Arditti, J. A. (1999). The ties that bind: Attachment between former spouses. *Family Relations, 48*, 243–249.

Madsen, B., Bond, A., Willoughby, B., Carroll, J., & Busby, D. (2012, October). *"Stayover couples": Are they a unique couple type?* Paper presented to National Council on Family Relations conference. Phoenix, AZ.

Mah, J. W., & Johnston, C. (2012). Cultural variations in mothers' acceptance of and intent to use behavioral child manage-ment techniques. *Journal of Child and Family Studies, 21*, 486–497. doi:10.1007/s10826-011-9502-z

Mahfouz, A. Y., Philaretou, A. G., & Theocharous, A. (2008). Virtual social interactions: Evolutionary, social psychological and technological perspectives. *Computers in Human Behaviour, 24*, 3014–3026.

Maholmes, V., Nicholson, C. E., Haverkos, L. M., & Boyce, C. A. (2007). Research directions in child neglect and exposure to violence. *Protecting Children, 22*(3 & 4), 10–19.

Mahon, R. (2004, November). *Early child learning and care in Canada: Who rules? Who should rule?* Discussion paper for the National Conference on Child Care in Canada, Canadian Council on Social Development, Winnipeg.

Mahoney, J., Harris, A. L., & Eccles, J. S. (2008, February). *The over-scheduling myth.* Retrieved from http://www.childtrends.org/Files//Child_Trends_2008_02_07_Myth.pdf

Mahony, T. H. (2010, June 29). *Police-reported dating violence in Canada, 2008.* Ottawa: Statistics Canada. Retrieved from http://www.statcan.gc.ca/pub/85-002-x/2010002/article/11242-eng.htm

Maidman, F. (1984). Physical child abuse: Dynamics and practice. In F. Maidman (Ed.), *Child welfare: A source book of knowledge and prac-tice* (pp. 135–181). New York: Child Welfare League of America.

Makarenko, J. (2007, January 1). *Same-sex marriage in Canada.* Retrieved from http://www.mapleleafweb.com/features/same-sex-marriage-canada

Makin, K. (2004, September 21). Lesbian divorcées speak out. *Globe and Mail*. Retrieved from http://www.globeandmail.com

Malat, J., Oh, H. J., & Hamilton, M. A. (2005). Poverty experience, race, and child health. *Public Health Reports, 120*, 442–447. Retrieved from http://www.publichealthreports.org/userfiles/120_4/120442.pdf

Malia, S. E. C. (2005). Balancing family members' interests regarding stepparent rights and obligations: A social policy challenge. *Family Relations, 54*, 298–319.

Malley-Morrison, K., & Hines, D. A. (2004). *Family violence in a cultural perspective: Defining, understanding, and combating abuse.* Thousand Oaks, CA: Sage.

Manitoba Agriculture, Food and Rural Initiatives. (2004). *The cost of raising a child: 2004.* Winnipeg: Author. Retrieved from http://www.gov.mb.ca/agriculture/homeec/coc2004/cba28s02.html

Mann, S. (2001, February/March). Love, gender, and Canadian history. *The Beaver*, 6–7.

Manning, C. L. (2003, November). *Information games: How ado-lescents exercise power in relationships with nonresident parents.* Poster presentation at the annual conference of National Council on Family Relations, Vancouver, BC.

Manning, W. D., Longmore, M. A., & Giordano, P. C. (2007). The changing institution of marriage: Adolescents' expectations to cohabit and marry. *Journal of Marriage and Family, 69,* 559–575.

Maranto, G. (1996, April). Embryo overpopulation. *Scientific American.* Retrieved from http://www.sciam.com/0496issue/0496infocus.html

Marcellus, J. (2012, July 30). Who are your caregiving employees? *Benefits Canada.* Retrieved from http://www.benefitscanada.com/benefits/other/who-are-your-caregiving-employees-30997

Marcia, J. E. (1966). Development and validation of ego-identity status. *Journal of Personality and Social Psychology, 3,* 551–558.

Marcia, J. E. (1983). Some directions for the investigation of ego development in early adolescence. *Journal of Early Adolescence, 3,* 215–223.

Marcia, J. E. (n.d.). *Identity, psychological development, and counselling.* Retrieved from http://www.iclass.info/docs/marcia_paper.pdf

Marcil-Gratton, N. (1998). *Growing up with Mom and Dad? The intricate family life courses of Canadian children* (Catalogue No. 89-566-XIE). Ottawa: Statistics Canada.

Marcil-Gratton, N., Le Bourdais, C., & Lapierre-Adamcyk, É. (2000). The implications of parents' conjugal histories for children. *Isuma–Canadian Journal of Policy Research, 1*(2), 32–40. Retrieved from http://www.isuma.net

Marcovitz, H. (2009). *The Obama family tree.* Broomall, PA: Mason Crest.

Marinkovic, K., Oscar-Berman, M., Urban, T., O'Reilly, C. E., Howard, J. A., Sawyer, K., & Harris, G. J. (2009). Alcoholism and dampened temporal limbic activation to emotional faces. *Alcoholism: Clinical and Experimental Research.* doi:10.1111/j.1530-0277.2009.01026.x

Mark, K. P., Janssen, E., & Milhausen, R. R. (2011, October). Infidelity in heterosexual couples: Demographic, interpersonal, and personality-related predictors of extradyadic sex. *Archives of Sexual Behaviour, 40*(5), 971–982. doi:10.1007/s10508-011-9771-z

Marks, L. D., Hopkins, K., Chaney, C., Monroe, P. A., Nesteruk, O., & Sasser, D. D. (2008). "Together we are strong": A qualitative study of happy, enduring African American marriages. *Family Relations, 57,* 172–185.

Marriage (Prohibited Degrees) Act. (1990). Retrieved from http://laws.justice.gc.ca/en/M-2.1/text.html

Marshall, K. (2003, March). Benefiting from extended parental leave. *Perspectives on Labour and Income* (Statistics Canada Catalogue no. 75-001-XIE), 5–10. Retrieved from http://www.statcan.gc.ca/

Marshall, K. (2006, July). Converging gender roles. *Perspectives on Labour and Income* (Statistics Canada Catalogue No. 75-001-XIE), 5–16.

Marshall, K. (2007, May). The busy lives of teens. *Perspectives on Labour and Income* (Statistics Canada Catalogue No. 75-001-XIE), 5–15.

Marshall, K. (2009, April). The family work week. *Perspectives on Labour and Income* (Statistics Canada Catalogue No. 75-001-X), 5–13. Retrieved from http://www.statcan.gc.ca/pub/75-001-x/pdf/10837-eng.pdf

Marshall, K. (2012). Youth neither enrolled nor employed. *Perspectives on Labour and Income* (Statistics Canada Catalogue No. 75-001-x). Retrieved from http://www.statcan.gc.ca/pub/75-001-x/2012002/article/11675-eng.pdf

Marsiglio, W. (2004). *Stepdads: Stories of love, hope, and repair.* Lanham, MD: Rowman & Littlefield.

Martel, L., & He, J. (2006). Part I—Current demographic situation in Canada 2003 and 2004. In A. Bélanger (Ed.), *Report on the demographic situation in Canada 2003 and 2004* (Statistics Canada Catalogue no. 91-209-XIE, pp. 13–76). Ottawa: Statistics Canada. Retrieved from http://www.statcan.gc.ca/pub/91-209-x/91-209-x2003000-eng.pdf

Martin, S. P. (1999). *Fertility trends among U.S. women who defer childbearing past age 30* (CDE Working Paper No. 99-11). Madison, WI: University of Wisconsin–Madison, Center for Demography and Ecology.

Martin, V., & Le Bourdais, C. (2009, September). *Stepfamily instability in Canada: New insights based on a comparison of male and female reports.* Poster presentation at the XXVI International Population Conference of the International Union for the Scientific Study of Population. Marrakech, Morocco. Retrieved from http://iuss2009.princeton.edu/download.aspx?submissionID=91699

Martin-Matthews, A. (2000). Change and diversity in aging families and intergenerational relations. In N. Mandell & A. Duffy (Eds.), *Canadian families: Diversity, conflict, and change* (2nd ed., pp. 323–360). Toronto: Harcourt Canada.

Martino, S. C., Collins, R. L., Elliott, M. N., Strachman, A., Kanouse, D. E., & Berry, S. H. (2006). Exposure to degrading versus nondegrading music lyrics and sexual behavior among youth. *Pediatrics, 118,* 430–441.

Masciadrelli, B. P., & Oswald, R. F. (2005, November). *Doing generativity: The non-parent and the navigation of generativity.* Paper presented at the annual conference of National Council on Family Relations, Phoenix.

Maslach, C. (1982). *Burnout: The cost of caring.* Englewood Cliffs, NJ: Prentice-Hall.

Mata, F. (2011). *Lone-parent status among ethnic groups in Canada: Data explorations on its prevalence, composition and generational persistence aspects.* Retrieved from http://mbc.metropolis.net/assets/uploads/files/wp/2011/WP11-17.pdf

Matas, R. (2008, May 3). Where "the handsome ones go to the leaders." *Globe and Mail,* pp. A10–A11.

Mathews, F. (2002). The forgotten child: The declining status of boys in Canada. *Transition, 33*(1), 3–6.

Maticka-Tyndale, E. (2008). Sexuality and sexual health of Canadian adolescents: Yesterday, today and tomorrow. *The Canadian Journal of Human Sexuality, 17*(3), 85–95.

Matjasko, J. L. (2002, November). *Single-father family typologies and adolescent functioning.* Poster presentation at the annual conference of National Council on Family Relations, Houston, TX.

Mattioli, D. (2009, September 23). Long haul for working couples. *Wall Street Journal.* Retrieved from http://online.wsj.com/article/5B10001424052970204348804574407270774616050.htm

Maume, D. J. (2006). Gender differences in restricting work efforts because of family responsibilities. *Journal of Marriage and Family, 68*, 859–869.

Maurier, W. L., & Northcott, H. C. (2000). *Aging in Ontario: Diversity in the new millennium.* Calgary: Detselig Enterprises.

Mauron, A. (1999, September). *Ethical aspects of gene therapy.* Geneva Foundation for Medical Education and Research, 9th Postgraduate Course for Training in Reproductive Medicine and Reproductive Biology. Retrieved from http://www.gfmer/ch/Endo/Lectures_09/ethical_aspects_of_gene_therapy.htm

Mayer, B., & Trommsdorff, G. (2010, September–November). Adolescents' value of children and their intentions to have children: A cross-cultural and multilevel analysis. *Journal of Cross-Cultural Psychology, 41*(5–6), 671–689. doi:10.1177/0022022110372195

Maylor, E. A., Reimers, S., Choi, J., Collaer, M., Peters, M., & Silverman, I. (2007). Gender and sexual orientation differences in cognition across adulthood: Age is kinder to women than to men regardless of sexual orientation. *Archives of Sexual Behavior, 36*(2), 235–249.

Maynard, R. (1987, June). Here come the brides. *Report on Business Magazine*, 24–30.

Maxwell, J. (2007, Spring). Let's start paying the debts we are leaving our grandchildren. *Transition*, 4–6.

McCoy, J. K., Brody, G. H., & Stoneman, Z. (1994). A longitudinal analysis of sibling relationships as mediators of the link between family processes and youths' best friendships. *Family Relations, 43*, 400–408.

McCoy, J. K., Brody, G. H., & Stoneman, Z. (2002). Temperament and the quality of best friendships: Effect of same-sex sibling relationships. *Family Relations, 51*, 248–255.

McCrae, R. R., Willemsen , G., & Boomsma, D. (2012, May 7). Are parental personality traits a basis for mate selection? *Journal of Research in Personality, 46*, 455–457.

McCubbin, H. I., & Patterson, J. M. (1983). Family transitions: Adaptation to stress. In H. I. McCubbin & C. R. Figley (Eds.), *Stress and the family: Coping with normative stress* (Vol. 1, pp. 5–25). New York: Brunner/Mazel.

McDonald, L. (2006). Gendered retirement: The welfare of women and the "new" retirement. In L. O. Stone (Ed.), *New frontiers of research on retirement* (Statistics Canada Catalogue no. 75-511-XPE, pp. 137–164). Ottawa: Statistics Canada.

McDonald, L., & Collins, A. (2000). *Abuse and neglect of older adults: A discussion paper.* Ottawa: Health Canada.

McDonald, M., & Quell, C. (2008, Spring). Bridging the common divide: The importance of both "cohesion" and "inclusion." *Canadian Diversity/Diversité canadienne*, 35–38. Retrieved from http://canada.metropolis.net/pdfs/Pgs_can_diversity_spring08_bridging_e.pdf

McDonald, R., & Skopp, N. A. (2007). Cultural diversity and children exposed to family violence: Issues in adapting interventions. *Protecting Children, 22*(3 & 4), 32–44.

McGoldrick, M. (1999a). Becoming a couple. In B. Carter & M. McGoldrick (Eds.), *The expanded family life cycle: Individual, family, and social perspectives* (3rd ed., pp. 231–248). Boston: Allyn & Bacon.

McGoldrick, M. (1999b). Women through the family life cycle. In B. Carter & M. McGoldrick (Eds.), *The expanded family life cycle: Individual, family, and social perspectives* (3rd ed., pp. 106–123). Boston: Allyn & Bacon.

McGoldrick, M., & Carter, B. (1999). Remarried families. In B. Carter & M. McGoldrick (Eds.), *The expanded family life cycle: Individual, family, and social perspectives* (3rd ed., pp. 417–435). Boston: Allyn & Bacon.

McGoldrick, M., Gerson, R., & Petry, S. (2008). *Genograms: Assessment and intervention* (3rd ed.). New York: W. W. Norton.

McGoldrick, M., Watson, M., & Benton, W. (1999). Siblings through the life cycle. In B. Carter & M. McGoldrick (Eds.), *The expanded family life cycle: Individual, family, and social perspectives* (3rd ed., pp. 153–168). Boston: Allyn & Bacon.

McHale, S. M., Kim, J.-Y., Whiteman, S., & Crouter, A. C. (2004). Links between sex-typed time use in middle childhood and gender development in early adolescence. *Developmental Psychology, 40*, 868–881.

McIntosh, R. (1987/88, December/January). Canada's boy miners. *The Beaver*, 34–38.

McIntyre, L., Connor, S., & Warren, J. (1998). *A glimpse of child hunger in Canada.* Hull: Human Resources Development Canada.

McKay, A. (2006). Trends in teen pregnancy in Canada with comparisons to U. S. A. and England/Wales. *Canadian Journal of Human Sexuality, 15*(3–4), 157–161.

McKay, A., & Barrett, M. (2012). Trends in teen pregnancy rates from 1996–2006: A comparison of Canada, Sweden, U.S.A., and England/Wales. *Canadian Journal of Human Sexuality, 19*(1–2), 43–52.

McKie, C. (1993). An overview of lone parenthood in Canada. In J. Hudson & B. Galaway (Eds.), *Single parent families: Perspectives on research and policy* (pp. 53–71). Toronto: Thompson Educational Publishing.

McKie, D. C., Prentice, B., & Reed, P. (1983). *Divorce: Law and the family in Canada* (Catalogue No. 89-502). Ottawa: Statistics Canada.

McLaren, A., & McLaren, A. T. (1997). *The bedroom and the state: The changing practices and politics of contraception and abortion in Canada, 1980–1997* (2nd ed.). Toronto: Oxford University Press.

McLaughlin, M. A. (1987). Homelessness in Canada: The report of the national inquiry [Special insert]. *Social Development Overview, 5*(1).

McWilliams, S., & Barrett, A. E. (2012, 11 Dec.). Online dating in middle and later life: Gendered expectations and experiences. *Journal of Family Issues* (online). doi:10.1177/0192513x12468437

Meadows, S. O., McLanahan, S. S., & Brooks-Gunn, J. (2007). Parental depression and anxiety and early childhood behavior problems across family types. *Journal of Marriage and Family, 69*, 1162–1177.

Meal Exchange (2006). *Hunger and food security in Canada.* Retrieved from http://www.mealexchange.com/index.php?option=com_content&task=blogcategory&id=18&Itemid=51

Medora, N. P. (2003). Mate selection in contemporary India: Love marriages versus arranged marriages. In R. R. Hamon & B. B. Ingoldsby (Eds.), *Mate selection across cultures* (pp. 209–230). Thousand Oaks, CA: Sage.

Meezan, W., & Rauch, J. (2005). Gay marriage, same-sex parenting, and America's children. *The Future of Children, 15*(2), 97–115. Retrieved from http://www.futureofchildren.org

Mehlsen, M., Platz, M., & Fromholt, P. (2003). Life satisfaction across the life course: Evaluation of the most and least satisfying decades of life. *International Journal of Aging and Human Development, 57*, 217–236.

Mersky, J. P., Topitzes, J., & Reynolds, A. J. (2009). Chronic neglect: Prediction and prevention. *Protecting Children, 24*(1), 67–77.

Métis National Council. (2012). *The Métis Nation.* Retrieved from http://www.metisnation.ca/index.php/who-are-the-metis

Miall, C. E. (1987). The stigma of adoptive parent status: Perceptions of community attitudes toward adoption and the experience of informal social sanctioning. *Family Relations, 36*, 34–39.

Miall, C. E., & March, K. (2005). Community attitudes toward birth fathers' motives for adoption placement and single parenting. *Family Relations, 54*, 535–546.

Michael, H. J., & Reitsma-Street, M. (2002). *A new era of welfare: Analysis of B.C.'s employment and assistance acts.* Retrieved from http://web.uvic.ca/spp/

Michaels, M. L. (2006). Factors that contribute to stepfamily success: A qualitative analysis. *Journal of Divorce & Remarriage, 44*(3/4), 53–66.

Michalopoulos, C., Tattrie, D., Miller, C., Robins, P. K., Morris, P., Gyarmati, D., et al. (2002). *Making work pay: Final report on the self-sufficiency project for long-term welfare recipients.* Ottawa: Social Research and Demonstration Corporation.

Michalski, J. H. (2003). The economic status and coping strategies of food bank users in the greater Toronto area. *Canadian Journal of Urban Research, 12*, 275–298.

Middlesex London Health Unit. (2011). *Health at work 4 all: Work–life family balance.* Retrieved from http://www.healthunit.com/articlesPDF/17229.pdf

Mihorean, K. (2006). Factors related to reporting spousal violence to police. In L. Ogrodnik (Ed.), *Family violence in Canada: A statistical profile 2006* (Catalogue No. 85-224-XIE, pp. 19–24). Ottawa: Statistics Canada. Retrieved from http://www.statscan.gc.ca

Milan, A. (2000, Spring). One hundred years of families. *Canadian Social Trends* (Statistics Canada Catalogue No. 11-008), 2–12.

Milan, A. (2003, Autumn). Would you live common-law? *Canadian Social Trends* (Statistics Canada Catalogue No. 11-008), 2–6.

Milan, A. (2011, July). *Fertility: Overview, 2008.* Ottawa: Statistics Canada. Retrieved from http://www.statcan.gc.ca/pub/91-209-x/2011001/article/11513-eng.pdf

Milan, A., & Hamm, B. (2003, Winter). Across the generations: Grandparents and grandchildren. *Canadian Social Trends* (Statistics Canada Catalogue No. 11-008), 2–7.

Milan, A., & Hamm, B. (2004, Summer). Mixed unions. *Canadian Social Trends* (Statistics Canada Catalogue No. 11-008), 2–6.

Milan, A., Maheux, H., & Chui, T. (2010, April 20). *A Portrait of Couples in Mixed Unions.* Ottawa: Statistics Canada. Retrieved from http://www.statcan.gc.ca/pub/11-008-x/2010001/article/11143-eng.pdf

Milan, A., & Peters, A. (2003, Summer). Couples living apart. *Canadian Social Trends* (Statistics Canada Catalogue No. 11-008), 2–6.

Milan, A., & Tran, K. (2004, Spring). Blacks in Canada: A long history. *Canadian Social Trends* (Statistics Canada Catalogue No. 11-008), 2–7.

Milan, A., Vézina, M., & Wells, C. (2007). *Family portrait: Continuity and change in Canadian families and households in 2006, 2006 Census* (Catalogue No. 97-553-XIE). Ottawa: Statistics Canada.

Milardo, R. M. (2005). Generative uncle and nephew relationships. *Journal of Marriage and Family, 67*, 1126–1236.

Miller, P. J. E., Caughlin, J. B., & Huston, T. L. (2003). Trait expressiveness and marital satisfaction. *Journal of Marriage and Family, 65*, 978–995.

Miner, H. (1939/1974). *St-Denis: A French-Canadian parish.* Chicago: University of Chicago Press.

Ministry of Children and Youth Services, Ontario. (2011, October 26). *How to adopt a child.* Retrieved from http://www.children.gov.on.ca/htdocs/English/topics/adoption/how/index.aspx

Ministry of Education, Ontario. (2013). *Healthy schools: Healthy Food for Healthy Schools Act.* Toronto: Author. Retrieved from http://www.edu.gov.on.ca/eng/healthyschools/lifestyle.html

Ministry of Health and Long-Term Care, Ontario. (2012, June 6). *Ontario's aging at home strategy.* Toronto: Author. Retrieved from http://www.health.gov.on.ca/en/public/programs/ltc/33_ontario_strategy.aspx

Mishra, V., & Smyth, R. (2010). Female labor force participation and total fertility rates in the OECD: New evidence from panel cointegration and Granger causality testing. *Journal of Economics and Business, 62*(1), 48–64. doi:10.1016/j.jeconbus.2009.07.006

Mitchell, B. A. (2006). *The Boomerang age: Transitions to adulthood in families.* New Brunswick, NJ: Aldine Transaction.

Mitchell, B. A. (2010). Happiness in midlife parental roles: A contextual mixed methods analysis. *Family Relations, 59*, 326–339. doi:10.1111/j.1741-3729.2010.00605.x

Mitchell, B. A., & Gee, E. M. (1996). "Boomerang kids" and midlife parental marital satisfaction. *Family Relations, 45*, 442–448.

Moen, P. (2006, June). Between the career mystique and reality: Mending the gap. *Family Focus*, F1–F3.

Mohs, A. (2012). *Choice v. equality: The legal recognition of unmarried cohabitation in Canada.* Retrieved from https://circle.ubc.ca/handle/2429/23487

Mollborn, S. (2009). Norms about nonmarital pregnancy and willingness to provide resources to unwed parents. *Journal of Marriage and Family, 71*, 122–134.

Money, J. (1986). *Lovemaps: Clinical concepts of sexual/erotic health and pathology, paraphilia, and gender transposition in childhood, adolescence, and maturity.* New York: Irvington.

Monserud, M. A. (2008). Intergenerational relationships and affectual solidarity between grandparents and young adults. *Journal of Marriage and Family, 70*, 182–195.

Montenegro, X. P. (2003). *Lifestyles, dating, and midlife singles.* Washington, DC: American Association of Retired Persons.

Montgomery, J., & Fewer, W. (1988). *Family systems and beyond.* New York: Human Sciences Press.

Montgomery, L. M. (c. 1935). *Anne of Green Gables.* Toronto: McClelland-Bantam.

Moogk, P. N. (1982). Les petits sauvages: The children of eighteenth century New France. In J. Parr (Ed.), *Childhood and family in Canadian history* (pp. 17–43). Toronto: McClelland & Stewart.

Moore, K. A., Redd, Z., Burkhauser, M., Mbwana, K., & Collins, A. (2009, April). *Children in poverty: Trends, consequences, and policy options* (Child Trends Research Brief #2009-11). Washington, DC: Child Trends. Retrieved from http://www.childtrends.org/Files//Child_Trends_2009_04_07_RB_ChildreninPoverty.pdf

Moore, K. A., Whitney, C., & Kinukawa, A. (2009, April). *Exploring the link between family strengths and adolescent outcomes.* Retrieved from http://www.childtrends.org/Files//Child_Trends_2009_04_16_RB_FamilyStrengths.pdf

Moore, M. (1988, Autumn). Female lone parenthood: The duration of episodes. *Canadian Social Trends,* 40–42.

Moore, T., & Thompson, V. (1987). Elder abuse: A review of research, programmes and policy. *The Social Worker/Le Travailleur social, 55*, 115–122.

Morris, M. B. (1987). Children's perceptions of last-chance parents: Implications of current trends toward late childbearing. *Child Welfare, 66*, 195–205.

Morissette, R., & Ostrovsky, Y. (2006, October). Earnings instability. *Perspectives on Labour and Income* (Statistics Canada Catalogue no. 75-001-XIE), 5–16. Retrieved from http://www.statcan.gc.ca/pub/75-001-x/11006/9501.pdf

Morissette, R., & Ostrovsky, Y. (2008, February). *How do families and unattached individuals respond to layoffs? Evidence from Canada* (Catalogue No. 11F0019 MIE–No. 304). Ottawa: Statistics Canada. Retrieved from http://www.statcan.gc.ca

Morissette, R., & Picot, G. (2005, April). *Summary of low-paid work and economically vulnerable families over the last two decades* (Catalogue No. 11F0019MIE–No. 249). Ottawa: Statistics Canada. Retrieved from http://www.statcan.gc.ca

Moore, N. B., & Davidson, J. K., Sr. (2002). A profile of adoption placers: Perceptions of pregnant teens during the decision-making process. *Adoption Quarterly, 6*(2), 29–41.

Morrissey, T. W. (2009). Multiple child-care arrangements and young children's behavioral outcomes. *Child Development, 80*, 59–76.

Morrison, A. (2004). Transracial adoption: the pros and cons and the parents' perspective. *Harvard BlackLetter Law Journal, 20*, 163–202. Retrieved from http://www.harvard.edu/students/orgs/blj/vol20/morrison.pdf

Moses, B. (2006). *Dish: Midlife women tell the truth about work, relationships, and the rest of life.* Toronto: McClelland & Stewart.

Moss, K. (2003). Witnessing violence—Aggression and anxiety in young children. *Supplement to Health Reports* (Statistics Canada Catalogue no. 82-003), 14, 53–66.

Mponda, F. (2009). *Madonna wins second Malawi adoption on appeal.* Retrieved from the Canada.com website http://www.canada.com/Life/Malawi+court+allows+Madonna+adopt+child/1689370/story.html

Mundy, L. (2007). *Everything conceivable: How assisted reproduction is changing men, women, and the world.* New York: Alfred A. Knopf.

Murdock, G. P. (1937, May). Comparative data on the division of labor by sex. *Social Forces, 15*(4), 551–553.

Murdock, G. W. (1949). *Social structure.* New York: Macmillan. Retrieved from http://archive.org/stream/socialstructure00murd#page/10/mode/2up

Murray, C. I., Toth, K., Larsen, B. L., & Moulton, S. (2010). Death, dying, and grief in families. In S. J. Price, C. A. Price, & P. C. McKenry (Eds.), *Families & change: Coping with stressful events and transitions* (4th ed., pp. 73–95). Los Angeles: Sage.

Murry, V. M., Harrell, A. W., Brody, G. H., Chen, Y.-F., Simons, R. L., Black, A. R., Cutrona, C. E., & Gibbons, F. X. (2008). Long-term effects of stressors on relationship well-being and parenting among rural African American women. *Family Relations, 57*, 117–127.

Musick, K., & Bumpass, L. (2012). Reexamining the case for marriage: Union formation and changes in well-being. *Journal of Marriage and Family, 74*(1), 1–18. doi:10.1111/j.1741-3737.2011.00873.x

Myers, J. B., Madathil, J., & Tingle, L. (2005). Marriage satisfaction and wellness in India and the United States: A preliminary comparison of arranged marriages and marriages of choice. *Journal of Counseling and Development, 83*(2), 183–190.

Myers, S., Buchanan, C., & Grzywacz, J. (2012, November). *Monitoring strategies and knowledge among diverse mothers of adolescents.* Poster presentation at the annual conference of the National Council of Family Relations, Phoenix, AZ.

Myles, J., Hou, F., Picot, G., & Myers, K. (2006). *Why did employment and earnings rise among lone mothers during the 1980s and 1990s?* (Catalogue No. 11F019MIE, no. 282). Ottawa: Statistics Canada. Retrieved from http://www.statcan.gc.ca

Myles, J., Hou, F., Picot, G., & Myers, K. (2008). *The demographic foundations of rising employment and earnings among single mothers in Canada and the United States* (Catalogue No. 11F0019M, no. 305). Ottawa: Statistics Canada. Retrieved from http://www.statcan.gc.ca/pub/11f0019m2008305-eng.pdf

Myers, S. M., & Booth, A. (1999). Marital strains and marital quality: The role of high and low locus of control. *Journal of Marriage and the Family, 61*, 423–436.

Nash-Nance, S. (2012, May 10). Five survival tips for parents with "boomerang" kids. *Forbes.* Retrieved from http://www.forbes.com/sites/sherylnancenash/2012/05/10/five-tips-for-surviving-the-boomerang-kids

National Abortion Federation. (2010). *History of abortion in Canada.* Retrieved from http://www.prochoice.org/canada/history.html

National Advisory Council on Aging. (2000). *The NACA position on enhancing the Canadian health care system.* Ottawa: Author.

National Advisory Council on Aging. (2005a). *Aging in poverty in Canada.* Ottawa: Author.

National Advisory Council on Aging. (2005b). *Seniors from ethno-cultural minorities*. Ottawa: Author. Retrieved from http://www.naca.ca

National Advisory Council on Aging. (2005c, Fall). The changing face of long-term care. *Expression, 18*(4), 1–8.

National Advisory Council on Aging. (2005d, Fall). The National Advisory Council on Aging demands improvements to Canada's long-term care institutions. *Expression, 18*(4), Insert.

National Advisory Council on Aging. (2006). *Seniors in Canada: 2006 report card* (Catalogue No. HP30-1/2006E). Ottawa: Author.

National Child Benefit (2007, February). *The national child benefit: Progress report*. Retrieved from http://www.nationalchild-benefit.ca/eng/pdf/ncb_pr05.pdf

National Clearinghouse on Family Violence (2008). *Sibling sexual abuse: A guide for parents*. Ottawa: Author. Retrieved from http://www.phac-aspc.gc.ca/nc-cn

National Council of Welfare. (2007a). *First Nations, Métis, and Inuit children and youth: Time to act* (Catalogue No. HS54-1/2007E-PDF). Ottawa: Author. Retrieved from http://www.ncwcnbes.net

National Council of Welfare. (2007b, Winter). *Solving poverty: Four cornerstones of a workable national strategy for Canada* (Catalogue No. HS4-31/2007E-PDF). Ottawa: Author. Retrieved from http://www.ncwcnbes.net

National Council of Welfare. (2008, December). *Welfare incomes, 2006 and 2007*. Ottawa: Author. Retrieved from http://www.ncwcnbes.net

National Council of Welfare. (2009, September). *Poverty profile 2007: Overview of poverty trends, 1976–2007*. Ottawa: Author. Retrieved from http://www.ncwcnbes.net/documents/researchpublications/ResearchProjects/PovertyProfile/2009/Poverty%20Profile%201%202007%20E.pdf

National Council of Welfare. (2011, Autumn). *The dollars and sense of solving poverty*. Ottawa: Author. Retrieved from http://publications.gc.ca/collections/collection_2011/cnb-ncw/HS54-2-2011-eng.pdf

National Institute of Justice. (1996). *The cycle of violence revisited*. Washington, DC: U.S. Department of Justice.

National Seniors Council. (2009). *The government of Canada and elder abuse: Breaking the silence*. Retrieved from http://www.seniorscouncil.gc.ca/eng/speeches/2008/080616.shtml

National Seniors Council. (2011). *Overview of the financial situation of Canadian seniors*. Retrieved from http://www.seniorscouncil.gc.ca/eng/research_publications/low_income/2009/hs1_9/page05.shtml

Neal, M. B., & Hammer, L. B. (2007). *Working couples caring for children and aging parents: Effects on work and well-being*. Mahwah, NJ: Lawrence Erlbaum.

Neff, L. A., & Karney, B. R. (2007). Stress crossover in newlywed marriage: A longitudinal and dyadic process. *Journal of Marriage and Family, 69*, 594–607.

Nelson, F. (1996). *Lesbian motherhood: An exploration of Canadian lesbian families*. Toronto: University of Toronto Press.

Nelson, M. K. (2006). Single mothers "do" family. *Journal of Marriage and Family, 68*, 781–795.

Nemr, R. (2009). Fact sheet—Police reported family violence against children and youth. In Statistics Canada, *Family violence in Canada: A statistical profile 2009* (Catalogue No. 85-224-X, pp. 32–41). Ottawa: Statistics Canada. Retrieved from http://www.statcan.gc.ca/pub/85-224-x/85-224-x2009000.eng.pdf

Nesteruk, O., & Gramescu, A. (2012). Dating and mate selection among young adults from immigrant families. *Marriage and Family Review, 48*, 40–58. doi:10.1080/01494929.2011.620732

Nett, E. M. (1988). *Canadian families: Past and present*. Toronto: Butterworths.

Neufeld, A., Harrison, M. J., Stewart, M., & Hughes, K. (2003, November). *Nonsupport and advocacy among family caregivers*. Poster presentation at the annual conference of National Council on Family Relations, Vancouver, BC.

Neugarten, B. L., & Neugarten, D. A. (1986). Changing meanings of age in the aging society. In A. Pifer & L. Bronte (Eds.), *Our aging society: Paradox and promise* (pp. 33–51). New York: W. W. Norton.

Neysmith, S. (2003). Caring and aging: Exposing the policy issues. In A. Westhues (Ed.), *Canadian social policy: Issues and perspectives* (3rd ed., pp. 182–199). Waterloo, ON: Wilfrid Laurier University Press.

Nguyen, L. (2012, September 20). Rising "grey divorce" rates create financial havoc for seniors. *Globe and Mail*. Retrieved from http://www.theglobeandmail.com/news/politics/rising-grey-divorce-rates-create-financial-havoc-for-seniors/article4553219

Nihmey, J., & Foxman, S. (1987). *The time of their lives: The Dionne tragedy*. Toronto: McClelland-Bantam.

Niren, M. (2009). *A look back at the history of divorce in Canada*. Retrieved from http://www.divorcesupport.ca/divorce-blog/divorce/a-look-back-at-the-history-of-divorce-in-canada

Noël, A., & Larocque, F. (2009, August). *Aboriginal peoples and poverty in Canada: Can provincial governments make a difference?* Paper prepared for the annual meeting of the International Sociological Association's Research Committee 19 (RC19), Montreal. Retrieved from http://www.cccg.umontreal.ca/RC19/PDF/Noel_A_Rc192009.pdf

Nomaguchi, K. M. (2006). Maternal employment, nonparental care, mother–child interactions, and child outcomes during preschool years. *Journal of Marriage and Family, 68*, 1341–1369.

Northcott, M. (2012). *Intimate partner violence risk assessment tools: A review*. Ottawa: Department of Justice. Retrieved from http://www.justice.gc.ca/eng/rp-pr/cj-jp/fv-vf/rr12_8/rr12_8.pdf

Novac, S., Brown, J., & Bourbonnais, C. (1996). *No room of her own: A literature review on women and homelessness*. Ottawa: Canada Mortgage and Housing.

Nowicki, S., Jr. (2003, February). The hidden language of relationships [Audiotape]. In J. K. Comeau (Ed.), *Family Information Services Professional Resource Materials*. Minneapolis: Family Information Services.

O'Brien, M. (2007). Ambiguous loss in families of children with autism spectrum disorders. *Family Relations, 56,* 135–146.

O'Connor, J. (2012, September 19). Trend of couples not having children just plain selfish. *National Post.* Retrieved from http://fullcomment.nationalpost.com/2012/09/19/joe-oconnor-selfishness-behind-growing-trend-for-couples-to-not-have-children

O'Donnell, V. (2008, Winter). Selected findings of the Aboriginal Children's Survey 2006: Family and community. *Canadian Social Trends* (Statistics Canada Catalogue No. 11-008), 65–72.

OECD. (2006). *Starting strong II: Early childhood education and care.* Paris: Author. Retrieved from http://www.oecd.org/dataoecd/14/32/37425999.pdf

Ogilvie, B. A. (2004). *Mother–daughter incest: A guide for helping professionals.* New York: Haworth.

Ogrodnik, L. (2007a). *Seniors as victims of crime, 2004 and 2005* (Catalogue No. 85F0033MIE, no. 14). Ottawa: Statistics Canada. Retrieved from http://www.statcan.gc.ca/pub/85f0033m/85f0033m2007014-eng.htm

Ogrodnik, L. (2007b). Spousal homicide or attempts and prior police contact for spousal abuse. In L. Ogrodnik (Ed.), *Family violence in Canada: A statistical profile 2007* (Catalogue No. 85-224-XIE, pp. 9–15, 19). Ottawa: Statistics Canada. Retrieved from http://www.statscan.gc.ca

Ogrodnik, L. (2009). Fact sheet—Family homicides. In Statistics Canada, *Family violence in Canada: A statistical profile 2009* (Catalogue No. 85-224-X, pp. 48–56). Ottawa: Statistics Canada. Retrieved from http://www.statcan.gc.ca/pub/85-224-x/85-224-x2009000.eng.pdf

Okazaki, E., & Yorgason, J. B. (2006, September). Individual and family adjustment to MS and ALS. *Family Focus,* F10, F12.

O'Keefe, M. (2005, April). *Teen dating violence: A review of risk factors and prevention efforts.* Harrisburg, PA: VAWnet, A Project of the National Resource Center on Domestic Violence/Pennsylvania Coalition Against Domestic Violence. Retrieved from http://www.vawnet.org

Okimoto, J. D., & Stegall, P. J. (1987). *Boomerang kids: How to live with adult children who return home.* Boston: Little Brown.

Oldehinkel, A. J., Ormel, J., Veenstra, R., De Winter, A. F., & Verhulst, F. C. (2008). Parental divorce and offspring depressive symptoms: Dutch developmental trends during early adolescence. *Journal of Marriage and Family, 70,* 284–293.

Olmstead, S., Roberson, P., Fincham, F., & Pasley, K. (2012, November). *First- semester college men's hookups: The role of pre-college risk behavior.* Paper presented at the National Council on Family Relations annual conference, Phoenix, AZ.

Olsen, C. S. (1997, Summer). Stepping stones for stepfamilies. *CFLE Network,* 5.

Olson, D. H. (1990). Commentary: Marriage in perspective. In F. D. Fincham & T. N. Bradbury (Eds.), *The psychology of marriage* (pp. 402–419). New York: Guilford.

Ontario Arts Council. (n.d.). *Aboriginal artists in schools.* Retrieved from http://www.arts.on.ca/Page2774.aspx

Ontario Ministry of Community and Social Services. (2000). *Making welfare work: Report to taxpayers on welfare reform.* Toronto: Author.

Ontario Ministry of Community and Social Services. (n.d.). *Frequently asked questions about searching for adoption records in Ontario.* Retrieved from http://www.accesson.ca/mcss/english/pillars/community/questions/adoption/

Ontario Women's Directorate. (1991). *Work and family: The crucial balance.* Toronto: Ministry of Community and Social Services.

Oppenheimer, V. K. (2000). The continuing importance of men's economic position in marriage formation. In L. J. Waite, C. Bachrach, M. Hindin, E. Thomson, & A. Thornton (Eds.), *The ties that bind: Perspectives on marriage and cohabitation* (pp. 283–301). New York: Aldine de Gruyter.

Option of Adoption Act. (2009). Georgia, 09 HB 388/AP. Retrieved from http://www.legis.ga.gov/2009_10/fulltext/hb388.htm

Orkin, M. M. (1981). *The great stork derby.* Don Mills, ON: General Publishing.

Ormond, K., & Ross, L. F. (2006). Ethical issues in reproductive medicine. In S. M. Miller, S. H. McDaniel, J. S. Rolland, & S. L. Feetham (Eds.), *Individuals, families, and the new era of genetics: Biopsychosocial perspectives* (pp. 465–485). New York: W. W. Norton.

Orrange, R. M., Firebaugh, F. M., & Heck, R. K. Z. (2003). Managing households. In P. Moen (Ed.), *It's about time: Couples and careers* (pp. 152–167). Ithaca, NY: Cornell University Press.

Osborne, C., Manning, W. D., & Smock, P. J. (2007). Married and cohabiting parents' relationship stability: A focus on race and ethnicity. *Journal of Marriage and Family, 69,* 1345–1366.

Osborne, C., & McLanahan, S. (2007). Partnership instability and child well-being. *Journal of Marriage and Family, 69,* 1065–1083.

Oswald, R. F., & Masciadrelli, B. P. (2008). Generative ritual among nonmetropolitan lesbians and gay men: Promoting social inclusion. *Journal of Marriage and Family, 70,* 1060–1073.

Owram, D. (1996). *Born at the right time: A history of the baby-boom generation.* Toronto: University of Toronto Press.

Pagelow, M. D. (1984). *Family violence.* New York: Praeger.

Pann, K. M., & Crosbie-Burnett, M. (2005). Remarriage and recoupling: A stress perspective. In P. C. McKenry & S. J. Price (Eds.), *Families & change: Coping with stressful events and transitions* (3rd ed., pp. 253–284). Thousand Oaks, CA: Sage.

Pappenheim, H., & Graves, G. (2005). *Bringing home the bacon: Making marriages work when she makes more money.* New York: William Morrow.

Parcel, D. L., & Dufur, M. J. (2001). Capital at home and at school: Effects on child social adjustment. *Journal of Marriage and Family, 63,* 32–47.

Parcel, T. L., & Menaghan, E. G. (1994). *Parents' jobs and children's lives.* New York: Aldine de Gruyter.

Parent, D., & Wang, L. (2007, May). Tax incentives and fertility in Canada. *Canadian Journal of Economics, 40*(2), 371–400.

Parker, K. (2012). *The boomerang generation: Feeling OK about living with mom and dad.* Pew Research Center. Retrieved from http://www.pewsocialtrends.org/files/2012/03/PewSocialTrends-2012-BoomerangGeneration.pdf

Parker, M. (2004, June). Meeting the needs of Southeast Asian elders. *Family Focus,* F10–F12.

Parsons, T., & Bales, R. (1956). *Family, socialization, and interaction process.* London: Routledge and Kegan Paul.

Pasley, K., & Lee, M. (2010). Stress and coping within the context of stepfamily life. In S. J. Price, C. A. Price, & P. C. McKenry (Eds.), *Families & change: Coping with stressful events and transitions* (4th ed., pp. 235–261). Los Angeles: Sage.

Patterson, J. M. (2002). Integrating family resilience and family stress theory. *Journal of Marriage and Family, 64,* 349–360.

Patton, M. Q. (1990). *Qualitative evaluation and research methods* (2nd ed.). Newbury Park, CA: Sage.

Patton, M. Q. (1996). Preface: A look at the mosaic of qualitative research. In M. B. Sussman & J. F. Gilgun (Eds.), *The methods and methodologies of qualitative family research* (pp. xvii–xxii). New York: Haworth.

Pawson, M. (2003). The battle with mortality and the urge to procreate. In J. Haynes & J. Miller (Eds.), *Inconceivable conceptions: Psychological aspects of infertility and reproductive technology* (pp. 60–72). New York: Brunner-Routledge.

Payne, J. D. (1986). Whither the broken family? *Transition, 16*(1), 4, 10.

Pederson, S. (2009, May 29). Personal communication with author.

Pennell, J., & Burford, G. (2008). Introduction: Principled diffusion of family group conferencing in Canadian child welfare. *Protecting Children, 23*(4), 3–8.

Pepler, D. J., Catallo, R., & Moore, T. E. (2000). Consider the children: Research informing interventions for children exposed to domestic violence. In R. A. Geffner, P. G. Jaffe, & M. Suderman (Eds.), *Children exposed to domestic violence: Current issues in research, intervention, prevention, and policy development* (pp. 37–57). New York: Haworth Maltreatment & Trauma Press.

Pepper, F. C., & White, W. A. (1996). *First Nations traditional values.* Retrieved from www.nautsamawt.org/support/resource-documents/language-a-culture/doc_download/15-traditional-first-nations-values

Perreault, S. (2009, May). *Criminal victimization and health: A profile of victimization among persons with activity limitations or other health problems* (Catalogue No. 85F0033M, no. 21). Ottawa: Statistics Canada. Retrieved from http://www.statcan.gc.ca/pub/85f0033m/85f0033m2009021-eng.pdf

Peter, K. (1987). *The dynamics of Hutterite society: An analytical approach.* Edmonton: University of Alberta Press.

Peterson, G. W., Hennon, C. B., & Knox, T. (2010). Conceptualizing parental stress with family stress theory. In S. J. Price, C. A. Price, & P. C. McKenry (Eds.), *Families & change: Coping with stressful events and transitions* (4th ed., pp. 25–49). Los Angeles: Sage.

Pew Research Center. (2006). *National polls not undermined by growing cell-only population: The cell phone challenge to survey research.* Retrieved from http://www.people-press.org/reports/pdf/276.pdf

Pew Research Center. (2007, January 9). *How young people view their lives, futures, and politics: A portrait of "Generation Next."* Washington, DC: Pew Research Center.

Phenice, L. A., & Griffore, R. J. (1996). Understanding ethnic minority families: An ecological approach. *Family Science Review, 9,* 5–12.

Picot, G., Hou, F., & Coulombe, S. (2007). *Chronic low income dynamics among recent immigrants* (Catalogue No. 11F0019, no. 294). Ottawa: Statistics Canada. Retrieved from http://www.statcan.gc.ca

Pillemer, K. (2005). Elder abuse is caused by the deviance and dependence of elderly caregivers. In D. R. Loseke, R. J. Gelles, & M. M. Cavanaugh (Eds.), *Current controversies in family violence* (2nd ed., pp. 207–220). Thousand Oaks, CA: Sage.

Pinderhughes, E. E., Nix, R., Foster, E. M., Jones, D., & The Conduct Problems Prevention Research Group. (2001). Parenting in context: Impact of neighborhood poverty, residential stability, public services, social networks, and danger on parental behaviors. *Journal of Marriage and Family, 63,* 941–953.

Pines, A. M. (1996). *Couple burnout: Causes and cures.* New York: Routledge.

Pines, A. M. (2005). *Falling in love: Why we choose the lovers we choose* (2nd ed.). New York: Routledge.

Pitrou, A. (2006). The irreplaceable third age: Between family, work, and mutual support. In L. O. Stone (Ed.), *New frontiers of research on retirement* (Catalogue No. 75-511-XPE, pp. 113–126). Ottawa: Statistics Canada.

Pixley, J. E., & Moen, P. (2003). Prioritizing careers. In P. Moen (Ed.), *It's about time: Couples and careers* (pp. 183–200). Ithaca, NY: ILR Press.

Plant, R. W., & Siegel, L. (2008). Children in foster care: Prevention and treatment of mental health problems. In T. P. Gullotta & G. M. Blau (Eds.), *Family influences on childhood behavior and development: Evidence-based prevention and treatment approaches* (pp. 209–230). New York: Routledge.

Pohlman, C., & Dulipovici, A. (2004). *Fostering flexibility: Work and family.* Canadian Federation of Independent Business. Retrieved from http://www.cfib.ca

Pollack, S. (2009). Creating submissive subjects: Lone mothers and social assistance regimes in Canada. *Journal of Poverty & Social Justice, 17*(3), 225–235.

Poncet, M. C., Toullic, P., Papazian, L., Kentish-Barnes, N., Timsit, J.-F., Pochard, F., ... & Azoulay, É. (2007). Burnout syndrome in critical care nursing staff. *American Journal of Respiratory and Critical Care Medicine, 175,* 698–704.

Pong, S.-l., Dronkers, J., & Hampden-Thompson, G. (2003, August). Family policies and children's school achievement in single- versus two-parent families. *Journal of Marriage and Family, 65*(3), 681–699.

Popenoe, D. (2007, July). The future of marriage in America. In *The state of our unions 2007: The social health of marriage in America* (pp. 5–12). Piscataway, NJ: Rutgers University, The National Marriage Project. Retrieved from http://marriage.rutgers.edu

Popenoe, D. (2008). *Cohabitation, marriage and child wellbeing: A cross-national perspective.* Piscataway, NJ: Rutgers University, The National Marriage Project. Retrieved from http://marriage.rutgers.edu/Publications/NMP2008/CohabitationReport.pdf

Portwood, S. G. (2008). Physical abuse in childhood (Ages 5–13). In T. P. Gullotta & G. M. Blau (Eds.), *Family influences on childhood behavior and development: Evidence-based prevention and treatment approaches* (pp. 267–292). New York: Routledge.

Postmedia News. (2011, November 23). B.C. Supreme Court rules polygamy ban is constitutional, but flawed. *National Post*. Retrieved from http://news.nationalpost.com/2011/11/23/b-c-supreme-court-rules-polygamy-law-is-constitutional

Potter, D. (2012, June). Same-sex parent families and children's academic achievement. *Journal of Marriage and Family, 74*, 556–571. doi:10.1111/j.1741-3737.2012.00966.x

Pottie Bunge, V., & Locke, D. (Eds.). (2000). *Family violence in Canada: A statistical profile 2000* (Catalogue No. 85-224-XIE). Ottawa: Statistics Canada.

Power, P. W., & Dell Orto, A. E. (2004). *Families living with chronic illness and disability: Intervention, challenges, and opportunities.* New York: Springer.

Preto, N. G. (1999). Transformation of the family system during adolescence. In B. Carter & M. McGoldrick (Eds.), *The expanded family life cycle: Individual, family, and social perspectives* (3rd ed., pp. 274–286). Boston: Allyn & Bacon.

Previti, D., & Amato, P. R. (2003). Why stay married? Rewards, barriers, and marital stability. *Journal of Marriage and Family, 65*, 561–573.

Price, S. J., Price, C. A., & McKenry, P. C. (2010). Families coping with change: A conceptual overview. In S. J. Price, C. A. Price, & P. C. McKenry (Eds.), *Families & change: Coping with stressful events and transitions* (4th ed., pp. 1–23). Los Angeles: Sage.

Primack, B. A., Douglas, E. L., Fine, M. J., & Dalton, M. A. (2009). Exposure to sexual lyrics and sexual experience among urban adolescents. *American Journal of Preventive Medicine.* doi:10.1016/j.amepre.2008.11.011.

Prince, B. (2004). *I came as a stranger: The underground railroad.* Toronto: Tundra.

Prince, M. J. (2009, Summer). Retirement (in)security for Canadians. *Transition*, 6–9.

Pronovost, G. (2007, Février). Le temps dans tous ses états: temps de travail, temps de loisir et temps pour la famille à l'aube du XXIe siècle. *Enjeux publics IRPP, 8*(1). Retrieved from http://www.irpp.org

Pruett, K. D. (2000). *Fatherneed: Why father care is as essential as mother care for your child.* New York: Free Press.

Pruett, M. K., Cowan, C. P., Cowan, P. A., & Pruett, K. (2009). Fathers as resources in families involved in the child welfare system. *Protecting Children, 24*(2), 54–64.

Public Health Agency of Canada. (2005). *The safe living guide: A guide to home safety for seniors* (3rd ed., Catalogue No. HP25-7/2008E). Ottawa: Public Health Agency of Canada, Division of Aging and Seniors.

Public Health Agency of Canada. (2007a). *HIV/AIDS Epi updates* (Catalogue No. HP37-7/2007E-PDF). Retrieved from http://www.phac-aspc.gc.ca/aids-sida/publication/index.html

Public Health Agency of Canada (2007b). *Spousal and partner abuse—It can be stopped.* Ottawa: Author. Retrieved from http://www.phac-aspc.gc.ca/ncfv-cnivf/publications/rcmp-grc/fem-partnrabus-eng.php

Public Health Agency of Canada. (2009). *Child sexual abuse.* Ottawa: Author. Retrieved from http://www.phac-aspc.gc.ca/ncfv-cnivf/publications/nfntsxagrsex-eng.php

Public Health Agency of Canada. (2010). *Canadian incidence study of reported child abuse and neglect, 2008: Major findings.* Ottawa: Author. Retrieved from http://www.phac-aspc.gc.ca/cm-vee/public-eng.php

Public Health Agency of Canada. (2012a, July 19). *At a glance—HIV and AIDS in Canada: Surveillance report to December 31st, 2010.* Ottawa: Author. Retrieved from http://www.phac-aspc.gc.ca/aids-sida/publication/survreport/2010/dec/index-eng.php

Public Health Agency of Canada. (2012b). *Curbing childhood obesity: A federal, provincial and territorial framework for action to promote healthy weights.* Ottawa: Author. Retrieved from http://www.phac-aspc.gc.ca/hp-ps/hl-mvs/framework-cadre/pdf/ccofw-eng.pdf

Public Health Agency of Canada. (2012c, May 15). *National clearinghouse on family violence e-bulletin: May 2012.* Ottawa: Author. Retrieved from http://www.phac-aspc.gc.ca/ncfv-cnivf/EB/2012/may-mai/index-eng.php

Pudrovska, T. (2008). Psychological implications of motherhood and fatherhood in midlife: Evidence from sibling models. *Journal of Marriage and Family, 70*, 168–181.

Quah, S. R. (2009). *Families in Asia: Home and kin* (2nd ed.) New York: Routledge.

Quam, J. K. (1993, June/July). Gay and lesbian aging. *SIECUS Report.* Retrieved from http://www.cyfc.umn.edu/Diversity/Gay/gayaging.html

Queen's Printer, Alberta. (n.d.). *Adult Interdependent Relationships Act, Chapter A-4.5.* Retrieved from http://www.qp.alberta.ca/

Raag, T., & Rackliff, C. L. (1998). Preschoolers' awareness of social expectations of gender: Relationships to toy choices. *Sex Roles, 38*, 685–700.

Raley, R. K., Crissey, S., & Muller, C. (2007). Of sex and romance: Late adolescent relationships and young adult union formation. *Journal of Marriage and Family, 69*, 1210–1226.

Raley, R. K., & Wildsmith, E. (2004). Cohabitation and children's family instability. *Journal of Marriage and Family, 66*, 210–219.

Ramarajan, L., Barsade, S. G., & Burack, O. R. (2008). The influence of organizational respect on emotional exhaustion in the human services. *Journal of Positive Psychology, 3*, 4–18.

Raphael, D. (2011, May). Poverty in childhood and adverse health outcomes in adulthood. *Maturitas, 69*(1), 22–26. Retrieved from http://dx.doi.org.ezproxy.usherbrooke.ca/10.1016/j.maturitas.2011.02.011

Rastogi, M. (2009). Asian Indians in intercultural marriages: Intersections of acculturation, gender and exogamy. In T. A. Karis & K. D. Killian (Eds.), *Intercultural couples: Exploring deversity in intimate relationships* (pp. 189–206). New York: Routledge.

Ray, A. J. (1996). *I have lived here since the world began: An illustrated history of Canada's Native people.* Toronto: Lester/Key Porter.

Rea, W., Yuen, J., Engeland, J., & Figueroa, R. (2008, January). The dynamics of housing affordability. *Perspectives on Labour and Income* (Statistics Canada Catalogue no. 75-001-X), 15–26. Retrieved from http://www.statcan.gc.ca/pub/75-001-x/2008101/pdf/10511-eng.pdf

Recker, N. (2002). *Before you say "I do" again.* The Ohio State University Extension. Retrieved from http://www.ohio-line.osu.edu/flm02/FS01.html

Recker, N. (2007, August). *In praise of older parents* [Fact sheet]. The Ohio State University Extension. Retrieved from http://ohioline.osu.edu

Reefhuis, J., Honein, M. A., Schieve, L. A., Correa, A., Hobbs, C. A., Rasmussen, S. A., et al. (2008). Assisted reproductive technology and major structural birth defects in the United States. *Human Reproduction.* Advance online publication. doi:10.1093/humrep/den387

Regan, P. C. (2008). *The mating game: A primer on love, sex, and marriage* (2nd ed.). Los Angeles: Sage.

Régie des Rentes Québec. (2013). Definition of spouse. Retrieved from http://www.rrq.gouv.qc.ca/en/vie_a_deux/couple/Pages/definition_conjoint.aspx

Regional Research Institute for Human Services. (2005, Summer). Resilience and recovery: Findings from the Kauai Longitudinal Study. *Research, Policy, and Practice in Children's Mental Health, 19*(1), 11–14.

Rehm, J., Baliunas, D., Brochu, S., Fischer, B., Gnam, W., Patra, J., Popova, S., Samocinska-Hart, A., & Taylor, B. (2006, March). *The costs of substance abuse in Canada 2002: Highlights.* Ottawa: Canadian Centre on Substance Abuse. Retrieved from http://www.ccsa.ca/2006%20CCSA%20Documents/ccsa-011332-2006.pdf

Reid, J. H. (1963). Principles, values, and assumptions underlying adoption practice. In I. E. Smith (Ed.), *Readings in adoption* (pp. 26–37). New York: Philosophical Library.

Reid, S. (n.d.). *Myths vs. facts about older people.* Fredericton, NB: St. Thomas University, Centre for Research on Youth at Risk. Retrieved from http://www.stthomasu.ca/research/youth/manual/myths.htm

Reilly, D. R. (2007, February 13). Surrogate pregnancy: a guide for Canadian prenatal health care providers. *Canadian Medical Association Journal, 176*(4), 483–485. Retrieved from http://www.cmaj.ca/cgi/reprint/176/4/483

Reinhold, S. (2007, December 20). *Reassessing the link between premarital cohabitation and marital instability.* Mannheim, Germany: Mannheim Research Institute for the Economics of Aging. Retrieved from http://client.norc.org/jole/SOLEweb/8197.pdf

Reiss, I. L. (1960). *Premarital sexual standards in America.* New York: Free Press.

Reiss, I. L. (1980). *Family systems in America.* New York: Holt, Rinehart & Winston.

Retirement in Elliot Lake. (n.d.). Retrieved from http://www.elliotlake.com/retire/

Revenue Canada. (2010). *Marital status.* Retrieved from http://www.cra-arc.gc.ca/tx/ndvdls/tpcs/ncm-tx/rtrn/cmpltng/prsnl-nf/mrtl-eng.html

Rhodes, A. R. (2002). Long-distance relationships in dual-career commuter couples: A review of counseling issues. *The Family Journal, 10*, 398–404.

Richards, J. (2008, October). *Closing the Aboriginal/Non-Aboriginal education gap* (Backgrounder No. 116). Toronto: C. D. Howe Institute.

Richards, J., & Brzozowski, M. (2006). *Let's walk before we run: Cautionary advice on childcare* (Commentary No. 237). Toronto: C. D. Howe Institute. Retrieved from http://www.cdhowe.org/pdf/commentary_237_english.pdf

Richardson, C., & Nelson, B. (2007). A change of residence: Government schools and foster homes as sites of forced aboriginal assimilation—A paper designed to provoke thought and systemic change. *First Peoples Child and Family Review, 3*, 75–83.

Richardson, R. A. (2005, November). *Anticipating adolescence: Separation anxiety in mothers of middle schoolers.* Poster presentation at the annual conference of National Council on Family Relations, Phoenix, AZ.

Risman, B. J., & Johnson-Sumerford, D. (1998). Doing it fairly: A study of post-gender marriages. *Journal of Marriage and the Family, 60*, 23–40.

Ristock, J., & Timbang, N. (2005). *Relationship violence in lesbian/gay/bisexual/transgender/queer [LGBTQ] communities.* Minnesota Center Against Violence and Abuse. Retrieved from http://www.mincava.umn.edu/documents/lgbtqviolence/lgbtqviolence.html

Roberts, D. F., & Foehr, U. G. (2008, Spring). Trends in media use. *The Future of Children, 18*(1), 11–37.

Roberts, K.C., Shields, M., de Groh, M., Aziz, A. & Gilbert, J. (2012). Overweight and obesity in children and adolescents: Results from the 2009 to 2011 Canadian Health Measures Survey. *Health Reports, 23*(3), 3–7 (Statistics Canada Catalogue No. 82-003-XPE). Retrieved from http://www.statcan.gc.ca/pub/82-003-x/2012003/article/11706-eng.pdf

Roberts, L. J., & McCrady, B. S. (2003). *Alcohol problems in intimate relationships: A guide for marriage and family therapists* (Publication No. 03-5284). Washington, DC: National Institutes of Health, National Institute on Alcohol Abuse and Alcoholism. Retrieved from http://www.niaaa.nih.gov/publications/niaaa-guide/

Roberts, L. J. (2005, March). Alcohol and the marital relationship. *Family Focus*, F12–F13.

Roberts, N. A., & Levenson, R. W. (2001). The remains of the workday: Impact of job stress and exhaustion on marital interaction in police couples. *Journal of Marriage and Family, 63*, 1052–1067.

Roberts, P. S. (2004, April 21). *Alleviating stress in clergy wives: The development and formative evaluation of a psychoeducational group intervention* (Doctoral dissertation, Virginia Polytechnic Institute and State University). Retrieved from http://scholar.lib.vt.edu/theses/available/etd-04272004-134248/unrestricted/RobertsDissertation2.pdf

Robinson, P. (2009, March). Profile of child support beneficiaries. *Juristat* (Statistics Canada Catalogue No. 85-002-X), *29*(1). Retrieved from http://www.statcan.gc.ca/

Robinson, T.R. (2008). *Health and welfare Canada—Section C: Social security.* Ottawa: Statistics Canada. Retrieved from http://www.statcan.gc.ca/pub/11-516-x/pdf/5220013-eng.pdf

Rodgers, K. B., & Rose, H. A. (2002). Risk and resiliency factors among adolescents who experience marital transitions. *Journal of Marriage and Family, 64*, 1024–1027.

Roer-Strier, D., & Ben Ezra, D. (2006). Intermarriages between Western women and Palestinian men: Multidirectional adaptation processes. *Journal of Marriage and Family, 68*, 41–55.

Rogers, S. J. (2004). Dollars, dependency, and divorce: Four perspectives on the role of wives' income. *Journal of Marriage and Family, 66*, 59–74.

Rolland, J. S. (2003). Mastering family challenges in serious illness and disability. In F. Walsh (Ed.), *Normal family processes: Growing diversity and complexity* (3rd ed., pp. 460–489). New York: Guilford.

Rooke, P. T., & Schnell, R. L. (1983). *Discarding the asylum: From child rescue to the welfare state in English-Canada (1800–1950).* Lanham, MD: University Press of America.

Root, M. P. P. (2001). *Love's revolution: Interracial marriage.* Philadelphia: Temple University Press.

Roper, S. O., & Jackson, J. B. (2007). The ambiguities of out-of-home care: Children with severe or profound disabilities. *Family Relations, 56*, 147–161.

Rosenthal, R., & Jacobson, L. (1968). *Pygmalion in the classroom.* New York: Holt.

Roscoe, B., Cavanaugh, L. E., & Kennedy, D. R. (1988). Dating infidelity: Behaviors, reasons, and consequences. *Adolescence, 23*, 35–43.

Rose, J. (1992). *From career to maternity: A feminist reconsiders the mommy track—Felice M. Schwartz.* Retrieved from http://findarticles.com/p/articles/mi_m1316/is_n7-8_v24/ai_12514473/?tag=content;col1

Rosenbaum, J. E. (2009). Patient teenagers? A comparison of the sexual behavior of virginity pledgers and matched non-pledgers. *Pediatrics, 123*, e110–e120. Retrieved from http://www.pediatrics.org

Rosenblatt, P. C. (2006). *Two in a bed: The social system of couple bed sharing.* Albany: State University of New York.

Rosenblatt, P. C. (2009). A systems theory analysis of intercultural couple relationships. In T. A. Karis & K. D. Killiam (Eds.), *Intercultural couples: Explaining diversity in intimate relationships* (pp. 3–20). New York: Routledge.

Ross, D. P., & Roberts, P. (1999). *Income and child well-being: A new perspective on the poverty debate.* Ottawa: Canadian Council on Social Development. Retrieved from http://www.ccsd.ca/pubs/inckids/

Ross, D. P., Roberts, P. A., & Scott, K. (1998). *Mediating factors in child development outcomes: Children in lone-parent families.* Ottawa: Human Resources Development Canada.

Ross, D. P., Scott, K. J., & Smith, P. J. (2000). *The Canadian fact book on poverty—2000.* Ottawa: Canadian Council on Social Development.

Ross, J. J., & Benson, M. J. (2005, November). *Dimensions of parenting and identity development in late adolescence.* Poster presentation at the annual conference of National Council on Family Relations, Phoenix, AZ.

Rotberg, I. C. (2012). *Balancing change and tradition in global education reform.* Lanham, MD: Rowman and Littlefield Education.

Rotermann, M. (2007a, May). Marital breakdown and subsequent depression. *Health Reports* (Statistics Canada Catalogue no. 82-003), 33–44. Retrieved from http://www.statca.gc.ca/

Rotermann, M. (2007b, February). Second or subsequent births to teenagers. *Health Reports* (Statistics Canada Catalogue No. 82-003), 39–42. Retrieved from http://www.statcan.gc.ca/

Rotermann, M. (2008). Trends in teen sexual behaviour and condom use. *Health Reports* (Statistics Canada Catalogue No. 82-003-XPE), *19*(3), 1–5.

Rothbaum, F., & Trommsdorff, G. (2008). Do roots and wings complement or oppose one another? The socialization of relatedness and autonomy in cultural context. In J. E. Grusec & P. D. Hastings (Eds.), *Handbook of socialization: Theory and research* (pp. 461–489). New York: Guilford.

Rothblum, E. D. (2006). Same-sex marriage and legalized relationships: I do, or do I? In J. J. Bigner (Ed.), *An introduction to GLBT family studies* (pp. 203–214). New York: Haworth.

Rothman, E. K. (1987). *Hands and hearts: A history of courtship in America.* Cambridge, MA: Harvard University Press.

Rowe, D. C. (1994). *The limits of family influence: Genes, experience, and behavior.* New York: Guilford.

Rowe, J. W., & Kahn, R. L. (1997, August). Successful aging. *Gerontologist, 37*(4), 433–40.

Royal Commission on Aboriginal Peoples. (1996). *People to People, Nation to Nation: Report of the Royal Commission on Aboriginal Peoples.* Ottawa: Aboriginal Affairs and Northern Development Canada. Retrieved from http://www.aadnc-aandc.gc.ca/eng/1100100014597/1100100014637

Roy, F. (2006, June). From she to she: Changing patterns of women in the Canadian labour force. *Canadian Economic Observer* (Statistics Canada Catalogue No. 11-010), 3.1–3.10. Retrieved from http://www.statcan.gc.ca

Roy, L., & Bernier, J. (2007). *Family policy, social trends and fertility in Québec: Experimenting with the Nordic model?* (Translation). Québec: Ministère de la Famille, des Aînés et de la Condition féminine. Retrieved from http://www.mfacf.gouv.qc.ca/publications/index_en.asp

Roy, N. (2005, January). *De facto union in Quebec.* Ottawa: Department of Justice Canada. Retrieved from http://www.justice.gc.ca/eng/pi/icg-gci/dfu-udf/index.html

Royal Bank. (1989, Winter). *Reporter.*

Rudman, L. A., & Glick, P. (2008). *The social psychology of gender: How power and intimacy shape gender relations.* New York: Guilford.

Rueter, M. A., & Conger, R. D. (1995). Antecedents of parent-adolescent disagreements. *Journal of Marriage and the Family, 57*, 435–448.

Ryser, L., & Halseth, G. (2011). Informal support networks of low-income senior women living alone: Evidence from Fort St. John, BC. *Journal of Women & Aging, 23*, 185–202.

Sabatelli, R. M., & Bartle-Haring, W. (2003). Family-of-origin experiences and adjustment in married couples. *Journal of Marriage and Family, 65*, 159–169.

Sailor, D. H. (2004). Influences on sibling relationships. *Education.com.* Retrieved from http://www.education.com/reference/article/influences-sibling-relationships

Saleem, S. (2003, August 30). Arranged marriages: A proposal I never thought I would consider. *Hamilton Spectator*, p. M3.

Salvation Army. (2009, May). *Poverty shouldn't be a life sentence.* Toronto: Salvation Army. Retrieved from http://www.

salvationarmy.ca/documents/salvationarmy_homeless-ness_study.pdf

Samuel, T. J. (1990, May/June). *Immigration of children as an element of immigration policy*. Paper presented at the joint meeting of Canadian Population Society and Canadian Sociology and Anthropology Society, Victoria, BC.

Samuels, E. J. (2001). The strange history of adult adoptee access to original birth records. *Adoption Quarterly, 5*(2), 63–74.

Sandel, M. J. (2007). *The case against perfection: Ethics in the age of genetic engineering*. Cambridge, MA: Belknap.

Sandness, G. (1983). The miracle of Molly. In L. Dunn (Ed.), *Adopting children with special needs: A sequel* (pp. 33–34). Washington, DC: North American Council on Adoptable Children.

Sarkisian, N. (2006). "Doing family ambivalence": Nuclear and extended families in single mothers' lives. *Journal of Marriage and Family, 68*, 804–811.

Sarkisian, N., & Gerstel, N. (2008). Till marriage do us part: Adult children's relationship with their parents. *Journal of Marriage and Family, 70*, 360–376.

Sarlo, C. (2008, May). *What is poverty? Providing clarity for Canada*. Fraser Institute. Retrieved from http://www.fraserinstitute.org

Sasaki, T., Hazen, N. L., & Holmes, E. K. (2005, November). *Distorted expectations across the transition to parenthood: A dyadic growth curve approach*. Poster presentation to the annual conference of the National Council on Family Relations, Phoenix, AZ.

Saskatchewan Education. (2001). *Aboriginal elders and community workers in schools: A guide for school divisions and their partners*. Retrieved from http://www.education.gov.sk.ca/aboriginal-elders-community-workers

Saskatchewan Women's Secretariat. (n.d.). *The changing workplace: Flexible working arrangements*. Retrieved from http://204.83.176.82/flexible%20working%20arrangements%20new.htm

Sassler, S. (2004). The process of entering into cohabiting unions. *Journal of Marriage and Family, 66*, 491–506.

Saul, S. (2009, February 12). Birth of octuplets puts focus on fertility clinics. *New York Times*. Retrieved from http://www.nytimes.com/2009/02/12/health/

Sauvé, R. (2006, December). *The effect of the changing age structure on households and families to 2026*. Ottawa: Vanier Institute of the Family. Retrieved from http://www.vifamily.ca/library/cft/age_waves.pdf

Sauvé, R. (2009a, January). *The current state of Canadian family finances: 2008 report*. Ottawa: Vanier Institute of the Family. Retrieved from http://www.vifamily.ca/library/cft/famfin08.pdf

Sauvé, R. (2009b). *Family life and work life: An uneasy balance*. Ottawa: Vanier Institute of the Family.

Savoie, J. (2007, September 25). Youth self-reported delinquency, Toronto, 2006. *Juristat* (Statistics Canada Catalogue No. 85-002-XPE), *27*(6). Retrieved from http://www.statcan.gc.ca

Sayeed, A. (1999). *Improving the National Child Benefit: Matching deeds with intentions*. Toronto: C. D. Howe Institute.

Schaeff, A. W. (1986). *Co-dependence: Misunderstood—mistreated*. San Francisco: Harper & Row.

Scharlach, A., Li, W., & Dalvi, T. B. (2006). Family conflict as mediator of caregiver strain. *Family Relations, 55*, 625–635.

Schatz, J. N., & Lounds, J. J. (2007). Child maltreatment: Precursors of developmental delays. In J. G. Borkowski, J. R. Farris, T. L. Whitman, S. S. Carothers, K. Weed, & D. A. Keogh (Eds.), *Risk and resilience: Adolescent mothers and their children grow up* (pp. 125–150). Mahwah, NJ: Lawrence Erlbaum.

Schellenberg, G., & Maheux, H. (2007). Immigrants' perspectives on their first four years in Canada: Highlights from three waves of the Longitudinal Survey of Immigrants to Canada. [Special issue]. *Canadian Social Trends* (Statistics Canada Catalogue no. 11-008).

Schellenberg, G., & Silver, C. (2004, Winter). You can't always get what you want: Retirement preferences and experiences. *Canadian Social Trends* (Statistics Canada Catalogue no. 11-008), 2–7.

Schindler, H. S., & Coley, R. L. (2005, November). *Fathers experience homelessness too*. Poster presentation at the annual conference of National Council of Family Relations, Phoenix, AZ.

Schlesinger, B. (1990, June). *The one-parent family*. Paper presented at the 2nd International Rural Mental Health and Addictions Conference, North Bay, ON.

Schlesinger, B., & Schlesinger, R. A. (2005, September). Young adult grandchildren's perceptions of their grandparents. *Family Focus*, F16, F19.

Schmeeckle, M. (2007). Gender dynamics in stepfamilies: Adult stepchildren's views. *Journal of Marriage and Family, 69*, 174–189.

Schmeeckle, M., Giarusso, R., Feng, D., & Bengston, V. L. (2006). What makes someone family? Adult children's perceptions of current and former stepparents. *Journal of Marriage and Family, 68*, 595–610.

Schneewind, K. A., & Gerhard, A.-K. (2002). Relationship personality, conflict resolution, and marital satisfaction in the first 5 years of marriage. *Family Relations, 51*, 63–71.

Schock-Giordano, A. M. (2013, January–March). Ethnic families and mental health: Application of the ABC-X model of family stress. *Sage Open* (online). doi:10.1177/2158244013478015

Schock-Giordano, A. M., & Gavazzi, S. M. (2010). Mental illness and family stress. In S. J. Price, C. A. Price, & P. C. McKenry (Eds.), *Families & change: Coping with stressful life events and transitions* (4th ed., pp. 163–183). Thousand Oaks, CA: Sage.

Schoppe-Sullivan, S. J., Schermerhorn, A. C., & Cummings, E. M. (2007). Marital conflict and children's adjustment: Evaluation of the parenting process model. *Journal of Marriage and Family, 69*, 1118–1134.

Shreck, K. H. (2001, September). Rethinking the family tree. *Adoptive Families*, 39–40.

Schroeder, V. M., & Kelley, M. L. (2008). The influence of family factors on the executive functioning of adult children of alcoholics in college. *Family Relations, 57*, 404–414.

Schulz, P. V. (1978). Day care in Canada: 1850–1962. In K. G. Ross (Ed.), *Good day care: Fighting for it, getting it, keeping it* (pp. 137–158). Toronto: Women's Press.

Schwartzberg, N., Berliner, K., & Jacob, D. (1995). *Single in a married world: A life cycle framework for working with the unmarried adult.* New York: Norton.

Sciadas, G. (2006). *Our lives in digital times* (Catalogue No. 56F0004MIE, No. 14). Ottawa: Statistics Canada.

Segalen, M. (1986). *Historical anthropology of the family* (J. C. Whitehouse & S. Matthews, Trans.). Cambridge: Cambridge University Press.

Segré, F. (2007, October 28). This is to inform you of our new life apart. *New York Times.* Retrieved from http://www.nytimes.com/2007/10/28/fashion/weddings/

Séguin, L., Nikiéma, B., Gauvin, L., Zunzunegui, M.-V., & Xu, Q. (2007). Duration of poverty and child health in the Quebec Longitudinal Study of Child Development: Longitudinal analysis of a birth cohort. *Pediatrics, 119,* e-1063–e1070. Retrieved from http://pediatrics.aappublications.org/cgi/reprint/119/5/e1063

Seligman, M., & Darling, R. B. (2007). *Ordinary families, special children: A systems approach to childhood disability* (3rd ed.). New York: Guilford.

Seltzer, J. A. (2004). Cohabitation in the United States and Britain: Demography, kinship, and the future. *Journal of Marriage and Family, 66,* 921–928.

Senate of Canada (2002, January). *The health of Canadians—The federal role.* Vol. 2: *Current trends and future challenges.* Ottawa: Author. Retrieved from http://www.parl.gc.ca/37/1/parlbus/commbus/senate/Com-e/soci-e/rep/repjan01vol2-e.pdf

Senate of Canada. (2008, June). *Poverty, housing and homelessness: Issues and options* (First Report of the Subcommittee on Cities of the Standing Senate Committee on Social Affairs, Science and Technology). Ottawa: Author. Retrieved from http://www.parl.gc.ca/39/2/parlbus/commbus/senate/Com-e/soci-E/rep-e/repfinaljun08-e.pdf

Senate of Canada. (2009a, December). *In from the margins: A call to action on poverty, housing, and homelessness.* Ottawa: Author. Retrieved from http://www.parl.gc.ca/40/2/parlbus/commbus/senate/com-e/citi-e/rep-e/rep02dec09-e.pdf

Service Canada. (2009b, May 21). *Employment insurance (EI) and maternity, parental and sickness benefits.* Ottawa: Author. Retrieved from http://www.servicecanada.gc.ca/eng/ei/types/special.shtml#Parental3

Service Canada. (2012a, August 8). *Overview of the Old Age Security Program.* Ottawa: Author. Retrieved from http://www.servicecanada.gc.ca/eng/isp/oas/oasoverview.shtml

Service Canada. (2012b, June 13). *Canada Pension Plan.* Ottawa: Author. Retrieved from http://www.servicecanada.gc.ca/eng/isp/cpp/cpptoc.shtml

Service Canada. (2012c, July 26). *Questions and answers regarding the changes to the Old Age Security Act.* Ottawa: Author. Retrieved from http://www.servicecanada.gc.ca/eng/isp/oas/changes/faq.shtml

Service Canada. (2012d, July 30). *Employment Insurance Compassionate Care Benefits.* Ottawa: Author. Retrieved from http://www.servicecanada.gc.ca/eng/sc/ei/benefits/compassionate.shtml

Service Canada (2012e, October 4). *Universal Child Care Benefit.* Ottawa: Author. Retrieved from http://www.servicecanada.gc.ca/eng/goc/universal_child_care.shtml

Shaffer, M. (1997). The battered woman syndrome revisited: Some complicating thoughts five years after *R. v. Lavallee. University of Toronto Law Journal, 47,* 1–33.

Shaienks, D., & Gluszynski, T. (2009, July). *Education and labour market transitions of young adults* (Catalogue No. 81-595-M, no. 075). Ottawa: Statistics Canada. Retrieved from http://www.statcan.gc.ca/pub/81-595-m/81-595-m2009075-eng.pdf

Shanahan, L., McHale, S. M., Crouter, A. C., & Osgood, D. W. (2008). Linkages between parents' differential treatment, youth depressive symptoms, and sibling relationships. *Journal of Marriage and Family, 70,* 480–494.

Shanly, M. L. (2001). *Making babies, making families: What matters in an age of reproductive technologies, surrogacy, adoption, and same-sex and unwed parents.* Boston: Beacon.

Shapiro, V. B., & Shapiro, J. R. (2006). The adoption of foster children who suffered early trauma and object loss. In K. Hushion, S. B. Sherman, & D. Siskind (Eds.), *Understanding adoption: Clinical work with adults, children, and parents* (pp. 91–114). Lanham, MD: Jason Aronson.

Sharp, E. A., & Ganong, L. (2007). Living in the gray: Women's experience of missing the marital transition. *Journal of Marriage and Family, 69,* 831–844.

Sharpe, T. H. (2003). Adult sexuality. *The Family Journal, 11*(4), 420–426.

Sharples, T. (2008, January 31). Bye bye, love. *Time,* 59–60.

Sheehan, N. W., & Petrovic, K. (2005, September). Great-grandparents, grandparents, and adult grandchildren in the 21st century. *Family Focus,* F15–F16.

Shelly, C. (2009, December 31). Another wrenching social issue, punted to the courts. *National Post.* Retrieved from http://www.nationalpost.com/story.html?id=2366032

Sherif Trask, B., Hamon, R. R., & Hepp, B. W. (2006, December). Families across the oceans: How transnational families and international adoption will further diversify families of the future. *Family Focus,* F14–F15.

Sherif Trask, B., & Koivunen, J. M. (2007). Trends in marriage and cohabitation. In B. Sherif Trask & R. R. Hamon (Eds.), *Cultural diversity and families: Expanding perspectives* (pp. 80–99). Thousand Oaks, CA: Sage.

Sherman, C. W., (2006, December). Remarriage and stepfamily in later life. *Family Focus,* F8–F9.

Shewell, H. (2004). *"Enough to keep them alive": Indian welfare in Canada, 1873–1965.* Toronto: University of Toronto Press.

Ship, S. J. (1997). *Our nations' Elders speak.* Retrieved from http://www.niichro.com/Elders/Elders7.html

Shreck, K. H. (2001, September/October). Rethinking the family tree. *Adoptive Families,* 39–40.

Sidwell, D. (2007, Autumn). Storytelling and community. *Transition,* 6–10.

Sieburg, E. (1985). *Family communication: An integrated systems approach.* New York: Gardner.

Silva, E. B. (1999). Transforming housewifery: Dispositions, practices and technology. In E. B. Silva & C. Smart (Eds.), *The new family?* (pp. 46–65). London, England: Sage.

Silverstein, M., & Ruiz, S. (2006). Breaking the chain: How grandparents moderate the transmission of maternal depression to their grandchildren. *Family Relations, 55,* 601–612.

Simons, L. G., & Conger, R. D. (2007). Linking mother–father differences in parenting to a typology of family parenting styles and adolescent outcomes. *Journal of Family Issues, 28,* 212–241.

Simons, R. L., Chao, W., Conger, R. D., & Elder, G. H. (2001). Quality of parenting as mediator of the effect of childhood defiance on adolescent friendship choices and delinquency: A growth curve analysis. *Journal of Marriage and Family, 63,* 63–79.

Simons, R. L., Lin, K.-H., Gordon, L. C., Conger, R. D., & Lorenz, F. O. (1999). Explaining the higher incidence of adjustment problems among children of divorce compared with those in two-parent families. *Journal of Marriage and the Family, 61,* 1020–1033.

Sinclair R. (2007). Identity lost and found: Lessons from the sixties scoop. *First Peoples Child & Family Review, 3*(1), 65–82. Retrieved from http://www.fncfcs/pubs

Sinclaire, M., & Storm, K. (2006). *First Nations culture and elders.* Winnipeg: University of Manitoba, Office of University Accessibility. Retrieved from http://www.umanitoba.ca/admin/vp_academic/accessibility/media/1_First_Nations_Culture_Areas_and_Elders.pdf

Sinha, M. (2012, May 22). *Family violence in Canada: A statistical profile, 2010.* Ottawa: Statistics Canada. Retrieved April 15, 2013, from http://www.statcan.gc.ca/pub/85-002-x/2012001/article/11643-eng.pdf

Sipe, A. W. R. (1990). *A secret world: Sexuality and the search for celibacy.* New York: Brunner/Mazel.

Skipper, J. K., Jr., & Nass, G. (1968). Dating behavior: A framework for analysis and an illustration. In M. B. Sussman (Ed.), *Sourcebook in marriage and the family* (3rd ed., pp. 211–220). Boston: Houghton Mifflin.

Skolnick, A. (2006, December). The family and its futures. *Family Focus,* F3–F4.

Slates, S. L., Alexander, K., Entwisle, D., & Olson, L. (2012, July). Counteracting summer slide: Social capital resources within socioeconomically disadvantaged families. *Journal of Education for Students Placed at Risk, 17*(3), 165–185. doi:10.1080/10824669.2012.688171

Slomkowski, C., Rende, R., Conger, K. G., Simons, R. L., & Conger, R. D. (2001). Sisters, brothers, and delinquency: Evaluating social influence during early and middle adolescence. *Child Development, 72,* 271–283.

Smith, D. E. (1993). The standard North American family: SNAF as an ideological code. *Journal of Family Issues, 14,* 50–65.

Smith, E. (2004). *Nowhere to turn? Responding to partner violence against immigrant visible minority women.* Ottawa: Canadian Council on Social Development. Retrieved from http://www.ccsd.ca/pubs/2004/nowhere/nowere_to_turn.pdf

Smith, J. Z., & Perry-Jenkins, M. (2005, November). *Predictors of role overload for working parents: A longitudinal analysis.* Poster presentation at the annual conference of National Council on Family Relations, Phoenix, AZ.

Smith, N. F., & Grenier, M. K. (1975). English- and French-Canadian children's views of parents. *Canadian Journal of Behavioural Science, 7,* 40–53.

Smith, S. R., & Ingoldsby, B. (2005, June). Hutterite families. *Family Focus,* F29–F30.

Smith, S. R., & Ingoldsby, B. (2009, July 2). The role of discipline in Hutterite child rearing. *Family and Consumer Sciences Research Journal, 37*(3), 284–297. doi:10.1177/1077727X08330685

Smock, P. J., Manning, W. D., & Porter, M. (2005). "Everything's there except money": How money shapes decisions to marry among cohabitors. *Journal of Marriage and Family, 67,* 680–696.

Smyke, A. T., Zeanah, C. H., Fox, N. A., Nelson, C. A., & Guthrie, D. (2010, January/February). Placement in foster care enhances quality of attachment among young institutionalized children. *Child Development, 81*(1), 212–223. doi:10.1111/j.1467-8624.2009.01390.x

Snell, J. G. (1991) *In the shadow of the law: Divorce in Canada, 1900–1939.* Toronto: University of Toronto Press.

Snell, G. (1992). "The white life for two": The defence of marriage and sexual morality in Canada, 1890–1914. In B. Bradbury (Ed.), *Canadian family history: Selected readings* (pp. 381–399). Toronto: Copp Clark Pitman.

Snyder, L. (2003). Workfare. In A. Westhues (Ed.), *Canadian social policy: Issues and perspectives* (3rd ed., pp. 108–127). Waterloo, ON: Wilfrid Laurier University Press.

Sobol, M. P., Daly, K. J., & Kelloway, E. K. (2000). Paths to the facilitation of open adoption *Family Relations, 49,* 419–424.

Social Technologies. (2007, September 10). *Helicopter parenting.* Washington, DC: Social Technologies. Retrieved from http://www.socialtechnologies.com

Soenens, B., Vansteenkiste, M., & Sierens, E. (2009). How are parental psychological control and autonomy-support related? A cluster-analytic approach. *Journal of Marriage and Family, 71,* 187–202.

Some notes on the prohibited degrees of marriage. (1984, February 22). Provided in 1995 by Raymond L. du Plessis, Law Clerk and Parliamentary Counsel, Senate of Canada.

Sorenson, S. B., & Thomas, K. A. (2009). Views of intimate partner violence in same- and opposite-sex relationships. *Journal of Marriage and Family, 71,* 337–352.

Spar, D. L. (2006). *The baby business: How money, science, and politics drive the commerce of conception.* Boston: Harvard Business School Press.

Spector, A. N., & Klodawsky, F. (1993). The housing needs of single-parent families in Canada: A dilemma for the 1990s. In J. Hudson & B. Galaway (Eds.), *Single parent families: Perspectives on research and policy* (pp. 239–252). Toronto: Thompson Educational Publishing.

Spitalnick, J. S., Younge, S. N., Sales, J. M., & Diclemente, R. J. (2008). Sexual abuse in childhood: The abused child. In T. P. Gullotta & G. M. Blau (Eds.), *Family influences on childhood behavior and development: Evidence-based prevention and treatment approaches* (pp. 293–324). New York: Routledge.

Spock, B. (1976). *Baby and child care.* New York: Pocket Books.

Sprecher, S., & McKinney, K. (1993). *Sexuality.* Newbury Park, CA: Sage.

St. Thomas University. (2005). *Myths vs. Factors about Young People.* Retrieved from http://www.stthomasu.ca/research/youth/manual/myths.htm

Stahl, P. M. (2007). *Parenting after divorce: Resolving conflicts and meeting your children's needs.* Atascadero, CA: Impact Publishers.

Stanley, S. M., Rhoades, G. K., & Markman, H. J. (2006). Sliding versus deciding: Inertia and the premarital cohabitation effect. *Family Relations, 55*, 499–509.

Stapleton, J. (2007, November). *Why is it so tough to get ahead? How our tangled social programs pathologize the transition to self-reliance.* Toronto: Metcalf Foundation. Retrieved from http://www.metcalffoundation.com/downloads/John%20Stapleton%20-%20why%20is%20it%20so%20tough%20to%20get%20ahead(1).pdf

Stapleton, J. (2009, October). *Why don't we want the poor to own anything? Our relentless social policy journey toward destitution for the 900,000 poorest people in Ontario.* Toronto: Metcalf Foundation. Retrieved from http://metcalffoundation.com/download/Why_dont_we_want_the_poor_to_own_anything.pdf

Stark, E. (1986, October). A grandmother at 27. *Psychology Today.*

Starkey, S. (2006). *Scaling the welfare wall: Earned income tax credits.* Ottawa: Library of Parliament. Retrieved from http://www2.parl.gc.ca/Content/LOP/ResearchPublications/prb0598-e.html

Statistics Canada. (1983). *Divorce: Law and family in Canada* (Catalogue No. 89-502). Ottawa: Statistics Canada.

Statistics Canada. (1998, Spring). Elders more likely than younger Canadians to agree with reasons to divorce. *Canadian Social Trends* (Catalogue No. 11-008). Ottawa: Statistics Canada.

Statistics Canada. (2002a). *Family history* (Catalogue No. 89-575-XIE). Ottawa: Statistics Canada.

Statistics Canada. (2002b). *Profile of the Canadian population by age and sex: Canada ages* (Catalogue No. 96F0030XIE2001002). Ottawa: Statistics Canada.

Statistics Canada. (2003). *Work, parenthood, and the experience of time scarcity* (Catalogue No. 89-584-XIE). Ottawa: Statistics Canada.

Statistics Canada. (2004a, May 4). Divorces 2000 and 2001. *The Daily.* Retrieved from http://www.statcan.ca/Daily/English/040504/d040504a.htm

Statistics Canada. (2004b). *Live births by age and marital status of mother, Table 102-4507 Canada annual, 2002.* Retrieved from http://www.statcan.ca

Statistics Canada. (2005a, February 7). Childcare. *The Daily.* Retrieved from http://www.statcan.ca/Daily/English/050207/d050207b.htm

Statistics Canada. (2005b). *Longitudinal survey of immigrants to Canada: A portrait of early settlement experiences* (Catalogue No. 89-614-XIE). Ottawa: Statistics Canada. Retrieved from http://www.statcan.gc.ca

Statistics Canada (2005c, February 21). National Longitudinal Study of Children and Youth: Home environment, income and child behavior. *The Daily.* Retrieved from http://www.statcan.ca/Daily/English/050221/d050221b.htm

Statistics Canada (2005d, June 28). Canada's Aboriginal population in 2017. *The Daily.* Ottawa: Statistics Canada. Retrieved from http://www.statcan.ca/Daily/English/050628/d050628d.htm

Statistics Canada. (2006a, October). *Measuring violence against women: Statistical trends 2006* (Catalogue No. 85-570-XIE). Ottawa: Statistics Canada. Retrieved from http://www.statcan.gc.ca

Statistics Canada. (2006b). *Women in Canada: A gender-based statistical report* (5th ed.) (Catalogue No. 89-503-XPE). Ottawa: Statistics Canada. Retrieved from http://www.statcan.gc.ca

Statistics Canada. (2007a). *2006 Census dictionary* (Catalogue No. 92-566-XWE). Ottawa: Statistics Canada. Retrieved from http://www12.statcan.gc.ca/englishcensus06/reference/dictionary

Statistics Canada. (2007b). *Census families by number of children at home, by province and territory (2006 Census) Canada.* Ottawa: Statistics Canada. Retrieved from http://www40.statcan.gc.ca/101/cst01/famil50a-eng.htm

Statistics Canada. (2007c). *Portrait of the Canadian population in 2006, by age and sex, 2006 Census* (Catalogue No. 97-551-XIE). Ottawa: Statistics Canada.

Statistics Canada. (2007d). *The evolving linguistic portrait, 2006 Census* (Catalogue No. 97-555-XIE). Ottawa: Statistics Canada. Retrieved from http://www.statcan.gc.ca

Statistics Canada. (2007e). Legal marital status (6), common-law status (3), age groups (17) and sex (3) for the population 15 years and over of Canada, provinces, territories, census metropolitan areas and census agglomerations, 2001 and 2006 Census—100% data (table). Topic-based tabulation. *2006 Census of population* (Catalogue No. 97-552-XCB2006007). Retrieved from http://www12.statcan.gc.ca/english/census06/data/

Statistics Canada. (2007f). *Women in Canada: Work chapter updates, 2006* (Catalogue No. 89F0133XIE). Ottawa: Statistics Canada. Retrieved from http://www.statcan.gc.ca

Statistics Canada. (2008a). *Aboriginal children's survey, 2006: Family, community, and child care* (Catalogue No. 89-634-X, No. 001). Ottawa: Statistics Canada.

Statistics Canada. (2008b). *Aboriginal peoples in Canada in 2006: Inuit, Métis, and First Nations, 2006 Census* (Catalogue No. 97-558-XIE). Ottawa: Statistics Canada. Retrieved from http://www.statcan.gc.ca

Statistics Canada (2008c). *Births, 2006* (Catalogue No. 84F0210X). Ottawa: Statistics Canada. Retrieved from http://www.statcan.gc.ca/pub/84f0210x/840210x2006-eng.pdf

Statistics Canada. (2008d). *Canada's ethnocultural mosaic, 2006 Census* (Catalogue No. 97-562-X). Ottawa: Statistics Canada. Retrieved from http://www.statcan.gc.ca

Statistics Canada. (2008e). *Induced abortion statistics* (Catalogue No. 82-223-X). Ottawa: Statistics Canada.

Statistics Canada. (2008f). *National longitudinal survey of children and youth (NLSCY).* Retrieved from http://www.statcan.gc.ca

Statistics Canada. (2008g, September). *Participation and activity limitation survey 2006: Families of children with disabilities in Canada* (Catalogue No. 89-628-X, no. 009). Ottawa: Statistics Canada. Retrieved from http://www.statcan.gc.ca

Statistics Canada (2008h). *Pregnancy outcomes, 2005* (Catalogue No. 82-224-X). Ottawa: Statistics Canada. Retrieved from http://www.statcan.gc.ca/pub/82-224-x/82-224-x2005000-eng.pdf

Statistics Canada (2008i, June 26). *Projected population by age group and sex according to a medium growth scenario for 2006, 2011, 2016, 2021, 2026 and 2031, at July 1.* Retrieved from http://www40.statcan.gc.ca/l01/cst01/demo23b-eng.htm

Statistics Canada. (2008j). *Report on the demographic situation in Canada, 2005 and 2006* (Catalogue No. 91-209-X). Ottawa: Statistics Canada.

Statistics Canada. (2008k). Selected collective dwelling and population characteristics (25) and type of collective dwelling (17) for the population in collective dwellings in Canada, Provinces and Territories, 2006 Census—100% data (table). *Topic-based tabulation, 2006 Census.* Ottawa: Statistics Canada. Retrieved from http://www12.statcan.gc.ca/english/census06/data

Statistics Canada. (2008l, May 23). Study: Life after teenage motherhood. *The Daily.* Ottawa: Statistics Canada. Retrieved from http://www.statcan.gc.ca/daily-quotidien/080523/dq080523c-eng.htm

Statistics Canada. (2008m, November 17). *Participation and activity limitation survey 2006: Families of children with disabilities in Canada.* Ottawa: Statistics Canada. Retrieved from http://www.statcan.gc.ca/pub/89-628-x/89-628-x2008009-eng.htm

Statistics Canada (2009a, July). *2007 General social survey: Care tables* (Catalogue No. 89-633-X). Retrieved from http://www.statcan.gc.ca/pub/89-633-x/89-633-x2008001-eng.pdf

Statistics Canada. (2009b). *Child and spousal support maintenance enforcement survey statistics 2007/2008* (Catalogue No. 85-228-X). Ottawa: Statistics Canada. Retrieved from http://www.statcan.gc.ca/pub/85-228-x/85-228-x2009000-eng.pdf

Statistics Canada. (2009c). *Deaths 2006* (Catalogue No. 84F0211X). Ottawa: Statistics Canada. Retrieved from http://www.statcan.gc.ca/pub/84f0211x2006000-eng.pdf

Statistics Canada (2009d). *Definitions.* Retrieved from http://www.statcan.gc.ca/pub/85-002-x/2009001/definitions-eng.htm#l1

Statistics Canada. (2009e, April 9). *Labour force survey, March 2009.* Ottawa: Statistics Canada. Retrieved from http://www.statcan.gc.ca/subjects-sujets/labour-travail/lfs-epa/lfs-epa-eng.pdf

Statistics Canada. (2009f, June). *Low income cut-offs for 2008 and low income measures for 2007* (Catalogue No. 75f0002M, no.002). Ottawa: Statistics Canada. Retrieved from http://www.statcan.gc.ca/pub/75f0002m/75f0002m-eng.pdf

Statistics Canada. (2009g). *More information on low income before tax cut-offs (LICOs).* Ottawa: Statistics Canada. Retrieved from http://www12.statcan.ca/census-recensement/2006/ref/dict/fam020a-eng.cfm

Statistics Canada. (2009h). *Persons with disabilities, by age group and sex.* Ottawa: Statistics Canada. Retrieved from http://www40.statcan.gc.ca/l01/cst01/health71a-eng.htm

Statistics Canada. (2009i, September 22). *2006 Census: Aboriginal peoples in Canada in 2006: Inuit, Métis and First Nations.* Ottawa: Statistics Canada. Retrieved from http://www12.statcan.gc.ca/census-recensement/2006/as-sa/97-558/p1-eng.cfm

Statistics Canada. (2009j, November 18). *Nuptiality and divorce.* Ottawa: Statistics Canada. Retrieved from http://www.statcan.gc.ca/pub/91-209-x/2004000/part1/divorce-eng.htm

Statistics Canada. (2010a, November 10). *National longitudinal survey of children and youth (NLSCY).* Ottawa: Statistics Canada. Retrieved from http://www23.statcan.gc.ca:81/imdb/p2SV.pl?Function=getSurvey&SDDS=4450&lang=en&db=imdb&adm=8&dis=2

Statistics Canada. (2010b, November 2). *Canada's ethnocultural mosaic, 2006 Census: National picture.* Ottawa: Statistics Canada. Retrieved from http://www12.statcan.ca/census-recensement/2006/as-sa/97-562/p2-eng.cfm

Statistics Canada. (2010c, September 9). Study: Marital trends and education. *The Daily.* Ottawa: Statistics Canada. Retrieved from http://www.statcan.gc.ca/daily-quotidien/100909/dq100909c-eng.htm

Statistics Canada (2010d). Household food insecurity, 2007–2008: Canadian Community Health Survey. *Health Fact Sheets.* Ottawa: Statistics Canada. Retrieved from http://www.statcan.gc.ca/pub/82-625-x/2010001/article/11162-eng.htm

Statistics Canada. (2010e, January 11). *Dependency ratio.* Ottawa: Statistics Canada. Retrieved from http://www.statcan.gc.ca/pub/82-229-x/2009001/demo/dep-eng.htm

Statistics Canada. (2011a, July 5). Study: Projections of the diversity of the Canadian population, 2006–2031. *The Daily.* Ottawa: Statistics Canada. Retrieved from http://www.statcan.gc.ca/daily-quotidien/100309/dq100309a-eng.htm

Statistics Canada. (2011b). Table 1.1—Average time spent per day on various activities, for the population and participants aged 15 and over, by sex, Canada, 2010. Ottawa: Statistics Canada. Retrieved from http://www.statcan.gc.ca/pub/89-647-x/2011001/tbl/tbl11-eng.htm

Statistics Canada. (2011c). *Portrait of families and living arrangements in Canada. 2011 Census,* Table 2—Distribution (number and percentage) and percentage change of census families by family structure, Canada, provinces and territories, 2011. Ottawa: Statistics Canada. Retrieved from http://www12.statcan.gc.ca/census-recensement/2011/as-sa/98-312-x/2011001/tbl/tbl2-eng.cfm

Statistics Canada. (2011d, September 29). *Residential care facilities, 2009–2012.* Ottawa: Statistics Canada. Retrieved from http://www.statcan.gc.ca/pub/83-237-x/83-237-x2012001-eng.pdf

Statistics Canada. (2011e, July 5). Women in Canada: Economic well-being. *The Daily.* Ottawa: Statistics Canada. Retrieved from http://www.statcan.gc.ca/daily-quotidien/101216/dq101216c-eng.htm

Statistics Canada. (2011f, July 5). Study: Consequences of long-distance caregiving. *The Daily.* Ottawa: Statistics Canada. Retrieved from http://www.statcan.gc.ca/daily-quotidien/100126/dq100126a-eng.htm

Statistics Canada (2011g). *Women in Canada: A gender-based statistical report* (Catalogue No. 89-503-X, 2011). Ottawa: Statistics Canada.

Statistics Canada. (2011h, May 17). Study: Violent victimization of Aboriginal women, 2009. *The Daily.* Ottawa: Statistics Canada. Retrieved from http://www.statcan.gc.ca/daily-quotidien/110517/dq110517b-eng.htm

Statistics Canada. (2012a, April 16). *Size of household.* Ottawa: Statistics Canada. Retrieved from http://www.statcan.gc.ca/concepts/definitions/hsize-tmenage-eng.htm

Statistics Canada. (2012b, April 16). *Census family.* Ottawa: Statistics Canada. Retrieved from http://www.statcan.gc.ca/concepts/definitions/c-r-fam-eng.htm

Statistics Canada. (2012c, April 16). *Visible minority of person.* Ottawa: Statistics Canada. Retrieved from http://www.statcan.gc.ca/concepts/definitions/minority-minorite1-eng.htm

Statistics Canada. (2012d, April 16). *Aboriginal ancestry of person.* Ottawa: Statistics Canada. Retrieved from http://www.statcan.gc.ca/concepts/definitions/aboriginal-autochtone1-eng.htm

Statistics Canada. (2012e, Dec. 20). Table 051-0042—Population by marital status and sex. Ottawa: Statistics Canada. Retrieved from http://www.statcan.gc.ca/tables-tableaux/sum-som/l01/cst01/famil01-eng.htm

Statistics Canada. (2012f, August 4). Table 051-00011—Estimates of population, by age group and sex for July 1, Canada, provinces and territories. Ottawa: Statistics Canada. Retrieved from http://www5.statcan.gc.ca/cansim/a26

Statistics Canada. (2012g). Table 061-0042—Estimates of population, by marital status or legal marital status, age and sex for July 1, Canada, provinces and territories, annual (persons), CANSIM (database). Ottawa: Statistics Canada. Retrieved from http/www.statcan.gc.ca/tables-tableaux/sum-som/l01/cst01/famil01-eng.htm

Statistics Canada. (2012h, August 10). Table 282-0087—Labour force survey estimates (LFS), by sex and detailed age group, CANSIM (database). Ottawa: Statistics Canada. Retrieved from http://www5.statcan.gc.ca/cansim/a26;jsessionid=925D7890EBB88405ED03776B1248974D

Statistics Canada. (2012i). Chart 6—Demographic estimates. Ottawa: Statistics Canada, Canadian Vital Statistics, Marriage Database and Divorce Database and Demographic Division.

Statistics Canada. (2012j, September 19). 2011 Census: Families, households, marital status, structural type of dwelling, collectives. *The Daily.* Ottawa: Statistics Canada. Retrieved from http://www.statcan.gc.ca/daily-quotidien/120919/dq120919a-eng.htm

Statistics Canada. (2012k, June 12). *Presence of children.* Ottawa: Statistics Canada. Retrieved from http://www12.statcan.gc.ca/census-recensement/2011/dp-pd/tbt-tt/Rp-eng.cfm?LANG=E&APATH=3&DETAIL=0&DIM=0&FL=A&FREE=0&GC=0&GID=0&GK=0&GRP=1&PID=102074&PRID=0&PTYPE=101955&S=0&SHOWALL=0&SUB=0&Temporal=2011&THEME=89&VID=0&VNAMEE=&VNAMEF=

Statistics Canada. (2012l, September 19). *Portrait of families and living arrangements in Canada.* Ottawa: Statistics Canada. Retrieved from http://www12.statcan.gc.ca/census-recensement/2011/as-sa/98-312-x/98-312-x2011001-eng.pdf

Statistics Canada. (2012m, May). *The Canadian population in 2011: Age and sex* (Catalogue No. 98-X2011001). Ottawa: Statistics Canada. Retrieved from http://www.statcan.gc.ca.

Statistics Canada. (2012n). Table 051-001—Estimates of population, by age group and sex for July 1, Canada, provinces and territories, annual (persons unless otherwise noted), CANSIM (database). Ottawa: Statistics Canada. Retrieved from http://www.statcan.gc.ca/cansim

Statistics Canada. (2012o). *Living arrangements of young adults aged 20 to 29* (Catalogue No. 98-312-x2011003). Ottawa: Statistics Canada. Retrieved from http://www12.statcan.gc.ca/census-recensement/2011/as-sa/98-312-x2011003_3-eng.pdf

Statistics Canada. (2012p, December 4). Study: Years to retirement, 1998 to 2009. *The Daily.* Ottawa: Statistics Canada. Retrieved from http://www.statcan.gc.ca/daily-quotidien/121204/dq121204b-eng.pdf

Statistics Canada. (2012q). *2011 General Social Survey: Overview of families in Canada—Selected tables on families in Canada.* Ottawa: Statistics Canada. Retrieved from http://www.statcan.gc.ca/pub/89-650-x/89-650-x2012001-eng.pdf

Statistics Canada. (2012r). *Fifty years of families in Canada: 1961 to 2011.* Ottawa: Statistics Canada. Retrieved from http://www12.statcan.gc.ca/census-recensement/2011/as-sa/98-312-x/98-312-x2011003_1-eng.pdf

Statistics Canada. (2012s, September 27). *Live births, by age of mother, Canada, provinces and territories, annual.* Ottawa: Statistics Canada. Retrieved from http://www5.statcan.gc.ca/cansim/a26?lang=eng&id=1024503&p2=46

Statistics Canada. (2012t, Oct. 18). *2011 General Social Survey: Overview of families in Canada* (Catalogue No. 89-650-XWE, no. 002). Ottawa: Statistics Canada. Retrieved from http://www5.statcan.gc.ca/bsolc/olc-cel/olc-cel?lang=eng&catno=89-650-X

Statistics Canada. (2012u, July 12). *National Household Survey, 2011. Aboriginal peoples in Canada: First Nations People, Métis and Inuit.* Ottawa: Statistics Canada. Retrieved from http://www12.statcan.gc.ca/nhs-enm/2011/as-sa/99-011-x/99-011-x2011001-eng.pdf

Statistics Canada. (2012v, June 18). Table 4—Market Basket Measure thresholds for reference family of two adults and two children, by MBM region. Ottawa: Statistics Canada. Retrieved from http://www.statcan.gc.ca/pub/75f0002m/2012002/tbl/tbl04-eng.htm

Statistics Canada. (2012w). Table 1—Low income cut-offs (1992 base) after tax. (Catalogue No. 75F0002MWE). Ottawa: Statistics Canada. Retrieved from http://www.statcan.gc.ca/pub/75f0002m/2012002/tbl/tbl01-eng.htm

Statistics Canada. (2012x, June 18). Table 202-01011—Distribution of earnings, by sex, 2010 constant dollars, CANSIM (database). Ottawa: Statistics Canada. Retrieved from http://www5.statcan.gc.ca/cansim/pick-choisir;jsessionid=B69426E53C4B433345A2E6966FBC2320

Statistics Canada. (2012y, September). *Living arrangements of seniors.* Ottawa: Statistics Canada. Retrieved from http://www12.statcan.gc.ca/census-recensement/2011/as-sa/98-312-x/98-312-x2011003_4-eng.pdf

Statistics Canada. (2013a). Figure 1—Censuses of population, 2001 to 2011. Ottawa: Statistics Canada. Retrieved from http://www12.statcan.gc.ca/census-recensement/2011/as-sa/98-312-x/2011001/fig/fig1-cng.cfm

Statistics Canada. (2013b, February 18). *Labour force survey*. Ottawa: Statistics Canada. Retrieved from http://www5.statcan.gc.ca/cansim/a47

Statistics Canada. (2013c, February 25). Violence against women, 2011. *The Daily*. Ottawa: Statistics Canada. Retrieved from http://www.statcan.gc.ca/daily-quotidien/130225/dq130225a-eng.pdf

Statistics Canada. (2013d, May 8). 2011 National Household Survey: Immigration, place of birth, citizenship, ethnic origin, visible minorities, language and religion. *The Daily*. Ottawa: Statistics Canada. Retrieved from http://www.statcan.gc.ca/daily-quotidien/130508/dq130508b-eng.htm

Statistics Canada (2013e). *2011 National Household Survey: Data Tables*. Ottawa: Statistics Canada. Retrieved from http://www12.statcan.gc.ca/nhs-enm/2011/dp-pd/dt-td/rp-eng.cfm?lang=e&apath=3&detail=0&dim=0&fl=a&free=0&gc=0&gid=0&gk=0&grp=1&pid=105396&prid=0&ptype=105277&s=0&showall=0&sub=0&temporal=2013&theme=95&vid=0&vnamee=&vnamef=

Statistics Canada. (2013f, July 11). *Immigration and ethnocultural diversity in Canada*. Ottawa: Statistics Canada. Retrieved from http://www12.statcan.gc.ca/nhs-enm/2011/as-sa/99-010-x/99-010-x2011001-eng.pdf

Statistics Canada. (2013g, July 11). *Fertility: Overview, 2009 to 2011*. Figure 1—Number of births, Canada, 1926 to 2011. Ottawa: Statistics Canada. Retrieved from http://www.statcan.gc.ca/pub/91-209-x/2013001/article/11784-eng.htm

Statistics Canada. (2013h). *Low income lines, 2011-2012*. Ottawa: Statistics Canada. Retrieved from http://www.statcan.gc.ca/pub/75f0002m/75f0002m2013002-eng.pdf

Statistics Canada. (2013i). *Generations in Canada*. Ottawa: Statistics Canada. Retrieved from http://www12.statcan.gc.ca/census-recensement/2011/as-sa/98-311-x/98-311-x2011003_2-eng.pdf

Statistics Canada. (n.d., a). Table 101-6501—Divorces and crude divorce rates, Canada, provinces and territories, annual, CANSIM (database). Ottawa: Statistics Canada. Retrieved from http://cansim2.statcan.gc.ca/cgi-win/cnsmcgi.exe?Lang=E&CNSM-FC=CII/CII_1-eng.htm

Statistics Canada. (n.d., b). Table 101-6512—Number of dependents in divorces involving custody orders, by party to whom custody was granted, Canada, provinces and territories, annual, CANSIM (database). Ottawa: Statistics Canada. Retrieved from http://cansim2.statcan.gc.ca/cgi-win/cnsmcgi.exe?Lang=E&CNSM=CII/CII_1-eng.htm

Statistics Canada. (n.d., c). Table 101-6516—Divorces by reason for marital breakdown, Canada, provinces and territories, annual (number), CANSIM (database). Ottawa: Statistics Canada. Retrieved from http://cansim2.statcan.gc.ca/cgi-win/cnsmcgi.exe?Lang=E&CNSM-Fi=CII/CII_1-eng.htm

Stearns, P. N. (2003). *Anxious parents: A history of modern childrearing in America*. New York: New York University Press.

Steidtmann, C. (2006, April 28). *The economist's corner: The graying of America*. New York: Deloitte Research. Retrieved from http://www.deloitte.com/dtt/

Steinberg, L. (2005). Cognitive and affective development in adolescence. *Trends in Cognitive Sciences, 9*, 69–74.

Steinberg, L. (2007). Risk taking in adolescence: New perspectives from brain and behavioral science. *Current Directions in Psychological Science, 16*, 55–59.

Steinberg, L., Blatt-Eisengart, I., & Cauffman, E. (2006). Patterns of competence and adjustment among adolescents from authoritative, authoritarian, indulgent, and neglectful homes: A replication in a sample of serious juvenile offenders. *Journal of Research on Adolescence, 16*(1), 47–58. doi:10.1111/j.1532-7795.2006.00119.x

Steinberg, L., & Lamborn, S. (1992, October). Impact of parenting practices on adolescent achievement: Authoritative parenting, school involvement, and encouragement to succeed. *Child Development, 63*(5), 1266–1281. doi:10.1111/1467-8624.ep9301210142

Steinberg, L., & Monahan, K. C. (2007). Age differences in resistance to peer influence. *Developmental Psychology, 43*, 1531–1543.

Steinmetz, S. K. (2005). Elder abuse is caused by the perception of stress associated with providing care. In D. R. Loseke, R. J. Gelles, & M. M. Cavanaugh (Eds.), *Current controversies in family violence* (2nd ed., pp. 191–205). Thousand Oaks, CA: Sage.

Stelle, C., Fruhauf, C. A., Orel, N., & Landry-Meyer, L. (2010). Grandparenting in the 21st century: Issues of diversity in grandparent-grandchild relationships. *Journal of Gerontological Social Work, 53*(8), 682–701.

Stevens, D., Kiger, G., & Riley, P. J. (2001). Working hard and hardly working: Domestic labor and marital satisfaction among dual-earner couples. *Journal of Marriage and Family, 63*, 514–526.

Stevens, G., McKillip, M. E. M., & Ishizawa, H. (2006, October 1). *Intermarriage in the second generation: Choosing between newcomers and natives*. Washington, DC: Migration Policy Institute.

Stevens, M., Golombok, S., Beveridge, M., & the ALSPAC Study Team. (2003). Does father absence influence children's gender development: Findings from a general population study of preschool children. *Parenting: Science and Practice, 2*, 47–60.

Stewart, A. J., & Torges, C. M. (2006). Societal, historical, and developmental influences on the psychology of the baby boom at midlife. In S. K. Whitbourne & S. L. Willis (Eds.), *The baby boomers grow up: Contemporary perspectives on midlife* (pp. 23–43). Mahwah, NJ: Lawrence Erlbaum.

Stewart, S. D. (2005). How the birth of a child affects involvement with stepchildren. *Journal of Marriage and Family, 67*, 461–473.

Stewart, S. H., & Wall, A. M. (2004, Summer). Drinking problems in Canada then and now. *Transition*, 8–10.

Stobert, S., & Cranswick, K. (2004, Autumn). Looking after seniors: Who does what for whom? *Canadian Social Trends* (Statistics Canada Catalogue no. 11-008), 2–6.

Stobert, S., Dosman, D., & Keating, N. (2006). *Aging well: Time use patterns of older Canadians, 2005* (Catalogue No. 89-622-XIE, no. 2). Ottawa: Statistics Canada.

Stobert, S., & Kemeny, A. (2003, Summer). Childless by choice. *Canadian Social Trends* (Statistics Canada Catalogue no. 11-008), 7–10.

Strasburger, V. C. (1993). *Children, adolescents, and the media: Five crucial issues.* Retrieved from http://www.cyfc.umn.edu/media/crissues.htm

Straus, M. A. (2005). Women's violence toward men is a serious problem. In D. R. Loseke, R. J. Gelles, & M. M. Cavanaugh (Eds.), *Current controversies in family violence* (2nd ed., pp. 55–77). Thousand Oaks, CA: Sage.

Straus, M. (2007, June). Do we need a law to prohibit spanking? *Family Focus*, F7, F19.

Straus, M. A., & Field, C. J. (2003). Psychological aggression by American parents: National data on prevalence, chronicity, and severity. *Journal of Marriage and Family, 65*, 795–808.

Strock, C. (2008). *Married women who love women* (2nd ed.). New York: Routledge.

Strohschein, L. (2005). Parental divorce and child mental health trajectories. *Journal of Marriage and Family, 67*, 1286–1300.

Strohschein, L. (2007). Challenging the presumption of diminished capacity to parent: Does divorce really change parenting practices? *Family Relations, 56*, 358–368.

Strohschein, L. (2011). A life-course approach to studying transitions among Canadian seniors in couple-only households. *Canadian Public Policy, 37*(s1), 57–71.

Strohschein, L., Gauthier, A. H., Campbell, R., & Kleparchuk, C. (2008). Parenting as a dynamic process: A test of the resource dilution hypothesis. *Journal of Marriage and Family, 70*, 670–683.

Strong-Boag, V. (2006). *Finding families, finding ourselves: English Canada encounters adoption from the 19th century to the 1990s.* Don Mills, ON: Oxford University Press.

Strong-Boag, V. (2011). *Fostering nation? Canada confronts its history of childhood disadvantage.* Waterloo, ON: Wilfrid Laurier University Press.

Struckman-Johnson, C., Struckman-Johnson, D., & Anderson, P. B. (2003). Tactics of sexual coercion: When men and women won't take no for an answer. *Journal of Sex Research, 40*, 76–86.

Stubblefield, A. (2007). "Beyond the pale": Tainted whiteness, cognitive disability, and eugenic sterilization. *Hypatia, 22*(2), 162–181.

Stuifbergen, M. C., Van Delden, J. J., & Dykstra, P. A. (2008). The implications of today's family structures for support giving to older parents. *Ageing & Society, 28*(3), 413–434.

Sturino, F. (2012). Intergroup relations. *Encyclopedia of Canada's Peoples/Italians.* Retrieved from http://www.multicultural-canada.ca/Encyclopedia/A-Z/i11/10

Subrahmanyam, K., & Greenfield, P. (2008, Spring). Online communication and adolescent relationships. *The Future of Children, 18*(1), 119–146.

Suddath, C. (2013, February 25). Why won't Yahoo! let employees work from home? *Bloomberg Businessweek.* Retrieved from http://www.businessweek.com/articles/2013-02-25/why-wont-yahoo-let-employees-work-from-home.

Suitor, J. J., Sechrist, J., Steinhour, M., & Pillemer, K. (2006). "I'm sure she chose me!" Accuracy of children's reports of mothers' favoritism in later life families. *Family Relations, 55*, 526–538.

Sumner-Mayer, K. (2006). Children in foster families. In L. Combrinck-Graham (Ed.), *Children in family contexts: Perspectives on treatment* (2nd ed., pp. 190–220). New York: Guilford.

Sun, Y., & Li, Y. (2002). Children's well-being during parents' marital disruption process. *Journal of Marriage and Family, 64*, 472–488.

Sun, Y., & Li, Y. (2008). Stable postdivorce family structures during late adolescence and socioeconomic consequences in adulthood. *Journal of Marriage and Family, 70*, 129–143.

Supreme Court approves same-sex marriage. (2004, December 9). CTV.ca. Retrieved from http://www.ctv.ca

Surrogate mother furious as couple rejects one of twins. (1988, April 24). *Toronto Star*, p. A24.

Swanberg, J. E., Logan, T. K., & Macke, C. (2005). Intimate partner violence, employment, and the workplace: Consequences and future directions. *Trauma, Violence, & Abuse, 6*, 286–312. Retrieved from http://tva.sagepub.com/reprint/6/4/286

Swanton, S. (2009, January). *Social housing wait lists and the one-person household in Ontario.* Ottawa: Canadian Policy Research Networks. Retrieved from http://www.cprn.org/documents/50959_EN.pdf

Swisher, R. (2008). Neighborhood and youth: How neighborhood demographics and social processes affect youth outcomes. *The Prevention Researcher, 15*(2), 7–11.

Sykes, S. (2008). *Life on the reef in the Canadian ocean: The "new" second generation in Canada.* Ottawa: Policy Research Initiative. Retrieved from http://www.policyresearch.gc.ca

Szinovacz, M. (2006). Families and retirement. In L. O. Stone (Ed.), *New frontiers of research on retirement* (pp. 165–198). Ottawa: Statistics Canada.

Tach, L., & Halpern-Meekin, S. (2009). How does premarital cohabitation affect trajectories of marital quality? *Journal of Marriage and Family, 71*, 298–317.

Tait, H. (1999, Spring). Educational achievement of young Aboriginal adults. *Canadian Social Trends*, 6–10.

Tanner, J. L., & Arnett, J. J. (2009). The emergence of "emerging adulthood": The new life stage between adolescence and young adulthood. In A. Furlong (Ed.), *Handbook of youth and young adulthood: New perspectives and agendas* (pp. 39–45). New York: Routledge.

Taylor, D. M., Frasure-Smith, N., & Lambert, W. E. (1978). Psychological development of French and English Canadian children: Child-rearing attitudes and ethnic identity. In L. Driedger (Ed.), *The Canadian ethnic mosaic: A quest for identity* (pp. 153–168). Toronto: McClelland & Stewart.

Taylor-Butts, A. (2009). Fact sheet–Police-reported spousal violence in Canada. In Statistics Canada, *Family violence in Canada: A statistical profile 2009* (Catalogue No. 85-224-X, pp. 24–31). Ottawa: Statistics Canada. Retrieved from http://www.statcan.gc.ca/pub/85-224-x/85-224-x2009000.eng.pdf

Teachman, J. (2008). Complex life course patterns and the risk of divorce in second marriages. *Journal of Marriage and Family, 70*, 294–305.

Telford, G. E. (2005, Summer). Aging in place. *Transition, 9*, 12–14.

Texas Medical Association. (2001). *Physician stress and burnout.* Retrieved from http://www.texmed.org/cme/phn/psb/

The Arc of the United States. (2008). *Policy statement: Sexuality.* Retrieved from http://www.thearc.org/NetCommunity/Page.aspx?pid=1375

Thiele, D. M., & Whelan, T. A. (2008, September 22). The nature and dimensions of the grandparent role. *Marriage & Family Review, 40*(1), 93–108.

Thomas, D. (2001, Summer). Evolving family living arrangements of Canada's immigrants. *Canadian Social Trends* (Statistics Canada Catalogue No. 11-008), 16–22.

Thomas, D. (2011, November 30). *Personal networks and the economic adjustment of immigrants.* Ottawa: Statistics Canada. Retrieved from http://www.statcan.gc.ca/pub/11-008-x/2011002/article/11592-eng.pdf

Thomas, E. M. (2004). *Aggressive behaviour outcomes for young children: Change in parenting environment predicts change in behaviour* (Catalogue No. 89-599-MIE). Ottawa: Statistics Canada.

Thompson, C. J. (2000). Parenting after divorce. In J. K. Comeau (Ed.), *Family information services: Professional resource materials* (pp. FI-P/CD 21–41). Minneapolis, MN: Family Information Services.

Thornton, A. (2009a). Historical and cross-cultural perspectives on marriage. In E. Peters, & C. M. Kamp Dush (Eds.), *Marriage and family: Perspectives and complexities* (pp. 3–32). New York: Columbia University Press.

Thornton, A. (2009b). Framework for interpreting long-term trends in values and beliefs concerning single-parent families. *Journal of Marriage and Family, 71*, 230–234.

Thornton, A., Axinn, W. G., & Xie, Y. (2007). *Marriage and cohabitation.* Chicago: University of Chicago Press.

Ting-Toomey, S. (2009). A mindful approach to managing conflict in intercultural intimate couples. In T. A. Karis & K. D. Killian (Eds.), *Intercultural couples: Exploring diversity in intimate relationships* (pp. 31–49). New York: Routledge.

Tonmyr, L., Fallon, B., & Trocmé, N. (2006). Overview of Canadian Incidence Study of Reported Child Abuse and Neglect (CIS), 2003. In L. Ogrodnik (Ed.), *Family violence in Canada: A statistical profile 2006* (Catalogue No. 85-224-XIE, pp. 35–39). Ottawa: Statistics Canada. Retrieved from http://www.statcan.gc.ca

Torjman. S. (2007, May). *Repairing Canada's social safety net.* Ottawa: Caledon Institute of Social Policy. Retrieved from http://www/caledoninst.org/Publications/PDF/631ENG.pdf

Torjman, S. (2008, October). *Poverty policy.* Ottawa: Caledon Institute of Social Policy. Retrieved from http://www.caledoninst.org

Toulouse, P. R. (n.d.). *Supporting aboriginal student success: Self-esteem and identity, a living teachings approach.* Retrieved from http://www.edu.gov.on.ca/eng/research/toulouse.pdf

Tower, C. C. (1989). *Understanding child abuse and neglect.* Boston: Allyn & Bacon.

Townson, M. (2009, September). *Women's poverty and the recession.* Ottawa: Canadian Centre for Policy Alternatives. Retrieved from http://www.policyalternatives.ca/~ASSETS/DOCUMENT/National_Office_Pubs/2009/Womens_Poverty_in_the_Recession.pdf

Tran, K., Kaddatz, J., & Allard, P. (2005, Autumn). South Asians in Canada: Unity through diversity. *Canadian Social Trends* (Statistics Canada Catalogue no. 11-008), 20–25.

Treas, J. (2008). Transnational older adults and their families. *Family Relations, 57*, 468–478.

Treas, J., & de Ruijter, E. (2008). Earnings and expenditures on household services in married and cohabiting unions. *Journal of Marriage and Family, 70*, 796–805.

Tremblay, R. E., Gervais, J., & Petitclerc, A. (2008). *Early learning prevents youth violence.* Montreal: Centre of Excellence for Early Childhood.

Trocmé, N., MacLaurin, B., Fallon, B., Daciuk, J., Billingsley, D., Tourigny, M., et al. (2001). *Canadian incidence study of reported child abuse and neglect: Final report* (Catalogue No. H49-151/2000E). Ottawa: Health Canada, National Clearinghouse on Family Violence.

Trost, J., & Levin, I. (2005). Scandinavian families. In B. Adams & J. Trost (Eds.), *Handbook of world families* (pp. 347–363). Thousand Oaks, CA: Sage.

Tucker, C. J., McHale, S. M., & Crouter, A. C. (2002, November). *Patterns of differential treatment: Links with parental stressors.* Poster session presented at the annual conference of National Council on Family Relations, Houston, TX.

Tuller, D. (2004, June 21). Sex and medicine: Gentlemen, start your engines. *New York Times.* Retrieved from http://www.nytimes.com/2004/06/21/health/

Turcotte, M. (2006a, Spring). Parents with adult children living at home. *Canadian Social Trends* (Statistics Canada Catalogue no. 11-008), 2–9.

Turcotte, M. (2006b, Winter). Seniors' access to transportation. *Canadian Social Trends* (Statistics Canada Catalogue no. 11-008), 43–50.

Turcotte, M. (2007, Summer). Time spent with family during a typical workday, 1986 to 2005. *Canadian Social Trends* (Statistics Canada Catalogue no. 11-008), 2–11.

Turcotte, M., & Schellenberg, G. (2007). *A portrait of seniors in Canada 2006* (Catalogue No. 89-519-XIE). Ottawa: Statistics Canada.

Turcotte, M., & Zhao, J. (2004). *A portrait of Aboriginal children in non-reserve areas: Results from the 2001 Aboriginal Peoples Survey* (Catalogue No. 89-597-XIE). Ottawa: Statistics Canada.

Turcotte, P. (1993, Summer). Mixed-language couples and their children. *Canadian Social Trends*, 15–17.

Turner, M. J., Young, C. R., & Black, K. I. (2006). Daughters-in-law and mothers-in-law seeking their place within the family: A qualitative study of differing viewpoints. *Family Relations, 55*, 588–600.

Twenge, J. M., Campbell, W. H., & Foster, C. A. (2003). Parenthood and marital satisfaction: A meta-analytic review. *Journal of Marriage and Family, 65*, 574–583.

Twiggs, J. E., McQuillan, J., & Ferree, M. M. (1999). Meaning and measurement: Reconceptualizing measures of the division of household labor. *Journal of Marriage and the Family, 61*, 712–724.

Tyyskä, V. (2007). Immigrant families in sociology. In J. E. Lansford, K. Deater-Deckard, & M.C. Bornstein (Eds.), *Immigrant families in contemporary society* (pp. 83–99). New York: Guilford.

Uecker, J. E. (2008). Religion, pledging, and the premarital sexual behavior of married young adults. *Journal of Marriage and Family, 70,* 728–744.

Unger, D. G., Cuevas, T., & Woolfolk, T. (2007). Human services and cultural diversity: Tenuous relationships, challenges, and opportunity ahead. In B. Sharif Trask & R. R. Hamon (Eds.), *Cultural diversity and families: Expanding perspectives* (pp. 173–193). Thousand Oaks, CA: Sage.

Unicef Canada. (2013). *About the Convention on the Rights of the Child.* Retrieved from http://www.unicef.ca/en/policy-advocacy-for-children/about-the-convention-on-the-rights-of-the-child

University of Bath. (2005, February). Internet dating is much more successful than previously thought, study shows (Press Release 14). Retrieved from http://www.bath.ac.uk/pr/releases/internet-dating.htm

Updegraff, K. A., McHale, S. M., Crouter, A. C., & Kupanoff, K. (2001). Parents' involvement in adolescents' peer relationships: A comparison of mothers' and fathers' roles. *Journal of Marriage and Family, 63,* 655–668.

Updegraff, K. A., Thayer, S. M., Whiteman, S. D., Denning, D. J., & McHale, S. M. (2005). Relational aggression in adolescents' sibling relationships: Links to sibling and parent-adolescent relationship quality. *Family Relations, 54,* 373–385.

Urquia, M. L., Frank, J. W., Glazier, R. H., & Moineddin, R. (2007, November). Birth outcomes by neighbourhood income and recent immigration in Toronto. *Health Reports* (Statistics Canada Catalogue no. 82-003), 1–10.

Usdansky, M. (2009a). Ambivalent acceptance of single-parent families: A response to comments. *Journal of Marriage and Family, 71,* 240–246.

Usdansky, M. L. (2009b). A weak embrace: Popular and scholarly depictions of single-parent families, 1900–1998. *Journal of Marriage and Family, 71,* 209–225.

Usita, P. M. (2007). Parent–child ties of culturally diverse aging families. In B. S. Trask & R. R. Hamon (Eds.), *Cultural diversity and families: Expanding perspectives* (pp. 154–169). Thousand Oaks, CA: Sage.

Vaillancourt, R. (2009). Fact sheet–Police-reported family violence against older adults. In Statistics Canada, *Family violence in Canada: A statistical profile 2009* (Catalogue No. 85-224-X, pp. 42–47). Ottawa: Statistics Canada. Retrieved from http://www.statcan.gc.ca/pub/85-224-x/85-224-x2009000.eng.pdf

Valois, J. (1993). *Sociologie de la famille au Québec.* Anjou, QC: Centre Éducatif et Culturel.

Valverde, M. (2006). A new entity in the history of sexuality: The respectable same-sex couple. *Feminist Studies, 32*(1), 155–162.

van Gelderen, L., Gartrell, N., Bos, H., van Rooij, F., & Hermanns, J. (2012). Stigmatization associated with growing up in a lesbian-parented family: What do adolescents experience and how do they deal with it? *Children and*

Youth Services Review, 34, 999–1006. doi:10.1016/j.childyouth.2012.01.048

Van Harten, P. (2004, July 22). Agency reconsiders moving foster kids. *Hamilton Spectator,* p. A3.

Vanderburgh, R. M. (1987). Modernization and aging in the Anicinabe context. In V. W. Marshall (Ed.), *Aging in Canada: Social perspectives* (2nd ed., pp. 100–110). Markham, ON: Fitzhenry & Whiteside.

Vanier Institute of the Family. (2007). *Peace of mind for working parents: Short term child care.* Ottawa: Author. Retrieved from http://www.vifamily.ca/library/social/stcc.html

Vanier Institute of the Family. (2008, December). Fertility intentions: If, when and how many? *Fascinating Families, 13.* Retrieved from http://www.vanierinstitute.ca/modules/news/newsitem.php?ItemId=187

Vanier Institute of the Family. (2010). *Families count: Profiling Canada's families.* Ottawa: Author. Retrieved from http://www.vanierinstitute.ca/include/get.php?nodeid=35

Vanier Institute of the Family. (2012). *Definition of family.* Ottawa: Author. Retrieved from http://30645.vws.magma.ca/node/2

Van Volkom, M. (2006). Sibling relationships in middle and older adulthood: A review of the literature. *Marriage and Family Review, 40*(2/3), 151–170.

Varela, V. C. (n.d.). *Couple dynamics in stepfamilies.* Bakersfield, CA: California State University. Retrieved from http://www.taftcollege.edu/faculty/varela/soc_paper-asa_example.pdf

Veenhof, B, (2006). *The Internet: Is it changing the way Canadians spend their time?* (Catalogue No. 56F0004MIE, no. 13). Ottawa: Statistics Canada.

Veenhof, B., & Timusk, P. (2009, August). Online activities of Canadian boomers and seniors. *Canadian Social Trends* (Statistics Canada Catalogue no. 11-008), 25–32. Retrieved from http://www.statcan.gc.ca/pub/11-008-x/2009002/article/10910-eng.pdf

Vézina, M. (2012). *2011 General Social Survey: Overview of Families in Canada—Being a parent in a stepfamily: A Profile.* Ottawa: Statistics Canada. Retrieved from http://www.statcan.gc.ca/pub/89-650-x/89-650-x2012002-eng.pdf

Videon, T. M. (2002). The effects of parent-adolescent relationships and parental separation on adolescent well-being. *Journal of Marriage and Family, 64,* 489–503.

Visher, E. B., Visher, J. S., & Pasley, K. (2003). Remarriage families and stepparenting. In F. Walsh (Ed.), *Normal family processes: Growing diversity and complexity* (3rd ed., pp. 153–175). New York: Guilford.

Voydanoff, P. (2004). The effects of work demands and resources on work-to-family conflict and facilitation. *Journal of Marriage and Family, 66,* 398–412.

Voydanoff, P. (2007). *Work, family, and community: Exploring interconnections.* Mahwah, NJ: Lawrence Erlbaum.

Wachtel, A. (1989). *Discussion paper: Child abuse.* Ottawa: Health and Welfare Canada.

Wachtel, A. (1999). *The "state of the art" in child abuse prevention, 1997.* Ottawa: Health Canada.

Wade, T., Veldhuizen, S., & Cairney, J. (2011). Prevalence of psychiatric disorder in lone fathers and mothers: Examining the intersection of gender and family structure on mental health. *Canadian Journal of Psychiatry, 56*(9), 567–573.

Waite, L. J. (2003). Why marriage matters. In M. Coleman & L. Ganong (Eds.), *Points & counterpoints: Controversial relationship and family issues in the 21st century: An anthology* (pp. 64–69). Los Angeles: Roxbury.

Walberg, R., & Mrozek, A. (2009, June). *Private choices, public costs: How failing families cost us all.* Retrieved from http://www. imfcanada.org/article_files/Cost%20of%20Family%20 Breakdown%20finalHR.pdf

Walker, C. (1977). Some variations in marital satisfaction. In R. Chester & J. Peel (Eds.), *Equalities and inequalities in family life* (pp. 127–139). London: Academic Press.

Walker, L. E. (2009). *Battered woman syndrome* (3rd ed.). New York: Springer.

Wallace, K. (2009, September 24). B.C. judge tosses polygamy charges. *National Post.* Retrieved from http://www.nationalpost.com/news/story.html?id=2026113

Wallerstein, J. (2007, December). Adult children of divorce speak out. *Family Focus,* F13–F14, F19.

Walsh, C. A., & Yon, Y. (2012). Developing an empirical profile for elder abuse research in Canada. *Journal of Elder Abuse and Neglect, 24,* 104–119. doi:10.1080/08946566.2011.644088

Walsh, D. (2001). *Dr. Dave's cyberhood: Making media choices that create a healthy electronic environment for your kids.* New York: Fireside.

Walsh, F. (1999). Families in later life: Challenges and opportunities. In B. Carter & M. McGoldrick (Eds.), *The expanded family life cycle: Individual, family, and social perspectives* (3rd ed., pp. 307–326). Boston: Allyn & Bacon.

Walsh, F. (2003a). Changing families in a changing world: Reconsidering family normality. In F. Walsh (Ed.), *Normal family processes: Growing diversity and complexity* (3rd ed., pp. 3–26). New York: Guilford.

Walsh, F. (2003b). Family resilience: Strengths forged through adversity. In F. Walsh (Ed.), *Normal family processes: Growing diversity and complexity* (3rd ed., pp. 399–423). New York: Guilford.

Walsh, F. (2006). *Strengthening family resilience* (2nd ed.). New York: Guilford.

Wang, Y., & Marcotte, D. E. (2007). Golden years? The labor market effects of caring for grandchildren. *Journal of Marriage and Family, 69,* 1283–1296.

Wannell, T. (2007, February). Young pensioners. *Perspectives on Labour and Income* (Statistics Canada Catalogue no. 75-001-XIE), 5–14.

Ward, M. (1978). Full house: Adoption of a large sibling group. *Child Welfare, 57,* 233–241.

Ward, M. (1979). The relationship between parents and caseworker in adoption. *Social Casework, 60,* 96–103.

Ward, M. (1984). *The adoption of native Canadian children.* Cobalt, ON: The Highway Book Shop.

Ward, M. (2005, June). When is a grandparent not a grandparent? *Family Focus,* F16–F17.

Ward, M., & Tremitiere, B. (1991, August). *How marriage and special-needs adoption coexist.* Paper presented at the annual conference of North American Council on Adoptable Children, Atlanta.

Ward, R. A., & Spitze, G. (1996). Will the children ever leave? Parent–child coresidence: History and plans. *Journal of Family Issues, 17,* 514–539.

Ward, R. A., & Spitze, G. D. (2004). Marital implications of parent–adult child coresidence: A longitudinal view. *Journal of Gerontology: Social Sciences, 59B,* 52–58.

Ward, R. A., Spitze, G., & Deane, G. (2009). The more the merrier? Multiple parent–adult child relations. *Journal of Marriage and Family, 71,* 161–173.

Waterman, J. (1986). Family dynamics of incest with young children. In K. MacFarlane, J. Waterman, & others (Eds.), *Sexual abuse of young children: Evaluation and treatment* (pp. 204–219). New York: Guilford.

Waters, L. E., & Moore, K. A. (2001). Coping with economic deprivation during unemployment. *Journal of Economic Psychology, 22,* 461–482.

Waters, L. E., & Moore, K. A. (2002). Predicting self-esteem during unemployment: The effect of gender, financial deprivation, alternate roles, and social support. *Journal of Employment Counseling, 39,* 171–189.

Waters, L. E., & Muller, J. (2003). Money or time: Comparing the effects of time structure and financial deprivation on the psychological distress of unemployed adults. *Australian Journal of Psychology, 55,* 166–175.

Watson, W. K., & Stelle, C. (2011). Dating for older women: Experiences and meanings of dating in later life. *Journal of Women & Aging, 23,* 263–275. doi:10.1080/08952841.201 1.587732

Weaver, C. M., & Akai, C. E. (2007). Understanding the cycle: Violence in the lives of at-risk children. In J. G. Borkowski, J. R. Farris, T. L. Whitman, S. S. Carothers, K. Weed, & D. A. Keogh (Eds.), *Risk and resilience: Adolescent mothers and their children grow up* (pp. 151–178). Mahwah, NJ: Lawrence Erlbaum.

Weeks, L. E., Nilsson, T., Bryanton, O., & Kozma, A. (2009). Current and future concerns of older parents of sons and daughters with intellectual disabilities. *Journal of Policy and Practice in Intellectual Disabilities, 6*(3), 180–188.

Weigel, D. J., & Ballard-Reisch, D. S. (1999). How couples maintain marriages: A closer look at self and spouse influences upon the use of maintenance in marriages. *Family Relations, 48,* 263–269.

Weil, E. (2006, March 12). A wrongful birth? *New York Times.* Retrieved from http://www.nytimes.com/2006/03/12/ magazine/

Weiss, R. S. (1979). Growing up a little faster: The experience of growing up in a single-parent household. *Journal of Social Issues, 35*(4), 97–111.

Weitzman, S. (2000). *"Not to people like us": Hidden abuse in upscale marriages.* New York: Basic Books.

Wentzel, K. R., & Looney, L. (2008). Socialization in school settings. In J. E. Grusec & P. D. Hastings (Eds.), *Handbook of socialization: Theory and research* (pp. 382–403). New York: Guilford.

Westfall, W. (1989). *Two worlds: The protestant culture of nineteenth-century Ontario.* Montreal & Kingston: McGill-Queen's University Press.

Whipple, V. (2006). *Lesbian widows: Invisible grief.* New York: Harrington Park.

White, J. M. (1989). Marriage: A developing process. In K. Ishwaran (Ed.), *Family and marriage: Cross-cultural perspectives* (pp. 197–211). Toronto: Wall & Thompson.

White, J. M., & Klein, D. M. (2008). *Family theories* (3rd ed.). Los Angeles: Sage.

White, L., & Peterson, D. (1995). The retreat from marriage: Its effect on unmarried children's exchange with parents. *Journal of Marriage and the Family, 57,* 428–434.

Whiteman, S. D., & Christiansen, A. (2008). Processes of sibling influence in adolescence: Individual and family correlates. *Family Relations, 57,* 24–34.

Whiteman, S. D., McHale, S. M., & Crouter, A. C. (2007). Longitudinal changes in marital relationships: The role of offspring's pubertal development. *Journal of Marriage and Family, 69,* 1005–1020.

Whiteside, M. F. (2006). Remarried systems. In L. Combrinck-Graham (Ed.), *Children in family contexts: Perspectives on treatment* (2nd ed., pp. 163–189). New York: Guilford.

Widom, C. S., & Maxfield, M. G. (2001, February). An update on the "cycle of violence." *Research in Brief.* Washington, DC: National Institute of Justice.

Wiehe, V. L., & Herring, T. (1991). *Perilous rivalry: When siblings become abusive.* Lexington, MA: Lexington Books.

Wight, R. G., LeBlanc, A. J., de Vries, B. & Detels, R. (2012). Stress and mental health among midlife and older gay-identified men. *American Journal of Public Health, 102,* 503–510. doi: 10.2105/AJPH.2011.300384

Wilken, C. S. (2005, September). Ethical dilemmas in caregiving. *Family Focus,* F23, F25.

Wilkie, K., & Bardahl, L. (2007, September). *Hard times: A portrait of street level social problems in western Canada.* Calgary: Canada West Foundation. Retrieved from http://www.cwf.ca

Wilkins, K. (2006, February). Predictors of death in seniors. *Health Reports* (Statistics Canada Catalogue no. 82-003), 57–67. Retrieved from http://www.statcan.ca

Wilkins, K. (2007, November). Work stress among health care providers. *Health Reports* (Statistics Canada Catalogue no. 82-003), 33–36. Retrieved from http://www.statcan.gc.ca/pub/82-003-x/2006011/article/10367-eng.pdf

Wilson, D., & Macdonald, D. (2010, April). *The income gap between Aboriginal peoples and the rest of Canada.* Retrieved from http://www.policyalternatives.ca/sites/default/files/uploads/publications/reports/dodo/Aboriginal%20Income%20Gap.pdf

Will Dunning, Inc., for Co-operative Housing Federation of Canada. (2007). *Dimensions of core housing need in Canada.* Retrieved from http://www.chfcanada.coop/eng/pdf/mediareleases/dunning_report.pdf

Williams, A. M., Eby, J., Crooks, V., Stajduhar, K., Giesbrecht, M., Vuksan, M., et al. (2011). Canada's Compassionate Care Benefit: Is it an adequate public health response to addressing the issue of caregiver burden in end-of-life care? *BMC Public Health, 11*(Suppl. 4), 335–349.

Williams, C. (2003, November). Finances in the golden years. *Perspectives on Labour and Income* (Statistics Canada Catalogue No. 75-001-XIE), 5–13.

Williams, C. (2004, Summer). The sandwich generation. *Perspectives on Labour and Income* (Statistics Canada Catalogue No. 75-001-XIE), 5–12.

Williams, C. (2005, Summer). The sandwich generation. *Canadian Social Trends* (Statistics Canada Catalogue No. 11-008), 16–21.

Williams, C. (2010, December). Economic well-being. *Women in Canada: A gender-based statistical report,* Ottawa: Statistics Canada. Retrieved from http://www.statcan.gc.ca/pub/89-503-x/2010001/article/11388-eng.pdf

Williams, P. H. (2006, September). Children's mental health: A family perspective on AD/HD. *Family Focus,* F2–F4.

Williams, S. K., & Dunne-Bryant, A. (2006). Divorce and adult psychological well-being: Clarifying the role of gender and child age. *Journal of Marriage and Family, 68,* 1178–1196.

Williams-Washington, K. N., Melon, J., & Blau, G. M. (2008). Childhood growth and development in a family context. In T. P. Gullotta & G. M. Blau (Eds.), *Family influences on childhood behavior and development* (pp. 21–38). New York: Routledge.

Wilson, B. J. (2008, Spring). Media and children's aggression, fear, and altruism. *The Future of Children, 18*(1), 87–118.

Wingard, J., McCormack, C. S., & Neigh, S. (2003). *Progress report on homelessness in Hamilton 2003.* Hamilton, ON: Social Planning and Research Council of Hamilton.

Wiseman, J. P. (1991). *The other half: Wives of alcoholics and their social-psychological situation.* New York: Aldine de Gruyter.

Wolfe, D. A., & Jaffe, P. G. (2001, September). Emerging strategies in the prevention of family violence. *Family Focus,* F1–F3, F5.

Wolin, S. J., & Wolin, S. (2010). *The resilient self: How survivors of troubled families rise above adversity.* Random House Digital.

Women's Health Research Institute (2011, April 28). *Contraception and abortion in BC: Experience guiding research guiding care.* Report of Proceedings.

Women's Issues and Social Empowerment (WISE). (1998). *Domestic violence information manual.* Melbourne, AU: WISE. Retrieved from http://infoxchange.net.au/wise/DVIM/

Wood, J. T. (1996). She says/he says: Communication, caring, and conflict in heterosexual relationships. In J. T. Wood (Ed.), *Gendered relationships* (pp. 149–162). Mountainview, CA: Mayfield.

World Health Organization. (2013a). *Global strategy on diet, physical activity and health: Childhood overweight and obesity.* Geneva: Author. Retrieved from http://www.who.int/dietphysicalactivity/childhood/en

World Health Organization. (2013b). *School policy framework: Implementation of the global strategy on diet, physical activity and health.* Geneva: Author. Retrieved from http://www.who.int/dietphysicalactivity/schools/en

World Health Organization. (2013c). *Global strategy on diet, physical activity and health: What are the causes?* Geneva: Author. Retrieved from http://www.who.int/dietphysicalactivity/childhood_why/en

Workershelp.ca. (2013). *Leaves of absence from work*. Retrieved from http://workershelp.ca/leaveofabsence.asp

Wright, D. L., & Aquilino, W. S. (1998). Influence of emotional support exchange in marriage on caregiving wives' burden and marital satisfaction, *Family Relations, 47*, 195–204.

Wu, Z. (1994). Remarriage in Canada: A social exchange perspective. *Journal of Divorce & Remarriage, 21*(3/4), 191–224.

Wu, Z. (1995). Premarital cohabitation and postmarital cohabiting union formation. *Journal of Family Issues, 16*, 212–232.

Wu, Z. (2007, October 31). *Shacked up: A demographic profile of nonmarital cohabitation*. Paper presented to Breakfast on the Hill Seminar Series, Ottawa.

Wu, Z., & Penning, M. J. (1997). Marital instability after midlife. *Journal of Family Issues, 18*, 459–478.

Xu, C. (2007). Direct and indirect effects of parenting style with child temperament, parent–child relationship, and family functioning on child social competence in the Chinese culture: Testing the latent models. (Doctoral dissertation, University of North Texas). Retrieved from http://digital.library.unt.edu/permalink/meta-dc-3592:1

Xue, L. (2007, June). *Portrait of an integration process: Difficulties encountered and resources relied on for newcomers in their first 4 years in Canada*. Ottawa: Citizenship and Immigration Canada. Retrieved from http://www.cic.gc.ca/english/pdf/research-stats/portrait-integr-process-e.pdf

Yalnizyan, A. (2009, April). *Exposed: Revealing truths about Canada's recession*. Ottawa: Canadian Centre for Policy Alternatives. Retrieved from http://www.policyalternatives.ca/reports/2009/04/reportsstudies2207/?pa=a2286b2a

Yoshikawa, H., Magnuson, K. A., Bos, J. M., & Hsueh, J. (2003). Effect of earning-supplement policies on adult economic and middle-childhood outcomes differ for the "hardest to employ." *Child Development, 74*, 1500–1521.

Youniss, J. (1980). *Parents and peers in social development*. Chicago: University of Chicago Press.

Zarit, S. H. (2004). Family care and the burden at the end of life. *Canadian Medical Association Journal, 170*, 1811–1812. Retrieved from http://www.cmaj.ca/cgi/reprint/170/12/1811

Zelizer, V. A. (1985). *Pricing the priceless child: The changing social value of children*. New York: Basic Books.

Zhang, Y., & Van Hook, J. (2009). Marital dissolution among interracial couples. *Journal of Marriage and Family, 71*, 95–107.

Zheng, W., Costigan, C., Feng, H., Kampen, R., & Schimmele, C. (2012). Change and stability in cohabitation and children's educational adjustment. *Journal of Comparative Family Studies, 41*(4), 557–579.

Zhou, Y. R. (2012). Space, time, and self: Rethinking aging in the contexts of immigration and transnationalism. *Journal of Aging Studies, 26*, 232–242.

Zimmer-Gembeck, M. J., Hughes, N., Kelly, M., & Connolly, J. (2012). Intimacy, identity and status: Measuring dating goals in late adolescence and emerging adulthood. *Motivation and Emotion, 36*(3), 311–322. doi:10.1007/s11031-011-9253-6

Zimmerman, K. (2005, September). Parenting again: Grandparents raising grandchildren. *Family Focus*, F18–F19.

Zolotor, A. J., Theodore, A. D., Chang, J. J., Berkoff, M. C., & Runyan, D. K. (2008). Speak softly—and forget the stick: Corporal punishment and child physical abuse. *American Journal of Preventive Medicine, 35*, 364–369.

Zukewich, N. (2003). *Work, parenthood and the experience of time scarcity 1998, no. 1* (Catalogue No. 89-584-MIE-No. 1). Ottawa: Statistics Canada. Retrieved from http://www.statcan.gc.ca/pub/89-584-m/89-584-m2003001-eng.pdf

Index